UNFORGETTABLE
SACRIFICE

RECONSTRUCTING AMERICA
Andrew L. Slap, series editor

Unforgettable Sacrifice

How Black Communities Remembered the Civil War

Hilary N. Green

Foreword by Edda L. Fields-Black

FORDHAM UNIVERSITY PRESS
NEW YORK   2025

Fordham University Press also publishes its books in a variety of electronic formats. Some content that appears in print may not be available in electronic books.

Visit us online at www.fordhampress.com.

Library of Congress Cataloging-in-Publication Data available online at https://catalog.loc.gov.

Printed in the United States of America

27 26 25   5 4 3 2 1

First edition

To my parents, who introduced me to the porch archives

Contents

Author's Note on Language and Sources

As a book on African Americans' remembrances and commemoration of the Civil War, I draw on archival materials and transcriptions of oral histories that reflect the racist and anti-Black attitudes of the men, women, and children who produced them and the racial terms and notions common to the period. The creators are not perfect. Instead of reifying the rhetorical violence on Black people and expressions of white Americans' denial of their humanity, I embrace an ethic of care when quoting and citing these sources. I have carefully chosen my words and use updated language conventions for speaking about slavery, wartime acts of resistance, and post–Civil War racial experiences.

I use the words "Black" and "African American" interchangeably and capitalize "Black." Whenever possible, I provide wartime status, military service, and genealogical connections to the Civil War generation. I have retained the original spelling, grammar, punctuation, and capitalization. All editorial interventions are enclosed in brackets. I also made specific decisions regarding how racial pejoratives appear in the text. Unless directly quoting an African American historical actor or publication, one common pejorative will appear as either the "n-word" or "n****r." My hope is to mitigate the effects on modern readers and African American descendant communities.

Foreword

Edda L. Fields-Black

In the long history of Black freedom, there are voices from which we haven't heard. They are African American ancestors who experienced the Civil War. We haven't heard their stories for a variety of reasons. Many were illiterate and did not write them down. Some memories which were enshrined in writing have been lost through the passage time. But there are traces. If we search, particularly for the people whose names we don't recognize, if we look in places and at sources that have not been examined, and if we listen very closely, we can still hear their voices. We can still feel their pain, their trauma, and their triumph. We can still learn from their stories.

Hilary Green's new book takes the reader on a journey to her ancestral lands both above the Mason-Dixon Line, to Gettysburg where General Robert E. Lee and the Confederate Army invaded the free state of Pennsylvania, capturing Black people who had been free before the Civil War, enslaved and re-enslaved them, Chambersburg, Pennsylvania, where John Brown met Frederick Douglass to discuss plans for his ill-fated raid on the US Arsenal at Harpers Ferry, and below the Mason-Dixon line, to Richmond, Virginia, the capital of the Confederacy, to Charleston, South Carolina, where the Confederate flag flew at the state house until after a white nationalist gunned down nine innocent people during a prayer meeting at Mother Emanuel's AME Church in 2015, and everywhere in between. She illuminates how African Americans from the well-known Bishop Henry McNeal Turner to the unknown Joseph Lane have remembered the American Civil War. They remembered the defeat and capture of Black soldiers and civilians, the suffering of slaves, civilians, and soldiers, and the triumph of battle as soldiers in the US Colored Troops, rescuers, liberators, freedom fighters, heroes, and heroines. In defeat and triumph, capture and freedom, African Americans remembered their ancestors as soldiers, citizens, contrabands, and slaves, the full array of Black peoples' Civil War experiences.

To hear the Black Civil War veterans, widows, descendants, and community members' voices, we have to look beyond the traditional archives. Throughout the US, approximately 83,000 Civil War veterans applied for military pensions in which they, their widows and dependents, and neighbors testified in their pension files about their military service. But over 100,000 Black men who served in the US Army during the Civil War did not receive pensions. Few left diaries or journals, letters or speeches, or other such written documents, though some of the Black Civil War veterans wrote songs, anthems and dirges, and poetry. Thus, privileging written sources limits what we know about the lives, events, places, and moments in time in the African Diaspora and on the African continent.

Many more told their stories the best and sometimes only ways they knew how, in the places where they safely could and which they knew best, and to those who were closest to them: on their porches to their family members, in their churches, in the curricula of segregated schools, and in their newsletters and journals, clubs, military organizations, mutual aid societies, and fraternal organizations. In order to see how Black people have remembered and commemorated the diversity of their Civil War experiences, the archive must be expanded and the "porch archives" collected, valued, interpreted, and preserved. Since the deaths of the generations who were born enslaved and experienced the Civil War, Black women have played very important roles in these critical processes, remembering, preserving, teaching, and disseminating Black Civil War memories. In the late twentieth and early twenty-first centuries, historical re-enactors have embodied Black Civil War experiences and memories.

We need to hear the voices of African Americans who experienced the Civil War to counter the Lost Cause fantasies about the institution of enslavement during the antebellum period, amnesia about Black men's military service during the Civil War, and falsehoods of heritage, not hate with African Americans' own heritage of freedom and history of sacrifice. Despite the inherent diversity within the African American community, Black people were violently and unanimously condemned when they told the stories of their and their ancestors' Civil War experiences in the public sphere. But they were united on the understanding that their Won Cause was not a Lost Cause; they were not victims; their ancestors as soldiers and citizens struggled, fought valiantly for freedom. Despite the inherent diversity of the African American community, Black folks agreed that people who were born enslaved and experienced the Civil War were heroes and heroines, living monuments of our forebearers' torture, oppression, and survival. Their stories tell the world there were no "happy slaves" and all enslaved people wanted to be free. They risked their lives and took advantage of any opportunity to seize their freedom and then risked their own freedom, their very lives so that other Black people who were still enslaved could also be free.

Black folks' efforts to honor our ancestors' Civil War experiences laid the cornerstone for broader public education, such as Negro History Month (which was first established by Dr. Carter G. Woodson in February 1926). We are all standing on their shoulders. Let their sacrifices not be in vain!

Unforgettable
Sacrifice

Porches

An Introduction

Now, if they come back, I'll tell you what to do,
We'll give them some grape, and canister too;
Let white and black all shoulder a gun,
And then, O Lord, won't we have some fun.
And now I'll bring this song to an end,
For I am always ready my services to lend,
And willing to aid, and my money to spend,
For that is what Father Abraham said.

—Joseph R. Winters, 1863

African American porches inspired this book.

I developed some of the questions surrounding the porch stories explored here when I was a young girl. Born in Boston, Massachusetts, in the late 1970s, I developed a deep appreciation of the Civil War and the role of African American soldiers' courage in creating a more inclusive society following the destruction of slavery. As a child, I became well acquainted with the Fifty-Fourth Massachusetts Regiment monument on the edge of the Boston Commons. I loved how the Black faces on the Augustus Saint-Gaudens bas-relief took on new dimensions when the shifting daylight uncovered some features while obscuring others. The gold top dome of the statehouse and the long walk up Beacon Hill always brought me joy. I knew that I would have the opportunity to see these proud Black men's faces marching forward in their Civil War fight for freedom, equality, and the destruction of slavery. Without their courage, I understood, even at a young age, that another world might have existed for me if they had never met the challenge demanded at times of war.

My family made annual pilgrimages to the rural border communities of south-central Pennsylvania and on occasion to the even longer drive to Charleston, South Carolina. Leaving the vibrant and diverse Boston area always felt like traveling to another time and place. My brothers and I experienced the cornfields, cows, and life in the rural Pennsylvania communities as well as the extreme heat, humidity, and Spanish-moss-laden oak trees dotting the Charleston lowcountry for one week each year respectively. My parents desired that we should know our familial roots by maintaining connections with a host of cousins, aunts, uncles, grandparents, and countless friends who constitute their network of individuals who influenced their lives. We toured the Gettysburg battlefield, regional museums, lowcountry plantations, slave markets, and other locales on the Civil War commemorative landscape. My passion for history, memory, and the Civil War flourished because I knew how it shaped both sides of my family in unique ways. As both free and enslaved, my family's roots were deeply intertwined with the nation's past and these communities. Thus, it was on two of these trips that this work's focus and major research question germinated.

On my maternal relatives' porches in Franklin County, Pennsylvania, my grandparents, great uncles, and other elders of the St. Paul African Methodist Episcopal Church shared the various stories of how the Black community survived the Civil War, the Confederate invasions, and the various migrations during and since the Civil War. Where children were seen and not heard, our role was clear. We were to listen and occasionally ask clarifying questions. They insisted that we knew and understood the family's antebellum free status and how some Black residents were stolen and enslaved during the Gettysburg Campaign. But never once could they answer my questions—what happened to the "stolen" ones? Did any of them return? In the process of writing this book, I discovered another Civil War ancestor who enlisted because of the "stolen ones," but the more colorful elements of his service (court-martial and subsequent imprisonment with a ball and chain) never trickled down to my mother, her siblings, or me in the stories shared by elder Franklin County residents.

In 1987, now ten years of age, I found myself on another porch in the Charleston lowcountry where a relative shared a newspaper clipping describing the chance discovery of a cemetery of twenty or so remains initially identified as members of the Fifty-Fourth Massachusetts (later correctly identified as predominantly members of the Fifty-Fifth Massachusetts regiment) during the construction on a Folly Beach, South Carolina, property. The next two years of family vacations saw the re-interment at the National Cemetery in Beaufort, the release of the film *Glory*, and the devastating effects of Hurricane Hugo. Yet this initial clipping and the many adult conversations circulating around me on the restoration of the CSS *Hunley*, national reception of the film *Glory*, and reburial process raised additional questions over the next two years of my family vacations—why were not these Black soldiers being discussed with the same passion as the *Hunley* crew? Why were they not buried in Charleston like the rediscovered Confederates?

With these questions filed away, I began my academic journey with the intent of eventually seeking answers to these lingering questions. I developed the language, methodologies, and knowledge for later exploration as well as heard more African Americans share their Civil War histories on their respective porches. Four years at Franklin and Marshall College in Lancaster, Pennsylvania, introduced me to other Black communities whose shared memory and material culture demonstrated the rich intra-racial diversity of Civil War memory. Two years in the MA program at Tufts University led me to David Blight's *Race and Reunion* as well as the then new *Valley of the Shadow* digital humanities project where I found my first sources that confirmed Pennsylvania family lore. When I had completed my graduate career at Chapel Hill and subsequently started my first tenure-track position at Elizabeth City State University, a public HBCU in northeastern North Carolina, I developed additional questions. The period also saw my increasing frustration at the dearth of Civil War memory studies that acknowledged the diversity of Black experience (let alone bothered to consider Black memory as more than counter-memory). Consequently, the field turned the richness of Black Civil War memory and the individuals essential to shaping collective memory into caricatures. Contrary to claims made in several conferences and social media posts, the study of Civil War memory is not dead. African American memory makes clear that the field has a long way to go. Indeed, the field has a race problem. We must reckon with the field of Civil War memory's racial origins, complex history, and persistent legacies. We must be intentional, precise, and self-reflexive.

African American porches serve as the entry point for Black Civil War memory. These African American oral traditions and subsequent archival research reveal the necessity of recovering and amplifying memories that have been ignored by scholars. Joseph R. Winters's haunting lyrical songs of the Gettysburg invasion (as in the epigraph to this chapter),[1] Bishop Henry McNeal Turner's biting commentary over the use of exclusionary Reconciliationist rhetoric at the expense of franchised African Americans, and William Howard Day's powerful oratory should be included in every Civil War history; however, these men, who left a rich archival record, are not included in Civil War history narratives. Words matter. Listening to their voices deepens our understanding of Black leaders who attempted to place into words the range of emotions and experiences defining their respective community's collective memory of the Civil War. Frederick Douglass's presence often eclipses these lesser-known Black male leaders; therefore, for many scholars, Douglass becomes the default Black perspective on the meaning of the Civil War. And although Douglass helped shape Black Civil War Memory, he is far from the only one. Rural communities and small urban centers serve as important loci of memory as do New York, Philadelphia, Richmond, and Washington, DC.

Most important, the diversity of the Black communities requires an intersectional approach.[2] By taking seriously the intersections of race, class, gender, and place, the voices of women come to the fore. See, for example, Priscilla Marshall who reunited with two of her stolen children after the Civil War. It also reveals the ways in which Perquimans County, North Carolina, women's networks contributed to the persistence of memory. For these women, we cannot merely look toward traditional Civil War organizations, such as the Woman's Relief Corps. Instead, we need to look at clubwomen and the women's auxiliary groups of several fraternal organizations. We also need to look at women who advanced Civil War memory within the twentieth-century Black History Movement.

Moreover, we, as practitioners of history, must be interdisciplinary. Class dynamics reveal a commemorative landscape that was simultaneously created but also constrained in the public forms of Black collective memory. We must move beyond monuments. While monuments proved too costly, Black communities embraced photography, song sheets, and parades. These visual and material cultural sources require a more expansive approach for understanding Black Civil War memory as more than counter-memory. We need to look at African American memory making on its own terms. African Americans prioritized their communities and raising the next generations. This explains the survival of oral traditions within segregated spaces as well as the disdain by some present-day African Americans for professional historians for ignoring their family and communal remembrances.

Civil War memory, therefore, has many years of scholarship that is yet to be written. By expanding the archive and ways of examining sources, the current scholarly Black Civil War memory categories may become as nuanced as those employed for understanding white Civil War memory. The tapestry of African American experiences and postwar remembrances demand such scholarly attention. *Unforgettable Sacrifice* is one attempt to understand everyday African Americans' memory of the Civil War from its wartime origins to the present.

The central question that I ask is the following: What are the various ways African Americans have remembered and commemorated the American Civil

War and its legacy? African Americans experienced the war as enslaved and free, but also as soldier, contraband, refugee, and/or civilian in both the United States and the Confederate States of America. As a result, geographic place, status before the war, gender, and wartime experience produced a rich tapestry of collective memories that are not neatly encapsulated within the traditional Civil War memory categories. Rather, the highlighted communities demonstrate the diverse commemorative traditions, commonalities, and evolution of Civil War memory among everyday African Americans. *Unforgettable Sacrifice* argues that African Americans, whether nationally, regionally, and/or locally, sought to preserve a more complex past that honored the service and sacrifice of veterans, the diverse wartime civilian experiences, and the destruction of slavery to advance communal notions of patriotism, democracy, and their full inclusion as American citizens.

Unforgettable Sacrifice expands existing Civil War Memory scholarship by embracing diverse African Americans as the preservers of memory and not merely the victims of the Lost Cause and Reconciliationist understandings of the Civil War. David Blight's *Race and Reunion* remains an essential text for transforming previous understandings of how Americans remembered the Civil War. He showed how a national memory based on the reconciliation of white Americans triumphed over the pro-Southern Lost Cause and the largely African American–supported Emancipationist traditions in the fifty years following the war's end. Blight concluded that reunion and the Reconciliationist impulse came at the expense of African Americans. Despite reunion, Blight also maintained that African Americans held onto an Emancipationist version of the Civil War that celebrated a war for freedom and equality; however, his limited chronology obscures the ways in which they did.

Subsequent scholars have refined and substantiated Blight's conclusions. Some have explored the role of white women, class dimensions, and the African American preservation of memory of slavery and emancipation in segregated institutions destroyed by urban renewal.[3] Some have shown the fluidity within each category.[4] Collectively, these works demonstrate the dynamism of white Civil War memory but also reveal in stark relief the treatment in African American memory. While race and its intersections with gender, class, and place are included in many of these works, African American memory is often presented as an underdeveloped counterpoint to dominant white memories that lost in the cultural wars to the Lost Cause and Reconciliation traditions.[5]

The post–*Race and Reunion* expansion of the Black Civil War memory to include the Won Cause is an exception. Barbara Gannon coined the term after reading Black newspapers that demonstrated that African Americans were more than an afterthought to the construction of Northern Union memory.[6] She showed how Black veterans and their auxiliary units' participation in Black-only and integrated units of the Grand Army of the Republic (GAR) reinforced both institutional and respective members' memory of interracial comradeship, the destruction of slavery, and veterans' wartime sacrifice in the victorious federal effort. Gannon's notion of the Won Cause better captures Black Northerners who do not neatly fit the Emancipationist category. It also creates space for understanding how Black women, children, and other community members played a role in veterans' organizations and activities. *Unforgettable Sacrifice* focuses on African Americans and their construction and preservation of memory using analytical categories established by Blight and Gannon as the bookends, but also showcases the spectrum of Civil War remembrance within diverse Black communities.

Unforgettable Sacrifice also contributes to the work of Black scholars and their allies who never forgot the contributions of United States Colored Troops (USCT) soldiers, and the collective memories established by the Civil War–era generation. These remembrances formed the basis of the public countermemory. The published scholarship written by Joseph T. Wilson, Luis F. Emilio, and William Wells Brown engaged in early public Civil War cultural wars. They actively fought against erasure even from the constructed official record.[7] The *OR*, the abbreviation for *The War of the Rebellion: The Official Records of the Union and Confederate Armies*, and its dissemination had a role in reconciliation.[8] Ex-Confederate General Jubal Early and others were co-conspirators in the project to reconcile lingering Civil War feelings. They willingly accepted white supremacist lies and myths of faithful slaves and Black Confederates.[9] However, Black Civil War veterans and early historians were either ignored or dismissed as being biased or unqualified to be trusted as authentic preservationists of the past.

Later academic scholars, specifically W .E. B. Du Bois and Carter G. Woodson, received their foundational beginnings in the porch archives of their relatives and other members of the Civil War generation in their overlapping communities.[10] Over the twentieth and early twenty-first centuries, Black women have taken up the charge. Some even expanded beyond the traditional North–South binary.[11] While not always focused on the Civil War itself, African American porches, storytelling, and communal archival practices served as important sources of Black knowledge and remembrances purposefully forgotten by academic historians wedded to whiteness as the source of expertise and knowledge production of how the Civil War has been remembered by Americans more broadly. For scholars who have been exposed to these Black sites of memory, the noise of the traditional archives used in our work cannot be easily ignored.[12]

In serving as a corrective to a body of literature that marginalized the African American experience, several scholars revealed the everyday ways by which African Americans employed memory to advance individual as well as communal notions of freedom, citizenship, and a postwar identity distant from their slave past. Some explored African Americans' active participation in assigning meaning to slavery and its destruction through parades, family reunification, and tourism.[13] Others showed how African Americans, primarily Southerners, created and sustained a counter-memory that facilitated their perseverance, activism, and a more positive remembrance of the Civil War and Reconstruction eras.[14]

Unforgettable Sacrifice builds on this scholarship by engaging with the origins, parameters, and evolution of Black Civil War memory. It intentionally recognizes the role of place, wartime experience, gender, and antebellum status in shaping collective memories over time and space. Collectively, African American alternative public spaces, whether the porch, church, or segregated classroom, served as important spheres of African American Civil War commemorative culture. By refusing to forget, everyday African Americans rejected local, regional, and at times, national impulses encouraging them to accept white understandings of the Civil War and their racial subordination in the politicized Civil War commemorative landscape. For African Americans, whether in south-central Pennsylvania or the Charleston, South Carolina, lowcountry, remembrance was simultaneously political, an act of survival, and a source of resilience in shaping a more just nation. Operating outside the white gaze, Black Civil War memory developed into a distinct commemorative culture with its own traditions, rituals, and community-based archives that persisted into the twenty-first century. It was more than counter-memory.

Much of the surviving porch archives remains outside of mainstream Civil War memory scholars' gaze. This traditional archival void, however, does not prevent the recovery process. Oral traditions thrived on porches, at reunions and other events celebrating Black history and commemorative culture. In recent years, digital humanities and revised post–Civil Rights Movement archival practices have made accessible carefully created community archives previously stored in families' and Black institutional attics, basements, and storage rooms. The Works Progress Administration slave narratives and other formal oral history projects have captured some of these porch archives but do not represent the totality of Black Civil War remembrances.

With the exception of Chapter 5, this book draws on porch archives for the entry point into the diverse communities explored. A double standard has existed for scholars and Civil War enthusiasts. Few question the veracity of sources or even the constructed nature of the *OR* and other archives for understanding the origins and evolution of the Lost Cause, Reconciliation, and white federal Civil War memory.[15] Sources of Black epistemology and cultural knowledge, however, have been routinely dismissed as false and illegitimate by white scholars. I treat Black porch archives as legitimate and authentic sources of communal Civil War understandings.

I also mined traditional archives for sources produced by African Americans for substantiating and clarifying gaps of remembrance. Black newspapers yielded the diversity of opinions, activities, and organizational efforts. These invaluable publications show how racism informed but not necessarily defined African Americans' efforts to remember and deploy Civil War memory in their everyday lives and politics. Advances in digital humanities has eased the recovery process.

In addition, close reading of written, visual, and sonic sources demonstrated how Black communities created both the mental and bodily muscle memory for sustaining Civil War memory. These sensory cues and ritual performances become important for communities intentionally rendered invisible. By embracing all senses, Black communities cultivated the traditions that promoted Civil War remembrance as a source of empowerment and resilience in the long struggle for citizenship.

Sound and its absence matters. Songs and poetry become more than written texts for simple literary analysis. The singing of songs could unite Black men into a voting bloc while also serving as aural resistance to monuments. The recitation of poems at events gave children, women, and nonveterans opportunities to contribute. The diverse Black commemorative soundscape also includes marching feet and windblown banners on parade routes. It not only includes the spontaneous applause during public addresses but also the collective struggle in mastering the shift in the low-high vocal range of the Black National Anthem. Silence and the absence of sound reveal how Black communities coped with trauma and protested the intentional collective forgetting. Instead of complicity, their silence often served as a survival tactic until the late twentieth century.

Black Civil War memory also engaged other senses. Photography, postcards, and ephemera reveal an alternative archive where the visual culture mattered in countering the anti-Black archival practices associated with white Civil War remembrance. The materiality of uniforms, scrapbooks, and other objects engaged touch as part of the embodied memory process. Monument-making in segregated cemeteries represented the geographies of counter-memory. The smells of post–Memorial Day picnics and family reunions as well as the taste of iced tea served on porches are also considered to be part of the process in which Black communities remembered the Civil War over generations.

Unforgettable Sacrifice adds precision to how ordinary African Americans encountered, influenced, and upended popular and historical Civil War commemorative traditions and landscapes. It connects emancipated Southerners with rural Black Pennsylvanians whose lived experiences shaped initial traditions and the intergenerational modern turn to audiovisual technologies and academic historians as Civil War remembrances pushed into the twentieth century. Drawing on these early efforts, African American beneficiaries engaged in the long political struggle over memory and meaningful inclusion in the American body politic.[16]

The work's significance is not merely for the academic scholars and historians of Civil War memory. The ways that scholars, including myself, have discussed Civil War memory still have consequences. Following the 2015 Charleston Massacre, Americans renewed debate over the Civil War commemorative landscape.[17] Some Confederate monuments received new interpretative panels. Others were removed. New African American sites of memory, notably the Reconstruction Era National Monument in Beaufort, South Carolina, opened.[18] These debates and modest commemorative changes led to the violent 2017 Unite the Right rally in Charlottesville, Virginia.[19] Amid these renewed debates, the lack of inclusion of diverse scholarly Black voices rendered visible the disconnect between scholars and African Americans desiring more nuanced understandings of Civil War memory. Instead of historians, these communities turned to Ta-Nehisi Coates for commentary. The past still informs the present.[20]

By treating Black Civil War memory as a dynamic and complex process, *Unforgettable Sacrifice* strives to make the scholarly field relevant for a twenty-first-century African American reading public and their allies whose education did not include this history. It is for individuals who took Black Studies courses while in college and kept their reading materials for circulation among their family and friends. It is for the family genealogists, community archivists, and local historians who sustained Civil War memory outside of the historical profession. Last, and more important, this book is for African American descendant communities of the Civil War generation, including my own. This book investigates these historical experiences and struggles over time and space.

This book embraces an organization that might seem jarring to some readers familiar with traditional Civil War memory scholarship. Each chapter explores a different community whose memory work does not follow a straightforward chronology. Scholars who have focused primarily on the intellectual architects, organizations, and archives of white federal, reconciliation, or Lost Cause proponents are not accustomed to the way Black communities' memory and commemorative landscapes operate. At times, Black commemorative work shared a common language, chronology, and commemorative calendar. Quite often, however, Black communities' conceptions of time and clear connections to regional or national trends lack easy categorization. Indeed, Black Civil War memory is a fluid, complex, regional, and gendered social process that simultaneously has political implications for diverse African American communities who collectively refused to accept whitewashed narratives of the Civil War.[21]

Organized into three sections, readers will find interspersed three different Porch Lessons. The Porch Lessons reveal how the personal is political. They serve not only as love letters to my family and community kinkeepers who inspired this work but how I listened to their insistent demands to be heard by the profession. The first Porch Lesson explores my Civil War ancestor Joseph Lane's world that included the communities explored in Part I. As a member of the Twenty-Second USCT, he was one of the many Black soldiers who entered Richmond, Virginia, in April 1865. His daughters' unique memory work shared the same impulses and goals of the Black women discussed in Part II. By connecting several generations of Lane descendants, I hope to reveal the methodological challenges of recovery and the ethics of care involved in doing this work. The last set of Porch Lessons focuses on my own education as a student of the post-*Roots* cultural renaissance. This informal education influenced my understanding of events witnessed as a child as well as several relatives' memory work in the Charleston, South Carolina, lowcountry.

Some readers might desire reading the loosely interconnected chapters traditionally. Some might want to read the Porch Lessons first before moving through the various chapters. For members of the highlighted communities, I give you permission to start with your community before reading the other chapters.

The four chapters of Part I draw upon the porches of my mothers' kinkeepers in south-central Pennsylvania.[22] Chapter 1 explores how a Confederate military policy of enslaving freeborn African Americans shaped the memory of the Gettysburg Campaign and two other raids in Franklin County. For Pennsylvania border residents, the enslavement of Black Pennsylvanians left scars that could not be easily forgotten. Thus, they developed a collective memory that acknowledged the Pennsylvanians forcibly removed, the trauma experienced by the civilians who remained, and regional-specific narratives of Black military enlistment. Moving to the state capital, Chapter 2 explores the November 1865 Grand Reception for returning Black soldiers in Harrisburg, Pennsylvania. From the parade to speeches, Garnet League members and Black Pennsylvanians challenged the all-white May 1865 Review of Armies by hosting their own event. Collective memories of the ongoing racism and the November reception shaped subsequent demands for equality, the franchise, and recognition of the Civil War liberators. Consequently, the acknowledgment of Black military service and sacrifice became an essential component of how Pennsylvanians commemorated the Civil War well into the twenty-first century.

Returning to Franklin County, Pennsylvania, Chapter 3 examines how Joseph Winters and rural Black Pennsylvanian men politicized Civil War memory. By harnessing memory of the Gettysburg Campaign, Winters's political activities and presidential campaign songwriting ensured that Franklin County men retained their unique Civil War experience as the point of entry for shaping the local, state, and national post–Fifteenth Amendment political landscape. Spanning both sides of the Pennsylvania-Maryland border, Chapter 4 explores how Black veterans cultivated the Won Cause tradition in the Cumberland Valley. Though small in numbers, these veterans marshaled their Grand Army of the Republic status into a tool of liberation. They established new traditions and leisure practices in the region. They also created another pathway into African American leadership for subsequent generations of war veterans.

The chapters in Part II draw specifically on the literal and figurative porches of communities who adopted me as kin. These kinkeepers (sometimes known as family by choice or fictive kin) show how African American memories of the Civil War survived independently in community-based spaces.[23] Chapter 5 explores Black Richmonders' attempts to define the memory of emancipation in the city, state, region, and nation through Emancipation Celebrations in 1866, 1890, and 1915. Throughout these events, Black Richmonders' diminishing power in shaping Civil War memory reflected the limits of the emancipationist category. Chapter 6 explores the critical role of Black women's memory work within their overlapping familial, religious, and professional educational networks. Whether writing a newspaper serial column, teaching the next generation, or erecting monuments, these women promoted a usable Civil War past that emphasized African American agency, achievements, and sacrifice. In the process, they empowered subsequent generations to draw on the Civil War memory in the continued struggle for civil and political rights over the twentieth century. Several late twentieth-century developments revealed the legacy of their work.

The chapters in Part III shift to the porches of my father's kinkeepers in the Charleston, South Carolina, lowcountry and events witnessed by the author. Chapter 7 examines how the rediscovery of a USCT cemetery on Folly Beach, South Carolina, and the cinematic release of *Glory* introduced new diverse audiences to African American Civil War military service. Both events encouraged the growth of a Black reenactment community which helped in dislodging the hegemony of Lost Cause understandings that had defined the region's past since the Jim Crow era. Civil War memory was no longer confined to segregated Black spaces. Chapter 8 takes seriously a Black USCT reenactor's bold prediction of a significant African American presence and meaningful incorporation of Black Civil War memory in the sesquicentennial Civil War commemoration by examining the debates and responses to four specific events— the Secession Ball, Fort Sumter, Battle of Fort Wagner, and Nat Fuller's Feast of 1865. While organizers sought redemption from the specter of the centennial, some challenged the neo-Reconciliation affair; however, their responses never fully dislodged the conscious embrace of more truthful understandings of the Civil War and its immediate aftermath. Ultimately, the murder of nine African Americans cemented the sesquicentennial celebration into more than a footnote in the city and nation.

After a brief conclusion, the epilogue explores the author's personal efforts to understand how the University of Alabama (UA) both remembered and disremembered the role of the enslaved Drum Corps and other enslaved people who labored at the institution during the Civil War era. By encouraging remembrance, the Hallowed Grounds tour disrupted campus narratives that did not fully engage the history of enslaved Civil War laborers, emancipation, and slavery's afterlives. The alternate campus tour offered a forum to reconcile UA's past with its diverse campus community.

Since I am a descendant of a Twenty-Second USCT veteran, a member of several communities, and a professional historian, this book is more than a personal exploration of a struggle for an "intergenerational self" desired by my parents and other family members by blood and by choice.[24] Rather, African American family and community histories, including my own, have largely existed "below and beyond the radar of professional scholarship."[25] These histories, however, offered a powerful catharsis for those African Americans of the Civil War era, their respective communities, and their descendants. By considering family histories, porch archives, and their overlapping community histories, this book is an attempt to move toward repair for those families and communities who fought to have their Civil War memories heard. In short, this work details the efforts of those engaged in the act of "re-membering—in piecing together the fragments left—and in reconciling" the Civil War.[26]

The remaining pages showcase the men, women, and children who fought against erasure through remembrance. They sustained oral traditions, created community and familial archives, and performed rituals of remembrance from parading to singing the Black national anthem. They countered anti–Black Civil War commemorative cultures and contradictions whenever necessary. Many summarily dismissed a distinct minority of African Americans whose racial performances contributed to the persistence of racial fantasies promoted by white adherents of the Lost Cause and Reconciliationist traditions. Defying the real and rhetorical threats to both community and personhood, they developed and sustained a complex African American commemorative culture that persisted into the twenty-first century. We, therefore, should disrupt the intentional silencing of their efforts and voices. We must listen to their demands for recognition of sacrifice, service, and patriotism from the depths of archival voids. They matter. The resulting commemorative culture should be understood not in terms of opposition to the traditional white Civil War commemorative traditions, but as its own distinct and foundational commemorative tradition bookended by the Emancipationist and Won Cause traditions.

As a scholar, I am the product of these underappreciated efforts of ordinary African Americans who did extraordinary things because they chose to remember the Civil War in a manner that has not been fully explored. Their names, experiences, commemorative traditions, and embrace of porches have been excavated from the margins and amplified over the pages to come. We, in the present, must tend to the Civil War memories that proved to be unforgettable by African Americans. Remembrance became their personal and communal politics.

I

PORCHES OF MY
MOTHER'S KINKEEPERS

Yes, the Blacks enjoy their freedom,
And they won it dearly, too;
For the life blood of their thousands
Did the southern fields bedew.
In the darkness of their bondage,
In the depths of slavery's night;
Their muskets flashed the dawning
And they fought their way to light.
They were comrades then and brothers,
Are they more or less to-day?
They were good to stop a bullet
And to front the fearful fray.
They were citizens and soldiers,
When rebellion raised its head;
And the traits that made them worthy,—
Ah! those virtues are not dead.

—PAUL LAURENCE DUNBAR, "THE COLORED
SOLDIERS," 1895, IN AFRICAN AMERICAN POETRY (1870–1927)

1   Remembering the Enslavement of Black Pennsylvanians

Corporal Samuel Nickless wrote and dedicated "The New Version of the Colored Volunteer" as a regimental song for the Twenty-Fourth United States Colored Troops (USCT). The Black Philadelphian had enlisted into the regiment as a private and rose through the ranks before penning the song.[1] Even though regimental songs were no longer in vogue among white troops, Nickless chose the tune of "The Bonnie Blue Flag," a popular Confederate song, rather than the popular Union anthems of "The Battle Cry of Freedom" or "John Brown's Body."[2] Both regimental members and Black Pennsylvanian audiences would have recognized Nickless's melodic intent with the following fourth verse and chorus:

> When the Rebels made a dashing raid into our noble State,
> We all became impatient, and for orders did not wait,
> But went unto the Governor, and took him unawares,
> For he did not know he'd find so many Colored volunteers.
> Give us the flag, all free without one slave,
> And we will defend it as fathers did so brave,
> Onward! boys, onward! it's the year of Jubilee,
> God bless America, the land of Liberty.[3]

When the free Black barber turned soldier composed the song, he paid homage to the events surrounding the creation of the regiment organized at Camp William Penn, Philadelphia, Pennsylvania. In mid-June 1863, Confederate troops crossed the Mason-Dixon line and waged warfare in the center part of the state without much resistance. They plundered communities for horses, material goods, and most significantly, free Black Pennsylvanians. Even as Governor Andrew G. Curtin requested volunteers, state enlistment policies thwarted Nickless and other Black Philadelphians who attempted to answer the call but were turned away for defense of the state.[4] Hamstrung by race, Nickless and other would-be defenders returned to their homes and stood by as Confederate raiders

seized an undetermined number of Black civilians in and surrounding Franklin County. Memory of these events weighed heavily in the minds of white and
Black Pennsylvanians in the organization of Camp William Penn. Through his
deliberate choice of melody, Nickless reclaimed and transformed "The Bonnie
Blue Flag" from a song of occupation, enslavement, and civilian trauma into one
of Black liberation and martial manhood.[5]

Black Franklin County residents would have recognized and found solace
in Nickless's regimental song. The seizure and enslavement of free and self-
emancipated African Americans represented a major aspect of the Gettysburg
Campaign, the second of three Confederate raids into the border Pennsylvania county.[6] The policy of "gathering up" African American men, women, and
children exposed their vulnerability. The policy also revealed local, state, and
federal government officials' inability to prevent such acts. Camp William Penn
represented a bittersweet yet positive development as a result of the shared suffering experienced. For others, the forced removal and enslavement contributed
to massive dislocation in the county as many fled for safety. Hence, Franklin
County residents collectively remembered the strong emotions associated with
loss, forced separation, and military occupation. Whereas seizures occurred
during the 1862 J. E. B. Stuart raid and the 1864 burning of the county seat, the
Gettysburg Campaign represented the largest number of individuals taken and
enslaved.[7] Rescue attempts proved futile. As their removal became permanent
losses, the effects reverberated throughout Franklin County. Memories of this
civilian trauma influenced African American military enlistment, reunification
efforts, the postwar commemorative landscape, and postwar African American
remembrances. Throughout, Black Franklin County residents fought against the
silencing of their Civil War memories that recognized the civilian trauma, enslaved Pennsylvanians, and soldiers.

Using contemporary accounts of white and Black Franklin County residents,
newspaper coverage, reunification attempts and early commemorations, this
chapter explores the effects of Confederate military policy in shaping collective
memory in the border community. The experiences and memory of rural Black
Franklin County residents reveal the importance of the intersections of place,
status before war, gender, and wartime experience in producing a collective
memory of the Civil War that is not neatly encapsulated within the traditional
scholarly categories. While national reconciliation impulses later silenced the
localized remembrance, the Gettysburg Campaign and seizure of free and self-
liberated African Americans marked a watershed moment. For Black Franklin
County residents, these African Americans remained stolen but not forgotten.

As a result, they embraced a complex collective memory of the Civil War that acknowledged African Americans removed and enslaved during the raids, the trauma experienced by the civilians who remained, and the individuals who eventually served in the US Army and Navy. Whether in songs, reunification efforts, parades, and oral traditions, Black Franklin County residents fought a dual war—one for the liberation of all African Americans and another over the memory of the stolen ones. They demanded recognition of their complex Civil War memory and subsequent inclusion as full citizens.

In the days before the Battle of Gettysburg, General Albert G. Jenkins's arrival ushered a wave of vulnerability and helplessness among white and Black Franklin County residents. Jenkins and his men began the massive search and seizure of free Blacks and self-emancipated persons on June 15, 1863. For over two weeks, Jenkins became one of many Confederate officers and soldiers who reduced Black residents to enslaved captives and white residents to bystanders throughout the county.[8] Major Charles Blacknell of the Twenty-Third North Carolina Infantry recounted the process in a letter to his brother about his exploits in Williamsport, Maryland, and Greencastle and Chambersburg, Pennsylvania: "We have also captured thousands of horses and many hundred slaves. I have several negroes, free and slave, in my hands but negroes are worth nothing at all. No kind of negroes will sell for more than one hundred dollars."[9] Though low return on the yield, Blacknell and others continued the practice as citizens remained "shut up in their houses and frightened nearly to death."[10]

Moreover, several Confederate and Union occupied Southern newspapers acknowledged the practice. Some newspapers distinguished these captured African American civilians by using the terms "contrabands" or "runaway slaves" instead of using the term "prisoners," commonly associated with the white civilians taken by Confederate troops.[11] The Daily Picayune, the Union-occupied New Orleans newspaper, went further than most Southern newspapers when it reprinted a letter written by a Chambersburg resident. The July 10, 1863, article noted, "Free negroes were seized as eagerly as contrabands, and those parts of the town where blacks live, were left to the hands of the spoiler."[12] Indiscriminately seizing men, women, and children of "four or five years old and upward," Confederate troops "rode off 'toward the Carolinas and southwardly'" with their bounty as the seized African Americans "bade farewell to liberty."[13] These contemporary accounts are essential for understanding the collective memory established in Franklin County. Both wartime participants and later supporters of the Lost Cause purposely forgot this publicly acknowledged practice and inadvertently contributed to the development of a localized collective memory shared by Black and white Franklin County residents. Residents actively remembered Gettysburg and the other raids for the civilians removed and enslaved. They also promoted accounts deemed as true and legitimate of their civilian experiences while dismissing ones that did not acknowledge their shared trauma.

Rachel Cormany and her diary offer a window into the seizure and enslavement of Black residents and contrabands in Chambersburg. Cormany, the Canadian-born wife of Samuel Cormany, vividly described the frantic pre-arrival of contrabands and refugees, seizures, and military occupation over the course of several diary entries. In the June 16, 1863, entry, she wrote that the Confederates

> were hunting up the contrabands and driving them off by droves. O! How it grated on our hearts to have to sit quietly and look at such brutal deeds—I saw no men among the contrabands—all women and children. Some of the colored people who were raised here were taken along—I sat on the front step as they were driven by just like we would drive cattle. Some laughed and seemed not to care—but nearly all hung their heads.[14]

Throughout, the raiders reduced Cormany to the role of a helpless spectator unable to prevent the seizure of Black townspeople and refugees. With her own husband serving as an officer in the Sixteenth Pennsylvania Cavalry, she could not have effectively mounted any resistance. She might have pleaded with the raiders. However, overwhelming fear drove her inaction and private contemplations in her diary. Her feelings of pain and vulnerability were equally echoed in the surviving journal accounts of Philip Schaff and Rev. Thomas Creigh on the effects of the raiders in Mercersburg.[15]

In a few instances, several white civic leaders and residents moved beyond inaction and actively attempted to rescue the seized Black residents and refugees. Often pleading with Confederate raiders, individuals attempted to prevent their removal. Mrs. Jemima Cree tried to stop the seizure of her servants Mag and Fannie but to no avail.[16] Jacob Hoke also met a similar outcome when he intervened on the behalf of two neighbors in Greencastle.[17] Fueled by anger, armed Greencastle residents rescued thirty to forty women and children from their Confederate captors on rear guard duty.[18] Benjamin S. Schneck, a prominent Reformed Church theologian, would have a distinct place in the shared collective memory for successfully negotiating the return of Esque Hall, Henry Dietrick, and Samuel Claudy.[19] While Hall was a longtime county resident, Dietrick and

Claudy worked for the Cumberland Valley Railroad as repairmen. Schneck appealed directly to Jenkins at his headquarters and secured their release.[20]

African American residents' reports emerged only when the perceived threat to their freedom abated. Many free Black residents sought refuge in the various secured locales throughout the area Underground Railroad network, including ones in and near Little Africa located in the western mountainous edge of the county.[21] Joseph R. Winters offers valuable insights on the African American experience. Winters was born free in Leesburg, Virginia, in 1816 to an African American bricklayer and a Native American mother. His grandmother, a Native American medical healer, raised him in Waterford, Virginia, while his parents labored as migrant workers. In the 1840s, his entire family relocated to Chambersburg, where he eventually became active in the Underground Railroad.[22] Winters escaped seizure by using the same caverns previously used for hiding antebellum enslaved freedom seekers. He composed the song titled "About Ten Days after the Battle of Gettysburg" in order to tell his experience.[23]

Winters refused to allow others to speak his truth. His song sheet serves as important cultural artifact for understanding African American residents' collective Civil War memory. Like the white Franklin County diarists, Winters detailed the occupation of Chambersburg and the seizure of material goods. See the third and fourth stanzas of his song:

In Chambersburg he took a stand
And sent out the scouts to scour the land;
The railroad track he did tear up,
Likewise tore down the railroad shop.
The stores they plundered, that you know,
For that they do wherever they go;
They bought their goods with Southern trash,
And that they got by the Southern lash.[24]

Winters shared his feelings of disgust toward the Confederate occupiers. These dishonorable Confederate soldiers employed force and destruction on a civilian population. Winters dismissed the payment of goods with Confederate currency or "Southern trash."[25] The guise of payment did not mask the destructive nature and trauma inflicted. In these stanzas Winters expressed the rage felt by survivors.

Winters then recounted the chaos experienced by free Black Pennsylvanians. They understood the threat to their freedom posed by the Confederate raiders.

Many simply fled. Winters noted their flight and efforts at concealment in the fifth stanza:

> The colored people all ran away,
> Likewise the composer of this song, they say—
> For if I hadn't, I don't know
> But I'd been in the South a'working the hoe.

The threat of "a'working the hoe" guided their actions. Rather than endure possible enslavement, they chose freedom. They hid until the military engagement at Gettysburg had ceased. As one Mercersburg resident later attested from his conversations with members of a Black Grand Army of the Republic post, "They knew what it was for them and their families to flee to the mountains or hide in cellars and garrets and caves for safety when Confederate soldiers raided the neighborhood."[26] For Winters, his song title signaled his own emergence after ten days. The threat of "a'working the hoe" proved too great. Sold as a song sheet, Winters gave voice to the Black experience unmediated by white Franklin County residents. These events deeply affected Winters and others who escaped seizure. Thus, this song sheet marked the emergence of Winters as an important contributor to the Black Franklin County collective memory and how Winters and other survivors used the collective memory of the Gettysburg Campaign for securing civil, political, and social rights from their wartime sacrifices after the Civil War. After Gettysburg, Winters regularly drew on his wartime experiences in crafting subsequent lyrical calls to action.[27]

Similarly, John Calimer passed down an oral historical account of his unique Gettysburg Campaign experience. The eighteen-year-old worked at the Caledonia Iron Company owned by Thaddeus Stevens. General Jubal Early and his calvary unit purposely targeted the site. According to a published oral history with his great-grandson, Calimer "jumped in a flour barrel."[28] However, a Confederate soldier quickly discovered him. He recounted that "a southern soldier came in and seen him in this barrel and went over and patted him on the head and told him, 'Come out the barrel, son. I'm not going to hurt you. We're not going to kill anybody.' So he got out of the barrel."[29] Yet the soldier did not carry him into slavery. This rare act of compassion does not negate the fact that three African American laborers were seized from Thaddeus Stevens's property by Confederate troops. In this instance, luck and compassion spared Calimer from enslavement. Oral traditions, though, afforded Calimer and other African American survivors with another venue for expressing their remembrances of the trauma experienced.[30]

Print media also documented the memories of African American men who liberated themselves from their military captors. Lewis Nelson, an itinerant minister on the Franklin County circuit, freed himself and relayed his ordeal to the *Franklin Repository*, a Republican newspaper published in Chambersburg.[31] Nelson and five individuals initially absconded to a wheat field following General Jenkins's arrival in the town. After several days, Confederate troops discovered and imprisoned them. Nelson's opportunity for freedom became apparent shortly after the commanding officer sent his men in search of other African Americans for seizure. According to the article,

> Our colored preacher thought it would be a good time now to achieve his liberty, and forthwith drew from his pocket a pistol and shot the officer, not inflicting however a dangerous wound. The two closed, and after a protracted tussel the negro succeeded in possessing himself of his enemy's carbine. By this time another of the Rebs had come up hot foot to the assistance of his comrade; but our black skinned hero raised his gun and said he'd shoot unless they'd promise to let him go. The promise was given with a "don't shoot Uncle," and away sped Lewis Nelson, with his trophy, glad and worthy of the freedom he had won by his own right hand.[32]

The bravery shown in this instance demonstrates how some refused to accept their possible enslavement. Nelson demonstrated the willingness to kill his captor in order to remain free. Rather than see him as a depraved individual, the *Franklin Repository* highlighted his heroism and the freedom "won by his own right hand."[33] Although few in number, these African American remembrances countered later depictions of victimization by showcasing the agency of African American men in their own liberation during the Gettysburg Campaign.

Others were not as fortunate. Neither negotiations nor armed rescues occurred for individuals like Alexander Lewis who was captured and enslaved in the kitchens of Castle Thunder, a Confederate military prison in Richmond, Virginia. Officials granted him parole in late March 1865. He eventually returned and secured employment at a Chambersburg hotel. A white Chambersburg resident later recalled his imprisonment at Castle Thunder and a chance meeting with "Alexander Lewis, a colored man, from this place, known to many of our citizens."[34] In addition to Lewis, historian Mark Neely Jr. also noted the imprisonment of other free Black Pennsylvanians at Castle Thunder as a direct consequence.[35] However, their fates remained unknown. The sights and sounds of men, women, and children left invisible scars on surviving Franklin County residents who were forced to bear witness to the abductions. As one poem published in the Greencastle *Pilot* expressed in the second verse: "The pris'nors, horses, negroes— all/ Are far away, beyond our call."[36] The sheer number of individuals whose fate remained unknown haunted the civilian survivors well after the Confederate defeat. The ghosts of those who remained "beyond our call" loomed over all later remembrances.[37]

Moreover, national newspapers amplified the civilian trauma endured by reprinting survivors' letters in their coverage of the Gettysburg Campaign. These letters detailed the indiscriminate seizure of African Americans. According to one letter published in the *Daily Alta California*, the author wrote:

> During their stay among us, all the negroes that could be found were carried off by them; even children of four years of age were carried behind the soldiers on their horses, their parents having to leave them and make their escape to the grain fields and other places of refuge. Free men and women of color, raised in our town, were driven before the cavalry like cattle, while little children astride the horses clung to their riders to retain their seats.[38]

The *Sacramento Daily Union* published another white eyewitness's letter detailing the raiders' gleeful attitude at inflicting pain and terror on the African Americans whom they rounded up in the county. The unknown author commented:

> During the afternoon the rebels amused themselves in stealing horses, picking up contrabands, and running down little darkies. Some scenes of an amusing character occurred. Others were most painful and humiliating. The terror of the poor negroes was intense. They could be seen fleeing in all directions, and concealing themselves in every suitable place. Many lay in wheat fields during the rebel visit, and were fed by the humanity of the farmers.[39]

Both authors sought to bring attention to county residents' immense suffering. As Confederate soldiers stole residents, horses, and material goods, local, state, and federal leadership as well as limited military defenses utterly failed. Neither residents nor readers could readily dismiss the events as they had done with the October 1862 raid by General J. E. B. Stuart. The white and Black hostages seized by Stuart and his brief occupation of Mercersburg paled in comparison for Dr. Philip Schaff and others who witnessed both events.[40] Schaff deemed the actions of the soldiers who "came to town on a regular slave hunt" as the "worst spectacle I ever saw in this war."[41] The Gettysburg Campaign revealed that the war was no longer confined to Southern battlefields but had reached Franklin County and much of southern Pennsylvania in a dramatic fashion.

The *Sun* elaborated on the immediate conditions experienced by the individuals removed. Confederate raiders "took with them when they left Chambersburg all the negroes which they had found there (the majority having fled towards Harrisburg) with the exception of two or three, who claimed that they had been set free by their masters."[42] The individuals were separated and confined based on potential threat level to their captors. While adults and teens were bound together in an "an extemporized coffle-gang," young children "were placed upon the horses which the rebels had stolen."[43] Though unspoken, residents as well as readers understood their fates as one of enslavement at an army camp, military prison, and/or private plantation in the Confederacy. It was not clear whether the seized individuals would experience a life of freedom again. As few returned to the county, it was most likely the last time that residents actually saw them.

Through these published accounts, many of the Black Franklin County men serving in the military learned about the raids, seizures, and individuals fleeing the county. Most had enlisted in regiments outside of the state as they were barred from enlisting in state regiments. At the time of the Gettysburg Campaign, Black Franklin County soldiers primarily served in the South Carolina lowcountry. They, like most other Northerners, read the accounts and immediately wrote to their remaining family for news. The absence of specific names in the published accounts prompted both worry and a sense of hopelessness. Mary Jane Demus, a Black Mercersburg resident, received letters from her husband and brother, both of whom served in the Fifty-Fourth Massachusetts Regiment. While her husband only inquired after her well-being, her brother expressed frustration at the lack of military protection during the Gettysburg Campaign and the later destruction of the town in 1864.[44] Her brother even intimated that Black soldiers, especially his regiment, would have done a better job in protecting civilians from the Confederate raiders.[45] However, distance and military orders regulated both men to spectators who relied on newspaper accounts and hope for their families and other Black civilians against seizure. In this regard, the helplessness experienced by Black soldiers mirrored that of white Franklin County civilians.

Following the experiences of the Gettysburg Campaign, Black military recruiters canvassed Franklin County. The raw memories of the seizures, helplessness, and reality of Confederate occupation made the work of Thomas Morris Chester quite easy. Though Chester, a USCT recruiter and *Philadelphia Press* correspondent, had recruited in Chambersburg, Mercersburg, and other Pennsylvania locales before the Gettysburg Campaign, he purposely traveled to Franklin County in late July 1863.[46] Upon arrival, he quickly found volunteers for the Fifty-Fourth and Fifty-Fifth Massachusetts Regiments in Greencastle, Mercersburg, and Chambersburg.[47] These impatient enlistees desired to be more active participants in the fight for their freedom. Hence, they refused to wait for the official organization and enlistment of USCT regiments in Pennsylvania.[48]

The experiences of the invasion and occupation swayed the governor toward the acceptance of Black draftees into USCT regiments organized in the state per General Orders 178. In the name of state defense, Governor Curtin called for 60,000 three-month volunteers in a mid-July 1863 proclamation, in which Franklin County had a quota for 840 individuals.[49] Too old to serve, Joseph Winters again turned to his pen and published "At the Time of the Draft for the Civil War."[50] As promised in the closing stanzas of his first Civil War song, Black Franklin County men would no longer remain potential victims or passive bystanders. Rather, they would fight in the USCT regiments.[51]

Like Frederick Douglass's "Men of Color, to Arms" address, Winters employed the recent Gettysburg Campaign memory in the recruitment song.[52] Therein, he criticized white Democrats' opposition to Black military enlistments. But he also chided potential soldiers to ignore the Copperheads and to prove their manhood: "About the Draft, you will make a heap of fuss; / But, to be drafted, that you must."[53] Furthermore, he implored them to think about their recent experience during the Gettysburg Campaign. Confederate raiders exposed the vulnerability of their very freedom and even resulted in the enslavement of community members. If they did not want to be social pariahs, the decision was simple—enlist. Or, as Winters espoused in the third verse:

> Dar is but one place ob which I know—
> And de old man wants some fire below;
> For if in dis war you don't want to fight,
> Go down dar and git out of sight.

His words were not mere bombast. African American men would prove their manhood by fighting back and not cowering in fear. Many paid heed. Winters even contributed a son to the war effort. Jacob Winters enlisted and served in Company D of the Twenty-Second USCT. The return of Amos Barnes, a free Black resident seized during the Gettysburg Campaign, boosted Winters's recruitment efforts.

In late December 1863, several local newspapers jubilantly announced Amos Barnes's return to Franklin County.[54] The *Franklin Repository* secured an interview with Barnes and provided the most detailed account of his experiences in its December 23, 1863, edition. According to the newspaper, Confederate soldiers seized and enslaved Barnes on July 2, 1863. He made the long trek to Richmond, Virginia, with other free and self-emancipated persons captured during the Gettysburg Campaign. Barnes labored around Castle Thunder and Camp Winder, a Confederate hospital, but escaped some of the harsh treatment common to the institution. The article noted: "He saw a number of free negroes tied up and flogged at different times; but he fortunately escaped by his adroitness and his successful efforts to please those who had charge of him."[55] After negotiations between white Mercersburg leadership, Rev. J. V. Moore of Richmond, and Confederate officials, Major J. H. Carrington released the "free negro, resident of Pennsylvania who was brought off by our troops" on account of a lack of "charges against him."[56] Moreover, Confederate officials made arrangements for his transfer on a "flag of Truce boat" in early December 1863.[57] Seen as an early Christmas present to a community still reeling from the effects of the Gettysburg Campaign, the newspaper coverage of Barnes's return and account of his brief enslavement became a powerful motivator for young Black men to become liberators of the enslaved individuals in the Confederacy and border Pennsylvanian communities.

Interestingly, Barnes's published account did not detail the circumstances resulting in his enslavement. This silence is revealing especially given the surviving Confederate documents pertaining to Barnes's seizure, enslavement, and release. Amos Barnes and another free African American aided Confederate troops under the command of Capt. John Hanson McNeill of the Eighteenth Virginia Calvary in the seizure process in exchange for maintaining their own freedom. Barnes and the other man "told them where they would find these runaways and piloted them to the place."[58] The two Black Pennsylvanians then accompanied the coffle of men, women, and children to Martinsburg, Virginia (now West Virginia), before their Confederate conspirators enslaved Barnes and his ally.[59] Barnes's collusion is understandable given the traumatic events of the Confederate invasion and occupation. This was the largest slave hunt seen in south-central Pennsylvania. Fear over the loss of freedom and the horrors of slavery caused many free Black Pennsylvanians to act in their own self-interest whether absconding in fields, barrels, and caverns and even aiding Confederate soldiers searching for African Americans. Such details, though, would not warrant a heroic return to Franklin County. Hence, Barnes and white leaders involved in his release purposely excluded this information in the newspaper coverage and shaped Barnes's place in the community's collective memory as a victim of Confederate military policy.

Nevertheless, Black men enlisted within days of Barnes's reported return. On Christmas Day 1863, Joseph Lane and others enlisted directly from Franklin County into USCT Regiments at Chambersburg. Some individuals enlisted out of Philadelphia and Carlisle.[60] Following this initial enlistment drive, Black residents were subjected to the formal draft calls as noted in local newspapers. Though serving in segregated units, the Civil War became more than a white man's fight during which Black Pennsylvanians watched on the sidelines. Emancipation for both seized free Blacks and Southern Blacks became a reality following the Gettysburg Campaign. For those who served in the Twenty-Fourth USCT, Nickless's fourth stanza would have truly resonated. For them and the other Black Franklin County men who enlisted following the eventful summer of 1863, the enslavement of free Black Pennsylvanians during the "dashing raid into our noble State" motivated their military service. Amos Barnes's harrowing narrative most likely emboldened their actions.[61] Rather than remain passive bystanders forced to hide in caverns, the false-walled room in the county prison's dungeon, barrels, and elsewhere, they chose donning the blue uniform. These Franklin County enlistees joined other Black volunteers for training at Camp William Penn before leaving for the battlefront in one of eleven USCT units. Ultimately, they became liberators of their enslaved Southern brethren and the free Black Pennsylvanians enslaved during the Gettysburg Campaign.[62]

With the war's end, Black Franklin County residents directly employed wartime memories in their attempts to reunite with their stolen family members. Since Pennsylvania bore the brunt of several Confederate Army raids, the state legislature passed three acts in which border county residents could submit claims for damages incurred. The lack of claims of personhood filed by African American residents of Franklin, Cumberland, and Fulton Counties demonstrates that this was not a valid space for restitution for the trauma experienced and the enslavement by Confederate soldiers. Agents received and provided compensation for claims of real property (i.e., livestock, crops, business expenses, and household goods) but not individual claims of one's personhood. Despite being treated like property by the Confederate Army, free Black border county residents could not seek reparations for themselves, family members, or employees from this state agency.[63]

Therefore, free Black Franklin County residents, specifically women, employed the resources of the federal bureaucracy, Black press, and postwar communication networks for navigating the gendered political landscape. In so doing, they secured reparations (real and symbolic) through their reunification efforts.[64] Letty Willis and Mary Ranson, both of Frederick, Maryland, placed Information Wanted advertisements in *The Christian Recorder*. Reverend Benjamin T. Tanner submitted and received information on Willis's behalf for her sister and brother-in-law, who had relocated to Chambersburg. The 1864 destruction caused either their seizure or migration from the area. Anxiety prompted Willis's decision to place the advertisement. Ranson, too, sought a reunification with Rose Jackson, her daughter who escaped from Harpers Ferry to Chambersburg in 1863. Both former slaves and Black Franklin County residents directly affected by the forced wartime separation sought reunification. Their efforts "were rarely fulfilled but the possibility kept them hoping, and intermittent stories of success kept them encouraged."[65] These women refused to allow their seized loved ones to be forgotten by state and federal officials. Hope, memory of loved ones, and the possibility of reunification served as the greatest motivator for their efforts.

Other free Black women turned to the Freedmen's Bureau for assistance. Established in March 1865, the Bureau of Refugees, Freedmen, and Abandoned Lands was originally designed as a temporary organization mandated by the United States Congress to assist freedpeople in their transition from slavery to freedom, deal with wartime abandoned lands possessed by the federal government, and aid displaced refugees.[66] In addition, bureau agents assisted with the location and reunification of Black Pennsylvanians. Sisters Lucy and Maria Meade applied for and secured their transportation from Winchester, Virginia, to Greencastle, Pennsylvania, in September 1865. In late December 1867, bureau agents coordinated the transportation for Martha Ann Marston's return to Chambersburg, where she reunited with her husband.[67] These services proved invaluable for families torn apart during the Confederate raids. The federal agency provided the necessary resources and networks that made reunification possible.

In addition, the Freedmen's Bureau courts offered a space in which Black Franklin County residents could sue for personal liability and the return of their stolen loved ones. Black women chose the postwar US military judiciary over civilian courts in a manner similar to that of emancipated Southern Black women across the former Confederacy. As argued by historian Sharon Romeo, these litigating Black women "chose to use the apparatus of the Union Army and the strategy of claiming national inclusion to maneuver for a better life and to construct a civic existence."[68] The Freedmen's Bureau courts, local agent offices, and even state headquarters served as venues for justice and restitution where the Pennsylvania Claims Office could not. Eliza Alesouth filed official complaints against Madison Leary and a slave trader simply identified as MacRichardson in early fall 1865. MacRichardson, a Bedford County, Virginia, slave trader, kidnapped Eliza and her three children from outside of Greencastle and sold them to Madison Leary during the 1864 raid that resulted in the burning of the county seat.[69] After vetting her claim, Freedmen's Bureau agents summoned Leary to appear before the court. Claiming that his travels away from Winchester prevented his appearance, Leary requested and presumably received a change in court date. Agents also attempted to bring MacRichardson before the court as well.[70] The final outcome against both men is unclear. By filing these claims, Alesouth voiced both her family's experience and particular Civil War memory as a Black civilian enslaved by a Virginian slave trader. Moreover, she demonstrated the gendered separation of the wartime seizures and internal slave trade. Military personnel and professional slave traders transported women and children for sale and enslavement in the nearby Shenandoah Valley, whereas able-bodied men traveled two hundred miles with their military captors and were directly transported to the Confederate prisons in Richmond, Virginia.[71] Unable to make their escape or secure a wartime parole, the memories of Alesouth and other more vulnerable Black populations rarely made it to the collective conscious documented in the local newspapers and later histories.

Unlike Alesouth, Priscilla Marshall found success in her dealings with the federal agency. She appealed directly to the Freedmen's Bureau for her three children, Rosa, Sallie, and Jack, taken during Jenkins's Raid.[72] Initially encountering unsympathetic Freedmen's Bureau agents, Marshall escalated her claim to General Orlando Brown, head of the Freedmen's Bureau in Virginia. She even went as far as to secure witness statements from six neighbors and presented them directly to General Brown in April 1866.[73] Marshall never accepted the permanency of the separation. She reunited with two of her three children. In her last documented letter to the Freedmen's Bureau, she not only refused to accept any assistance for transportation costs from the federal agency, but she also expressed hope that her children could provide information on the third child. Marshall's use of Civil War memory and federal agencies enabled her to secure reparations. She successfully reunited with two of her three children. Although she never reunited with her third child, Marshall still remade a world according to her gendered notions of freedom and justice in postwar America.[74]

After the Civil War, Franklin County residents, Black and white, sought to establish the truth of their unique war experience through published accounts and official county histories. Sadly, Gettysburg would not be the last time in which Confederate soldiers inflicted harm on Black and white residents. In late summer 1864, General McCausland and his men set Chambersburg ablaze. Consequently, both events would become conflated in local collective memory as "the rebel hordes who had so often made it the valley of our National Humiliation."[75] Chambersburg also becomes viewed as ground zero of Confederate soldiers' wrath over the other communities in both the 1863 and 1864 raids.[76]

Local commemorative efforts, therefore, entailed formally documenting the shared wartime traumatic civilian experiences. Jacob Hoke's 1884 reminiscences as well as the county history written by Samuel Bates and J. Fraise Richard chronicled the African Americans removed, the heroic rescue efforts of white emancipators, and the individuals who returned after their seizure during the Gettysburg Campaign and other raids.[77] The accounts often characterized African Americans as the victims of the Confederate raiders and poor Pennsylvanian leaders who did not adequately protect them from the raids. Though flawed in their victimization depictions, the published accounts of Hoke, Bates, and Richard offered a corrective to the Confederate reminiscences, which were devoid of any discussion of the indiscriminate seizure of free Blacks and self-emancipated individuals.[78] The proliferation of Lost Cause accounts hardened Black and white Franklin County residents' attitudes toward national reconciliation attempts that excluded their experiences.

Furthermore, Lost Cause accounts encouraged the active promotion of a shared local collective memory. Franklin County chroniclers regarded the Confederate raiders as neither chivalrous nor honorable men. Rather, residents considered them as something much worse. In a serial poem published less than a month after the Gettysburg Campaign, Hudibras elaborated on the plight of free Blacks as they attempted to escape capture by Confederate troops in the fifth verse before writing the following opening of the eighth verse:

Jenkins and his horse-thief men,
Passed through to Chambersburg, and then
We thought that we again were free
From Southr'n rule and chivalry.[79]

This nineteenth-century insult leveled at Jenkins and his men by poet Hudibras may seem innocuous to twenty-first-century ears. However, "horse stealing and 'negro stealing' were linked" as major detractions against one's honor and identity.[80] Like individuals who obtained stolen horses, the purchase of a person "knowing him to have been stolen . . . makes the slave buyer and the slaveholder a man-stealer."[81] Therefore, Jenkins and his men became villains who committed the most unforgivable crime on the rural communities. Both white and Black residents used the terms horse-thieves and man-stealers interchangeably as they remembered the Civil War, especially the three major raids into Franklin County.

Thus, the published accounts of Hoke, Bates, and Richard actually named specific individuals taken during the Gettysburg Campaign and in some instances recounted the experiences of individuals who returned up to fifteen years after seizure. By saying their names, the official chroniclers provided restorative justice for the shared trauma experienced by all Franklin County residents, white and Black.[82] These accounts elevated the names of John Filkill, Findley Cuff, Amos Barnes, Esque Hall, and other African American men. Some of their names were later placed on a private historical marker in downtown Mercersburg alongside the names of white citizens imprisoned for ransom in the same Confederate prisons.[83] However, these accounts marginalized Joseph Winters's Civil War songs and removed the names of the women and children seized from the collective conscious. By promoting a racialized, classist, and gendered Civil War memory, Black women's postwar reunification efforts did not fit. Though not sufficient to eliminate postwar racial and gender discrimination, Black and white Franklin County residents collectively agreed to never forget the enslaved Pennsylvanians. The power to define the public commemorative landscape and traditions, though, rested in the white male leadership of Franklin County.

Black Franklin County residents, however, employed their local churches, a Grand Army of the Republic chapter, and contributions to regional and national Black newspapers for promoting a particular memory that honored military service of veterans as well as civilian sacrifices. They challenged the narrative of victimhood and impotency as they made postwar claims of full citizenship. More important, emancipation took on a new significance in Franklin County. The wartime raids and the forced enslavement facilitated the embrace of Emancipation Day celebrations throughout Franklin County and surrounding border counties affected by wartime seizures.

Before the Civil War, Black Franklin County residents had prided themselves on their free status over their Southern brethren and even newly emancipated individuals who had migrated to the area. Free status, Native American ancestry, colorism, educational attainment, and economic status were crucial markers for distinguishing one's place in the community. Black residents previously fought for the opportunity to liberate their Southern brethren from slavery, destroy the institution confined outside of the Pennsylvania border, and subsequently secure their rights and privileges as full citizens. The Gettysburg Campaign, however, brought occupation, seizure, enslavement, and dislocation. In short, the events of 1863 made them reassess emancipation, Abraham Lincoln's wartime proclamations, and their understandings of freedom that they had taken for granted in shaping their identity as a border county citizen.

In January 1864, Black Franklin County residents and refugees celebrated the first anniversary of the Emancipation Proclamation's passage with a watch night ceremony and a midnight parade through the streets of Chambersburg "with their voices blending in harmony, [as they] sang a welcome to the first anniversary of emancipation."[84] The roughly one hundred participants celebrated the individuals who escaped enslavement, honored the men permitted to enlist in the US Army, and mourned those who had their freedom stolen. Even white residents recognized the importance of the first Emancipation Day celebration for Black participants and themselves. In his January 4, 1865, editorial, Alexander K. McClure recounted the previous year's significant events, including the first Emancipation Day celebration and the destruction of the county seat. He wrote: "To them and their posterity the first day of each new year will be sacred, because it will be the anniversary of the day which witnessed the overthrow of their great oppressor, while all will hail it as the anniversary of the day which witnessed the grandest act of the century, the *liberation of millions of human beings from a degrading bondage* [emphasis original]."[85] Indeed, Lincoln's wartime proclamations resonated with the Black community. January first was one of many dates commemorated as Emancipation Day celebrations. Such occasions allowed Black residents to assert their claims of citizenship. In this regard, Black residents employed the rhetoric and commemorative tradition associated with Black Southerners. They used Emancipation Day celebrations to promote a new racially inclusive postwar order.[86]

By 1865, Emancipation Day celebrations encompassed the preliminary Emancipation Proclamation, the Final Emancipation Proclamation, and the three major raids into south-central Pennsylvania. Most African Americans celebrated multiple dates throughout the months of July, September, and October, to the chagrin of the *Valley Spirit*. A writer for the Democratic Party newspaper published in Chambersburg complained: "It strikes us that they have celebrated the emancipation proclamation eight or ten times this year already, and we presume they intend to run it up to a round dozen before the year closes."[87] Nevertheless, Black Franklin County residents celebrated with Black-only events, including church services, picnics, watch night services, parades, and grand balls, complete with hired musicians and special orations for the occasion. The commemorations of Stuart's Raid, the Gettysburg Campaign, and the 1864 destruction of Chambersburg afforded them the opportunity to address the real consequences of the enslavement of free Black Pennsylvanians. Black residents' commemoration of these raids as Emancipation Day celebrations overlapped with the broader Civil War commemorative landscape. These public commemorative events embodied the shared trauma endured without minimizing Black Civil War memory.

While rumors of another Confederate raid made for a more somber first anniversary of the Gettysburg Campaign, Franklin County residents marked the first anniversary of the 1864 destruction of Chambersburg with an elaborate parade, series of orations, and services in the local churches.[88] The *Franklin Repository* reported that the festivities occurred "on the 30th as had been announced" in the July 26, 1865, edition.[89] Unlike the Black-only nature of Emancipation Day celebrations, the inaugural celebration involved all residents, irrespective of race, gender, class, and age from throughout the county and neighboring counties. Beginning at the Public Square, musicians performed "The Storm Gallop"; effigies of Early and other Confederate generals were carried; several participants carried banners proclaiming, "Hope, for a season, bade the world farewell"; and others carried relics from the destruction.[90] Nine African American men and forty-three youth (thirty-four boys and nine girls) participating in the parade represented the individuals forcibly removed from the county.[91] Even Eliza Alesouth, who did not find justice in the Freedmen's Bureau's courts, would have found comfort. The inclusion of the African American participants, though symbolically, recognized her pain and trauma endured at the hands of MacRichardson and Madison Leary.[92]

Overall, the entire affair recognized the trauma endured by the scarred community. Directly preceding the returned white and Black veterans, the procession featured the residents who bore witness and survived. Following the procession, Rev. Moore, who was instrumental in the return of Black and white civilians from Confederate prisons and enslavement, delivered a sermon at the Associate Reformed Church, which was damaged in the fire.[93] Throughout, white and Black Franklin County residents were viewed as victims in the third major Confederate raid. Organizers commemorated the survivors, the removed citizens, and Civil War veterans, while casting blame on the Confederate military amid the ruins and rebirth of Chambersburg. The biracial nature of the celebration set the tone for subsequent celebrations over the next fifty years. Although effigies did not extend beyond the first commemoration, the other traditions continued. Parades processed throughout Public Square and in front of rebuilt buildings;

white and Black residents participated in the procession, and Civil War veterans remained a core parade group until their dwindling numbers prevented their participation.[94]

Parades and other community celebrations, separate and integrated, facilitated the development of an oral and written tradition that acknowledged the stolen ones, those who escaped capture, reasons for Black military enlistment, and the relatively small number of individuals who returned. Issues of gender and purposeful silences shaped the nature of the memory formed, rituals developed, and the power to educate later generations. Veterans and women, to be discussed in later chapters, also played a major role in shaping and promoting Civil War memory in the border Pennsylvania communities. Though the communities saw an increase in African Americans because of postwar migration from Virginia, Maryland, and North Carolina, the overall Black population remained small in numbers but not in terms of using Civil War memory to advance their notions of citizenship and identity through overlapping civil, social, and familial networks. The sacrifices of civilians, veterans, and the individuals who were forcibly removed became an essential component of African American memory of the Civil War. This counternarrative and its persistence reveal that national reconciliation did not mean repression of memory. Black Franklin County residents boldly asserted their humanity and inclusion in the county, state, and nation by not forgetting the civilian trauma, the circumstances of military enlistment, and veterans' service.

Beyond its military significance, the Gettysburg Campaign left an indelible mark on Franklin County, Pennsylvania. The seizure and enslavement of free African Americans removed the veil of security previously enjoyed by most white and Black residents. Confederate policy of "gathering up" both free Blacks and fugitives exposed the vulnerability of individuals as well as government officials' inability to prevent such acts. Rachel Cormany and other white residents became spectators to the Confederate raiders, as few could muster the courage to thwart the seizures. Joseph Winters and other African Americans fled to safe spaces and tried to prevent their possible enslavement. Regardless, the forced removal of African Americans produced strong emotions and memories associated with the separation and loss. Although Camp William Penn emerged as a positive outcome, neither the acceptance nor training of African Americans in the state prevented later raids in the county. Camp William Penn still provided some solace to white and Black Pennsylvanians as well as Northerners who were deeply affected by Confederate invasion, occupation, and seizure of Black residents during the campaign.

By examining the experiences of rural African Americans in a border community, another perspective of African American memory of the Civil War emerges.
Black Franklin County residents experienced the war as free individuals whose
very freedom was threatened and in some instances taken by Confederate soldiers, and local leadership proved unable to protect their rights of citizenship.
Moreover, some experienced the war as soldiers, self-emancipated contrabands,
and/or civilians in both the United States and the Confederate States of America.
Understanding this diverse experience requires an intersectional approach that
considers the role of place, status before the war, gender, and wartime experience. Such an approach demonstrates the fluidity of the spectrum of African
American memories ranging from Emancipationist to the Won Cause traditions.

Therefore, Black Franklin County residents developed a usable past that honored the men, women, and children enslaved by the Confederate army, the service and sacrifice of veterans, the diverse wartime civilian experiences, and the
destruction of slavery to advance communal notions of patriotism, democracy,
and their full inclusion as American citizens. This rural Black memory sometimes coincided with the wider dominant white memory of the Gettysburg and
two other raids, while at other times it remained distinct. Black Franklin County
residents developed a complex collective memory of the Civil War that acknowledged enslaved Pennsylvanians, civilians' trauma, and the men who eventually served in the US Army and Navy. After the Civil War, they wielded this
memory for social, political, and economic purposes and made claims of full
citizenship. They engaged in a new struggle over defining the contours of public commemorative landscape. More important, they ensured that subsequent
generations would never forget the stolen Franklin County residents by sharing oral and commemorative traditions transmitted in safe African American
spaces. Their efforts contributed to the development of local commemorative
memory particular to south-central Pennsylvania recognized by local museums,
historical markers, and tourist pamphlets. Their complex Civil War memory of
enslaved Pennsylvanians, civilian trauma, and soldiers persists into the twenty-
first century.

Honoring Liberators and the Grand Reception in Harrisburg, 1865

On February 9, 2010, Diana Fishlock informed readers of *The Patriot News* of another grand spectacle honoring Black Civil War soldiers in the Pennsylvania capital. When "black soldiers who fought in the war were not invited [in May 1865]," Fishlock reminded readers how Black Harrisburg men and women "declared public outrage, and then held their own grand review, officially sanctioned by the US Army."[1] The November 1865 reception saw hundreds of Black soldiers parade from Soldiers Grove through downtown and then to former Secretary of War Simon Cameron's mansion on Front Street. Yet as one Harrisburg SusqueCentennial Commission organizer, remarked: "This city really has made a mark on our nation. There are so many things that happened here or started here that people don't know about."[2]

During the first weekend in November, the city planned a "reenactment of the grand review and exhibitions" as part of the city sesquicentennial celebration. As part of the November 2010 review, a citywide parade of Black reenactors embodied specific USCT soldiers on the re-created route. Several actors also reenacted the major white and Black speakers from the original November 1865 event. Portraying Thomas Morris Chester, Harrisburg SusqueCentennial Commission researcher Calobe Jackson Jr. explained: "No other US city held a grand review honoring the 180,000 free blacks and freed slaves who reinforced the Union army in the final two years of the Civil War."[3] Twenty-first-century planners encouraged USCT descendant families to "form walking teams to march behind the actors playing their ancestors."[4] By celebrating this previously unappreciated Civil War commemorative event, organizers hoped to "connect descendants to their legacies and build and interpret their stories."[5] Indeed, this 2010 commemoration and recovery effort of Black Civil War memory honored not only the Civil War veterans and their descendants but the original organizers.

One hundred and forty-five years earlier, ordinary Black Pennsylvanians did the extraordinary. The Garnet League and various Pennsylvania State Equal Rights League chapters organized a grand reception for the returning Black soldiers who defended their freedom from Confederate raiders but also liberated their Southern brethren living under the yoke of the short-lived Confederate nation committed to sustaining slavery and white supremacy. Black men, women, and children used this opportunity to celebrate their patriotic contributions to the US victory and their support of the Black men who valiantly served in the federal army and navy. Yet this event was not one without issues.

After the May 1865 Grand Review of Armies excluded Black USCT soldiers, Black Pennsylvanians agreed on three things. First, Black military service and their collective sacrifices in securing federal victory would be actively remembered and celebrated. While selectively forgetting the racial conditions of their enlistment and service, the returning men became heroes in the broader freedom struggle. Second, they would activate collective memory of Black military service for advancing civil, political, and social rights in the anti-Black state and nation. Civil War memory served as an effective strategy for actualizing the goals of the first Civil Rights Movement.[6] Third and most important, Black Pennsylvanians publicly embraced a pragmatic activist approach that stressed "unity over allegiance to a particular activist strategy or ideological dogma."[7] This activist strategy emerged in the abolitionist movement. Activists continually refined the strategy over the late nineteenth century and routinely deployed it during twentieth-century Black History Civil Rights and Black Power movements.[8] As a unified front, Black Pennsylvanians fought for their vision of a more just society through Civil War memory. Their early remembrances enshrined essential commemorative traditions and strategies for countering ongoing anti-Blackness. As such, they crafted the non-negotiable tenets of Black Civil War memory. They also stubbornly chose remembrance as the nation demanded collective disremembrance. Their stubbornness, moreover, laid the groundwork for the 2010 reenactment and other additions to Civil War commemorative landscape from the late nineteenth century to the 2020 unveiling of a new State Capitol Grounds monument.

Outside the white gaze, however, Black Pennsylvanians fiercely disagreed over strategy and leadership and worked toward a public-facing consensus. This closed-ranks strategy epitomized the November 1865 reception in Harrisburg. Undeterred by racism, discrimination, and significant internal statewide community strife, this chapter examines the citywide celebration of the "Liberators of the Race" by African Americans gathered for the 1865 Grand Review held in Harrisburg, Pennsylvania. From the parade, speeches, and regimental representation, this early commemoration focused on the service and sacrifices of men who served in Blue and contributed to the destruction of slavery and Union victory.

By centering the celebration around Black veterans and martial manhood, Black Pennsylvanians promoted a particular Civil War memory that enabled the articulation of demands for equality, inclusion in the body politic, and improved race relations. Consequently, the acknowledgment of African American military service and sacrifice would become an essential component of how African Americans remembered and commemorated the Civil War. The fruits of their specific efforts were neither fully accepted by white Pennsylvanians nor immediate. Perseverance and a strong communal commitment to upholding solemn promises made to Civil War veterans grounded their celebration in November 1865 and beyond.

The Grand Review of Armies of May 1865 and the myth of the Civil War as a white man's war inspired the public Black Pennsylvanian response in Harrisburg. Newspapers announced the public spectacle in early May. Following the inspection, most white soldiers would muster out. Military officials promised that the remaining troops were "sufficient to take care of Texas, if necessary, and do garrison duty throughout the pacified States."[9] Special Order No. 239 clarified for those who read the May 18, 1865, missive. The parade route passed by the Capitol to Pennsylvania Avenue and other streets before ending at a specially constructed inspection stand.[10] After the collective mourning of the assassinated Lincoln, this event offered a necessary balm by celebrating the victorious armies before President Andrew Johnson, congressional leaders, and General U. S. Grant. There were cheers and windblown banners. The Drum Corps's syncopated beats melded together with the sounds of shoed-hooves and the rhythms of the feet of the military on the earthen parade route. The parade lasted for six hours on both May 23 and 24, 1865.[11]

White school administrators closed city schools for the two-day review. The white and Black Washington, DC, youth who "scaled the shade trees to steal more commanding views" witnessed the white returning soldiers serving in the Armies of the Potomac, Tennessee, and Georgia under Generals Meade and Sherman instead of completing their schoolroom lessons in the waning days of the academic year.[12] From their vantage point, these Black scholars eagerly waited for their Black heroes to appear in view but experienced disappointment at their absence. After actively serving in Lincoln's funeral ceremonies in late April, Black spectators expected to see at least the Twenty-Second USCT. Selected for their discipline, the Black soldiers performed their solemn duties before actively hunting Lincoln's assassins.[13] Neither the Twenty-Second USCT nor other Black soldiers appeared in the May 1865 review. Older Black children, their parents, and community leaders who witnessed the spectacle probably regretted becoming the unwitting pawns to a victory parade that sowed the seeds of whitewashed Civil War memory and collective amnesia.

Some Civil War historians have understood the May review as one of race relations, the transformation of the common soldier to veteran, general nineteenth-century militarism, and the preservation of the nation during the crisis of 1861–1865. I agree with these scholarly assessments. The two-day celebration had multiple meanings of the Civil War for the organizers, participants, and attendees. However, race and the exclusion of African American soldiers cannot be divorced from the event. For African Americans and the Harrisburg reception organizers, whiteness and the perceived erasure of Black military service mattered.[14] The racial politics of the May 1865 review gave them purpose. They objected to the racial expectations demanded of them. They refused to remain subservient silent witnesses in the emerging Civil War memory culture war. Black Pennsylvanians responded in kind with an all-Black soldier review held in November 1865.

The May 1865 Grand Review set the stage for a particular racial performance of Civil War memory. Few newspapers questioned the overwhelmingly white public spectacle and inclusion of stereotypical African American parade participants.[15] The New York Times coverage provided detailed coverage of what it considered the "comic relief" offered by African American women and children liberated by the armies. In its May 25, 1865, coverage, the major New York daily reported: "It was a most nonchalant, grotesque spectacle—two very diminutive white donkeys bestrode by two diminutive black contrabands."[16] After describing the other roughly dozen pack animals carrying "camp equipage on one side and boxes of hard tack on the other," The New York Times reporter added how a "half-a-dozen contraband females on foot" and "a dozen contraband males leading the mules" were supervised by "a white solider or two on horseback, to see that everything was all right."[17] Replicating antebellum white overseer-Black enslaved relationships on the parade route, this grouping was followed by "the servants of the mess."[18] All of which, the reporter informed readers, "brought laughter and cheers from end to end of the avenue."[19] While not going into as extensive detail as the New York Times, one Gettysburg newspaper mentioned the "two contraband boys riding diminutive white donkeys" following the Second Division of the Twentieth Corps.[20] Therefore, Black Washingtonians and other Black visitors' attendance and even their cheers for federal troops would have been viewed as tacit agreement by some. For others, the Black attendees and few parade participants served as evidence bolstering "Lost Cause" revisionist myths of the war combatants, loyal camp servants, and Black Confederates.[21] For the African American witnesses to the May 1865 spectacle, their heroes—returning US Colored Troops—had been slighted. And the May 1865 Grand Review spectacle reinforced racial scripts in which the Civil War commemoration, along with "laws, customs, and props [that] transformed the racial geography," forced African Americans "to play the servile role convincingly in public spaces."[22]

The Grand Review was a decidedly white affair. The May events attempted to reinforce the pre-1863 interpretation of the Civil War as a "white man's war" while ignoring the realities of African American military contributions and those of the Choctaw and Chickasaw. Even the USCT soldiers that had connections to the predominantly white regiments of the Armies of the Potomac and James of 1864 and 1865 did not participate. Although *The Christian Recorder* did not draw attention to the USCT absence, the Philadelphia-based AME Church publication expressed hope that veterans "will never cease to receive their pay in the gratitude of generation after generation of those whose government they have so nobly delivered from its peril."[23] One poet inserted the absent USCT men in a re-reimagined "'second review' of the miraculously restored armies of the republic."[24] This second fictionalized review "not only included the dead, but also, quite tellingly, the many brigades of African-American soldiers excluded from the first review."[25] By remembering the "dusky martyrs of Pillow's fight," the poet attempted to remember their role and sacrifices made in securing the federal victory.[26] These poetic reimaginations did little to address the hurt, anger, and disappointment felt by Black Americans and USCT veterans, including Pennsylvanians who actively participated in the Overland, Petersburg, and Richmond campaigns. Embracing the lyrics of "The Enlisted Soldiers; or, The Negro Battle Hymn," Black USCT soldiers demonstrated their manhood, bravery, and patriotism to the nation. Proclaiming "We call for valiant hearted men / Who're not afraid to die," they contributed to defeating the Confederate nation and earned their place in the Washington, DC, celebration.[27]

In May 1865 many Black soldiers served as the occupying military force in the conquered Confederate states. Some also began mustering out. Others petitioned for furloughs. Many officers and common soldiers desired returning to their communities. Writing on behalf of men in the Forty-Fourth, Sixteenth, and Eighth USCT, one anonymous soldier wrote to the secretary of war because the men's "wives is scatered abut the world without pertection" and they had "not seen there Faimlys for two years & more."[28] While serving in Texas, several First US Colored Cavalry men petitioned for either the chance to muster out or to secure a furlough out of a concern for the well-being of their spouses.[29] Family letters to soldiers also conveyed the desired soldiering kin's return. For instance, Emily Waters informed her husband of the harassment experienced and the threat of eviction when an ex-Confederate officer returned to the Louisiana plantation. She hoped that he could "get a furlough as soon as you can . . . and find a place for us to live."[30] She closed her July 16, 1865, letter with a plea to her husband: "Come home as soon as you can."[31] Some served a court-martial sentence before returning home. These men and their communities never expected imprisonment as the conclusion to their military service.[32] Yet they fought for a pension for themselves and surviving kin by relying on the collective memory of Black men's military service and their collective familial sacrifices.[33] The pension served as a form of inheritance born out of the wartime sacrifices that allowed for the survival of spouse, families, and communities.[34] Despite how the Civil War ended, all Black soldiers, their families, and their communities desired an end to Black soldiers' military service and the collective embrace of them as national heroes.

Few newspapers proved more pointed in their rebuke. One *New Orleans Tribune* correspondent noted: "Much surprise has been felt, and indignation expressed, at the absence of the colored troops from the ranks of the Army of the Potomac."[35] After debunking the post-review excuses for their absence, the correspondent praised General Benjamin Butler for encouraging a medal to be given to the approximate 200 "meritorious colored soldiers" who served in the Army of the James.[36] While insufficient in nature, the proposed medal attempted to atone for the slight shown to Black veterans and their communities at the Grand Review. This racial incident served as one of many reminders of how the Civil War did not resolve racism and anti-Blackness. Black veterans and their allies still "felt obliged to defend their manly honor."[37]

Butler's allyship extended beyond the medal. Other newspapers reprinted Butler's June 1865 speech made in Lowell, Massachusetts, where he reminded audiences of USCT soldiers' Grand Review exclusion. Butler hoped that federal government would fulfill its duty to the African American veterans through the distribution of confiscated land, the franchise, and other civil rights. Quoting his remarks in full, the *Liberator, San Francisco Bulletin*, and the *Daily Picayune* reported Butler's dismay. In a series of questions, he asked the assembled crowd: "Is there no reward to be given to him? Shall we forget him?"[38] Hoping that "this country will never be guilty of such ingratitude," Butler advocated for Black suffrage and full citizenship rights.[39] "Indeed, as Johnson raced toward conciliation," according to one biographer, "Butler's speeches consistently, eloquently, and uncompromisingly made clear that he was moving in the opposite direction, which thrilled those who were similarly troubled by Johnson's leniency."[40]

In the process, he further endeared himself to Black Americans at the Lowell monument dedication ceremony. His 1865 Lowell speech and the minting of the "Butler Medal," validated African Americans' feelings about the ongoing racism directed toward Black military service and the hurt felt by their exclusion at the May celebration. During Reconstruction, African Americans considered Butler to be "a hero—their hero—and an increasingly rare source of hope."[41] In addition to John Brown, Black Pennsylvanians celebrated Butler as an important ally in the Black freedom struggle. These national sentiments, transportation networks, and military logistics influenced the reception for returning Black soldiers in Harrisburg, Pennsylvania. General Butler and other white allies had minor but significant roles in the counter Harrisburg review.

By late summer 1865, Black Harrisburg residents remained dissatisfied. Their military heroes had not received the recognition that they earned. Thomas Morris Chester, a Harrisburg native who emigrated to Liberia in 1853, must have especially felt the ongoing slight. Born to George and Jane Chester on May 11, 1834, Chester provided a valuable in-home education. His mother taught him the horrors of slavery. Born in Virginia, she self-liberated from Maryland to York, Pennsylvania, in 1825. She worked as a domestic servant before meeting her future husband George in Harrisburg, Pennsylvania, where they established their family. His father operated a restaurant and catering business near the courthouse. With parents active in the abolitionist movement, Chester learned about the major political issues of the day.[42] His parents cultivated Chester's and his siblings' love of education and their activist spirit. He received his education at Allegheny Institute (later Avery College) in Pittsburgh. Racism, American Colonization Society (ACS) public lectures, and the negative consequences of the Fugitive Slave Law of 1850 influenced his emigration to Liberia.[43] After attending the Alexander High School in Monrovia and Thetford Academy in Vermont, Chester became an educator and superintendent of the ACS sponsored Receptacle, a re-acclimation institution for recaptured Africans from American vessels and American emigrants in Liberia.[44]

In January 1862, Chester returned to the United States when the Civil War promised the possibility of improved social, civil, and political rights for African Americans either in the nation or in Liberia. Emancipation in the District of Columbia gave him hope. Returning to Harrisburg, Chester notably solicited Simon Cameron, then secretary of war, for federal assistance in postwar migration to Liberia. Chester saw the African country as the "only true and natural home of our race."[45] Following the final Emancipation Proclamation, Chester turned his energies toward the enlistment of Black soldiers. He actively recruited across the state for the Fifty-Fourth and Fifty-Fifth Massachusetts regiments. After Confederate raiders came within miles of the Pennsylvania capital, Chester again recruited Black Pennsylvanians for the state militia in the defense of the city. After raising two regiments, Chester received and accepted the rank of captain in the Pennsylvania militia. The end of the threat posed by the Gettysburg Campaign saw the militia regiments dismantled and many of the men incorporated into the Third and Eighth United States Colored Infantry (USCI).[46]

In addition to recruitment, Chester became a Philadelphia *Press* war correspondent. By providing valuable news of Black men's military service, he helped to cement the Black collective memory on display at the November 1865 event. In his wartime dispatches, according to one biographer, Chester "paid specific attention to the actions of black soldiers in the field" while admonishing "white commanders of black troops who refused to treat 'a negro patriot as a man'" and praising "those who did."[47] After reporting on Black men's April 1865 entry into Richmond, he witnessed liberated Black Richmonders' jubilant reception of the Black Pennsylvanians and other soldiers. The prolonged lack of public reception of Black soldiers and veterans became personal.[48]

Chester joined other Black Harrisburg residents in the Garnet League formed in late August and early September of 1865.[49] Honoring the Black abolitionist Henry Highland Garnet, who served as a chaplain to the Twentieth, Twenty-Sixth, and Thirty-First USCT on Riker's Island, New York, the November reception served as the organization's first major public event that attracted audiences outside of Harrisburg as well. As the corresponding secretary, Chester advanced the organizational goals. As a relatively new organizations, the Garnet League righted the wrongs perpetuated at the May 1865 Grand Review of the Armies and celebrated Black Pennsylvanians' military service.[50]

In addition to planning the November reception, the Garnet League represented Harrisburg residents' concerns to the Pennsylvania State Equal Rights League, an umbrella organization committed to advancing social, civil, and political rights for all Black men, women, and children in Pennsylvania. The purpose of the Garnet League, according to President Rev. John E. Price, was "to promote the interest of our people at home, to encourage mental improvement and moral rectitude, and to defend our race when assaulted in the person of any colored man and woman."[51] They planned lectures, advocated for full and equal citizenship, and lobbied for the restoration of the franchise to all Black Pennsylvanians. One early protest contributed to a major concession made for a Fourth Ward school for Black children on South Street. They also investigated attacks on Black veterans by roving white gangs and secured justice. At its physical headquarters, the organization made the building available not only for its general activities but also as a communal "meeting place for literary and dramatic associations" and a job employment clearinghouse.[52] The organization brought the popular orator William Howard Day to the city in October 1865 as part of a series of fundraising lectures for the November event and other initiatives. Based on the reception of his October address, the Garnet League selected Day as the keynote speaker for the November 1865 reception.[53]

The Garnet League's fall 1865 lecture series leveraged Civil War memory into one fundraising strategy for the reception. Over two days in mid-October, the organization sponsored several "pay lectures" with leading religious, community, and popular orators.[54] Rt. Rev. Joseph J. Clinton, African Methodist Episcopal Zion (AMEZ) church bishop of Philadelphia and president of the Freedmen's American and British Commission, delivered the first address in the packed Wesley Union AMEZ Church. Clinton reported on the conditions of Southern freedpeople and the current state of the Reconstruction project. Responding with "enthusiastic applause," attendees contributed books, money, and other items for the church missionary efforts in the Southern states.[55] Rev. David R. Stephens, a former Thirteenth USCT chaplain and a member of the Garnet League Board of Directors, echoed the plea for money, educational materials, clergy, and teachers by offering his own experiences with liberated Southern African Americans. Stephens urged the Black veterans in the audience to "form organizations for their improvement, and to assist the freedmen in every possible manner."[56]

During the next day, the Garnet League used another lecture for announcing the reception to the community and beginning the planning efforts in earnest. With Chester serving as the chairman, a fundraising committee and committee of arrangements were organized and given their respective tasks. Both committees and total league membership of 150 men and women received encouragement from *The Christian Recorder* correspondent, who reported to readers: "The prospects are very flattering for its being the most brilliant affair ever held among the colored people of this State."[57] *The Christian Recorder* and other Black newspapers circulated the proposed date of the reception. The Black press served as an important source for articulating and using Civil War memory as an extension of previous wartime activism for civil and political rights in the state and nation by USCT veterans, their communities, and the postwar freedom struggle. Without the Black press, the Harrisburg reception would have not been able to draw the widespread support of Black Pennsylvanians and prominent white allies necessary for publicly countering the ongoing racism and perceived disrespect shown to solders at the May 1865 Grand Review.

Before the evening lecture on the second night, the Garnet League welcomed seventy Black veterans who were invited for the occasion. Of the named regiments, veterans in attendance represented the Fifty-Fourth Massachusetts, Twenty-Fourth USCT, 127th USCT, and Fifteenth USCT.[58] Before its largest celebration in November honoring Black veterans, this smaller celebration demonstrated the organization's commitment to remember and honor Black Civil War soldiers. More important, Black Harrisburg residents drew on Civil War memory for advancing social justice at the state and federal level. They insisted that this celebration and the later November reception would eliminate "the crude and vulgar ideas of the colored citizens' inferiority to whites."[59] The personal invitations and special program before the evening lecture reinforced their commitment to the living Civil War monuments in their midst. After the singing of John Brown's favorite hymn, Chester introduced William Howard Day.[60]

William Howard Day was born to John Day and Eliza Dixon Day, free People of Color, on October 16, 1825, in New York City. Day developed his oratory skills through connections to significant antebellum religious, educational, and political circles. Bishop James Varick, an AMEZ institutional founder, baptized him in New York.[61] He attended New York city public schools and a private high school in Northampton, Massachusetts. This education prepared his entry into Oberlin College, where he earned an undergraduate and master's degrees. After the Civil War, he eventually earned a DD degree from Livingstone College in Salisbury, North Carolina.[62] Before the Civil War, Day became a popular speaker in the Colored Conventions Movement, committed to advancing abolition, equality, and full citizenship rights. He operated the *Aliened American*, a Cleveland weekly that bore the name of a popular Black abolitionist song.[63] He must have felt like the aliened American after the passage of the Fugitive Slave Law of 1850. During the mid-1850s, Day emigrated to the Black settlement of Buxton, Ontario, Canada, where he briefly taught Black immigrants and Afro-Canadians before embarking on an abolitionist lecture tour with the African Aid Society in the United Kingdom from 1859 to 1863. Returning to the United States, Day rejoined the lecture circuit. Notably, Day delivered a major address remembering Abraham Lincoln at a Fourth of July 1865 event held on the Presidential Grounds in Washington, DC.[64] Day later returned to the Pennsylvania community as a significant educational reformer and newspaper editor in the early 1870s. He became the first elected African American member on the Harrisburg School Board in 1878 and even served as the board president from 1891 to 1893.[65] In Fall

1865, Day's public introduction to the Harrisburg community and event organizers had lasting effects on the November celebration and collective remembrance from 1865 to the twenty-first century.

Day's lecture enthralled the attendees. He gave a short history of the plight of African Americans in the nation beginning with slavery. Yet Day reminded the audience how African Americans responded during the Civil War "when defeat came to humiliate the nation's pride—when the disaster of the first Bull Run fell with crushing weight on the national ardor."[66] Day added, "Thereafter, on many well contested battle-fields, the African had fairly attested his valor and established his ability to fight. Having exhibited his ability, having established his power in assisting to preserve the Government, why should he not be invested with equal rights in participating in the control thereof?"[67] The popular orator concluded his remarks by appealing to Black Harrisburg residents' resolve to make the sacrifice of the Black veterans in attendance and across the nation meaningful. He demanded: "Political equality might not be conceded to the negro of today, or tomorrow, or in a year hence—but equality before the law would come—*must come*—BECAUSE GOD RULES ON EARTH AS WELL AS IN HEAVEN!"[68] Following Day's rousing remarks, Rev. John Walker Jackson, a major white ally of Locust Street Methodist Episcopal Church, and Captain David R. Stephens gave brief remarks before closing with the collective singing of "John Brown's Body."[69]

With a clear statement of intent, the Garnet League began the work in earnest. They had the support of *The Christian Recorder*. They secured Day as their keynote speaker. Governor Andrew G. Curtin even had a reversal of opinion toward Black Civil War soldiers, their service, and collective sacrifice. After refusing "to accept blacks to the state militia" until the Gettysburg Campaign, Curtin now endorsed the celebration and agreed to review the soldiers.[70]

Some Black Philadelphians voiced their dismay over the host city and principal host organizer. As a member of the Philadelphia-based Social, Civil, and Statistical Association (SCSA), William Still, a noted Black abolitionist connected to the Underground Railroad, opposed giving money. During the September 4, 1865, meeting, Still felt such a financial contribution "would take away from their own efforts."[71] Several prominent SCSA members did not follow Still's lead. Alfred M. Green, William Forten, Octavius Catto, and other members actively served in both organizations and provided financial support. While remaining "at the center of almost everything that the SCSA did," Still abstained from participating in the statewide effort involved in the November 1865 celebration.[72] It is not clear whether he attended the celebration of returning Black soldiers. Neither the newspaper coverage nor final report noted his attendance.[73] Rather,

Still supported local efforts for the care and education of orphaned children of Black Civil War soldiers.[74] These activities still honored the Black USCT dead and memories of their service without sacrificing his primary goal of advancing the collective of the Pennsylvania Anti-Slavery Society (PASS) and abolitionism over the late nineteenth century. Abolition and not Civil War memory mattered more for this Black abolitionist.[75]

The confluence of state railroads, the presence of the former Twenty-Second USCT commander Joseph B. Kiddoo, and military logistics kept the reception in Harrisburg.[76] In terms of Civil War memory, Harrisburg and south-central Pennsylvania directly experienced the war in their backyards. The Gettysburg invasion, occupation, and enslavement of Black Pennsylvanians had convinced many returning soldiers to enlist. This second major Pennsylvanian invasion even shaped Chester's own wartime contributions as recruiter, militia officer, and reporter. Black Philadelphians could not make such claims that justified them to serve as the host city. Governor Curtin's approval also helped in defusing claims of holding the reception outside of Harrisburg. Although criticism persisted, Harrisburg remained the host city, and organizers ignored the "influence of that dangerous class" who attempted to "defeat the noble efforts."[77] Newspapers began advertising accordingly.[78] For their efforts, one letter to the editor of *The Christian Recorder* commended the organizers. Drawing on recent memory of the enlistment and military service of Black Pennsylvanians, L'Overture, an editorialist who embraced the pen name of a Haitian Revolution leader, urged active participation and attendance "in this grand re-union of the citizens of Pennsylvania."[79] This reception permitted them to pressure the Harrisburg mayor and governor to reflect on the past wrongs of initially rebuffing Black men's military service until Confederate soldiers almost captured the city during the Gettysburg Campaign, and participate in a decisively Black celebration honoring returning Black soldiers.[80]

Scholar P. Gabrielle Foreman has shown how Colored Conventions Movement sites, including the host city for the 1865 reception, required "elaborate institutional frameworks" and a "broad set of logistical skills to support and accommodate the meeting held in their cities, neighborhoods, and homes."[81] Local chapters determined initial transportation logistics. The Garnet League expected county delegates to ensure veterans' attendance. At a meeting held at Avery Mission Church, one Pittsburgh newspaper reported on the committee formed to support the participation of "the colored soldiers of Allegheny . . . and to give all the soldiers who may be in that city upon the occasion a public dinner."[82] Across the state, Pennsylvania State Equal Rights League members embarked on similar processes that engaged entire Black communities. Black men and women raised the funds for transportation, lodging, and meals for individuals who had already returned home. Their efforts ensured that any financial difficulties would not be a barrier to attendance to this reunion of living Black heroes while mourning the Black wartime dead. Without the existing Colored Conventions Movement's infrastructure, the November 1865 celebration would not have been possible.[83]

To this end, the Garnet League, in coordination with the Pennsylvania State Equal Rights League, secured discounted tickets on all major railroad companies to the Harrisburg event. They cemented another feature of the Black Civil War memory in Pennsylvania—the railroad network functioned as a Won Cause community network. The train shaped Black Pennsylvanians' military experience. Enlisted Black men took the train to Camp Meigs in Readville, Massachusetts, and Camp William Penn outside of Philadelphia for training. They took the train and then other modes of transportation to the warfront and federal camps. And now they boarded trains for the grand reception held in Harrisburg. Their arrival in the Pennsylvania capital on November 13 and 14 attracted much attention by all observers.[84]

Once in Harrisburg, the Garnet League activated host arrangements. Arriving soldiers quickly crowded the streets surrounding the train station. While meandering the main streets of the Black Harrisburg community of the Eighth Ward, they saw evergreen arches and wreaths, bunting, and banners welcoming them. One banner proclaimed: "HE WHO DEFENDS FREEDOM IS WORTHY OF ALL ITS FRANCHISES."[85] They encountered Black residents and visitors who cheered and even celebratorily waved handkerchiefs from their windows. Some shook their hands while others toasted them. The arrival of the Twenty-Fourth USCT Drum Corps prompted an impromptu performance to the satisfaction of Jacob Compton, a Twenty-Fourth USCT veteran, and Black Harrisburg welcome committee members, while drawing the ire of the white Harrisburg *Patriot* reporters. Many displayed American flags at their front doors and from their windows. For many of the veterans, these simple celebratory actions re-created earlier experiences with Black public audiences during the various military processions of 1863 and 1864. Black women, children, and men celebrated these USCT men as they had when they departed for battlefield. They returned as heroes who had saved the nation.[86] Some eventually stopped by the Soldiers' Rest for a quick meal. Here, veterans, food servers, and civilian onlookers communed over food. "In these surroundings," according to scholar Psyche Williams-Forson, "food brought together those who could and would tell distinctly Black stories in places where alliances and allegiances could be forged and renewed and particular in-group intimacies could be shared."[87] To the chagrin of the Harrisburg *Patriot*, the celebratory mood continued late into the night. Others moved toward the major Black boardinghouses and hotels hosting them.[88]

In terms of accommodations, Black soldiers and veterans would have stayed at one of three Black-operated hotels: Garnet House, Bradley House, and Jones House. William Battis and Alfred Garner operated the Garnet House at the corner of Sixth and South streets.[89] Battis owned and operated a variety of businesses. He later became an alderman representing the Eighth Ward.[90] Garner, a self-liberated Virginian, also served on the Garnet League's Board of Directors.[91] The other two locations also offered comfortable accommodations and professionalism. Henry Bradley operated a three-story brick hotel located on Elder Street. He also owned and operated a popular barbershop near the *Harrisburg Telegraph* offices.[92] Dr. William M. "Pap" Jones operated the Jones House. Born in Luzerne County, Pennsylvania, Jones was a founding member of the Wesley Union AMEZ Church and a well-known abolitionist who helped self-liberating individuals on the Underground Railroad before and after the Fugitive Slave Law of 1850.[93] As a respected community member, Jones welcomed Black Civil War veterans and other guests at the large, wooden multistory hotel on the corner of South Street and the West Alley.[94]

These three Eighth Ward Black-owned hotels offered convenient lodging for the African American soldiers and veterans in attendance. The parade starting location of Soldier's Grove was within easy walking distance. Moreover, these facilities had been used to catering to white and Black Civil War soldiers and their families traveling to and from Camp Curtin in Harrisburg and Camp William Penn.[95] As such, the hotels and alternate boarding houses offered "intimate access to the conversations, debates and deliberations" but also functioned as spaces for reminiscing, fellowship, and comradeship with other Black veterans. The celebrated Black Civil War soldiers also relayed stories and personal testimonies of their service, wartime sacrifice, and postwar visions of citizenship and equality that became the "recorded gaps" in the archival record but added to the jubilant mood of the celebration.[96]

Despite the warm Black Harrisburg community's hospitality, the pre-reception arrivals and early decorations offended some white residents. There were minor racial incidents that almost derailed the celebration. One incident involved two veterans who thwarted vandals from destroying the various arches and decorations welcoming the soldiers on the evening of November 13, 1865. When vandals targeted the welcome arch, two USCT veterans guarded the arch and Garnet House with armed muskets. Instead of investigating the vandalism, Harrisburg police arrested them. Neither the men's veteran status nor uniforms had changed the racist policing typical of antebellum urban Northern communities. Officers placed the two men in the city jail and released them in time for their attendance at the reception in the morning. These minor acts, however, could not prevent the grand spectacle of November 14, 1865.[97]

At ten o'clock, the parade worked its way through the Harrisburg streets. The procession moved down South to Fifth and then moved down Fifth to Market Street. Once at Market, the parade participants moved up Market to Front and moved down Front.[98] Once reaching Simon Cameron's Front Street residence, the procession paused. Illness prevented Governor Curtin from participating in the spectacle. Cameron, former secretary of war in the Lincoln administration, provided brief remarks from his Front Street residence as Bvt. Major General Kiddoo and Brig. Gen. John P. Brisbin stood next to him.[99]

Cameron opened by thanking the African American soldiers for their service. Although claiming to "never doubted that the people of African descent would play a great part in this struggle," he acknowledged the early refusal by the nation and state to embrace Black men as soldiers.[100] The Gettysburg invasion and the direct threats to Harrisburg prompted a change in sentiment. Their bravery and sacrifice endeared them to the state and nation. He told them: "Your services, offered in the early part of the war, were refused; but when the struggle became one of life and death, then the country gladly received you, and thank God, you nobly redeemed all you promised."[101] Applause broke up his remarks at this point. The men understood the nature of the apology by this former official in the Lincoln administration and approved of it.

Through their applause, Simon had received their forgiveness. When he added that "you will have all the rights you ask for, all the rights that belong to human beings" shortly thereafter, applause deafened.[102] And Cameron quickly concluded this section. With sincerity, he expressed his heartfelt thanks: "I can only say again that I thank you from my heart for all that you have done for your country, and I know the country will hold you in grateful remembrance."[103]

In the closing, Cameron called on Black Pennsylvanians to trust President Andrew Johnson. He had faith that the president would not only extend full rights of citizenship, but he would also not allow former rebellious states to return without conditions. He, therefore, demanded their patience. The contours of the post-emancipation nation needed time for resolution. With faith in the president and God, Cameron ended by drawing on recent Civil War memory: "Remember, when the war began, there were 4,000,000 of slaves in this country, protected by law. Now all men are made free by the law. Thank God for all this! For He alone has accomplished the work!"[104]

Immediately following Cameron, Bvt. Major General Kiddoo spoke. Attendees welcomed Kiddoo's presence and remarks because of his Civil War record in a USCT regiment. Meade inspected his former Twenty-Second USCT regiment as they left Camp William Penn for Fortress Monroe where they joined Butler's forces in February 1864. After the Civil War, Kiddoo oversaw the decommissioning of white and Black soldiers at Harrisburg and eventually became the assistant commissioner of the Freedmen's Bureau in Texas.[105] For his service among one of the Camp William Penn USCT regiments, parade participants and attendees called him to the podium and cheerfully welcomed his brief address. Shortly after the reception, Kiddoo presided over the mustering out and celebratory dinner of the 640 men serving in the Twenty-Second USCT.[106] Sadly, Kiddoo's Harrisburg remarks have not been carefully preserved.

The parade then resumed and headed toward the Capitol grounds for the addresses given at the makeshift platform for the next portion of the reception. After a brief introduction by Chester, Rev. John Walker Jackson opened with a prayer. The white minister thanked God for how their service, though marred by discrimination, saved both African Americans and the nation. He then remembered "the dead of all classes and conditions, who have fallen on the battlefield" before recalling the sacrifice of "the greatest martyr, the dead President of the United States."[107] By reminding all of the wartime dead, Jackson's prayer set the tone for the living veterans, their kin, and their respective communities who witnessed the next section of the program. Other Black speakers reminded attendees of Black soldiers' valor and role in victory as justification for expanding citizenship and freedom to all Americans and the restoration of the franchise for Black Pennsylvanians. The reading and approval of resolutions articulated this vision for Civil War memory.[108] As one unified voice, Black Pennsylvanians emphatically declared: "We, therefore, as colored native born citizens, claim for ourselves all the rights, privileges and franchises enjoyed by our fellow-citizens of another race."[109] In effect, this reception signaled the Garnet League's claims to full citizenship and the advancement of a more just postwar society though arguments grounded in their understanding of what the war and Black military service meant.

Following this bold declaration, the public reading of letters received from Generals Meade and Butler had special meaning for the soldiers and attendees. These letters represented their white allies' endorsement of Black Pennsylvanians' collective remembrance of Black Civil War service and claims for broader rights of citizenship. Major newspapers and the final post-reception debriefing report republished the letters sent by the Civil War generals in full.[110] While a Garnet League member read other letters received from Maj. George L. Stearns, a white recruiter for three Massachusetts and several USCT regiments, Sen. Charles Sumner, and Secretary of State William H. Seward, this military and federal recognition corrected the most egregious perceived wrong committed during the May 1865 review.[111] Butler's letter further showed how this major Civil War general disagreed with postwar treatment of Black soldiers and agreed with their use of memory for advancing social, civil, and political rights. Collectively, these letters added legitimacy to the Harrisburg reception and Black Pennsylvanians' understanding of Civil War memory centered on the military service of Black men.[112]

Day's keynote addressed reinforced Black Pennsylvanians' means of honoring Black military service beyond the November reception.[113] Unlike his earlier address, neither the newspaper coverage nor final post-event report provided details or quotations. The Garnet League and newspapers had hoped to get an official copy from Day, but he never supplied it. As result, a general summary with paraphrased quotes survived. Day argued that Black men "had indeed shown their manhood," and cited many examples "of personal daring among members of the African race for the last hundred years." Day reportedly surmised that through their sacrifices and bravery "they had demonstrated the fact that they were fit to be free and to take part in the Government. He welcomed the soldiers of the Republic, soldiers of loyalty and liberty, of truth and justice, against rebellion and slavery. They were thrice welcome."[114] He closed by acknowledging and thanking the Harrisburg organizers "for the energy and zeal they had evinced in inaugurating and carrying forward the reception to success."[115] For these remarks, the civilian and military attendees gave their "rapt attention" and periodically offered "bursts of applause."[116]

The Black, Republican Party–leaning and abolitionist newspapers overwhelmingly offered positive coverage. From state and national publications, many accounts captured the mood, activities, and celebratory nature of the day.[117] The *Harrisburg Telegraph* and Philadelphia newspapers provided the most comprehensive accounts. In the final debriefing report, the Garnet League heavily relied on the *Philadelphia Inquirer, Philadelphia Press*, and *Harrisburg Telegraph* for recounting event details.[118]

Not all newspapers celebrated the Harrisburg reception. Blending portions of the Harrisburg *Patriot* with their own anti-Black commentary, state Democratic-leaning newspapers used the Black soldiers' exclusion in the May 1865 for their accounts and the language deployed in shaping their commentary about the returning soldiers, white participants, and the event itself. The Harrisburg *Patriot* set the tone for other critical media reports of the reception. In the opening paragraph, the *Patriot* reporter established the reception in terms of anti-Black racism and the non-revolutionary nature of the Civil War and emancipation: "The much talked off celebration in 'honor of de nigs that fought in dis war,' naturally claimed some attention from us as public journalists. We therefore 'gove de subject, our 'tention.'"[119] From there, the *Patriot* reporter disparaged the event. The white reporter mocked the selected hotels and the Black Harrisburg residents and visitors who unabashedly welcomed the Black soldiers. The resulting account also depicted the returning soldiers and even the Twenty-Fourth Drum Corps as still novice soldiers ineptly performing military drills and parade maneuvers instead of disciplined, battle-tested veterans.[120]

Suggesting that the parade "fell far short" of expectations, the *Patriot* reporter took pains to further discredit the parade and Day's keynote address.[121] He significantly undercounted the participants in the parade and overall audience size. While accurately addressing the parade route, the reporter significantly condensed Cameron's remarks. The *Patriot* reporter also mocked Cameron by calling him the "Winnebago Chief" who was followed by several "white trash" which included Rev. John Walker Jackson, Kiddoo, and "three or four other mule contracts."[122] The *Patriot* reporter also mentioned Day's speech using stereotypical anti-Black language. Surprisingly, the letters received by Generals Benjamin Butler, George Meade, and others were not detailed. The evening events were not described. From racial slurs to attacks on the prominent white participants, the *Patriot* provided the template and even the title for other critical coverage across Pennsylvania.[123]

Some Black Pennsylvanians privately criticized the event. They found fault with the Harrisburg organizers and their execution of the grand celebration. Black Philadelphians still felt that the event should have occurred in their city and perhaps at Camp William Penn. Emilie Davis captured their disappointment in her pocket diary. Unable to attend herself, Davis felt it necessary to record the sentiments of others in her close circle. On November 15, 1865, this working-class Black Philadelphian wrote: "Quite warm this morning the Harrisburg folks arrived to Day they were quite Disappointed in the reception."[124] Unlike the *Patriot* and other state newspapers, Black Pennsylvanians limited their criticism in spaces outside of the white gaze. Private correspondence, pocket diaries, and in-person conversations became the venues of their criticism. Based on the vitriolic anti-Black commentary, they understood how any public statements might be weaponized against them in their ongoing social justice movement. Post-reception raw emotions required a shoring up on intra-community politics to move forward.

Within the Garnet League's final post-event debriefing report, emotions remained raw. The report extensively reprinted the overwhelmingly positive newspaper coverage of the November event, provided the financial statement, and defended the organizers in a publication written by and for Black Pennsylvanians. Anti-Black media coverage in the Democratic Party–leaning newspapers had no place in the first part of the report. The report also showcased all individuals who made the event possible. Building on the reception momentum, the report ended with an appeal from the organization to support its other endeavors and a full listing of officers.[125]

Addressing the charge of fiscal mismanagement, Garnet League organizers provide a full fiscal statement for readers. The organization collected money from an array of individuals, chapter treasurers, and church congregations throughout the state. The financial statement also noted the role of Black women and their expansive financial networks. Building upon a legacy of wartime fundraising efforts, Jane Chester and other Black Harrisburg women raised more money than the Garnet League, Garnet House, and all other Pennsylvania State Equal Rights League chapters. These Harrisburg women expressed their rage at the May 1865 event by opening their purse strings.[126] The grassroots fundraising and Garnet League stewardship contributed to a small surplus. Despite this transparency, allegations forced some at the heart of the fraud questions to issue clarifying statements reprinted for report readers. The Garnet League reassured readers and Pennsylvania State Equal Rights League activists that there were only errors of judgment made by the Hollidaysburg and Norristown chapter treasurers.[127] Rumors and allegations persisted despite their best efforts. Leadership responded with "Resolutions of Vindication." Published as part of the final report as well as a separate 1866 pamphlet, internal problems took longer to reconcile, but never reached the level of the white partisan anti-Black critique.[128]

Ultimately, the Garnet League found the reception to be an overwhelming success. They thanked the "patriotic population" of Black Pennsylvanians who attended. As one publicly unified voice, they collectively celebrated Black soldiers and mourned the dead. In recognition of their military service in securing federal victory, they demanded the "unqualified recognition of their humanity…in thunder tones to the throne of Eternal Justice, shouting GLORY TO GOD AND THE COLORED VOLUNTEER."[129] They also demonstrated their rejection of the anti-Blackness displayed in May and set the tone for future Civil War commemorations. The service and sacrifice of Black soldiers, dead and living veterans, would not be forgotten.

Remembrance shaped Black Pennsylvanians' politics. They pledged their ongoing commitment to advancing the democratic ideals and nation that they fought for during the Civil War. Remembrance shaped their commemorative traditions, including Memorial Day celebrations, activities of an all-Black Grand Army of the Republic (GAR) post, monuments, and oral traditions from 1865 to the 2010 reenactment. In short, the military service and sacrifices of Black Civil War soldiers would not be in vain. Race, ongoing racism, and anti-Black treatment of Civil War veterans strengthened Black Pennsylvanians' resolve and grounded their commemorative traditions in Harrisburg and state.

Unfortunately, Black Pennsylvanians did not immediately see the expected returns of the event. The Garnet League and Pennsylvania State Equal Rights League continued their fight for equality, full citizenship rights, and the franchise. Immediate hurt and disappointment eased into a more unified campaign for maximizing the legacy of Black men's service. The organization and its local chapters met regularly to define how the war and its memory might benefit all Pennsylvanians and their Southern brethren. The Garnet League expanded on Rev. David R. Stephens's educational philanthropy request by becoming a major benefactor for several Freedmen Schools in Tennessee and North Carolina.[130] The organization even commissioned Chester to raise funds for its Southern educational efforts in the United Kingdom and Europe. At every public occasion, the organization recognized the veterans in their midst and pledged to remember them through direct action for civil and social rights.[131]

Pay lectures for popular Black speakers remained a major activity throughout the post-reception existence of the Garnet League. Organization leaders and members welcomed back Day. In his January lecture, Day spoke on the "advancement of the colored race, their education and promotion to civil rights and political franchises."[132] The organization also hosted former Benjamin Butler, who had offered a letter of support for the November reception. Of course, several newspapers praised these lectures and their efforts while the Harrisburg *Patriot* derided the organization and its white allies.[133] These later events and continued Garnet League activism had little effect. The newspaper still rejected Black Pennsylvanians' citizenship claims boldly articulated at the November 1865 reception. Only the ratification of the Fifteenth Amendment caused a minor shift in coverage of the franchised Black Pennsylvanians but not its anti-Black editorial stance.[134]

After the ratification of the Fifteenth Amendment, the Garnet League and Pennsylvania State Equal Rights League shifted from previous political strategies to electoral politics.[135] Old hurts and perceived internal wrongs of the November 1865 reception were forgotten as Black men, women, and children again crowded Harrisburg during the 1872 Pennsylvania State Equal Rights League convention. Transitioning to Grant and Wilson Clubs, the various chapters, including the Garnet League, mobilized Black men's electoral activism in the Republican Party.[136] Convention delegates heard another keynote address by Day who reminded them that "you are for Grant, not because he led our armies to victory; but because these men are the representative men of the party of human rights, of the party of loyalty, of the party of progress."[137] They also celebrated the second anniversary of the Fifteenth Amendment with another citywide parade. Public unity prevailed at the convention hall and on the city streets. This intra-racial unity translated into the transformation of the Harrisburg political landscape from a Democratic to Republican Party stronghold over the decade. Although the Garnet League and Pennsylvania State Equal Rights League ended, Black Harrisburg residents' Civil War remembrances continued in new organizations, annual events, and segregated cemeteries. With the franchise secured, they engaged in the preservation of Black Civil War memory for future generations.[138]

The David R. Stephens GAR Post, No. 520, represented one new organization. Black Civil War veterans had originally named the post after Octavius V. Catto at its founding June 1886 meeting. By Memorial Day 1887, the Harrisburg veterans quickly changed the name from the Black Philadelphian abolitionist, educator, and postwar activist killed on Election Day 1871 to the Thirteenth USCT chaplain as their namesake. They regarded Stephens's Civil War experiences, Garnet League leadership, and religious prominence as most deserving of the honor.[139] The Harrisburg GAR comrades also embraced the railroad network for cultivating a veterans' network throughout Pennsylvania and neighboring states.[140]

Through monument making and ritual, Black Harrisburg residents forged communal understandings of Black Civil War military service and the November 1865 reception at the segregated Lincoln Cemetery. Black Harrisburg women led the early monument-making efforts. They erected and dedicated a monument honoring Civil War veterans buried at the cemetery, which served as the final resting place for many veterans and former abolitionists of the Harrisburg area.[141] This Civil War soldier monument was placed near a mound of the graves of the re-interred African Americans removed from the Herr Street cemetery where a color line reinforced racial hierarchies before the creation of the Lincoln Cemetery in 1877.[142] Through Black women's memory work, this monument became an essential location in later Memorial Day celebrations conducted at the cemetery. These annual occasions allowed Black residents to educate the next generations of the historic November 1865 celebration and communal Civil War collective memories. Ordinary Harrisburg and Dauphin County residents ensured Black Civil War soldiers and veterans received their laurels. Over the late nineteenth century, the David R. Stephens GAR post and its women's auxiliary took over the planning of the annual celebration. By 1920, communal and fraternal organizations took over the duties. These annual celebrations cemented local Black Civil War memory that included remembrance of the November 1865 reception.[143]

Until the last veteran's death in the early 1940s, Civil War veterans participated alongside other war veterans in community events. Combined with other intentional Black memory-making efforts, the aged Black Civil War veterans' presence and oral traditions added to the persistence of memory. For instance, GAR comrade Ephraim Slaughter (Thirty-Seventh USCT and Third NC Colored Infantry) attended every Memorial Day celebration until his last one in 1941. The entire Harrisburg community, white and Black, mourned his death at the age of ninety-seven.[144]

Following Slaughter's death, the Black community still celebrated the Civil War generation and reception participants. On Memorial Day 1950, W. E. B. Du Bois and other speakers recalled the November 1865 reception during a monument dedication to William Howard Day at the historic Lincoln Cemetery. "It is our duty," Du Bois reminded attendees of the monument dedication, "as men and women living in this new day to understand and understand thoroughly what has taken place since the death of William Howard Day."[145] He hoped that Day's achievements and legacy might inspired the twentieth-century activists attending the ceremonies. "But doing this work we cannot forget the full life and real service of this intelligent, busy and unselfish servant of man," Du Bois closed his Memorial Day speech.[146] While the nation forgot Day and others celebrated in November 1865, Black Harrisburg residents and national Black leaders never forgot their legacy.[147]

Locally, Black Harrisburg residents and organizations chose remembrance until the early twenty-first century. Their efforts were ignored. The city, state, and nation preferred forgetting and the intentional whitewashing of the Harrisburg reception, if remembered. Black Harrisburg residents and their allies' commemorative additions, however, laid the foundation for a twenty-first-century reenactment of the 1865 Grand Review.[148] The 2010 reenactment of the Grand Review celebrated the November 1865 event with a parade, speeches, lectures, and other activities centering the historic African American graveyards that served as the final resting place for hundreds of Black Pennsylvanians who served in the Civil War.[149]

By all accounts, the November 2010 reenactment successfully reconnected the city residents, visitors, academics, and descendant communities. Charles Thompson, a *Patriot-News* reporter, reflected a reversal of opinion shared by his 1865 counterpart. Thompson discussed the event in terms of one of reconciliation and community healing through celebrating the November 1865 reception. He wrote: "Harrisburg, a city bedeviled by a spate of current-day troubles, set aside its civic strife today to re-create, re-teach and just plain celebrate one of its brightest days: the Nov. 14, 1865, Grand Review of the United States Colored Troops."[150] His short article captured the mood of the event for many attendees. Attendees witnessed young and older African Africans reenact specific USCT soldiers who either attended the original event or had Pennsylvania roots. For many it was the first time to witness Black Civil War reenactors and even learn about another Civil War historical event other than the Gettysburg Campaign. After federal officials "spurned proper recognition of these Union soldiers in the nation's capital during its 'Grand Review of the Armies' in May 1865," attendees learned how the city "welcomed them."[151] And on this Saturday, the governor and entire community again hosted a grand celebration commemorating Black Civil War memory.

Other celebrations allowed attendees to learn about Black Pennsylvanians who served in the Civil War, the original event, and the Garnet League while engaging with members of the descendant communities. Organizers intentionally reached out to USCT descendant communities in the publicity and personally. In a supplement to *ShowcaseNow! Magazine*, organizers asked: "Do you recognize any of the names below? Is your ancestor listed here?"[152] Anita Wills, descendant of Henry Green and Uriah Martin, responded. She shared her families' history and the role of her mother who had "passed the history of our ancestors through stories she told, when we were children."[153] During the November reenactment, genealogists and community activists introduced many to various projects dedicated to researching the history and preserving the various African American cemeteries where many Civil War veterans, abolitionists, and other prominent Black Pennsylvanians of the Civil War and Reconstruction era were interred.

On November 14, 2010, several communities continued the momentum of the reenactment by hosting celebrations at several historic African American cemeteries. At the Lancaster event, Black reenactors portrayed two significant Lancaster residents during the celebration held at the Shreiner-Concord cemetery.

A. Lee Brinson portrayed Sgt. Jonathan Sweeney, a Third USCI veteran who was interred in the cemetery.[154] Darlene Colon portrayed Lydia Hamilton Smith, the long-time housekeeper and confidante of Thaddeus Stevens, who is interred in the racially segregated Black section of the Shreiner-Concord cemetery.[155] As one of three descendants of Abraham J. Quamony, a Twenty-Fourth USCT veteran interred at the cemetery, Colon reminded how her family never forgot this history. Millersville University Professor Leroy Hopkins, Michael Laverty, and the president of the Thaddeus Stevens Society also spoke at both events held at Shreiner-Concord cemetery and Stevens-Greenland.[156] Other celebrations recognized the other interred Civil War veterans in the various historic cemeteries.[157] In short, the 2010 Grand Review became a wider celebration of the previously unacknowledged history and thus Black Civil War memory moved to the center of many Pennsylvanians' consciousness. By remembering the November 1865 reception, diverse Pennsylvanians have worked to develop a more inclusive commemorative landscape. For the original organizers and participants, the legacy of their work has been enshrined in the form of a bronze memorial at the Pennsylvania Capitol Complex grounds.

Dedicated in 2020 during the national reckoning of Confederate monuments, *A Gathering at the Crossroads* monument was built to commemorate Black Civil War efforts. The life-size, immersive monument features William Howard Day, Thomas Morris Chester, Frances Ellen Watkins Harper, and Jacob Compton, a Twenty-Fourth USCT veteran. Three of the four honorees participated in the November 1865 reception. Becky Ault, co-founder of ART Research Enterprises of Lancaster, Pennsylvania, realistically captured the four individuals' likeness, dress, and personalities using a wax casting method. In its final form, the twenty-first-century monument built on the original legacy laid in the November 1865 reception for advancing equality and social justice for all Pennsylvanians. Now enshrined in the centrally located bronze monument, the Garnet League's vision for Civil War memory has persisted.[158]

For the Civil War memory on display at the Pennsylvania Capitol Complex grounds, several generations of Black men, women, and children created new traditions and means of memory making and sustained a vibrant and diverse Civil War memory culture in Harrisburg, the state, and the nation. They worked together to realize the political aims of the Black men's military service. Restoration of the franchise became paramount for Black Pennsylvanians. With the passage of the Fifteenth Amendment, older organizations embraced political mobilization as part of their mission and new political clubs emerged. By voting, Black men remembered and honored Black Pennsylvanian soldiers whose sacrifices contributed to the civil and political rights defined by the Thirteenth, Fourteenth, and Fifteenth Amendments. Black veterans used the Grand Army of the Republic for cultivating a Won Cause culture that normalized Memorial Day celebrations and the care of the Civil War burial spaces that the twenty-first-century celebrations relied on. From oral tradition to community archival practices, Black women served as essential memory makers who turned the porch into archival spaces while using their familial, educational, and religious networks for transmitting knowledge over several generations.

These ordinary men, women, and children did the extraordinary. They ensured the persistence of Civil War memory that remembered Black USCT military service and the sacrifices of during and after the Civil War. Remembrance became their personal and communal politics. As a result, Black Pennsylvanians and others nationally never forgot when others intentionally did. And we, in the present, should applaud their tenacity and memory-making efforts which facilitated the twenty-first-century reenactment and monument.

3   Joseph Winters's Songs for Self-Made Men

Following the assassination of President Abraham Lincoln, Joseph R. Winters of Chambersburg, Pennsylvania, captured the mood of the nation and African Americans, whether freeborn, newly emancipated, former refugees, widowed, orphaned, or enlisted soldier, in poetic verse. Instead of celebrating Confederate defeat and the destruction of slavery, the civilian Gettysburg invasion survivor and wartime songwriter eulogized the murdered Commander-in-Chief:

> Our country is all in morning
> Our President is Dead
> By assassin booth. he was slain
> And in his coffin lain.[1]

From this opening verse, Winters briefly described the events that occurred at Ford's Theatre before demanding the capture, conviction, and death of the assassins. But he also turned his gaze toward the future of African Americans in Franklin County, Pennsylvania. During the war, his community had survived three Confederate raids that resulted in the seizure and enslavement of freeborn Pennsylvanians and self-liberating refugees who fled the Northern state. He and other civilian survivors hoped that Lincoln's assassination and Confederate defeat might contribute to the expansion of the franchise and other rights of citizenship. Winters imagined a postwar future where Lincoln's ultimate sacrifice could benefit African American USCT soldiers and civilian survivors when he wrote "That the poor may live as well as rich / In this free and prosperous land."[2] His death should not be in vain. In this moment, the shrewd observer and chronicler of the African American wartime experience bemoaned how "Father Abraham is dead and gone."[3] And Winters, African Americans who made the Lincoln White House their house, and other African Americans across the nation shared a Civil War experience that defined their subsequent memory work. Collectively, they "mourned, as a race, when their champion fell under the assassin's bullet."[4]

From 1870 to 1916, Winters turned his grief into action. Through political songs, voting, and participation in party politics, Winters advanced new notions of manhood and citizenship centered on the franchise. In the process, Winters harnessed Civil War memory and Frederick Douglass's concept of self-made men to enact a new political reality for Black men in Franklin County, the state of Pennsylvania, and the nation. As a contemporary of Henry McNeal Turner, Winters's own political party affiliations also shifted but not his usage of Civil War memory for mobilizing Black voters. Although scholars usually focus on Douglass, Turner, elected politicians, formerly enslaved Southerners, and urban Northern communities, Winters and rural Black Pennsylvanians also drew upon collective memories of the Civil War for transforming the postwar political landscape.

With the ratification of the Fifteenth Amendment, this chapter contends that Winters represented other Black Franklin County men who hoped the memory of the Civil War could bring meaningful change. Winters actively engaged in the political realm but experienced disappointment with the limits of postwar politics to fully include African Americans in party affairs, elected positions, and patronage. Yet the new post-Fifteenth Amendment political ethos allowed for the creation of new organizations, community engagement, and the persistence of Black Civil War memory into the twentieth century. The Civil War, as Winters and Black men remembered it, transformed them into self-made men.

Winters remained a consistent political voice. He never forgot the Gettysburg Campaign and other Confederate invasions; they appear in his political party work, editorials, and presidential campaign songs. His work complemented other national African American leaders, specifically Frederick Douglass and Henry McNeal Turner. Yet his complex understanding of the Gettysburg Campaign and coalition building represented rural Black Pennsylvanians' experiences and their unwillingness to allow others to speak their truth. Thus, Winters's political biography shows how rural Black Pennsylvanian men contributed to the postwar Black politics rooted in new notions of manhood, the franchise, and a politicized Civil War memory. Despite his complicated legacy, Winters ensured that Franklin County men retained their unique Civil War experience as the point of entry for shaping the local, state, and national post-Fifteenth Amendment political landscape.

The celebration of the ratification of the Fifteenth Amendment marked the political debut of Winters and other Franklin County men as self-made franchised men. Across Franklin County and the nation, African Americans and their white allies patiently waited until enough states had ratified the constitutional amendment expanding the African American male franchise. The date occurred on

February 3, 1870.[5] Soon after, Chambersburg newspapers announced the intended plans for a grand celebration. Winters and many future members of the Republican Party gave eloquent speeches at a mass meeting before unanimously adopting a series of resolutions for the celebration. The assembled March 1870 mass meeting attendees declared "it essential that we celebrate appropriately That Day which was given franchise to our so long benighted race."[6] Indeed, the committee in charge of arrangements organized a grand public spectacle celebrating the franchise and the Fifteenth Amendment.

Held in Chambersburg, Winters and other Franklin County residents took to the streets. The parade officers and acknowledged procession members represented veterans, community leaders, and several militias and fraternal orders led by Civil War veterans.[7] The parade also recognized several individuals seized during the Civil War who had returned home. Alexander Lewis, one of the Black Pennsylvanians enslaved by Confederate forces, served as the adjutant of the event. In front of the Court House, Winters delivered the first address in an "an able manner" before three other chosen orators "made a few well-timed remarks."[8] In addition to these speeches, the displayed banners hinted at Black men's political allegiance—"We are Grant's Rough and Ready Boys," "Virtue, Liberty and Independence," and "Grant & Colfax." Following the parade, the celebration continued at the Repository Hall with a formal ball. Joseph Winters again delivered one of the many speeches made for the occasion. Overall, the celebration reportedly "passed off quietly, pleasantly, and without any disturbance."[9]

As self-made men, newly franchised Franklin County men capitalized on their collective electoral power following the celebration. The Democratic Party–leaning *Valley Spirit* reported the registration of 228 Black voters in Chambersburg. Black men now represented a sizable portion of the electorate, making up one-sixth of the total number of voters in the county seat and roughly one-fourth of the Republican voters.[10] Antrim, Montgomery, and other county communities saw similar numbers added. Thus, the *Valley Spirit* expected Black men to fully claim representation in party affairs. The Chambersburg newspaper also predicted a similar political outcome across the American South The Republican Party, at the county and state level would receive "the solid negro vote."[11]

The *Valley Spirit* prediction came to fruition. County Republicans embraced African Americans into the fold. At a political rally held at a local African American church, the integrated affair saw county would-be officeholders court Black voters. Winters was one of three African American speakers who gave remarks before Thaddeus Maclay Mahon, a white candidate for the Pennsylvania

legislature, addressed the crowd.[12] The former abolitionist seized on the economic emancipationist language described by historian Matthew Stanley. By
linking labor with emancipation memory, Mahon promised to "stand up for liberty, justice, right and equality in spite of prejudice."[13] Moreover, he hinted at the
possibility of a future political slate with both white and Black candidates. Black
men did not need to support a third party, such as Greenbacks, Socialist Labor,
and/or the National Labor Union. They also did not have to follow the lead of
Black Bostonians who split politically and began considering an independent
political strategy over the traditional two-party system during the 1872 election
season. After some prodding by Douglass and others, Bostonians ultimately supported Grant, as did the majority of Black men in Franklin County and the nation. The Republicans accepted Black voters as valuable members essential for
ensuring electoral success and expanding the party's political reach through officeholding in Black-majority enclaves.[14]

Like other African Americans, Winters saw the franchise as the foundational
extension of the revolutionary consequences of the Civil War. Actively participating in the county and state Republican party, Winters mobilized Black men
by marshaling collective memories of the Civil War dead and the sacrifice of veterans, including his own son Jacob. The party allowed him and other Black men
to express civic virtue and manhood through voting, organizing political clubs,
and shaping party affairs. Winters hoped that such party loyalty would eventually extend to patronage positions and officeholding.[15] His leadership as well as
his antebellum connections to Frederick Douglass most likely contributed to the
first major Republican Party campaign event in Chambersburg.

On March 1, 1872, Frederick Douglass delivered his popular "Self-Made Man"
speech at Repository Hall. While written before the Civil War, Douglass's lecture
was "in frequent demand after the conflict."[16] Eagerly paying fifty cents, citizens
overflowed the popular Chambersburg venue. Both Black and white attendees
"listened intently to the very close [of the speech]."[17] The famed abolitionist and
Civil War recruiter's speech kicked off the election season in which Black Franklin County men would cast ballots in their first presidential and state gubernatorial races. The reception and aftermath of the speech revealed how Winters,
Black Franklin County men, and their white counterparts understood Black
men's political uses of Civil War memory for advancing an inclusive and just
postwar society.

After offering perfunctory introductory remarks, Douglass defined and outlined the characteristics of self-made men in the first section. Douglass considered self-made men as those "who, under peculiar difficulties and without the

ordinary helps of favoring circumstances, have attained knowledge, usefulness, power and position and have learned from themselves the best uses to which life can be put in this world, and in the exercises of these uses to build up worthy character."[18] Race, wealth and/or birth status did not automatically secure one's entry into the coveted class. Black military service and African American communal sacrifices provided them with the necessary traits for becoming self-made men. Whether civilian, soldier, slave, or self-liberated refugee, the Franklin County men and other African Americans had to overcome "unfavorable conditions, to hew out for themselves a way to success, and thus to become the architects of their own good fortunes."[19] In this context, at the start of the 1872 presidential and Pennsylvania gubernatorial election season, these newly franchised African Americans had earned the political, social, and economic rights secured by the Civil War victory and three Reconstruction Amendments. Of the postwar developments, the franchise and ability to shape local, state, and national politics allowed them to truly live meaningful lives and honor the sacrifices of Black military service remembered within the Emancipationist and Won Cause traditions. For Douglass and Franklin County men, the Civil War and its immediate memory created new gendered understandings of Black manhood and intra-community relations.

Out of the ashes of the Confederacy, Black men could now fully reach their highest potential without the stain of slavery and prewar second-class Black citizenship status. The war, Black military service, and recent Reconstruction history had allowed Douglass to situate his concept of the Black self-made man within the predominantly white canonical tradition. He showed how Black men would rise to the occasion of freedom irrespective of region and Civil War experience. Work, the franchise, and equality, all secured by the Civil War, would allow for racial progress.[20] After providing United States and Atlantic World models of Black self-made men, Douglass expressed hope in the national Reconstruction project. The Fifteenth Amendment eliminated another major obstacle impeding African American success. "With equal suffrage in our hands, we are beyond the power of families, nationalities or races," Douglass told the audience."[21] In his closing, he cautioned them against hero worship of past, present, and future self-made men. Self-made men could be flawed. And African American men, flawed or otherwise, still categorically fit the new definition of manhood defined by the self-made men ethos. Even past wrongs and enemies of African Americans and white allies laid the foundation. Antebellum anti-Blackness rhetoric, policies, and historical experiences provided a valuable education for the moving forward in the new political landscape.[22]

Media responses proved mixed. The nature of the commentary shaped how rural Black Pennsylvanians navigated their first presidential campaign. The *Public Opinion* praised Douglass's lecture and oratory skills. The white Chambersburg reporter positively summarized the lecture for readers: "The subject was treated in a philosophical yet popular manner. The thoughts were sensible, conservative and elegantly expressed, and despite some manifest want of animation and careless tripping an occasional sentence, it gave general satisfaction."[23] Instead of going into extensive detail on the speech, the local Democratic Party–leaning newspapers took pains in discussing a racial incident involving Douglass after the Chambersburg lecture in nearby Carlisle. At his local accommodations, the proprietor did not allow Douglass to eat at the same table with other white boarders.[24] Extensively quoting Douglass's account of the incident, the Carlisle *American Volunteer* openly questioned Douglass's age, perceived racial heritage, and in turn, his ability to shape Black men's political activism.[25] The white author then deemed Douglass's account as being "simply silly and wicked" and dismissed his entire lecture for its promotion of "social equality nonsense" to the audience.[26] For white Pennsylvanians, Douglass's Chambersburg lecture and the Carlisle racial incident became fodder for ridicule of African Americans' claims of equality and participation in shaping local and national politics as self-made men.

For Winters and other Black Franklin County men, however, Douglass's notion of self-made men unified them into a single voting bloc. The different Civil War experiences—civilian, veteran, slave, or self-liberated refugee—did not matter in actualizing the promise achieved through the Civil War sacrifices. The 1872 election season allowed them to become the self-made men characterized by Douglass. In the process, they transformed the Douglass lecture into a real political strategy and countered white Pennsylvanians' dismissal of the African American military service and Civil War collective memories for political action. Despite the anti-Black racist treatment of Douglass, the success of the March 1, 1872, event reflected the early strength of the biracial Republican Party in Franklin County. The event not only affirmed African American allegiance to the party but also cemented Winters's position as a significant party leader.

After the Douglass lecture, Winters helped to mobilize Black Republicans in the Colored Grant and Wilson Club of Franklin County. The political organization's leadership included both veterans and non-veterans who had played a role in the Ratification celebration. The future Martin Delany GAR post commander Thomas L. White, Fifty-Fifth Massachusetts veteran, served as the head of the organization. Winters served as co-vice president with Ashford Collins. Collins had enlisted in the Forty-First USCI as a private in September 1864 and mustered out as a corporal in September 1865.[27] Alfred (Albert) Bradford, a Twenty-Fourth USCI veteran served as the sergeant in arms. The future inaugural vice commander of the Delaney GAR post also led the Independent Blues militia at the Fifteenth Amendment ratification parade.[28] Both Corresponding Secretary William H. Middleton and Recording Secretary Edward M. Thompson were known community leaders active in the Fanset Lodge, No. 1497, of the Odd Fellows. Thompson used his leadership in the Grant and Wilson Club as a stepping-stone for future leadership in the local Black Republican Party affairs.[29] During the 1872 election season, Winters and these organizational leaders mobilized Black Franklin County men through speeches, rallies, and other activities.

The diverse Civil War experiences of veterans, civilians, self-liberated, and formerly enslaved persons extended to the entire membership. Of the named individuals within published news accounts of the Colored Grant and Wilson Club activities, several Civil War veterans participated. Several had self-liberated from Virginia before enlisting out of Pennsylvania and later joined the local GAR post.[30] Franklin County natives, such as David Nelson Little of Chambersburg, enlisted once racial barriers had been removed.[31] Serving in places far away from Franklin County, Pennsylvania, these veterans established families and formed strong community organizations. Now, these franchised veterans transformed their military service and communal collective memories of their wartime sacrifices into shaping local and national politics in the Grant and Wilson Club.

The Colored Grant and Wilson Club also encompassed formerly enslaved Virginians who migrated to Franklin County. Some had previous community leadership positions before their service in the various club subcommittees. Armstead Baltimore, for instance, was a leading figure in the Hope Presbyterian Church and a member of the Odd Fellows.[32] Emigrating from the Shenandoah Valley, Royal Christian established himself as a major religious and community leader. His daughter later chronicled these contributions in her 1956 Black History series published in the mainstream Franklin County newspaper.[33] These new county residents' Civil War experiences did not prevent them from shaping the organization. They worked alongside veterans in cementing their support for the Grant reelection bid and defining the Black postwar political landscape through a politicized understanding of Civil War memory.

Collectively, these Grant and Wilson Club members articulated new notions of manhood, citizenship, and leadership. Rural Franklin County men emerged as a significant voting bloc for shaping local and national affairs. Whether veteran, formerly enslaved, civilian, or self-liberated, these known Grant and Wilson club members embodied the postwar franchised role models. As self-made men, Winters's leadership and songwriting helped to unify them in their first two presidential elections.

At the inaugural meeting of the Colored Grant and Wilson Club, Winters helped draft the resolutions affirming their political commitment. The meeting format reflected tried and true Black formalist tradition. After reports read by the committee tasked with the creation of the club, the initial officers were named and approved by consent.[34] With confirmed leadership, the work of approving the resolutions got underway. For the Franklin County men, the memory of the Civil War and postwar political actions of the opposing party shaped the resolutions explaining their support of Grant's reelection. Offered by Club President Thomas L. White and "adopted with great demonstration of applause," the assembled men passed the following resolutions:

> We, the colored citizens of Chambersburg, declare our hostility to our common foe, the Democratic party, which has been from its organization down to the present time, the unrelenting enemy of our race, as is seen in its united opposition to the acts of emancipation, our civil rights and enfranchisement; therefore—
>
> *Resolved*, That its infamous record in causing a bloody war, with all its consequences, is not by us forgotten.[35]

Democrats were the postwar enemy. Congressional Republicans had in their estimation secured their constitutional rights of citizenship. The Franklin County men pledged their support of the entire Republican Party slate in the closing.[36] With the resolutions adopted, White appointed Winters as one of the local delegates to the statewide Pennsylvania State Equal Rights League meeting in Harrisburg.[37]

Given his prominence in the community, Winters was a natural choice for representing the Franklin County club interests at the statewide Pennsylvania State Equal Rights League convention held in Harrisburg on August 20, 1872. He and other Franklin County men found common ground with other Pennsylvania State Equal Rights League delegates. The convention organizers proclaimed: "The enemies of our rights, our citizenship, our race, under a new leader and with a new name, are mustering to fight for power, position, and the National government."[38] They were concerned, according to their published *Harrisburg Telegraph* announcement, that "the crack of the slave-whip echoes in their camp, and the clanking of new forged chains for our limbs may be heard amidst treacherous deliberations." They, therefore, called on all "Men of Pennsylvania. Awake! Arise!" Winters and other delegates took special trains to Harrisburg and solidified a unified campaign in support of Grant's reelection and other Republican candidates.[39]

The statewide convention also celebrated the second anniversary of the Fifteenth Amendment ratification with a large parade and public speeches. The Black Harrisburg community again hosted a parade that featured three divisions of marshals, civic and fraternal organizations, militias and drum corps, and carriages carrying the featured speakers and members of the Pennsylvania State Equal Rights League. Several parade banners announced their preferred presidential and gubernatorial candidates of Grant and John F. Hartranft. After navigating the Harrisburg streets, William Howard Day and other speakers addressed the assembled crowd on Independence Island.[40] This large public spectacle reminded all Pennsylvanians of Black men's constitutional right to participate in their first postwar presidential and gubernatorial elections. As self-made men, convention delegates, visitors, and eligible parade attendees fully planned on exercising their political rights. The Civil War political gains would not be wasted. They would cast their ballots en masse for the Republican Party.

The September 10, 1872, Grant and Wilson Club meeting established the template for future meetings. After Winters's report on the Harrisburg convention, the attendees received and sang the official 1872 Republican Song appealing to African American voters "with great spirit and enthusiasm."[41] Members heard a special address by Frederick Henninger. Club members worked in subcommittees and presented reports on their progress. After the September meeting, club members regularly met. Through regular meetings, special addresses, and singing the official 1872 song, the men cemented their self-made political status as Republican voters.[42]

For Winters, however, the official 1872 Republican campaign song for Black voters did not capture the Pennsylvania border communities. Written by Elijah W. Smith, the nine-verse "The Colored Voters' Song" encouraged Black men to vote for Grant's reelection.[43] Set to the tune of "Tramp, Tramp, Tramp," Smith opened in the first two verses with clear use of Civil War memory of how Black soldiers' military service under General Grant's leadership secured emancipation. A vote for Grant would "bless the chieftain brave / Who our native land did save, / And we'll keep him in the presidential chair."[44] As a proven ally, Smith suggested that Black men should not be duped by either the Democrats or Liberal Republicans appealing for their ballot. The second verse would have felt alien to the Franklin County club members, except perhaps the formerly

enslaved Virginians who migrated to the Pennsylvania border county. A victory
for Greeley, one of Grant's opponents, might reverse emancipation and postwar
gains: "Though foul slavery's course is run / And the jubilee begun, / Yet the foe-
man's muttered curses fill the air. /" By voting, Black men would "bury out of
sight / All the wrong, the shame, the blight." The references to slavery failed to
capture the diverse Civil War experiences of potential Franklin County voters.
National Republican Party leaders saw the African American electorate consisting of primarily Southern freedpeople and USCT veterans. Winters and other
civilian Franklin County survivors of three Confederate raids did not neatly fit
in their political imaginary of the electorate.[45]

The failure to address Gettysburg and the flattening of Civil War experiences
to either slave or soldier most likely motivated Winters's first presidential campaign song, which he wrote four years later in support of Rutherford B. Hayes.
In 1876, Winters purposefully drew on his memories of the sights, sounds, wartime allegiances, and civilian traumas experienced during Gettysburg. Unlike
the other campaign songs, his songs addressed the self-made men who saw their
victory in 1872 as a hopeful start in their political emancipatory efforts to reshape
local, state, and national politics. Winters turned his songwriting skills into a tool
for political mobilization from 1876 to 1912.[46]

By the mid-1870s, the county and state Republicans expanded Winters's role in
the party. Party officials embraced Winters's skills as a songwriter in their local
campaign efforts for the national presidential election candidates. Winters had
gained notoriety with two wartime songs. One captured the African American
experience during the Gettysburg Campaign.[47] The other song encouraged Black
men's enlistment into the various USCT regiments that trained at Camp William Penn.[48] In the surviving Republican Party campaign songs of 1876 and 1880,
Winters drew on the complex African American memory and expectations for
patronage and rights for all African Americans. He intentionally deployed Civil
War memory as a central tenet of the new Black political ethos of Black Franklin
County men.

Winters's earliest surviving campaign song supported Rutherford B. Hayes
and his running mate William A. Wheeler in the 1876 presidential election.
Throughout, Winters urged Black men to vote to prove their manhood in the
new postwar fight for African American citizenship. By supporting the Twenty-
Third Ohio Infantry veteran turned presidential nominee, moreover, they affirmed their status as self-made men.[49] With "the foe is in our land," Winters
urged them to

Come, girdle on your armor;
Be ready at command,
To march with Hayes and Wheeler
Into the promised land![50]

In the opening verse, Winters appealed directly to postwar Black religious understanding of the Civil War embraced in the AME and AMEZ churches in the
Pennsylvania border community. As USCT soldiers had worn the blue uniform
for securing emancipation, Franklin County men as self-made political men and
Christians had to resist racial subjugation as God's chosen people.[51] They had to
stop efforts to undo their newly acquired rights and the other anti-Black policies of the Democratic Party seeking to redeem the nation of the Reconstruction
constitutional amendments. Voting represented their collective electoral power
of "emancipation's eschatological significance."[52] As political citizens, Franklin
County men had only one option: cast a ballot for the Hayes and Wheeler ticket.
      In the second verse, Winters drew on Black men's memories of the three Civil
War invasions in the Pennsylvania border community. These Confederate raids
resulted in the enslavement of African American residents and the 1864 burning of Chambersburg. Winters's inclusion of the second verse would have held
meaning for Black Franklin County men. He wrote:

For Tilden and his army,
With Hendricks in command,
Are marching, brother freeman,
Your right to countermand.
We see their rebel pickets,
We hear their cannons roar,
Like Herod and his army,
We'll see to see no more.[53]

Winters and other civilians who survived the three invasions would have recalled how the sounds of cannons forced them into hiding. They had witnessed
the seizure of community members by Confederate soldiers. Few of these stolen
residents returned. As freemen, they had to fight against their political enslavement and a return to second-class citizenship as experienced prior to the passage
of the Fifteenth Amendment. They had to destroy this new political army led by
Tilden and his supporters.

If Black men needed further encouragement, Winters urged them to honor Lincoln's memory by voting for the Republican Party in the third verse. Extending his April 1865 eulogy to the campaign song, Winters encouraged singers to remember:

Our good, old Father Abraham
Has safely brought us through
From slavery and oppression,
We know we now are free.[54]

Lincoln's memory still unified Black Franklin County men. It had yet to become a tokenized symbol used by white Republicans for securing Black men's political loyalty. Winters later abandoned such imagery. In his second campaign song, however, Winters urged:

Come, let us join together
In a band of unity.[55]

A vote for the Republican presidential slate would honor the slain president who made the ultimate sacrifice for African Americans in the state and nation.

Therefore, Winters demanded that Black men demonstrate their manhood by voting for the Hayes and Wheeler ticket. Like his 1863 recruitment song, Winters questioned whether Black men were cowards or self-made men. Winters demanded Black men's courage in this political struggle in the last verse:

We call for valiant soldiers
Who are not afraid to stand;
To go on next November
And vote for honest men.[56]

He saw the Republicans as critical allies in the fight for meaningful African American equality. With the ballot, they no longer had to rely on others to speak on their behalf. Now, Black Franklin County voters could address the perceived socioeconomic and political challenges facing the nation as had Black USCT soldiers who had responded to his and Douglass's call to arms in 1863. Now they had to demonstrate their political manhood by voting for Rutherford B. Hayes. Otherwise, they would be political cowards who allowed for the retreat of their postwar political, economic, and social rights. Simply put, Black men had to step up.

And they paid heed. As a voting bloc, Black Franklin County men overwhelmingly supported the Republican ticket as had Frederick Douglass, their mentor.[57]

Following the success of the 1876 presidential election, Winters composed another campaign song. The 1880 presidential election pitted Civil War veteran Winfield Scott Hancock of Pennsylvania against another Civil War veteran James A. Garfield of Ohio. As the Democratic Party candidate, Hancock, veteran of the Army of the Potomac, had earned his reputation as a war hero at Gettysburg.[58] He appealed to Southern Democrats by supporting home rule, decrease in the use of the military in civilian affairs, and the repudiation of the "great fraud of 1876–77."[59] The party platform not only called into question the Hayes presidency following the Compromise of 1877 but also the politicized use of Garfield's Civil War wartime legacy as evidence of his inability to lead. Instead, Democrats drew on their candidate's military record and suggested that a Hancock victory would "preserve the country from the horrors of a civil war, submitted for the time in firm and patriotic faith that the people would punish this crime in 1880."[60] Garfield, veteran of the Forty-Second Ohio Infantry, accepted the candidacy after a contested nomination process.[61] He promised the strengthening and expansion of biracial, inclusive democracy for reconciling the ongoing post–Civil War tensions. "But it is certain that the wounds of the war cannot be completely healed," Garfield wrote in his letter accepting the nomination, "and the spirit of brotherhood cannot fully pervade the whole country, until every citizen, rich or poor, white or black, is secure in the free and equal enjoyment of every civil and equal right guaranteed by the constitution and the laws."[62] While the Greenbacks waged a third party campaign, the 1880 presidential election served as a referendum on Civil War memory and Black political participation in the national body politic. In this contest over memory and shaping national political identity, Winters deployed his skills for the Garfield-Arthur candidacy. His song became one of many written for the Republican ticket. Winters, however, tailored his appeal to the self-made man identity and collective memories of Black Pennsylvania border county residents.[63]

Set to the tune of "We are Marching through the Gates," Winters again called upon the service of Black men in a fight for postbellum African American political gains and Civil War memory. He provocatively suggested that pro-Confederate raiders had invaded the southern Pennsylvanian county for a fourth time. "Come to arms! brother Freeman! / The foe is in our land," Winters warned in the opening two lines.[64] Unlike the Civil War invading generals, the Democratic candidates of Winfield S. Hancock and William H. English served as "the commanders of their band" under the direction of "a solid South united" and British industrialist support.[65] Hancock's embrace of Southern Democrats concerned him. Southern Democrats' violent return to power and retrenchment of Southern Black gains, according to Winters, intended to reduce all African Americans to a state of slavery and second-class citizenship. In this fourth Pennsylvanian invasion, Winters raised the alarm that Black men had to defend the nation in the 1880 presidential election struggle.

By intentionally using "call to arms" in the first verse, Winters also wanted Black Franklin County men to recall a similar order posed by Frederick Douglass in his recruitment editorial. Douglass reminded Black men of their duty to country and African American community, free and enslaved, in his USCT recruitment efforts.[66] As Douglass demanded twenty-seven years earlier, Winters called men into a new fight for country and African American community under the threat posed by a possible Hancock presidency. Once again, he felt that Black Pennsylvanians had to serve as liberators of the race and nation and secure their "gratitude . . . and best blessings" by voting for the Garfield-Arthur ticket on November 2, 1880.[67]

The next two verses drew on the collective memories of the previous invasions. Winters and other Franklin County residents had experienced immense trauma. They had had to evade seizure and enslavement. They had lost community members. Instead of waving the bloody shirt as white Republicans, Winters drew on their collective understanding of the sights, sounds, and experiences of the Gettysburg Campaign. "We have seen their rebel pickets, / We have heard their cannons roar," Winters reminded them in the second verse.[68] During the Gettysburg Campaign occupation, Winters added how they endured "lies and condemnation."[69] Yet these ex-Confederates lost. Defeat and Reconstruction brought justice for Franklin County residents' suffering. A Hancock victory, however, would bring the "mercy now they [Southerners] crave."[70] Black men, therefore, must fight. They must emphatically protest the embrace of these ex-Confederates by Lost Cause and Reconciliationist sympathizers, including a hero of Gettysburg seeking the presidency. His win would leave African Americans, whether in Franklin County or nation, "comfortless."[71] According to Winters, they had to defeat "General Hancock and his army" who sought the overturning of the postbellum gains achieved by African Americans. "With GARFIELD in command," their political service as self-made men would prevent both African Americans and "American labor" from becoming "subjects of foreign lands."[72]

Over the final two verses, Winters again cajoled Black men into action. Black Americans could not remain idle in this new political fight. They had to fight to remain self-made men instead of political slaves. Their "prize," as suggested by

Winters, would be the continued benefits of the Reconstruction Amendments. Their self-made men status remained "just in view" because the Republican nominees "will carry us safely through."[73] The proven Civil War commander would not disappoint them if they pledged their ballots. By going with "GENERAL GARFIELD," Winters assured Franklin County men that a victory would ensure "a Freeman's Land."[74] By drawing on Civil War memory, Winters convinced them. Again, Black Franklin County men overwhelmingly supported the Republican ticket and propelled Garfield to the presidency.

After a decade of Republican party allegiance, Winters voiced his disappointment at the failure of his party to advance a fully inclusive political order. In return for Black votes, he expected that party officials would provide patronage positions and more leadership opportunities in the county, state, and national party apparatus. Black men's sacrifices—by civilians, veterans, and those who had died in the war—failed to materialize real change. Not quite ready to abandon the Republicans, Winters drafted a warning to party leadership. In the published article titled "Information Wanted," he questioned white Republicans' insistence that Black men should wait

> until the very eves of election, to have a halter placed around our necks to be led to the political altars of this country as a lamb to the slaughter, there to surrender all rights of manhood to partyism, without the right to exercise our political judgment according to our own dictates of partyism, because we were once slaves held in bondage to a tyrannical power for over two hundred years by the white man of this free America, which only by the results of the late rebellion between the North and South and a war necessity to power, etc., we are free to-day, or so called to be?[75]

Demanding that they prioritize Black manhood over party, Winters did not mince his words. Black men saved the nation. Black men's military service and civilian patriotism allowed for the defeat of "Jefferson Davis and his followers of the Southern Confederacy" and secured the "rights of franchise."[76] Yet white Republicans only considered them as compatriots on the eves of elections. Winters no longer accepted without question white Pennsylvanians who claimed "to love us and our freedom for political purposes" while expecting them to wait for leadership positions.[77]

State party officials' appeal to a shared memory of Abraham Lincoln also irritated Winters. Simplistic collective memories of the assassinated president no longer connected Winters with white Republican officials. Winters countered with a more nuanced understanding of Abraham Lincoln. Instead of the "Great Emancipator," Winters recalled that Lincoln sought to preserve the nation; he didn't prioritize abolition or full African American citizenship. Winters chastised his white Republican brethren who promoted simplistic understandings because of preconceived stereotypical views of Black men as childlike, uneducated, and uninformed voters who unquestionably followed the party of Lincoln. In this public forum, Winters refused to accommodate such lazy usage of Lincoln's emancipationist memory for securing Black men's party loyalty. Speaking for all Black Pennsylvanians, Winters asked his white Republican brethren "under what tie of political subservience are we bound to party or partyism?"[78] For Winters, African American manhood and Civil War memory should not be placed on hold for existing party exclusionary practices.

Such appeals to simplistic Emancipationist collective memories rang especially hollow for Winters who remembered the civilian trauma incurred during the three Confederate invasions. He debunked the common election appeal that Republicans "fought, bled and died in the late cruel war only for the black man, North and South," by reminding them of the Gettysburg Campaign in the final paragraph of the article.[79] During the invasion and occupation of central Pennsylvania in June 1863, white Pennsylvanians rejected the service of Black Pennsylvanians who traveled to Harrisburg. After offering "their lives before the altar of his country for the preservation of this Union," the rebuffed able-bodied Cumberland Valley men, including Winters and four other Franklin County men who "went to Harrisburg, the Capital of the State of Pennsylvania, and there joined the company under Captain Bradley for the [defense] of this Union as well as our fireside."[80] But "on the same day the rebel army was marching on to the Capital of the State," Winters reminded Republican leaders how he and other Black Pennsylvanians built "a defense for the Capital of the State without a gun or the right to use, with the rebel outposts in view."[81] Winters questioned party leadership in his closing: "Are these they who fought, bled and died for us, the black man? God forbid that we have eyes but see not, ears but hear not, understanding but understand not, tongues to speak but speak not the things of our mind of a just cause."[82] By drawing on African American memory of Gettysburg, including Black men's defense of Harrisburg, Winters effectively cautioned them. Reform or African American voters would look for a party that fully appreciated their electoral support. White Republican leaders' memory of the Civil War will no longer guarantee their allegiance. Like other urban African Americans, Winters felt that race, manhood, and Black Civil War memory mattered more than party.

Winters's criticism and frustration mirrored the views of disillusioned urban Black men and national leaders. Winters used his editorials for enlightening his former white Republican allies who branded them "ungrateful" and "renegade Republicans" for considering their "political future" whether as Independents or Democrats.[83] In an open letter to the *Valley Spirit,* Winters and five other Black Franklin County men informed readers that "we will not bow down to our political masters, as sheep before their slayers, to be instruments for defeat."[84] They furthered added: "Defeat has marked the candidacy of every one of our colored men. . . . [They] have been made martyrs by votes of the party that today charges the colored man with defeat of his colored brother when he runs office."[85] Even William Still defied most Black Philadelphian voters by openly supporting Grover Cleveland's candidacy for president in 1884. Still's disillusionment began a decade earlier, and he attempted independent politics before embracing the Democratic Party.[86] The failure of the Republican and Democratic parties reflected white Americans' betrayal of Black voters and their communities. Political independence, though risky, allowed Black Bostonians to remain committed to racial solidarity and secure the desired material gains, patronage, and political appointments, and Black Baltimoreans' "organizing tradition" advanced postwar Black politics, equality, and citizenship.[87] In the process, Black men and women sustained citizenship rights and the franchise by positioning themselves as the best "safeguard against political corruption, oppression and disorder" in the Maryland city.[88] Winters's memory of the Gettysburg Campaign, however, distinguished his criticism from urban Black politicos: Winters carved out a space for rural Black Pennsylvanians and added their voices to the broader political landscape locally, regionally, and nationally.

Winters abandoned the Republican Party within the decade. His departure reflected the decisions of other Black men who sought a new political landscape that fully accepted African Americans as full and equal citizens. For many, the failed Republican promises motivated their actions. Black Baltimoreans, for instance, opted for organizations like the Mutual United Brotherhood, a late nineteenth-century civil rights organization whose legal strategy for challenging threats to Black citizenship predated the National Association for the Advancement of Colored People (NAACP).[89] Black Bostonians chose political independence and moved between Democrats, Republicans, and third-party movements. Winters and other Black men navigated the political landscape by pursuing a collective understanding of what emancipation and the Civil War meant as the nation moved toward political realities defined by the Lost Cause and Reconciliationist traditions.[90] Some embraced the various third party movements and their class reconciliationist politics that combined "aspects of emancipationist memory, which insisted that slavery's destruction was the primary legacy of the of war, and reconciliation memory, rooted in sectional rapprochement."[91] Winters, therefore, could have chosen political independence or supported one of the many third parties. Instead, Winters officially joined the Democratic Party. He felt that the local and state Democratic party best allowed him to actualize his understanding of Civil War memory as an expression of Black manhood and citizenship. Despite the party's stance nationally and within the South, Pennsylvania Party officials offered both leadership and actual power in shaping local affairs.[92]

Winters announced his new political allegiance in a dramatic fashion. With the Democratic victory in major state offices, county and state Democrats promised addressing former President Grover Cleveland's tariff reform message and statewide election reform. In the victory parade speeches, William Rush Gillan, who had been elected to the Pennsylvania House of Representatives, reminded the crowd of "the assistance received by the Democratic party from honest Republicans" like himself and vowed to "labor with all his strength for the enactment of such measures as would insure the integrity and secrecy of the ballot."[93] By taking a prominent position in the Gillan victory parade, Joseph Winters officially joined the Democratic Party.

Winters's political defection did not escape the notice of either the *Valley Spirit* or county Republicans. Using Civil War memory in mobilizing Black voters, Winters and other Franklin County men expected full inclusion. The county Republican Party simply failed to extend officeholding and patronage positions to its Black constituency. Black men's electoral support resulted in only two positions.[94] In addition to not receiving any material benefits from their political support, party leaders had ignored Winters and other men's warning to not take the Black electorate for granted. Ultimately, Winters chose race and his self-made man status over party.

County Democrats accepted and listened to the former Republican. He remained committed to the self-made man ethos but found a political home that fully embraced Black men in different ways. He led the local Democratic Party club for African American men for roughly twenty-five years.[95] He felt heard by white party leaders. His disappointment and political transformation were shared by others, but not all Black Franklin County men. As a result, rural Black Pennsylvanians reflected the split political allegiances consistent with the urban North. They chose political parties that best fit their vision wrought by veterans and wartime dead. While remaining committed to Douglass's notion, Black

Franklin County men were no longer unified since obtaining the franchise in the Fifteenth Amendment. For Winters, sectional reconciliation and Republican efforts to attract white voters grounded in Black political exclusion proved unacceptable. Winters would die as a Democrat.

Democratic Party leaders, as their Republican counterparts, benefited from Winters's songwriting skills even though Winters no longer held as much influence over the entire African American electorate. By the time of his defection, Winters remained one of the wealthiest African American residents in the county. He had secured a patent for an improved fire escape.[96] He also expanded his businesses to including drilling and mining while still maintaining a successful gunsmith shop in Chambersburg. Ultimately, party officials recognized how his Republican campaign songs helped in securing victory for both Hayes and Garfield.

Then Winters penned several Democratic Party campaign songs before his death in 1916.[97] The surviving songs for the presidential election campaigns of 1900, 1904, and 1912 mirrored his earlier Republican versions. He set the lyrics to the tune of "We Are Marching through the Gates." Like other songwriters of the era, Winters drew on Franklin County men's "musical knowledge" of his earlier campaign songs, which provided the "fastest way . . . to learn and spread song words" when "set to familiar melodies."[98] Winters still employed Civil War memory and African American wartime sacrifice for mobilizing Black voters. Some tropes remained similar, specifically phrasing, urgency of the moment, and complex understandings of Civil War memory. These songs remained political calls to arms. He continued to demand Black men to don their political armor and recall the sacrifices of the USCT soldiers during the Civil War.[99] The opening of the pro–Democratic Party songs marked a significant difference in the three surviving songs. With the revamped opening, Winters merely substituted the candidates' names in the chorus and promoted national Democratic candidates over the Republicans and Third Party options. Throughout, he advanced the necessity for Black men to fight for economic and political freedom and not their enslavement as dependent second-class citizens.[100]

Of these songs, Winters's 1900 campaign song and political transformation aligned with the views of AME Bishop Henry McNeal Turner, a Civil War veteran who served as a Reconstruction-era politician in Georgia. Both men openly campaigned for William Jennings Bryan in the election of 1900. Turner's own understanding of his military service, political expectations, and political use of Civil War memory brings into sharp relief how and why Joseph Winters's surviving Democratic songs reflected both rural Pennsylvanian and

national trends in the divided African American political and Civil War commemorative landscapes.

After his election to bishop in the AME Church, Turner, who served as the
chaplain of the First USCT Regiment, used his position and various Black newspaper outlets for leveraging Black political power in the late nineteenth century.
Like Winters, Turner expressed hope for the national Reconstruction project
following the ratification of the Fifteenth Amendment. "This Amendment is an
ensign of our citizenship, the prompter of our patriotism, the bandage that is
to blindfold Justice while his sturdy hands hold the scales and weighs out im-
partial equity to all, regardless of popular favor or censure," Turner explained.[101]
The outcome of the 1876 presidential election, the terms of the Compromise
of 1877 deal, and violent Southern redemption politics frustrated him. Over
the 1880s, Turner lost faith in the Republican Party, which chose the political expediency of whiteness over Black Southerners' political participation. The
Arthur administration's mishandling of the post–Supreme Court *Civil Rights
Cases of 1883* decision, which overturned Reconstruction-era social gains and
other failed promises, encouraged Turner's shift away from the Republicans to
the Democrats and independent politics.[102] In his mind, the Republican party
failed to live up to the African American political ethos rooted in Black Civil
War understandings.

Turner formally left the Republican Party by the end of the decade. He turned
his attention to emigration but still wrote several controversial editorials that
focused on major political issues shaping the Black community.[103] Turner, liked
Winters, coped with intergenerational conflict over the political strategies for
staving off the retreat from Reconstruction and the growing Reconciliationist
impulse that did not place value on either African American historical experiences or collective Civil War memorial traditions for shaping the American
political landscape.[104]

In the 1900 presidential election, Turner openly campaigned against William
McKinley's candidacy for reelection. He was a vocal critic of the white Twenty-
Third Ohio Infantry veteran who served under Rutherford B. Hayes during the
Civil War.[105] Turner criticized McKinley's limited interaction with Black Americans during his first term and unleashed an attack on McKinley's foreign policy,
specifically the involvement in the Spanish-American War and its imperialistic
expansion with the Filipino War. Seeing the wars as evidence of an American
imperial campaign, Bishop Turner criticized Black military involvement in the
conflict. He even rejected the popular Black communal sentiment that Black
soldiers' defense of the nation would secure African American rights at home

as it had been supposed to for the Civil War generation.[106] Unlike other Black leaders, Turner did not mince his words when voicing his opposition. Turner contended: "As the Filipinos belong to the darker human variety, the Negro is fighting against himself. Any Negro soldier that will cross the ocean to help subjugate the Filipinos is a fool or a villain."[107] Signaling his "solemn protest against the unholy war of conquest," Turner endorsed Democratic candidate William Jennings Bryan for president.[108]

Across the nation, Turner drew heavy criticism. For many African Americans, Turner had gone too far in supporting a political party that had historically proven to be a haven for anti-Black, pro-white supremacist, and pro–Lost Cause ideologues. His critics questioned his loyalty to the race and the Emancipationist tradition. By supporting Bryan, some felt Turner had approved the extension of Southern Black disfranchisement to the entire country. Some AME ministers also leveled pointed attacks against him at pro-McKinley political rallies. Neither his Civil War veteran status nor his leadership in the AME Church shielded Turner from intra-Black community attacks over the usage of Civil War memory as the foundational strategy of Black politics in the late nineteenth century. Democrats remained the enemy. Turner's critics pledged their political allegiance to the party of Abraham Lincoln; and therefore, they split from the prominent Civil War veteran for his pro-Bryan support and anti-Black Spanish-American War service stance.[109]

Using the *Voices of the Mission*, Turner responded to these attacks using Civil War memory for justifying his political decision. In the process, Turner stood in stark contrast to the national Republican Party's embrace of sectional reconciliation as a strategy adopted during the 1896 presidential campaign and continued during his reelection bid.[110] In one October 1900 editorial, Turner reminded readers of his own Civil War service when some suggested that since Lincoln and the Republican Party emancipated Southern bondspeople, they should solidify their political allegiance in the late nineteenth century. On this charge, he countered his critics in a series of rhetorical questions. Turner asked: "Where were they before the war between the states, when we were pleading for their freedom? Where were they during the war when as a United States chaplain, we were leading regiments into battle and inspiring tens of thousands to die for the freedom of our race?"[111] For Turner, political allegiance should rest with the collective memory of the African Americans who served and the veterans who survived. The Republican Party did not free them. Black men did. It should be the memory of these men and their sacrifices and not political inheritors of Lincoln's memory that should matter in deciding the election. In short, Black voters should listen to the Civil War veteran and not his detractors. In the end, his critics and *Voices of the Mission* readers remained unconvinced.[112]

Winters's 1900 presidential campaign song took a different approach than Turner's in his appeal to Black men. Winters again urged Black men to don their political armor in the fight for Civil War memory as a strategy for racial uplift.[113] In the second verse, Winters agreed with Turner's characterization of the effects of the Republican incumbent's economic policy for African Americans. "For the rich men with their millions" had not only exploited the "trust and combinations" but also had conspired to "take your rights away."[114] McKinley's economic policy had worsened the stability and future of African American communal and personal economy. For Winters, trusts and other aggressive business practices blocked competition, innovation, and wealth distribution. Combined with federal economic inaction, the trust question loomed large in the Black political landscape.[115] Winters then likened the economic plight to that of the Israelites led by Moses. He encouraged them to join the Democrats and "leave old Pharaoh and his host/In Egypt's land."[116] Winters felt that McKinley's economic policies had reduced them to slaves of the corporations and white business elite. Drawing on the Old Testament references, Winters appealed to both old and new Black voters to recall the political jubilee of the Fifteenth Amendment ratification. The Jubilee, as the community called the 1870 parade, had not been undone. It required another struggle, active campaigning among the undecided, and a unified front to combat the modern Pharaoh in the White House seeking reelection. Winters and other anti-McKinley supporters still believed in "a faith that at least since 1863 time, God, and the weight of history might be on their side."[117] Civil War memory, even if not explicitly stated, still motivated Winters's verse.

Instead of "old Pharaoh and his host," Winters called on Black voters to support Bryan.[118] He saw the 1900 presidential election as a major event in determining African Americans' trajectory in racial progress. Without mentioning any specific candidate or Black leaders, Winters demanded in the third verse:

Now come, follow up your leaders
For your rights of liberty,
And be ready to march over
At the parting of the seas.[119]

He, like Turner, implored Black men to not just blindly accept the Republican Party candidate. They should instead listen to him, Turner, and other Black leaders who saw alternate political parties as encouraging continued racial uplift and protection of African American citizenship writ large. "Now when you're safely over"—Winters believed that a vote for Bryan and Stevenson would see "Old Hanna and McKinley / At the bottom of the sea."[120] If they had any doubts, Winters reminded them of the Prophet Elijah and how all will work out for the best. Otherwise, the African American community's well-being in the Jim Crow imperial nation would continue to decline. They must act and vote against McKinley and his brand of anti-Black sectional reconciliation politics.[121]

Ultimately, McKinley defeated Turner's and Winters's preferred candidate. McKinley reiterated sectional reconciliation in his second inaugural address. While McKinley remained "comfortable accepting the state of racial politics that he had inherited," the small but vocal opposition of the reelection had some effect. McKinley turned post-1900 election visits to Black colleges and universities into racial theater for assuaging any lingering Black concerns.[122] An anarchist assassin's bullet did what Confederate minié balls could not, killing McKinley. National mourning muted Turner, Winters, and other Black leaders' previous opposition expressed during the 1900 election.[123]

Before the fateful events in Buffalo, New York, Turner and Winters differed in their responses to McKinley's reelection. Turner grew increasingly disenchanted with the nation who betrayed the Civil War generation. With his pen, oratory, and his standing as a national leader, the Civil War veteran remained "the prophet that African Americans needed. His pessimistic hope was to uplift the race by telling the truth about their situation."[124] In contrast, Winter composed two additional presidential campaign songs. Winters did not allow either the 1900 campaign defeat or his age to prevent his continued use of Civil War memory for the political mobilization of Black men. Through his pen, aged body, and status as a county leader, Winters, like others of the Civil War generation, symbolized the self-made man ethos proclaimed earlier by Douglass's 1872 speech in Chambersburg, Pennsylvania. Even as the nation opted for collective forgetting, white supremacy, and Black men's political removal from the body politic, Winters and other Franklin County men chose remembrance and defiance of the national political expectations of them. They deployed Civil War memory as an electoral strategy on their own terms.

For the 1904 presidential election, Winters endorsed Alton Parker of New York over the incumbent Theodore Roosevelt who became president following McKinley's assassination. With Parker as the nominee, Democrats affirmed the fundamental principles for ensuring national "peace, safety and progress" and outlined its objectives in eradicating corruption in public service, economic policy reforms, and limiting executive power in the platform adopted on July 6,

1904.[125] Democrats also called for limiting American imperialism in Cuba and the Philippines and pledged to "construct the Panama Canal speedily, honestly, and economically."[126] The Republican platform again appealed to sectional reconciliation by acknowledging the fiftieth anniversary of the party founding, Lincoln's election in 1860, and its national leadership over the long Reconstruction era.[127] Republicans celebrated their achievements, including economic recovery, the gold standard adoption, and success as an imperial nation. A vote for Roosevelt, according to the platform adopted on June 21, 1904, would honor the memory of the assassinated Civil War veteran turned president, and uphold the new Roosevelt corollary to the Monroe Doctrine which promised US military intervention to restore political stability in any country in the Western hemisphere.[128] Many of these platform themes and campaign talking points appear in Winters's song. Specifically, he drew on the issue of effects on trusts and combinations on ordinary men and Roosevelt's imperialistic policy that eroded the "constitutional rights of Americans," especially Black Americans.[129]

Winters suffered another defeat as Pennsylvania and the national electorate overwhelmingly supported Roosevelt over the Democratic Party and Third Party candidates. Roosevelt easily won with 336 electoral votes and the popular vote. Parker secured the solid South vote where disfranchisement effectively removed Black men from the electoral process. It seemed that both the Reconciliationist and Lost Cause commemorative traditions unified the Jim Crow nation more than Black Civil War collective understandings.[130]

As the president of Colored Democratic Club, Winters wrote his final presidential campaign song in support of Woodrow Wilson.[131] The 1912 Democratic Party platform promised "New Freedom" with an emphasis on tariff reform, banking reform, state rights, and individualism.[132] Keeping a similar opening as the 1900 and 1904 songs, Winters referred to many of the platform themes and appealed to the common man, irrespective of race and meager employment in the coal mines, on the "raging seas" or toiling the farmland. He also ignored the Socialist Party campaign. He only discussed the traditional two-party candidates and avoided mentioning Eugene Debs, which he had also done in the 1904 song. But in terms of tone and verse, Winters slightly modified the 1904 presidential campaign song.[133]

Winters exploited the division among those in the Republican Party in the song. He encouraged Black men to trust neither former President Theodore Roosevelt, who ran under the newly formed Progressive Party, nor Howard Taft, the Republican candidate. While Booker T. Washington endorsed Taft, Winters was more aligned with "a number of younger black leaders of the National

Independent Political League and the NAACP."[134] W. E. B. Du Bois, son of a Civil War veteran, even criticized Roosevelt and the Progressive Party on their collective silence on the issue of African American civil and political rights.[135] After considering "Roosevelt, our Lord Emperor," Winters dismissed Taft as among the "bands of Combination / Of our Government Robbers Pack."[136] The impact of either Roosevelt or Taft, if elected, would be dire. Winters warned in the fourth verse:

> By Taft and Roosevelt's Combination hands,
> That would for selfish honor and gain
> Our constitutional rights destroy
> That he might be called Lord Emperor
> And we his children's toys.[137]

He, therefore, implored Black Franklin County men to vote for "good Christian men." Wilson and his running mate, according to Winters in the second to last verse, would "drive the forces of imperialism / Away from our freedom's Land."[138] By electing these Democratic Party candidates, Winters concluded the verse:

> That the poor may live as well as rich,
> Let him be White, Red or Black,
> And not be bound by poverty
> With Starvation at his back.[139]

Winters composed the song on July 4, 1912, and again declared his self-made man ethos for using Civil War memory as a political strategy for achieving an inclusive, more just society on the eve of the fiftieth anniversary of the Gettysburg Campaign. The inclusion of the July Fourth date in the signature reminded both new generations in the state and nation of the aging Fifteenth Amendment generation of African American political leaders' presence, and their collective political usage of Civil War memory in the ongoing fight for social and political justice. He and others remained resolute in their commitment to equality and full citizenship wrought by the Civil War and Reconstruction-era constitutional gains.

With Wilson's victory, Winters's presidential campaign songwriting career ended as it had begun. His preferred candidate easily defeated the Republican, Progressive, and Socialist candidates. Wilson won forty states and secured 435 electoral votes. Roosevelt emerged in a distant second with six states and only 88 electoral votes. Taft won only Vermont and Utah. After exceeding electoral expectations, Debs would run again during the \next presidential cycle.[140]

Advanced age and declining health prevented Winters from writing another campaign song. In late November 1916, Winters died. His family produced and distributed photographs of his headstone in the historic Lebanon Cemetery, where many Civil War veterans and prominent Black leaders were interred.[141] Chambersburg and other Pennsylvanian newspapers covered his death. The newspaper tributes mentioned his age, scientific achievements, business success, and longtime membership in Hope Presbyterian Church. Newspaper coverage also mentioned his friendship with Frederick Douglass, his role in facilitating John Brown's August 1859 meeting in the city, and his Native American heritage, which contributed to his nickname "Indian Dick." Notably, no one discussed his songwriting and contributions to local presidential campaign efforts. The press only mentioned that he was a self-educated "writer of prose and poetry."[142] This erasure ensured Winters's disappearance from the scholarly and popular understandings of Civil War memory for advancing notions of the franchise, citizenship, and the political imaginary over the twentieth century.

Winters's death marked an end of a Black Franklin County political era. His activism spanned the antebellum to early Jim Crow eras. The community lost an important leader who not only helped define Black politics rooted in Civil War memory, but also ensured that the local Black community's political concerns received a hearing at the local, state, and national levels. The memory of the man and his political activism faded among white Pennsylvanians and became the subject of mythmaking in Black Franklin County residents' oral tradition. Edna Christian Knapper, daughter of a founding Grant and Wilson Club member, and other Black women played a significant role in shaping Winter's legacy and Civil War memory over the twentieth century more broadly.

As a result, his various campaign songs became scattered across the network of informal Black community archives and the formal institutional archives of Stanford University, Temple University, and the Franklin County Historical Society. Occasionally, his songs appear on eBay and other online auctions. Sadly, his autobiography titled after his Gettysburg Campaign song does not appear to have survived.

By piecing these archival traces, we can see Winters's political use of Civil War memory more clearly. He, as others of Franklin County and the Pennsylvania–Maryland border, never forgot the Gettysburg Campaign, the two other Confederate invasions, and the postwar transformation of the county's African American demographics. Using the trope of self-made men, Winters's activism and songwriting bridged the diverse Black population into a signifi- cant voting bloc recognized by both major political parties in Pennsylvania. Even Frederick Douglass recognized their potential strength when he spoke in Chambersburg during the 1872 election season. To fully understand Black Civil War memory and its complex political uses, it is necessary to firmly understand Joseph Winters, his political transformation over his long life, and his surviving presidential campaign songs. Black Civil War memory and its complex political uses were more than offering simple references to slavery, emancipation, and Abraham Lincoln for securing the Black electoral support.

Winters was a complicated man who did not settle. He found a political party that served his needs and politicized understanding of the Civil War. Looking beyond Frederick Douglass, Henry McNeal Turner, and other prominent leaders living in urban centers and within the South, we find Civil War memory used in a diverse and at times contentious manner. We must contend with these men's contemporaries, including Winters and the rural Black Northern experience, as important collective memory makers and politicos who advanced new political definitions of race, manhood, and Civil War memory.

4   Cumberland Valley Veterans and the Grand Army of the Republic

In her 1890 poem, Charlotte Forten Grimké, former abolitionist and South Carolina freedmen's school educator, paid homage to aging Black Civil War veterans. Like her earlier schoolgirl diary entries during the capture and trial of Anthony Burns, she offered poignant commentary with her poetry.

> And when at last our country's saviors came,—
> In proud procession down the crowded street,
> Still brighter burned the patriotic flame,
> And loud acclaims leaped forth their steps to greet.
>
> And now the veterans scarred and maimed appear,
> And now the tattered battle-flags uprise;
> A silence deep one moment fills the air,
> Then shout on shout ascends unto the skies.
> Oh, brothers, ye have borne the battle strain,
> And ye have felt it through the ling'ring years;
> For all your valiant deeds, your hours of pain,
> We can but give to you our grateful tears![1]

Grimké over several verses captured the soundscape of the Grand Army of the Republic (GAR) parade from the rising anticipation as the column advanced closer into view to the cheers from appreciative observers. Though aging, the men still elicited jubilant praise for their sacrifice, service, and resulting bodily and mental pain. But Grimké's "The Gathering of the Grand Army" did more than simply extol the courageous service performed by the men. At the thirty-fifth anniversary of the Confederate defeat, the nation had proven ungrateful and was betraying the wartime promises offered to those who had sacrificed with their military service and blood. Yet Black Pennsylvanians refused to follow in the nation's stead. The Black GAR veterans deserved the "grateful tears" and the "silent blessings from our full hearts."[2]

This chapter examines the Black GAR posts of the Cumberland Valley and how their presence influenced Black Civil War memory as expressed in Charlotte Forten Grimké's poem. Spanning both sides of the Pennsylvania-Maryland border, African American veterans organized and sustained the Lyon Post No. 31 of Hagerstown, Maryland, Delany Post, No. 494 of Chambersburg, Pennsylvania, and Corporal Jesse G. Thompson Post, No. 440 of Carlisle, Pennsylvania. Collectively, the three GAR posts connected veterans across towns in Franklin, Cumberland, and Washington Counties and throughout the lower Cumberland Valley for roughly forty years. They cemented the Won Cause culture of the Grand Army of the Republic through meetings, attendance at major interracial commemorative events, and creation of new Black community traditions.

Established in 1866, the Grand Army of the Republic organized federal Civil War veterans in a fraternal network. Nationally, the organization and its local posts established Memorial Day as a national holiday, lobbied for pensions, and advocated for an array of issues affecting Civil War veterans and their families. Historian Barbara Gannon surveyed the national veteran organization that linked Union men, irrespective of race, through a notion of comradeship in her essential text.[3] However, the lofty organizational aims were not evenly applied throughout its history. At major events, state encampments, and national reunions, white veterans welcomed their fellow Black comrades and auxiliary services. Their professed comradeship did not always extend to local activities. In the Cumberland Valley, the mere existence of three African American GAR posts alongside white GAR posts in the same communities, the names adopted for the local posts, and individual acts of racism occasionally expressed toward African American comrades demonstrate the uneven application. Yet even with these realities, white and Black Cumberland Valley posts attended one another's events, attended funeral services of fallen comrades, mutually performed Memorial Day rituals in segregated cemeteries, and even sang camp songs in blended harmony of voices.

While neither perfect nor consistent, Cumberland Valley GAR comrades found fulfillment on their own terms. They could and did reject their marginalization by their white counterparts through their mere existence, hosting of separate events, and upholding the organizational claims for cementing their own leadership positions within their respective communities. They also advanced their understanding of the Won Cause by attending biracial events and supporting other Black posts. They provided care for aging veterans, offered funeral rights for deceased veterans, and organized other activities in and beyond the Cumberland Valley. For individual members, the GAR served diverse needs.

Some held post leadership positions. Many enjoyed the leisure activities sponsored by the three posts. Some found redemption among the Cumberland Valley comrades. Despite its limits, these Black GAR men marshaled their veteran status as a tool of liberation and established the Won Cause commemorative culture as a defining feature of Civil War memory while providing a framework for subsequent generations of Black veterans.

Before the Lyon, Delany, and Jesse G. Thompson GAR posts formally organized, African American veterans actively engaged in diverse political and fraternal efforts. They participated in Memorial Day celebrations, political parades, and other commemorative events as unaffiliated participants since the ending of the Civil War. Veterans had a major presence at Emancipation celebrations and other events on the African American commemorative calendar. The Colored Conventions Movement, fraternal organizations, and militias served as significant outlets for veterans engaged in the broader communal struggle for postwar citizenship. These fraternal and political outlets saw Black men and women auxiliary members using memory of their wartime patriotism and military service for attaining full rights of citizenship, politically, socially, and economically. Instead of veteran status, gendered notions of citizenship united them.

The Colored Conventions Movement afforded some Cumberland Valley veterans with the opportunity for forging a network that spanned the Pennsylvania and Maryland border. The region's veterans participated in the 1868 Colored Border State Convention in Baltimore, Maryland. By claiming a border identity, Cumberland Valley men joined others from several states. As part of the multi-day convention, William Howard Day and Frances Ellen Watkins Harper delivered rousing addresses. The assembled participants also produced an open letter calling for universal suffrage and correcting the wrong "that citizens, even in States for many years free, are systematically deprived of suffrage, the first, the crowning right of citizenship."[4] While none of the future Lyon, Delany, and Jesse G. Thompson GAR comrades had a significant role, their presence as both veterans and leaders in their respective communities was welcomed. Together, they fought for the franchise, election of Grant and Colfax, the continuation of the Freedmen's Bureau, and other rights of full citizenship. The GAR later expanded this political network for unifying Cumberland Valley veterans, their families, and respective communities.[5]

Prince Hall Freemasonry and other fraternal organizations served as important GAR precursors. Postwar freemasonry created spaces for Black men to articulate notions of the ideal Black masculinity in a society where the politics of race, class, and gender excluded Black men from positions of power and leadership. Moreover, Prince Hall Freemasonry's "disciplinary individualism" appealed to Cumberland Valley USCT veterans.[6] Dress, ritual, lodge design, and public performance of the Black masculine ideal aligned with veterans' desire to continue notions of martial manhood for enacting postwar systemic change. Prince Hall Masons fought to extend the symbolic citizenship of "the masculine body politic" to securing meaningful civil and political gains in the postwar nation.[7] Nationally and locally, the fraternal organization flourished alongside the Odd Fellows and Knights of Pythias. These organizations functioned as both fraternal "gathering places" and a training ground for advancing notions of citizenship, politics and equality.[8] The various women's auxiliary groups also created spaces and leadership opportunities for Black Cumberland Valley women, albeit opportunities not necessarily free from patriarchy.[9] Collectively, fraternal organizational leaders and members claimed their role as essential partners in reconstructing the nation and facilitating freedpeople's transition from slavery to freedom. African American fraternal orders, however, never achieved a color-blind brotherhood. Simply put, Confederate defeat and emancipation failed to "bring Masonic brotherhood to the Union."[10] Race, class, and gender remained irreconcilable barriers despite African American activism and support by some white allies in the fraternal organizations. The Won Cause promoted by the GAR, therefore, appealed to veterans by allowing them to connect with other veterans, imagine the possibility of a different racial future, and develop a new form of political leadership rooted in their shared Civil War military service.

Many Cumberland Valley veterans also participated in the militia movement. The Cumberland Guards of Carlisle offered several future GAR members with a sense of purpose, the power to enact change, and maintain military readiness if again needed by the state and nation. Organized in May 1870, the Carlisle militia was part of a larger African American militia movement after the Civil War. Unlike their Southern brethren, the Cumberland Guards membership, according to a 1910 published historical account, included many Civil War veterans who "enjoyed all the privileges of the State Militia."[11] Yet memories of African American military prohibition in both Pennsylvanian and federal units, civilian trauma, and emasculation during the three Confederate invasions shaped its formation. Civil War military service and postwar optimism for the national Reconstruction project also motivated the veterans' participation. Over its four-year tenure, the Cumberland Guards had six officers, a fife and drum corps, and thirty-nine men among its membership. From its officers to its members, the Cumberland Guards "enjoyed a large patronage" before Special Order No. 38

officially disbanded the militia on November 24, 1874.[12] When comparing the membership rosters, Civil War veterans' experiences in the Cumberland Guards influenced the later Carlisle GAR post, specifically its pageantry, structure, community reception, and everyday performance of Civil War memory.

These alternative organizations, however, lacked the comradeship and understanding of the Civil War experiences offered by the GAR. To be sure, African American veterans did not abandon these other outlets. GAR members often remained active in in militias and fraternal organizations. The common vision of African American fraternal orders, churches, and the GAR encouraged collaboration in the struggle for racial progress. Overlapping membership proved quite common in these rural communities. Therefore, the Cumberland Valley fraternal, religious, and veteran networks saw extensive collaboration, coordination of events, and multi-organization racial uplift campaigns. Masons, Odd Fellow members, and GAR comrades attended one another's events, hosted them in their respective fraternal spaces and churches, and the surviving published rosters show individuals who served as leaders in multiple organizations. These overlapping networks reflect the various ways that African American men and women found fulfillment, created meaning, and developed safe spaces for their complex and diverse lives. As a Civil War veteran organization, however, the GAR simply filled a void not being served by their churches, fraternal organizations, and local militias. The formation, naming decisions, and diverse activities of the Lyon, Delany, and Jesse G. Thompson posts, therefore, represented a shift in how Black veterans mobilized Civil War memory for forging community and articulating claims of veteranhood, citizenship, and community leadership.

The formation of the Cumberland Valley posts drew local media attention. William Chapman, prominent African American and Twenty-Second UCST veteran, organized the Carlisle post during the Gettysburg anniversary celebration. It is fitting that Chapman picked July 2, 1884. The choice of date recognized the enslavement of free Black Pennsylvanians, the racism that stymied Black men from defending their communities and state during the Confederate invasion, and a shared Civil War experience which motivated many Cumberland County comrades' enlistment.[13] Franklin County veterans announced their plans to organize a GAR post during a reunion attended by African American veterans from the Cumberland Valley. Held in Chambersburg, this inaugural August 1885 event featured a citywide parade and public entertainment held at the Repository Hall.[14] Attracting about two hundred attendees, the event received praise from the local newspapers. Within a few weeks, the Chambersburg newspapers announced the formal organization of the Delany Post, the inaugural officers, and the weekly meeting location.[15]

Individual post names also shed light on how the GAR comrades defined and advanced the Won Cause commemorative culture. In the Cumberland Valley, white veterans named their local posts after local soldiers who died during the Civil War or held a ranked military position. Following this model of local and national naming practices, Black GAR members were intentional. While the namesake of the Lyon Post, No. 31 of Hagerstown, Maryland, remains elusive, the other two posts purposely chose African American veterans who had local Cumberland Valley connections. In so doing, they defined and elevated them into the pantheon of great men and martyrs in the African American freedom struggle. Though often noted as "colored" in local news coverage, the promoted post names prevented their erasure from white Civil War memory.[16]

Franklin County men named their post after Martin R. Delany. Born to a free African American mother and enslaved father in 1812, his mother relocated the family to Chambersburg in 1822 before his father joined them a year later after purchasing his freedom. At nineteen, Delany left the county seat in pursuit of education at Reverend Lewis Woodson's school. The ardent abolitionist encouraged emigration as a means for achieving true equality and not remain a "nation within a nation."[17] Delany abandoned emigration as a solution to become a full-time recruiter for the Fifty-Fourth and Fifty-Fifth Massachusetts regiments. In February 1865, he became the first African American commissioned field officer in the federal army. The combination of local connections and distinguished military service guided the post members' naming decision over one of many local options at a September 1885 meeting.[18]

The men also elected the first officers of the Major Martin R. Delany Post, No. 494. They chose Thomas L. White as post commander, Isaac Giles as senior vice commander, and Alfred Bradford as the junior vice commander. For the adjutant, quartermaster, and chaplain positions, the men selected William Little, John Butler, and James Crunkleton respectively. Gilbert Braxton, John Ukkerd, and Joseph Smith filled the remaining positions of officer of the day, officer of the guard, and sergeant. With weekly meetings held above a Chambersburg grocery store, the Black comrades began their work.[19]

For its namesake, Cumberland County GAR members chose Corporal Jesse G. Thompson. After organizing in 1884, William Chapman, the first post commander, and other comrades felt that that their namesake epitomized an individual worthy of commemoration.[20] Born to Benjamin and Mary Thompson in 1844, the Cumberland County native served as a paid servant for a white captain before enlisting as a private in the Thirty-Second USCT regiment in February 1864. He rose to the rank of corporal before mustering out and returning to Carlisle in August 1865. Thompson died before seeing the political gains reaped by his military service but was interred at the Carlisle Barracks.[21] By choosing Delany and Thompson, Cumberland Valley GAR members rejected their marginalization by their white counterparts and carved out a space within the Civil War commemorative landscape. The post names functioned as stark reminders of the role that African American military service had in securing Union victory and emancipation.

Even white veterans and residents took notice of the Cumberland County choice in post name. During the 1885 Fourth of July celebrations, Alexander Brady Sharpe, a white veteran of the Seventh Pennsylvania Reserve Corps, presented a banner to the organization at an event held at the Carlisle Opera House. The Carlisle *Sentinel* reprinted his address in which he eulogized the post's namesake at the post's first anniversary celebration.[22] After briefly discussing Thompson's service as a hired camp servant, the Captain Colwell GAR Post member praised his decision to enlist when his employer was wounded in action. "He was born on free soil, of free parents," Sharpe reminded them, "but he had blood of his race in his veins; a race which beyond a line almost within call, was 'living without a right, without a hope, for which the future had no dawn, no star, nothing but ignorance and fear, nothing but work and want.'"[23] Sharpe surmised:

> No wonder, therefore, that he threw in his lot with the side of freedom, marched to the music of Union, and in the everglades of Florida slew with his own hand, three of four of the oppressors of his race, that met him in a breach from which his comrades had retreated.[24]

Thompson sacrificed his freedom for the liberation of the enslaved as well as preserving the nation which did not fully appreciate African Americans' patriotism. White Americans oppressed both free and enslaved alike. Yet Thompson put aside any animosity and fought to secure the nation. In other words, Thompson epitomized the Won Cause. As a member of the "hero-martyrs," Sharpe hoped: "Let us who inherit these inestimable blessings, prove ourselves worthy of them."[25] Moreover, the detailed Carlisle newspaper coverage of Sharpe's address in the presentation of a banner to the post was not an anomaly. Local newspapers rarely shortened the post name to just Thompson's last name as commonly done with the Lyon, Delany, and other GAR posts irrespective of race. Media coverage routinely covered the officer elections, annual Memorial Day and Emancipation

Day celebrations, and participation in joint-celebrations with the white GAR posts for several decades. Despite the "colored designation," the African American comrades were welcomed additions.[26]

Together, the three Cumberland Valley posts actively participated in joint GAR public commemorations. Their presence helped stave off what Frederick Douglass had feared about reconciliation between the "the loyal North" and the "slaveholding South."[27] Following the Supreme Court's ruling in the *Civil Rights Cases of 1883*, Douglass raised the alarm over former Civil War combatants' willingness to "shake hands over the bloody chasm" to the detriment of Black Americans.[28] By organizing after the Supreme Court decision, the Cumberland Valley veterans rejected the pessimism of Douglass but understood the threat posed by the Reconciliationist impulse. They also rejected the calls for emigration by another Civil War veteran. Bishop Henry McNeal Turner felt that the Supreme Court decision "de-citizentized [*sic*]" African Americans and rendered them "uncivilized and outlawed."[29] Where Turner saw "no 'peaceful future' in America for Black people," the Cumberland Valley veterans chose the Won Cause.[30]

The official GAR designation empowered them. Black GAR members' participation now had a different meaning as well as urgency. In parades, Black GAR members marched in the middle but never at the end of the parade columns, where unaffiliated Black veterans were typically placed. Whether at indoor or outdoor celebrations, Black GAR members stood alongside white veterans and forced observers to acknowledge their sacrifice and status. Many were freeborn and did not share the experiences of their Southern brethren emancipated by their service. They survived the various Confederate invasions that saw the enslavement of free and self-liberated African Americans. They enlisted in the USCT regiments when race blocked their service in state regiments. Their mere presence, therefore, "represented powerful and undeniable evidence that African Americans had been among those brave men."[31] Interracial unity advanced by the GAR as well as Black struggle for a new inclusive body politic was on full display in these joint celebrations.

The Lyon Post, for instance, regularly participated in the Antietam celebrations. As the site of a national cemetery, the Lyon Post often was the sole African American representation at the solemn events until the turn of the twentieth century. Like other Black Maryland veterans, Lyon GAR members "often connected the policies of emancipation with Antietam."[32] As the "birthplace of emancipation," Black GAR representation mattered at these Antietam National Cemetery commemorations.[33] Hagerstown and Baltimore newspapers routinely noted their presence over the mid-1880s and 1890s. Representatives from the

Delany and Thompson Posts as well as unaffiliated veterans from the Pennsylvania, Maryland, and West Virginia border communities sometimes joined them.[34] The Lyon Post comrades also witnessed the 1896 dedication of the Pennsylvania Brigade Association monument on the Hagerstown turnpike near Dunker Church. As white veterans moved toward a national reconciliation, Black comrades' physical presence stood as reminders to observers, invited dignitaries, and regional newspaper readership of Black sacrifices in the Civil War.[35]

George B. McClellan, therefore, would have been hard-pressed to ignore Lyon Post members and other African American veterans at the 1885 Memorial Day celebration. The former general had strong opinions regarding African American military service. Following Antietam, President Lincoln's announcement of the preliminary Emancipation Proclamation strained his relationship with the commander in chief and facilitated his removal. Indeed, in his failed 1864 presidential campaign McClellan promised an end to the Civil War without abolition.[36] His wartime anti-Black notions facilitated the development and promotion of a Civil War memory in which Black veterans did not fit in either the Lost Cause or Reconciliationist understandings of either the Antietam National Cemetery or the war itself.[37] Yet as he spoke to the assembled 1885 Memorial Day crowd at the Antietam National Cemetery and Battlefield, McClellan could not easily ignore the sable faces of the Lyon Post and other African American veterans who traveled on special trains from Pennsylvania and West Virginia.[38] He also could neither ignore their voices as they sang "Our Patriot Dead" with white veterans and other organizations during the festivities. Nor could he avoid the African American veterans and residents who "paid their respects" at the public receptions at the Baldwin House and Col. Douglass residence.[39] By regularly attending these Antietam celebrations, Lyon Post comrades normalized their inclusion, bolstered the professed GAR comradeship, and challenged any Civil War memorial traditions that excluded them.

Even at state and national encampments, Black GAR veterans and auxiliary members promoted an alternative memory in separate celebrations. Amid the 1896 statewide encampment held in Chambersburg, Black and white veterans enjoyed an address by O. O. Howard at the Rosedale Opera House on the evening before the opening ceremony.[40] In their invitation, encampment organizers specifically requested Howard to lecture on Meade's campaign, including the Battle of Gettysburg.[41] The exact text of the address does not survive, but it is most likely that Howard delivered a version of a Memorial Day address made in 1894.[42] Therein, Howard focused primarily on General George Meade and the Battle of Gettysburg. This would have been appropriate for the occasion as

encampment participants made a brief excursion to Gettysburg for the unveiling of battlefield monuments to Meade and Hancock.[43] Although Howard does
make a brief reference to CSA General Albert Jenkins and his "saucy brigade,"
Howard never discussed Confederate soldiers' seizure and enslavement of free
and self-liberated African Americans,.[44] The brevity of the reference might have
been overlooked by white audience members. African American veterans in the
audience, though, would have connected the reference to the untold suffering
and sacrifices of their families and neighbors during the campaign as well as
Howard's significant postwar role in remaking the nation that recognized African American freedom and citizenship.

Yet such subtle references did not stop the Black veterans assembled from
holding a separate service spearheaded by the Delany Post at the local cemetery.
Like the 1888 Chambersburg GAR encampment, the Chambersburg Post again
chose to hold separate ceremonies apart from their white comrades. Instead
of their regular post room, they gathered around the gravesites of their fallen
brethren.[45] Amid other veterans, Black veterans and community members still
remembered those who were stolen, the sacrifices of those left behind in the border community, and the valiant service of individuals who served. In short, they
promoted a complex, inclusive, and intersectional counter-memory even when
participating in formal state and national GAR events.

Local Memorial Day events further magnified the uneven Won Cause application throughout the Cumberland Valley. During the most important day of the
Won Cause calendar, African American GAR posts served as the principal organizers of the segregated events before the culminating integrated, community-
wide afternoon celebrations in the various Cumberland Valley cities and towns.
Comrades and their community partners coordinated the graveyard cleanup
ceremonies and solicited floral donations for the annual decoration of Civil War
soldiers' graves. They determined the keynote orator of the day, hired bands for
the parade, and secured the participation of Black fraternal orders and other
civic organizations in the separate parade preceding the formal grave decoration
ceremony. County newspapers noted the numbers, the parade route taken, the
names of local GAR leaders, African American religious leaders, civic leaders
who gave remarks, and the keynote orator's remarks at the grave decoration ceremony. Although media coverage expanded following the creation of the Cumberland Valley posts, newspapers did not always cover the segregated events.
The Hagerstown newspapers, for instance, failed to report on the pre-Antietam
celebrations of the Lyon Post except for one article covering the combined 1891
celebration with the white Reno Post at the Rose Hill cemetery.[46] Between 1886

and 1920, however, these public spectacles cemented Black Won Cause traditions into the commemorative landscape.

As part of the Memorial Day celebrations, local pastors delivered sermons for the GAR comrades, their families, and community members. Local newspapers typically announced the occurrence but rarely offered detailed coverage to their readers. In 1885, however, the Carlisle *Sentinel* printed the remarks delivered by Rev. Lorenzo D. Blackson, a self-educated minister who gained acclaim following the 1867 publication of *The Rise and Progress of Kingdoms of Light and Darkness; or, The Reign of Kings Alpha and Abadon.*[47] Blackson's Memorial Day sermon celebrated these white and Black Cumberland Valley comrades as "Soldiers of Light" who served God or the "Kingdom of Light [that] had himself freed the sons of Africa."[48] Delivered at the Carlisle AMEZ church, his speech marked the first Memorial Day celebration following the creation of the Jesse G. Thompson GAR post.

Blackson's Memorial Day sermon probably made some of the white attendees uncomfortable. He opened by praising their role in putting down the "Slaveholders' rebellion," and giving "liberty to our nation, as well as to the millions of my race, who were held in a bondage worse and more cruel and unjust than the world ever before knew."[49] Despite expressing gratitude, Blackson reminded them of the racial prohibitions placed on African American military enlistment. He also chided the white federal veterans for being "ignorant of the fighting qualities of the negro, but now you white comrades as well as those you fought against, know to the contrary."[50] After summarizing the key major battles in which African American soldiers had fought, he encouraged the attendees to rise to their feet in remembrance of those who died or were wounded during the Civil War. Blackson prayed that "the good Lord bless these veterans, the survivors of the grand and great army of the republic, and all their comrades who are not here tonight, as well as you who are."[51] Blackson then devoted the rest of the sermon to remind them of their ongoing essential service in fulfilling God's plan for the Civil War. In this fight, GAR comrades, regardless of race, had a special role, but only if they don "the whole armor of God" for eradicating ongoing racism.[52] From parades to Memorial Day sermons, the GAR comrades defined the Won Cause and provided a model for future generations of veterans, families, and residents in the Cumberland Valley communities.

African American GAR veterans also collaborated with white GAR post members outside of Memorial Day celebrations in the Cumberland Valley. The Rhial GAR post of Greencastle commemorated the anniversary of their namesake's death, Delany, and Lyon Post members participated in the reinterment ceremony, public parade, and evening campfire held at Fleming's Grove.[53] The Greencastle event, as the *Valley Spirit* extensively reported, reminded the comrades of the organization's purpose of ensuring burial rites of all members and sustaining the Won Cause collective memory through the singing of "Tramp, Tramp, Tramp" and other Civil War camp songs, sharing a communal meal, and reminiscing with fellow comrades.[54] At this event, the last line of the "Tramp, Tramp, Tramp" chorus would have resonated with both white and Black comrades deeply affected by the invasion, occupation, and military engagement of the Gettysburg Campaign. Since a Confederate bullet fired by a member of CSA General Jenkins's cavalry brigade killed Cpl. William H. Rhial, memories would have turned to the shared trauma, grief, and sacrifice when they sang: "And beneath the starry flag we shall breathe the air again, Of the free land in our own beloved home."[55]

At the Waynesboro centennial celebration, Lyon Post veterans made the journey to the border Pennsylvania town for the occasion attended by members of four white GAR posts, governors of Pennsylvania and Maryland, other local dignitaries, and area residents. In the parade, they were positioned immediately in front of the Waynesboro GAR post.[56] Delany GAR members also attended the funeral of Capt. George Miles and mourned with their white Housum GAR comrades.[57] These African American GAR participants were not merely "space invaders" who disrupted traditional white Civil War commemorative spaces. Rather, the Won Cause was not superficial. The comradeship seemed genuine at these occasions. Memories of wartime service, drudgery of camp life, suffering from visible and invisible wounds, and postwar rituals bound these men together.[58]

The Won Cause also was not one-sided. In Carlisle, white GAR members occasionally attended events hosted by their Black comrades. Several Captain Colwell GAR members attended Rev. J. M. Taylor's "War a Good Warfare" sermon at Pomfret St. AME Church alongside their African American comrades in the Corporal Jesse G. Thompson Post. Following the death of a 107th Pennsylvania Volunteers veteran, his mother presented her deceased son's sword to the Delany GAR members in an elaborate ceremony. The collaboration between the white and Black GAR posts as well as with the Sons of Veterans group grew over time and became a regular occurrence.[59]

Beyond these public commemorative events, Black GAR posts organized member-only meetings and services. The Hagerstown *Herald and Torch Light* noted the annual election results and general meetings for the Lyon Post.[60] Local Pennsylvania newspapers, specifically the Chambersburg *Valley Spirit*, the Carlisle *Sentinel*, and *Carlisle Weekly Herald*, also provided annual leadership and other information for the Delany and Jesse G. Thompson posts.[61] These newspapers also provided insights onto the broader Black GAR network in the Cumberland Valley. The Frederick newspaper noted the hospitality of the Lyon Post for the Black Frederick GAR veterans visiting its August 1893 meeting. On this "fraternal visit," *The News* informed readers that the men "were handsomely entertained by the local post."[62] The Lyon Post held a reunion specifically for African American GAR members living in Maryland and surrounding states at Fort Frederick in July 1895.[63] Shared post events also included the presentations of flags and other gifts to area African American posts. For instance, Mercersburg GAR members presented a flag to the Lyon Post.[64] Through such practices, members sustained a Black GAR network within the Cumberland Valley. This network proved important in influencing communal notions of racial uplift, politics, and gendered expectations.

The Delany Post advanced postwar notions of manhood that challenged the narrative of victimhood and impotency in Franklin County. During its inaugural year, the regional Black newspaper noted the pageantry associated with a post-sponsored lecture in Chambersburg. The veterans entered the Zion AMEZ Church wearing ceremonial black suits and white gloves for a lecture delivered by Rev. Major Hillery Decoursey Ross.[65] The veteran of the 109th New York Regiment, church pastor, and fellow comrade in arms explored the "heroic deeds of colored soldiers during the revolutionary and civil wars" in the "Our Fallen Heroes" lecture.[66] Later published in pamphlet form with another sermon delivered in Washington, DC, a contemporary reviewer strongly recommended the publication for its views on contemporary political and social issues. Even the Democratic Party–leaning Chambersburg newspaper acknowledged the pamphlet, which included the speech given to local African American veterans.[67] The spectacle nature of the procession defied prevailing stereotypes of Black masculinity as undeserving of political citizenship. The finely dressed veterans and the accompanying lecture defined Black manhood in contrast to their antebellum lack of citizenship in the border Pennsylvania community. The veterans had proven themselves on the battlefield and contributed to the postwar Black community as leaders worthy of emulation, honor, and published accolades whether in news columns or pamphlet form. Moreover, this event demonstrated the layered GAR performances of new postwar notions of Black masculinity. As a veteran and spiritual leader, the chosen speaker of the day allowed the GAR post to use his church for this event. Therefore, his lecture as well as the GAR veterans embedded the sacrifice of the veterans and wartime dead within a Black Christian theological framework.

Beyond Chambersburg, the Carlisle post also employed local African American churches for major events. In 1909, the organization installed Noah Pinkney as post commander and other members at Third Presbyterian Church. Rev. W. W. Walker provided an address for the occasion. Roughly a month later, the post celebrated Lincoln's birthday with an elaborate service.[68] Although the post often conducted their normal meetings in secular spaces, Lincoln's birthday celebration warranted additional space. Surviving GAR members, the Woman's Relief Corps (WRC), and the Sons of Veterans crowded the church sanctuary to hear Rev. R. H. Shirley deliver an address titled "Abraham Lincoln, His Moral Grandeur, His Use of the Bible, His Religious Life, Why He Was Not a Church Member, and His Lasting Memorial."[69] The organization regularly alternated major events, such as Lincoln's birthday commemorations, Emancipation Day celebrations, and Memorial Day services, at Bethel AME, Third Presbyterian, and West Street AMEZ churches. For these events, the regular meeting space of Jordan Hall proved insufficient for both the space and nature of the occasion celebrated.[70]

GAR veterans and African Americans framed their post–Civil War socioeconomic and political experiences through a particular religious lens. They, as shown by historian Matthew Harper, applied Black religious thought to locate themselves "within God's plan for human history—past, present, and future."[71] African American remembrances of emancipation served as evidence that "divine justice could descend upon a realm of earthly injustice."[72] Thus, hope for both the end of racial discrimination and the "special role for the African race within Christian history" became defining features of Black Protestantism.[73] This worldview was not limited to Black Southerners. It encompassed the lived experiences of Civil War veterans, GAR leadership, church leaders, and the congregants of churches where public Civil War commemorative events occurred. Through biblical stories, postwar Black religious thought empowered people to resist racial subjugation and inspired belief in themselves as God's chosen people.

African American religious thought also created a space for veterans, religious leaders, and political leaders to coexist within postwar African American leadership. African American soldiers fulfilled biblical prophecy and reenacted the Hebrew past during the Civil War. As veterans, new pathways for leadership opened. Often, veterans who had theological training obtained local GAR leadership positions.[74] Such religious training and church affiliation, however, were not prerequisites for GAR leadership or community leadership. As Harper argues: "The divine act of emancipation spoke louder than any subsequent event;

that is, in Black Christian theology, freedom was always more significant than lynching, disfranchisement or segregation."[75] As veterans, their leadership did not compete with AME and AMEZ leadership. By hosting GAR events in local churches, church leaders shared their authority and space with these Civil War emancipators. Memorial Day services and other public GAR commemorative events, therefore, cemented rather than diminished the power of "emancipation's eschatological significance."[76]

By embracing postwar Black religious thought, Black GAR members expanded opportunities for women beyond the Woman's Relief Corps (WRC). Unlike the GAR, the women's auxiliary organization personified a gendered, racialized, and classist struggle over Civil War remembrance. White women rejected a sisterhood with African American WRC members. White women also rejected the national reconciliation impulse and made little effort to participate in the Blue and Gray veteran reunions.[77] African American women still participated in the WRC. Carlisle had an active WRC while the other GAR posts did not. The women's auxiliary of the Corporal Jesse G. Thompson Post initially had fifteen members with Eliza Jackson, Mrs. Jamison, and Mrs. Alexander serving as the inaugural officers. Once incorporated, WRC No. 17 membership expanded.[78] These Carlisle WRC members actively waged battles against the racism, classism, and regionalism within the expanding Civil War commemorative landscape and public consciousness. They maintained an active public role in the fight for pensions, veterans' care, and crafting histories accurately detailing their experiences.[79] However, Black women's involvement was not limited to this organization. The other posts relied on Black women's familial, religious, and educational networks for sustaining many of the services associated with veteran care and commemoration. For these women, Civil War memory work represented one component of their racial uplift activism.

In this regard, the women's religious organizations and auxiliary groups of the Masons and Odd Fellows played a significant role in advancing the Won Cause. All Black women's auxiliary groups engaged in the "documentary impulse" for advancing Civil War memory in their respective organizations.[80] Although the produced volumes never shared the reach that their white counterparts did, Black women documented, produced, and disseminated knowledge and alternate historical publications as a form of homemade citizenship to their communities through their segregated libraries, literary societies, classrooms, and other segregated spaces. Veteran connections allowed some to obtain leadership status, but it was not the only pathway available. A shared commitment to racial uplift, shared religious understanding of emancipation, and hope for a better future unified these diverse women.[81] Both the Lyon and Delany posts would have heavily relied on these networks in the absence of a formal WRC chapter. Thus, Black women, regardless of direct GAR affiliation, had an important role in shaping the Won Cause in the Cumberland Valley.

In addition, Black GAR posts organized community events and defined respectable leisure practices in the Cumberland Valley. As postwar leisure expanded beyond wealthy elites, African Americans fought for the right to participate in a range of recreational activities and access to recreational spaces. Aspiring postbellum members of the leisure class, irrespective of class backgrounds and locality, sought equal access and participation without violence in tourism and other recreational activities. Representing power dynamics, citizenship, and community control, African Americans made claims of economic citizenship for engaging in post–Civil War leisure activities.[82] Yet they endured segregated facilities and limited tourist destinations. This recreational segregation and limited access extended nationally and was not a product of Southern exceptionalism. Beaches, amusement parks, circuses, and other facilities remained off limits or limited in hours, access, and seating to African Americans except as waiters, bellhops, and other service industry employees. As a result, activists fought against local, regional, and national restrictions while defining forms of leisure acceptable within late nineteenth-century Victorian culture.[83]

Unlike other recreational activists and early tourists, GAR post members sought to promote nationally the rhetoric of colorblind comradeship. As GAR veterans and community leaders, they engaged in recreational activities and tourism in a concerted effort to forge community with other veterans, their families, and respective communities throughout several states and Washington, DC. Recreational segregation, as defined by "policies, privatization and violence," created both the need and a viable market.[84] The three GAR posts addressed the limited leisure and entertainment options in rural communities. By setting the tone, they provided respectable leisure alternatives to dance halls, vice, and other forms of working-class (and in turn, not respectable) recreation in the Cumberland Valley.[85]

GAR-sponsored concerts, musicals, and other public performances countered minstrelsy and vaudeville entertainment, which not only promoted stereotypical depictions of African American life but provided fodder for the Lost Cause and Reconciliationist proponents. Instead of Sam Sandford, a local favorite African American minstrel entertainer, the Jesse G. Thompson comrades offered concerts and operas that featured local Cumberland Valley talent. While serving as essential fundraising opportunities, these annual events offered affordable, respectable entertainment that typically included "addresses, orations, recitations, choruses and solos."[86] These annual events proved so popular that the Carlisle newspaper characterized them as "first-class" and hoped "no effort will be spared to make [them] a success."[87] At the 1888 Delany GAR fundraising fair, attendees competed over several coveted donated items in the silent auction while enjoying other entertainment in its Post headquarters. Coinciding with George Washington's birthday celebration, the GAR fundraiser laid claim to the Founding Father's legacy as a Won Cause event. Through their military service, GAR comrades saw their service as contributing to the second founding of the nation and affirming the spirit of the American Revolutionary war hero. Washington's birthday served as another important date in the Won Cause commemorative calendar.[88] These African American commemorative events were good business for building goodwill between the posts and their communities. These GAR-sponsored events also advanced their Won Cause claims as respectable tastemakers committed to providing entertainment offerings "by, for, and about black people."[89]

By inviting the African American Steelton, Harrisburg, and Carlisle GAR posts, Lyon Post comrades turned the twenty-second preliminary Emancipation Proclamation anniversary into a major Won Cause celebration. The GAR hosts graciously welcomed all residents and those who traveled for the occasion. The event was marked by a parade, speeches, and a picnic in September 1885.[90] Post Commander Shadrack Campbell served as the parade marshal, and other Lyon comrades appeared at the head of the procession, which consisted of the various GAR posts, bands, fraternal organizations, and several wagons "containing a number of little girls dressed in white and adorned with wreaths of evergreen and flowers" representing the states and the "Goddess of Liberty." Following this procession, Newton Cook, a Hagerstown lawyer, and Rev. Daniel Draper provided speeches before "the remainder of the day was spent in picnic pleasures."[91] The *Baltimore Sun* remarked that the grand parade throughout the main Hagerstown thoroughfares presented "an imposing appearance," while the local newspaper praised the entire celebration.[92] The Hagerstown celebration provided a framework for the 1888 and 1889 Emancipation Day events organized by the Delany and Jesse G. Thompson posts. Both posts opted for speeches and musical performances for their community-wide affairs instead of a parade.[93] Generous community support for these GAR-sponsored Emancipation celebrations helped solidify the GAR leadership by continuing to offer entertainment that advanced the Won Cause tradition.

Drawing on the extensive Cumberland Valley railroad networks, GAR-sponsored excursions became another popular activity among African American comrades and their families and communities. Railroads offered an affordable option for solidifying the Won Cause network throughout the Cumberland Valley but also to posts in Pennsylvania, Maryland, West Virginia, and Washington, DC. In this regard, the three posts expanded on existing African American religious, fraternal, and political networks defined by churches, Masons, and the Colored Conventions Movement. The regional railroad network further united the veterans who had previously traveled for wartime training and moved to the Civil War front. In the pursuit of leisurely comradeship, Lyon, Delany, and Jesse G. Thompson comrades solidified the bonds to one another as excursionists.

The short leisure excursions served two functions. First and foremost, the day trips and other short excursions connected the African American comrades to one another. When hosting one another, they reflected on their shared military experiences, attended to veteran issues such as medical care and pensions, and extended the GAR comradeship beyond reunions and the commemorative calendar. Second, the GAR-sponsored excursions offered safe and respectable tourist activities for rural members of the GAR circle who lacked consistent entertainment options. Leaving in the morning, the excursionists arrived by the afternoon. Often, the trip included a visit to the local post meeting space, performance by the GAR drum corps and musicians, sightseeing, a luncheon, and conversations with fellow comrades before returning home on an evening train. Rarely did the excursions extend more than one day. If so, an evening banquet, concert, or other form of entertainment occurred. This pattern typified the experiences of the Lyon and Delany comrades.

The Lyon comrades exploited the leisure comradeship afforded by the extensive regional railroad networks. Most often, Lyon comrades traveled and connected with other Cumberland Valley veterans and their respective communities. In July 1884, the Hagerstown post traveled to Harrisburg, Pennsylvania, for a local GAR sponsored fundraising concert held in Brady Hall. The men as well as Shepherdstown, West Virginia, cornet band provided some of the entertainment for the evening event, which consisted of "addresses by prominent colored gentlemen in Hagerstown and music by the band."[94] The Lyon comrades enjoyed a banquet held in their honor, stayed overnight in local Black hotels, and left the next day on an afternoon train. Due to the nature of this excursion, the Harrisburg newspaper favorably looked upon the Hagerstown excursionists for providing a "great attraction for the colored population during their sojourn in this city."[95] The men occasionally hosted visitors from Pennsylvania and Maryland. They most often connected with other regional comrades as excursionists.[96]

The Delany comrades proved especially adept at hosting visiting comrades. In July 1886, Black Baltimoreans traveled to Chambersburg for the dedication of the Franklin Hall meeting space. Their large presence drew the ire of the *Valley Spirit*. The roughly one thousand visitors with the Empire Band in tow simply overwhelmed the downtown Chambersburg businesses. One newspaper writer bemoaned how the group allegedly terrorized "all of the business men on the Diamond."[97] These African American GAR excursionists, however, laid claim to leisure as a form of citizenship. They had both the time and discretionary money to participate in such practices, whether to the dedication celebration with the Delany Post or the annual preliminary Emancipation Proclamation celebrations hosted by the all-Black GAR post in Gettysburg, Pennsylvania, from the 1880s to World War I. Moreover, this GAR-sponsored excursion celebrated the success of the Delany Post when it dedicated a new meeting space. The new location, furthermore, had the capacity to accommodate large tourist groups while providing a dedicated space for the African American veterans and their families. Both the large African American tourist group and new permanent meeting space could not be ignored by even white critics.[98]

Collectively, the three GAR posts defined respectable leisure practices. They provided alternatives to leisure options associated with working-class African American culture. While vice and nonrespectable activities still occurred, the children and grandchildren of the Civil War generation learned respectable habits and expectations for access to safe recreational spaces from these African American comrades.[99] The fundraising concerts remained an important tradition. Now, the proceeds benefited veterans of Spanish-American War, World War I, and other military engagements while cementing these veterans as "leaders in and heroes to the black communities."[100] These respectable leisure activities offered an outlet to shore up resilience for the fight against racism in the Cumberland Valley while providing community-based social services and relief to veterans not provided by the state. Automobiles, Black resort enclaves, the Negro Motorist Green Book, and safe recreation options created by Black entrepreneurs for Black patrons expanded leisure possibilities in the twentieth century. African Americans also had access to safe, segregated resorts, beaches, theaters, and other recreational venues.[101] Despite rejecting older entertainment forms for modern ones, this GAR legacy influenced how subsequent veterans used similar organizations for comradeship, leisure, and community building. This legacy shaped both later generations' participation but also their fight for expanded access at swimming pools, amusement parks, and other recreational facilities during the long Civil Rights Movement.[102]

The main duty of the GAR posts was to celebrate fallen Civil War veterans. Obituaries acknowledged both leaders, general members, and unaffiliated veterans. The former adjutant of the Lyon Post received an elaborate death notice in the mainstream Hagerstown newspaper. The 1892 notice characterized his death as "a serious [loss] to the organization of which he was an honored and useful member."[103] The men and the GAR circle attended funerals and traveled widely throughout the Cumberland Valley in their service. Past and current post commanders often eulogized the deceased. For some members, like Thomas E. W. Henry, the post paid for the burials.[104] With dwindling numbers, members drafted letters of condolences for inclusion in the ceremonies. For the 1906 funeral of Richard Harrison, surviving Lyon Post members had a letter read in their absence.[105] In memory of John Butler, Delany GAR members held a memorial service where Rev. H. R. Phoenix delivered "an exceedingly able" sermon at St. James AME Church.[106] Similarly, the Corporal Jesse G. Thompson Post ensured that members had detailed death notices, letters of condolences read, and members in attendance at funeral services. All Cumberland Valley posts provided elaborate burial rites for GAR leadership.[107] In death, the three Black GAR posts honored the men who contributed to Emancipation, Confederate defeat, and Civil War memory. Regardless of GAR membership, Cumberland Valley comrades remembered their brothers in arms.[108]

Black GAR members also acknowledged the deaths of WRC members and other women connected to prominent Civil War veterans. Jane Williams's death garnered special attention for her active service in the WRC of the Corporal Jesse G. Thompson post. Members of the WRC, No. 114 conducted the funeral services held in John Lane's residence in Carlisle. As the junior vice commander of the Carlisle GAR post, Lane and other comrades helped James Williams in mourning his spouse's death and assisted the WRC with the funeral and other burial rites.[109] As the daughter of a prominent 127th USCT veteran, Miss Harriette Rebecca Demas garnered an elaborate obituary in the Carlisle *Sentinel*.[110] Rebecca Demas, widow of Jacob Demas, equally received significant attention. Her funeral occurred at the Pomfret Street AME Church, a regular GAR event locale. Both mother and daughter were interred at Zion Union Cemetery.[111] Serving as the final resting place for approximately forty Civil War veterans, including Jacob

Demas, the historic Mercersburg cemetery was a prominent location in annual Memorial Day and other Civil War commemorative traditions.[112] Though not mentioned in the news coverage, surviving GAR members would have been in attendance and sent letters of condolence, as all Black GAR members assisted in locating and marking the graves of all deceased veterans whom they honored. Ensuring proper burials rites extended to the immediate family members of GAR members and non-affiliated veterans.

Overall, the three GAR posts advanced the Won Cause as a major component of African American Civil War memory. The men established new traditions and rituals that later generations of veterans adopted. They created new pathways for leadership and defined leisure practices in the late nineteenth and early twentieth centuries. They also ensured that Black Civil War veterans received dignity in death even though racism shaped their postwar lives socially, politically, and economically. Veteran status and GAR membership, however, did not shield them from postwar racial, gendered, and classist realities. The Won Cause had limits despite Black men's efforts.

Cumberland Valley GAR veterans provided a leadership model that carried forward to subsequent war veterans. The American Legion, Odd Fellows, and other secular and religious groups took up the mantle of organizing Memorial Day celebrations. While still having a role, the dwindling GAR and Civil War veteran numbers required this transition. By 1910, Charles Leeds estimated that "79 percent have joined the 'silent majority'" in the Jesse G. Thompson post alone.[113] Often unable to march, the aging Civil War generation rode in carriages and automobiles. Two years later, the Memorial Day parade featured the drum corps performance of "Onward Christian Soldiers" as remaining Carlisle GAR comrades, Prince Hall Masons, and women's auxiliary, schoolchildren, and other community groups processed to the grave of Corporal Jesse G. Thompson in the North Pitt Street cemetery. Attendees heard an address by the Rev. James Harvey Anderson, the presiding elder of the AMEZ Church who served in the Civil War as a hired servant of a lieutenant in the Thirteenth New Jersey Regiment, before the singing of "America." Bugler Henry Smallwood closed by playing taps.[114]

The Won Cause tradition endured beyond the death of the last Civil War veterans and into emergence of new traditions honoring US veterans. Newspapers continued to report on the persisting Memorial Day and veterans' celebrations by the various Cumberland Valley communities once served by the three GAR posts. As a result, Charlotte Forten Grimké's description of these Won Cause parade attendees' appreciation remained apt.

> Ah, no! again shall rise the people's voice
> As once it rose in accents clear and high—
> "Oh, outraged brother, lift your head, rejoice!
> Justice shall reign,—Insult and Wrong shall die!"
>
> So shall this day the joyous promise be
> Of golden days for our fair land in store;
> When Freedom's flag shall float above the free,
> And Love and Peace prevail from shore to shore.[115]

Grimké's concluding verses held sway as the next generation stepped in the footsteps established by Black GAR members. The Civil War generation cemented veteran status and not color, antebellum status, educational attainment, and/or class as entry into local Black leadership. By subtly rejecting their marginalization through the creation of separate GAR posts and child-rearing practices, they proved worthy as role models for those continuing to fight for justice at home and abroad. In this regard, later veterans fulfilled Grimké's promise made in the conclusion of "The Gathering of the Grand Army."[116]

Porch Lessons I

Rebel, Father, and Veteran

The veteran of the Civil War best known to me was my father, James Henry Woodson. . . . In the years that followed I met hundreds of Civil War Veterans, but fortunately, or unfortunately, I had attended college where I was directed toward definitive history—away from the personal narrative and the romantic aspects of the conflict.

—CARTER G. WOODSON, "MY RECOLLECTIONS OF VETERANS OF THE
CIVIL WAR" (1944)

The Civil War did not end well for my Civil War ancestor. After enlisting on Christmas Day 1863, Joseph Lane, a private in the Twenty-Second United States Colored Troops (USCT) regiment, found himself in a federal prison with a ball and chain around his right leg. Released in late November 1865, Lane returned home to his south-central Pennsylvania border community without the grand pageantry shown other returning "Liberators of the Race" only days earlier at the Reception of Colored Troops in Harrisburg, Pennsylvania.[1] His youthful rebellious spirit plagued him and subsequent collective memory. His court-martial and postwar decisions forever shaped how his community, his descendants, and scholars have remembered his Civil War experience.

Yet this unlikely Civil War hero would be instrumental in the promotion of rural Black Civil War collective memory and its persistence into the twentieth century. Lane employed his overlapping familial, religious, and veteran networks in remembering and commemorating the Civil War in both Franklin and Cumberland Counties. But his greatest contribution was that of a parent who raised the next generation committed to sustaining Black Civil War memory. Lane's complicated biography reveals the necessity of placing the rural Northern Won Cause experience in conversation with large urban Northern and even Southern African American communities.[2]

Born free in Franklin County, racial discrimination was a major influence in Joseph Lane's life. Indeed, race defined his entire wartime experience and much of his life. Like other freeborn Black residents, he had a limited education and worked a variety of low-waged agricultural jobs. State law also denied him the franchise. Racial politics had reduced him to a second-class citizen. Race also determined the timing of his enlistment, military duties performed, and even his six-month imprisonment following a court-martial. State and federal enlistment policies stymied his enlistment too. When Confederate soldiers enslaved many free Black Pennsylvanians during the 1863 Gettysburg Campaign, Lane successfully hid from capture. He did not initially answer the post-campaign call for service in the Fifty-Fourth and Fifty-Fifth Massachusetts regiments. Following the celebrated return of Amos Barnes from enslavement in a Richmond prison, however, Lane enlisted in Chambersburg, Pennsylvania, on Christmas Day 1863 and headed to Camp William Penn, outside of Philadelphia, for training. Signing with his mark, Lane and other Black Franklin County enlistees wanted to prove their manhood and secure better futures by donning the federal uniform.[3]

While serving in the Twenty-Second USCT, Lane witnessed several major battles and campaigns in the eastern theater. He fought for country and for enslaved African Americans. He also fought for Black Pennsylvanians who survived the Gettysburg Campaign with their freedom and those who had it stolen. He did what Joseph Winters, Frederick Douglass, and T. Morris Chester had asked of him and other able-bodied Black men.

Racial discrimination, though, followed Lane into the service. A fateful encounter on US Steamer *Western Metropolis* resulted in his court-martial. In May 1865, officials charged him with attempted mutiny and for striking his commanding officer. According to the court-martial documents, while the steamer was on the James River, Lane was trying to "rescue . . . an enlisted man" from being thrown off the vessel. In the process, he struck Capt. Joseph B. Reed of the Nineteenth USCT "with his clenched hands," and actively resisted placement in the hold by saying, "Let me alone. Damn you let me go."[4] Although pleading not-guilty, Lane was tried, convicted, sentenced to six months of hard labor without pay, and confined with a ball and chain attached to his right leg in a Norfolk, Virginia, prison. In late November 1865, Lane returned to Franklin County after receiving his discharge.[5]

Lane's rebellious streak did not end upon his return to Franklin County. His veteran status yielded neither economic nor social mobility. He worked a series of low-paying jobs as a part-time farm laborer, fruit picker, and road maintenance worker. Despite marrying Irene "Aurine" Howard, a former enslaved Virginian, Lane "lived a rather unrestrained life after his return from the war and, to some extent, his waywardness was a carryover from the war. He knew suffering and hardship and was frequently in and out of difficulty with the law."[6]

In 1878, Joseph Lane supplied the music at a house party hosted by the Anderson family who had recently purchased a modest home in the Wolfstown neighborhood of Chambersburg. During the December 17, 1878, party, Rachel Butler, the hostess's sister, rebuffed the advances of Peter Swingler. A fight ensued. John Anderson physically defended his sister-in-law. Egged on by Lane to defend his honor, Swingler left the party with Lane. Swingler retrieved his rifle and returned. When Lane opened the door for his friend, Swingler fired his weapon into Anderson's midsection. He immediately killed John Anderson.[7] Both Lane and Swingler were arrested and thrown in Chambersburg jail cells.

After being arrested, jailed, and acquitted of murder, Joseph Lane experienced a religious conversion. As recalled by elderly Black residents in the 1950s to a Shippensburg Historical Society member, Lane "prayed so hard that the doors of the Franklin County Jail opened."[8] Published accounts of this latter experience show a Won Cause collective memory that selectively remembered the lack of socioeconomic material benefits of Black military service, not-so-respectable working-class leisure pursuits, and the real reasons behind Lane's post-acquittal transformation. Local oral tradition held that Lane's prayer resulted in his freedom. Drawing on community remembrances, scholars have linked the court-martial, acquittal, and post-acquittal transformation to his Civil War service. As a result, rebel is often used when explaining the collective memory of Joseph Lane.

Swingler proved less fortunate. He was convicted and sentenced to death by hanging. Pennsylvanian courts denied his appeals. On June 5, 1879, the state executed him.

None of the trial coverage mentioned Lane's military service. With the expansion of constitutional protections, collective memory of the USCT military service secured citizenship rights for African Americans writ large. Indeed, the Civil War helped transform Lane and other Black Pennsylvanians into self-made men. Yet neither his military service nor veteran status mattered to many of his white counterparts and newspaper writers.[9] National and local media coverage stereotypically portrayed both men as other late nineteenth-century Black men. They were simply criminals whose actions at a house party in the predominantly African American neighborhood contributed to the death of another African American homeowner. One of whom was acquitted.[10] While having his life spared, the press and their predominantly white readership regarded him as a savage "who could never achieve true civilized manliness because [his] racial ancestors had never evolved that capacity."[11] As such, local, state, and national newspaper writers judged him through the racialized and gendered terms of manhood and civilization and not as a venerated Civil War veteran.[12]

The circumstances of this murder and acquittal appear to have made Lane a pariah in the wider Black Chambersburg community. Lane and his entire family relocated to Shippensburg in neighboring Cumberland County. The tight-knit Black Cumberland County community offered Lane and his family with a fresh start. The Lane family was representative of the postwar migration to Shippensburg. Like other Cumberland Valley communities, Shippensburg saw a significant increase in its Black population. Veterans and other migrants from the border communities of Pennsylvania, Maryland, and Virginia sought new lives in the rural town and employment with the railroad industry. These migrants added new "blood" to the existing Black community. The population grew from 176 in 1860 to 241 in 1870.[13] The Locust Grove/N. Queen Street cemetery served as the final resting place for at least twenty-six Civil War veterans. Of the twenty-one Black veterans buried in the older section of the cemetery, only eight were from Shippensburg. The rest, including Joseph Lane, had migrated to Shippensburg from other places."[14] At its height, the Black community boasted four Black churches, a Prince Hall Masonic Lodge, an Odd Fellows Lodge, an American Legion Post, and several Black-owned businesses.[15] The new demographic reality contributed to the robust Civil War commemorative traditions developed by the Black Shippensburg community and surrounding Cumberland County.

In short, Black Shippensburg residents overlooked Lane's less than perfect past and embraced him as they did other veterans in their midst. He participated in the Carlisle Grand Army of the Republic (GAR) post events. Like other Shippensburg veterans, he traveled the distance for camaraderie afforded by the Black GAR network.[16] He regularly represented the organization in Shippensburg's segregated Memorial Day and Emancipation Day celebrations. His participation as well as coverage of these early Black commemorations "escaped the notice of the white newspaper reporters."[17] While never serving in the GAR leadership, he became a fixture in the civic, fraternal, and African Methodist Episcopal (AME) religious communities of Shippensburg. Lane reinvented himself as a God-fearing, respectable family man, and honorable Civil War veteran. He, however, could never fully escape the collective Civil War memory of his previous colorful life. He would be remembered in the community for his court-martial and acquittal who found religion before settling down in the Shippensburg Civil War veteran networks.[18]

Never rising to local leadership or within the GAR ranks, fatherhood served as Lane's greatest contribution to Black Shippensburg Civil War memory. As a father of nine surviving children, Lane and his wife instilled in their children, specifically their daughters, the importance of honoring the memory of Black military service. Lane, as other parents, passed down stories of his wartime experiences and how the Civil War contributed to changes in education, politics, and social mobility. It is not clear how much he shared about his court-martial and postwar troubles with the criminal justice system.

Beyond these family oral traditions, Lane and his wife exposed their children to other GAR members, non-affiliated veterans, and civilian survivors in Franklin and Cumberland Counties who shared their experiences. These veteran elders were essential to reinforcing home lessons on their porches and sustaining a vibrant Civil War commemorative culture in their communities.[19] Moreover, Lane's children assisted with decorating graves in the Locust Grove/N. Queen Street cemetery. They marched in the various parades with their schools and/ or church youth groups. Their parents ensured their ongoing participation and prepared them for future work of caring for aging veterans and their families. Their public schools, church, and other community institutions reinforced these essential home lessons. Through parenting, Lane and his wife facilitated the persistence of memory into the twentieth century by raising the next generation. Neither Joseph Lane nor his wife would live to see how several daughters applied these lessons upon reaching adulthood. But the traditions and values instilled continued after their death in 1894 and 1895 respectively.

The Lanes' child-rearing practices mirrored other African American veterans' families in and beyond the Cumberland Valley. The instruction received by Black children at home, school, church, and other Civil War commemorative spaces allowed for the persistence of Black Civil War memory. Since African Americans "never forget their own innate humanity," these child-rearing practices instilled self-worth and racial pride. Civil War memory became one of many oppositional teachings necessary for survival, resistance, and culture.[20] Similar to the parenting and racial instruction during the Jim Crow era, Black parents employed a variety of resources and strategies for socialization, including isolation, avoidance, and education.[21] This meant that African American parents, including veterans, as well as survivors of both slavery and civilian survivors of the Confederate raids, ensured socialization and race pride in a degree of safety by delaying difficult questions and encouraging a culture of silence around the discrimination endured, harsh realities of slavery, and postwar struggles.[22]

The politics of respectability grounded these diverse family strategies practiced by Lane and other families on both sides of the Mason-Dixon line.[23] By claiming respectability, African Americans of diverse economic, educational, religious, and even geographic locales redefined self-identity and community-identity in relation to the dominant white culture and wielded Civil War memory as a political tool for continued struggle for civil and political rights nationally. Respectability, therefore, informed child-rearing practices. Historian Jennifer Rittenhouse has explained that "respectable black child-rearing emphasized the need for individual blacks to define or redefine themselves and their race in the public eye."[24] Parents also employed its second purpose: "to teach children to be self-defining in their own minds."[25] In so doing, the outcome would result in children's maturing into self-assured adults capable of "defin[ing] themselves, to develop their own sense of identity, regardless of how whites attempted to circumscribe and define them."[26] More important, Rittenhouse suggests: "They would possess not only the emotional strength to carry the unavoidable psychological baggage of racism but also the self-assurance and sense of purpose they needed in order to achieve in public and private life and contribute to the betterment of humanity."[27] Black veterans' promotion of the Won Cause, therefore, became one of many strategies employed in respectable child-rearing practices. Lane and other veterans raised the next generation through ritual, oral traditions, and modeling of Black leadership within GAR activities to persevere and fight for the betterment of family and community over individual advancement.

Veterans, parents, and community leaders viewed children as both living monuments of the diverse African American Civil War experience and future defenders of Black Civil War memory. This was not unlike the way the United Daughters of the Confederacy (UDC) and pro–Lost Cause parents instilled white supremacy in their children. Careful instruction inside and outside of the home was essential.[28] The efforts of African American parents permitted the evolution of the Civil War traditions and support services to include later veterans, specifically Memorial Day and Armistice Day, but also aided in their ongoing civil rights struggle. Black Civil War memory had a significant role defining Black identity at the Pennsylvania–Maryland border over the twentieth century. For these reasons, the Veterans' Graves Recognition project recognized the GAR and unaffiliated Civil War veterans interred at the Locust Grove/N. Queen Street cemetery. On the eve of World War II, the 1940 Memorial Day parade featured the sons of Civil War veterans laying of flowers on graves and performing graveside services. The Won Cause vision of Lane and other veterans continued to hold sway over Cumberland Valley traditions.[29]

As with any individual, Joseph Lane was complex. It is easy to focus on the less-than-stellar and sensational aspects of his life. He was a court-martialed USCT

veteran who "prayed the jail cell open" when accused of murder. The public notoriety of his military service and acquittal could make for mythic legends for
scholars and still be hidden among later twenty-first-generation descendants. He
and his immediate descendants could never fully escape his colorful past. Yet the
collective memory of youthful rebellions failed to capture Lane's most important post–Civil War roles—father and kinkeeper of the rural Pennsylvania USCT
experience.

In Shippensburg, Lane found redemption and respectability among the Cumberland Valley comrades. The Black veterans' network provided him with a
community and a purpose. He and other USCT veteran kinkeepers cultivated
the spirit of the Won Cause culture in the next generation of his biological and
chosen family. This work had lasting consequences for my own maternal family and others who benefited from his mode of kinkeeping. Three of his daughters imparted those lessons to my maternal grandmother who in turn reared my
mother, aunts, and uncles on the distant Civil War ancestor's kinkeeping lessons.
As a result of Lane's reinvention, the collective memory about him expanded so
that he was seen as a respectable USCT veteran.

Lane was a rebel. He also was a husband, father, and respectable USCT veteran who inspired generations. He epitomized the rural Won Cause experience
at the Pennsylvania–Maryland border. And I am proud of my own personal connection to my great-great-grandfather.

II

PORCHES OF MY ADOPTED KINKEEPERS

Think you that John Brown's spirit stops?
That Lovejoy was but idly slain?
Or do you think those precious drops
From Lincoln's heart were shed in vain?
That for which millions prayed and sighed,
That for which tens of thousands fought,
For which so many freely died,
God cannot let it come to naught.

—JAMES WELDON JOHNSON, "FIFTY YEARS, 1863–1913," 1917

5

The Limits of Emancipationist Memory in Richmond

Thomas Morris Chester, African American correspondent for the Philadelphia *Press*, captured the reception of the Thirty-Sixth USCT when it entered Richmond on April 3, 1865. Chester described to his readers in his April 4, 1865, dispatch: "Tears of joy ran down the faces of the more aged."[1] The sight of the Black soldiers garnered deep emotions from elderly African Americans who anxiously awaited their arrival: "'You've come at last;' 'We've been looking for you these many days'; 'Jesus has opened the way'; 'God bless you'; 'I've not seen that old flag for four years'; 'It does my eyes good'; 'Have you come to stay?'; 'Thank God'; and [other] similar expressions of exultation."[2] Richmond had been liberated. Cheers and cries of joy, according to Chester, meshed with the sounds of "Yankee Doodle" and "Shouting the Battle Cry of Freedom" performed by the Thirty-Sixth USCT drum corps. Jubilee had arrived in the Confederate capital on April 3.[3]

When the remaining USCT regiments of Brevet Brigadier General Alonzo Draper's brigade arrived, they included numerous Franklin County and other Cumberland Valley, Pennsylvania, USCT soldiers. They entered the Confederate capital as liberators of African Americans and military occupiers of the individuals who supported their perpetual racial subordination.[4] They avenged freeborn Pennsylvania-Maryland border residents enslaved in Richmond and throughout the Confederacy. More important, they vindicated those Pennsylvanian civilians who successfully escaped capture during the three major border raids only to have their worlds turned upside down once they emerged from their hiding spots. Before the hard work of rebuilding the nation began in earnest, the seeds of the Richmond Emancipationist tradition had already been sown.

For Black Richmonders, April 3 became a significant date in the Civil War commemorative calendar. Beginning in 1866, they took to the streets through formal parades and marked the day with speeches, music and other activities. They celebrated their freedom and post-emancipation progress but also used their experiences within the former Confederate capital for claiming the power to define local, state, and national Emancipationist traditions. Yet their claims of authority were not widely accepted. White Richmonders, federal officials, and even some African Americans periodically challenged Black Richmonders' efforts to celebrate the April third anniversary of emancipation.

Three celebrations—1866, 1890, and 1915—offer windows onto the forces shaping the Richmond emancipation celebrations and the ability of Black Richmonders to shape local, regional, and national celebrations. In 1866, residents planned a parade that recognized the first anniversary of emancipation and Union victory; however, white opposition contributed to a more subdued event. In 1890, a conference on a possible national day of Thanksgiving again threatened the primacy of the April third date for emancipation celebrations within the national Black commemorative tradition and revealed Black Richmonders' diminishing power to shape such debates. In both instances, Black Richmonders' ability to define and remember the April 3 emancipation date as a central part of Civil War memory was challenged. These early challenges informed the last significant effort by Black Richmonders to define a national Jim Crow–era Emancipationist commemoration for African Americans writ large in the summer of 1915. Predating the post–Civil Rights and Black Power Movements embrace of Juneteenth as a national celebration, Black Richmonders organized a month-long spectacle celebrating emancipation and fifty years of African American progress. While applying valuable lessons learned from 1866 and 1890, even these Richmond Emancipationist adherents could not overcome the issues of race, public memory, the national reconciliation impulse, and changing African American demographic shifts to northern urban centers.

Collectively, these events show the various forces and processes shaping how Black Richmonders remembered and attempted to commemorate their April 3, 1865, Emancipation Day. Recognizing that not all African Americans embraced a single memory of the Civil War, these episodes shed light on the limits of Emancipationist commemorative tradition as a singular and unifying collective Civil War memory despite the concerted efforts of Black Richmonders.

In April 1866, African American community leaders wanted to celebrate the anniversary of their emancipation with a parade and events at the local schools. Organizers planned the event through a series of meetings held primarily at the First and Second African Baptist Churches. As in other mass meetings, the diverse attendees engaged with the main organizers. All saw the Emancipation Day celebration as another opportunity to remember the Civil War as a political strategy for shaping the debates over African American citizenship in the postwar city.[5] In response to the proposed celebration, Richmond government officials and white elites adamantly refused to permit the proposed celebration. Fearing possible violence to their homes, churches, and schoolhouses, event organizers appealed directly to white Richmonders through leaflets and broadsides. The event was not intended "to celebrate the failure of the Southern confederacy, [as] it has been stated in the papers of this City." Rather, the celebration, according to the organizers, simply marked "the day on which GOD was pleased to Liberate their long-oppressed race."[6] While willing to limit the scale of the event, Black Richmonders refused to cancel the event. As ordained by God, the April 3 parade represented Jubilee—the one-year anniversary of their physical and figurative freedom from the chains of slavery with several USCT regiments having a significant role in the liberation of Richmond. Organizers' assurances and revised plans, however, did not sway local leaders.

White Richmonders saw the proposed Emancipation Day event as one flagrantly celebrating Confederate defeat and the consequence of their wartime loyalties to the short-lived nation. The proposed event caused white Richmonders to remember USCT regiments entering the city as oppressors who freed their enslaved property without compensation, the flight of Confederate leadership, and the ultimate collapse of the Confederacy. They also had to recall their initial anger at the sight of the occupying United States Army, the Freedmen's Bureau agents, and individuals facilitating freedpeople's post-emancipation transition. Such sights had caused Julia P. Read and other elite women to express fits of rage in 1865. Now, a year later, the proposed festivities would have forced them to recall how the war's outcome had upended their antebellum household status and power in society.[7] Feeling forced to remember the totality of April 3, 1865, and its aftermath, white Richmonders saw the inaugural Emancipation Day celebration as being too much and too soon.

Elite white Richmonders quickly escalated their attempts to prevent the parade from a local to a national issue. John H. Gilmer, ex-Confederate and Richmond attorney serving in the Virginia Senate, sent a confidential telegram to President Andrew Johnson. The brief missive raised the alarm of violence if the African American residents celebrated the anniversary on April 3.[8] With this telegram, Gilmer and other white elites sought action from the Tennessean whom they regarded as an ally to prevent the parade. Indeed, Johnson's February 1866 remarks during an interview with a delegation consisting of Frederick Douglass and other African American leaders and his February 19, 1866, veto message for the Freedmen's Bureau Bill made clear his attitudes toward the newly freed African Americans in the former Confederate States of America.[9] In appealing to the president, Gilmer and other white Richmonders sought an executive order prohibiting the Emancipation Day celebration. Assured by a Washington newspaper that presidential action was forthcoming, the *Richmond Whig* reported: "It could not have been otherwise than distasteful to the whole white community. . . . In every point of view, they have acted wisely in concluding not to have their celebration. They will be just as free without it as with it, and far more comfortable."[10] Beyond Richmond, other newspapers prominently covered the possible federal intervention on the proposed Richmond celebration and prematurely reported: "President Johnson unequivocally refused to allow the freedmen of Richmond to parade on or celebrate the 3d instant, and issued an order to that effect, directed to the proper military authorities."[11] Contrary to these reports, Johnson did not block the parade. Instead, Johnson committed his leading military generals to the matter.

Federal military officials responded to the potential crisis posed by the planned Emancipation celebration with diplomacy and preparedness for the possibility of violence. Between March 29 and April 3, 1866, a series of telegrams between Major General Alfred Terry, Brigadier General John A. Rawlins and Lieutenant General Ulysses S. Grant reveals the attempts to defuse a possibly violent clash between anxious white residents and defiant Black residents celebrating the Emancipation anniversary. Terry first attempted to persuade the community leaders not to have the celebration. Terry's advice against the celebration only emboldened African Americans to proceed. He explained to Rawlins: "I now find that the great mass of them are determined to celebrate the day and that great numbers are coming in from the country to join them."[12] In seeking advice for his next steps, Terry expressed that he did not want to engage in military action against the white civilian population and was willing to suppress the African Americans' emancipation celebration for the sake of peace. Moreover, the planned celebration would have occurred during an authorized leave of absence. Grant responded to Terry to either "put a stop to it or take steps to suppress the disorder as you deem most advisable." But most important, he ordered Terry to delay the start of his leave until after the planned celebration.[13]

As April 3 neared, it became evident that Black Richmonders remained committed to the parade. Terry attempted to calm white anxieties and fears. He focused on the happiness of white Richmonders and not the African American community's desires to celebrate emancipation. When Terry arrived months earlier, Black Richmonders had different expectations of the "Republican, military hero, and wartime commander of both black and white troops."[14] Terry's personal racial bias and unquestioned adherence to the Johnson administration's anti-Black policies shaped his attempts to curb the April 3 celebration. His efforts were not helped by African American organizers' published statements. The parade would occur. Hence, Grant sent the following telegram at 11:00 am on April 3, 1866:

> If the colored peoples celebration takes place to day close all drinking houses in the city and use patrols to arrest for the day, all parties black or white, who are threatening in their manner, or who are intoxicated.[15]

Based on the flurry of telegrams, federal military officials feared the worst possible outcome and attempted to mitigate the potential crisis. Terry, Rawlins, and Grant acted like white Richmonders in trying to curb the Emancipation commemoration. Black Richmonders not only had to fight against white Richmonders, but also against their supposed military protectors tasked with the promotion of white sectional reunification and peace in the former Confederate capital.[16]

The parade occurred as scheduled, although arsonists destroyed the Second African Baptist Church on the night before the event. Black Richmonders astutely understood this violent attack as one challenging their Emancipation celebration. The city had burned following the entry of white and USCT regiments. Now, arson destroyed a major symbol of African American citizenship but not Black Richmonders' resolve. Amid the smoldering ashes of Second African Baptist Church, Black Richmonders and their white allies celebrated the inaugural Emancipation Day celebration before the rebuilding efforts began in earnest. By late May 1866, the congregation placed the cornerstone on the new church building. But on April 3, 1866, in response to the terrorist attack on their church, they defiantly marched.[17]

According to William D. Harris, an African American Freedmen's School educator, approximately two thousand participants representing 163 military guards and 15 different fraternal and other social groups proceeded to Capitol Square in "Military precision."[18] Both the *Daily Dispatch* and the *Richmond Whig* disparaged the precision of the parade participants, but they could agree with Harris on the grand parade that traversed from the Fair Grounds through the main streets and neighborhoods (Broad, Main, First, Grace Streets) and ended in Capitol Square. The banners proclaimed messages of African American achievement since Confederate defeat and the ushering in of Black freedom on April 3. One banner read *"Peace, Friendship, and Liberty with all mankind"* while another noted, according to the *Daily Dispatch*, *"Union Liberties Protective Society, organized February 4, 1866,* with the unnecessary postscript, *Peace and good-will towards men"* (emphasis original).[19] The roughly 12,000 to 15,000 Black observers who lined the streets made it impossible for even white elites to ignore the grand demonstration of African American commemoration of their emancipation and the Confederate defeat in their city. Shouting "emancipated," the crowd took the streets and proudly watched the procession. For Black Richmonders, as the *Richmond Whig* surmised, "the day was a holiday."[20]

Upon reaching their destination, Reverend J. W. Hunnicutt, a local white Republican, delivered the main address before a crowd of fifteen thousand observers. Addressing "fellow-citizens," Hunnicutt encouraged education, hard work, and a life grounded in religion as the means of postwar advancement. He informed the crowd: "Work hard and work steadily, . . . and then, indeed, you can *command* respect and position. With education you may become creditable doctors, lawyers, skilled mechanics, or clergymen, . . . and without it you will be nothing."[21] Following these remarks, an unknown Black community leader spoke briefly before dispersing the crowd. Harris considered the event as the "most respectable orderly and sensible demonstration" that he had ever seen. In the wake of the pre-event local and national opposition, Harris saw the entire affair as African Americans recapturing the city of Richmond for a "second time."[22]

White spectators and leaders made different observations. Terry reported to his commanding officers: "The celebration today passed off in peace & quiet except for a dubious report that the procession was fired upon by a white man from a window—I have heard of no disorders."[23] While begrudgingly noting the lack of violence, the white Richmond press still found fault with Black Richmonders' inaugural Emancipation Day celebration. The media coverage criticized the small number of attendees and promoted stereotypical characterizations of the Black Richmond leaders' clothing and speech. Considered as a betrayal of whiteness, Hunnicutt's use of "fellow-citizens" grated on the *Richmond Dispatch* reporter, who counted all "sixty-three" instances of the honorific previously afforded to solely white citizens. The reporter also peppered his transcription of Hunnicutt's Emancipation Day speech with asides that mocked Black Richmonders' more prominent white ally. Overall, the more subdued event than originally planned reflected how white elite Richmonders successfully exerted their authority over African Americans' public expressions of Civil War memory.

The April 1866 commemoration revealed the limits of Black Richmonders' authority to define and publicly commemorate their collective memory of emancipation and in turn Confederate defeat. From Terry's actions to the media coverage, white Richmonders usurped the Emancipationists' claims by arguing that the lack of violence resulted from their leadership and restraint and not from

Black Richmonders' skillful leadership and organization. Instead of a "'diabolical deed' of some irate youth," white Richmonders minimized the act of terrorism and agreed with the *Daily Dispatch* coverage of the fiery destruction of Second African Baptist Church that it was an accidental event that coincidently occurred on the eve of the inaugural Emancipation anniversary celebration. White Richmonders saw the parade as a temporary demonstration of African American claims of freedom and citizenship, and ultimately, an Emancipationist event that did not overturn the racial hierarchies being redefined in the postwar city.[24]

White public opinion affected subsequent Emancipation Day celebrations on April 3. Later parades remained restricted to the African American neighborhoods and on occasion traversed from one neighborhood to another through the center of town. Although white public opinion restricted subsequent parade routes, African Americans and their allies did not tone down their speeches.[25] For instance, at the 1867 celebration, parade attendees heard political speeches by Reverend J. W. Hunnicutt, Peter Randolph, a popular Black minister, and Lewis Lindsay, an African American bandleader. Lindsay's speech encouraged parade attendees to "be steadfast, fight the good fight, be strong, get your diplomas. Be peaceable and wait until you get to the ballot-box before your proclaim your political sentiments. Then vote for a good man without regard to color. But whatever you do, don't cast your vote for a rebel."[26] Lewis's words reflected the community's adoption of strategies to cope with the limits placed on African American expression of freedom by white Richmonders. These coping strategies permitted the community's perseverance until they could freely express themselves, whether at the ballot box, in the classroom and during the annual Emancipation Day celebrations.

Over the next two decades, white opposition declined except for a few grumbles in the local newspapers and gave way to a power struggle among African American leaders over the best means to commemorate emancipation and postbellum racial progress. Black Richmonders positioned themselves as national trendsetters due to their unique Civil War history within the former Confederate capital. Yet an 1890 celebration and conference revealed the ways that the burgeoning Lost Cause commemorative landscape and diverging African American political interests stymied Black Richmonders' ability and power to influence the commemorative emancipation traditions on a national stage.

In October 1890, Black Richmonders hosted a three-day Emancipation celebration aimed at creating a National Thanksgiving Day for Freedom. The Indianapolis *Freeman* informed its readers of the date and the topic for the assembled national African American leaders to discuss: "A 'National Thanksgiving Day' is the name of a natal day celebration which the wide awake Afro-Americans of Richmond, Va., are endeavoring to establish. Their idea is to perpetuate the emancipation of the slaves in this country, and to establish one day which will be regarded as a national day for this purpose."[27]

George Williams Jr. proposed and spearheaded the celebration with Black Richmond educated elite. Born on May 23, 1856, to George Williams Sr. and Clara Williams, his enslaved parents raised him on a Pittsylvania County, Virginia, planation until emancipation. After the Civil War, he did agricultural work with his parents before relocating to Manchester, Virginia (now part of the city of Richmond). He then secured an education and operated as a junk dealer for a brief time, according to Williams's own account published in the *Richmond Planet*.[28] Williams later served as the president of the Virginia Industrial, Mercantile, Building and Loan Association headquartered in Richmond before becoming the president of the National Industrial Beneficial Endowment Company in Lynchburg after the 1890 celebration. In addition to these leadership roles, Williams proved especially adept at organizing railroad tour excursions for middle-class African American tourists. He brought these skills and tour operator connections with the local and regional railroad companies to the planning process.[29]

In late July 1890, the Manchester leader approached Black Richmonders about "establishing a national Thanksgiving Day for the whole people." Other event organizers were individuals who had come of age during Reconstruction and who rose to the ranks of middle-class leadership following their graduation from Richmond Colored Normal and High School.[30] Williams and fellow Emancipationists hoped that their celebration would appropriately honor "the issuing of that immortal document by that martyred man, Lincoln" and cement their role as national commemorative leaders. Assuring readers that "no political signification will be attached to this gathering," Williams Jr. proclaimed: "This is to be 'Our Great Thanksgiving Day,' and, doubtless, Richmond will see and feel the proudest day of her life."[31]

To ensure success Richmond organizers enlisted former Reconstruction Congressman John Roy Lynch and former Senator Blanche K. Bruce to lead a delegation to the White House. The delegation personally invited President Benjamin Harrison to the October 1890 celebration. President Harrison declined the invitation, but Black Richmonders planned a multi-day celebration consisting of a meeting, a grand parade, speeches by George T. Downing, Joseph C. Price, and Congressman John Mercer Langston, and literary performances by several Black

Richmonders.[32] After the theatrics of the Lee Monument unveiling in May 1890, organizers even sent a request to the Virginia governor that "Richmond How-itzers . . . fire . . . a salute during the Emancipation celebration in that city." The governor summarily denied the request; he didn't want to see white Virginians donning "their uniforms [to] shoot off their guns in honor of emancipation."[33]

And so Richmond hosted yet another grand Emancipation celebration—this one in the form of a convention in early October 1890 to plan future celebra-tions. Convention delegates represented the diversity of Virginia's political and community leadership as well as national African American leaders. Several lo-cal African American communities organized through their local Republican Party and elected official delegates to attend the convention determining the formal Emancipation holiday date. Even the Emancipation Association of Dan-ville, a town that endured significant election violence in the Readjuster Party overthrow several years earlier, elected delegates to be in attendance. Attendees arrived from across Virginia and the nation through the regional and national railroad network.[34]

Several national African American newspapers sent correspondents to cover the multi-day celebration. The parade and speeches drew significant praise. The *Washington Bee* considered this "Emancipation Celebration in Richmond, Vir-ginia," to be "one of the greatest events in the history of the Virginia people."[35] The correspondent commended the *Richmond Planet* editor who served as the chief marshal of the Emancipation parade. Black Richmonders had successfully organized an "imposing celebration" for Black people by Black people that was enjoyed by all in attendance.[36] According to *Richmond Planet* editor John Mitch-ell Jr., city streets "were thronged with visitors, all present to witness the Emanci-pation exercises, pertaining to the setting a day to be forever commemorated of the Emancipation of the slaves in the country. Nearly all of the places of business by colored men were decorated with flags and bunting."[37] Some marchers used the occasion to promote their preferred national Emancipationist celebration dates on their banners. These banners did not distract from the "gala day" as the parade succeeded by "celebrating all that had been achieved" since Confederate defeat.[38]

This spectacle did encourage some criticism from a small Baltimore religious weekly. In response, the national *New York Age* directly engaged with the Balti-more newspaper in its coverage and countered the anti-Black criticism leveled at the Emancipation parade and other festivities. "Almost in every great celebra-tion by the whites you will notice the presence of the black man; he is there for nothing but a laughing stock," the *New York Age* correspondent remarked.[39] He then juxtaposed the racial composition at the Lee Monument unveiling with the October celebration: "At General Lee's monument unveiling last spring the daily papers of Richmond and adjacent cities made special mention of the fact that a number of ex-slaves, some quite aged, had come hundreds of miles to join their former masters in the process and celebration to keep green the memory of one who sacrificed his life fighting for the perpetuation of slavery."[40] Possibly taking aim at the white attendees of the Lee monument unveiling, the reporter surmised: "Certainly some of the old ex-masters ought to have returned the compliment at this time and united with the ex-slave in his emancipation celebration, especially since one good turn deserves another."[41] Despite this minor criticism, media coverage acknowledged but still remained defiant of the competing Lost Cause commemorative tradition. In this predominant Black and relatively safe space, the performative Emancipationist traditions and rituals reined in the former Confederate capital.

Many enjoyed the parade, festivities, and speeches by prominent national Black leaders, but the date of the proposed new national Emancipation event caused fierce debate. This portion of the October celebration almost marred the entire festive spirit. Indeed, the *Richmond Planet* reported: "There is quite a difference of opinion existing among our people as to the proper day to be observed."[42] Some participants proposed January 1 (for the Emancipation Proclamation), April 9 (Lee's surrender), or September 22 (Lincoln's signing of the preliminary Emancipation Proclamation). Whereas these dates would have facilitated a sectional reconciliation over the official date for celebrating Emancipation, several organizers insisted on April 3. Black Richmonders advocated at both the last major planning meeting and actual celebration that the fall of the Confederate capital should be the proper date to celebrate the abolition of slavery. As William Bell eloquently stated: "I am in favor of April 3d when Richmond fell, because that was the day that I shook hands with Yankees."[43]

It may seem inconsequential for Black Richmonders to engage in this Civil War cultural war. Their fight for the fall and liberation of Richmond as a national holiday reflected their concerns over the broader fight against the emerging regional hold of the Lost Cause. When considering the Lee Monument unveiling, Black Richmond leaders' defense of April 3 as the proposed date represented a response to the hardening of the Lost Cause geographical boundaries.

Weeks before this national meeting of African American leaders, the unveiling of the Lee Monument on the burgeoning Monument Avenue occurred on Memorial Day, a Won Cause tradition embraced by white and Black veterans and communities. The unveiling attracted National Guard units, Confederate veterans, and other Lost Cause proponents from across the city and several states.[44] As part of the celebrations, several revelers documented their presence with studio photography. While scholars have noted the intentional involvement of white children in these festivities, Captain M. F. Wyckoff of Company D, Second Regiment, West Virginia National Guard posed with a barefoot African American boy for a souvenir photograph. As one of his first public events as a commissioned captain, Wyckoff noted the living prop in the verso inscription to his brother. "I am Cap. of a Militia Co. This is my little n****r waiter. I weigh 214 lbs. in my shirt sleeves. I brought my Co. to the unveiling of Lee's statue that was a great time."[45] Neither Black Richmonders' Reconstruction-era gains nor Emancipationist collective memories meant anything to the white West Virginia National Guardsman. Representing a state admitted to the United States during the Civil War, the Lee Monument unveiling allowed him to enact the Lost Cause fantasy of the faithful slave trope. Elderly African American men and women often served as living props at Confederate monument unveilings. Some African Americans willingly played the part at these public events and even applied the Lost Cause racial logics in their Confederate pension application. Financial considerations and fear often motivated these actors, as discussed by historians Kevin Levin and Adam Domby. This waiter, however, was too young to have served as a Civil War camp servant. Born after emancipation, the African American youth's motivation is unclear, except possibly cash payment. Yet Wyckoff commanded his faithful camp servant's performance and perpetuated the lie to his brother who received the staged photograph. Both the photograph and the inscription demonstrate the emerging racial power dynamics and selective whitewashed remembrances being resisted by Black Richmonders.[46]

In this culture war, Black Richmonders saw the defense of April 3 as part of a larger, multifaceted struggle over Civil War memory. They firmly understood the threats faced on the local, regional, and national level. Each required different tactics. The *Richmond Planet* offered an outlet for the criticism of the Lee Monument. John Mitchell Jr. decried the "emblems of the 'Lost Cause,' many of which had been perforated by Union bullets" on the display at the unveiling. The *Richmond Planet* editor criticized the revelers on the front page of the May 31, 1890, edition: "The South may revere the memory of its chieftains. It takes the wrong steps in doing so, and proceeds to go too far in every similar celebration."[47] He considered the spectacle as an anti-modern celebration in the former Confederate capital. He concluded: "It serves to retard its progress in the country and forges heavier chains with which to be bound. All is over."[48]

Mitchell and other Black Richmonders could not afford to lose any ground to Wyckoff, the Ladies Lee Monument Association, and other white Virginians implementing the Lost Cause commemorative landscape locally. Their minor struggle over the April 3 date with national African American leaders was a fight that they could cede territory to influencing the Emancipationist tradition at the national level. For the sake of unity and the reality of multiple options, convention delegates agreed on January 1, the date of the final Emancipation Proclamation, "as the most fitting for the celebration to be observed in future."[49] By choosing a date of freedom, and one that privileged President Abraham Lincoln, convention delegates unwittingly lost an opportunity to counter the Lost Cause tradition. April 3 and even April 9 would have celebrated the failure of the Confederacy as a national project and permitted additional opportunities to celebrate African American USCT soldiers and naval personnel who contributed to the fiery destruction of slavery. Either of these dates would have been a bolder statement of the national Emancipation holiday. Unlike the chosen date, pro–Lost Cause proponents would have been forced to remember their defeat, failed nationalism, and the national elevation of African Americans from property to citizen. January 1 permitted the continuation of the Lost Cause fantasy of the Civil War, emancipation, and subjugated role of African Americans in the postwar nation. Lost Cause proponents could and did ignore the African American tradition. If recognized, Abraham Lincoln and not African Americans became the center of the selective remembrance of the date.

Despite failing to name April 3 as the national Emancipation Day date, Black Richmonders could and did celebrate a successful parade. The GAR posts marched in the front, prominent position in front of the members of the State Guard, Attucks Guard, Union Guard of Richmond, and the three guard units from Petersburg. Among the civic societies, the Lincoln Beneficial Club was signaled out for its elaborate banner featuring "Abraham Lincoln after breaking the slavery chains and raising the slaves."[50] The grand spectacle of music, military organizations, Civil War veterans, and civic organizations was much more elaborate than the 1866 celebration, featured more speakers, and earned extensive praise.

This event highlighted the limits of Black Richmonders' authority to define national Emancipationist commemorative traditions. To be sure, Black Richmonders do not abandon the practice of celebrating April 3 with parades. These traditions served as powerful statements of African Americans' claims to public spaces as evident in the well-known photograph of the 1905 parade.[51] However, the Richmond Emancipationists' claims of authority to define the meaning of emancipation both locally and nationally continued a downward trajectory. As national Emancipationist leaders, Black Richmonders simply could not elevate the April 3 commemoration onto the national stage. They remained aspirational Emancipationist trendsetters among African Americans nationally while trying to stave off the consequences of the Lost Cause landscape and Jim Crow segregation following the Lee Monument unveiling. In both endeavors, they failed.

By the fiftieth anniversary of the Civil War, Monument Avenue demarcated the expanded racial boundaries of the Lost Cause commemorative landscape. The 1907 larger-than-life monuments of J. E. B. Stuart and Jefferson Davis towered over the city. The later Stonewall Jackson (1919) and Matthew Fontaine Maury (1929) monuments enshrined the "know-your-place aggression" in the Lost Cause commemorative landscape. The now disenfranchised Black Richmonders firmly understood "the reactionary nature of white supremacy and the violence that necessarily accompanie[d]" anti-Blackness as a daily lived experience in the Jim Crow city.[52] By continuing the April 3 celebrations, however, Black Richmonders voiced their discontent. Their annual claims to public space reflected their refusal to accept the Lost Cause landscape. Few white Richmonders, however, "had any interest in listening."[53] Instead, they embraced fabrications, whitewashed narratives, and a cultural landscape grounded in white supremacy and widespread collective forgetting. In the former Confederate capital, the Lost Cause proponents encouraged the destruction of Black Richmonders' Emancipationist tradition and post-emancipation success "while claiming it never existed" as part of an intentional and coordinated political agenda. The resulting Civil War commemorative landscape privileged the Lost Cause tradition over all other traditions and defined "who matters within a community, who should matter, and who can be ignored."[54]

As their power waned, Black Richmonders remained committed Emancipationists who claimed the authority to define this component of Black Civil War memory. While the April third anniversary remained sacrosanct, they applied the lessons learned from the 1866 and 1890 events during the fiftieth anniversary of the fall of Richmond. The commemoration afforded them with one last opportunity to shape Civil War memory on a national stage.[55]

In its 1914 debut issue, the Richmond *Industrial Advocate* informed readers of the "great exposition to be held at Richmond, in the spring of 1915, the opening day of which will be the 4th of July celebration."[56] In addition to securing the support of President Wilson, the author boasted of the event's significance, peppering the word "great" in the title and throughout the article. He wrote, "A great deal has been said and written by both white and colored, and especially by the white daily papers, who are giving their aid and support to the promotion of this great enterprise."[57] From the inaugural issue of the *Industrial Advocate* to the exposition's opening day, exposition organizers attempted to use this event to shore up Black Richmonders' standing in the national arena of influencing Civil War memory and racial uplift progress. By executing a "Great Exposition and Celebration," they sought to minimize previous missteps in commemorating Emancipation.

Since 1866, Black Richmonders' had attempted to define the collective memory of emancipation in the city, state, region, and nation through Emancipation parades and celebrations. By the fiftieth anniversary celebration, Black Richmonders in the Negro Historical and Industrial Association had learned valuable lessons. Intense white opposition and contested national debates over the meaning of emancipation, and the racial realities of the Reconstruction and Jim Crow eras dictated their acquiescence to internal and external forces. Yet they still insisted on a national exposition celebrating emancipation and fifty years of African American achievement nationally beginning July 4, 1915. Even after securing congressional funding and organizing a grand month-long spectacle in the Richmond area, adherents of the Emancipationist tradition could not overcome the issues of race, public memory, the national reconciliation impulse, and changing African American demographics. When I surveyed the efforts of Giles B. Jackson (committee chair), African American newspaper coverage, and actual reception, I found that the 1915 Emancipation Exposition signaled the closure of Black Richmonders' relevancy in shaping the Emancipationist tradition, but also how national realities encouraged new organizations and forms of commemorative traditions to emerge in its wake.

Giles B. Jackson, lawyer and civil rights advocate, served as the principal organizer of the Emancipation Exposition. Born to Hulda and James Jackson in 1853, the former enslaved Goochland County, Virginia, native served as the body servant for his enslaver Charles G. Dickerson before self-emancipating himself after federal troops landed at City Point. After the Civil War, Jackson worked for a prominent white Richmond family as a laborer before becoming a domestic worker in a Washington, DC, household. While in Washington, DC, he married Sarah E. Wallace in November 1874.[58] By the 1880 census, he relocated his growing family to Richmond, where he studied law under a local attorney. In 1887, he became the first African American lawyer certified to practice law before the Virginia Supreme Court of Appeals. In addition to maintaining a law office, he advocated for civil rights and racial uplift in the years prior to the 1915

Emancipation Exposition. In 1901, President Theodore Roosevelt made him an honorary colonel. His connections to President Roosevelt and Booker T. Washington provided Jackson both credentials and opportunity to head the organizing committees for the Jamestown Ter-Centennial and later the Richmond Emancipation Exposition.[59]

Unlike other exposition organizers working on the Emancipation Exposition, Jackson had previous experience in organizing an exposition. He helped organize the Negro Exhibit at the Jamestown Ter-Centennial Exposition of 1907 at the Norfolk fairgrounds; that exposition celebrated the three hundredth anniversary of the establishment of Jamestown by English colonists. From April 26 to November 30, the segregated event showcased the history and achievements of Black Virginians in the two-story Negro Building from their 1619 arrival as captured Africans through the Civil War and post-emancipation. From the exhibitions to the August 3 address by Booker T. Washington during "Negro Day," African Americans flocked to the exposition in large numbers.[60] They purchased the souvenir postcard of the Negro Building. Instead of mailing the commemorative postcard, some attendees carefully preserved the memento in their scrapbooks as an act of counter-archival resistance. Some even posed for souvenir tintype photographs placed in a special commemorative cardboard sleeve. Unlike the living prop used in the Wyckoff souvenir photograph, African Americans embraced the inexpensive technology for capturing their status as modern citizens and racial progress achieved since emancipation.[61] The Ter-Centennial celebration also inspired poetry read during the 1919 celebrations honoring the arrival of the first Africans on the White Lion ship at Point Comfort. Carrie Williams Clifford, an African American suffragist, poet, and clubwoman, published "Tercentenary of the Landing of Slaves at Jamestown 1619–1919" as part of her Widening Light collection. Over the fourteen lines, she traced the trajectory from "helpless slaves" who arrived at Jamestown to their "brave, patriotic" descendants who served "America in her crucial hour."[62] Although the exposition failed to bring in the expected revenue, Black Virginians saw the Ter-centennial exposition as a major success for celebrating African American achievements and contributions to the state.[63]

The New York Age concurred. The African American newspaper offered an extensive and frank post-exposition assessment for its readers. R. W. Thompson praised the Jamestown exposition for disarming anti-Black proponents "who have made the wholesale accusation that the Negro race is incapable of achievements that require intelligent initiative, scientific skill, original methods, business acumen and unceasing application."[64] Recognizing the historic 1619 arrival "in chains," Thompson, commended the Negro Building exhibitions for serving as "a 'star witness' in support of the Negro's claim to full-fledged American citizenship" while remaining critical of the "Jim Crowing" of their racial achievements as separate from the "main body of the Jamestown Exposition."[65] Thus, the Black press heralded Jackson for his leadership and organization skills.

Following this successful event, Jackson and Daniel Webster Davis, a Richmond public schoolteacher, minister, and civil rights activist, published *The Industrial History of the Negro Race of the United States* (1908). This volume embraced an essential tenet of the Emancipationist tradition—African American post-emancipation progress demonstrated a people on the rise from its dark slave past. These Jamestown Ter-Centennial credentials made Giles Jackson seem like a natural choice to organize the Emancipation Exposition.[66]

Jackson began preparations for the fiftieth Emancipation celebration months before the *Industrial Advocate* debuted. He wanted the event to succeed where efforts in 1866 and 1890 had not occurred as originally planned. Since intense white opposition and interference by President Andrew Johnson resulted in a scaled-back event in 1866, Jackson received President Woodrow Wilson's endorsement for a national exposition on Emancipation despite the concerted efforts of Mississippi Senator James Vardaman, a Jim Crow propagandist who embraced a Lost Cause understanding of the Civil War and Reconstruction. Jackson also secured the support of Virginia governor H. C. Stuart. With prominent white support, Jackson hoped to minimize any white opposition to the event.[67] Moreover, he assembled a group of local and national African Americans to serve on the organizing committee. This team reflected in part an attempt to have Black Richmonders serve as the principal organizers and restore their place in shaping Civil War memory nationally and not solely in the city and state. Whereas 1890 saw Black Richmonders make concessions over the April 3 date as a national holiday, the 1915 celebration featured city leaders spearheading the Negro Historical and Industrial Association and planning a national celebration hosted in their own community.[68]

With these previous concerns addressed, Jackson launched an ambitious media campaign through the *Industrial Advocate*. Debuting in late October 1914, the inaugural issue of this newspaper announced "the plans and purposes of the great exposition to be held at Richmond" and the planned opening during the Fourth of July festivities. The lead article noted Jackson's credentials, reception of the Jamestown Ter-Centennial Celebration, congressional appropriations secured, and prominent white federal, state, and local officials who endorsed the celebration.[69] Other articles reprinted the entire report in the *Congressional Record* approving the appropriations, correspondence with prominent white supporters, initial plans for the location, dates for the exposition, and the submission process for items, displays, and other exhibits. Proceeds from the short-lived newspaper sales contributed to the overall budget. The reprinting of articles in the major Black newspapers nationally contributed to publicity and support for the event's success.[70]

In addition, the inaugural edition of the "Official Organ of the Negro Exposition Celebration of the Fiftieth Anniversary of Emancipation" presented this event as one that directly challenged the prevailing Lost Cause narrative enveloping the state, region, and nation. Writing from Houston, Virginia, one letter to the editor extolled Jackson's efforts to celebrate fifty years since emancipation. The paper reprinted a letter written by someone using the name "Dr. Socrates" that was originally published in the *St. Luke Herald* on October 17, 1914. Dr. Socrates drew clear connections to the failed Confederate nation and how its defeat contributed directly to emancipation. He wrote:

> But when the Confederate hosts, those ragged and hungry troopers who had put up for four years the most magnificent fight the world had ever seen, grounded their arms and furled their flags and sheathed their swords, then, and not until then was liberty proclaimed throughout the land and unto all inhabitants thereof.[71]

Therefore, Dr. Socrates saw the exposition as a fitting event to commemorate this revolutionary period in American history. Calls for reunion and the Lost Cause reality in Richmond and other Southern communities demonstrated the urgency of the moment. Jubilee had to be celebrated on a national scale. Any Civil War tradition devoid of emancipation and USCT contributions had to be defeated. By the using the Emancipationist rhetoric understood by other national African American leaders, Dr. Socrates concluded:

> And so "it is meet and right" as the Prayer Book says, for this fiftieth year of actual freedom to be celebrated in a befitting manner, for fifty years, come next April the 9th, the Negroes came out of Egypt, out of his house of bondage, and he should hallow the fiftieth year; it should be a jubilee unto him, and every Negro, North, South, East, West, should join in to make the exposition a grand and glorious success, for, till April, 1865, there was not a free Negro from New York to California, from Maine to Texas.[72]

For a celebration of such national importance, according to Dr. Socrates, Giles Jackson was the only choice to lead this event. He implored Virginians to put aside any differences over questions of leadership and embrace the emancipation celebration. He closed: "Yes, let all Virginians, black and white, especially black, rally to our Colonel who brings things to pass."[73] By publishing this letter, the editors of the *Industrial Advocate* reminded readers of the necessity to support this event by honoring those who fought for their freedom and the progress made following slavery's destruction. In other words, failure to support the exposition and Jackson would be seen as betrayal of both Civil War soldiers and those African Americans who had benefited socially, politically, and economically over the last fifty years.

Another letter to the editor echoed these sentiments. The letter writer called on African Americans to come together and support the exposition. Under the name of Reformer, the supporter urged: "All petty jealousies should be buried and all should unite in the effort to show the people of Virginia and the country the progress the colored people have made along all useful lines in 50 years, despite the many handicaps that have and that now stand in the way of material advancement of the race from so many sources."[74] Like Dr. Socrates, Reformer reminded readers of how Richmonders were among the first to propose such a celebration during President William McKinley's administration. With federal support, it was time for Black Virginians and all African Americans to close ranks and support this event. But, more important, the celebration must demonstrate to all attendees and national observers that emancipation had not been in vain. Reformer proclaimed: "Let the exposition be by and for the people, and let it be a grand and magnificent display of what the race has done and is doing to elevate itself to a higher plane of usefulness among the other races for the good of our common country."[75] Encouraging attendance by all African Americans, event organizers and Black Richmonders, more broadly, understood that failure would have negative consequences for Black Richmonders to make a difference in terms of national leadership and possibly encourage a backlash from white officials who had entrusted Jackson and the city to host the exposition. Therefore, they strove for success. as all eyes were on Giles Jackson and Richmond's entire African American community.

Beyond the *Industrial Advocate*, African American newspapers publicized the Emancipation Exposition across the nation. Some newspapers, such as the *Denver Star*, *Cleveland Gazette* and Pittsburg, Kansas *Uplift*, wholeheartedly endorsed the exposition. They reported on the white support received, progress made on the event, and encouraged their readers to attend the month-long event in Richmond.[76] One California newspaper encouraged readers to witness the grand affair but also the activism for racial justice being done by the African

American community leadership. As a city on the rise, fair attendees would see for themselves the community work done by emancipation's beneficiaries, notably John Mitchell Jr., Maggie Lena Walker, and Giles B. Jackson.[77] Some African Americans paid heed. By the time the exposition opened, African Americans had contributed items, displays, and exhibitions from across the nation. Special transportation had been arranged for attendees traveling to and within the state.[78]

However, some newspapers expressed skepticism. The Indianapolis *Freeman* scoffed at Jackson's "big exposition event" in terms of fundraising and ability to create a spectacular event with a $55,000 budget given by Congress. One editorialist bluntly stated: "Smoke up, Mr. Jackson, make a noise like an exposition."[79] The Chicago *Broad Ax* outright told readers to attend the 1915 Lincoln Jubilee in Chicago instead of the Richmond Exposition. Deeming the Jamestown Ter-Centennial and the Richmond Exposition as "dismal failures," they reminded readers that the event held in the state of the "sainted emancipator" would serve as the perfect embodiment of Emancipationist memory by calling "the attention of the people and the country to what the Negro has accomplished . . . in his fifty years of freedom."[80] Giles Jackson, members of the organizing committee, and the *Industrial Advocate* publicity campaign never convinced these early critics, who used their respective newspapers in voicing their concerns over the exposition.

Even the *Richmond Times-Dispatch*, the city's white newspaper, publicized the event in the weeks leading to opening day, daily events, and aftermath. A closer analysis reveals that the pre-exposition coverage came directly from the publicity arm of Jackson's Negro Historical and Industrial Association. However, the *Richmond Times-Dispatch* promoted the same message to its readership as had supportive African American newspapers—attend the exposition, celebrate the fifty years of racial progress made since emancipation in the city, region, and nation, and celebrate Richmond's role in the national Emancipation celebration.[81]

Opening on July 5, 1915, and lasting until July 28, 1915, the Emancipation Exposition simply failed to live up to expectations. Low attendance plagued the event. While prominent state officials attended, President Wilson did not uphold his original promise of attending the exposition. The event closed with a significant overage in expenses. This overspending and under-budgeting prompted national criticism that Giles Jackson and members of the Negro Historical and Industrial Association mismanaged the exposition funding and extravagantly spent the large appropriations on themselves. The Chicago *Broad Ax* declared in a front-page above-the-fold headline: "Col. Giles B. Jackson and His Fifty Years of Freedom Celebration at Richmond, Virginia, Has Turned Out to Be a Ranked Failure."[82] Although placing the event's failure on Jackson's shoulders, the *Broad Ax* writer suggested that the failed event was one that should not extend to the progressive Richmond African American community, "who usually make a success of any undertaking." The author turned the failed event into a cautionary tale for white Southerners who expected a certain type of "old antebellum Negro" leadership. For success in the future emancipation events, white Southern leadership needed to embrace a younger and more modern generation of African American leaders. Foretelling the New Negro Movement, he concluded that the "old Antebellum Negro . . . is not the kind of Negro who will suit nowadays, to foster and conduct great enterprises, which call for experience and wisdom of a commanding order."[83]

Ultimately, the failed exposition served as a referendum on Black Richmonders' ability to have a national role in shaping Civil War memory. Jackson and his generation had established the necessary traditions and modes of collective memory essential for the spread of the Emancipation tradition. However, they could never unite all African Americans under the mantle. The limits of the Emancipationist tradition were exposed and laid bare in front of the entire nation. As an Indianapolis *Freeman* editorial surmised: "Mr. Jackson's failure is also a race failure, since the affair was projected in the name of the race, standing for fifty years of progress since freedom."[84] This aged Civil War generation had lost to the progress of time and shifting demographics because of the Great Migration. A new generation of activists and leaders emerged in new organizations such as the National Association for the Advancement of Colored People (NAACP) and promoted a more militant style under the New Negro Movement. In the transition from the older Civil War generation to the younger generation, new modes of memory and traditions were forged within the overlapping cultural and historical movements discussed by historians W. Fitzhugh Brundage, Jeffrey Aaron Snyder, and Treva Lindsey.[85]

Black Richmonders were not the only group trying to influence the Emancipationist tradition. Another Virginian folded African American Civil War memory within a larger coherent Black History Movement following his successful appearance at the 1915 Lincoln Jubilee in Chicago. As a child, Carter G. Woodson heard firsthand accounts from his father and other Civil War veterans. James Henry Woodson expected his son to listen to the oral history shared within his Won Cause circle, be empowered by the diverse Civil War collective memory, and use it in everyday life. His son did not disappoint him. By learning about the "trials and battles of the Negro for freedom and equality" from these Civil War veterans, Woodson recalled how his "interest in penetrating the past of my people was deepened and intensified."[86] He supplemented this rich oral tradition by reading Joseph T. Wilson's *Black Phalanx* and other scholarly accounts. More important, Woodson's attendance at public events showcased African Americans' "recalled past" and afforded him and others the opportunity "to learn, invent, and practice a common language of memory."[87] Woodson presented his first monograph *Education of the Negro* at the Negro History Building of the Lincoln Jubilee. His first major effort to present Black history to a broader audience was a resounding success. Within weeks of the Chicago exposition, the Association for the Study of Negro Life and History (ASNLH) emerged as an organization and the *Journal of Negro History* soon debuted.[88]

Building on the spirit of early Emancipationists, Carter G. Woodson folded these earlier Civil War memorial traditions within the modern Black History Movement. From its Washington, DC, headquarters, Woodson and ASNLH's meetings, publications, and Negro History Week celebrations made the study of African American life and history and not solely of the Civil War into "the cause" that linked its members and audiences.[89] African American military service and collective remembrance by earlier generations functioned as role models for the ongoing civil rights struggle during the New Negro Movement and the later Civil Rights Movement.[90] Rather than privileging the Gettysburg 1913 celebration and its politics of racial exclusion, it is ASNLH and the New Negro Movement that signaled the death knell to Black Richmonders' efforts to have a national influence and not merely a local and state influence in terms of Civil War memory. These modern turns of African American history linked community activism and the study of the past within segregated African American free spaces.[91] Embracing fugitive pedagogy, teachers supplemented their Lost Cause curriculum and hand-me-down Jim Crow–era textbooks from the white schools with the *Negro History Bulletin* and other ASNLH publications in their segregated classrooms. Replacing Emancipation Day celebrations, Negro History Week celebrations, specifically the pageants, incorporated the Emancipationist traditions within the broader African American experience with a shared cultural past rooted in Africa. The Civil War and the Emancipationist memory tradition became one of the components and not the defining component of understanding a people with "a shared past, a shared struggle, and a shared culture."[92]

The 1866, 1890, and 1915 Emancipation celebrations offer windows onto the overlapping forces limiting residents of the former Confederate capital seeking to shape national African American national debates over the Emancipationist collective memory and the Civil War memory culture war. African Americans outright rejected the hegemonic Lost Cause and Reconciliation traditions that privileged whiteness and demanded their racial subordination as second-class citizens. While streamlining the 1866 event, they defied white Richmonders and federal officials seeking a speedy reconciliation. They rejected the racist challenge to their freedom, citizenship, and right to remember a day marking their emancipation. The wartime destruction of slavery, Confederate defeat, Black military service, and emancipation were significant components, but did not represent the totality of how everyday African Americans remembered, commemorated, and deployed memory in an ongoing civil rights struggle. Ordinary African Americans did, however, often disagree over who should lead endeavors, the appropriate commemorative form, and how to reconcile the reality of the Lost Cause landscape emerging in a nation committed to white supremacy, racial violence, and Jim Crow segregation. In the public disagreements between Black Richmonders and other African Americans during the 1890 and 1915 episodes, it is possible to see the limits of the Emancipationist tradition beyond the abject racism shown by white Richmonders and federal officials in the 1866 celebration and expose the overlapping role of turn-of-the-twentieth-century African American politics, regionalism, and national African American leadership. In addition, time, generational change in leadership, veterans of later wars, and shifting demographics from the former Confederate States to the industrial North, West, and Midwest shaped Richmond's failed exposition. But African Americans' use of Civil War memory continued. It merely shifted within newer forms and traditions, including Veterans Day, Negro History Week, and ASNLH events while remaining a fluid, complex, regional, and gendered process that had political implications for identity in a postwar racially inclusive body politic. It is, therefore, not as simple as labeling Black Richmonders' adherence to the Emancipationist tradition as a "counter-memory" to the Lost Cause. Instead, Black Richmonders' memory work was part of a robust narrative of Black uplift, struggle, and accomplishment.

As part of the modern turn to the Black History Movement, African American women would have a larger role in the perseverance of diverse African American collective memories of the Civil War over the twentieth century. They served as community archivists who collected the material culture of African American military experience and post-emancipation progress that challenged the intentional propaganda that minimized, fabricated, and even erased African American history for sustaining a nationally accepted Civil War memory grounded in white supremacy. As educators, whether in the public classroom, church Sunday School, home, and other segregated spaces, they taught several generations an alternative collective understanding of the Civil War and emancipation promoted by ASNLH. Black women served as essential griots and kinkeepers who enriched the K-12 curriculum by supplementing the *Journal of Negro History*, *Negro Bulletin*, and African American literary works with oral history. They also employed the African American press, radio, photography, scrapbooks, and other technologies for documenting African American memory as a form of homemade citizenship discussed by Koritha Mitchell. Black women's efforts revealed "a deep sense of success and belonging" independent of "civic inclusion or mainstream recognition."[93] As organizational, community, and familial leaders, they challenged the previous African American male-dominated Civil War traditions by creating a seat at the table. In short, Black women collected, preserved, and disseminated African American memory of the Civil War through their familial, educational, and religious networks under the guise of "women's work." The next chapter explores the importance of their labor in the persistence of Civil War memory beyond the parades, expositions, and the lives of the dwindling Civil War veteran population throughout the twentieth century.

Without Black women's memory work, Black Civil War remembrance might have remained unthinkable and unrecoverable as white Lost Cause memory proponents and academic historians suggested. Like the Haitian Revolution, as Michel-Rolph Trouillot reminds us, neither Lost Cause proponents could conceive of Black women challenging their white supremacist project nor could white academic historians engage with the archives, traditions, and narratives sustained within Black women's familial, educational, and religious narratives. The Civil Rights and Black Power Movements allowed for the recovery of Black Civil War memory from the margins of public consciousness. In Richmond, the recovered Black Civil War memory allowed for the 1996 monument to Arthur Ashe, a twentieth-century African American tennis player. This compromise quieted some of their objections to the daily indignities experienced whenever encountering the silent Lost Cause symbols on Monument Avenue.[94] The 2020 murder of George Floyd, however, resurrected the Emancipationist arguments articulated at the Lee Monument unveiling and National Thanksgiving Celebration by Black Richmonders. While securing delayed justice for the *Richmond Planet* editor and the April 3 celebration defenders, the removal of several Monument Avenue memorials occurred. Community activists reclaimed and recontextualized the Lee Monument base with colorful vernacular public art as the courts deliberated its fate.[95] Several historians, including the author, contributed amicus briefs throughout the legal process culminating at the Supreme Court of Virginia. After rendering decisions in *Gregory v. Northam* and *Taylor v. Northam*, construction crews removed the Lee Monument on September 8, 2021. Unable to foresee the twenty-first-century Monument Avenue developments, Black Richmonders responded by claiming public spaces every anniversary but also turned to Black women for sustaining their Civil War memory understandings locally and nationally.[96]

6   Black Women and the Persistence of Memory

In her 1911 poem "America," clubwoman and poet Carrie Williams Clifford expressed the rage of African American women. By the fiftieth Civil War anniversary, both the Lost Cause and Reconciliationist traditions had embraced collective amnesia regarding Black military service. African American military contributions and wartime sacrifices no longer had a place in much of the nation's public consciousness. To remember African American USCT men, it would have required a recognition of the importance of these men's service, bodies, and sacrifices in securing Confederate defeat. Collective forgetting, outright lies, race, and violence mattered more in the construction of the Jim Crow nation. Clifford decried this intentional erasure and elevation of unpatriotic white Confederate sympathizers to positions of power while disenfranchising Black veterans:

> When devastating war stalked through the land,
> And dangers threatened you on every hand,
> These sons whose color you cannot forgive.
> Did freely shed their blood that you might live
> A nation, strong and great. And will you then
> Continue to debase, degrade, contemn
> Your loyal children, while with smiling face
> You raise disloyal ones to power and place?[1]

These USCT contributions and living African American veterans deserved praise; however, race, class, and gender created a society that willingly embraced white supremacy, myths, and lies instead of truthful and inclusive Civil War understandings. Clifford and others refused to forget these race liberators, and they also called out the betrayal by their nation. Refusing to remain complicit in the national Civil War memory project, Clifford demanded action. She turned to Black women for their service, leadership, and overlapping networks of race work. In her poem "Duty's Call," Clifford, therefore, issued Black women their marching orders: "Come, all ye woman, come! / Help 'till the work is done."[2]

Black women listened to Clifford's call to arms by expanding their race work and activism for civil, socioeconomic, and political rights to include Civil War remembrance. In short, Civil War memory work was race work. Remembrance of the Black military service could be used to support Black claims of having earned full citizenship; and therefore, it was inherently political, gendered, classist, and an act of recovery from erasure.

Clifford also served as a model in the endeavor. Her subsequent poetry collection, *The Widening Light*, published in 1922, expanded her discussion of important Civil War–era figures beyond William Lloyd Garrison. She had originally read "Lines to Garrison" at the centennial celebration of his birth in Cleveland, Ohio, before publishing it alongside "America" in her 1911 collection *Race Rhymes*. The later collection commemorated Frederick Douglass, Abraham Lincoln, and the emancipated freedman and presented them as role models for new audiences. She also condemned the *Birth of a Nation* film for its depiction of the Civil War and Reconstruction. Her poetry directly challenged the Lost Cause commemorative culture being imprinted in the landscape and popular culture. She also provided alternate curricular materials for use in segregated classrooms, Memorial Day celebrations, and other Black History celebrations.[3]

Instead of forgetting the role of USCT soldiers, freedpeople, and emancipation, which white Civil War memory makers insisted upon, Clifford and other African American women rejected the Lost Cause and Reconciliationist impulses. They defied the "know-your-place aggression" promoted by white Southern women who erected Confederate memorials and monuments in the landscape as well as the less violently oppressive but still subordinated roles offered by white Northern women of the Woman's Relief Corps (WRC). Civil War remembrance served as their personal and communal politics. Their Civil War memory work created and sustained a usable past deployed by numerous activists in the struggle for civil rights and creation of the post–Civil Rights Movement political reality.[4]

Among the ways that the past was remembered and preserved within the African American community was through oral traditions shared on porches and reinforced in segregated public spaces and commemorations. As monument builders, Perquimans County, North Carolina, women organized and erected a monument honoring Black Civil War veterans and their military contributions in the heart of the Black community before white UDC women placed a Confederate monument on the county courthouse grounds in Hertford, North Carolina. Acting as community archivists, Black women carefully documented African American memory in scrapbooks, photograph collections, and published community histories. More important, they taught future generations of African

Americans the Civil War commemorative traditions and community histories in both Sunday School and K-12 classrooms.

Subsequent generations reveal the important legacy of this and other early women's memory work. During the Civil Rights Movement, late nineteenth and early twentieth-century Black women's memory work allowed for Edna Christian Knapper and Zadie Jones to move this preserved history out of segregated safe spaces into the public amid the Civil War centennial commemoration planning. Both women used newspapers for engaging activists in the fight for dismantling Jim Crow segregation. Following the post–Civil Rights Movement gains, several community historians, professional scholars, and other beneficiaries pushed Black Civil War memory from the margins and encouraged its reemergence in the wider American public consciousness.

By employing their familial, educational, and religious networks, Black women's embrace of Civil War remembrance became part of their everyday politics and race work, which ensured the persistence of African American memory beyond the death of the Civil War generation. These women made the African American porch, home, church, and schoolhouse into essential sites for transmitting Civil War memory.

Perquimans County women's Colored Union Soldiers Monument directly responded to Southern women invested in the Lost Cause ideology. These women did not limit their efforts to the porches. Rather, they embarked on a rare public challenge. After the Civil War, women, regardless of region and race, worked to care for the wartime dead, whether reinterments, the placement of headstones, burials, and commemorative celebrations. Southern white women viewed their work within the lens of Confederate defeat and vindicating those who supported the short-lived Confederate States of America. Often formally organized in the Ladies Memorial Association, these women expanded their early work to include monument building and annual commemorative events centered in these cemeteries. When the Ladies Memorial Associations evolved into the United Daughters of the Confederacy (UDC), the Lost Cause commemorations shifted from private to public spaces.[5] Established in 1894, UDC members devoted their efforts to "tell of the glorious fight against the greatest odds a nation ever faced, that their hallowed memory should never die."[6] They promoted the Lost Cause tradition through the construction of physical monuments and the education of subsequent generations of white children. The encompassing nature of their memory work has eclipsed the rare public challenge made by Black North Carolinians amid Jim Crow segregation. To understand the boldness of African

American women's claims to the Civil War commemorative landscape in north-eastern North Carolina, a discussion of the Southern white women's memory work and Black commemorative culture is necessary.[7]

White Southern women had an instrumental role in the spread of the Lost Cause commemorative culture. Determined to assert women's cultural authority over virtually every representation of the region's past, the UDC women lobbied for state archives and museums, national historic sites, and historic highways; compiled genealogies; interviewed former soldiers; wrote history textbooks; and more important, erected monuments in town centers, courthouse lawns, and other public spaces.[8] These monumental additions forced Southern African Americans "who had no stake in celebrating the Confederacy . . . to share a cultural landscape that did."[9] With access to state-sanctioned violence and lynch mobs, UDC women suppressed dissent and enacted their Lost Cause commemorative vision over the late nineteenth and twentieth centuries. In short, without the work of these white Southern women, Perquimans County Black women might not have entered the monument cultural wars with their 1910 contribution in Hertford, North Carolina.

Dedication speeches and unveiling ceremonies reinforced the UDC message of racial exclusion, white supremacy, and the Lost Cause commemorative landscape. At nearly every Confederate monument dedication, white women actively participated in the fundraising and dedication ceremonies. At the University of North Carolina at Chapel Hill and other southern universities, unveilings often occurred during graduation ceremonies which bridged past Civil War–era alumni with newly minted defenders of the Lost Cause and Jim Crow segregation. The NC Division of the UDC president gave an address at the 1913 dedication of Silent Sam, a Confederate monument. Another presented the monument to the university president while a group of women unveiled the monument.[10] By placing the monument at the segregated North Carolina flagship university campus, UDC women made an "intentional statement about who made laws and who enforced them," but also how the state university system cultivated new generations of government officials, lawyers, judges, and Lost Cause defenders working to uphold white supremacy. Like the Civil War generation, UDC women saw southern universities and colleges as co-partners in the endeavor of developing and sustaining pro–Lost Cause intellectual thought and racial geographies. Previously, these institutions had a major role in the spread of pro-slavery thought. Now, UDC women turned to these institutions for remembering their Confederate roots with monuments and furthering the work of the Civil War–era student body.[11]

Julian Shakespeare Carr, a University of North Carolina student who enlisted in 1864 before becoming a New South industrialist, delivered a memorable address that epitomized the gendered and racist dimensions of the UDC monument project in North Carolina. Carr acknowledged both women and the Lost Cause ideology epitomized in the monument. Carr extolled: "And as the gods transformed Niobe into a marble statue, and set this upon a high mountain, so our native goddesses erect this monument of bronze to honor the valor of all those who fought and died for the Sacred Cause, as well as for the living sons of this grand old University."[12] After discussing the numbers and various roles held by the institution's students and alumni, he reminded the audience of the necessity of the UDC monument building campaign. Silent Sam and the other monuments where he delivered the dedication speeches justified the violence and politics of Redemption and necessitated the Jim Crow–era of racial subordination of African Americans. Though emancipated, African Americans did not have a place except as university laborers, second-class citizens, and the acceptable victims of racial violence in North Carolina.

Frequently embellishing his Civil War–era experiences, Carr made explicit the racial politics embodied in the UDC monument at Carolina and expected behavior for African American women. He recounted an alleged incident that occurred within feet of the monument's placement. He shared: ·

> I trust I may be pardoned for one allusion, howbeit it is rather personal. One hundred yards from where we stand, less than ninety days perhaps after my return from Appomattox, I horse-whipped a negro wench until her skirts hung in shreds, because upon the streets of this quiet village she had publicly insulted and maligned a Southern lady, and then rushed for protection to these University buildings where was stationed a garrison of 100 Federal soldiers. I performed the pleasing duty in the immediate presence of the entire garrison, and for thirty nights afterwards slept with a double-barrel shot gun under my head.[13]

His unabashed recounting circulated throughout the state. Any Black woman (or any Black North Carolinian for that matter) who heard about Carr's speech understood the threat leveled at them. According to Carr, Black women's resistance to the North Carolina white supremacist project deserved brutal suppression. For Lost Cause defenders, African American women's memory work, moreover, should be ignored or destroyed. Black women's gender did not exempt them from such racial violence, whether real or rhetorical.

Instead, Carr and other Lost Cause proponents embraced African American women who willingly participated in promoting the Black Confederate myth and faithful slave fantasies.[14] Both these living monuments and stone monuments to the "Mammy" figure, such as the Fort Mill, South Carolina, monument, the Moses Ezekiel monument to the Confederate dead in Arlington National Cemetery, and a failed UDC mammy memorial, upheld the white supremacist logics and extended the know-your-place aggression by offering Black North Carolinians with acceptable models in the state's racial order.[15] For African American women who challenged white women as had the unknown African American woman mentioned in the Silent Sam dedication speech, however, Carr made clear that they deserved to be horsewhipped, raped, and/or lynched. Carr wanted the next generation to know that such violence would be warranted. None in the audience disagreed with him at the time. African Americans did.

Across the region, African American communities objected. Black youth had a special role in the resistance movement to white Southern women's commemorative efforts. Officials in Charleston, South Carolina, bemoaned how some Black children openly mocked the first Calhoun statue. Others regularly threw rocks and shot bullets at the Calhoun monument. Andrew Haig, an African American youth, explained to the police officers who arrested him for using the monument for target practice: "I shoot at Mr. Calhoun wife, and I when I hit 'um he sound like a gong."[16] Mamie Garvin Fields's remembrances encapsulated the anger of the children who experienced the transition to the Confederate memorial landscape of the Jim Crow era in her autobiography. She and other African Americans "took that statue personally."[17] The future public schoolteacher explained how whenever she passed by the Calhoun monument she saw that "Calhoun looking you in the face and telling you, 'Nigger, you may not be a slave, but I am back to see you stay in your place.'"[18] Therefore, she and her peers "used to carry something with us, if we knew we would be passing that way, in order to deface that statue—scratch up the coat, break the watch chain, try to knock off the nose—because he looked like he was telling you there was a place for 'niggers' and 'niggers' must stay there."[19] These Lost Cause monuments were never neutral and produced visceral responses from Haig, Fields, and other African American children and adults.

Black Charlestonians' resistance contributed to the replacement of the first Calhoun monument. The widespread daily acts of resistance troubled both the monument builders and local officials trying to maintain segregation. When a second monument featuring a standing Calhoun atop a large pedestal replaced the first commemorative attempt, Black Charlestonians celebrated. Fields proudly remembered: "Children and adults beat up John C. Calhoun so badly that the whites had to come back and put him way up high, so we couldn't get to him. That's where he stands today, on a tall pedestal. He is so far away now until you can hardly tell what he looks like."[20] In this instance, Black Charlestonians secured a minor victory. They successfully encouraged a revision to the city's Lost Cause commemorative landscape. Most Southern communities did not see similar results. Since Jim Crow governments ignored Black protest, African American opposition did not result in any substantive changes.

In neighboring North Carolina, some African Americans responded with vandalism as they did not have option to voice their opinions in a democratic manner under segregation. Vandalism and other acts of resistance often encouraged the possibility of state-sanctioned violence by pro–Lost Cause segregationists. When unknown individuals applied shoe polish to the recently unveiled courthouse monument, Chatham County officials threatened to lynch them in the widely circulated 1907 "Hanging Too Good, For Miscreant Who Defaced Confederate Monument" article. Predating the Hertford monument by three years, the article reflected how willing use of state-sanctioned violence, lynching, and other acts of extralegal violence curbed widespread African American protest of the UDC commemorative landscape. Black North Carolinians valued their lives and community's survival in their everyday navigations of the new white supremacist project's geographic, political, and social realities. In the absence of political discourse that accepted Black North Carolinians' voices as full and equal citizens, those without political, civil, and social rights responded with tactics deemed appropriate. Vandalism served as one of many protest tactics. Darkness afforded them with a degree of safety for expressing their opposition.[21]

Through Emancipation Day parades, African Americans aurally and physically resisted the UDC monumental landscape. Participants and spectators laid claim to public spaces in these annual events. The parade routes intentionally passed by the monuments before ending in African American communal spaces. The soundscapes created by the parade participants' feet traveling the parade routes, wind hitting the banners and American flag displays, clopping of the horse hooves on the ground as they pulled the wagons and carriages of prominent guests added to the aural and physical resistance to the Lost Cause commemorative landscape. Even these nonviolent public displays could cause a white supremacist backlash and threats of violence in North Carolina communities.[22]

Nevertheless, Emancipation Day celebrations persisted in northeastern North Carolina into the twentieth century. Participants and spectators, too, continued "traveling great distances" by beginning "their long trek a day or even two, in advance of the actual celebration."[23] In later parades, however, African American educators, especially women and Elizabeth City State Colored Normal personnel, had increased roles in sustaining the Civil War commemorative tradition. Scholar Kathleen Ann Clark has demonstrated that these turn-of-the-twentieth-century Black women "saw eye-to-eye with their male counterparts on many issues of racial progress and uplift, and leading men and women worked together to ensure that women's roles in public ceremonies reinforced—rather than challenged—contemporary middle-class ideologies."[24] They, as their white counterparts, recognized and engaged with race work as co-partners with African American men and veterans. The later Emancipation Day parades reflected the combined effort of their race work as Civil War memory work and the continuation of these essential annual traditions across the region.[25]

In addition to these everyday acts of resistance and annual events, the Perquimans County USCT veterans sustained a robust Won Cause culture. The number of USCT and US Navy veterans had fluctuated since the end of the Civil War. By 1890, approximately fifty African American veterans lived in Perquimans County, North Carolina, with about thirteen living in the county seat. Many of the men represented the First and Second US Cavalry, First North Carolina Colored Volunteers, and several USCI regiments, specifically the Thirty-Fifth, Thirty-Sixth, Thirty-Seventh, Thirty-Eighth, Fortieth, and Forty-First. At least one identified individual had served in the US Navy.[26] Most of the men mustered in and out as privates. John Gordon of the First USCT received a promotion to sergeant. His regiment participated in General Edward A. Wild's eastern North Carolina expedition that resulted in the burning of a Confederate camp in Hertford.[27] These veterans routinely traveled for Emancipation Day celebrations, Memorial Day ceremonies and other GAR events throughout northeastern North Carolina and Hampton Roads, Virginia.[28] In 1898, Perquimans County men traveled to Elizabeth City, North Carolina, for the Department of Virginia and North Carolina GAR encampment. White and Black comrades celebrated at the courthouse before the UDC women claimed the space as the sole Civil War memory permissible with its 1911 monument.[29] Elizabeth City's encampment also occurred just months before white supremacists led the Wilmington Massacre, a coup d'état culminating a statewide white supremacist campaign to overthrow biracial governance in the state.[30]

The Wilmington Massacre had a chilling effect on subsequent Civil War remembrances in the state. The coup d'état, however, did not stop African American veterans, community leaders, literary authors, and women from engaging in memory work in segregated spaces and public events deemed acceptable.

Collective amnesia, segregation, and periodic acts of violence rendered them invisible to Lost Cause proponents, radical class-based political coalitions, and scholars until post–Civil Rights Movement gains encouraged the resurgence of African American memory in public discourse.[31]

Perquimans County veterans also served as important monument builders. The placement of headstones and the creation of designated veterans burial sections typified their work. By using African American cemeteries, large and small, Black communities ensured dignified burial spaces for the Civil War veterans and offered safe spaces for sustaining the Won Culture throughout the twentieth century.[32] In Virginia, James E. Fuller, the first African American member of the Norfolk City Council designated section 20 of the West Point Cemetery for burial of African American Civil War veterans in 1885. He appointed the directors of the Union Veterans Hall Association for overseeing the burial of Civil War veterans and the proposed monument. Due to their Won Cause connections, the Perquimans County veterans helped their Virginia brethren in the fundraising.[33] The Norfolk Memorial Association dedicated the base that featured a simple inscription on Memorial Day in 1906. A statue of Sergeant William Carney of the famed Fifty-Fourth Massachusetts Regiment and recognition of World War I veterans was added in 1920. It remains unclear whether the Perquimans County women drew inspiration from this successful campaign, but it seems likely.[34]

This Norfolk monument became one of the few erected by African American veterans and communities in the nation. These monuments, especially the Norfolk monument, Portsmouth monument, Shaw Memorial, and the Lincoln Emancipation Memorial of Washington, DC, and Boston, are better known because of the existence of a rich archival base and for their focus on the African American veterans and Abraham Lincoln.[35] Located in the county seat of Hertford, the Perquimans County monument, therefore, becomes even more important as African American women opted to add a third monument in the region. Their work, moreover, contributed to the early twentieth-century race work done by Black women in the struggle against the Lost Cause commemorative landscape and further advanced the monument building work previously done by Black Civil War veterans.

Perquimans County veterans also employed their aging bodies as living monuments at subsequent events held at the West Point Cemetery in Norfolk, Virginia. At a 1910 encampment, the remaining Civil War veterans of Perquimans County, northeastern North Carolina, and Hampton Roads dressed in their finest clothing adorned with their GAR medals and posed for a group photograph. One proudly served as the color bearer and held the US flag; the other veterans stood on either side of him. The veterans looked boldly, defiantly, and directly into the photographer's lens. Unlike the lynching tableaus of African American men in circulation at the time, these men dared viewers to deny their existence.[36] The veterans directly challenged the Lost Cause and Reconciliationist impulses even as the UDC monumental campaign intentionally erased African American military service in sounding the death knell of both slavery and the Confederacy. The Perquimans County veterans' continued sacrifice and service in the Civil War memorial culture wars as well as the history of regional counter-memory and resistance influenced the Perquimans County women's memory work.

By adding another USCT memorial, Black Perquimans County women built upon the region's Won Cause culture and monument building traditions established by their fathers, uncles, brothers, and other community members. Since the conclusion of the Civil War in 1865 and the establishment of the First Baptist Church congregation in 1866, the monument builders mostly likely heard of the veterans' exploits of garrison duty, experiences during the siege of Petersburg, and triumphant entry into Richmond after it fell. They also learned about their experiences in liberating their people from slavery and their crucial role in securing federal victory and emancipation. The monument builders viewed the veterans as living heroes who deserved a monument.[37]

Organized in the United Daughters of Veterans (UDV), Black women challenged the hegemony and vision of the UDC Lost Cause monument project. Of the almost eighty members at the inception of the UDV, these Perquimans County women, many of whom were also members of the Sisters Missionary Union for First Baptist Church in Hertford, North Carolina, were directly related to the surviving veterans residing in Hertford and surrounding Perquimans County. Thus, it was Emily Bembry, Jennie Burke, Clarissa Reid, A. L. Hudgins, Emma Lassiter, Esther Wood, Fannie Hall, Sarah Barnes, and other women in both the UDV and the Sisters Missionary Union who placed this monument honoring the service and sacrifice of the African American men who served in the US Army and Navy during the Civil War.[38] As their white UDC counterparts, these Black women sought the promotion of their understandings of Civil War memory "unto the third and fourth generations."[39] Instead of encouraging white supremacy and racial violence, Perquimans County women encouraged the continued use of African American memory as a usable past in the ongoing Civil War cultural wars and activism against Jim Crow segregation.

The final Colored Union Soldiers monument demonstrated the strength of the African American women's networks. Unlike white UDC women, the UDV women did not have the support of the national organization for the design, fundraising, fabrication, and erection. They also did not have the support of local governments to place the final monument on public lands and support of tax funds for subsequent maintenance. They had to rely on their much smaller networks. Yet they secured the necessary contributions. As one member later recalled, there was "hardly a family that did not take part in the monument."[40] Indeed, it was a community effort spearheaded by the African American women of Hertford and Perquimans County. The Perquimans County women and local monument funders firmly understood, as did their white UDC counterparts, the importance of imprinting their vision of the Civil War memory onto the physical landscape of the town. White and Black residents would be forced to negotiate the cultural landscape defined by the monument.[41] While the final costs remain elusive, the UDV monument did not cost as much as the downtown Confederate monument erected in 1912.[42]

The resulting monument appeared more like the early Civil War monuments located in cemeteries. It consists of a headstone-like obelisk mounted atop two concrete blocks, perhaps to increase the overall height of the piece. The inscription read: "Erected by the United Daughters of Veterans." One side featured two flags inscribed on it. The rear panel is blank. The modest monument complemented the two other monuments in the Hampton Roads, Virginia, area.[43] UDV members countered the local UDC chapter's memory. They vindicated Black Civil War veterans who resided in Hertford and Perquimans County. They did not want future generations of children to forget the "Colored Union Soldiers Who Fought in the War of 1861–1865."[44] The final UDV monument celebrated the men's wartime sacrifice, role in slavery's destruction, and their postwar contributions as veterans.

Moreover, the UDV women embedded Civil War memory in a space purchased by six African American residents in the heart of the African American community in Hertford. Its placement on community-owned property out of sight of the UDC's monument meant that their Civil War monument could not be easily torn down or removed. It also did not directly compete with the downtown Confederate monument. Instead, it co-existed and yet provided a concrete alternative public Civil War memory that challenged the Lost Cause memory of the Confederate monument erected two years later in downtown Hertford. As a result, the monument became part of the everyday routine of African Americans who traveled en route to the First Baptist Church located across the street as well as the school, library and fraternal lodge located in the surrounding neighborhood.[45]

As Black North Carolinians were being eliminated from the political and commemorative landscape, the UDV monument offered solace. Passing by the monument, community members could receive reassurance that the sacrifice and service of the Civil War veterans had not been in vain. The monument, as described by historian David Blight, was imbued with a worldview held by African Americans to "embrace a long view, a faith that at least since 1863 time, God, and the weight of history might be on their side."[46] This worldview guided these women's efforts and subsequent use of the final monument to empower those engaged in the long Civil Rights Movement struggle in North Carolina, the South, and the nation. By negotiating the monument in their daily movements, African Americans would be least likely to forget the service of Civil War veterans and could find inspiration in their historical service for their present lives.

Through the UDV monument, Perquimans County women chose remembrance of African American military service as a public and overtly political act. They rejected the romanticization of the Confederacy that simultaneously disparaged African American military participation and emancipation in the United States. They understood how collective forgetting, an essential component of the UDC Lost Cause monument project, served as a strategic expression of power by those with the authority to shape the meaning of the Civil War. Memory construction, selective remembrance, and intentional forgetting shaped the Black women's use of Civil War memory.[47] Like other early twentieth-century Black women, Perquimans County women used their "position at the forefront of memory making" for claiming "cultural authority and political power well before woman suffrage" and defining "who belonged to the nation."[48] Thus, Black women successfully created an important community fixture in the geographic center of the Black Hertford community. This UDV monument became the bedrock of subsequent Civil War commemorations and other community events in the area.

After the dedication of the monument, Perquimans County women disbanded the UDV chapter. The sole purpose of organizing had been the placement of the monument. With its dedication, the short-lived organization no longer served a purpose in the race work of northeastern North Carolina. The women resumed their Civil War memory work out of the women's church organizations, schools, and community organizations. Civil War remembrance continued within the school on Academy Green, a Black communal space in Hertford, services and events held at the First Baptist Church, and within the homes of the various members and residents.[49] In short, the UDV women returned to the most common loci of Black women's memory work.

Most Black women did not operate within recognizable Civil War memory organizations. The politics of race, class, and region shaped their decision whether
to join the WRC and other fraternal auxiliary groups. Regardless of their decision, Black women's commemorative efforts failed to prevent the anti-Black
turn in Civil War memory. After being pushed from the public sphere, African
American porches increasingly functioned as important archival repositories
and informal educational spaces. Black women transformed the home, church,
and schoolhouse into sites of resistance and minimized the worst effects of Civil
War collective forgetting and whitewashed narratives. In these segregated spaces,
Black women's memory work persisted until conditions proved favorable. Not
until the modern Civil Rights Movement would Americans witness a biracial
coalition united in a shared struggle for a usable Civil War memory for advancing racial justice.

After World War II, Black women engaged with print and other media technologies for advancing Civil War memory. Instead of traditional Civil Rights organizations, the Association for the Study of Negro Life and History (ASNLH)'s Black
History Movement became the vehicle for their activism for the dismantling of
racial segregation, formal and informal, in the political, social, and commemorative landscape.[50] Using their local newspapers, Edna Christian Knapper of
Chambersburg, Pennsylvania, and Zadie Jones of Tuscaloosa, Alabama, pushed
the oral traditions from segregated spaces to the forefront of public consciousness. Knapper, a retired educator and descendant of former enslaved Virginians,
published a 1956 Black History series in the *Public Opinion*, the mainstream
Chambersburg newspaper. She hoped that this memory would encourage activists in their struggle against persistent discrimination endured in the Pennsylvania-Maryland border community. Likewise, Jones, a descendant of Jeremiah
Barnes, wrote a two-part biographical sketch of her ancestor for the *Alabama
Citizen*, a Black newspaper published in Tuscaloosa. Jones hoped that Black Tuscaloosa residents would employ this collective memory in their demands for a
more inclusive public commemorative landscape that recognized their emancipationist tradition. As the preservers of Civil War memory, these Black women
played an essential role. They exploited the persistent oral tradition, the press,
and the national Civil Rights Movement for advancing Civil War memory as a
tool in struggle for achieving social justice. In the process, these women shaped
late twentieth-century Civil War memory understandings.

In the early twentieth century, the combined national efforts of white Americans excised the Emancipationist and Won Cause traditions with surgical

precision from the public commemorative landscape and popular consciousness except for segregated African American safe spaces. As the centennial commemoration approached, Black activists deployed Civil War memory again on a
national stage. By connecting Civil War memory with the modern social justice
struggle, they made plain how "African American success has always emerged in
an environment that seeks to prevent it, to destroy it and to obliterate evidence
that it ever existed."[51] Knapper and Jones produced short histories that reminded
white Americans and their communities of their presence, their citizenship, and
alternate Civil War memory in the burgeoning Civil Rights Movement. They
challenged both Lost Cause and Reconciliationist traditions and articulated their
notions of homemade citizenship.[52] Cold War realities, the burgeoning Civil
Rights Movement, and centennial Civil War preparations made their activism
have a new urgency.

The women's choice of media technology is telling. Television afforded new
means of attracting large and diverse audiences. But in rural and small-town
broadcasting markets, race determined access to the limited airtime available.
State, national, and international news and events of nearby Harrisburg, Baltimore, and Washington, DC, dominated along with popular entertainment
programs that appealed to the predominantly white border Pennsylvania community.[53] In contrast, Southern communities yielded airtime to broadcasting
pro-segregationist advocates who wielded the Lost Cause and the threat of Com-
munism as anti-American rhetoric for preventing racial progress and the end
of Jim Crow segregation. For instance, the media coverage of Autherine Lucy's
admission to the University of Alabama and the mob violence resulting in her
expulsion garnered much attention; it was akin to contemporary Sinclair media conglomerate's shaping how Americans receive their news in the twenty-first
century.[54] Depending on market, the Civil Rights Movement gained the sympa-
thy for either the activists or segregationist defenders. Television had a significant role in shaping the movement; however, neither Knapper nor Jones chose
this medium.[55]

These women also could have opted for radio technology. African Americans
immediately embraced the medium. In major Alabama cities, religious leaders,
announcers, and select programs "appeared on white-owned stations in scheduled blocks reserved for Black listeners" until the post–World War II emergence
of African American radio "as a broadcasting format."[56] But this medium afforded African Americans with another venue to promote Civil War memory as
part of the broader Black History Movement advanced by Carter G. Woodson's
ASNLH. From the content to the use of "Lift Every Voice and Sing," other Negro

History Week radio specials helped advance African Americans' "politics of representation in local broadcasts as well as national ones."[57] Radio programs, like NBC Chicago's *Destination Freedom*, challenged whitewashed Lost Cause myths and popular American historical understandings devoid of inclusive Black history.[58] Black representation and Civil War memory mattered. The popularity of the Black History programming even spurred Langston Hughes's recording *The Glory of Negro History* for Folkway Records. Such sound recordings allowed for use in segregated classrooms and worked with other ASNLH curricula to advance empowering narratives to schoolchildren.[59] These popular media technologies disrupted expressions of Black formalism as solely the "property of the elites"; radio and sound recordings of Black History Movement programming appealed to diverse African American audiences even if production occurred at white-owned spaces during the 1940s and 1950s.[60]

By opting for the *Public Opinion* and *Alabama Citizen*, however, Knapper and Jones tapped into an established print media culture where class barriers might have made their message inaccessible to the desired audiences who lacked either a television, radio, or quality broadcasting reception in the rural communities. They also engaged in a still dominant medium in the Black History Movement. As Black women, Knapper's and Jones's contributions "forged connections between national freedom and black emancipation" in the quest for ensuring full African American integration in the body politic while ensuring the persistence of African American Civil War collective memories to mid-twentieth-century audiences.[61] Collectively, print, television, and radio contributed to the "shifts in public opinion that in turn determined changes in legislated public policy" and became powerful tools in the struggle for civil rights and racial equality.[62] These ordinary women offered a local perspective to small town African American readership who still preferred commercial print media for local news coverage, community-focused features, and community personalities as well as *Jet*, *Ebony*, and other Black periodicals. Thus, they contributed to the mass media culture by inserting local Civil War memory into the fight for racial equality. By moving private and personal porch stories to the public realm, Knapper and Jones published Civil War memory as an activist strategy and not simply for the act of preservation as had John E. Washington and the Federal Writer's Project testimony of Priscilla Joyner and other former enslaved informants. These porch stories had a new urgency on the eve of the centennial Civil War commemoration.[63]

Knapper took advantage of her networks and local porch archives in her 1956 "Outstanding Colored Citizens of Chambersburg—Past and Present" series for the *Public Opinion*. Knapper was born on November 6, 1892. Her parents, Royal

Christian and Mary Galloway Christian, secured their freedom following Confederate defeat. Her father chose a name that signified his emancipation. He adopted his former enslaver's last name as his first name and extended his original enslaved name of Chris to Christian as a surname. Her mother, too, experienced the Civil War as a young girl on a Virginia plantation. Marrying in the early years of Reconstruction, the Christians relocated to Chambersburg from Virginia and quickly became involved as institutional builders in the St. James AME Church while raising their children. Her parents' memories of slavery and the Civil War left an indelible mark.[64] From her parents, she and her siblings developed their love of education because slavery had kept their father from obtaining a formal education. While her brother published a memoir of his World War I exploits, Edna Christian taught the next generation. By 1953, Edna Christian had married John Henry Knapper, raised a family, and retired from teaching. Knapper's own familial, educational, and religious networks provided her valuable insights into the complex Civil War memory sustained in Chambersburg.[65]

Between January 17 and May 2, 1956, the fifteen *Public Opinion* installments brought the previously segregated African American memory to new audiences of white and Black readers. While still serving as a substitute teacher, Knapper had the time to promote a subject that she enjoyed. She recalled in a 1976 published interview: "I know Negro history from A to Z. I could go back into the classroom and teach it."[66] Each column educated *Public Opinion* readers of the profiled Black Chambersburg residents and their contributions to the community and nation. Like John E. Washington's *They Knew Lincoln* (1942), Knapper "challenged people's tendency to exclude or diminish the testimony of African Americans."[67] Since her gaze rested on the county seat, Knapper excluded other Franklin County communities except for those connected to the profiled prominent families and individuals. In the process, she institutionalized understandings of African American memory that overemphasized her own familial, educational, and religious network's contributions in this popular series.

Knapper advanced twentieth-century understandings of local Black Civil War memory throughout the series. Several installments showcased the Civil War military service of Black Chambersburg residents. In the eleventh installment Knapper discussed how William H. Little's military service in Company D of the Fifty-Fourth Massachusetts regiment, wartime promotion to sergeant, and his antebellum Lincoln University degree allowed him to become the first Black Chambersburg policeman following his August 1865 discharge.[68] Writing about Elias Craig, Knapper emphasized his childhood as one of the free African American families who lived in the St. Thomas township before the Civil War. Upon his discharge, Craig married Lucy Little and lived in Chambersburg where he worked at a popular restaurant.[69] These accounts not only revealed a long history of African American military service but reminded white residents of the significant role of these USCT soldiers in securing Confederate defeat amid Civil War centennial anniversary celebration planning.

Despite their enslavement in Virginia, Knapper also acknowledged the diverse Black kinkeepers who shaped local Civil War memory. In her February 22, 1956, column, Knapper profiled Isaac Page, who migrated to Chambersburg after self-liberating during the 1862 First Battle of Winchester. The warm welcome received by Black Chambersburg residents convinced him to settle in the community.[70] A month later, in the thirteenth installment, Knapper profiled Cango Ransom, who had been enslaved before the war. Her biography explored how his geographical knowledge contributed to the destruction of slavery. When US troops arrived on his plantation, Ransom, like so many other enslaved Virginians, offered essential military intelligence of the mined roads and Confederate troop movements to them. Knapper celebrated his actions as an example of one of the many formerly enslaved kinkeepers living in Chambersburg.[71] But it would be her own mother's contributions that eclipsed the other acts of slave resistance discussed in the series. Although a child at the start of the Civil War, Knapper recounted for readers in the May 1956 column how her mother "could amusingly recall the raid on the plantation by the northern army."[72] During this Civil War encounter, Knapper wrote: "The [slaveholding] family, having been warned of the approach of the northern army, was busy hiding everything of value, and when the soldiers appeared Mary was equally as busy showing them where everything was hidden."[73] In this final installment, Knapper showcased her own family's Civil War experiences and memories as noteworthy. Her mother had helped the Union cause and harmed the enslavers' cause. In these accounts, Emancipationist understandings had permeated the Chambersburg community through oral porch stories. Parenting and the communal sharing of these formerly enslaved Virginians' memories melded with those of the antebellum freeborn community's experiences whether soldier or civilian. Together, the resulting Civil War memory defied popular whitewashed understandings of the Lost Cause and Reconciliationist traditions.

Knapper also reminded *Public Opinion* readers of the civilian trauma endured during the Gettysburg invasion and other Confederate raids. After self-liberating to Chambersburg, Isaac Page temporarily relocated to Harrisburg and avoided re-enslavement alongside the enslavement of freeborn African Americans enslaved by Confederate soldiers. He returned to the community that offered him a haven once "all danger of recapture had passed."[74] Collective memories of the Civil War seizures and enslavements affected how Taylor Curtis "enjoyed telling of the Confederate attack on Chambersburg." Knapper informed readers: "This story was always followed by the song 'Wait for the Wagon' which Taylor sang with accordion accompaniment."[75] Through the stories about Page and Curtis, Knapper helped readers recall how the Civil War affected all Chambersburg residents. African American memories, like their community contributions, deserved equal footing. She was keenly aware of the planning for the Civil War centennial and the likely erasure of Black Pennsylvanians' experiences during the Gettysburg anniversary. She deployed the persistent African American memory of the Civil War memory at a critical moment of the Black History movement for advancing broader civil, social, and economic rights from the nation and white Pennsylvanians.[76]

Knapper's inaugural column about Joseph Winters is striking when compared with her other columns. Her treatment erased Winters's wartime songs. Instead, she highlighted his relationship with John Brown and his role in setting up a meeting between Brown and Frederick Douglass when he spoke in Chambersburg in the first installment. She also recounted how his political campaign songs rallied African American voters. His 1880 Garfield-Chester campaign song served as an important "call to arms."[77]

Her public treatment of Joseph Winters sheds light on how the politics of representation sometimes differed from the vernacular intra-African American community's commemorative politics. Winters's acerbic personality, unwillingness to serve as a community banker, and abandonment of the Republican Party did not endear him to Black Chambersburg residents. Except for his connections to John Brown and post–Fifteenth Amendment presidential campaign songs, her profile focused on Joseph Winters's mixed-race heritage, knowledge of community events and histories, and scientific contributions. Her silences demonstrate a public performance of memory for meeting post–*Brown v. Board of Education* Black History movement goals. For Knapper, Winters's Civil War songs did not merit inclusion. Within the Black Chambersburg community, however, Knapper and other African Americans engaged with advancing false memories of Winters as someone who actively assisted slavecatchers in the search, capture, and transportation of their human cargo to Southern enslavers.[78] This myth had its origins after Winters's death but gained salience over the century. Her column and vernacular memory later became accepted as legitimate historical truth retold and reprinted over the second half of the twentieth century. Yet her public column also facilitated the placement of a historical marker of Winters. All could agree on his scientific contributions. But the false memory of his reverse Underground Railroad involvement persisted as contested memory within the Black Chambersburg community.

Notwithstanding Winters, Knapper succeeded in using Civil War memory as a tool for advancing a less racist community for Black Franklin County residents engaged in combating the myth of absence. She moved African American oral tradition from porches and segregated spaces to public spaces using print technology. From the bravery shown by enslaved Virginians, soldiers, and civilians, Knapper recounted a tapestry of Civil War memories that shaped the Chambersburg community. Consequently, Knapper's *Public Opinion* series profiles had a significant influence on how later generations understood the Civil War and its legacy. By the late twentieth century, the effects of her series would become apparent.

Knapper was not the only Black woman seeking to highlight Black oral histories in the 1950s. Zadie Jones employed an African American newspaper published in Tuscaloosa, Alabama, to tell the story of the formerly enslaved Jeremiah Barnes. Jones likely hoped to inspire Civil Rights activists in their campaign for dismantling Jim Crow with modern histories of seemingly overlooked Black heroes. Like Knapper, Jones moved the oral African American memory traditions from the porch to the printed page. She, however, ensured that the Emancipationist memory would receive a favorable audience in the relatively safe space afforded by a newspaper catering to the Black community. In February 1954, just months before the *Brown v. Board of Education of Topeka* decision would shake the country, her two-part biographical sketch introduced to a new generation of activists the former enslaved property of Judge Washington Moody. As a boy, Barnes had been the enslaved playmate of Judge Moody's son. Before and after the war, he occasionally worked on the University of Alabama (UA) campus. Barnes's successful afterlife of slavery reached new ears because of a Black woman's efforts to remember what UA and the broader white Tuscaloosa power structure opted to forget.[79]

The first installment focused on Barnes's enslaved past and immediate postemancipation experiences. Jones emphasized Barnes's Tuscaloosa roots and slave past. "Jeremiah Barnes was born not 'before the stars fell' as our forefathers computed time; but, eleven years after, February 28, 1844," Jones informed readers.[80] Not shying away from the rape of enslaved women, she added: "His mother was a slave on a plantation along the Black Warrior River, eight miles west of Tuscaloosa. His father was the white over-seer."[81] Jeremiah Barnes could neither be dismissed as an outside agitator nor could his connections to the prominent

Tuscaloosa family and UA benefactor be denied by white Alabamians. His connections to Judge Moody inspired his resistance and later contributions to African American public schools. As an enslaved domestic laborer in the Moodys'
Tuscaloosa household, Jones explained how Barnes learned to read and write
through his association with the white children of the family. Despite "knowing
that education was forbidden to slaves," Barnes rebelled. Discovery of his self-ed-
ucation prompted his relocation to the Moody plantation.[82] This punishment did
not stop Barnes. The self-taught rebel shared "his stolen secrets with his mates"
and operated his first school for enslaved students while "keeping the "Blue Back
Speller" as his companion."[83] Jones concluded the first installment by discussing
his temporary relocation to Selma after emancipation and his marriage on June
18, 1865, to Dema Mark, a formerly enslaved woman who worked as nurse in a
white Selma family household. Despite his slave past, Jones established Barnes as
a freedom fighter who used education for empowering himself and others. With
emancipation, Barnes continued this journey as a free, educated family man
committed to building and strengthening the Black Tuscaloosa community.[84]

In the second installment, Jones established Barnes as a hero for mid-twentieth-century activists fighting for civil and political rights. Jones reminds readers
how Barnes served as a Tuscaloosa alderman. His pioneer status should earn
their respect as no other African American "before or since has ever been known
to hold the position in the city of Tuscaloosa."[85] Barnes also proved to be a pioneer in the city schools; he advanced African American education more broadly
by sending his five children to Tuskegee. Only his four sons earned degrees. His
daughter married and left before earning her degree. Here, Jones showed how
Barnes's relationship with Booker T. Washington enabled the Tuskegee president's only official visit to Tuscaloosa. It was the formerly enslaved Barnes and
not the UA administration or Jim Crow city leadership who facilitated this visit,
which was extensively covered by the mainstream Tuscaloosa newspaper at the
time.[86] Jones also established Barnes as an institutional builder as a Prince Hall
Mason, Odd Fellow, and one of the founding members of the AME Zion church
in Tuscaloosa. She closed by imploring activists to use his example: "To the world
he supplied an example for the old and young alike to follow. It is just another
illustration that life with people is as with vegetation. The earth gives generous
measures to proper cultivation."[87] The adjacent columns reinforced Jones's di-
rective to activists. Barnes laid an important foundation for African American
education in Tuscaloosa. By making her familial Civil War memory available for
public consumption, Jones promoted Barnes's legacy as a source of inspiration in
their campaign to name the new African American high school.[88]

Tuscaloosa activists embraced Jones's suggestion that Barnes provided them with the ideal candidate for the building name. In a 1953 editorial, activists attempted to remake the Civil War public landscape to include African American collective counter-memories by using the *Alabama Citizen* to make their case that the "founder of Negro education in Tuscaloosa" should have the new high school named after him.[89] Activists rallied behind him for two reasons. First, Barnes brought the gains of Educational Reconstruction seen in Mobile, Alabama, and other larger communities to Tuscaloosa. He overcame the obstacles posed by a hostile white community. Second, and most important, his lifelong commitment to African American education had a lasting effect in the racial progress achieved in the Alabama community. From slavery to his death, Barnes remained committed to Black education as a right of citizenship. He also contributed to the growth of the Black middle-class in Tuscaloosa. Through his words and actions, Barnes embodied the Emancipationist memory of the Civil War.[90] For these reasons, activists and the *Alabama Citizen* editorial staff encouraged readers to present their case to Tuscaloosa school administrators. Barnes High School would "serve as a living reminder of one [who] contributed so much to our progress."[91]

Jones's two-part biographical sketch based on stories told to her by elders provided activists with the crucial ammunition in their campaign. She humanized her Civil War–era ancestor and made his memory available for the early Civil Rights Movement, which needed local historical examples. Her contribution, though limited to the Alabama college town, added to the larger chorus of the Black History Movement devoted to school desegregation on the eve of the *Brown* decision. Despite drawing on the Emancipationist memory of Jeremiah Barnes, Tuscaloosa administrators remained unmoved by African American activists' arguments for the suggested school name. Instead of Barnes High, as desired by the African American community, the city chose the singularly uninspired Druid High when the school opened in 1955.[92]

While experiencing a setback, Black Tuscaloosa residents had been successful in naming the segregated YMCA branch after his son. Benjamin Barnes had attended the Tuscaloosa schools before earning a degree from Tuskegee University. With these credentials and his father's position, Barnes found employment in the Tuscaloosa schools. Like his father, Benjamin had been active in local fraternal and religious organizations.[93] Comprised of Black Tuscaloosa residents, the Branch Board of Management announced their decision in the *Alabama Citizen*.[94] The Tuscaloosa YMCA executive committee then approved the fundraising and construction of "the much-needed and long-awaited Negro branch of the Young Men's Christian Association."[95] Although suffering a defeat with Barnes High, the Civil Rights activists continued their struggle into the next decade with a new Black cultural institution.

Scholars often overlook both Jones's efforts and these early Civil Rights Movement campaigns as the practical extension of Civil War memory at the mid-twentieth century. The UA desegregation struggle has earned much attention. Autherine Lucy's failed desegregation attempt and George Wallace's infamous stand at the Foster Auditorium eclipsed these early local civil rights efforts.[96] Anti-Black violence directed toward three Stillman College students and one high school student by a white bus driver and Bloody Tuesday, an attack on activists on June 9, 1964, have also overshadowed the high school naming campaign and success achieved with the naming of the YMCA branch.[97]

By offering Barnes as a historical freedom fighter, and role model, Jones tapped into the post–World War II shift in the Black History Movement toward meaningful integration. Barnes helped desegregate the Tuscaloosa educational landscape by providing a quality public school education to African American children. The formerly enslaved Barnes overcame the odds posed by racialized Reconstruction-era violence in Tuscaloosa.[98] He empowered generations to fight on a new terrain and emancipated generations from the shackles of post–Civil War realities. Now, in the fight to dismantle Jim Crow's foothold, Black Tuscaloosa residents drew inspiration from the Emancipationist memory; and in the process, mid-twentieth-century activists found the will and resiliency necessary to persevere in a UA community wedded to the Lost Cause commemorative landscape and anti-Black violence.

The work of Edna Christian Knapper and Zadie Jones is important for understanding how African Americans deployed Civil War memory as a tool during the burgeoning Civil Rights Movement. The published short history articles reminded white Americans and their communities of the presence and citizenship of Black Americans. In the process, Knapper and Jones not only challenged the know-your-place aggression of the Lost Cause and Reconciliationist traditions but inspired a new generation of activists and community documentarians as had the Perquimans County women intended with their early Civil War memory work.[99] Black Civil War memory offered a potent strategy for advancing societal change. The fruits of these Black women's memory work became apparent after the gains of the Civil Rights and Black Power movements.

The Civil Rights and Black Power movements of the 1960s and 1970s marked an important shift in Black Civil War memory. Activists and their white allies began openly questioning the Confederate commemorative landscape. The placement of UDC monuments on courthouses and other prominent public spaces encouraged activists' reclamation of the spaces in their protest for civil, social, and political rights. Activists and even observers would be unable to ignore the juxtaposition of the competing visions for the nation in the Southern freedom struggle.[100] Some even openly defaced these symbols. In Tuskegee, Alabama, HBCU students protested the murder of Samuel Younge at the Macon County monument. Aural resistance and occupation of space initially defined their efforts. Following the acquittal of Younge's murderer, they openly defaced the UDC monument with black paint and the words of "Black Power" and "Sam Younge."[101] Activist Scott Smith recalled: "When the paint hit, a roar came up from the students. Every time the brush hit, *wham*, they'd roar again."[102] Threats of violence and pro-UDC monument defenders could not stop these challenges. Communities now operated openly and defiantly against those committed to the Confederate monumental landscape and its white supremacist racial logics.

The challenges continued in the post–Civil Rights and Black Power political landscape. The spirit of Black resistance spilled onto desegregated state flagship university campuses in North Carolina, Alabama, and Missouri.[103] Petitions and attempts to use more inclusive democratic processes appeared before more diverse Southern governments. Harvey Gantt and other elected officials used their power as elected officials to thwart the Confederate landscape expansion while promoting inclusive understandings. African Americans expanded their voices in the once denied political process and did not stop the subversive activism where spray paint served as the principal tool.[104] While drawing the ire of pro–Lost Cause monument defenders, emboldened African Americans and their allies pushed for a different Civil War commemorative landscape. In this environment, Black women's previous efforts facilitated the reemergence of Black Civil War memory in the late twentieth century.

Over the twentieth century, the Perquimans County women's efforts successfully fostered a counternarrative. The UDV monument helped counter negative portrayals of African American contributions to the Civil War in a landscape dominated by the UDC memory project. Subsequent African American residents made sure that the Won Cause symbol persisted. When the base showed its age, the community attempted to repair the monument. By shoring up the base, the preservation attempt caused the rotation of the obelisk from its original placement. The text originally faced the First Baptist Church, according to a descendant of Augustus Reid, who explained the restoration attempt. Despite this modification, residents still embraced the monument in their events. During the 110th anniversary of the church, Rev. Loudon, congregants, and other participants "went across the street to participate in a short service at the monument to the Civil War Black soldiers" and concluded with the George W. Carver Floral Club and the local American Legion placing wreaths at the monument.[105] They remembered the USCT and US Navy veterans, the UDV women, and commemorations around the monument through special events and oral tradition held in segregated safe spaces. In reflecting on the monument for the 1976 anniversary celebration, one church member commented: "We've come a long way, but look America, we have a long way to go before the country realizes its dream of equality, not only for blacks, but for all Americans."[106] Indeed, the country had changed.

The publication of Alex Haley's *Roots* and the successful television mini-series provided the impetus of furthering the pioneer work of Edna Christian Knapper. Stella Fries, Janet Gabler, and C. Bernard Ruffin expanded the original Knapper series through additional interviews and community histories in *Some Chambersburg Roots*. Civil War memory had a central place in the 1980 publication. The community historians presented the collective memories of USCT soldiers and veterans explored in the 1956 newspaper series, *Roots*, and the 1979 sequel, *Roots: The Next Generation*.[107] They featured the names of all Civil War veterans and Delany GAR members interred at the historic African American cemetery, an account of Robert E. Lee's visit to Mrs. Berry's farmhouse, and the 1930 pension application of Rachel Cato Starks Little seeking relief as the widow of David Little of the Forty-Fifth USCT. They also showed how collective memories of the Gettysburg Campaign helped mobilize African American men to enlist in USCT regiments and later their vote in presidential elections. The volume included reprints of three Joseph Winters's songs and Knapper's original profile of the songwriter.[108]

The community historians also perpetuated the contested collective memory of Joseph Winters and the reverse Underground Railroad myth. When promoting *Some Chambersburg Roots*, Stella Fries recounted the reverse Underground Railroad myth to the local newspaper: "Well, Joe Winters played a role. They did harbor a lot of slaves in this area."[109] The inclusion in the volume of an oral history by Mary Jones Carter corroborated Fries's published remarks. "He was a slave trader," Carter recalled. She explained how Winters "would entice the runaway slaves to his house on the back way to the cemetery. He had a basement or cellar and put them in there and then sell them back to their masters."[110] When Carter claimed that "all the old people used to say that about him," it is most likely that her own mother's poor relationship with Winters's daughter had helped with this strong recollection kept alive within the Black community.[111] Subsequent publication of oral histories with Anna Blondine Jones Bruce and May Anderson Lewis have continued the Winters myth while Mary Lee Williams Barnett contested it by sharing alternate memories of him. To date, Joseph Winters's collective memory has remained divided. Now, the vernacular collective memory has moved beyond the porch and the African American community into the public consciousness of all Chambersburg residents and scholars seeking information on the African American experience and memory of the Civil War era.[112]

Other Franklin County communities also drew inspiration from Knapper's legacy. Mercersburg documentarians researched and publicized their findings in the *Public Opinion* during the early 1990s. Their work focused on the Civil War military and civilian experience and drew attention to the men who served in the Fifty-Fourth and Fifty-Fifth Massachusetts regiments.[113] With the popularity of the Hollywood film *Glory*, these military connections as well as ties to the Underground Railroad and community freedom struggle of the Civil War era captured readers' attention. The resulting coverage also unsilenced Black Mercersburg community's diverse contributions, originally absent in the 1956 series, and introduced the sustained history to another generation.[114] By correcting the narrative of Black Pennsylvanians' contributions, local newspapers and media outlets remained important venues for communities who demanded the inclusion of their histories and Civil War memories.

In Hertford, the UDV monument and sustained oral traditions helped Dorothy Spruill Redford in her campaign to correct a Civil War Trails wayside marker erected in the early twentieth century. An incorrect dedication date and other misinformation contextualizing the rarity of the Hertford monument drew sharp criticism from community members. In her email to Jeffrey Crow, deputy secretary of the North Carolina Office of Archives and History, Redford summarized: "Local historians (black and white) agree the wayside information is incorrect, but seem to be allowing their anger to fester rather than pursuing having the wayside changed."[115] The executive director of Somerset Place, a historic plantation museum that contextualizes the enslaved experience in its exhibits, descendant reunions, and other outreach, provided her research notes as an email attachment. She hoped that Crow and other North Carolina Department of Natural and Cultural Resources personnel would make the necessary corrections. "After reviewing my notes," Redford urged in her closing, "you will understand why I fiercely embrace historians who choose not to rewrite history in ways that diminish the accomplishments of African Americans."[116]

Michael Hill, research supervisor, quickly responded. His apologetic email assured "that the sign will be changed to correct any errors."[117] The rest of the email, though, sheds light on the wayside marker placement process. The Perquimans County Restoration Association, with input of a First Baptist Church member, had initiated the original effort. A Civil War Trails historian drafted the text based on the information provided and additional research. No one in the original project questioned the information provided. "To my regret we did not have a reason to question the dedication date or the name of the sponsor organization," Hill wrote.[118] The combined research resulted in the errors presented on the original wayside marker.

The Civil War Trails historian corroborated Hill's account. He addressed the three points of contention—the incorrect dedication date, incorrect name of African American women's organization, and the inclusion of a Hertford UDC Confederate monument photograph placed on the wayside marker. He, like Hill, explained how he did not doubt the information provided by the local sponsoring organization. He took blame for naming the incorrect organization and the inclusion of the photograph despite "considerable discussion" with Hill and Mark Moore who "advised against it."[119] He, too, promised to partner with Redford on the correction process in the concluding section. After expressing appreciation for "calling these mistakes to our attention," he closed by stating, "We look forward to working with you to correct and improve the marker."[120] And they did.

Redford proposed a symposium to kick off the sesquicentennial Civil War celebration at First Baptist Church. She chose January 31, 2011. because it marked the "date the 13th Amendment was proposed." Her choice of location, like that of the original Hertford monument builders, would bring "deserved attention and on the WOMEN who had it erected in the segregated south of 1910" (emphasis original).[121] For speakers, she desired African American historian Heather Andrea Williams and other appropriate speakers selected by Chris Meekins. Ultimately, Redford desired using the corrected marker to bring attention to the African American Civil War monument and the memory work of the Perquimans County women as the nation entered the sesquicentennial celebrations. She closed her email by writing: "I will be retired, but am **passionate** about bringing attention to the brave Hertford women" (emphasis original).[122] Redford's passion and recovery work built on the legacy of early Perquimans County women. She successfully reeducated a new generation of African Americans about this Civil War memorial before the sesquicentennial commemoration began. The Northeastern North Carolina African American Festival organizers celebrated the Perquimans County monument in a June 2007 public celebration.

Attendees enjoyed a Civil War reenactment, a performance of African dancers and drummers, a jazz band performance, and other festivities over the daylong celebration.[123]

More important, Redford's efforts contributed to a more inclusive Civil War sesquicentennial celebration in North Carolina. The proposed 2011 conference did not occur. Instead, Redford presented the "Forced to Aid Enemy's Cause" lecture as one of two inaugural Civil War 150 Commemoration events at the Somerset Place State Historic Site on January 15, 2015. In addition to this event, forty-nine libraries hosted the *Freedom, Sacrifice, and Memory* traveling photography exhibit across the state. The North Carolina African American Heritage Commission revealed a new guiding document, *Envisioning the Future of African Americans in North Carolina,* for incorporating the African American experience into historical sites and interpretation throughout the state. Three new highway historical markers recognized African American historical contributions in early 2011.[124] By correcting this wayside marker, Redford harnessed the sustained African American memory for change. She introduced new audiences to the rare example of African American Civil War monuments in a landscape dominated by the UDC monument project and reminded the state of the continued role of African American women in sustaining Civil War memory in the twenty-first century.

Far from being lost, there remains a robust memory of the Civil War within the African American community. Once conditions changed, later twentieth-century activists reintroduced their assumed lost Black Civil War understandings. Both the Colored Union Soldiers monument and the Barnes YMCA Branch persist in the present. Several Black Pennsylvanians extended Edna Christian Knapper's legacy by publishing communal histories that reached new audiences. Dorothy Spruill Redford and other scholars have ensured the presentation of accurate public history in historical markers, museum exhibitions, and other public history sites. These later efforts reflected the power and legacy of previous Black women's work in sustaining Black Civil War memory. They took the memories that had been kept private within local Black communities and brought them to the wider world.

The nation's betrayal of the African American military service, emancipation, and Reconstruction served as the starting point of Black women's memory work. They rejected the Lost Cause and Reconciliationist demands to forget what the war was about and accept the children of "disloyal ones" to resume their "power and place."[125] By maximizing their overlapping networks, the diverse women of this chapter defied expectations of race, class, education levels, religious levels, and geographies of Civil War memory. As the preservers of Civil War memory, Black women saw their memory work as race work. As such, they promoted nuanced understandings of the Civil War that countered the accepted whitewashed national public understandings. They sustained a usable past for generations that could be tapped into at any time for enacting reform and change in their communities. Redford, Franklin County community historians, and Tuscaloosa civil rights activists drew on this past and rendered visible African American women's work in meaningful ways. The labor of these ordinary women, therefore, contributed persistence of memory now being recovered by late twentieth- and twenty-first-century communities seeking more inclusive narratives of the Civil War in the commemorative landscape.

By answering Clifford's call to arms in "Duty Call," ordinary Black women performed extraordinary feats. Simply put, they preserved the African American memory of the Civil War generation's contributions and unforgettable sacrifices. They did not accept their marginalization by white women's Civil War memory organizations or the know-your-place aggression. Perquimans County women, Edna Christian Knapper, and Zadie Jones instead preserved and returned these memories to the Black public sphere. They forged their own pathway in the collective struggle of Black women keeping Civil War memory accessible and relevant by deciding when and where they entered in the Civil War cultural wars. Civil War remembrance became their politics.[126]

The twentieth- and twenty-first-century inheritors of Black women's memory work ensured its reemergence when conditions made it possible. African American activists, community historians, and museum professionals drew on the early work to great effect. They have worked to bring more accurate and inclusive understandings of the Civil War in public spaces, publications, documentaries, and other public venues. Black Civil War memory was no longer confined to porches and segregated spaces. By engaging new audiences, this latter work has influenced the growth of new traditions as well as the development of a more inclusive sesquicentennial commemoration.

Porch Lessons II

More Than Names on a Page

And ages yet uncrossed with life,
As sacred urns, do hold each mound
Where sleep the loyal, true, and brave
In freedom's consecrated ground.

—Frances E. W. Harper,
"The Massachusetts Fifty-Fourth," 1863

C ivil War scholars and genealogists told me it would be easy. It was not. It took five years to receive a copy of my Civil War ancestor's pension file from the US Department of Veterans Affairs in early 2022. The National Archives did not have the pension file of Joseph Lane, a Twenty-Second United States Colored Troops (USCT) veteran as it did for other Civil War soldiers' files. After relocating his family from Chambersburg to Shippensburg, Pennsylvania, his file was among the pensions transferred to Veterans Affairs. As a result, the process required a Freedom of Information Act (FOIA) request with an elaborate justification of why the request should be granted. It also required patience, time, and perseverance. Ironically, COVID-19 eased some of the bureaucratic red tape. So, I, as well as my mother, aunts, siblings, and cousins, were elated by my persistence.[1]

As I opened the file, one word listed on the widow's pension application stopped me in my tracks. Rejected. The neat lettering of the blue ink stamp clarified some of the unanswerable questions from previous porch lessons of my maternal and adopted kinkeepers' porches.

White pension agents denied Irene Lane's widow pension application. Their actions created chaos in the Lane household. The children immediately had a white Shippensburg woman appointed as their guardian. Lane's widow, Irene Lane, simply wanted to place a headstone for her husband. Yet she would not live to see its placement. Her parental authority over her children's financial security had been removed and placed in the hands of a white middle-class woman. Her claims to her husband's service and sacrifice were denied. She died shortly after with her last infant child conceived with her husband. While her widow's pension was denied, the eligible children received dependent pensions until they aged out. And I, a twenty-first-century descendant of Joseph Lane, experienced similar reactions and processes described by historians Holly Pinheiro, Brandi Brimmer, and James G. Mendez.[2] My anger and disappointment forced me to take a mental break from the file. I had the duty of informing my mother and interested family members of the file contents. And I prepared myself for their emotional responses.

Lane and his family subjected themselves to the intrusive, racialized, and gendered bureaucratic process because their family's survival depended on it. Yet the memory work of the Lane children did not end with the stamping of rejection on their mother's widow's pension application. On the porches of my adopted communities of Richmond, Virginia, northeastern North Carolina, and Tuscaloosa, Alabama, I gained clarity. A patchwork of traditional archives documented some of the Lane children's memory work, specifically that of Nora, Bessie, and Avis. The impact on my aunt, mother, and surviving descendants only become visible when one considers porch archives and the lived consequences on listeners.

At the same time Black women challenged the public memory work of the United Daughters of the Confederacy, three daughters of Joseph Lane used their familial, religious, and communal networks for sustaining the Won Cause tradition independent of the Woman's Relief Corps (WRC). While the North Carolina women opted for the United Daughters of Veterans, Nora, Bessie, and Avis Lane applied their parental lessons received as children in the preservation of Civil War memory among the next generation of Shippensburg, Pennsylvania. Joseph Lane's daughters defied many obstacles and expectations of race, gender, and class through their everyday politics of Civil War memory. Yet like the Perquimans County women, the Lane sisters sustained a usable Won Cause past until conditions allowed for fuller appreciation in the Shippensburg commemorative landscape.

Joseph Lane's death followed by that of his wife, Irene, brought chaos to the Lane family. Despite his wartime court-martial, Joseph Lane secured a pension. The Civil War reversed previous understandings of determining freedom status from the presumed enslaved Black mother to the emancipated Black father. While never enslaved, Lane and other Northern Black men's parental authority was not considered equal to that of white fathers. With Confederate defeat and abolition, each African American man, especially if a USCT veteran, gained "new legal and social power over his wife and children."[3] The process also heavily relied of individual and communal memory for convincing federal bureaucrats of applicants' claims. Lane succeeded where other Black veterans did not.[4]

Lane's widow, however, failed. Her experience was quite common. White women had better success than Black widows. The Pension Bureau rejected her application on the grounds of alleged "adulterous cohabitation."[5] Irene appealed but died in the process. Josephine Nevin was appointed as official guardian of the surviving eligible children. With a white guardian in place, Lane's children retained their inheritance of the children's pension based on their father's service. Sadly, Florence, the youngest child whose existence resulted in the rejected widow's application, died shortly after the approval of the minor's pension.[6] Moreover, Avis Lane successfully applied for and secured extended pension benefits. Her older siblings and many of the informants used in Joseph Lane's pension application testified to her disability and need for the extended benefits. Her father's service and status as a "helpless child" entitled her to material support from the pension office until her death in May 1966. Her extended services contributed to the five-year process to secure Joseph Lane's pension file.[7] The surviving pension file documents reveal how the placement of a white guardian created uncertainty for the Lane children. Unable to afford a headstone, they buried their mother in the Locust Grove Cemetery in an unmarked grave as was a common practice for Black Shippensburg residents.[8] Josephine Nevin, the designated guardian, and the federal pension office determined both their income and ability to keep the family intact.[9]

This period also must have been one of hardship and struggle. As the oldest sibling still living in the household, adulthood came quickly for Nora Lane. Although several Lane children had established their own households in Philadelphia and Shippensburg, these elder siblings could not financially provide a home for their younger siblings. The 1900 Federal Census listed the twenty-two-year-old Nora as the head of the household and responsible for her younger siblings ranging in age from eight to nineteen years old. Avis, age eleven, and Bessie, age thirteen, may have regarded Nora as a mother figure more than a sister. As a domestic servant, Nora stretched her meager income to the fullest.[10]

One year later, tragedy struck the family again. Oscar Lane, their brother, was murdered. A disputed dice game at the Cumberland Valley Railroad yard and depot escalated and turned deadly after Oscar Lane and Arthur Robinson left this popular space for "relaxation after long days of labor."[11] Robinson struck Lane with a baseball bat. Lane did not immediately die from the head injury. Attempting to deescalate the situation, Nora Lane persuaded her brother to return home where the injury became more severe. Nora sent for a local doctor who employed Oscar Lane. After the doctor assessed "his case very critical," Oscar Lane died. Young Nora had to cope with keeping the family together and another burial.[12]

Their brother's murder and media coverage revealed the extent that the Lane siblings' economic plight reflected the difficult situations of other Shippensburg children of Civil War veterans. The initial court proceedings saw the testimony of Nora Lane and other veterans' children. As in other rural counties, postwar socioeconomic success "had stalled."[13] Although these veterans' children retained the franchise, few economic opportunities existed. Their status also did not exempt them from popular stereotypical understandings of African American men and women engaged in criminal behavior, vice, and unrespectable behavior.[14] Robinson received a sixteen-year sentence in Eastern State Penitentiary, a Philadelphia prison plagued by "overcrowding, corruption and routine scandals."[15] During the court proceedings, the Lane siblings buried their brother. The funeral attracted "quite a number of relatives and friends."[16] The extensive media coverage suggested that their father's legacy extended to his children. Amid the regional news coverage, one brief article noted that Lane had an insurance policy that provided his eldest sister Nora with a modest bequest. Familial ties, the church, and Civil War memory provided the Lane sisters with a different legacy.[17]

Even though Nora functioned as the head of the Lane household, Josephine Nevin still played a role in the family. Nora got her brother John Palmer Lane (who went by Palmer to family and friends) enrolled at the Pennsylvania Soldiers' Orphans Industrial School (later renamed Scotland School for Veterans Children) located in Franklin County. Created by the Pennsylvania legislature as an industrial residential school in 1893, the Scotland school offered primary, intermediate, grammar, and high school classes and prepared students in at least one employable trade. As veterans' children, the school also instilled "patriotism and discipline by incorporating military drill, pageantry, and physical culture."[18] Palmer and other students, therefore, participated in Memorial Day celebrations throughout Franklin County and in the state capital. Joseph Lane's military service and sense of "patriotic debt" secured Palmer with an education that prepared him for better socioeconomic opportunities after graduation. Indeed, he found employment in Philadelphia, married, retained his African Methodist Episcopal church affiliation, and modeled the Scotland School vision for its graduates.[19] At death, the surviving Lane sisters interred him in Locust Grove Cemetery. Nora Lane successfully deployed her family's Civil War memory to get him an education and ensured a better future for her brother. By being a graduate of veterans' school, there was recognition of Lane's service and an erasure of those aspects of

Joseph Lane's career that were less than stellar. Yet two official reports listed Josephine Nevin and not Nora Lane as the guardian responsible for the education of the youngest Lane sibling received at the Scotland school.[20]

Although Palmer benefited from Joseph Lane's memory, his three sisters who remained in Shippensburg struggled. Marriage, births, tragedy, and the establishment of different households shaped the Lane sisters over the next twenty years. In July 1903, Nora Lane married Daniel E. Collins, a widower with a young son, whom his deceased wife's family raised.[21] Born to a formerly enslaved mother in Staunton, Virginia, Collins regularly contributed to the family's income by enlisting in several US military engagements. He served in the Spanish-American War, Mexican border crisis engagements, and World War I, and attempted to enlist in World War II.[22] His salary, enlistment bonuses, and pensions supplemented the family's finances. Collins also contributed to the military culture of African American manhood as race work against racism and the struggle for citizenship in the Jim Crow nation. As discussed by historian Le'Trice Donaldson, Collins's military service carried social, political, and economic capital within the broader Shippensburg community.[23] When not in the employ of the US Army, he worked for the Cumberland Valley Railroad and other local businesses. Nora added to the family income by selling food to individuals traveling to and from the train depot. She also continued to serve as the de facto parent of the younger siblings.[24]

After being labeled a "helpless child," Avis Lane benefited from her father's Civil War pension but still suffered economic and personal hardships. She became an unmarried mother raising two sons fathered by different men. Her eldest son's death in a February 1926 railroad accident precipitated her raising her then one-year-old granddaughter, Margaret, and youngest son John Leroy Green.[25] She supplemented her pension payments by operating a boardinghouse adjacent to her brother James Garfield Lane's home and St. Peter's AME church. By taking in boarders, she sometimes dealt with negative police interactions for allegedly operating a "disorderly house" and not as an entrepreneur engaged in a long history of African American boardinghouses.[26] African American women operated such businesses that addressed the needs of the Colored Conventions Movement, high rental costs, and the lack of short-term lodging options. Like many white women of the era, African American boardinghouses, though fewer in number, enabled women to support their families and achieve a degree of financial independence. Their decision, though, also could subject them to police violence, cycles of debt, and negative association with prostitution.[27]

Bessie Lane worked as a domestic for a prominent white Shippensburg lawyer and family. Her employment not only afforded her a decent income but also provided the sisters with access to legal advice and services. This was crucial in Nora's effort to become the official guardian of her younger siblings.[28] Bessie neither married nor had any children. By all accounts, the Lane sisters were not wealthy but among the working African American poor in the rural community. Their sisterly bonds strengthened as they lived in households within the same town, attended the same church, and raised the next generation.

The three Lane sisters were instrumental members of a tight-knit Black community committed to honoring Civil War veterans in their midst and promoting the Won Cause traditions to the next generation. Bessie Lane served as a leader in the Parent Teacher Association in the racially segregated African American elementary school, despite an 1881 state law prohibiting racially segregated public schools. As part of the welfare committee, she investigated the school conditions and proposed reforms to the elementary schooling of African American children for their entrance into the integrated high school. She remained an active member of the organization until the mid-1930s when actual enforcement of the 1881 law occurred in Shippensburg and other south-central Pennsylvania communities.[29] She also helped with the planning of Memorial Day celebrations, as her father had instilled the importance of them in her and her siblings. As her grand-niece, nephews, and nieces obtained their education in the Shippensburg public schools, Bessie Lane's service ensured a quality education but also continued training the next generation to keep alive Civil War memories. Both Avis and Bessie ensured that Margaret Lane's home education reinforced the annual school children's Black History Movement lessons and participation in the Won Cause traditions. Instead of the WRC and United Daughters of Veterans, the Lane sisters applied the Won Cause lessons instilled by their father and his USCT networks in their overlapping networks. In the process, the Lane sisters remembered and celebrated their father and other Civil War veterans through their communal memory work.[30]

Given their familial and geographical proximity to the Locust Grove/N. Queen St cemetery, the Lane sisters were very much a part of the sustained Won Cause commemorative traditions over the first half of the twentieth century. Black residents still embraced the Won Cause tradition of Memorial Day as one to honor Civil War veterans and subsequent war veterans. Memorial Day, like other Black holiday calendar events, "began and ended at African-American churches."[31] In 1923, Bessie served as one of the organizers for Memorial Day festivities. The event acknowledged and celebrated the three surviving Civil War veterans—John Hinton, John Barnitz, and John Brown—with a parade, music provided by a Hagerstown, Maryland, band, and school children decorating "the graves of veterans in Locus Grove Cemetery and the old cemetery of Queen street."[32] Although not always named, Nora, Bessie, and Avis Lane also helped organize grave decorations, picnics, and children performances through their women's church groups. Their church and secular communities would have also recognized them as the children of Joseph Lane, his service in the destruction of slavery, and his interment in the Locust Grove cemetery.

The sisters were also involved with the Black Parade, a separate non-Memorial Day parade honoring Black veterans that developed in the early twentieth century. In 1931, the last two surviving Civil War veterans from the town joined other veterans in the public spectacle. According to one report, "The Shippensburg Band led the procession, followed by the American Legion firing squad, sons of colored veterans, the Cheer-Up Dramatic Club, 'other folks in automobiles,' and children carrying bouquets of flowers to place on veterans' graves. The Reverend Joseph Robinson delivered the Memorial Day address on the grounds of the old North Queen Street Cemetery."[33] The circumstances regarding this expansion by the Black Shippensburg community is unclear, but the traditions reflected Civil War commemorative roots. The claims of public space still served as reminders to white Shippensburg residents of their commemorative traditions, existence, and citizenship. White residents, however, opted for derision of the continued practices by characterizing the event as the "N****r Parade" that ended at St. Peter's AME church and Memorial Day parades ending at the "N****r Hill" cemetery. Instead of celebrating Black Civil War commemorative traditions, white Shippensburg residents had fully embraced the color line and white privilege embedded in the Reconciliationist traditions.[34]

It is in this context that the Lane sisters make a considerable contribution to the community's collective Civil War memory. After the 1931 Black Parade, John Y. Smith returned to Shippensburg from Pittsburgh, Pennsylvania. He preferred dying in the Shippensburg community than alone. Without any direct family relations, the Lane sisters provided the necessary end-of-life care for the elderly Civil War veteran. It is not known exactly why Avis provided him accommodations in her South Penn Street home while Nora and Bessie helped with food and convalescent care.[35] In some respects, John Y. Smith was like their father. The Franklin County resident enlisted in Company C of the Twenty-Fifth USCT regiment on January 7, 1864, less than two weeks following the Christmas Day enlistment of Joseph Lane. He, too, migrated to Shippensburg after the Civil War. Unlike their father, Smith lived off and on in the community due to employment as a Pullman porter. Neither the sisters nor Avis's granddaughter Margaret openly acknowledged this selfless act to subsequent generations.

Rather, they stressed the memory and sacrifice of Civil War veterans and the commemorative traditions, specifically participation in parades, picnics after cemetery cleanup, grave decorations, and membership in church-related women's groups.[36]

The sisters, like other Black women discussed by historian Evelyn Brooks Higginbotham, considered their work in shaping familial, religious, and community networks as important toward building strong communities without assistance of the state and to contribute to racial uplift. These "unheralded women worked together in quotidian fashion" for the care and uplift of all community members, including elderly veterans.[37] The sisters did not rely on the exclusionary practices of the WRC. Rather, they internalized the lessons of their parents and Civil War veterans in the community and enacted a different type of rural Civil War memory work as their politics. They also embraced the call demanded of them by African American poet and suffragist Carrie Williams Clifford. As Black women, the Lane sisters simply labored until "the work is done," and in the process, contributed to the ongoing Civil War cultural wars as their white counterparts engaged in similar memory work.[38] Simply put, a housewife, domestic, and boardinghouse operator challenged the know-your-place aggression as well as the class dynamics influencing educated, middle-class African American women's memory work.[39]

The Lane sisters' memory work did not end with the end-of-life care of Smith. The women continued to engage with the Memorial Day celebrations and other community events. By the late 1930s, Civil War commemorative events were fully incorporated into the Black History Movement. Walter Foust, a Lancaster County prison warden and former Shippensburg resident, drew on the memories of John Brown and Abraham Lincoln as martyrs to the African American struggle against white supremacy and growing global fascism in his 1938 Memorial Day address. He concluded his address by telling the audience gathered at the Locust Grove cemetery "to use your citizenship."[40] The 1939 Memorial Day keynote speaker reinforced Foust's message. Rev. Fred Norris urged the audience to "honor the principles and ideals in which those men and women believed and which they thought were so worthwhile that they were willing to die for them."[41] Instead of merely criticizing social faults, Norris proposed that current residents rededicate themselves to fight for change as citizens and "continue to make America the land of the free and the home of the brave."[42] On the eve of World War II, the Memorial Day speech deployed the collective memories of USCT military sacrifice to encourage attendees' participation in the ongoing civil rights struggle at home and abroad.

Following the death of Nora Collins in 1942, Bessie and Avis Lane continued to use their overlapping familial, religious, and communal networks. Of the two sisters, Bessie had a more active role. She had a memorial window dedicated to her parents at St. Peter's AME Church. Presided over by Rev. George McCrory, the special dedication service on June 30, 1946, saw one window presented in memory of William and Sarah Carter and the other of Joseph and Irene Lane.[43] The Chatterbox column, a dedicated *News-Chronicle* feature of African American community news written by Lillian Daniels, regularly reported Bessie Lane's activities and travels to visit family and attend the annual AME conference in Philadelphia. Both sisters remained active in the annual Memorial Day planning and activities. They also helped to sustain the Won Cause traditions and oral histories and provided community members engaged in the Civil Rights Movement with historical role models and connections to the long community social justice struggle.[44]

The surviving Lane sisters' less publicized women's memory work reflected some intentional silencing. For instance, Edna Knapper's editorial decision of privileging her networks accounted for the absence of Joseph Lane and his descendants in the "Outstanding Colored Citizens of Chambersburg" series. By 1956, Avis Lane and Bessie Lane still resided in Shippensburg. Margaret Lowman, granddaughter of Avis Lane, had relocated with her husband and raised her growing family, including the author's mother, in Waynesboro. Neither Joseph Lane nor the Waynesboro family connections were included in Knapper's commemorative gaze. This silencing has influenced how Black Franklin County contributions to the Civil War era and memory construction are presented in subsequent county histories.

The Lane sisters also crafted another type of silencing of their Civil War memory work. They purposefully avoided the negative aspects of their father's wartime and postwar experiences except for private recollections. They actively remembered the soldiers' service, returning veterans, and the civilians seized and enslaved by Confederate troops in annual Won Cause events, church programs, and school activism. These aspects remained the essential components of how they remembered and commemorated the Civil War. The Lane sisters actively wrote themselves out of familial and communal collective memory of the Civil War and its legacy.[45] If not for a white Shippensburg Historical Society member, the women's efforts might had been lost except for the memories of those who encountered the preservers of Civil War memory within their networks.

In 1960, William H. Burkhart, a Shippensburg newspaper editor, World War II veteran, and active Shippensburg Historical Society member, presented a research paper detailing the Black Civil War veterans of Shippensburg for the historical society members. Burkhart began this project during his own campaign to place flags in front of the Civil War veterans' graves during the 1949 Memorial Day celebration. The deteriorating state of the headstones piqued his own memory recovery work. He explained to the audience: "In the years that followed, I gathered all available information I could locally on these Queen Street veterans, partly to identify their graves for a map and record and partly out of curiosity."[46] As part of his research process, Burkhart interviewed several members of the elderly African American community beginning in March 1958.

Of the fifteen families interviewed by Burkhart, it is likely that Bessie and Avis Lane were included. His interview notes do not shed light on the complete list of his informants. As private individuals, Burkhart respected the wishes of individuals who chose not to be named in the acknowledgments even though "all . . . showed a friendly interest in the project."[47] From the surviving notes and the paper's acknowledgments, however, it is clear that Burkhart interviewed Daniel Collins, the widower of Nora Lane, and other members of the sisters' religious, educational, and familial networks.[48]

Several Black Shippensburg residents detailed the experiences of the Civil War veterans and commemorative traditions for the white interviewer. During his interview with Daniel Collins, Joseph Lane's rather interesting exploits dominated the conversation; but he also revealed the daughters' care of John Y. Smith. Burkhart wrote in the 1960 paper:

> Elderly residents would recall bit by bit and tell me of days gone by while we talked together after services, on Memorial Day and just about anywhere we happened to meet. One excellent place was their N. Queen Street Cemetery while we repaired stones.
>
> On my last visit with Dan Collins in his living room [in] July, 1960, he strained hard at his memory to tell me something about: Henry Galloway and Wilson Carmichael. But he could not remember them. No one can. They were two men who lived to themselves.[49]

With this paper and the compiling of research for the Shippensburg Historical Society, Burkhart sealed the Civil War memory of Lane and others interred at Locust Grove cemetery. The Lane sisters' contributions were significantly reduced and are casually mentioned while the Civil War veterans and their wartime records remained the center of the paper's focus and analysis. The move from African American porches to the institutional archival repositories ensured that the men's contributions, the community archival processes, and Won Cause traditions persisted in the wider community consciousness into the second half of the twentieth century. These memories also survived the deaths of Joseph Lane's remaining children in the 1960s. Bessie Lane died in 1962. Avis Lane died in 1966 at the Cumberland County Nursing Home in Carlisle.[50]

By entrusting community histories with Burkhart, the impact of their decision becomes apparent as the presented paper forged the bedrock of subsequent public history research by Steven Burg, a Shippensburg University historian, and Shippensburg Historical Society members. Thus, the collective scholarship and research of Burkhart, Burg, and Shippensburg Historical Society members have influenced how African American Civil War military service and veteranhood are understood in the present. Locust Grove Cemetery has received a historical marker and designation as a historic African American cemetery.[51] By the Shippensburg community and historians, Joseph Lane is remembered for his enlistment, court-martial, and postwar acquittal. He is also commemorated at every major holiday with grave decorations, cemetery cleaning events, and now through Shippensburg University student research projects. When vandals destroyed his headstone in 2005, Matthew and Ellen Whitsel ensured its replacement through the department of Veterans Affairs after reading the *Shippensburg Sentinel* coverage.[52] The honor and sacrifice of USCT soldiers and returning veterans continue to be commemorated in this rural Pennsylvania community. Yet Joseph Lane's three daughters, all of whom are interred in the same cemetery, remain in the shadows of Black Civil War memory, as they had intended. In the process, they overcame the lack of sisterhood of the WRC and maximized their overlapping familial and communal networks in extraordinary and lasting ways.

The work of a historian often involves translation. As I shared the pension file with my mother, I carefully explained the formal pension process that the Lane family went through and how it compared with the experience of other USCT families. She, too, had a physical reaction when seeing the rejected widow's pension. During her long pause, I quickly explained how Avis Lane found success in the pension office and the other parts of the pension. Then she stopped me. "Avis is not just a name in this file. She was my mother's grandmother."[53]

My mother was a teenager when Avis Lane, daughter of Joseph Lane of the Twenty-Second USCT, died. Her own mother lived with her grandmother during John Y. Smith's final months and actively participated in Black Parade and Memorial Day celebrations. For my mother, Avis Lane's struggle and success were more than words on a page. She was a family member whom she regularly visited; she told family stories and received an education about the communal history not taught in the Waynesboro, Pennsylvania, K-12 schools. And yet the original widow's rejection gave both my mother and me a new appreciation for her struggles and other Black women who kept Black Civil War memory alive over the twentieth century.

My mother's reprimand forced me to recall another episode in the process of researching this book. During the summer of 2016, I traveled to several Pennsylvania archives. During my trip to the Shippensburg Historical Society, I answered a common question when asked about my research—"who is your family?" On this visit, a white elderly man had more questions after I explained my ties to Joseph Lane and the Lanes buried in the historic Locust Grove Cemetery. He then had a photograph of Bessie Lane pulled from the manuscript collection of her former employer. He also gave me a tour of where she worked and other downtown locales that she frequented. His generosity and memories of a distant relative helped in connecting the archival traces and porch archives and gave me more insights into the Lane family ancestor.

Later that evening, I explained what happened to my aunts and cousin. As I showed the picture to Aunt Bea (Barbara Lane Hill) in her nursing home bed, she exclaimed, "That's Aunt Bessie," before telling me more about her and her sisters.[54] Aunt Bea was the family historian. She also encouraged my educational pursuit through the doctoral process and beyond in the academy. This photo tucked into a manuscript collection and not a family photo album showed another legacy of Joseph Lane's daughters. Aunt Bea died less than a month after this research trip.

As kinkeepers, Bessie and Avis Lane were more than what I had recovered from the archives. They had different identities. They were aunts, community mothers, grandmothers, great-aunts, and even beloved employees. How does one combine porch archives with traditional archives while maintaining an ethics of care for descendants? My mother's response to Joseph Lane's pension file, however, raised another crucial question: How do I ensure that these women and others are more than names on a page?

III

Porches of My Father's Kinkeepers

Stony the road we trod,
Bitter the chastening rod,
Felt in the days when hope unborn had died;
Yet with a steady beat,
Have not our weary feet
Come to the place for which our fathers sighed?

—James Weldon Johnson,
"Lift Every Voice and Sing," 1900

Porch Lessons III

The Other Syllabus

I really want to make as big an impact as I can among younger black people about the vital importance of us going to our oldest people and talking with them and finding what they know about our families. The black history untold in the memories of the hundreds of thousands of grandmothers, grandfathers, great aunts, great whatever. Nobody asks them.

—ALEX HALEY, INTERVIEW FOR *THE BLACK SCHOLAR*, (1976).

I asked.
  I listened and watched.
  I read.

Born in 1977, I am a Xennial. I am part of the micro-generation between Generation X and millennials who saw the transition to digital from analog. I even graduated from college in 1999. I am my father's daughter—well-read, curious, and a legacy graduate of Franklin and Marshall College. I am also a student of the African American porch stories from Pennsylvania to my adopted communities of North Carolina, Virginia, Alabama, and the Charleston, South Carolina, lowcountry. As an African American woman whose family desegregated their suburban block, I am the product of the post-*Roots* cultural renaissance.

Alex Haley's *Roots*, and the miniseries based on it, inspired a cultural renaissance that affirmed and reimagined Civil War memory for late twentieth-century audiences nationally and internationally.[1] Storytelling served as a critical mode for sustaining Black Civil War memory over the nineteenth and twentieth centuries. As shown in preceding chapters, songwriting served as Joseph Winters's preferred storytelling form for remembering the Gettysburg invasion. Songs and public performance shaped Black men's political culture and participation in the formal tradition while allowing the next generations of African American children to learn about the Civil War generation at commemorative events like Memorial Day and during Black History movement events. Poetry, short stories, novels, and community histories also empowered African American men and women to remember the Civil War in a way that defied national expectations for collective forgetting and the acceptance of the anti-Black commemorative traditions of the pro-Southern Lost Cause and pro-white sectional Reconciliationist traditions. The Black History Movement also motivated Edna Knapper, Zadie Jones, and other mid-twentieth-century activists to turn to newspapers for advancing Civil War memory as an activist strategy in the Civil Rights Movement struggle. The storytelling of *Roots*, however, "offered ways to bring intimate experiences of oppression into the overarching narrative of U.S. historical knowledge."[2] The effects of *Roots* rippled through the African American literary and cinematic imaginaries. As a result, *Roots* inspired a significant change in Black Civil War memory.

In the post-*Roots* cultural landscape, film, television, and literature encouraged the shift from storytelling confined to porches and segregated spaces to more diverse scholarly and non-academic audiences. This diversification allowed for the recovery of Black Civil War memory from the margins of public consciousness. While still struggling against both Lost Cause myths and to get the attention they deserved, the greatest spreaders of Black Civil War memory have not been historians but rather communities, novelists, and filmmakers.[3] These Black cultural producers were often inspired by what they learned on porches and safe segregated spaces.

When two white Civil War relic hunters discovered an unmarked USCT hospital cemetery on Folly Island, South Carolina, in 1987, I witnessed how this post-*Roots* cultural renaissance helped set the stage for the reemergence of Black Civil War memory beyond mere counter-memory status. It also shaped my own and South Carolina relatives' responses to the 1989 Hollywood film *Glory*. We could see the magnitude of the *Roots*-esque cultural renaissance for not only recentering of Black Civil War memory into popular and scholarly understandings but how it also laid the foundation for dislodging Lost Cause understandings in Charleston, South Carolina, and the surrounding lowcountry as the dominant tradition expressed during the Civil War sesquicentennial celebrations. In the land where my father and his kinkeepers' "sighed," African American porches opened new opportunities for storytelling and revising whitewashed Civil War narratives.[4]

As Alex Haley wanted for readers and audiences of *Roots,* I asked. I listened. I read. I watched. And I learned the power of storytelling and witnessing as essential means for advancing Black Civil War memory. In a sense, the informal post-*Roots* syllabus of key texts, films, and documentaries left an indelible mark on this Xennial historian.

Rural Black Pennsylvanians' porches and traditional historical research influ-enced David Bradley's award-winning *The Chaneysville Incident* (1981). While writing a history of African Americans in the Pennsylvania-Maryland border county in 1969, his mother rediscovered that "there were thirteen unmarked graves on the property of a local landowner."[5] This knowledge, according to Bradley, "took on the force of fact."[6] Expanding on this archival trace, Brad-ley learned to move beyond the American exceptional myths. "I began to read and really understand American history, to go beyond the myths I'd ac-cepted without examination—Lincoln's role as the 'great emancipator,' for one," Bradley recalled.[7] He researched antebellum slavery, the slave trade, and the enslaved people's world of the Civil War era and complex afterlives in rural Pennsylvania.

The novel was inspired by Black collective memories. The Bedford, Pennsyl-vania, native told the *New York Times* how his childhood was filled with stories surrounding local participation in the Underground Railroad and other racial incidents. He recalled:

> All during the time that I was growing up I heard stories about the under-ground railroad that had run through Bedford. There were people in town who were descendants of slaves who had escaped by that route. I'd also heard about a group of 13 slaves who had escaped and when they learned that they were about to be recaptured asked to be killed.[8]

Bradley turned to the literary form for reimagining the motivations and expe-riences of the thirteen African Americans buried in the unmarked graves in southern Bedford County. He used a familiar commemorative tradition in Civil War memory but reimagined the storytelling form for national and international audiences. In the process, Bradley's memory work advanced African American porches as critical archival spaces and shared them more widely.[9]

Readers of the book follow John Washington, a toddy-drinking academic his-torian of African American history who returned home for the end-of-life care of a beloved uncle. John Washington travels from his West Philadelphia home with white psychiatrist girlfriend to the racially segregated Hill community in rural Pennsylvania. In the process, he discovered the truth of the area's Underground Railroad history, post–Civil War race relations by those who "didn't know the Civil War was over, or, at leastways, didn't know which side won," and his father's suicide.[10] The journey of rediscovery led to the protagonist's questioning the role of family lore within the history profession. "The stories were endless. . . . But somewhere along the line it had occurred to me that the stories were not just stories. They were something else: clues."[11] As a historian, he attempted to fill in the gaps while knowing that "the unknown are never filled, never can be filled, for they are larger than data, larger than deduction, larger than induction."[12] Yet the clues within Old Jack's stories aided the protagonist's journey of rediscovery of community history, his father's death, and his sense of self.

The historical reality of the thirteen unmarked graves inspired the plot. Introduced as a flashback, John Washington remembered how Old Jack

> had told me the story twenty times by then . . . of a dozen slaves who had come north on the Underground Railroad, fleeing whatever horrors were behind them, and who got just north of the Mason-Dixon Line, somewhere in the lower reaches of the County.[13]

His uncle's death and recalled childhood stories forced him to confront the past. While cleaning the cabin that "stank of dying," the protagonist received confirmation. He stumbled across his father's notes and personal archive.[14]

Instead of ignoring this inherited archive, John Washington filled in the gaps contained within Old Jack's stories. "Finally I decided to use them to record the information contained in the documents Moses Washington had constructed his final fiction to protect, because he thought them valuable," he proclaimed.[15] Previous family stories combined with his historical research skills led to his obsession to find the truth of his father but also the fate of the twelve self-liberating Virginians, and his own relative's role in their 1859 escape. He embraced the dual roles of family storyteller and dogged historian in search of the past. He understood the frustration of these competing identities. He confided to his girlfriend: "I want to know everything *now*. But history doesn't work that way; the truth is usually in the footnotes, not in the headlines."[16] By discovering the fate of the thirteen, the novel concluded with Washington's reconciling with his father's suicide, his birthplace, and his relationship with his girlfriend, who aided him in the journey. In effect, porch stories and an ethic of care in the recovery process permitted healing.[17] For this reader in a college classroom, the fictional journey helped break down the artificial barrier between porch archives and the ones privileged by historians.

Although Bradley's book may not have gotten as much attention as *Roots,* he was part of a wider movement. Toni Morrison's Pulitzer Prize–winning work *Beloved* (1987) similarly drew on archival traces for her own effort to shape memory of the Civil War era. She retold the true story of Margaret Garner to show the

horrors endured by enslaved mothers on the eve of the Civil War. In 1856, Garner self-liberated with her entire family and others from northern Kentucky by
fleeing to Cincinnati over the frozen Ohio river. When US Marshals attempted
recapture under the provisions of the Fugitive Slave Law of 1850, Garner made
a fateful decision. Hoping to spare her children from a life of slavery, Garner
nearly decapitated her daughter Mary with a knife and attempted to kill her other
daughter Cilla with a shovel.[18] Arrested, tried, and convicted of filicide, Garner's
well-publicized case in contemporary newspapers inspired Toni Morrison, who
showed a new generation of scholars the possibility of recovery and revising
whitewashed collective understandings of the Civil War era. The book's popularity and cultural impact are hard to overstate.

When editing the 1974 anthology, *The Black Book*, Morrison included a
newspaper account that revealed how the Garner case unfolded in the 1850s.
This account, additional historical research, and Morrison's masterly storytelling resulted in the 1987 novel centered on a former enslaved family coping with
the ongoing spectral hauntings during Reconstruction.[19] As in the other novels,
Morrison moved beyond the white gaze in understanding Garner's maternal
decisions and brought a more nuanced understanding of enslaved women's experiences. "In moments like these, Morrison takes a people deemed simplistic
by whites, and reveals the worldview they've created, the theories, philosophies,
analyses, and ethics they invented and lived by," according to literary scholar
Farah Jasmine Griffin. "As with the chorus in Greek tragedy, these moments of
communal revelation comment on the action but also contain the community's
values. She honors the meaning these people have given to their lives."[20] The
1998 Hollywood film adaptation further advanced Morrison's storytelling approach embraced by the diverse reading public seeking deeper understandings
of the Civil War era. Oprah Winfrey portrayed Sethe, a fictionalized version
of Margaret Garner, grappling with the daughter that she had killed during
slavery. Film audiences proved receptive and added to the overall box office
earnings.[21]

Success of these post-*Roots* cultural works inspired new adaptations of classic
Civil War–era texts on the small screen. Directed by Stan Lathan, the modern
made-for-television movie adaptation of Harriet Beecher Stowe's *Uncle Tom's
Cabin* debuted on Showtime Networks Inc, a cable network station, known as
simply Showtime, on June 14, 1987. The film featured well-known popular African
American actors. Avery Brooks played the title role of Uncle Tom with Phylicia
Rashad, Samuel L. Jackson, and Endyia Kinney-Sterns costarring.[22] Through-
out, the director kept a sensitivity to source material while not replicating

stereotypical Black caricatures. "I liked the challenge this production presented: a black man's interpretation of a white woman's interpretation of black reality— a reverse of 'The Color Purple,'" Lathan explained in a *New York Times* interview.[23]

This made-for-cable-television film built on the legacy of *Roots* and its 1979 sequel *Roots: The Next Generations*, a seven episode mini-series focused on the African American military experience and postwar disappointment during World War I and World War II.[24] On the screen and in Haley's original source material, the series addressed race, the racialized and gendered limits of military service, and the pursuit of American democratic ideals shared with the Civil War generation but within the context of the national Jim Crow white supremacist project.[25] Resilience, familial persistence, and the legacy of wartime sacrifice showed how African Americans of the Civil War generation and their post-emancipation progeny "responded to, resisted, and often overcame powerful forces."[26] Collectively, the *Roots* sequel and *Uncle Tom's Cabin* (1987) demonstrated the function of collective memories of the African American Civil War–era experience for shaping the long struggle for freedom, equality, citizenship, and social justice. Each generation fought under new political conditions, but the persistent legacy of anti-Blackness demanded both vigilance and role models for perseverance. While imperfect, the Reagan-era political and racial climate created a sense of urgency for such reminders among Black Generation X and Xennial viewers.

The controversial figure of John Brown—and his connections to race relations, sectionalism, and the politics of memory—has influenced statues, songs, public murals, and even Jacob Lawrence's "The Legend of John Brown" screen print series. For white Americans, John Brown was either a fanatical zealot or a martyr for the abolitionist cause. African Americans have typically viewed him as a freedom fighter who used violence for equality and social change.[27] James McBride's contribution to this aspect of Civil War memory took the form of 2013 novel, *The Good Lord Bird*. His treatment fell solidly within the long African American commemorative tradition in literature and popular understandings.[28] As professional historians debated the legacy of John Brown, McBride interjected. Unconcerned about the scholarly practices of which archival knowledge received inclusion in the footnotes, Black authors' fictional imaginations and storytelling again served as an important foundation for the reemergence of Black Civil War memory.

Throughout the National Book Award–winning novel, McBride deftly melded historical accounts of John Brown's exploits and enslaved people's experiences with his own literary imaginings. McBride introduced readers to Henry

Shackleford by following genre conventions of the slave narrative. Shackleford opened the account by providing some of his pre-liberation life history in Kansas Territory. McBride, however, disrupted the familiar narrative convention in the first sentence: "I was born a colored man and don't you forget it. But I lived as a colored woman for seventeen years."[29] When an altercation results in the death of his father, Henry becomes Henrietta (nicknamed "Little Onion") to survive. Afraid, without kin, and a witness to his father's brutal death, Henry-Little Onion eventually found his surrogate father in John Brown and his chosen family among the white and Black members of Brown's army. Happenstance allowed the protagonist to meet Frederick Douglass and Harriet Tubman during Brown's pre–Harpers Ferry recruitment tour of the eastern United States and Canada.[30] By the final section, Little Onion's inclusion in real historical events appeared natural in the fictional Civil War–era world crafted by McBride. The unfolding events of Harpers Ferry saw Henry-Little Onion's escape so that he can "tell the stories" to future generations.[31]

In the concluding pages, McBride returned to real historical events of the trial, the hanging of Brown and his army, and early African American remembrances of Brown and Harpers Ferry at the Pennsylvania-Maryland-West Virginia border. For generations, these rural Black communities sustained John Brown's legacy as a freedom fighter. James McBride intentionally recognized and celebrated the ordinary African Americans "who, over the years kept the memory of John Brown alive."[32] His acknowledgment served as a powerful reminder of the African American porches to Civil War memory, which had escaped the gaze of most white Americans. McBride, too, found inspiration on Black porches.

In the fall of 2020, Showtime again dramatized another Black Civil War historical fiction for modern audiences by turning the *Good Lord Bird* into a multi-episode miniseries starring Ethan Hawke, Daveed Diggs, and Joshua Caleb Johnson.[33] Not all people—audiences and critics—were impressed with the Showtime adaptation. Black creatives offered some nuanced critiques of the white-savior narrative typified in the series. African American critic and podcast creator Carvell Wallace offered a layered critique in *The New York Times*. Wallace praised McBride's source material. "McBride excels at viewing the "peculiar institution" of slavery from multiple perspectives," he wrote.[34] He appreciated how "McBride's version of John Brown is a complex character—a man whose absolute certainty of mission combines with a bumbling presence, and whose ability to reframe every misfortune as a Gift from the Lord sits alongside an absolutely savage capacity for bloodshed."[35] But he bristled at the Ethan Hawke–centered adaptation and Hollywood's inadequate ability to capture the messiness and complexity of the Civil War era. Wallace asked: "Can a white person ever usefully tell a slave story—or, more specific, can they tell a story that is useful to the descendants of the enslaved, rather than to their own egos or cinematic fantasies?"[36]

In his layered review, Wallace also acknowledged the 2019 Hollywood film *Harriet*, starring Cynthia Erivo in the title role. Directed by African American filmmaker Kasi Lemmons, the film ends with Tubman leading USCT soldiers, under the command of Col. James Montgomery, along the Combahee River. Her leadership and navigation of the marshy South Carolina lowcountry contributed to the liberation of more than seven hundred enslaved individuals.[37] Viewers leave the film understanding Harriet Tubman, a self-liberated woman, nurse, and scout, as the savior of these Black South Carolinians. By commanding Black soldiers, Tubman, and not a white officer, becomes the heroine in this Civil War memory project. Unlike the earlier *Glory*, director Kasi Lemmons demonstrated the centrality of Black women in the USCT experience and the wartime destruction of slavery.[38] Sadly, Harriet Tubman could not make similar inroads as the Black male-centered military film *Glory*.

This movie about a real-life Civil War–era heroine did not attract the hoped-for audiences. Wallace questioned the disappointing box office returns for *Harriet*. "How, precisely, one 'gets it right' when it comes to the intersection of slavery and Hollywood is at this point unclear."[39] He felt that the *Good Lord Bird* series, like *Harriet*, represented solid attempts but fell short of telling the "African-American perspective on the white savior."[40] He acknowledged that the resulting 2020 series offered "a complicated work; it asks questions, refutes facile narratives and plays with contradictions, as much art does."[41] Ultimately, Wallace remained unsatisfied in the context of the post–George Floyd racial reckoning moment of the mass anti-racist protests against policing and contested Confederate and settler colonial monuments. While some found solace "in watching good TV dramas, reading books that educate you about racism, shopping at black-owned businesses or putting up the right yard signs," Wallace pointedly surmised: "Whether you think that's enough, it would seem, depends how much Onion is in you, and how much John Brown."[42] If produced before the 2020 national reckoning, Wallace's nuanced review might have been different. The political landscape mattered for use of films and cultural works in advancing Civil War memory to twenty-first-century audiences who had asked more sophisticated questions of the medium, and its limitations. Yet they understood the need for presenting authentic Black perspectives of the Civil War era, including prominent white allies like John Brown. Unfortunately, some questions remained unanswered: Are white saviors enough? Without the help from white saviors, will Black women ever be recognized as lead protagonists within the cinematic landscape of Civil War memory?

Modern Black storytellers continue to build on the post-*Roots* renaissance and Black women historians. In *Carolina Built* (2022), Kianna Alexander added to the legacy of the post-*Roots* cultural renaissance while addressing growing demands for nuanced depictions of the Civil War era. The Black North Carolina native offered a fictional account of Josephine L. Leary, a real Black North Carolinian woman born into slavery who built extensive real estate holdings as a post–Civil War inheritance for her children. Capitalizing on the post-*Roots* cultural renaissance cultural works, Alexander found inspiration from a social media post discussing Leary and the recovery work by Dorothy Spruill Redford, the former Somerset Place director who spearheaded the correction of a wayside marker of a rare Black Civil War monument in Hertford, North Carolina.[43] By detailing a Black woman from rural northeastern North Carolina, Alexander upended the white savior narrative by showing how emancipation memories of the Civil War shaped her real estate holdings.

Drawing on Leary's personal papers contained at Duke University and other historical research, Alexander firmly rooted her novel in the history of Black women's economic strategies and activities as a form of Civil War memory. Emancipation defined her actions. Her memories of the extractive labor, violence, and harsh living conditions motivated how she navigated the post-emancipation landscape. She acquired an education in the local Freedmen's School. She acquired middle-class lifestyle alongside her husband who operated a barber shop. Yet emancipation shaped her dreams for her daughters, her parenting style, and even marital spats over her real estate holdings. As freedom's children, to borrow from historian Mary Niall Mitchell, Leary ensured that her daughters would not share her childhood experiences.[44] Her children "represented the possibility of a future dramatically different from the past, a future in which black Americans might have access to the same privileges as whites: landownership, equality, autonomy."[45] As the remaining pages show, Leary's vision prevailed. She ensured that the entire family would benefit from the rental property income "that will serve this family after we finally retire."[46] In effect, she created an inheritance that allowed for the transmission of generational wealth denied to her before emancipation.

Moreover, Alexander's account allowed Leary to challenge white women's Lost Cause claims to the commemorative landscape. While it is not clear whether Leary contributed to the Hertford, North Carolina, monument honoring Black Civil War veterans, Alexander included a scene in which Leary stymied local

Ladies Memorial Association efforts for establishing a social club. After winning another property at a local auction, Alexander detailed:

> Mrs. Anderson stands up, her free hand curled into a fist. "Why I'd planned to set up my social club for Confederate widows in that building!"
>   The auctioneer shrugs. "Sorry, darlin'. You've been outbid."[47]

Auctions created another means for Black women to challenge white women's desires for implementing a Lost Cause landscape. Leary created a real estate empire throughout northeastern North Carolina because of emancipationist Civil War understandings. In the process, she defied the victimization narrative of Black women losing to Lost Cause proponents. Ultimately, she purchased and created her own monument in the form of the J. N. Leary Building in downtown Edenton, North Carolina. To date, Leary's multistory brick monument stands while Lost Cause monuments have been removed following the Charleston Massacre, Charlottesville 2017, and George Floyd's national reckoning of 2020.[48]

Although a fictional account, Alexander sought to share Leary, her life, and cultural legacy for her family, community, and contributions to the diversity of the Civil War era experience. She included a detailed bibliography of the sources. She provided readers with a selection of both historic and contemporary photographs of Josephine Leary and the existing J. N. Leary Building. She also developed a series of questions for facilitating discussion among African American reading circles and other book clubs. Recognizing her diverse audience, Alexander responded with additional resources for cultivating new understandings of Black women's memory making beyond monuments to include economic activities as part of the rich tapestry of Black Civil War memory. She, too, found inspiration from the long history of memory work by northeastern North Carolinian women and Dorothy Spruill Redford.

The post-*Roots* cultural landscape coincided with the history I witnessed, specifically the fateful rediscovery of an unmarked USCT hospital cemetery on Folly Island, South Carolina, and the theatrical release of *Glory*. Instead of entering the discussion from a point of counter-memory, the post-*Roots* cultural renaissance influenced the reception of the 1989 Hollywood film and even Governor Michael Dukakis's Memorial Day speech. While white South Carolinians devoted their energies to the rediscovered CSS *Hunley*, Black South Carolinians continued to advance Civil War memory but to newer and accepting audiences because of the post-*Roots* cultural and Civil Rights Movement political landscapes. The restoration of Black Civil War memory eventually disrupted Lost Cause understandings in Charleston, South Carolina, and the surrounding lowcountry as the dominant commemorative tradition. Without the *Roots* effect, the recent shift toward a more inclusive Civil War commemorative landscape would have been different.

In short, this post-*Roots* fiction, films, and television series did more for restoring Black Civil War memory to the public consciousness than professional historians. Writers and filmmakers spread recovered Black memories of the Civil War in ways historians have failed to do. Through storytelling, writers, filmmakers, and other cultural producers prepared the ground later claimed by historians, museums, and even Black Civil War reenactors over the late twentieth century. Without this cultural movement, it is impossible to understand not only the reception of *Glory* but how reinvigorated Black commemorative traditions allowed Charleston and the South Carolina lowcountry to re-remember its Black Civil War era past.

Many Black Generation X and Xennial scholars, including myself, received our first exposure to this storytelling as children. My own parents incorporated these works in my summer reading diet. These film adaptations filled in the holes left by Ken Burns's *The Civil War* series and unanswered questions of the war's aftermath on the lived experiences and commemorative traditions for activists showcased in *Eyes on the Prize* I and II. All three acclaimed Public Broadcasting System (PBS) documentaries were essential viewing in my childhood home. (And I later had to the opportunity to work with the now-late Gerald Gill who advised *Eyes on the Prize* as a master's student at Tufts University.) Courses in African American literature and Civil War fiction at Franklin and Marshall College introduced the *Chaneysville Incident* and *Beloved* alongside *The Killer Angels* (1974) and *Cold Mountain* (1987) as part of the American literary canon exploring the Civil War era.[49] A part of a new generation of academic and popular audiences, we reimagined spaces where the African American porch flourished and transformed traditional, predominantly white spaces that once dismissed such knowledge as biased, unworthy of academic study, and/or forever lost to the traditional archives.

On the porches of my father's kinkeepers, I learned the power of storytelling for revising whitewashed Lost Cause narratives embraced in the Charleston lowcountry. I also witnessed the history of the transformation by those inspired by the post-*Roots* cultural landscape and the Hollywood film *Glory*. As both a witness and historian, I became better equipped to connect my seemingly disparate communities—descendant of Joseph Lane, professional historian, and a native Bostonian with South Carolina lowcountry paternal roots—into the driving force of my scholarship. These concluding chapters, therefore, return to the land where my father's family labored on rice plantations and retained their Gullah Geechee heritage before securing their freedom at the end of the Civil War. Often living on heirs' property, these kinkeepers' porches offered another personal and more intimate education rooted in porch stories and the post-*Roots* cultural landscape. Because I asked, listened, and watched, I could better appreciate the reemergence of Black Civil Memory and how Black remembrance became a defining feature of the sesquicentennial commemoration.

7

Delayed Honor in the Charleston Lowcountry

On Memorial Day 1989, a unique Civil War commemoration occurred in South Carolina. Over 140 Civil War reenactors marched through the Beaufort National Cemetery to the sounds of a "somber drum roll and plaintive fife."[1] These men, however, portrayed Black USCT soldiers. The gathering served as the formal reburial of primarily Fifty-Fifth Massachusetts and First North Carolina Colored Infantry soldiers found at a Folly Island, South Carolina, construction site. Massachusetts Governor Michael Dukakis addressed the crowd: "These black soldiers of the Massachusetts 54th and 55th regiments fought for their liberty, to grasp their own freedom, and to ensure both for others of their own race."[2] He also reminded the largely South Carolinian crowd how some "had been slaves. But all were heroes for their race and for their cause, joined with Col. Shaw together in the democracy of death."[3]

Several African American attendees offered interesting perspectives of the day. Some commented on the large turnout of white attendees at the reinterment ceremonies. Traditionally Memorial Day had been a celebration within the Emancipationist and Won Cause traditions of Black Civil War Memory. With the annual Confederate Memorial Day observance popular among many white South Carolinians, the mixed audience did not escape their notice. "It's always been a black celebration," one African American woman reflected. "After the Civil Rights movement, more whites began to participate."[4] While some Black South Carolinians considered the composition of the crowd as unusual, George Coblyn, whose grandfather served in the Fifty-Fourth Massachusetts Regiment, had a different response: "This brings closure to the events of the Civil War," Coblyn remarked to a *Boston Globe* reporter.[5] But to the *Washington Post*, Coblyn elaborated in an extended interview: "I feel like my grandfather is watching this from somewhere." While wearing his own wartime uniform adorned with medals, including two Purple Hearts and three Bronze Stars from World War II and Korea, Coblyn added after a brief pause: "It's a final endorsement of black soldiers everywhere in the struggle to be recognized."[6] Indeed, the day had been special. By showcasing the recovered USCT soldiers' ultimate wartime sacrifice in securing federal victory, both the ceremony and processional united everyday residents, USCT descendants, and Massachusetts politicos. This decidedly Black Civil War commemoration marked a shift away from a white neo-Confederate emphasis.

Happenstance led to this late twentieth-century Civil War commemoration. Two years earlier, two white Civil War relic hunters stumbled across a previously unknown USCT cemetery outside of Charleston, South Carolina. Archaeological excavations revealed that the remains had military roots in the Fifty-Fifth Massachusetts and First North Carolina Colored Infantry regiments. Political gains of the modern Civil Rights-Black Power Movements allowed for such a gathering. The meaning of the event and diverse audience had been shaped by the post-*Roots* Black cultural renaissance, which generated scholarly and popular interest in the Black Civil War experience and collective memory traditions. From the presence of the Massachusetts governor to the large audience of white and Black, Northern and Southern Americans, this chapter explores how the discovery of USCT soldiers' remains marked the beginning of a significant shift in Civil War memory.

These Civil War heroes became the subject of cultural memory war over patriotism, honor, and manhood in Charleston, South Carolina, Massachusetts, and the nation. While the Lost Cause politics of the CSS *Hunley* memory might have initially won the battle, the impressive reinterment ceremony amid the backdrop of the cinematic release of *Glory* afforded them another Appomattox. A new generation of everyday Americans learned about and came to remember the essential role of African American military service in the Civil War. The 1989 Hollywood film became another entry into the post-*Roots* Black cultural renaissance, which advanced Civil War memory. With its gaze solely on the Civil War, this film generated diverse national and international as well as scholarly attention for understanding Black Civil War commemorative and oral traditions. In its wake, new monuments, new voices, and a Black Civil War reenacting group emerged.

By the late twentieth century, African American porch stories and other traditions were no longer confined to predominantly African American audiences. This shift encouraged the reemergence of Black Civil War memory from the margins and helped in dislodging the Lost Cause understandings that had defined the regional past since Jim Crow. This new Civil War commemorative landscape allowed for a rare acknowledgment by the South Carolina governor of the event that allowed for the reemergence of Black Civil War memory in Charleston and the surrounding lowcountry.

In May 1987, Robert Bohrn, a white native Charlestonian who operated a popular restaurant, and his friend Erik Croen rediscovered a USCT cemetery at

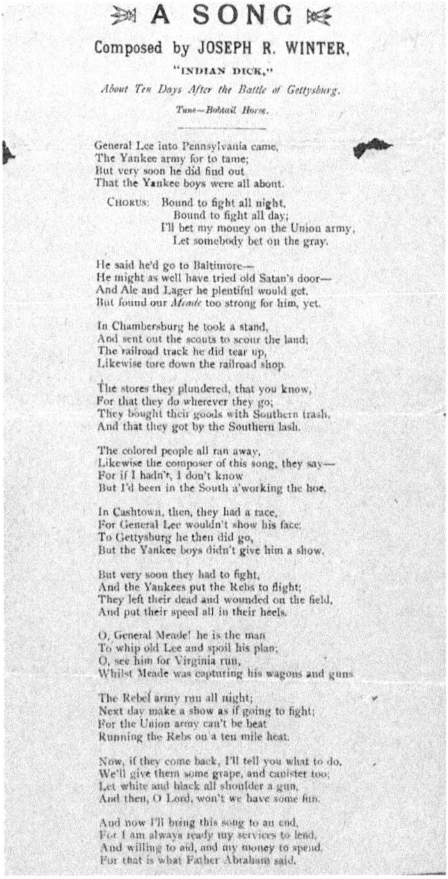

A SONG

Composed by JOSEPH R. WINTER,

"INDIAN DICK,"

About Ten Days After the Battle of Gettysburg.

Tune—Bobtail Horse.

General Lee into Pennsylvania came,
The Yankee army for to tame;
But very soon he did find out
That the Yankee boys were all about.

CHORUS: Bound to fight all night,
Bound to fight all day;
I'll bet my money on the Union army,
Let somebody bet on the gray.

He said he'd go to Baltimore—
He might as well have tried old Satan's door—
And Ale and Lager he plentiful would get,
But found our *Meade* too strong for him, yet.

In Chambersburg he took a stand,
And sent out the scouts to scour the land;
The railroad track he did tear up,
Likewise tore down the railroad shop.

The stores they plundered, that you know,
For that they do wherever they go;
They bought their goods with Southern trash,
And that they got by the Southern lash.

The colored people all ran away,
Likewise the composer of this song, they say—
For if I hadn't, I don't know
But I'd been in the South a'working the hoe.

In Cashtown, then, they had a race,
For General Lee wouldn't show his face;
To Gettysburg he then did go,
But the Yankee boys didn't give him a show.

But very soon they had to fight,
And the Yankees put the Rebs to flight;
They left their dead and wounded on the field,
And put their speed all in their heels.

O, General Meade! he is the man
To whip old Lee and spoil his plan;
O, see him for Virginia run,
Whilst Meade was capturing his wagons and guns.

The Rebel army run all night;
Next day make a show as if going to fight;
For the Union army can't be beat
Running the Rebs on a ten mile heat.

Now, if they come back, I'll tell you what to do,
We'll give them some grape, and canister too;
Let white and black all shoulder a gun,
And then, O Lord, won't we have some fun.

And now I'll bring this song to an end,
For I am always ready my services to lend,
And willing to aid, and my money to spend,
For that is what Father Abraham said.

Figure 1. Joseph R. Winters, "About Ten Days after the Battle of Gettysburg," song sheet, 1863. Courtesy of the Department of Special Collections, Stanford University Libraries.

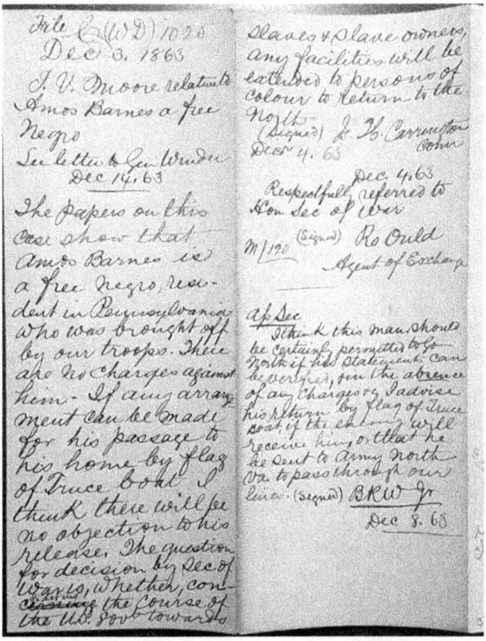

File (WD) 1020
Dec 3. 1863
J. V. Moore relative to Amos Barnes a free Negro
See letter to Gen Winder Dec 14, 63

The papers on this case show that Amos Barnes is a free Negro, resident in Pennsylvania who was brought off by our troops. There are no charges against him - If any arrangement can be made for his passage to his home by flag of Truce boat I think there will be no objection to his release. The question for decision by Sec of War is, whether, considering the course of the U.S. Govt towards slaves & slave owners, any facilities will be extended to persons of colour to return to the North
(Signed) J. H. Carrington Comr
Decr 4. 63

Dec. 4, 63
Respectfully referred to Hon Sec of War
M/190 (Signed) Ro Ould
Agent of Exchange

A/Sec
I think this man should be certainly permitted to go North if his statements can be verified, in the absence of any charges vs. I advise his return by flag of Truce boat, if the enemy will receive him, or that he be sent to Army North Va. to pass through our lines. (Signed) BKW Jr
Dec 8. 63

Figure 2. Release papers of Amos Barnes. National Archives.

(Top) Figure 3. 24th USCT at Camp William Penn. The Library Company of Philadelphia.

(Bottom) Figure 4. *A Gathering at the Crossroads* monument. *Pennsylvania Heritage*/Pennsylvania Historical & Museum Commission (PHMC).

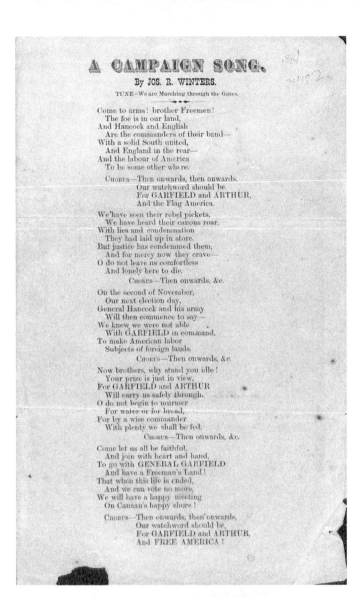

A CAMPAIGN SONG.

By JOS. R. WINTERS.

TUNE—We are Marching through the Gates.

Come to arms! brother Freemen!
  The foe is in our land,
And Hancock and English
  Are the commanders of their band—
With a solid South united,
  And England in the rear—
And the labour of America
  To be some other where.

    CHORUS—Then onwards, then onwards,
      Our watchword should be,
        For GARFIELD and ARTHUR,
        And the Flag America.

We have seen their rebel pickets,
  We have heard their canons roar,
With lies and condemnation
  They had laid up in store.
But justice has condemned them,
  And for mercy now they crave—
O do not leave us comfortless
  And lonely here to die.

    CHORUS—Then onwards, &c.

On the second of November,
  Our next election day,
General Hancock and his army
  Will then commence to say—
We knew, we were not able
  With GARFIELD in command,
To make American labor
  Subjects of foreign lands.

    CHORUS—Then onwards, &c.

Now brothers, why stand you idle!
  Your prize is just in view,
For GARFIELD and ARTHUR
  Will carry us safely through.
O do not begin to murmer
  For water or for bread,
For by a wise commander
  With plenty we shall be fed.

    CHORUS—Then onwards, &c.

Come let us all be faithful,
  And join with heart and hand,
To go with GENERAL GARFIELD
  And have a Freeman's Land!
That when this life is ended,
  And we can vote no more,
We will have a happy meeting
  On Canaan's happy shore!

    CHORUS—Then onwards, then onwards,
      Our watchword should be,
        For GARFIELD and ARTHUR,
        And FREE AMERICA!

(Top) Figure 5. Joseph R. Winters, "A Campaign Song," ca. 1880. Courtesy of the Department of Special Collections, Stanford University Libraries.

(Bottom) Figure 6. Joseph Lane headstone, Shippensburg, Pennsylvania. Author's personal collection.

Figure 7. M. F. Wyckoff with unidentified African American youth at the Lee Monument Unveiling, 1890. Author's personal collection.

Figure 8. Unidentified African American mother and daughter, Jamestown Ter-Centennial souvenir photograph, Norfolk, 1907. Author's personal collection.

Figure 9. Giles J. Jackson, 1911. Virginia Museum of History and Culture (VMHC).

(Left)Figure 10. Colored Union Soldiers Monument, Hertford, Perquimans County, North Carolina. Author's personal collection.

(Bottom) Figure 11. Edna Christian Knapper's concluding column in the "Outstanding Colored Citizens of Chambersburg—Past and Present" series.

OUTSTANDING COLORED CITIZENS OF CHAMBERSBURG—PAST AND PRESENT

This is the fifteenth and last of a series of weekly articles on some of the outstanding colored citizens of Chambersburg, past and present. The series has been prepared by Mrs. Edna Christian Knapper, retired school teacher, of 621 S. Main St.

THE CHRISTIAN FAMILY

By EDNA CHRISTIAN KNAPPER

Royal Christian Sr. was born a slave on a plantation owned by the Royal estate in Lynchburg, Va. He was thirteen years old when the Civil War began. Many of the slaves were pressed into service, but because of his youth Royal's one task was to help carry the wounded off the battlefield following the Battle of Lynchburg. His name was originally Christian Royal, it being the custom in some sections of the South for slaves to take the name of their master.

ton Heights Chamber of Commerce.

Alfred Barbour is owner and operator of the Barbour Wine and Liquor Store in North Tarrytown, N. Y., and is also engaged in the real estate business. He is a Mason of high degree. His colonial ranch house, which he built himself, is one of the showplaces of that section.

Sergernia Christian Jackson, a product of our local schools spent twenty - four years as waitress and

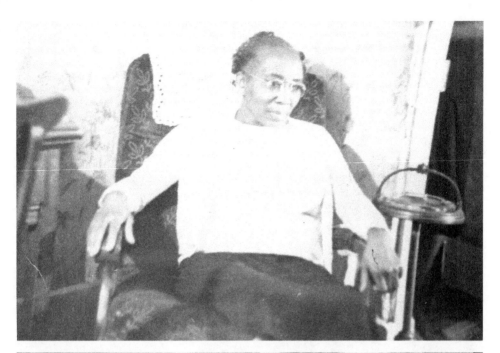

(Top) Figure 12. Bessie Lane, 1948. Shippensburg History Center Collection.

(Bottom) Figure 13. Author, brother, and maternal grandmother, ca. 1983. Author's personal collection.

Figure 14. 1961 Corolla "Student Life" section break. The University of Alabama Libraries Special Collections.

Figure 15. Author conducting a Hallowed Ground Tour.

a construction site on Folly Island. During a routine outing, Bohrn and Croen searched for Civil War artifacts in an area located between two known federal Civil War camps. The area had been rewarding for the men before this particular day and often yielded the desired Civil War relics. With freshly cleared land, the pair grabbed their metal detectors and shovels. This pre-dusk outing would be different. After "my metal detector went crazy," Bohrn located "a general issue enlisted man's button. This one, though, instead of being in great shape like other finds, was corroded and had bits of black clothlike material clinging to it. Several other buttons were there also, all in a small group."[7] Croen, however, found a human femur. They had found a gravesite. Before leaving for the evening, the pair temporarily covered the site out of respect for the interred soldier. Assuming their discovery was an isolated burial, Bohrn and Croen intentionally erased "all traces of our being there" out of fear that another collector might "come along and destroy the grave, if in fact that's what it was."[8]

When they returned the following day, Bohrn and Croen planned to reinter the soldier's femur a short distance away from the original discovery point. When their shovels unearthed "four vertebrae, a button and some more clothlike material," the men realized that they had found a Civil War–era cemetery.[9] The men had been aware of the federal camp existence. This area had served as a prime relic collecting spot. But this discovery proved different. "I knew right then we had found a graveyard. What else would account for finding two graves that far apart? It was really an eerie feeling," Bohrn explained.[10] While understanding the Civil War significance of the discovery, the white relic hunters simply wanted the exhumation and reburial of the soldiers in a national cemetery. Neither Bohrn nor Croen imagined that their discovery would upend popular Lost Cause understandings and bring Black Civil War memories to the fore of the public consciousness.

On May 11, 1987, Bohrn contacted state archaeologists in Columbia.[11] By contacting the South Carolina Institute of Archaeology and Anthropology (SCIAA), Bohrn and Croen unleashed a series of events contributing to the recovery and reburial of the USCT soldiers in Beaufort, South Carolina. Three days later, Steven D. Smith, the deputy state archaeologist, met the relic hunters. Smith then contacted the corporate property owner Ravenel Elserhardt Securities, the Charleston County coroner, the medical examiner's office, and Folly Beach council members.[12] Although the South Carolina State Historic Preservation Office determined that no "legal obligation to stop construction" existed, positive media coverage had generated a lot of public interest.[13] This publicity resulted in the month-long construction delay necessary for the salvage recovery and excavation work. On May 19, eight days after the initial notification, phase one of the two-year process began at the USCT cemetery.[14]

Designated as site 38CH920, the SCIAA team's work quickly expanded beyond the original scope. Initially, the agency had two goals. First, the team would "collect an archaeological sample of the burial," and second, "take the sample from roadbed where they would otherwise be destroyed or looted."[15] Between May 19 and 29, 1987, the team unearthed fourteen burials and other archaeological samples. Their work revealed the necessity of a formal 42-acre survey and simultaneous preparation of a nomination for a National Register of Historic Places designation. The property owner again gave permission for the expanded archaeological work. As SCIAA prepared the final report on the May 1987 excavations, Bohrn found additional remains near the sewer line construction project on the property. This discovery and the previous work done made clear that "a major Civil War occupation existed in the area."[16] Phase two excavations focused on three additional sites, which resulted in the discovery during the summer of 1988 of one additional burial and archaeological evidence of the entire campsite for white and Black federal soldiers on the island during the summer of 1988. All archaeological fieldwork followed normal discipline-specific protocols.[17]

Funding affected all aspects of the two-year project. Straining its budget, SCIAA paid for all phase one work. SCIAA and First Coastal Properties Inc. funded phase two excavation work conducted by Lisa D. O'Steen's team.[18] In order to finish the project, the SCIAA team approached two state senators for additional appropriations. Their efforts initially failed.[19] Such financial considerations did not extend to the CSS *Hunley*. When the Hunley Museum opened in 1967, the publicly funded Charleston Museum branch featured a replica of the Civil War submarine. When located off the Charleston coast in 1995, state legislators willingly opened state coffers for the eventual recovery and subsequent preservation efforts. Few questioned the expenditures until millions had been spent.[20] Ultimately, the search, recovery, and preservation of the CSS *Hunley* and elaborate reburial of the Confederate crew mattered more than the USCT cemetery and federal Civil War campsite. South Carolina officials and the power elite chose the Lost Cause and recovery of the Confederate submarine. The agency persisted with the cemetery project and "filled in the financial gap."[21] Eventually, a special appropriation from the Contingency Fund allowed SCIAA to complete the archaeological work and laboratory analysis before drafting the final report. These funding challenges revealed a lack of commitment by the state who remained wedded to Lost Cause understandings of the siege of Charleston.[22]

Based on their work, SCIAA determined the burials primarily represented soldiers from the Fifty-Fifth Massachusetts and First North Carolina Colored Infantry. For each of the eighteen burials, team members noted the orientation, condition, and completeness of the skeletal remains, sex, height, race, and approximate age. The men were approximately sixteen to thirty years old. Miscellaneous human bones formed the nineteenth burial.[23] Consistent with federal Civil War burial patterns, Smith and team characterized the initial archaeological site as "an abandoned brigade cemetery . . . [consisting of the graves of men] who were buried there as a result of death due to sickness and disease."[24] The site was located next to the known Fifty-Fifth Massachusetts camp on the island from November 1863 to February 1864. None buried in the new cemetery had any battle wounds. The men's documented non-combat service contributed to their deaths and burials in the racially segregated cemetery.[25] The archaeological evidence corroborated the Civil War historical record and Black oral history. Twenty-seven of the soldiers died while in the winter camp: two Second US Colored Infantry, ten First NC Colored Infantry, and fifteen Fifty-Fifth Massachusetts.[26] While drafting the final report for publication, Smith and other SCIAA colleagues prepared the remains for reburial at Beaufort National Cemetery.[27]

Ultimately, a cross-regional, state-federal-private coalition prevailed. The archaeological work brought local, national, and scholarly attention to the Black USCT military experience and federal Civil War camp activities on Folly Island. SCIAA's efforts also afforded full military honors to the Black Civil War soldiers reburied at the Beaufort National Cemetery. The Memorial Day 1989 reburial and Governor Dukakis's speech would not have been possible without two relic hunters and diligent archaeologists committed to the truth.[28]

Fulfilling the relic hunters' original desires, the recovered USCT remains finally received their final resting place at the Beaufort National Cemetery on Memorial Day 1989. Once on the opposing sides of the Civil War, some South Carolinians and Massachusetts residents found common commemorative ground by participating in the elaborate events honoring Black Civil War soldiers. The South Carolina political leadership was noticeably absent, but Massachusetts Governor Michael Dukakis had an active role in the Memorial Day ceremonies. In April 1989, the *Beaufort Gazette* announced Dukakis's planned attendance. The governor's press office spokeswoman Mindy Lubber stressed, "We had to work pretty hard to make sure he was everywhere he was supposed to be but this ceremony is something he felt pretty strongly about so he's looking forward to it."[29] Several living African American descendants of the Fifty-Fourth and Fifty-Fifth Massachusetts regiments also planned their attendance.[30] Other special guests included African American extras from the movie *Glory* being filmed in the South Carolina-Georgia area. These Black reenactors would have a central role in the Memorial Day parade and reburial ceremonies at Beaufort National Cemetery. According to the May 26, 1989, press release, the cemetery portion would be "conducted according to Union Army Regulations of 1863 and feature the 55th's colors, as well as earth from historic Massachusetts military burial grounds."[31] The planned Memorial Day 1989 ceremonies would give fitting honors for the forgotten African American heroes.

Drawing on twentieth-century Northern understandings of Civil War memory, Governor Dukakis's speech showcased the uniqueness and historic nature of the occasion. In previous Civil War cultural wars, attendees might not have fathomed such an occasion. He acknowledged in the opening: "It is particularly fitting that I should come here today to honor the memory of Massachusetts men who died on Carolina soil."[32] But he stressed how race, sacrifice, and death defined experiences of the men being honored. He told them how "these Black soldiers of the Massachusetts 54th and 55th regiments fought for their own liberty, to grasp their own freedom; and to ensure both for others of their own race."[33] Dukakis reminded the crowd that nonetheless: "They were unwanted."[34] Lincoln, his cabinet, and even the US Congress scoffed, rebuffed, and thwarted serious discussions regarding Black men's enlistment in the federal army. In this fray, the "voices of Massachusetts, at least some of the more powerful ones, persisted, and Governor Andrew was finally allowed to recruit and train two Black regiments—the 54th and the 55th Massachusetts, made up of free Negroes from his own state and others."[35] Even then the enlisted men of the Massachusetts regiments remained in Dukakis's estimation: "Grand, yes, and strange, perhaps, but unwanted. . . . But not for long."[36] Here, Dukakis launched into an extended discussion of the more famous Fifty-Fourth Regiment whose bravery and sacrifice at Fort Wagner secured "the respect and admiration of those who had previously been among their detractors, including General Seymour."[37]

Dukakis used this extended history lesson for explaining the twentieth-century legacy of the Black men's sacrifice in his state. He shared his experiences during a visit to the Sgt. William H. Carney Memorial Academy in New Bedford, Massachusetts. He remarked on how the public school's racial demographics as "half Black and half white . . . and happily integrated" showed how the Black soldiers' sacrifice and death had not been in vain.[38] He attributed the success to the school's Black principal. This experience moved him to understand the weight of these Black soldiers who served in South Carolina and for those reburied at Beaufort National Cemetery. "As I stand here today, on the soil of South

Carolina where Sergeant Carney shed his blood, I see the face of Doctor Waters, and the faces of those eager and bright-eyed students at the Carney Academy," he concluded.[39]

In closing, Dukakis surmised that this educational legacy marked the future of how this Northern Black Civil War memory can inspire, heal, and shape future relations. He implored all to

> hear not only the voices of Massachusetts past, and the cannon of Fort Wagner, but the warm promise of our nation, of the blood of its men and women, Black and white, alive with a love of our beautiful land and with homes for a future of great promise—for those children at Carney Academy—and the children everywhere.[40]

His remarks received praise by the attendees and largely positive reception in the national media coverage.[41]

Following Dukakis's remarks, attention moved to the three rows of nineteen flag-draped coffins. Two descendants of the Massachusetts Fifty-Fourth and Fifty-Fifth Regiments assisted Governor Dukakis in laying a wreath. Other Massachusetts state officials placed small state flags next to the individual coffins. After a group of women placed Massachusetts soil in each coffin, two buglers played *Taps*, and the *Glory* film extras performed a forty-gun salute.[42]

George Coblyn, a descendant of Eli George Biddle of the Fifty-Fourth Massachusetts, saw the occasion as one of closure. The festivities reminded him of his attendance with his grandfather at the 1938 Blue and Gray reunion held in Gettysburg. When a white Confederate veteran shook the teenager's hand, he recalled the white Confederate veteran's words: "'I was looking to shoot you, and you were looking to shoot me. Thank God we both missed,' as their hands clasped together."[43] His grandfather died two years later at the age of ninety-four. "He [Biddle] was an inspiration to me," Coblyn shared with reporters.[44] While offering closure, the event also allowed the decorated World War II and Korean War veteran to share how the Civil War generation ensured the memory transmission on display that day: "Before he died, we used to march together in Memorial Day parades in Boston until I was 12 or 13. I wore a sailor suit my mother made and he'd always say, 'Stick your chest out! Be proud, be proud!'"[45] At this new Gettysburg-esque reunion held in South Carolina, the reinterment of the nineteen USCT coffins allowed Coblyn to introduce new audiences to his and the community's porch stories for understanding their experiences. In the process, the ceremony allowed descendants to redefine the 1913 and 1938 Gettysburg reunions of their Civil War ancestors as an inclusive Black Civil War tradition.[46] The active use of the *Glory* film extras not only added to the mood and reception of the reinterment ceremonies, but increased interest for the film later released in theaters.

Directed by Edward Zwick, the award-winning film dramatized the experiences of Robert Gould Shaw, the white commanding officer of the Fifty-Fourth Massachusetts regiment and his African American soldiers, from enlistment to their July 1863 assault on Fort Wagner. Matthew Broderick and Cary Elwes portrayed Colonel Shaw and Major Cabot Forbes respectively.[47] Despite calling the conflict "The War Between The States," the opening scenes evokes a white-savior narrative. Historian Gary Gallagher has suggested that "Shaw's voice-over from a letter written early in the war when he served with a white regiment from Massachusetts sets the tone (and also eliminates the complexity and racial ambiguity present in Shaw's correspondence)."[48] Broderick's portrayal added a layer of empathy for the underrecognized USCT regiment and the white commanding officers who led them. By commanding the all-Black volunteer regiment, viewers come to understand his personal wartime maturation from initial cowardice at Antietam, to questioning whether to accept the position to his willingness to risk bodily harm, to a refusal of military protocols by Confederate military who promised a different treatment for white officers of USCT regiments.[49]

While Broderick had the leading role, the talented cast of Black supporting actors firmly placed the film within the post-*Roots* cultural renaissance. Morgan Freeman, an award-winning actor, producer, and US Air Force veteran, played Sgt. Maj. John Rawlins. His character is introduced as a gravedigger burying the dead following Antietam and rousing an unconscious Shaw.[50] Andre Braugher, an award-winning actor, portrays Cpl. Thomas Searles, an educated Black Bostonian and abolitionist friend of Shaw and Forbes. Denzel Washington portrayed Pvt. Trip.[51] Relatively early in Washington's film career, *Glory* represented his second movie set during a war. In the critically acclaimed *A Soldier's Story* (1984), Washington played a villain in the World War II murder mystery set in a racially segregated Southern army base before departing for Europe.[52] Race and racism in the US military unified his roles. Washington's Oscar-winning role in *Glory* portrayed a self-liberating enlistee in the Fifty-Fourth Massachusetts.[53] In total, Zwick deployed 125 Civil War reenactors to provide historical accuracy. For Stanley Slater, the filming of *Glory* encouraged his own participation in the Memorial Day 1989 reburial at Beaufort National Cemetery. By developing "a personal connection with, and interest in, the men of this historic regiment," Slater later donated his uniform to the Smithsonian Museum and continued to educate in-terested audiences during reenactments and elementary school visits.[54]

Instead of drawing on known Fifty-Fourth Massachusetts soldiers and non-commissioned officers, most of the Black supporting cast played composite his-torical characters reflecting the diversity of the enlistees' backgrounds. Gerard Horne and other scholars questioned the decision and other storytelling licenses. Audiences did not seem to mind. The movie offered them an introduction to this previously unknown history absent from their K-12 education.[55] The film de-tailed the men's training struggles against racial discrimination at Camp Meigs, the Readville, Massachusetts, training camp. The film also highlighted their ra-cial and gendered pride as uniformed soldiers marching through the streets of Boston with cheers and Black women waving their handkerchiefs and the sights of Frederick Douglass and Governor John Andrew's celebrating their service. While not depicted, Douglass would have celebrated his own son's service in the regiment and another son who served in the Fifth Massachusetts Cavalry.[56] For Northern freeborn African Americans, the regiment's arrival in South Caro-lina lifted the veil on slavery and enslaved brethren whose liberation they fought for. For enslaved South Carolinians, the uniformed African American soldiers marked the coming of the jubilee long hoped and prayed for.[57] The regiment's cohesion and sense of civil-religious duty strengthened over early engagements at Darien, Georgia, and James Island, South Carolina, before the film concludes with the more well known Morris Island, South Carolina, on July 18, 1863.[58]

Before the fateful battle at Fort Wagner, songs, prayers, and an almost religious revival-esque atmosphere girded the courage of the Black soldiers who fought for freedom, manhood, and citizenship. The film turned to a discussion between Trip and Shaw who understood that the next day would most likely mark their deaths. And it did.[59] The film ended with Shaw, Trip, and other characters among the 272 men who were killed, wounded, and missing during the assault on Fort Wagner.[60] By dying for their understandings of the federal cause, soldiers and officers shared a common reality—burial in an unmarked open grave with no distinction made between race, class, or rank. When federal officials attempted to recover Shaw's remains, a Confederate officer responded: "We have buried him with his n*****s."[61] The film does not include this pejorative response; but viewers see Broderick and Washington being rolled into the mass grave. This lack of military honors in death now received a correction for the cinematic monument and the earlier reinterment ceremonies in Beaufort National Cem-etery. These men—Black and white—were heroes who had the support of the twentieth-century nation for their collective service, sacrifice, and commitment to building the perceived post-racial nation.[62] The film "reached far more people than any monograph could have" on the African American military experiences and contributions during the Civil War.[63] And this reality set into motion new scholarship, public commemorations, and monuments centered on the African American military experience and Civil War memory.

In the wake of the film and Memorial Day ceremonies, the national African American Civil War Memorial in Washington, DC, became one of the new commemorative additions. Its location embodied Black Civil War memory. Situated in a historic Black neighborhood named for Colonel Robert Gould Shaw, the new memorial was placed near Howard University, whose namesake was another Civil War general and Freedmen's Bureau commissioner Oliver Otis Howard. Beyond this symbolism, Black Fifty-Fourth Massachusetts reenactors and descendants added to the site dedication ceremony's gravitas.[64] When asked about his thoughts about the site dedication celebration, Richard Burbridge, a descendant of Sgt. Maj. Thomas Burbridge of the 114th USCT, reflected on the original May 1865 Grand Review of the Armies that excluded Black soldiers. Focusing on the delayed justice for USCT soldiers, Burbridge stated: "The story of the 185,000 soldiers is being told. That's the most important thing."[65] Marking the end of the first phase of the new monument, the National Park Service also used the occasion for the release of a searchable database of the names of Black soldiers and sailors, their respective regiment or unit, and brief regimental histories.[66] Within two years, the unveiling of the final bronze memorial occurred to much fanfare and approval by African American descendants, politicos, and general attendees of the culminating multi-day celebration. The unveiling events featured public lectures, parades, reenactments, and a memorial service at Arlington National Cemetery.[67] For those in attendance, the final memorial deserved the praise and its place alongside other Civil War monuments in the city.

Also known as the "The Spirit of Freedom," the African American Civil War Memorial, honors the over 200,000 soldiers and sailors who served in federal uniforms during the Civil War. "The Spirit of Freedom" was sculpted by Ed Hamilton. The base has an inscription acknowledging the USCT honorees. It reads: "Civil War to Civil Rights and Beyond. This Memorial is dedicated to those who served in the African Units of the Union Army in the Civil War. The 209,145 names inscribed on these walls commemorate those fighters of freedom."[68] On the granite walls with the honorees' names, another quote is inscribed. The text seamlessly continues with the sentiments expressed on the base. The named individuals served because, according to the Frederick Douglass, who is quoted here, "who would be free themselves must strike the blow, better even die free than to live slaves."[69] Featuring three uniformed USCT infantrymen and a sailor posed for action, Hamilton also included a home front scene of a soldier leaving his family for the defense of home, nation, and abolition.[70] By situating the monument in a neighborhood defined by the memorialization of two white Civil War generals viewed as significant allies, the monument and nearby museum that opened a year later made an important statement.[71] These ordinary USCT men deserved the same honor and respect as the white military freedom fighters. As such, monuments, museums, and other commemoration of the African American military contributions required equal footing. This set the stage for changes in Charleston and surrounding lowcountry.

By the late twentieth century, national post–Civil Rights Movement political and cultural developments ushered the return of a more inclusive Civil War commemorative understanding in Charleston. The Folly Beach discoveries, the blockbuster success of *Glory*, and the new national Civil War monument encouraged two important developments. The first involved the reintroduction of Mamie Garvin Fields as an important voice for understanding Black Civil War memory over the late nineteenth and twentieth centuries. The second saw the growth and normalization of Black Civil War reenactors. These legacies allowed for the reemergence and normalization of Black Civil War memory in Charleston, South Carolina.

In collaboration with her granddaughter sociologist Karen Fields (and sister of Civil War era historian Barbara Fields), Mamie Garvin Fields published her memoir in 1983. The project began as a series of letters written for Fields's granddaughters. As more African American families began documenting their histories, Karen Fields began recording the conversations with her grandmother during the late 1970s. The final memoir details Fields's experiences of growing up during the fading years of Reconstruction and implementation of the Lost Cause commemorative landscape in Charleston.[72]

Born in 1888, Mamie Garvin Fields stated how her Civil War memory and family remembrances of slavery, the Civil War, and Reconstruction shaped her adult life. She recalled how "anything that smelled of slavery" and "discrimination about color" brought rare expressions of anger from her mother.[73] Although attending the Robert Gould Shaw School, whose namesake infamously died at Fort Wagner, Fields found that her formal education resulted in a cognitive dissonance with her porch lessons. Unlike her Claflin High School classmates, "who had teachers of our race [and] came better prepared," Fields learned the "Rebel tradition" through required recitations of "Under the Blue and Gray" and the singing of "Dixie," "My Kentucky Home," and other pro–Lost Cause songs."[74]

If not for her cousin Anna Eliza, affectionately known as Lala, the Lost Cause–centered curriculum would have had different consequences. As a member of the first graduating class of Avery Normal Institute, Lala taught important lessons in Black history and Civil War countermemory at Miss Anna Eliza Izzard School.[75] By adopting a fugitive pedagogy, Fields recalled: "It was from her that I learned about slavery as our relatives had experienced it and what it meant. . . . She taught us how strong our ancestors back in slavery were and what fine people they were."[76] Coupled with these home lessons, Fields quickly understood how the implementation of Governor Ben Tillman's Jim Crow legislation "made friends into enemies overnight."[77]

Jim Crow and the public pro-Confederate culture gave impetus to Fields's activism. As a young girl, she challenged the daily slights from other white children as she traveled to and from school. Her strong reactions produced by seeing the John C. Calhoun monument reflected her rejection of the Lost Cause landscape.[78] Jim Crow and public Confederate culture contributed to her embrace of the Fourth of July celebration on the Battery, a seawall and promenade in Charleston, South Carolina. This annual Black countertradition featured food, community speeches, readings of the Emancipation Proclamation, and other pieces honoring Abraham Lincoln and Frederick Douglass, and collective singing of "The Battle Hymn of the Republic" and "Lift Ev'ry Voice and Sing."[79] "I don't think the Battery was ever so alive as on the Fourth," Fields remembered before adding after some thought, "Long years after emancipation, this special picnic was the Fourth of July to us."[80]

The consequences of the Black counter-commemorative resistance to Confederate public culture influenced Fields's own contributions to the fugitive pedagogy that empowered her Black students attending the Jim Crow–era schools. She embraced subtle empowering acts, such as teaching and having her students perform "America, the Beautiful," and challenged the UDC-friendly curriculum because her "school was in the United States, after all, and not the Confederacy."[81] Outside the classroom, Fields's clubwomen activism fought against all aspects of the racial logics embedded in the Confederate commemorative landscape in Jim Crow–era South Carolina. Adding authenticity to the Black Charlestonian experience, Fields's memoir also gained traction among scholars of slavery and Civil War memory for understanding the suppressed Black collective memory as a form of resistance.[82]

Interestingly, Charleston's overreliance on the tourist industry aided Fields's reintroduction to wider audiences. After *Roots* and *Glory*, African American tourists and others were interested in understanding the non-whitewashed Black experience in Charleston and the surrounding lowcountry. In the 1980s, two African American heritage tours pioneered an important shift. Robert Small and Alada Shinault-Small created the Living History Tours. Alphonso Brown began the Gullah Tours a few years later.[83] Drawing on both archival research and African American collective memories, these alternate tours brought Black memory from the margins and porches to diverse audiences.[84] Beyond these African American heritage tours, behind-the-big-house tours at area plantations, revised National Park Service interpretations of Forts Sumter and Moultrie, and the purchase of the Old Slave Mart Museum and McLeod Plantation by the city and the Charleston County Parks and Recreation Commission respectively brought nuance, inclusivity, and truthfulness to the area's past.[85] No longer confined to area porches, tourism has shaped the complex ways in which Charlestonians, white and Black, have remembered and at times purposefully forgotten the totality of its antebellum and Civil War pasts.

Yet tourism did not resolve all issues. Historians Ethan Kytle and Blain Roberts astutely point out the persistence of willful docents who ignore the revised scripts and the tours of the antebellum homes occurring without any discussion of slave housing and outbuildings unless probed. Some myths persist despite the 2011 revision of official tour guide training manual.[86] The industry remained available to tourists desiring either a whitewashed or more-inclusive cultural memory of slavery. The Folly Beach discoveries expanded the Charleston tourist industry's gaze to the African American perspective of the Civil War and not merely counternarratives of the city's slave past. In the process, tourists willingly purchased Fields's memoir as a souvenir.

In addition to Fields's reintroduction, the Charleston Civil War reenacting community diversified. Fearing another erasure, Black reenactors became a regular presence after the Beaufort reburial and the release of *Glory*. By donning the blue uniform, these men and women reinserted USCT history and collective remembrances into the Lost Cause stronghold and introduced new audiences to the African American experience. Like Black veterans who advocated the Won Cause over the nineteenth and early twentieth centuries, these reenactors served as living monuments who corrected myths through education, immersive reenactments, and ceremonial duties. They refuse to allow the collective forgetting of the rediscovered history. Through public performance, they naturalized Black Civil War understandings in the commemorative landscape.

Inspired by the film *Glory*, the formation of Company I, Fifty-Fourth Massachusetts Re-Enactment Regiment represented a significant development. White relic hunter turned amateur historian of the USCT regiments joined forces with

Joseph McGill in the early 1990s. National and local interest facilitated the emergence of the collective brotherhood that disrupted the predominantly white pastime.[87] A brief *Charleston Chronicle* announcement discussed the organizers' intent and encouraged anyone "interested in joining the newly formed unit" to attend a meeting held at the Fort Moultrie Visitor Center on Sullivan's Island.[88] Early members came from all over the state and not just the Charleston, South Carolina, lowcountry. Men and women, Black and white, wanted to deepen popular understandings of the essential role of Black Civil War soldiers. From these beginnings, the group of "living historians portraying brave Black Union troops who fought to end slavery" quickly made their presence felt in the Civil War commemorative landscape in and around Charleston.[89]

Living history events, specifically the annual Fort Wagner commemorations, allowed for sharing this history to diverse publics while preserving endangered Civil War battlefields against development and erosion. Donning their respective uniforms, white and Black enthusiasts re-created the July 1863 events. The participants also laid a wreath honoring the soldiers who died in the engagement. Joseph McGill, former Charleston Police Chief Reuben Greenburg, and other Company I, Fifty-Fourth Massachusetts reenactors also educated spectators. These living monuments ensured that next generations learned about Black Civil War memory and history.[90]

Early living history events also showed the diversity of the group. Fred Holsclaw, a Jewish reenactor who portrayed a white Company I Captain, participated alongside the predominantly Black reenacting group. Black women also portrayed women as nurses, seamstresses, and laundresses at these events.[91] By representing the other South and diverse USCT experience, they dispelled Lost Cause myths regarding African Americans, USCT military service, and white USCT officers.

In addition to the annual events, the Company I, Fifty-Fourth Massachusetts Re-Enactment Regiment has participated in major commemorations and monument unveilings around the state and region. Their presence at the 2001 dedication of the controversial African American History Monument in Columbia served as an attempt to smooth over tensions and fierce debate over the place of Black South Carolinians' contributions among the statuary promoting the Lost Cause, enslavers, and white supremacists on the State House grounds. In the process, the men became embroiled in another aspect of the Civil War culture war—the Confederate monument debates.

The contentious debate over the Confederate Battle Flag atop the South Carolina State House dome shaped the monument origins. Rallying around removal,

NAACP activists encouraged allies to boycott the state. Flag supporters decried the perceived outside interference. Civil War–era scholars even weighed in with their opinions about the fray.[92] In this moment, Black lawmakers saw an opportunity to establish a more permanent Black historical presence in the South Carolina State House commemorative landscape. When Governor David Beasley wanted a rural economic development bill, Darrell Jackson and Glenn McConnell found a suitable compromise. Together, the men built a biracial, bipartisan coalition. In supporting the monument, the coalition agreed that the Confederate battle flag could remain until another compromise saw the relocation from the State House dome to the Confederate soldier monument in 2000.[93] Republican John "Jake" Knotts of Lexington strongly objected to the quid quo pro deal. Under the guise of fairness, Knotts's anti-Black counterarguments of potential monuments to the Ku Klux Klan and other ethnic minorities angered both white and Black lawmakers alike while making McConnell seem like a moderate. After appealing to the public, Knotts stalled the entire economic platform of Governor Beasley over the proposed monument. This action prompted a special legislative session to resolve both the rural economic development and monument legislation.

The biracial, bipartisan coalition overcame the opposition. By separating the issues, procedural maneuvers secured passage. All state senators unanimously voted for the monument. With nineteen absent members, the House approved the measure in an 88–16 vote.[94] Celebrating the victory, Glenn McConnell captured the mood: "There are two great themes to South Carolina history: State's rights and civil rights. Both sides should be told."[95] Despite the flag remaining, the State House grounds would have a new monument devoted to the African American experience. However, not all South Carolinians celebrated the first of its kind monument.[96]

Black South Carolinians voiced their concerns and competing ideas over the project. Some desired Modjeska Simkins and other Black South Carolinians to be highlighted for their contributions to the modern Civil Rights Movement. Cleveland Sellers, a Civil Rights activist who served as the University of South Carolina (USC) African American Studies department chair, proposed Denmark Vesey and Robert Smalls. Sellers, a notable Civil Rights activist and survivor of the Orangeburg Massacre, however, wanted the final memorial to "reflect the true history of the struggle in South Carolina."[97] Others feared that a generic monument "that encompasses everything in African-Americans' past, present and future is too broad to have much meaning." Many raised a common concern about the most likely American exceptional narrative that would be told. [98]

USC Assistant Professor Ernest L. Wiggins leveled the clearest critique over the proposed monument. The African American professor of Journalism and Mass Communications saw the proposed monument as a misguided performative diversity measure. In terms of scope and possible reparative work, Wiggins felt the new State House Grounds memorial itself would be "woefully inadequate."[99] Wiggins instead suggested a different use of state funds—invest in community centers and organizations doing critical work. He felt that the proposed monument funding would be better served through increasing visibility of the Penn Center on St. Helena Island and transforming Modjeska Simkins House into a cultural center. "Such tributes would have greater resonance, for we best honor those who have gone before by respecting and protecting their most cherished legacy, their offspring," he wrote.[100] The monument legislation did not stop the debate within and outside the African American community. These differing opinions shaped the entire process and reception of the completed monument.

The commission charged with site selection and monument design reflected the partisan politics and competing interests at play. Of the four Republican members, one voted against the bill authorizing the monument creation. Another led the contentious fight to keep the Confederate Battle Flag atop the State House. Senate President Pro Tempore Glenn McConnell also supported the flag but became an unlikely ally in the monument vote and commission. The white Charleston attorney who also operated a Confederate memorabilia store bridged competing interests. With the flag debate temporarily out of the equation, McConnell worked across the aisle with Gilda Cobb-Hunter of Orangeburg, who played a significant role.[101] Monument bill sponsor, Darrell Jackson of Richland County also served alongside John Scott and McKinley Washington. As the ninth member, Governor Beasley appointed Jesse Washington, executive director of the Greater Columbia Human Rights Council. Competing interests and partisan politics defined all remaining aspects of the monument building process.[102]

Holding six public hearings, the commission sought community input throughout the state. The commission also considered other Black heritage projects of interest to individual members. In contemplating an African American museum in Charleston, members debated its merits while considering which era—either pre-1865 history or the Civil Rights Movement history—should be the focus of the proposed museum.[103] After the careful review of forty-six submissions received, the commission selected Ed Dwight, an African American sculptor who designed a Hank Aaron statue for the Atlanta Braves stadium. They, however, disagreed over the design. Specific references to Denmark Vesey's attempted rebellion were removed. A panel featuring hooded Klansman lynching

Black South Carolinians and other aspects of the Jim Crow era were toned down to include only words and phrases of the major developments. With the moderated design, the South Carolina legislators approved the memorial, and the next phase of construction and fundraising began in earnest.[104]

Unlike other State House monuments and statuary, private donations and corporate sponsorships funded the $1.2 million dollar project. Legislators gave no state appropriations. Subsequent memorials followed the funding precedent established by the African American History Monument.[105] A fundraising blitz kicked off the funding drive during the groundbreaking ceremony. Contributions came in from all over the state. BMW and the South Carolina legislative Black Caucus gave the maximum donation of $25,000. Most donations were more modest. W. G. Saunders Middle School students gave slightly over $500.[106] While some Blacks and whites complained about the funding process, the Columbia monument attracted diverse funders, large and small, white and Black. The project moved forward. The project overcame weather-related delays, partisan politics, and persistent criticism from both white and Black South Carolinians.[107]

After the contentious and racialized debates over the State House grounds and monument, the dedication was a grand spectacle. Attendees, participants, and politicians emphasized the event as one of healing and a possible end to the Civil War cultural wars. Even Republican Governor Jim Hodges encouraged South Carolinians to embrace the new memorial. The Company I, Fifty-Fourth Massachusetts Re-Enactment Regiment had a major role in the ceremony. The men proudly presented the colors. Recalling the burning of the original State House, Black reenactor Marvin Nicholson understood the significance of his involvement and the monument. "This just proves for me the complexities and the intricacies of our state. Just a few months ago, we were going through this thing with the flag. Today we're dedicating the monument," Nicholson told reporters.[108] African American poet Nikky Finney delivered an inspiring poem written for the occasion, tracing the history rendered visible in bronze. But as the daughter of South Carolina Supreme Court Justice Ernest Finney, she kissed his bronze likeness during the unveiling.[109] Ed Dwight, the sculptor, who was in attendance, remarked how the memorial "was a story that had to be told."[110] Indeed, newspapers extensively described the ceremony, location, the panels, and the overall scale of the monument itself. It was a rare celebration embraced by most South Carolinians.[111]

The final monument captivated. The completed memorial is impressive in scale and scope. A twenty-three-foot-tall obelisk is flanked by two twenty-five-foot curved granite walls that hold twelve bronze panels. In front of the obelisk and panels, visitors encounter a re-creation of the slave ship *Brookes* with slightly raised bronze hull embedded in the foreground. Without glossing over the means of transportation, visitors then engage with a counter-height platform that has an engraved map of where most Black South Carolinians originated in Africa. Representing Senegal, Sierra Leone, Ghana, and the Republic of Congo, the Dwight wanted visitors to touch the four stones, view the accompanying map, and gain a deeper appreciation of Black South Carolinians' African roots visually and physically.[112]

Two plaques adorn the obelisk. The front plaque recognized the artist, memorial title, and the dedication year. On the opposite side, the second plaque list the names of commission members, relevant sub-committee members and their dedication of the monument to the "people of South Carolina." On the two granite walls, the twelve bronze bas-reliefs depict important scenes from shackled slaves on the auction block to important twentieth-century Black South Carolinians. On several panels, Dwight carved bronze figures that come away from the wall as if they were stepping out of the past into the present.[113]

Black understandings of the Civil War and its aftermath anchor the historical narrative told in the carved bronze panels. Beginning with Black South Carolinians' arrival, the last three panels of the first carved flank celebrate the Civil War era. Black men planned their path toward freedom. Huddled in a slave cabin, the freedom seekers' intent becomes clearer in the next panel depicting the First South Carolina Volunteer Infantry (later renamed the Thirty-Third USCT) in a full charge led by a Black sergeant.[114] Often inviting floral tributes on his pronounced kepi, the flagbearer's gaze reveals a steely determination and pride in carrying the regimental colors. Dwight's sculpture captured his grizzled full beard, intense countenance, and firm grip on the flagstaff. The final panel signaled the result of the Black soldiers' martial manhood. Broken shackles, jubilant shouts, and praying men and women celebrate their emancipation and their answered prayers of a federal victory.[115]

The opening panel of the second curved section depicted Black political power realized during the Reconstruction era. Given the monument's proximity to the USC campus, more informed visitors would connect the power of the Black political majority that brought biracial, inclusive democracy to the flagship university. Even with the moderated design, the next panel made clear the violent closure of this brief period in state history. The remaining four panels moved through the twentieth century from the Great Migration to the renowned Black South Carolinians who made their mark in the judiciary, athletics, music, and space exploration.[116] By referencing "lambswool hair blowing like liberation flags," Nikky Finney's dedication poem acknowledged the centrality of the Civil War era in the final bronze memorial: "We were never slaves. We were enslaved."[117] The Civil War broke the cycle of slavery and changed the course of history and the lived experienced of Black South Carolinians. Most praised this commemorative narrative told.

Nevertheless, controversy still shaped the dedication. Cobb-Hunter boycotted the affair. A last-minute change to the commission composition meant the addition of Sen. Robert Ford's name on the monument plaque. Yet the Charleston Democrat had a minimal role.[118] As a Black woman, Cobb-Hunter tapped into the tradition established by previous generations of Black women who built both physical and living Civil War monuments. Like previous Black women's monument work, Cobb-Hunter solicited funds, regardless of the amount, from schools, African American church congregations, and Black neighborhoods. She campaigned among white colleagues who never respected her presence due to her race, gender, and urban legislative district. After planning every detail of the dedication ceremony, including the presence of the USCT reenactment regiment, her boycott should not be read in the frame of the angry Black woman trope. Rather, it reflected her refusal to allow politics to shape future understandings of the monumental achievement, secure future electoral votes from constituents, and in the process, trivialize her work by including the last-minute commission addition on the permanent plaque naming the commission members. For Cobb-Hunter, the political power play undermined the process. While McConnell applauded her service, he approved the late commission addition and revised the plaque listing the names of both Cobb-Hunter and Ford. McConnell contributed to the continued undercutting of Black women's memory work in the turn of the twenty-first century.[119]

While an important step to African American commemorative culture, neither the monument nor the presence of the Black reenactment regiment at the dedication could compete with the dominant narratives celebrating the Lost Cause, white supremacy, and other uncritical understandings of the African American experience on the State House grounds. Scholar Lydia M. Brandt astutely surmised that the African American History Monument does not "directly confront these other monuments in its design or narrative."[120] While adding diversity, the monument had existed in perpetual tension with the fraught commemorative landscape. It is tucked into the lower slope of the State House grounds. Although substantial in height, Confederate and other racial exclusionary monuments still dwarf it. The Confederate flag flew until 2015. Dwight's monument could not fully correct the State House grounds. The South Carolina

State House grounds remain a shrine to white supremacy and the Lost Cause.[121] The process of remaking the pro–Lost Cause, white supremacist landscape has been difficult, fraught, and inadequate in resolving a long history of erasure and selective remembrances.

Despite the controversy surrounding this early Company I, Fifty-Fourth Massachusetts Re-Enactment Regiment event, the unit focused on educating students, adults, scholars, and non-academics. Reenactors visited area schools. They traveled and participated in events where the Fifty-Fourth Massachusetts served. Acknowledging their expensive hobby, these activities enabled "them to fill a void in the history books."[122] On St. Helena Island, the group participated in a reenactment of the court-martial of Sgt. William Walker of the Third South Carolina Volunteer Infantry for leading a mutiny of Black soldiers "who refused to serve without equal pay" at the "Liberation of Port Royal, S.C.—A Civil War Reenactment" held at the Penn Center.[123] For this portion of the two-day October 1996 living history event, the group developed the script using the trial record, Civil War regulations, and other documents. Instead of donning his Confederate uniform, State Sen. Glenn McConnell performed Walker's legal defense at the re-creation of the federal court-martial.[124]

During the Charleston County Library's Magical History Tour, eight reenactors participated in a Black History Month event. They educated visitors about the role of the Massachusetts regiment in the Civil War from the lawn of the St. Andrew regional library. In one instance, captured by the *Post and Courier* photographer, a nine-year-old Black youth handed back a historic rifle to a Fifty-Fourth Massachusetts reenactor.[125] When asked about their craft, James Brown, a Sol Legare, South Carolina, reenactor, acknowledged the rarity of the Black reenactors and their purpose. "What we're trying to do is educate our white brothers and sisters on the history on the black soldiers. What they did enabled me to be here," Brown answered.[126] At a Black History Month event that showcased Gullah musical performers, African drummers, and a local hip hop group, the reenacting regiment kept the history alive and staved off another erasure in the local and national collective memory of the Civil War.[127]

On July 16, 2010, Company I, Fifty-Fourth Massachusetts reenactors marked the 147th anniversary of the Battles of Sol Legare Island and Fort Wagner. The group set up their tents off of Sol Legare Road for part of the day. Before the Battle of Fort Wagner, the regiment saw fourteen killed in action and twenty-nine wounded or missing in one of its first major Civil War engagements.[128] The celebration also included a short boat ride to Morris Island. Unlike earlier events, attendees paid a modest admission charge for events commemorating

Fort Wagner. On this day, roughly ten reenactors honored the soldiers killed by laying a wreath. They educated attendees on this history and "talked with dozens of people who turned out to celebrate a special chapter of black history that played out several miles from downtown Charleston."[129]

Discussions surrounding the sesquicentennial swirled around the July humid air. Most noted how the celebration would be different from the centennial celebration. Instead of a form of counterprotest, Black Civil War memory would be incorporated as part of the celebration.[130] The restored Seashore Farmers Lodge No. 176 would attract eager attendees who wanted to view the old National Park Service diorama depicting the historic assault on Confederate forces at Fort Wagner. The James Island, South Carolina African American history museum and cultural center planned to have a central role in the upcoming celebration.[131] For Joseph McGill, the group's upcoming events carried a different meaning. "We will not be relegated to the back pages of history. We will not be a footnote," he proclaimed.[132] Indeed, his bold prediction came true. Charleston and the surrounding lowcountry experienced a Civil War anniversary unlike all previous ones. Revised historical scholarship, the Folly Beach USCT archaeological discovery, a more inclusive reenactment community, and new audiences demanded a different celebration. The restored Black Civil War memory encouraged more complete public understandings and debate over how to remember the conflict and its legacy.[133]

On February 11, 2021, hell froze over. South Carolina Governor Henry McMaster and State Representative Spencer Wetmore, a Folly Beach Democrat, awarded Robert Bohrn the Order of the Silver Crescent. His accidental discovery proved sufficient for receiving one of the highest civilian honors in South Carolina, but it also rewrote history in the recent Civil War memory culture war.[134]

The Charleston white power structure minimized this initial discovery because it was not part of the Lost Cause narrative packed for tourists. It was not convenient to fully recognize these African American veterans, their Northern regiment origins, and contributions to the Civil War. The CSS *Hunley* and the Lost Cause mattered more. The success of *Glory* and the Beaufort reburial as well as changing historical narratives contributed to the dislodging of non–Lost Cause understandings up until the sesquicentennial.

Black Civil War understandings had regained their original standing. Even so, the CSS *Hunley* and Lost Cause understanding retain a foothold, albeit a less firm one, in the Charleston public memory. The sesquicentennial, as will be discussed in the next chapter, revealed a more diverse but not quite unified Civil

War memory in Charleston and the Palmetto State. Black Civil War understandings were no longer relegated to the margins or easily erased.

Amid the mishandling of the COVID-19 pandemic, Governor McMaster's Black History Month performative action only mentioned the Massachusetts regiment and not the North Carolina USCT regiment also discovered in this mass grave. In this recasting, Bohrn became the sole hero of the narrative. The state archaeologists, entire excavation team, and even Bohrn's companion in the 1987 relic-hunting adventure received no mention.[135] The process of reburial, including the absence of white South Carolina political elite and Governor Michael Dukakis's stirring Memorial Day speech were either glossed over or erased. Rather, Bohrn and his Friends of the 55th Massachusetts foundation get the accolades for the 1987 discovery and 2011 placement of a historical marker recognizing the USCT soldiers in the Folly River Park.[136] In his remarks, Governor McMaster proclaimed: "You're quite deserving of this recognition."[137]

Ironically, Bohrn expressed concern for the preservation of history, including his fateful rediscovery of USCT cemetery on Folly Island. "You can't forget history. These men didn't have a whole lot to gain but a whole lot to lose," Bohrn told local reporters. "They gave their lives for not just the Union, but also their families. Their contributions are not recognized as much as they should be."[138] And yet the 2021 ceremony and media coverage did just that. The African American men, the archaeologist team, and Black Charleston lowcountry efforts, did not fit the white savior narrative promoted. For McMaster, he could accept this white relic hunter as an ally. He bestowed on him the honorific of "historian" while presenting the state honor. Ignorance and escapism might have convinced some uninformed readers and ceremony attendees. For African Americans and their white allies, however, they saw through the lies and myths. McMaster could have learned from Massachusetts Governor Dukakis who thirty-two years earlier, expressed a call to the nation to honor the USCT men as national heroes who did not need contemporary white saviors. Instead, McMaster issued the terms for the next phase of the Civil War culture wars on the eve of the 160th anniversary in Charleston and the state.

8

"More Than a
Footnote" during the
Sesquicentennial

On the eve of the sesquicentennial commemoration of July 1863 events,
a *Charleston City Paper* reporter raised an important question with
Joseph McGill, the African American co-founder of the Company I,
Fifty-Fourth Massachusetts Reenactment Regiment.[1] After 150 years, the reporter asked: "Why continue to rehash a terrible time in our nation's history,
rather than let it be forgotten?"[2] Remembering the previous major Civil War
anniversary, McGill responded: "At the centennial, African Americans were still
fighting for our own rights."[3] Fifty years earlier, Charleston journalists would not
have asked an African American for his opinion on the events. If asked, Mc-
Gill's perspective would have been rejected outright in a city and state whose
officials doubled down on pro-Confederate understandings amid the national
Civil Rights Movement. Rejecting the Lost Cause understandings, Charleston
organizers, journalists, and historians drew on twentieth-first-century Reconciliationist understandings of the Civil War. McGill, his predominantly Black
Civil War reenactment group, and twenty-first-century Black Civil War memory
understandings had an essential role in the sesquicentennial commemoration,
which encouraged fuller, inclusive, and more truthful understandings of the
causes of war and its immediate aftermath.

The Civil War centennial legacy loomed over the entire commemoration.
Some rejected the inclusive commemoration. Some white Charlestonians clung
to the pro-Confederate sentiments. Challenging the city's efforts, a private gala
celebrated the sesquicentennial anniversary of the South Carolina declaration of
secession. Despite this early controversy, the Fort Sumter–Fort Moultrie Trust
and Charleston organizers laid the foundation for a Civil War commemoration
unlike any other previous ones held in South Carolina. The April 2011 celebration
recognized the diversity of the Civil War experiences but not without some Black
South Carolinians' reluctance to accept the inclusive sesquicentennial goals. The
2013 Fort Wagner anniversary continued the historic commemoration with the
full embrace of the post-*Roots* and *Glory* developments in the Charleston lowcountry. African American Civil War memory received its proper recognition

in a city once committed to the Lost Cause. This public stage of the once marginalized Black Civil War memory influenced the concluding Nat Fuller's Feast
in 2015. Controversy again arose when some questioned the historic record of
whether the reconciliation dinner occurred in spring 1865.

Previous controversies were minor in comparison; the horrific Charleston
Massacre dampened the seemingly successful four-year Civil War commemoration. The murder of nine African Americans marred collective understandings
of the sesquicentennial celebration. As African American reenactor Joseph Mc-
Gill predicted, Black Civil War memory would be "more than a footnote" during
the sesquicentennial celebration in Charleston and the surrounding lowcountry.[4]

After race had a defining role during the 1961 centennial, Charleston sought
redemption during the Fort Sumter sesquicentennial. White commentators recalled how Jim Crowism led to a showdown between pro-segregationist Charlestonians against the pro–Civil Rights Movement Kennedy administration over
the treatment of Madaline Williams, one of three African Americans who served
in statewide Civil War Centennial Commissions. By shifting a meeting from the
segregated Francis Marion Hotel to the federal naval base, white Charlestonians
used politicized Lost Cause understandings of Fort Sumter in their pro-segrega-
tion and pro–state rights' defense against the perceived federal encroachment.[5]
Now, Charleston organizers, journalists, and historians intentionally drew on
inclusive understandings of Civil War memory promoted by the federal government. Instead of a foe, the National Park Service (NPS) became a major ally in
the sesquicentennial commemoration.

The Civil War sesquicentennial lacked a national commission. While lessons from the centennial commemoration most likely informed this decision,
the reality of an African American president of the United States and racialized
partisan politics over a national health care plan further complicated the possibility of a dedicated national committee. As a result, NPS coordinated a patchwork of events with local and state organizations under the Rally on the High
Ground mandates. Starting with the April 2011 commemoration of Fort Sumter,
Charleston organizers' vision drew heavily on the revised federal public interpretations. Specifically, they no longer denied that slavery lay at the root cause
of the Civil War.[6]

The post–Civil Rights Movement political realities forced redress of previous
intentional silences and collective forgetting at NPS Civil War battlefields. After
visiting several NPS Civil War sites, Illinois Congressman and House Appropriations Committee Chair Jesse L. Jackson Jr. directed Secretary of the Interior

Bruce Babbitt, who oversaw the NPS, "to encourage Civil War battle sites to recognize and include in all of their public displays and multimedia educational
presentations the unique role that the institution of slavery played in causing the
Civil War."[7] By offering a more truthful and fuller narrative of the Civil War, Jackson saw the NPS as performing the necessary work of "build[ing] a more perfect
union for all Americans" while preserving the endangered Civil War battlefields.[8]

The resulting NPS Rally on the High Ground report and symposium was
more than a self-congratulatory checking off a box. It became a reflective framework for moving forward. In his introduction, Robert Sutton briefly explored
how the previous Reconciliationist impulse allowed for the collective forgetting
and intentional erasure of slavery as a cause of the Civil War and the role of African American soldiers. "So, the war was over, the nation was healing itself, but
the country had defaulted on its down payment toward emancipating the former
slaves," he argued.[9] The federal agency acknowledged the centrality of slavery to
the Civil War. It acknowledged the motivations of Black soldiers, families, and
communities as being more unified in their focus on freedom, abolition, and
full citizenship. For white Americans, however, the agency promised a more nuanced portrayal of the various motivations than previously presented. Gender,
class, ethnicity, education, and regional attitudes mattered.[10] In this regard, the
final report and its published scholarly essays "serve as a primer to help develop
a new paradigm for interpreting our Civil War battlefields."[11] From the centrality
of slavery to more intersectional understandings of the combatants' motivations,
the assembled scholars offered ways to reinterpret the Civil War that appealed to
existing NPS visitors and potential new audiences who had been uninterested in
previous NPS interpretations.[12]

As stewards of these American resources, NPS affirmed the federal government's commitment to more truthful storytelling of the nation's Civil War past.
As co-partners with Charleston and state agencies, moreover, NPS represented
federal government's sesquicentennial interests without a national commission.
The decentralized commemoration, however, did not prevent a showdown over
states' rights, federal intervention, and the collective public meaning of the Civil
War in Charleston, South Carolina.[13]

The privately funded December 2010 Secession Ball soundly rejected the neo-
Reconciliationist federal framework for the Charleston sesquicentennial commemoration. At a $100 per person, co-organizers Confederate Heritage Trust
and the Sons of Confederate Veterans planned a gala featuring a play dramatiz-
ing the historic signing, period dancing, and a dinner at the Gaillard Municipal
Auditorium.[14] When criticized by the National Association for the Advancement

of Colored People (NAACP) and others, organizers took pains to reassure South Carolinians that they celebrated heritage instead of the purported claims of slavery, white supremacy, and anti-American sentiments. The verbal sparring also brought national attention. Organizers retreated by not responding to media requests and finalizing plans.[15] When the anniversary celebration occurred, the Secession Ball had been reduced to a fundraiser where "heritage and not hate" Confederate rhetoric attracted more than four hundred ticket purchasers.[16]

The planned NAACP protest allowed organizers to play the role of the aggrieved victims. Familiar neo–Lost Cause talking points framed the local and state media coverage. Under the guise of heritage, organizers turned the event from a contested debate over states' rights versus federal overreach into a debate over racial politics.[17] Despite being organized by Charleston and state NAACP members, the white Lost Cause event proponents decried the perceived outside agitators who sought to force their notions of political correctness onto individuals merely celebrating their Confederate heritage. Some even claimed both-sides-ism arguments in an attempt to regain the high ground.[18] Collectively, Secession Ball proponents' arguments represented the eight characteristics of Confederate rhetoric defined by scholar Stephen M. Monroe. They hoped to neutralize the concerted diversity efforts of the Civil War sesquicentennial commemoration by claiming a space for their neo–Lost Cause celebration. But the tone and acrimonious nature of the pro–Secession Ball arguments, however, failed to convince others.[19]

Event organizers failed to grasp how much had changed. The Lost Cause no longer had its hegemonic foothold in the city, even among some local white Charlestonians. Both the post-*Roots* and *Glory* cultural realities wrought a more inclusive Civil War commemorative landscape. White South Carolinians agreed with the NAACP. Capturing the feelings of many, one *Charleston City Paper* columnist challenged a local radio personality's defense of the private event:

> I don't know about you, but when a group is hosting a bash to "celebrate" the secession of South Carolina—and by extension the start of the Civil War— well, it's not too difficult to see why the civil rights organization, not to mention the Holy City's black population and most of its white one as well, would take issue with it.[20]

City political leaders concurred. Charleston Mayor Joseph Riley questioned the Sons of Confederate Veterans (SCV) publicity stunt that might jeopardize the city's planned April 2011 commemoration of Fort Sumter. Riley publicly declared: "I won't be going."[21] After calling the planned private gala "unfortunate," Riley then reminded press conference attendees how the Secession Ball was not "a sanctioned event," but "a private activity."[22] He and others distanced themselves from the December celebration. For these white Charlestonians, the Secession Ball represented a relic of its Civil War commemorative past and not its future.

NPS and Fort Sumter-Fort Moultrie Trust co-partners also reinforced the Charleston mayor's commitment to a redemptive sesquicentennial celebration. The latter organization issued a public statement declaring that it had "not supported or contributed to the Secession Ball as the Trust does not see it as part of its mission."[23] The trust president even pledged a willingness to "work with groups in a constructive manner" when pressed by the media.[24] An NPS representative affirmed its Rally on the High Ground framework by pledging "a different commemoration" than the centennial.[25] In response to the Secession Ball, the sesquicentennial coalition presented a united front in their opposition of the divisive pro–Lost Cause commemoration.

Black South Carolinians also challenged the Secession Ball organizers. Warren Bolton, African American editorialist for *The State*, rejected the neo–Lost Cause event. In his "What's There to Celebrate" editorial, Bolton captured the attitudes of Black South Carolinians and their white allies in the opening: "I just don't get it. And I never will."[26] He then proceeded to raise a series of questions for all South Carolinians to consider when coming to terms with the strong African American reaction to the proposed event. He pointedly asked:

> What's so joyous about a state that thrived off the enslavement and degradation of human beings deciding to withdraw from a contract to living under a common union just to continue those mean-spirited, malicious and evil acts? What's there to dance about? What's there to celebrate? What, pray tell, is there to get dressed up and prance around about? What's there to be proud of?[27]

In the rest of the editorial, Bolton summarily debunked arguments for holding the controversial commemorative event. While agreeing that the day should be noted by South Carolinians, Bolton strongly disagreed with the entire premise. "But the folks who assemble in Charleston won't be just whistling 'Dixie' as they dance to it," he concluded before adding, "They're romanticizing a period of this state's history that should not be romanticized and, in the process, continuing the fantasy that slavery was not the cornerstone of secession."[28] Thus he rejected the

Lost Cause fantasy rooted in "fabrications" as the start of the important sesqui-centennial commemoration.[29]

On the actual anniversary, Bolton again questioned the neo-Confederate gala. By creating "more wedges between our people," event organizers and not the pre-dominantly Black NAACP protesters had acted in bad faith.[30] Bolton hoped that future sesquicentennial events would allow the "sons of slave owners and sons of slaves to come together to rebuild, redirect and resurrect South Carolina."[31] In-stead of debating the history of the original secession ordinance, Secession Ball, and the causes of the Civil War, Bolton saw the controversy as an opportunity for building a better and more just South Carolina.

Although most attention focused on the NAACP protest, African American public opinion was mixed. Instead of protesting the event, one Black Orange-burg resident suggested that Black South Carolinians should concentrate on planning upcoming pro–Black Civil War commemorations. Alluding to the 2013 Fort Wagner commemoration, he felt that NAACP and Black South Carolin-ians should not worry over the Secession Ball but rather focus their energy on these later events.[32] One former HBCU professor living in Lexington called for continuing the moral path toward reconciliation and racial healing by resolving the "unfinished business."[33] Divergent opinions over tactics always existed. They had been previously ignored by white South Carolinians or confined to the Black counter-public sphere. The sesquicentennial merely allowed for a more public airing of diverse Black perspectives to wider audiences. The pro–Lost Cause cel-ebration produced mixed emotions in a weary African American community.

Historians have discussed the various consequences of the Secession Ball con-troversy over the April 2011 commemoration of Fort Sumter and other sesquicen-tennial events. Some have discussed how nonacademic Americans' ambivalence and opposition resulted in an underwhelming sesquicentennial commemora-tion. They questioned whether the NPS framework and the focus on slavery and emancipation contributed to the ambivalence by some and opposition by others.[34] Some focused on the overall tone of the Fort Sumter commemoration and multi-year celebration in comparison to the centennial celebration. Unlike the centennial that "repackaged the bloody struggle into a noble fight," historian Ethan Kytle characterized the Fort Sumter events as "sober, reflective, and inclu-sive."[35] Yet white Americans' ambivalence encouraged a change in the NPS com-memoration theme amid the actual commemoration from "Holding the High Ground" to "Civil War to Civil Rights."[36]

When one considers Black South Carolinians' diverse responses, another pic-ture emerges. Fort Sumter coalition organizers failed to account for how much

Black collective memory of the centennial commemoration would shape their response to the sesquicentennial commemoration. While anticipating neo–Lost Cause criticism, few organizers and local media expected African American hesitancy and refusal to participate in the April 2011 commemorative events. Reconciliation of this Civil War past and the Secession Ball fallout required time and community-building and not merely promises of a more diverse commemoration. In the weeks between the Secession Ball and the April 12, 2011, commemoration, the various events, media coverage, and lack of targeted community relations sowed the seeds for the African Americans' mixed responses, including their decisions to stay home.

Following the Secession Ball, concerns over the April 2011 commemoration prompted another debate: Should President Barack Obama attend or not? Organizers proposed this idea during an early spring 2010 meeting. Mayor Joseph Riley extended the invitation. However, fallout from the December private gala renewed debate out of concern for potential violence surrounding the presence of the first African American president. One white *Charleston City Paper* journalist feared that his presence would prompt an "'incident' that would embarrass the state and haunt the city for years to come."[37] He understood the possible outcome of the fraught optics. Even for the pro-diverse sesquicentennial ally, he argued that the "image of a black president from a Northern state gazing out over Fort Sumter and delivering an elegy to Abraham Lincoln might be too much for some susceptible minds to endure."[38] Drawing on lessons from American history of mass shootings in the twentieth and early twenty-first century, he encouraged the president to "stay away on April 12."[39] The fallout of the Secession Ball, political rancor, and the specter of the Civil War centennial past allowed for such pleas out of concern over possible violence by neo–Lost Cause South Carolinians willing to resurrect the April 1961 ghosts. By appealing to these extreme white sentiments, however, his words and overall tenor of media coverage over the potential Obama presence in April 2011 shaped Black Charlestonians' attendance.

In the weeks leading to the anniversary, the *Post and Courier* introduced readers to revised interpretations of local Civil War history. Between December 12, 2010, and April 24, 2011, the newspaper published a twenty-installment series written by Brian Hicks.[40] Often prominently featured on the front page, the various "Civil War: 150 Years" columns covered an array of topics from secession and the firing on Fort Sumter to the Battle of Fort Wagner, sinking of the CSS *Hunley*, and the fall of the city.[41] Hicks also wrote non-series articles. One discussed the centrality of slavery and the domestic slave trade in the city and surrounding lowcountry plantations. Another explored a twenty-first-century reunion between two descendants whose Civil War ancestors served on opposing sides during the Battle of Secessionville on James Island.[42] By publishing these pieces, the *Post and Courier* educated readers on why they should care about the Civil War and engage with the sesquicentennial commemorations beginning with the April 12, 2011, anniversary of the firing on Fort Sumter.

The weekly independent *Charleston City Paper* also attempted to salvage the April 2011 commemoration after the Secession Ball controversy. Notably, the April 6 special issue of the *Charleston City Paper* educated the broader Charleston area public on the event, and the consequences for the city, state, and nation in a series of articles. From its graphic cover to its title, the independent weekly moved educational strategy from the traditional *Post and Courier* subscription readers to the masses who read the free publication. Several personal pieces appealed to white Charlestonians who either rejected or remained ambivalent about the planned celebration. Daniel Gidick, a high school teacher and Palmetto Guard reenactor, encouraged readers' participation in the planned events. He recognized the answers to the pressing question "What do we hope to accomplish from this observance?" was "different, as different, perhaps, as to why each man fought during the Civil War."[43] Gidick hoped that education and reflection could bridge previous divisions and push toward a better future.[44] Regular contributor Chris Haire shared his personal journey as an ex-neo-Confederate to having a more nuanced understanding of his grandfather and those who weaponized the Confederate battle flag under the mantle of "heritage not hate."[45]

Other *Charleston City Paper* articles provided fresh insights into how the Charleston elite and newspaper editors responded to the firing on Fort Sumter. One article explored the elite white Charlestonians who chose to seek refuge in Flat Rock, North Carolina. Their class privilege exempted the Charlestonians and other white Southerners who found refuge with some of their slave property in the Blue Ridge Mountains. They benefited from military protection against their white neighbors who viewed them with suspicion and anger.[46] Instead of an idyllic sanctuary, white Charlestonians craved news from home when Flat Rock became "almost entirely cut off from the rest of the Confederacy."[47] By exploring the *Charleston Mercury* editorial stance on the eve of the Civil War, Greg Hambrick also made explicit the role of slavery in the conflict. He reminded readers, using their own words, of the paper's April 11, 1861, article predicting the sectional war as "proof of the earnestness of our intentions and our manhood. Experience shall be their teacher. Let them learn."[48] Through these two pieces, Hambrick laid out two core principles of the NPS Rally on the High Ground framework to diverse readers. White Southern responses were more complex than previously understood. The centrality of slavery was not a myth crafted by revisionist scholars, but a cause clearly understood at the time of the conflict by the Charleston editors and reading public.

Michael Smallwood's piece showed how the afterlives of slavery shaped later public understandings at the Old Slave Mart Museum. Historians Ethan Kytle and Blain Roberts have shown how the original museum served as the pet project of Miriam P. Wilson. When she died, two white women kept Wilson's Lost Cause mission alive before selling the museum to the city in 1987. Under new management, the museum reopened with more truthful understandings of the institution than the previous Lost Cause public interpretation.[49] Smallwood encouraged readers to not shy away from the history of the domestic slave trade. "If we don't expose that scar to fresh air," Smallwood closed with the ominous warning, "it will never heal properly."[50] He therefore encouraged readers to visit the Old Slave Mart during the Fort Sumter sesquicentennial programming.

Appealing to nonacademic audiences, the *Charleston City Paper* informed its readers of other less esoteric events. The musical *Civil War Voices* dramatized "both sides of the historic conflict."[51] Several local galleries and museums showcased the works of African American artist Leo Twiggs, ex-Confederate soldier turned painter Conrad Wise Chapman, and restored Library of Congress photographic images of Charleston during the Civil War.[52] By highlighting these events, the special issue coverage helped to curry favor with the non–*Post and Courier* reading public who might not have attended the various sesquicentennial events.[53]

The Lowcountry Civil War Sesquicentennial Observance officially opened on April 8, 2011, with a series of events. The Fort Sumter-Fort Moultrie Historical Trust, in conjunction with the NPS and the Fort Sumter National Monument, sponsored a multi-day lecture series where scholars reflected on the diverse motivations and attitudes of Americans who decided their allegiances and level of Civil War engagement whether on the home front or battlefield. Each academic lecture also drove home the centrality of slavery to the conflict. St. Stephen's Episcopal Church saw remarks made by historians Catherine Clinton and Stephen Berry before a moderated discussion led by Amy McCandless.[54] The following night featured the public viewing of the first two episodes of the Ken Burns documentary at the Fort Johnson Marine Center on James Island. African American historian Daniel Littlefield moderated a discussion focused on John Brown's Raid with author Tony Horwitz and his work *Midnight Rising* at a Jewish synagogue in Charleston.[55] On the eve of the sesquicentennial celebration of the firing on Fort Sumter, Robert H. Dallek moderated a panel discussion with Edward Ayers and Emory Thomas at the First Scots Presbyterian Church in Charleston. The final lecture was delivered by noted Civil War historian James McPherson at the Gibbes Museum of Art. Vernon Burton gave the introductions while Marcus Cox served as moderator for the later discussion. Through the choice of locations, featured speakers, and themes, this portion of the Charleston sesquicentennial marked a significant departure from the centennial celebration. Diversity mattered.[56]

Charleston officially marked the actual anniversary with two grand events. The first observance occurred in the early hours of April 12, 2011, from the location where one hundred and fifty years earlier white Charlestonians watched the shelling on the federal fort. However, this occasion featured remarks, music, and participants in a more inclusive neo-Reconciliationist affair. With Mayor Joseph Riley serving as the emcee, the "Voices from the Civil War" program highlighted the diversity of Civil War experiences.[57] Attendees witnessed the melding of diverse military experiences with an updated reenactment of a military review performed by white and Black reenactors of the Palmetto Battalion and Company I, Fifty-Fourth Massachusetts Regiment.[58] Following this neo-Reconciliationist nod, musicians performed a Civil War medley. Instead of President Obama, SC president pro tempore Glenn McConnell delivered remarks before the performance of Aaron Copeland's "The Lincoln Portrait" and Stephen Foster's "Hard Times Come Again No More."[59] The concluding portion recognized the centrality of African American history to the American Civil War. The Ebenezer AME Church pastor delivered the benediction. After his words, two spiritual groups performed the Black National Anthem before the retiring of the colors.[60] Throughout, the city shed its Lost Cause centennial past. As one Charleston journalist remarked, "Such a sight would have been unthinkable 50 years ago."[61] This event was more inclusive and representative of a more honest telling of the Civil War past for a city viewed as the cradle of the Confederacy.

Held at the Fort Sumter National Monument, the evening observance reflected a more traditional commemoration of music and formal remarks. The Citadel Color Guard presented the colors before the laying of wreaths and performance of "My Country 'tis of Thee."[62] The various speakers reflected the diverse coalition involved in the planning. NPS Southeast regional director, NPS chief historian, and the former NPS director delivered remarks. Locally, Mayor Riley and a Moultrie High School teacher reflected on the occasion. Adding to the racial diversity, College of Charleston professor Bernard Powers again reinforced the inclusive nature of the sesquicentennial celebration and centrality of slavery to the Civil War origins. The NPS Park superintendent gave closing remarks. A military salute ended the event.[63] Whereas the morning celebration was filled with music, the evening program was circumspect. By adhering to tradition, the program took pains to commemorate and not celebrate the anniversary. And on this federal property, the diversity of platform speakers and sober account reinforced key lessons learned from the centennial. Charleston had presented a Civil War commemoration like no other.

In the minds of most white observers, Charleston had redeemed itself from its Lost Cause centennial past. *Charleston City Paper* columnist Will Moredock praised the Fort Sumter organizers, participants, and attendees. He likened the Fort Sumter commemoration to a family reunion "where everyone waited for the crazy drunk uncle to start raving about some long-ago indignity, which all others had forgotten."[64] In his estimation, he proclaimed: "In 2011, the crazy uncle held his peace, and the reunion went on without interruption or embarrassment."[65] By embracing diversity over white segregationist exclusionary practices, no large-scale protests occurred. The NAACP did not take to the streets as it had done several weeks earlier in response to the Secession Ball.

Indeed, no significant neo–Lost Cause counterprotest occurred. Unable to predict the later actions of Dylann Roof, Moredock recognized how even the *Post and Courier* "acquitted itself admirably" through the article series by Brian Hicks, Robert Rosen, and others. He also praised the various events. Appreciating the diverse scene at the *Voices from the Civil War* concert, Moredock, therefore, closed on a hopeful tone for the remaining sesquicentennial events and future bicentennial Civil War commemoration. The successful Fort Sumter "family reunion" lulled Moredock and other Charlestonians into a sense of a stress-free redemptive commemoration. This inclusive beginning to a multi-year commemoration did not completely atone for the past. Instead of a "drunk uncle," it would be a neo-Confederate cousin who brought the reunion to a violent end in 2015.[66]

But in 2011 one group remained skeptical. Despite the inclusive neo-Reconciliationist tone, most Black Charlestonians were not convinced. They, too, understood the history of the Civil War commemoration as predominantly Lost Cause affairs. Despite reassurances, some could not overlook the inclusion of Confederate reenactors and retellings of whitewashed (albeit toned-down) Civil War understandings. Rev. Joseph Darby best articulated this concern: "I think it's very painful and raw," he explained before adding, "If you're going to be authentic in the war you re-create it, it would be hard to filter out the triumphal air of the firing on Fort Sumter."[67] These painful recollections resulted in only one African American woman attending the intentionally designed inclusive NPS events near the Fort Sumter boat deck.[68]

This sesquicentennial protest recalled an earlier protest movement. In the 1960s, African American NAACP members engaged in direct protest of the centennial celebration of Fort Sumter. Executive secretary Roy Wilkins used the controversy over Madaline Williams for the call to arms for its Black members in the city and across the nation. Wilkins and other members did not leave unchallenged how the centennial Charleston events "overlook[ed] the real meaning" of the American Civil War.[69] With the support of the national leadership, the state NAACP president sponsored a rally rejecting "a version based on [the] alleged inferiority of the Negro, upholding the Confederacy and repudiating the great moral issue which lay at the bottom of the Civil War."[70] Morgan State University historian Benjamin Quarles, Madaline Williams, and others emphasized Black Civil War memory as a weapon in their counterprotest but also in their fight in the Civil Rights Movement. They rejected the professed minimization of slavery as a cause of the Civil War. They celebrated the failure of the Confederacy, which was rooted in enslavement and white supremacy, in front of an audience of roughly three hundred individuals. While small in numbers, these Black activists voiced their discontent while "raising public awareness of the movement and its principles."[71] In 2011, the Charleston NAACP branch drew on this recent past in articulating the protest by some of their members.

Charleston NAACP branch President Dot Scott voiced the concerns of her members. They rejected the neo-Reconciliation tone. Scott contended: "It's almost like celebrating with the enemy."[72] While she applauded the efforts of NPS and local organizers, she and many Black Charlestonians could not overlook the past. After holding a "well-attended 'teach-in'" at the College of Charleston, NAACP branch members as well as most Black Charlestonians embraced a wait and see attitude. Neither the participation of Company I, Massachusetts Fifty-Fourth Reenactment Regiment, African American singers, and historian Barbara Fields (granddaughter of Mamie Garvin Fields) nor the inclusive design was enough. It took a few more years to convince them.[73]

The Fort Wagner sesquicentennial festivities represented the full embrace of Black Civil War memory in the city and nation. No longer confined to the margins and intentional silences, Fifty-Fourth Massachusetts reenactors and their white allies took center stage with other traditional white institutions having supporting roles. Unlike the previous May 1865 Grand Review of Armies, this anniversary effectively was a Black commemorative celebration.[74] The post-*Roots* cultural renaissance, Beaufort reinterment, and the emergence of African American Civil

War reenactors reinserted and normalized this African American tradition as part of the Charleston commemorative landscape.

In the days leading to the anniversary, Charleston newspapers again educated the public about the event, and the consequences for the city, state, and nation. Several articles educated Charlestonians on the previously untaught Civil War history at the heart of the commemoration. Charleston attorney turned historian Robert N. Rosen provided several pieces detailing the Confederates' successful defense of the Confederate installation but also the role played by Frederick Douglass's sons, Luis F. Emilio and others in the Black regiment led by Robert Gould Shaw.[75] Both *Post and Courier* writer Brian Hicks and Associated Press writer Bruce Smith contextualized the July 18, 1863, events to the eventual siege and fall of Charleston for readers of the various South Carolina newspapers.[76] These pieces served an important role in filling in the gaps of the previously un-taught Civil War history for would-be attendees. The re-education proved neces-sary for understanding the history of African American military experience and the direct consequences of the failed Fifty-Fourth Massachusetts engagement for the city.

In addition, other pieces announced the intended program for the multi-day celebration consisting of living history events, lectures, round table discussions, a historical marker unveiling, and two public screenings of the 1989 film *Glory*. For African American attendees who might have felt uncomfortable in down-town Charleston, the restored Seashore Farmers Lodge Museum and Cultural Center hosted the first screening.[77] Storytelling, reenactments, and living history demonstrations educated attendees about the Battle of Grimball's Landing on Sol Legare Island and the assault on Fort Wagner held at the NPS Fort Moultrie. Fol-lowing these two major full-day commemorations, Massachusetts Fifty-Fourth reenactors moved to the Old City Jail for two evening events that culminated with the group members honoring the "men who were imprisoned there after the assault" by sleeping inside the old cells.[78]

Throughout, Joseph McGill and other Black USCT reenactors became the principal subjects profiled. Much of the coverage focused on McGill's personal journey to Civil War reenactment, his understanding of the Civil War military engagements, and expectations for the sesquicentennial commemorations. Be-fore the 1989 release of *Glory*, McGill disliked the predominantly white Civil War reenactments. For him, he told a *Charleston City Paper* reporter: "They were reenacting part of a history that wasn't really fair to my ancestors."[79] The 1989 Hollywood film revealed a history, that, as a National Park Service ranger for Fort Sumter, he felt the "information should be readily available to me."[80] That moment inspired his co-founding of the Massachusetts Fifty-Fourth reenacting group. He understood the historical significance of South Carolina military engagements as providing the "war a new reason for being."[81] The spirit of the Black men's service and sacrifice motivated his own work to reinsert and naturalize this history in the dominant Lost Cause commemorative landscape.

In 2013, all eyes were on Charleston. Failure was not an option. After acknowledging McGill's role in President Obama's inauguration, the *Post and Courier* captured the high stakes felt by McGill: "We need to shine, just as those men did 150 years ago in proving to the world they could be soldiers."[82] But for the *Charleston City Paper*, McGill was more explicit. "There was an enemy, and they fought for things too, and there's an opportunity to tell their part of the story, but for so long, the stories of the 200,000 African-American soldiers who served have not been told," he explained before concluding: "Right now, we've got the stage, we've got the microphone, and we're going to use it."[83] Black reenactors' performance would determine whether Black Civil War memory became a permanent inclusion in the neo-Reconciliation tradition or remain a mere sesquicentennial commemorative experiment. NPS community partnership specialist Michael Allen echoed these concerns expressed by McGill. "This is bringing things to the forefront that will increase the understanding of the roles different people played in the Civil War," Allen informed the *Post and Courier*. He, too, acknowledged and reminded readers how much has changed since the centennial: "That's not always been the case, but that was then. This is now."[84] In this moment, academic scholarship, collective memory of the centennial, and high expectations of the sesquicentennial commemoration collided during the 2013 events honoring the Massachusetts regiment.

New voices, specifically Black voices, had a central role in the Charleston commemoration. In reflecting on the pending commemorations, other Fifty-Fourth Massachusetts reenactors offered additional thoughts of the two major anniversaries being celebrated. US Navy veteran and middle school history teacher Marlene Lemon recognized the positive effects of the history for enslaved and free Black South Carolinians and the twenty-first-century descendants. The presence of Black soldiers at Grimball's Landing and Fort Wagner "gave hope" to the Civil War generation; however, the martial manhood and courage shown in the July 18 assault allowed twenty-first-century inheritors to "grow up today feeling less disenfranchised than their parents and grandparents did."[85] Reenactor James Brown viewed the men as the "first civil rights workers," who chose to die as men "with hope" rather than remained enslaved.[86] For Ernest Parks, however, the rich history of the Fifty-Fourth Massachusetts deepened his work in understanding his own Gullah-Geechee heritage, reenacting with the McGill group, and even his restoration of the Seashore Farmers Lodge. After an education focused on Fort Sumter and Lost Cause understandings, Parks's attendance at the Fort Wagner living history event almost a decade earlier convinced him and a neighbor to join the reenacting group.[87] All prepared to engage with other Fifty-Fourth reenactors and interested attendees in the special commemoration of the African American men who fought and died in the Charleston area. They understood their role as storytellers, educators, and living monuments to the Black Civil War past.[88]

On July 18, Fifty-Fourth Massachusetts reenactors and white members of the Tenth South Carolina Regiment reenactors participated at the living history event at Fort Moultrie. Earlier in the day, the annual laying of a wreath occurred. NPS rangers also educated attendees about the history as the men prepared for the rifle demonstration. Following the demonstration, storytelling took center stage.[89]

Traveling from within the state and across the nation, the diversity of the over fifty Black reenactors was striking. Several had performed in the 1989 film. Others caught the reenactment bug because of the film. A few, such as social science educator Donavin White, participated in their first event because of the milestone anniversary.[90] Kharson McKay was among the youngest reenactors present. The eleven-year-old descendant of David Miles Moore shared his family's history after the rifle demonstration. His Civil War ancestor served as a drummer in the regiment. McKay felt obligated to share these family history connections with attendees. He "had to honor him."[91] From the familial to textbook Civil War history, all used storytelling as an invitation to understand the shared collective Civil War historical past to new and diverse audiences. All understood their essential role in making the sesquicentennial Black Civil War celebration a success.

These individuals chose not to participate in the smaller Boston celebration where Governor Deval Patrick presided. With the Augustus Saint-Gaudens memorial in the background, the first African American Massachusetts governor laid a wreath at the monument base and then addressed the crowd.[92] Governor Patrick reminded attendees of his decision to hang a portrait of John Andrew in his office. His remarks reflected on his Civil War predecessor's bold idea. He told the audience how "bringing enlistees into the US Army [was] a radical idea, but one whose time had come."[93] After reading a letter convincing Robert Gould Shaw's father to have his son serve in the Black regiment, he drew connections to Nelson Mandela, whose birthday coincided with the sesquicentennial anniversary.[94]

Governor Patrick's words and the entire ceremony acknowledged the descendants of soldiers and white Boston abolitionists in the audience. Governor John Andrew's idea led a thirteen-year-old African American drummer to witness history. Ninety-one-year-old Winfred Monroe, living descendant of Henry Monroe, heard her grandfather's words read at the affair. "Like a slumbering volcano," Monroe recalled how Fort Wagner in South Carolina "awoke to action and poured forth sheets of flame from ten thousand rebel fires, and earth and heaven shook with the roar of a hundred pieces of artillery."[95] By hearing her Civil War ancestor's remembrance recognized at the celebration, she felt pride for her grandfather who survived the assault. By being "here for the 54th today," Monroe proudly represented all Black Fifty-Fourth Massachusetts men and their families alongside the descendants of Lt. Col. Norwood Penrose Hallowell, William Lloyd Garrison, and African American abolitionist John J. Smith.[96] While smaller in scale, the Boston commemoration paid tribute to the state's role in the Charleston, South Carolina, area military engagement and the legacy for both the descendants and city in the present.

From reenactors to storytelling, McGill's prediction came to fruition. The sesquicentennial celebration of Fort Wagner stood in stark contrast to the centennial. Fifty years earlier, Charleston celebrated their domination over the African American soldiers and their white commanding officer in the failed assault. One Charleston newspaper praised Confederate intelligence and the defenders who staved off the federal attack by the "Negro regiment, the Fifty-fourth Massachusetts," while incurring few casualties.[97] Such Lost Cause narratives advanced the politicized use of memory for the pro-segregationist defense against federal incursion during the Civil Rights Movement.

In 2013, the Fort Wagner celebrations marked the full ascendancy of Black Civil War memory from the margins. Black reenactors and their scrutinized performance did not disappoint. Through the active presence and storytelling, Black Civil War memory was no longer an afterthought. Their work succeeded in advancing more inclusive and fuller narratives in the former Lost Cause stronghold; but it did not change African American public opinion nationally.[98]

In April 2015 the City of Charleston marked the end of the sesquicentennial commemoration with a re-creation of Nat Fuller's Feast. After the criticism of the December 2010 Secession Ball, organizers, politicos, and others sought redemption through the inclusive capstone reconciliation dinner event that remembered Nat Fuller, an African American chef who hosted a dinner for white and Black diners celebrating emancipation and the end of the Civil War in the city.[99] University of South Carolina English professor and heirloom foodways expert David Shields conceived of the celebration when working on his book. Shields worked with white and Black chefs, local farmers, and scholars in the creation of the menu held on the 1865 site of Fuller's restaurant.[100] The 2015 reenactment reinforced the neo-Reconciliationist commemoration in the city. Fifty-Fourth Massachusetts reenactors led the procession through the Charleston streets to the restaurant. Attendees enjoyed the feast prepared by famed restaurateur and James Beard winner Sean Brock and others. Local, state, and national newspapers praised the dinner held at McCrady's restaurant.[101] Through food and ritual, however, the neo-Reconciliationist event celebrated a myth rooted in "a third-hand account, a story gleaned from a story gleaned from a story written by one northern journalist."[102] Few questioned the myth's veracity. One historian did.

Historian Ethan Kytle debunked the myth of the alleged "miscegenation dinner."[103] He meticulously tracked down the evidence after local news coverage piqued his interest. The surviving archival traces raised more questions than answers. By following the footnotes to the original source, he identified the myth's origins in a personal letter written by Mrs. Abby Louisa Porcher, a white Charlestonian married to "a wealthy Charleston cotton and rice broker and Confederate officer who had signed the South Carolina Ordinance of Secession."[104] He also rediscovered that Porcher's letter heavily drew on white journalist James Redpath's reporting. "Whatever the case," according to Kytle, "Porcher's characterization of Fuller's feast as a miscegenation dinner also betrays her fears about the post-emancipation breakdown of social barriers between whites and Blacks—fears she shared with much of the white South."[105] The April 2015 reenactment sustained the myth. While Shields has since shifted his understanding of the alleged 1865 event (due to Kytle's work), the popular embrace of it has continued to grow and become accepted as fact.[106] As a "disservice to the recovery of Charleston's African American history," the persistent Fuller feast myth, according to Kytle, "reinforces paternalist myth of interracial harmony" that has allowed for self-congratulatory narratives of "unity and forgiveness" in the wake of the Charleston Massacre.[107] Instead of the reconciliation dinner, the Charleston Massacre became the real capstone event. Eclipsing Nat Fuller's Feast, the actions of an extremist neo–Lost Cause white supremacist brought the Civil War sesquicentennial commemoration to a brutal end.

Drawn to Charleston's complex racial past, the twenty-one-year-old Columbia, South Carolina, native rejected the neo-Reconciliationist-staged sesquicentennial celebration. His published manifesto and handwritten draft read at the later trial reflected his embrace of neo–Lost Cause understandings advanced in the modern white power movement discussed.[108] Peppered with the n-word and other pejoratives, Dylann Roof's formal and informal education taught him important lessons of white privilege. "Modern history classes instill a subconscious White superiority complex in Whites and an inferiority complex in blacks," Roof argued before expressing his hatred of desegregation for reducing white Americans "to the level of brute animals."[109] The demise of Jim Crow and the post–Civil Rights landscape, moreover, fueled another hatred. He detested "scared White people running" to suburban enclaves.[110] After the lengthy "Blacks" section, Roof shared his racialized thoughts about American Jewish, Latinx, and Asian communities, and the patriotic reverence given to American veterans who served in post-Vietnam military engagements.[111]

In closing, Roof explained his intended actions in the city, which had recently ended its inclusive multi-year sesquicentennial commemoration. He wanted a race war akin to the Civil War. "I have no choice," Roof rationalized. "I chose Charleston because it is the most historic city in my state, and at one time had the highest ratio of blacks to Whites in the country."[112] Because "[we] have no skinheads, no real KKK, no one doing anything but talking on the internet," drawing on South Carolina's first to secede heritage at the close of the sesquicentennial Civil War celebration, Roof decided to take a stand and "have the bravery to take it to the real world, and I guess that has to be me."[113] On June 17, 2015, Roof moved beyond talking and white supremacist, neo–Lost Cause cosplaying at various South Carolina historical sites, including a burial site of enslaved persons at McLeod Plantation on James Island. Roof enacted his plan at the historic Emanuel African Methodist Episcopal Church.[114]

Shortly after 8 p.m., Roof entered the church. South Carolina State Legislator and Rev. Clementa Pinckney and other congregants welcomed the would-be killer. Seated next to Rev. Pinckney, he participated in the traditional religious routine—prayer, reading of biblical verses, and discussion. After an hour, Roof announced his intent. He executed Pinckney. After his first victim, Roof murdered eight others. Spewing hate and racial epithets, Roof's opening salvo in the intended racial war lasted several minutes. Upon reaching Polly Sheppard, a seventy-year-old church trustee, he spared her life. Nine victims were killed. The men and women ranged in age from twenty-six to eighty-seven years old.[115] They were grandparents, parents, sons, daughters, church leaders, and valued community members. Their church leader also represented the region in the state legislature. All became martyrs in the new Civil War cultural war. All were subsequently remembered for the cause of their deaths and not the fullness of their lives lived. Roof exited the building and fled. The city, state, nation, and world grappled with the heinousness of his actions.[116]

Historian Robert J. Cook provocatively characterized President Barack Obama's influence on Civil War memory as "Abraham Obama."[117] While the author failed to meaningfully discuss pre-Obama cultural developments shaping the reemergence of Black Civil War memory from the margins, this notion becomes useful in understanding the violent conclusion of the sesquicentennial commemoration in Charleston. By taking seriously the "Abraham Obama" image, Obama's 2015 Gettysburg Address honored the latest victims of the sesquicentennial Civil War cultural war dead. Held at the College of Charleston, the first African American president eulogized the assassinated South Carolina state legislator and Emanuel AME Church minister Clementa Pinckney. His words attempted to console the victim's families, church congregation, and stunned nation.[118]

Harkening to the Black prophetic tradition laid by Reverend Henry McNeal Turner and others, Obama stated the occasion in his opening. He honored the man who "set an example worthy of his position, wise beyond his years, in his speech, in his conduct, in his love, faith, and purity."[119] In the immediate aftermath, media coverage focused on understanding the white supremacist youth's background, radicalization process, and rationale for entering Emanuel AME Church. His victims and their previous lives and dreams became lost in the coverage. Thus, Obama reminded the audience of the man. Obama felt that Pinckney, as a state senator, "embodied a politics that was neither mean, nor small."[120] Obama reminded the audience how Reverend Pinckney, as a religious leader,

> embodied the idea that our Christian faith demands deeds and not just words; that the "sweet hour of prayer" actually lasts the whole week long—(applause)—that to put our faith in action is more than individual salvation, it's about our collective salvation; that to feed the hungry and clothe the naked and house the homeless is not just a call for isolated charity but the imperative of a just society.[121]

Through his intentional language choice, Obama connected Pinckney to the region, state, and shared Christian collective faith. His use of "our" appealed to not only African American Christians but all Americans in a secular national faith. In this regard, Pinckney died as a Christian soldier whose faith defined his praxis and worldview in building a more just society. Pinckney welcomed all, including his own murderer. Therefore, Obama had the momentous task of eulogizing a martyred Christian public servant killed "in his sanctuary with eight wonderful members of his flock."[122]

In the next section, Obama recognized the other victims by name. Obama characterized these murdered men and women as decent, God-fearing individuals. These Christian foot soldiers died in a place that served as the "beating heart" of African Americans' quest for freedom, citizenship, and social justice in Charleston.[123] Affectionately known as Mother Emanuel, the church and its congregants fought for abolition, survived anti-Blackness laws and norms, and laid an important foundation for the twentieth-century Civil Rights Movement. Obama honored them by situating the deaths within the long historical arc of adversity and struggles of previous church members. Their freedom struggle reflected the entire African American experience in the nation.[124]

Obama then shifted to the Emanuel Nine's murderer. Without directly naming him, Obama questioned whether Roof understood the unintended consequences of his actions. Like Fort Sumter, few predicted a four-year Civil War that allowed for post-emancipation Mother Emanuel's rise like "a Phoenix from the ashes."[125] African Americans' love and the capacity of the post-emancipation Black Church did not result in the intended race war. Instead, white and Black Charlestonians, South Carolinians, and the Americans responded, "not merely with revulsion at his evil act, but with big-hearted generosity and, more importantly, with a thoughtful introspection and self-examination that we so rarely see in public life."[126] God's grace, according to Obama, removed the blinders of the pain caused by the previous Lost Cause understanding of its cloth symbols. Roof's weaponization of the Confederate symbols revealed the necessity for the removal of the Confederate flag from the South Carolina State House grounds. Erected during the centennial, as discussed in the previous chapter, late twentieth-century boycotts and legislative compromises shaped Roof's reading of a whitewashed history and emboldened him. The first African American US president called on pro-flag defenders in the state legislature to remove the Confederate battle flag. Removal would serve a "modest but meaningful balm for so many unhealed wounds."[127] Coupled with policies and laws addressing systemic oppression, the president also called for removal as an expression of the religious faith embraced by Pinckney and other victims. The blood shed on June 17, 2015, might allow for the necessary collective reckoning of the Civil War past and its afterlives in the twenty-first century. Pinckney's sacrifice would not be in vain. As long as the flag waved, collective healing remained impossible.

In his closing, Obama issued a call to the city, state, and nation. After sing-talking "Amazing Grace," he closed by recognizing the Charleston Massacre victims. He further immortalized the names of the men and women murdered during their Bible study. Obama reminded the world:

Clementa Pinckney found that grace.
Cynthia Hurd found that grace.
Susie Jackson found that grace.
DePayne Middleton-Doctor found that grace.
Tywanza Sanders found that grace.
Daniel L. Simmons, Sr. found that grace.
Sharonda Coleman-Singleton found that grace.
Myra Thompson found that grace.[128]

By calling their names, President Obama connected their sacrifice within the neo-Reconciliationist frame established by the Civil War commemorations in the city, state, and nation. Through their spilled blood caused by a neo-Confederate white supremacist high school dropout, Obama hoped for the nation to heal as Lincoln did previously at the Gettysburg National Cemetery. Instead of the white military sacrifice on a Pennsylvania battlefield, these ordinary African American men and women might allow "God to shed His grace on the United States of America."[129] Charleston and the state of South Carolina responded to the president's call.

The Charleston Massacre renewed calls for the removal of the Confederate battle flag from the South Carolina State House grounds. The flag had previously encouraged some African Americans to boycott the sesquicentennial events in Charleston. Roof's brazen photographic embrace of the flag and the murders of the Emanuel Nine enflamed the calls by Black South Carolinians and their diverse allies for removal of the Confederate battle flag and shaped the ensuing public debate.[130] The Post and Courier reminded readers of the flag's Civil War origins and its postwar legacy as a white supremacist "rallying banner" against the Civil Rights Movement, anti-federal policies, and in anti-Black violence.[131] "In the spirit of reconciliation," one Post and Courier editorial supported removal as a means of honoring the Emanuel Nine. The June 21, 2015, piece demanded: "Do it to honor of the nine people who were killed at Emanuel AME Church. Do it now."[132] Within news coverage and letters to the editors in the state's three largest newspapers, removal supporters framed the issue as a reparative act. Other reasons supporting removal included political leaders' support, shame, and possible decline in corporate and tourist interest.[133] Opposition centered on arguments of heritage, the 2000 Heritage Act compromise, and the inability to resolve racial tensions.[134]

With the full support of the state and national Republican leadership, South Carolina Governor Nikki Haley called on state legislators for the immediate removal of the flag on June 22, 2015. The first woman governor of South Carolina and of Indian American descent explained: "There is a place for that flag. It's not in a place that represents all people in South Carolina."[135] She also drew on recent South Carolina history surrounding previous compromises over the Confederate flag on the State House grounds. Channeling Governor Beasley's earlier strategy, Haley threatened a special legislative session if agreement could not be found. Her greatest obstacle came from Representative Mike Pitts of Laurens County. He led the opposition and stalled the proceedings as Jake Knotts had done in the compromise resulting in the African American History Monument discussed in the previous chapter.[136]

When the legislative debate stalled, Bree Newsome became a post–Charleston Massacre icon. The Black North Carolinian activist scaled the flagpole where it hung following the 2000 Heritage Act compromise. As she removed the Confederate cloth symbol, Newsome exclaimed: "You come against me with hatred and oppression and violence. I come against you, in the name of God. This flag comes down."[137] Citing scripture, she descended with the flag in tow. Police arrested her for her defiant act of civil disobedience. Black feminist scholar Brittany Cooper called Newsome a "shero."[138] In her 2015 "On the Pole for Freedom," Cooper praised Newsome for challenging the Lost Cause symbol and the impotence of state legislators contemplating its removal. For Cooper, Newsome spoke for all grieving Black Charlestonians, Black South Carolinians, and Black Americans writ large. She became an icon to them. "A Black girl with the trophy of white supremacy in her clutches is the only sermon on freedom I'll ever need," Cooper concluded her *Crunk Feminist Collective* piece.[139] Indeed, Newsome ignored the calls for patience and forgiveness. She reclaimed the power of the refusal. She claimed her trophy without waiting for state-sanctioned approval. Her bold act of civil disobedience made her an icon.

The deafening calls for removal of the Confederate battle flag proved victorious. State legislators overcame the opposition led by Pitts and approved removal. Governor Haley signed the law in a special ceremony with several family members of the Charleston Massacre victims in attendance. On July 10, 2015, the Confederate flag came down from its prominent perch on the State House grounds. Many praised Governor Haley for her leadership in the process.[140]

For the actual removal, state leaders again called on African American poet Nikky Finney to capture the moment in verse. Drawing on Black Civil War memory, she exclaimed in a poem composed for the occasion: "Let us put the cannons of our eyes away forever. Our one and only Civil War is done. Let us tilt, rotate, strut on. If we, the living, do not give our future the same honor as the sacred dead—of then and now—we lose everything."[141] Years of African American protest had little effect on the fate of the political Confederate cloth symbol. Compromise often resulted in tepid responses and concessions designed to placate African American discontent. Following the death of one of their legislative members and eight others, this 2015 compromise resulted in removal and placement in the South Carolina Confederate Relic Room and Military Museum in Columbia, South Carolina. Sadly, it took the murder of nine African Americans, one of whom was a state legislator, to bring about the change.[142]

As African American Civil War reenactor Joseph McGill predicted, the Charleston Civil War sesquicentennial commemoration proved memorable. Rejecting the Lost Cause understandings, organizers actively promoted fuller, inclusive, and more truthful understandings of the causes, the war, and its immediate aftermath. Their decision encouraged a significant place for twenty-first-century Black Civil War memory understandings in the neo-Reconciliationist affair. Not all accepted this shift.

White Charlestonians' backlash and public appeals to minimize the post–Secession Ball fallout contributed to African Americans' hesitancy to engage with the intentionally diverse commemoration. By 2013, the Fort Wagner commemoration reduced some of the hesitancy and encouraged a more positive response for the Black Civil War commemoration. At the sesquicentennial end, neo-Reconciliation myths surrounding the Nat Fuller's Feast cause some minor controversy. However, the neo-Reconciliation and pro–Black Civil War commemoration failed to fully address white Charlestonians' discontent, which manifested in the Charleston Massacre on June 17, 2015.

Dylann Roof's opening salvo in the next phase of the Civil War culture wars not only made the Charleston sesquicentennial memorable but also pushed the fight onto college and university campuses. Once the intellectual homes of the Lost Cause ideology, desegregation allowed for the chipping away at old traditions, monuments, and anti-Black building naming practices. Roof's actions as well as other national events in Charlottesville and Minneapolis turned campus spaces into incubators for how to reckon with the lingering Lost Cause pasts in higher education and the national Civil War commemorative landscape. Here, African American scholars and their diverse campus constituents entered the fray and responded creatively and cogently.[143]

Toward Black Civil War Memory Studies: A Conclusion

The one who came to start the next Civil War
speaks to her directly. *Have I shot you yet?*
There is no one else left to answer. In the church
basement all are dead or bleeding out. Miss Polly,
half on her knees, is askew, tilted, her last angle, . . .
No, you have not.

> —NIKKY FINNEY, "MISS POLLY IS AKIMBO UNDERNEATH
> THE MOTHER EMANUEL COLLECTION TABLE," 2020

Unlike other Civil War memory categories, Black Civil War memory lacks a single author. It lacks a single text or set of texts that captures the totality of how everyday African Americans chose to remember and commemorate the Civil War. Even previous scholarly attempts have failed. Since David Blight and Barbara Gannon have published their masterly works, few have seriously considered the memory work of African Americans beyond a chapter or a handful of pages.[1] To date, there has yet to be one comprehensive monograph exploring the history of African American Civil War remembrance. None has explored the memory of Black women. By privileging certain middle-class leaders, communities, and Civil War veteran organizations, historians have missed the everyday African Americans showcased in this book.

African Americans experienced the war as enslaved and free, but also as soldier, contraband, refugee, and/or civilian in both the United States and the Confederate States of America. As a result, geographic place, status before the war, gender, and wartime experience matter. These African Americans defy the traditional scholarly Civil War memory categories. Whether nationally, regionally, and/or locally, African Americans sought to preserve a complex past that honored the service and sacrifice of veterans, the diverse wartime civilian experiences, and the destruction of slavery to advance their full inclusion as American citizens. In the process, they collectively built a commemorative culture and traditions recognizing the diverse experience while countering white anti-Black collective Civil War remembrances that reduced them to stereotypes and second-class American citizens.

Since the Black Civil War experience was not monolithic, this book has made a case for new methodologies, sources, and approaches for understanding the scope of African Americans' Civil War commemorative culture. So, what, therefore, is Black Civil War memory?

When one expands the archives to include African American porches, it is possible to see Black Civil War memory as a collectively defined tradition in which the Emancipationist and the Won Cause bookend the expressions of the diverse commemorative culture. Even with hyperlocal and regional variations, African Americans collectively agreed on several essential components for Black Civil War memory. The defining traits are as follows:

First, the Civil War generation's sacrifice deserved full and unquestioned veneration as heroes and heroines. USCT veterans received their laurels during and after their lifetime. By surviving, USCT military service afforded them entry into community leadership. Veterans functioned as living monuments. They were visible reminders of the Black Civil War sacrifice in their communal commemorative holidays and veteran encampments. The children, widows, and other kin also received recognition. Black community members offered witness statements for pensions. They provided end-of-life care and other assistance whenever necessary. Annually, communities tended to the gravesites of USCT soldiers and veterans' gravesites. They erected monuments in spaces important to the Black community. Without the military service of African Americans, a federal defeat of the Confederacy, abolition, and expansion of US constitutional protections would have been impossible. Any perceived slight to Black USCT veneration received a swift public rebuke.

Veneration did not stop with USCT veterans and collective understandings of their military service and sacrifice. Northern civilians, including those who endured Confederate raids, received recognition for their sacrifice. They ensured that the military service of USCT soldiers did not go in vain. They petitioned for equal pay and better treatment. Some provided material relief for soldiers and their families. Some actively recruited for the US Army. These civilians ensured a warm welcome for returning soldiers in Harrisburg, Pennsylvania, but also in their local communities. For their sacrifice at the federal home front, they, too, received recognition.

Slavery survivors embodied the Jubilee on earth. The Civil War resulted in their liberation from slavery and life in the failed Confederate nation-state. Black military service cemented the destruction of slavery as a foundational US institution. While predominantly focused on the majority of Southern African

Americans, this category also proved flexible. It extended to self-liberating individuals who became refugees in the federal contraband camps, free Black Southerners who remained a nation rooted in white supremacy, and those enslaved by Confederate soldiers in border communities. With slavery's destruction and the support of Black soldiers and Northern civilians, God had meted justice against the national sin of slavery. Their sacrifice had not been in vain. Subsequent generations praised them accordingly.

Together, these veterans, Northern civilians, and slavery survivors were living monuments whose kinkeeping practices collectively helped define a core component of Black Civil War memory.

Second, a shared calendar of commemorative holidays allowed for the reinforcement of the common Black Civil War Memory components. This alternate calendar prevented collective forgetting and erasure. The events had certain traditions and rituals that persisted into the late twentieth century. Parades, church services, and public speeches served as public acts of Black remembrance. Performances by school-aged children, music, and sharing of food. Some holidays had specific traditions. For instance, Memorial Day celebrations always included the decoration of graves, a communal meal, and formal addresses. The post–Civil Rights and Black Power movements disrupted some of the widespread celebrations that occurred in segregated safe Black spaces. Some holiday rituals, such as the singing of the Black national anthem, persisted. Other traditions expanded. Juneteenth, a Texas Emancipation Day celebration, moved from a local celebration to a state holiday in 1980 to a federal holiday under the Joseph Biden administration in 2021.[2] New traditions emerged in the post–Civil Rights and Black Power movement cultural landscape. Annual reenactment of the July 18, 1863, assault on Fort Wagner by white and Black reenactors is a new addition to the commemorative calendar. While centered in the Charleston, South Carolina, lowcountry, participants travel from across the nation for the celebration.

Even with the common dates, flexibility allowed for hyperlocal and regional additions. Specific liberation dates of Southern communities, such as April 3 or pre-twenty-first-century Juneteenth commemorations had their places as did the Shippensburg's Black Parade.

Third, a collective rejection of racist definitions and categories of slavery, the Civil War, and its aftermath prevailed. White supremacist myths of faithful slaves, loyal college servants, Black Confederates, and other white racial fantasies had no place in Black Civil War commemorative culture. While understanding the existence of complex circumstances, the racial performances of African Americans sustaining myths and fantasies neither represented nor defined their commemorative culture.

Fourth, Black Civil War veteran networks and auxiliary organizations were more far-reaching than membership in traditional Civil War veterans' organizations. Class and gender mattered. GAR comrades, lapsed dues-paying GAR comrades, and non-affiliated veterans always gained acceptance in Black GAR post meetings and events. Comradeship extended to all USCT veterans. Moreover, Prince Hall Masons, Odd Fellows, local militias, and other Black fraternal organizations offered alternative models of comradeship for those who lived in communities without a formal post or where professed GAR values failed; the alternative models provided veterans with access to the respective women's auxiliary groups. Religious, familial, and educational networks also filled in the gap of Black veterans' networks. Black veteran networks proved more expansive than traditional organizations and established post-service life models for later Black war veterans.

Fifth, Black women and their overlapping networks had an essential role in sustaining Black Civil War memory. They built monuments in the segregated cemeteries and other community spaces. Their clubwomen activism mirrored the work of white women in advancing Civil War memory. With an eye to the third and fourth generation of Black youth, Black women performed their memory work as acts of homemade citizenship. They created and sustained community archives. They preserved oral traditions beyond the death of the Civil War generation members and veterans. Black women's embrace of new print and media technologies aided their preservation efforts. They taught the next generation of Black children in K-12 classrooms and guaranteed their participation in commemorative events. They saw Civil War memory work as a natural extension of their activism over the nineteenth and twentieth centuries. Without Black women, like their white counterparts, much of Civil War memory would not have persisted. They instilled the original Civil War kinkeepers' lessons to the next generation as mother, aunts, community leaders, and educators.

Above all, African Americans collectively agreed to remember the Civil War on their own terms. They rejected white Americans' calls to forget. They rejected erasure by making the porch and other spaces into counter-publics of Black Civil War memory. They sustained public expressions by claiming the streets during annual parades and publicizing their holiday events in local newspapers, radio programming, and television. However, much of the work has remained outside of the white gaze. Racism and anti-Black policies shaped African American participation in the federal military and home front. The Civil War ended slavery, but it did not end racism. As such, Black Civil War memory has embraced a radical hope for a better and inclusive future where race no longer mattered.

By not forgetting, Black Civil War memory formed a way of life for living in the post–Civil War world. It shaped parenting, modes of community building, voting patterns, and activism until favorable conditions emerged. Yet with the Civil Rights and Black Power movements, Black Civil War memory continues as a source of faith and hope for a better America.

In short, twenty-first-century inheritors still have much in common with those in 1865. Since the cultural wars over Civil War memory continue unabated, Black Civil War remembrance remains political. By remembering an inclusive Civil War, African Americans and their white allies reject calls for forgetting and acquiescing to other predominant white traditions.

Our collective goal must be toward a new future in Black Civil War Memory Studies. Scholars must take seriously African American porch archives and lessons. Currently, non-institutionalized African American porch archives are endangered. Community collections not donated to archives or libraries might become lost forever or broken up for sale on eBay. With the passing of elderly Black kinkeepers, the oral traditions might not continue to current generations, and therefore, preservation of porch archives must be paramount. We need mass-scale oral tradition projects akin to the Depression-era Works Progress Administration interviews of former enslaved people. Mass digitization, oral history efforts, and accessible Digital Humanities (DH) projects are needed and are easily adaptable for current courses and institutional projects.

More important, scholars must fully develop Black Civil War Memory Studies as its own distinct subfield. Borrowing from Michel-Rolph Trouillot, this book uncovers how Black Civil War memory became unknowable, like the Haitian Revolution, to academics and public audiences; and yet collective memories persisted within Black communal spaces.[3] This book should serve as a model and not an end to the work that remains to be done. The field of Civil War Memory Studies has a race problem. It is not the responsibility of Black and other scholars of color to fix it. Allyship also cannot be limited to the few who have been brave.

This book demonstrates what can be learned when scholars incorporate porch archives and traditional archives into their historical scholarship using intersectional and interdisciplinary frameworks. The first step remains the same as in any other scholarly historical endeavor. Our research questions must include diverse Black people as subjects without objectification and more than an afterthought in Civil War memory. The showcased men, women, and children deserve our attention, empathy, and application of our academic historical training.

I, however, have not given up hope.

Locating Neal, Crawford, and Gabe: An Epilogue

To accept one's past—one's history—is not the same thing as drowning in
it. An invented past can never be used; it cracks and crumbles under the
pressures of life like clay in a season of drought.

—JAMES BALDWIN, *THE FIRE NEXT TIME*

This book ends as it began. I offer another personal journey into the continuing the work of ordinary African American men, women, and children in the promotion of Civil War memory. Instead of a question asked
on my maternal grandparents' porch, it was a Black male student's comment
raised in a classroom at the University of Alabama.

"But, Dr. Green, slavery did not exist here," said the junior enrolled in my
Nineteenth-Century Black History course during spring 2015.

His comment and implicit questioning of the course content shocked me. Almost a year earlier, a historical marker for the Little Round House/Guard House
helped convince me to accept a position at the University of Alabama. When
I read the marker text, I knew that the campus had made progress since the
mob violence blocked Autherine Lucy's 1956 desegregation attempt and George
Wallace's infamous stand at Foster Auditorium in June 1963.[1] I had yet to learn
about the 2004 institutional apology for slavery and 2006 placement of a slavery
apology marker. But one sentence changed my perception: "Until 1865, it also
housed the University Drum Corps, which was composed of rented slaves."[2] This
sentence guided my decision to join the faculty. It also sparked my intellectual
curiosity. Who were the enslaved drummers? What were their experiences? His
comment, though, made me painfully aware that the Little Round House/Guard
House marker, institutional apology, and slavery apology marker had done little
to change campus myths regarding slavery and the Civil War.

These persistent myths still erased the experiences and names of the University Drum Corps and other enslaved campus laborers. These myths still caused
harm to Black students and other marginalized communities who walk the
grounds. These myths had continued to cause much discomfort for many Black
Tuscaloosa residents who refuse to step foot on the campus. These whitewashed

myths still affected all who encountered the space and prevented the majority from seeing the real campus.

After turning the comment into a teachable moment, I sought the source. I took the official admissions tour. After several tours, I could no longer fault the student. This collective forgetting had been reinforced in the use of servants instead of slaves while official tour guides also proclaimed, "Sadly, we lost," and "Yankee invaders," when discussing the Civil War, and even characterized the surviving slave quarters as "garden sheds." After some action on my part, tour participants no longer hear such proclamations. The use of servants and the noncontextualized buildings named for enslavers, proslavery apologists, and segregationists masked the long history of African Americans at the university. Visitors were encouraged to appreciate the aesthetic campus beauty instead of interrogating who actually constructed and labored in the surviving antebellum buildings. The tours never discussed the bold institutional examples—Little Round House/Guard House historical marker, institutional apology, and slavery apology marker—to future students, their parents, and other constituents. Rather, the markers and apology empowered the collective forgetting of an institutional history hidden in plain sight by allowing those who knew better to do no more. As one white male STEM faculty member told me on my Hallowed Grounds tour with the Faculty Senate Executive Board and Provost in Spring 2017—"We gave them a marker."[3]

Since 2006, a "We gave them a marker" culture undergirded the student's comment and catapulted me into the process of recovering and telling fuller campus narratives. I shared the same sense of urgency to recover and tell new inclusive narratives of the Civil War past to the next generations of the UA community as had the individuals discussed in the preceding chapters. Unlike these men, women, and children, I had the language, tools, and doctoral training to guide the recovery process.

Individual curiosity about a specific Civil War site of memory gave way to a purposeful recovery of the memory of slavery and its fiery wartime destruction. The resulting work represented my refusal to accept the collective forgetting of this aspect of the campus history. It meant the restoration of the names and experiences of the enslaved University Drum Corps and others who labored at the University of Alabama from its original construction until April 4, 1865. This impulse meant the active act of remembrance and fight against the violence inflicted by myths accepted without question. The student's offhand remark revealed the real ways in which the Lost Cause project promoted by the United Daughters of the Confederacy (UDC) and other proponents continued to shape current students, especially students of color.

As a scholar committed to amplifying the experiences of ordinary Americans, especially people of African descent, over the long nineteenth century, I asked how might I be part of the solution of revising old narratives? How might I promote newer inclusive narratives of the enslaved campus laborers and their Civil War memory and legacy in the wider Tuscaloosa community? In effect, how might I contribute to an ongoing project that moves from "historical recovery to rigorous and responsible creativity" for exploring the campus's past, present, and future?[4] The work would require correcting the collective forgetting embedded in the "we gave them a marker" culture.

In this work, I have been mindful that the archives were not designed for my recovery efforts. When one explores the racial history of one's employer, the Lost Cause and resulting white supremacist project is no longer an abstract concept that I taught. Previous University of Alabama administrators' decisions shaped my daily experiences. They naturalized the Lost Cause and its myths as the inevitable and proper consequence of the Civil War in the built campus landscape, curriculum, and student body.[5] For my project, I turned to the recent work of slavery scholars but also digital humanities scholars who called for an expanded archive. They also encouraged the use of digital, multidisciplinary, and multidimensional methods and tools, such as 3-D digital modeling of historic plantations no longer physically present. But it was the provocations raised by Marisa Fuentes and others that convinced me to be brave.[6]

Ultimately, I knew that I could not have African American students enter my classroom, eventually graduate, and continue to sustain the Lost Cause myths about institutional slavery and the enslaved experiences. James Baldwin's words continue to haunt: "History is not the past. It is the present. We carry our history with us. We are our history."[7] And at the University of Alabama, the collective forgetting of the full institutional racial past of slavery, the Lost Cause, Jim Crow exclusion, and Civil Rights Movement continue to shape all aspects of one's experiences. As a faculty member, I became part of the long history of African Americans on campus. I feared that my efforts would become like those of other Black women who dared to remember a different Civil War past. Black women's memory work easily gets subsumed when deemed necessary by administrative and other political powerbrokers. I had plenty of historical examples; and in the process of doing the work, acquired personal examples of the intentional silencing of the Black institutional past at the University of Alabama. I still pushed forward.

So I created an alternate campus tour.

I originally designed the Hallowed Grounds tour to be conducted in a seventy-five-minute class period. The tour covered the untold history of slavery through the lives of the enslaved and complicated institutional legacy. Tour stops included the surviving antebellum campus buildings, the ruins of Franklin Hall transformed into The Mound, and postwar campus sites connected with its legacy. My tours ended at the slavery apology marker. I did a test run in my Summer 2015 course in the intense Alabama heat. During the Fall 2015 semester, my Nineteenth-Century Black History students walked the campus. Interest quickly spread. I adopted the 2016 Black History Month theme for its name and did my first set of tours for the public. Due to high demand, I later developed self-guided tour options. I regularly did public tours throughout the academic year and offered additional tours during Black History Month celebrations. Like the porches and other safe spaces within the African American community, the Hallowed Grounds tour transformed the campus into an important space for telling the narratives of the enslaved drummers and other buried histories.

Oral tradition supported by deep archival work became my vehicle for revising campus Lost Cause and self-congratulatory post-desegregation myths. To gain legitimacy, I knew that I had to convince a university community in a state with a motto proclaiming, "We Defend Our Rights." I recognized how the weaponization of the "we" and the "our" had been defined by race, class, gender, ability, and historical power hierarchies and how it operated at the campus. I, therefore, intentionally built the tour and subsequent Hallowed Grounds Project using sources readily obtained on campus before expanding to non-UA held sources.

I also tackled sources that had been previously underappreciated by most scholars. I initially avoided the diaries of Basil Manly, second campus president, enslaver, and Confederate chaplain. Some faculty skeptics felt that I would not find anything new because several scholars had over-prioritized the collection.[8] Instead, I explored the nondigitized early records of administrators, faculty, and the last president overseeing slavery at the university. I then tracked formerly enslaved campus laborers and their post-emancipation contributions in Tuscaloosa. My goal was to acknowledge their humanity by documenting and saying their names to tour participants and other willing audiences. In the process, I rediscovered Neal, Crawford, and Gabe.

The drummers' names were easily found in the third president's papers. Gabe and Neal were enslaved by Judge Watson and Mrs. Watson of Montgomery. A surviving pass revealed the permission granted for them to visit family in Montgomery and Mobile while the cadets were on break. Mrs. Watson, moreover, rebuffed President Garland's attempt to purchase the drummers and then increased her rate for their subsequent hire.[9] The surviving quartermaster ledger showed that they were paid from the "Music Fund" and not the "Servant Fund" used for other slave hires.[10] They were not also impressed like the thirty-eight men used in the construction of earthenworks between December 9, 1863, and January 18, 1864.[11] Officials boarded them off campus during the construction of the Little Round House/Guard House.[12] Crawford replaced Neal per President Garland's request in 1864.[13] On April 3, 1865, Gabe and Crawford stood on the steps and alerted students of the approaching federal forces as ordered. They participated in the retreat from campus. Their post-retreat fates remain unclear. Yet the ease of discovery of their names and insights into their campus experiences raised questions regarding the wartime slave cabin. Why and how did the University of Alabama erase the names of the three drummers while employing the site for the promotion of the Lost Cause memorial landscape and ideology before desegregation?

The University of Alabama had plenty of opportunities to remember Neal, Crawford, and Gabe. While repurposing the structure, the Little Round House/ Guard House became a potent Lost Cause symbol. Students and student organizations used it as a backdrop for Hallowed Grounds their yearbook photographs. The structure became a regular building featured throughout the yearbook pages and cover art during significant Civil War anniversaries. The politics of racial exclusion and the United Daughters of the Confederacy project encouraged collective forgetting and selective remembrance in the Jim Crow–era yearbooks.[14]

The UA *Corollas*, the student yearbooks, reflected an institutional commitment to a pro-Confederate culture centered on the wartime building. The 1912 *Corolla* best highlighted its function. It reminded students of the Old University destroyed on April 4, 1865; and like the phoenix, the modern university emerged out of the ashes. The caption incorrectly idenitified the structure as the "only remaining building of the old university."[15] The President Mansion and outbuildings, Maxwell Hall, and the Gorgas House also remained. The Little Round House/Guard House, however, was the only true military building to survive the wartime destruction. Beyond this incorrect fact, students chose to forget the names and presence of Neal, Crawford, and Gabe. Instead, they remembered romanticized slaves in their reminiscences and illustrations. The 1927 *Corolla* featured enslaved individuals picking cotton on front and back endsheets.[16] They rarely remembered the actual history of campus slavery until after desegregation.[17] Early yearbook poetry instead promoted Ed Gould and Dan Spencer as representative loyal Civil War–era slaves who maintained their fidelity to the university after emancipation.[18] Students found comfort in sustaining these myths over remembering the three enslaved drummers who labored in and around the Little Round House/Guard House.

I quickly discovered that the University of Alabama actively involved its entire Jim Crow–era campus community and not only the yearbook staff. A 1923 *Crimson White* article promoted an alternative tour of the Lost Cause commemorative landscape to the current student population. The growth of the modern university heightened fears about a loss of institutional memory of the Civil War. The Jim Crow–era tour showcased the Civil War structure, the Mound, and other locales "that bring tender memories of the old Confederacy" as an integral part of their education.[19] The university community also embraced the United Daughters of the Confederacy as a campus stakeholder. After elaborate unveiling ceremonies, the campus accepted two UDC memorials—the Boulder and a signed Tiffany Memorial Window. They also had their meetings on campus.[20] Like the Little Round House/Guard House, these UDC additions and its organizational presence became part of daily campus activities. In 1915, for instance, the Jasons, an honor society, claimed the Boulder and its original mound for its yearbook presence. Society members later appropriated the Little Round House/Guard House into its campus headquarters.[21] The alternate campus tour, UDC chapter, and student organization did not mention the enslaved drummers, nor did they discuss enslaved wartime workers hired out, directly owned and/or impressed by the university.

Early historians and campus chroniclers reinforced and naturalized Lost Cause narratives in their histories. James A. Anderson, a longtime postmaster who became a university archivist, normalized the erasure of the names and slave status of the drummers in his various historical accounts.[22] He never named Neal, Crawford. and Gabe even when discussing the wartime introduction of a fife and drum corps.[23] James B. Sellers continued this broader Lost Cause historical project but with two notable exceptions. He acknowledged the role of local African Americans who successfully guided federal troops en route to Tuscaloosa and others who openly welcomed the federal liberators. While not naming the drummers, Sellers documented in his 1953 official campus history: "From the guard rooms the Negro drum corps responded to the order of beating the 'long roll' announcing the arrival of federal troops.[24] Both early campus histories formed the basis for the account used in the Sons of the Confederate Veterans chapter's centennial and sesquicentennial celebration pamphlets describing the early April 1865 events.[25] As a consequence, these histories contributed to remembrance of the wartime structure and the simultaneous erasure of the names and sometimes status of the University Drum Corps members. Like their antebellum predecessors, their efforts had its intended effect in the education of the next generation of segregation defenders.

Students weaponized the memory of the Little Round House/Guard House into a symbol of white resistance in the 1961 *Corolla*. Appearing five years after a mob successfully blocked the desegregation attempt of Autherine Lucy, the yearbook coincided with centennial Civil War celebration amid the Civil Rights Movement. With UA history professor Albert B. Moore as the chief architect of the Alabama centennial commission, yearbook editors and staff deployed Lost Cause memory throughout.[26] The cover boasted a white outline drawing of the wartime slave cabin on a gray background with a colorized Confederate battle flag and American flag above it. The numbers 1861 and 1961 are imprinted in white font underneath the Confederate flag.[27] The dedication reminded the segregated campus community: "In 1961 the University again faces great problems and again as in 1861, a new University is being built to meet the challenges."[28] Race once again clearly played a role with the obvious references to desegregation efforts. Instead of abolition, the enrollment of African American students posed the greatest perceived threat. If the messaging remained unclear, yearbook editors then used the cover motif as the background of the various section breaks. Readers were encouraged to open the flap to reveal a modern photograph. For the "Campus Life" section, a male Alabama cheerleader was depicted literally jumping for joy on top of the wartime slave cabin and in turn, in defense of keeping the university as a white-only space.[29]

Two years later, George Wallace's failed stand outside of Foster Auditorium resulted in the enrollment of James Hood and Vivian Malone.[30] Desegregation contributed to a more diverse campus community uninterested in sustaining Lost Cause memory. UA administrators placed the historical marker, which signaled the site's importance in the post-desegregated campus. These developments intrigued me on my campus interview. Elevated to the same status as the UDC Boulder and Mound, the Little Round House/Guard House even currently has a no-tailgate zone during Alabama football home games. Previously, many white Alabama football fans drank their chosen beverage from the steps of the Civil War era slave structure. As the second stop on the Hallowed Grounds tour, participants learn this complex commemorative past; but they also say the names of the members of the University Drum Corps. This form of restorative justice allowed me to push this history from the margins to the present for students, faculty, staff, and others who continue to engage with campus either on a regular, temporary, or virtual basis.

After I secured tenure and promotion, the tours became an integral component of the Hallowed Grounds Project. This ongoing, multifaceted project remains committed to engaging the university community and wider public who
are interested in learning more about the history of slavery and the experiences
of enslaved campus laborers. The project consists of the in-person tour, accessible
self-guided versions, a simple digital humanities site, and several publications.
With every tour, lecture, and publication, I helped revise the commemorative
landscape to include these African American voices, experiences, and memories.
Between 2015 and 2022, I conducted in-person tours to more than 5,500 individuals. After my departure, University of Alabama students have continued the
in-person regular tours.

Interestingly, the Hallowed Grounds Project reclaimed the campus UDC
chapter motto—"Least We Forget"—and placed it firmly within the African
American commemorative tradition.[31] The current University of Alabama community will no longer easily forget the names and contributions of the University Drum Corps. Neither will they disremember Crawford and Gabe, who
retreated into the archival void when President Garland abandoned the campus
after encountering federal forces. Nor will the campus forget Claiborne Garland,
Jeremiah Barnes, and others emancipated on April 4, 1865. These survivors embodied the emancipationist Civil War tradition in their lives and community
institutions in Tuscaloosa. Some, like the named men, became occasional paid
university employees. They used their wages and institutional connections for
the betterment of Black Tuscaloosa. They also sustained a countermemory of the
Civil War and emancipation into the twentieth century.[32]

Because of the 2015 student comment, I had different types of conversations. I
no longer encountered students questioning slavery's existence, its fiery wartime
destruction, and its legacy for the current campus and wider Tuscaloosa communities. Rather, they wanted to know more about the school, explore the afterlives of slavery, and understand the institutional legacy. In short, the Hallowed
Grounds Project revealed the inadequacy of previous institutional attempts at
undoing the intentional silencing of the UA slave past. Within five years, the
names, experiences, and workspaces of Neal, Crawford, and Gabe mattered for
both tour participants and the campus community who regularly walked by the
historic wartime slave cabin.

More important, the Hallowed Grounds Project has resulted in a significant
revision to the campus landscape. The 2017 Charlottesville Unite the Right rally
events brought an awareness of the divisive Confederate monument and other
iconography in the campus landscape. The UDC Boulder became visible to

diverse stakeholders whether on their own volition but most often in a class-room setting or on a Hallowed Grounds tour. The privilege to ignore became impossible. As the contemporary inheritors of the Lost Cause campus landscape, twenty-first-century undergraduate and graduate students, faculty, staff, and ad-ministrators grappled with the monument builders' intent. They, like "Southern blacks, who had no stake in celebrating the Confederacy, had to share a cultural landscape that did."[33]

In response to the 2020 George Floyd murder amid a global COVID-19 pandemic, concerned graduate and undergraduate students drafted yet an-other petition demanding a revised campus landscape defined by slavery, the Lost Cause, and Jim Crow segregation. Petitioners insisted on the relocation of the UDC Boulder and two Confederate plaques to university archival collec-tions. They also demanded hiring of diverse faculty, a robust retention strategy for faculty, staff, and students, and campus policing reform. These students un-derstood how Lost Cause symbols embodied the burden of a festering "wound that has not been allowed to heal."[34] This institutional slave past influenced not only the placement of the UDC Boulder but the decision to remain a white educational space where the Tuscaloosa descendant communities could only find low-paying employment until 1963. These students and signatories un-derstood the necessity for an institutional reckoning. Based on previous ad-ministrative inaction, students hoped administrators would listen but did not expect them to.

On June 8, 2020, the UA Board of Trustees and administration defied expecta-tions. They announced a UA system commission tasked with reconsidering prob-lematic building names and the removal of three Confederate memorial places. Prior to the official notification, two plaques on the Amelia Gayle Gorgas Library and the UDC Boulder plaque had been removed and placed in the archives. The following day, more importantly, a facilities crew hoisted the 110-year-old UDC Boulder off its pedestal and removed it from the centrally located Quad to an un-disclosed location.[35] Fresh sod and careful landscaping have since made it impos-sible to recall its existence. It is unclear how much of the decision was based on the overwhelming petition response received, fear of widespread campus protest once students returned from summer break, or institutional performative ally-ship that offered temporary redress. The university has subsequently renamed six buildings. Only one drew campus-wide protest when trustees attempted to ap-pease protesters with a new hyphenated building name that recognized both the original namesake of a Ku Klux Klan Grand Cyclops with a Civil Rights pioneer. Within a week, the Civil Rights pioneer became the sole building namesake.

Autherine Lucy Hall now adorns the College of Education building. At present, the campus now has fewer whitewashed Lost Cause symbols.[36]

The work of the Hallowed Grounds Project remains necessary even though I am no longer on the University of Alabama faculty. The names, experiences, and descendants of the enslaved drummers and other enslaved campus laborers still must be meaningfully and sustainably reinserted into the landscape. Even as UA reconsiders its problematic campus landscape, there has been no mention of placing a new plaque bearing their names on the surviving Civil War–era building where the University Drum Corps labored. There also has not been any discussion of renaming buildings or adding new memorials to the enslaved campus laborers. As long as these enslaved individuals are excluded from the built landscape, self-congratulatory narratives and platitudes will remain inadequate in reconciling the Lost Cause landscape. Instead of reparative justice, removal might encourage the embrace of a "we removed and renamed problematic symbol" culture.

As a result, I will continue to share this complicated Civil War memory. Moving from the porch outside my office in the renamed Manly Hall to Davidson College during the summer of 2022, my scholarship, teaching, and digital spaces remain crucial sites of engagement.[37] Institutional leaders and some former colleagues would prefer if I did not continue. Erasure, whitewashing, and intentional silencing of Black women's labor remains engrained. I, however, understand my role. I am building on the legacy of the countless number of African Americans who chose the active act of remembrance.

Lest we forget the enslaved University Drum Corps members as well as the ordinary African Americans who persisted and sustained a complex Civil War memory into the twentieth and twenty-first centuries. We, in the present, must find a place for them in the American Civil War commemorative landscape, develop new scholarly understandings of the breadth and contours of their Civil War remembrances, and prevent the continued erasure of the role of African Americans in the American collective consciousness.

Acknowledgments

This book has been a labor of love. I benefited from a summer research grant from the University of Alabama and a sabbatical leave as the 2020–2021 Vann Professor of Ethics in Society at Davidson College. Annual APUSH reading events, invited talks and workshops, and work on an NPS-OAH historic resource study funded the writing of this book. The broader issues of humanities research, such as funding, sabbaticals, and gatekeeping, affected all aspects of this project. Unfortunately, self-funding remains the rule and not the exception in producing many historical monographs.

Nevertheless, I persisted.

While funding proved elusive, I am grateful for my editor Andy Slap and everyone at Fordham University Press who always had faith in the project. This book benefited from the generosity of scholars who helped at every stage. Some read early drafts. Others helped me think through the various chapters. All sustained me. I am indebted to Ed Ayers, Catherine Bateson, Lauren Cardon, Deidre Cooper-Owens, Karen Cox, Adam Domby, Le'Trice Donaldson, Greg Downs, Jim Downs, Crystal Feimster, Mike Fitzgerald, Elaine Frantz, Nishani Frazier, Megan Gallagher, Barb Gannon, Judy Giesburg, Sharony Green, Thavolia Glymph, Marja Humphrey, Christy Hyman, Brian Matthew Jordan, Ryan Keating, Kelly Kennington, Ethan Kytle, Ashleigh Lawrence-Sanders, Kevin Levin, Kate Masur, Utz McKnight, Jessy Ohl, Holly Pinheiro, Paul Quigley, John Quist, Blain Roberts, K. T. Shively, David Silkenat, Brooks Simpson, Sara-Maria Sorrentino, Erin Stoneking, Rose Stremlau, Frank Towers, Tara White and Kidada Williams. Conference presentations at African American Intellectual Historical Society (AAIHS), American Historical Association (AHA), Association for the Study of African American Life and History (ASALH), British American Nineteenth Century Historians (BrANCH), the Nau Center for Civil War History's Signature Conference, Organization of American Historians (OAH), Society of Civil War Historians (SCWH), the Southern Historical Association (SHA), and Society of Military Historians (SMH) offered additional refinement. Chapters 1 and 5 benefited from feedback received at the University of Edinburgh's American History Seminar and SHA Second Book Workshop. Invited talks at the City University of New York Graduate Center's National Endowment for the

Humanities (NEH) Summer Institute of the Visual Culture of the American Civil War and Its Aftermath, Ford's Theatre, Gettysburg National Military Park, and Youngstown State University clarified my audience and arguments.

Archivists, research librarians, and genealogists proved invaluable. During the COVID-19 lockdowns, however, certain chapters would not have been possible without archival scans made at Special Collections at Stanford University Libraries, Temple University's Charles L. Blockson Afro-American Collection, Massachusetts State Archives, and the Western Reserve Historical Society. Again, thank you for your essential labor and expertise throughout this journey.

This book is my attempt to honor the collective memory work and activism that kept Black Civil War memory alive across the generations. My parents introduced me to their community's kinkeepers. They filled in the archival silences with additional insights. They also provided feedback on the various drafts. Words cannot capture my gratitude for your time, patience, and faith in me. My brothers, sister-in-law, aunts, uncles, and cousins listened to my updates and offered their unwavering support. Dorothy Redford and other community kinkeepers shared their preserved archival collections. Some retraced their commemorative geographies with me. Sadly, several have departed this world, but their legacy continues through me.

The presidential cats (Rutherford B. Hayes, James A. Garfield, and Crete) and I thank you.

Notes

Porches: An Introduction

1. Joseph R. Winters, "About Ten Days after the Battle of Gettysburg," song sheet, 1863, VF-Winters, Franklin County Historical Society, Chambersburg, PA.

2. Kimberlé Crenshaw, "Mapping the Margins: Intersectionality, Identity Politics, and Violence against Women of Color," *Stanford Law Review* 43 (July 1991): 1244–1245.

3. See Karen L. Cox, *Dixie's Daughters: The United Daughters of the Confederacy and the Preservation of Confederate Culture* (Gainesville: University Press of Florida, 2003); Bruce Baker, *What Reconstruction Meant: Historical Memory in the American South* (Charlottesville: University of Virginia Press, 2009); W. Fitzhugh Brundage, *The Southern Past: A Clash of Race and Memory* (Cambridge, MA: Belknap Press of Harvard University Press, 2008).

4. See Anne E. Marshall, *Creating a Confederate Kentucky: The Lost Cause and Civil War Memory in a Border State* (Chapel Hill: University of North Carolina Press, 2010); Caroline E. Janney, *Remembering the Civil War: Reunion and the Limits of Reconciliation* (Chapel Hill: University of North Carolina Press, 2013); and Anne Sarah Rubin, *Through the Heart of Dixie: Sherman's March and American Memory* (Chapel Hill: University of North Carolina Press, 2014).

5. See William Blair, *Cities of the Dead: Contesting the Memory of the Civil War in the South, 1865–1914* (Chapel Hill: University of North Carolina Press, 2004); Brian Matthew Jordan, *Marching Home: Union Veterans and Their Unending Civil War* (New York: W. W. Norton, 2014); Christopher Phillips, *The Rivers Ran Backward: The Civil War and the Remaking of the American Middle Border* (New York: Oxford University Press, 2016); Matthew E. Stanley, *The Loyal West: Civil War and Reunion in Middle America* (Urbana: University of Illinois Press, 2017).

6. Barbara Gannon, *The Won Cause: Black and White Comradeship in the Grand Army of the Republic* (Chapel Hill: University of North Carolina Press, 2011).

7. See Joseph T. Wilson, *The Black Phalanx: A History of the Negro Soldiers of the United States in the War of Independence, the War of 1812 and the Civil War* (Hartford, CT: American Publishing Company, 1888); Luis F. Emilio, *The Assault on Fort Wagner, July 18, 1863: The Memorable Charge of the Fifty-fourth Regiment of Massachusetts Volunteers, Written for "The Springfield Republican"* (Boston: Rand Avery Company, 1887); William Wells Brown, *The Negro in the American Rebellion: His Heroism and His Fidelity* (Boston: Lee and Shepard, 1867).

8. Yael A. Sternhall, *War on Record: The Archive and the Afterlife of the Civil War* (New Haven, CT: Yale University Press, 2023), 8–9.

9. Sternhall, *War on Record*, 188, 207–209, 213–217; See Kevin M. Levin, *Searching for Black Confederates* (Chapel Hill: University of North Carolina Press, 2020); Adam

H. Domby, *The False Cause: Fraud, Fabrication, and White Supremacy in Confederate Memory* (Charlottesville: University of Virginia Press, 2020); Micki McElya, *Clinging to Mammy: The Faithful Slave in Twentieth-Century America* (Cambridge, MA: Harvard University Press, 2007).

10. The informal and formal education of Du Bois, Woodson, and other Civil War veterans' children cannot be overlooked. It inspired their academic scholarship challenging white supremacy and the racial myths sustaining Jim Crow segregation. See David Levering Lewis, *W. E. B. Du Bois: Biography of a Race, 1868–1919* (New York: Henry Holt, 1993), 11–149; Carter G. Woodson, "My Recollections of Veterans of the Civil War," *Negro History Bulletin 7*, no. 5 (February 1944): 103, 104, 115–118.

11. Susie King Taylor, *Reminiscences of My Life in Camp With the 3rd United States Colored Troops Late 1st S.C. Volunteers* (Boston: Self-Published, 1902) and Thavolia Glymph, "'Liberty Dearly Bought': The Making of Civil War Memory in Afro-American Communities in the South," in *Time Longer Than Rope: A Century of African American Activism, 1850–1950*, ed. Charles M. Payne and Adam Green (New York: New York University Press, 2003), 111–139. For expansion beyond the North–South binary, see Kendra Taira Field, *Growing Up with the Country: Family, Race, and Nation after the Civil War* (New Haven, CT: Yale University Press, 2018), 6–10, 15–18; Alaina E. Roberts, *I've Been Here All the While: Black Freedom on Native Land* (Philadelphia: University of Pennsylvania Press, 2021), 1, 57–58, 137–141; Annette Gordon-Reed, *On Juneteenth* (New York: Liveright, 2021), 11–14; 135–137; Fay Yarbrough, *Choctaw Confederates: The American Civil War in Indian Country* (Chapel Hill: University of North Carolina Press, 2021), 115, 124–125, 132, 180–201.

12. Michel-Rolph Trouillot, *Silencing the Past: Power and the Production of History*, with a new foreword by Hazel V. Carby (Boston: Beacon Press, 2015), 1–30; Saidiya Hartman, "Venus in Two Acts," *Small Axe* 12 (June 2008): 1–14; Stanley H. Griffin, "Noises in the Archives: Acknowledging the Present Yet Silenced Presence in Caribbean Archival Memory," in *Archival Silences: Missing, Lost, and Uncreated Archives*, ed. Michael Moss and David Thomas (London: Routledge, 2021), 84–86, 95.

13. See Kathleen Ann Clark, *Defining Moments: African American Commemoration and Political Culture in the South, 1863–1913* (Chapel Hill: University of North Carolina Press, 2005); Heather A. Williams, *Help Me to Find My People: The African American Search for Family Lost in Slavery* (Chapel Hill: University of North Carolina Press, 2012); James Oliver Horton and Lois E. Horton, eds., *Slavery and Public History: The Tough Stuff of American Memory* (Chapel Hill: University of North Carolina Press, 2006); Leslie Schwalm, *Emancipation's Diaspora: Race and Emancipation in the Upper Midwest* (Chapel Hill: University of North Carolina Press, 2009); Tiya Miles, *Tales of the Haunted South: Dark Tourism and Memories of Slavery from the Civil War Era* (Chapel Hill: University of North Carolina Press, 2015).

14. See Brundage, *The Southern Past*; Karen L. Cox, *Dreaming of Dixie: How the South Was Created in American Popular Culture* (Chapel Hill: University of North Carolina Press, 2013); Reiko Hillyer, *Designing Dixie: Tourism, Memory, and Urban Space in the New South* (Charlottesville: University of Virginia Press, 2014); Ethan J. Kytle and Blain Roberts, *Denmark Vesey's Garden: Slavery and Memory in the Cradle of the Confederacy* (New York: New Press, 2018).

15. Sternhall, *War on Record*, 1, 6–9.

16. See Daniel Thorp, *Facing Freedom: An African American Community in Virginia from Reconstruction to Jim Crow* (Charlottesville: University of Virginia Press, 2017), 3–4; Amy Murrell Taylor, *Embattled Freedom: Journeys through the Civil War's Slave Refugee Camps* (Chapel Hill: University of North Carolina Press, 2018), 15–18; Field, *Growing Up with the Country*, 6–15.

17. Chad Williams, Kidada E. Williams, and Keisha N. Blain, *Charleston Syllabus: Readings on Race, Racism, and Racial Violence* (Athens: University of Georgia Press, 2016), 1–5, 7–8.

18. Hilary Green, "2 Shifting Landscapes and the Monument Removal Craze, 2015–20," *Patterns of Prejudice* 54, no. 5 (December 2020): 487–488; Barack Obama, Establishment of the Reconstruction Era National Monument by the President of the United States of America: A Proclamation, January 12, 2017, https://obamawhitehouse.archives.gov/the-press-office/2017/01/12/presidential-proclamations-establishment-reconstruction-era-national.

19. Louis P. Nelson and Claudrena N. Harold, eds., *Charlottesville 2017: The Legacy of Race and Inequity* (Charlottesville: University of Virginia Press, 2018), xiv–xvi, 1–14.

20. See Ta-Nehisi Coates, *Between the World and Me* (New York: Spiegel and Grau, 2015), 99–107, 131–132.

21. Trouillot, *Silencing the Past*, 23.

22. In her essential 1985 article, sociologist Carolyn J. Rosenthal defined the term of kinkeeper as "the position filled by the family task specialist" who has the responsibility of "keeping family members in touch with one another" through social occasions, communication networks, family and community genealogy, and bridging home and family disrupted by migration or significant interpersonal events. The work is not limited to blood relatives and often includes chosen family members. I embrace this concept for understanding my relationship to my family, the communities where I researched, lived, and/or worked, and the individuals who shared their porch archives explored in the book. See Carolyn J. Rosenthal, "Kinkeeping in the Familial Division of Labor," *Journal of Marriage and Family* 47, no. 4 (November 1985): 965–966, 969.

23. See Carol B. Stack, *All Our Kin: Strategies for Survival in a Black Community* (New York: Harper and Row, 1974), 59–61, and Margaret K. Nelson, "Fictive Kin, Families We Choose, and Voluntary Kin: What Does the Discourse Tell Us?" *Journal of Family Theory and Review* 5 (December 2013): 261–274.

24. Field, *Growing Up with the Country*, x.

25. Field, *Growing Up with the Country*, 15.

26. Clint Smith, *How The Word Is Passed: A Reckoning with the History of Slavery across America* (New York: Little, Brown, 2021), 7; Lauret Savoy, *Trace: Memory, History, Race, and the American Landscape* (Berkeley, CA: Counterpoint, 2015), 2.

1. Remembering the Enslavement of Black Pennsylvanians

1. Samuel Nickless, "The New Version of the Colored Volunteer," American Song Sheets collection, David M. Rubenstein Rare Book & Manuscript Library, Duke University, Durham, NC; Record for Samuel Nickless, Film Number M589 Roll 64, Civil War

Soldiers and Sailors System (CWSS), http://www.itd.nps.gov/cwss/, accessed November 17, 2017; *Compiled Military Service Records* of Samuel Nickless, Ancestry.com. *U.S. Colored Troops Military Service Records, 1863–1865* [database online], Provo, UT, USA: Ancestry.com Operations Inc, 2007, accessed November 17, 2017.

2. Christian McWhirter, *Battle Hymns: The Power and Popularity of Music in the Civil War* (Chapel Hill: University of North Carolina Press, 2012), 73–77, 132–35, 158–162.

3. Nickless, "The New Version of the Colored Volunteer"; McWhirter, *Battle Hymns*, 59–60.

4. Erica Armstrong Dunbar, *A Fragile Freedom: African American Women and Emancipation in the Antebellum City* (New Haven, CT: Yale University Press, 2008), 149–150; Judith Giesburg, ed., *Emile Davis's Civil War: The Diaries of a Free Black Woman in Philadelphia, 1863–1865,* transcribed and annotated by the Memorable Days Project Editorial Team (University Park: Pennsylvania State University Press, 2014), 47; Karsonya Wise Whitehead, *Notes from a Colored Girl: The Civil War Pocket Diaries of Emilie Frances Davis* (Columbia: University of South Carolina Press, 2014), 39–40.

5. Nickless, "The New Version of the Colored Volunteer"; McWhirter, *Battle Hymns*, 131.

6. Scholars have provided some discussion of the seizure and enslavement of free Blacks in relation to the Gettysburg Campaign and/or the wartime of destruction of Chambersburg. This chapter is in conversation with these works but offers careful attention to the experiences and memories of Black Pennsylvanians and county residents. See Edward L. Ayers, *In the Presence of Mine Enemies: The Civil War in the Heart of America* (New York: W. W. Norton, 2003); Edward L. Ayers, *The Thin Light of Freedom: The Civil War and Emancipation in the Heart of America* (New York: W. W. Norton, 2017); Ted Alexander, "A Regular Slave Hunt: The Army of Northern Virginia and Black Civilians in the Gettysburg Campaign," *North and South* 4, no. 7 (September 2001): 82–89; Edwin B. Coddington, *The Gettysburg Campaign: A Study in Command* (New York: Charles Scribner's Sons, 1984); Mark Neely Jr., *Southern Rights: Political Prisoners and the Myth of Confederate Constitutionalism* (Charlottesville: University Press of Virginia, 1999), Megan Kate Nelson, *Ruin Nation: Destruction and the American Civil War* (Athens: University of Georgia Press, 2012), and David G. Smith, *On the Edge of Freedom: The Fugitive Slave Issue in South Central Pennsylvania, 1820–1870* (New York: Fordham University Press, 2013).

7. J. E. B. Stuart to Robert E. Lee, October 12, 1862, MSS 448, Albert and Shirley Small Collections Library, University of Virginia, Charlottesville, VA; Smith, *On the Edge of Freedom*, 182, 191–192; Ayers, *The Thin Light of Freedom*, 45–52, 200–201.

8. Edwin B. Coddington, *The Gettysburg Campaign: A Study in Command* (New York: Charles Scribner's Sons, 1984), 160.

9. Major Charles Blacknall, 23rd NC Infantry to brother George, June 18, 1863, printed in the *(NC) Carolina Watchman,* July 13, 1863, 2, Gettysburg Library File V7-NC23, Gettysburg National Park Library and Research Center, Gettysburg, PA.

10. Blacknall to George, June 18, 1863; Smith, *On The Edge of Freedom*, 188–191.

11. "Telegraphic to the Northern Press," *Weekly Arkansas Gazette*, July 4, 1863, 3; "Untitled," The Daily Progress (Raleigh, NC), July 13, 1863, 2.

12. "Scenes at Chambersburg," *Daily Picayune*, July 10, 1863, 1.

13. "Scenes at Chambersburg."

14. Rachel Cormany Diary (1863), June 16, 1863, entry, in The Valley of the Shadow, University of Virginia, Charlottesville, VA, http://valley.lib.virginia.edu. Both Edward L. Ayers and Ted Alexander extensively employed the Cormany diary in their respective works. Ayers, *The Presence of Mine Enemies*, 405 and Alexander, "A Regular Slave Hunt," 85.

15. Alexander, "A Regular Slave Hunt," 85–86; J. D. Edmiston Turner, "Civil War Days in Mercersburg as Related in the Diary of the Rev. Thomas Creigh, Kittochittiny Historical Society, February 29, 1940," in Valley of the Shadow; Philip Schaff, DD, "The Gettysburg Week," *Scribner's Magazine* 16, no. 1 (July 1894): 21–30.

16. Alexander, "A Regular Slave Hunt," 85.

17. Ayers, *The Presence of Mine Enemies*, 406.

18. Alexander, "A Regular Slave Hunt," 86; Ayers, *The Presence of Mine Enemies*, 406–407.

19. Ayers, *The Presence of Mine Enemies*, 406; Jacob Hoke, *Historical Reminiscences of the War: Incidents Which Transpired in and about Chambersburg, During the War of the Rebellion* (Chambersburg, PA: M. A. Foltz, Printer and Publisher, 1884), 38–39.

20. Hoke, *Historical Reminiscences of the War*, 38–39.

21. Robert Grier Stephens, *Intrepid Warrior: Clement Anselm Evans Confederate General from Georgia: Life, Letters, and Diaries of the War Years* (Dayton, OH: Morningside House, 1992), 218.

22. M. L. Marotte III, "The Story of Joseph Winters, 1816–1916: Citizen, Pioneer, Inventor, Gunsmith, Machinist, Land Owner, and Born a Free Man" (Chambersburg: M. L. Marotte III, 1999), 3, accessed in VF—Winters, Franklin County Historical Society, Chambersburg, PA; Stella M. Fries, Janet Z. Gabler, and C. Bernard Ruffin, eds., *Some Chambersburg Roots: A Black Perspective* (Chambersburg: Stella Fries, 1980), 235–238.

23. Joseph R. Winters, "About Ten Days after the Battle of Gettysburg," song sheet, 1863, VF-Winters, Franklin County Historical Society, Chambersburg, PA.

24. Winters, "About Ten Days after the Battle of Gettysburg."

25. Winters, "About Ten Days after the Battle of Gettysburg."

26. *Old Mercersburg Revisited: Civil War to Bicentennial* (Mercersburg, PA: Woman's Club of Mercersburg, 1987), 236.

27. Winters, "About Ten Days After the Battle of Gettysburg."

28. "Larry Dean Calimer, b. 1938, interview," in *Voices of Chambersburg: An Oral History of the African American Community of Franklin County, Pennsylvania*, vol. 1 of 4—*Interviews*, by C. Bernard Ruffin (Greencastle, PA: Allison-Antrim Museum, 2011), 130.

29. Calimer interview.

30. Max Woodhull to Orlando Brown, December 18, 1865, Valley of the Shadow.

31. "Gossip with Friends," *Franklin Repository*, March 30, 1864, 5.

32. "Gossip with Friends."

33. "Gossip with Friends."

34. Alexander, "A Regular Slave Hunt," 88.

35. "Paroled," *Franklin Repository*, April 5, 1865, 3; Mark Neely Jr., *Southern Rights: Political Prisoners and the Myth of Confederate Constitutionalism* (Charlottesville: University Press of Virginia, 1999), 139–140.

36. Hudibras, "The Rebs in G____; or, Incidents of the Invasion," *Pilot*, August 18, 1863, 1. Exact numbers are hard to determine as both free Blacks and fleeing contrabands were present in the county. Also, many simply migrated out of the county to Harrisburg, Carlisle, Lancaster, and Philadelphia. I believe that William Heyser offers the best estimate of individuals seized from Chambersburg as 250 and from other accounts probably another 150–200 individuals from other Franklin County towns, villages, and hamlets. The Gettysburg Campaign represented a major dislocation of the African American community from south-central Pennsylvania.

37. Hudibras, "The Rebs in G____; or, Incidents of the Invasion."

38. "The Foray on Chambersburg," *Daily Alta California*, July 15, 1863, 1. The letter was also reprinted and published in "List of Letters Received since Our Last," *Pacific Appeal*, July 18, 1863, 2.

39. "From Chambersburg—What Jenkins Did—The Place Literally 'Cleaned Out,'" *Sacramento Daily Union*, July 18, 1863, 2.

40. Coddington, *Gettysburg Campaign*, 179; J. E. B. Stuart to Robert E. Lee, October 12, 1862, Special Collections, Albert and Shirley Small Collections Library, University of Virginia, Charlottesville, Virginia; Samuel P. Bates and J. Fraise Richard, *History of Franklin County, Pennsylvania: Containing a History of the County, its Townships, Towns, Villages, Schools, Churches, Industries, etc.; Portraits of Early Settlers and Prominent men, Biographies; History of Pennsylvania, Statistical and Miscellaneous Matter, etc.* (Chicago: Warner Beers, 1887), 356–360; Schaff, "The Gettysburg Week," 21.

41. Schaff, "The Gettysburg Week," 24.

42. "The Late Visit of the Confederates to Chambersburg, &c.," *The Sun*, June 20, 1863, 1.

43. "The Late Visit of the Confederates to Chambersburg, &c.," 1.

44. David Demus to Mary Jane Demus, October 7, 1863, and Jacob Christy to Mary Jane Demus, August 10, 1864, in Valley of the Shadow

45. Jacob Christy to Mary Jane Demus, August 10, 1864, in Valley of the Shadow.

46. "Colored Recruits," *Village Record*, March 27, 1863, 2; "Negro Recruits," *Village Record*, May 8, 1863, 2; "Negro Soldiers," *Patriot and Union*, May 7, 1863, 3, clipping, Dauphin County Historical Society, Harrisburg, PA.

47. *Old Mercersburg Revisited*, 236.

48. Smith, *On The Edge of Freedom*, 187.

49. Addresses of the Hon. W. D. Kelley, Miss Anna E. Dickinson, and Mr. Frederick Douglass, at a Mass Meeting held at National Hall, Philadelphia, July 6, 1863, for the Promotion of Colored Enlistments, Special Collections, Albert and Shirley Small Collections Library, University of Virginia, Charlottesville, Virginia. "Fall In!," Mercersburg Journal, July 17, 1863, 3.

50. Joseph R. Winters, "At the Time of the Draft for the Civil War." song, VF—Winters.

51. Winters, "About Ten Days after the Battle of Gettysburg"; Cooper Wingert, "Fighting for State Citizenship in the US Colored Troops," *Civil War History* 69, no. 3 (September 2023): 25–26.

52. Frederick Douglass, "Men of Color, to Arms," March 3, 1863, Frederick Douglass Papers, Library of Congress, Washington, DC, https://www.loc.gov/item/mfd.22005/.

53. Winters, "At the Time of the Draft for the Civil War."

54. See "Discharged from Richmond," *Franklin Repository,* December 23, 1863, 8, "Just from Dixie," *Mercersburg Journal,* December 25, 1863, 2.

55. "Discharged from Richmond," *Franklin Repository,* December 23, 1863, 8.

56. File C (WD) 1025, Dec. 3, 1863. J. V. Moore related to Amos Barnes a free Negro, in Correspondence and Reports Relating to Federal Citizens, Clerks, and Sutlers Confined in Castle Thunder Prison, RG 249 Records of the Commissary General of Prisoners, box 1, NM 68 131, National Archives, Washington, DC.

57. File C (WD) 1025, Dec. 3, 1863. J. V. Moore related to Amos Barnes a free Negro.

58. File C (WD) 1025, Dec. 3, 1863. J. V. Moore related to Amos Barnes a free Negro.

59. File C (WD) 1025, Dec. 3, 1863. J. V. Moore related to Amos Barnes a free Negro.

60. William H. Burkhart, Samuel L. Daihl, J. Houston McCulloch, Dr. George Kaluger, Mrs. Elizabeth Roler, and Mrs. Howard A. Ryder. *Shippensburg, Pennsylvania in the Civil War* (Shippensburg: Burd Street Press, 2003), 214–217.

61. Nickless, "The New Version of the Colored Volunteer."

62. Ron Gancas, *Fields of Freedom: United States Colored Troops from Southwestern Pennsylvania* (Soldiers and Sailors Memorial Hall and Trust, 2004), 46, accessed at the Pennsylvania State Archives, Harrisburg, PA; *Old Mercersburg Revisited,* 236.

63. RG-2, Damage Claims Applicants for Cumberland and Franklin Counties, roll 6161, Pennsylvania State Archives, Harrisburg, PA.

64. Martha Minow, *Between Vengeance and Forgiveness: Facing History after Genocide and Mass Violence* (Boston: Beacon Press, 1998), 93–94, 117.

65. "Notice," *Christian Recorder,* February 11, 1865; "Information wanted of Rose Jackson," *Christian Recorder,* August 14, 1869; Heather A. Williams, *Help Me to Find My People: The African American Search for Family Lost in Slavery* (Chapel Hill: University of North Carolina, 2012), 168. For more on the use of newspapers and church publications, see Williams, *Help Me to Find My People,* 153–156

66. Eric Foner, *Reconstruction: America's Unfinished Revolution, 1863–1877* (New York: Harper and Row, 1988), 69; Randall M. Miller, "Introduction: The Freedmen's Bureau and Reconstruction: An Overview," in *The Freedmen's Bureau and Reconstruction: Reconsiderations,* ed. Paul A. Cimbala and Randall M. Miller (New York: Fordham University Press, 1999), xvii–xviii.

67. Captain W. Storer How to Colonel Orlando Brown, September 9, 1865, and Anthony Marston to Thomas P. Jackson, December 2, 1867, in the Valley of the Shadow.

68. Sharon Romeo, *Gender and the Jubilee: Black Freedom and the Reconstruction of Citizenship in Civil War Missouri* (Athens: University of Georgia Press, 2016), 3.

69. Capt. W. Storer How to Capt. R. S. Lacey, November 10, 1865, in the Valley of the Shadow, University of Virginia.

70. Kensie to Madison Leary, November 8, 1865, and [Shipley] to Kensie in Records of the Field Offices for the State of Virginia, Bureau of Refugees, Freedmen and Abandoned Land, 1865–1872, M1913, National Archives at Atlanta, Morrow, GA; How to Lacey, November 10, 1865.

71. Smith, *On the Edge of Freedom,* 191–192.

72. Albert Ordway to Orlando Brown, February 1, 1866, and Priscilla Marshall to Orlando Brown, April 4, 1866, Valley of the Shadow.

73. Marshall to Brown, April 4, 1866.

268   NOTES TO PAGES 30–34

74. Priscilla Marshall to H. S. Merrill, March 18, 1866, and Ann Gibbons to H. S. Merrill, March 18, 1866, in Registers of Letters Received, vol. 1, microfilm roll 164, Records of the Field Offices for the State of Virginia, Bureau of Refugees, Freedmen, and Abandoned Lands, 1865–1872, M1913 (Washington, DC: National Archives and Records Administration, 2006) accessed at the National Archives at Atlanta, Morrow, GA; Romeo, *Gender and the Jubilee*, 81–84.

75. "Untitled," *New Orleans Tribune*, October 15, 1864, 2; Thomas E. Cochran, *Address delivered at McSherrysville, Lower Chanceford Twp., York County, Pennsylvania, on the fourth day of July, 1865, by Thomas E. Cochran* (Lancaster: Pearsol & Geist, Printers, 1865), 11.

76. For the conflation of the two events and supremacy of Chambersburg, see W. S. Everett, Esq., "An Address: Delivered on the 4th of July, 1865, to the Returned Soldiers," *Franklin Repository*, July 19, 1865, 3.

77. Hoke, *Historical Reminiscences of the War*, 33–83 and Bates and Richard, *History of Franklin County, Pennsylvania*, 360–382.

78. See Sir Arthur James Lyon Fremantle, *Three Months in the Southern States: April, June 1863 by Lieut-Col. Freemantle, Coldstream Guards* (Mobile: S. H. Goetzel, 1864); John B. Gordon, *Reminiscences of the Civil War* (New York: Charles Scribner's Sons, 1904); John Singleton Mosby, *The Memoirs of Colonel John S. Mosby, Edited by Charles Wells Russell with Illustrations* (Boston: Little, Brown, 1917); and Louis Leon, *Diary of a Tar Heel Confederate Soldier* (Charlotte, NC: Stone Publishing Company, 1913).

79. Hudibras, "The Rebs in G____; or, Incidents of the Invasion," *Pilot*, August 11, 1863, 1.

80. Sylviane A. Diouf, *Slavery's Exiles: The Story of American Maroons* (New York: New York University Press, 2014), 234.

81. Diouf, *Slavery's Exiles*, 234.

82. Minow, *Between Vengeance and Forgiveness*, 90.

83. "Citizens Seized," historical marker, Mercersburg, PA, The Historical Marker Database, http://www.hmdb.org/marker.asp?marker=8030, accessed October 28, 2016.

84. Alexander K. McClure, "Untitled," *Franklin Repository*, January 4, 1865, 3.

85. McClure, "Untitled," *Franklin Repository*, January 4, 1865, 3.

86. Kathleen Ann Clark, *Defining Moments: African American Commemoration and Political Culture in the South, 1863–1913* (Chapel Hill: University of North Carolina Press, 2005), 30–33.

87. "Negro Celebration," *Valley Spirit*, October 10, 1867, 3. For additional Emancipation Day coverage, see "The Colored Troops Fought Bravely," *Valley Spirit*, August 14, 1867, 3; "Negro Celebration," *Valley Spirit*, August 28, 1867, 3; "Colored 'Turn Out,'" *Village Record*, August 30, 1867, 2; "Grand Celebration," *Mercersburg Journal*, September 24, 1869, 2; "Emancipation Ball and Jubilee," *Valley Spirit*, September 27, 1871, 3; and "Untitled," *Public Opinion*, July 23, 1872, 3.

88. Few local newspapers noted the first anniversary of Confederate occupation. Rather, the communities planned celebrations and services for the Fourth of July. However, rumors of a possible Confederate invasion into the south-central Pennsylvania caused white and Black residents to hurriedly prepare for defense and temporary flight

out of the county rather than enjoy traditional Fourth of July celebrations and fireworks. See "A Year Ago," *Pilot*, June 14, 1864, 2; "Last Year," *Pilot*, June 21, 1864, 2; "Fourth of July in Chambersburg!" *Franklin Repository*, July 6, 1864, 1.

89. "Gossip with Friends," *Franklin Repository*, August 2, 1865, 3.

90. "Gossip with Our Friends," *Franklin Repository*, July 26, 1865, 3.

91. "Gossip with Our Friends," *Franklin Repository*, July 26, 1865, 3.

92. Capt. W. Storer How to Capt. R. S. Lacey, November 10, 1865, Valley of the Shadow.

93. "Gossip with Our Friends," *Franklin Repository*, July 26, 1865, 3.

94. "Parade of Autos Marks Beginning of Old Home Week," *Harrisburg Telegraph*, July 27, 1914, 1; "Secret Order Day with Great Parade Marks Celebration," *Harrisburg Telegraph*, July 28, 1914, 1; Ann Hull and Franklin County Historical Society-Kittochtinny, *Cumberland Valley: From Tuscarora to Chambersburg to Blue Ridge* (Charleston, SC: Arcadia Publishing, 2011), 24–26.

2. Honoring Liberators and the Grand Reception in Harrisburg, 1865

1. Diana Fishlock, "Pennsylvania Will Honor Black Civil War Soldiers Again," *Patriot News*, February 9, 2010, https://www.pennlive.com/life/2010/02/post_1.html.

2. Fishlock, "Pennsylvania Will Honor Black Civil War Soldiers Again."

3. Fishlock, "Pennsylvania Will Honor Black Civil War Soldiers Again." After careful consideration, the Pennsylvania Tourism office selected one hundred Black Pennsylvanians who served in the USCT regiments, crafted short biographies, and had Black reenactors tell each person's story at the event. For a full listing with biographies, see House Divided Project, "'100 Voices,' Pennsylvania Grand Review: Honoring African American Patriots, 1865/2010," https://housedivided.dickinson.edu/grandreview/category/individual-stories/, accessed September 4, 2022.

4. Fishlock, "Pennsylvania Will Honor Black Civil War Soldiers Again."

5. Fishlock, "Pennsylvania Will Honor Black Civil War Soldiers Again."

6. See Stephen Kantrowitz, *More Than Freedom: Fighting for Black Citizenship in a White Republic, 1829–1889* (New York: Penguin Books, 2013); Van Gosse, *The First Reconstruction: Black Politics in America from the Revolution to the Civil War* (Chapel Hill: University of North Carolina Press, 2021); Kate Masur, *Until Justice Be Done: America's First Civil Rights Movement* (New York: W. W. Norton, 2021).

7. E. James West, *Our Kind of Historian: The Work and Activism of Lerone Bennett Jr.* (Amherst: University of Massachusetts Press, 2022), 63.

8. August Meier and Elliott Rudwick, *From Plantation to Ghetto*. Rev. ed. (New York: Hill and Wang, 1970), 147–149.

9. "Grand Review of the Victorious Union Armies," *New York Herald*, May 2, 1865, 1; "The Grand Review," *Evening Union* (Washington, DC), May 18, 1865, 1; "The Disposition of Our Armies," *Daily National Intelligencer* (Washington, DC), May 4, 1865, 3.

10. Cecily N. Zander, "'Victory's Long Review': The Grand Review of Union Armies and the Meaning of the Civil War," *Civil War History* 66, no. 1 (March 2020): 49.

11. Brian Matthew Jordan, *Marching Home: Union Veterans and Their Unending Civil War* (New York: Liveright, 2014), 14; Zander, "'Victory's Long Review,'" 48–55.

12. Jordan, *Marching Home*, 10; Caroline E. Janney, *Remembering the Civil War: Reunion and the Limits of Reconciliation* (Chapel Hill: University of North Carolina Press, 2013), 69.

13. Maj. Gen. G. Weitzel to Col. E. W. Smith, Assistant Adjutant-General, April 17, 1865, OR, ser. 1, v. 46, pt. 3, 816; "The Funeral of President Lincoln. The Great Crowds. Services at the White House. Funeral Sermon and Prayers. The Procession. The Body Lying in State at the Capitol," *Chicago Tribune*, April 20, 1865, 1; "The Colored Troops," *Philadelphia Inquirer*, April 20, 1865, 8; Bob Luke and John David Smith, *Soldiering for Freedom: How the Union Army Recruited, Trained, and Deployed the US Colored Troops* (Baltimore: Johns Hopkins University Press, 2014), 102–104.

14. Zander, "'Victory's Long Review,'" 45–48; Jordan, *Marching Home*, 15–40; Janney, *Remembering the Civil War*, 69–71.

15. Zander, "'Victory's Long Review,'" 59–64; Janney, *Remembering the Civil War*, 71. African American participation in the Grand Review fed into the Black Confederate myth and erasure of Black federal service. See Kevin M. Levin, *Searching for Black Confederates: The Civil War's Most Persistent Myth* (Chapel Hill: University of North Carolina Press, 2019), 72–99, and Adam H. Domby, *The False Cause: Fraud, Fabrication, and White Supremacy in Confederate Memory* (Charlottesville: University of Virginia Press, 2020), 104–131, 136–141.

16. "Review of the Armies," *New York Times*, May 25, 1865, 8; Janney, *Remembering the Civil War*, 70–71. Janney suggests that there were a "few black pioneers who marched with Sherman's men." But surviving accounts reveal that these pioneers were the camp servants and contrabands of war who provided comic relief. If these individuals had appeared, it would have moderated Black Harrisburg residents' and other African Americans' critique of the whiteness on display at the Grand Review of Armies.

17. "Review of the Armies," *New York Times*, May 25, 1865, 8.

18. "Review of the Armies," *New York Times*, May 25, 1865, 8.

19. "Review of the Armies," *New York Times*, May 25, 1865, 8.

20. "The Grand Parade: Review of the Army of the Potomac," *Adams Sentinel* (Gettysburg, PA), May 30, 1865, 4.

21. Levin, *Searching for Black Confederates*, 3–11, 70–76, 84–90.

22. Jordan, *Marching Home*, 11; Stephen A. Berry, *The Jim Crow Routine: Everyday Performances of Race, Civil Rights, and Segregation in Mississippi* (Chapel Hill: University of North Carolina Press, 2015), 33.

23. Barbara Krauthamer, *Black Slaves, Indian Masters: Slavery, Emancipation, and Citizenship in the Native American South* (Chapel Hill: University of North Carolina Press, 2013), 98–100, 103–118; Fay A. Yarbrough, *Choctaw Confederates: The American Civil War in Indian Country* (Chapel Hill: University of North Carolina Press, 2021), 93–105, 115–150; Alaina E. Roberts, *I've Been Here All the While: Black Freedom on Native Land* (Philadelphia: University of Pennsylvania Press, 2021), 29–39; Jordan, *Marching Home*, 13–19; "The Grand Review," *Christian Recorder*, June 3, 1865, 3.

24. Jordan, *Marching Home*, 19.

25. Jordan, *Marching Home*, 19.

26. Jordan, *Marching Home*, 19.

27. See William A. Dobak, *Freedom by the Sword: The US Colored Troops, 1862–1867* (New York: Skyhorse, 2013), 335–422; Richard M. Reid, *Freedom for Themselves: North Carolina's Black Soldiers in the Civil War* (Chapel Hill: University of North Carolina Press, 2008), 111–185; Noah Andre Trudeau, *Like Men of War: Black Troops in the Civil War, 1862–1865* (Boston: Back Bay Books, 1998), 201–251, 283–309, 415–434; Kevin M. Levin, *Remembering the Battle of the Crater: War as Murder* (Lexington: University of Kentucky Press, 2017), 7–32; Earl J. Hess, *Trench Warfare under Grant and Lee: Field Fortifications in the Overland Campaign* (Chapel Hill: University of North Carolina Press, 2007), 35, 136; Elizabeth D. Leonard, *Benjamin Francis Butler: A Noisy, Fearless Life* (Chapel Hill: University of North Carolina Press, 2022), 138–139, 142–154; Mat Callahan, *Songs of Slavery and Emancipation*. Introduction by Robin D. G. Kelley (Jackson: University Press of Mississippi, 2022), 63.

28. Ira Berlin, Barbara Fields, Steven F. Miller, Joseph P. Reidy, and Leslie S. Rowland, *Free at Last: A Documentary History of Slavery, Freedom, and the Civil War* (New York: New Press, 1992), 528.

29. Berlin, Fields, Miller, Reidy, and Rowland, *Free at Last*, 533–535.

30. Berlin, Fields, Miller, Reidy, and Rowland, *Free at Last*, 525.

31. Berlin, Fields, Miller, Reidy, and Rowland, *Free at Last*, 525–526.

32. Trudeau, *Like Men of War*, 455–462; Dobak, *Freedom by the Sword*, 422–454; Douglas R. Egerton, *Thunder at the Gates: The Black Civil War Regiments That Redeemed America* (New York: Basic Books, 2016), 279–304; James K. Bryant, II, *The 36th Infantry United States Colored Troops in the Civil War: A History and Roster* (Jefferson, NC: McFarland, 2012), 121–124; For Black Pennsylvanians' response to the delayed demobilization of USCT soldiers and consequences for their families, see Holly A. Pinheiro Jr., *The Families' Civil War: Black Soldiers and the Fight for Racial Justice* (Athens: University of Georgia Press, 2022), 76–80; Jonathan Lande, "Trials of Freedom: African American Deserters during the US Civil War," *Journal of Social History* 49, no. 3 (Spring 2016): 700–704.

33. Elizabeth Regosin, *Freedom's Promise: Ex-Slave Families and Citizenship in the Age of Emancipation* (Charlottesville: University of Virginia Press, 2002), 3–20; Pinheiro, *The Families' Civil War*, 110–114,124–141; and Brandi Brimmer, *Claiming Union Widowhood: Race, Respectability, and Poverty in the Post-Emancipation South* (Durham, NC: Duke University Press, 2020), 77–122.

34. Regosin, *Freedom's Promise*, 114.

35. G. F. H., "From Boston," *New Orleans Tribune*, June 7, 1865, 1.

36. G. F. H., "From Boston."

37. Donald R. Shaffer, *After the Glory: The Struggles of Black Civil War Veterans* (Lawrence: University Press of Kansas, 2004), 185.

38. "General Butler on Confiscation," *The Liberator*, June 23, 1865, 98; "Gen. Butler on Negro Suffrage Boston, June 18, 1865," *San Francisco Bulletin*, July 18, 1865, 1; "Butler on Confiscation," *Daily Picayune*, June 25, 1865, 1.

39. General Butler on Confiscation."

40. Leonard, *Benjamin Francis Butler*, 160.

41. Millington W. Bergeson-Lockwood, *Race over Party: Black Politics and Partisanship in Late Nineteenth-Century Boston* (Chapel Hill: University of North Carolina Press, 2018), 40–44, 55–85; Leonard, *Benjamin Francis Butler*, 161–162, 197.

42. R. J. M. Blackett, *Thomas Morris Chester, Black Civil War Correspondent: His Dispatches from the Virginia Front* (Boston: Da Capo Press, 1989), 4–5; Katie Wingert McArdle, "Jane M. Chester," in *One Hundred Voices: Harrisburg's Historic African American Community, 1850–1920*, ed. Calobe Jackson Jr., Katie McArdle, and David Pettegrew (Grand Forks: The Digital Press at the University of North Dakota, 2020), 33–34; For more on the vibrant Black Harrisburg community that the Chesters were connected with, see Gerald G. Eggert, "'Two Steps Forward, a Step-and-a-Half Back': Harrisburg's African American Community in the Nineteenth Century," *Pennsylvania History: A Journal of Mid-Atlantic Studies* 58 (January 1991): 2–18.

43. Blackett, *Thomas Morris Chester, Black Civil War Correspondent*, 8–13; R. J. M. Blackett, *The Captive's Quest for Freedom: Fugitive Slaves, the 1850 Fugitive Slave Law, and the Politics of Slavery* (New York: Cambridge University Press, 2018), 42–87.

44. Blackett, *Thomas Morris Chester, Black Civil War Correspondent*, 16–31; Chester, Thomas Morris," *Biographical Encyclopedia*, 256, clipping, VF-Thomas Morris Chester, Dauphin County Historical Society; Blackett, *The Captive's Quest for Freedom*, 125–134.

45. "Chester, Thomas Morris"; Blackett, *Thomas Morris Chester, Black Civil War Correspondent*, 33–36; "T. Morris Chester," clipping, VF-Thomas Morris Chester, Dauphin County Historical Society; Cooper Wingert, "Fighting for State Citizenship in the US Colored Troops," *Civil War History* 69, no. 3 (September 2023): 16–17; Thomas M. Chester to Hon. Simon Cameron, April 23, 1862, VF-Thomas Morris Chester, Dauphin County Historical Society.

46. Richard L. Kearns, "T. Morris Chester," clipping, Thomas Morris Chester VF, 38–38 accessed at the Dauphin County Historical Society, Harrisburg, PA; Eggert, "'Two Steps Forward, a Step-and-a-Half Back,'" 14–16; Wingert, "Fighting for State Citizenship in the US Colored Troops," 20–24.

47. Blackett, *Thomas Morris Chester, Black Civil War Correspondent*, 40.

48. Blackett, *Thomas Morris Chester, Black Civil War Correspondent*, 41–42.

49. The precise founding of the organization is unclear. R. J. M. Blackett, biographer of Thomas Morris Chester, suggests August 1865. While Todd Mealy, biographer of William Howard Day, argues for September 1865. I intentionally noted the general time period of the founding here.

50. Sterling Stuckey, *Slave Culture: Nationalist Theory and the Foundations of Black America* (New York: Oxford University Press, 1987), 166–212; Blackett, *Thomas Morris Chester, Black Civil War Correspondent*, 47; Todd Mealy, *Aliened American: A Biography of William Howard Day, 1825 to 1865*, vol. 1 (Baltimore: Publish America, 2010), 368–369, accessed at Dauphin Historical Society; For a complete listing of the Garnet League officers, see Garnet League, *Ceremonies at the Reception of Welcome to the Colored Soldiers of Pennsylvania in the City of Harrisburg, November 14th, 1865, By the Garnet League: Together With the Report Of The Committee of Arrangements, and the Resolution of Vindication by the Garnet League Defining Its Position with Reference to the Pennsylvania State Equal Rights League* (Harrisburg, PA: Telegraph Steam Book and Job Office, 1866), 28.

51. Quoted in Blackett, *Thomas Morris Chester, Black Civil War Correspondent*, 46.

52. Blackett, *Thomas Morris Chester, Black Civil War Correspondent*, 46–47.

53. Blackett, *Thomas Morris Chester, Black Civil War Correspondent*, 47; Mealy, *Aliened American*, 367.

54. Mealy, *Aliened American*, 364–367; "Our Harrisburg Letter," *Christian Recorder*, October 21, 1865, 2.

55. Blackett, *Thomas Morris Chester, Black Civil War Correspondent*, 47; "Our Harrisburg Letter."

56. "Our Harrisburg Letter."

57. "Our Harrisburg Letter."

58. "Our Harrisburg Letter."

59. Quoted in Blackett, *Thomas Morris Chester, Black Civil War Correspondent*, 48.

60. "Our Harrisburg Letter."

61. R. J. M. Blackett, "Day, William Howard, Educators, Newspaper Editors/Publishers," in *American National Biography Online* (New York: Oxford University Press, 2000), https://doi.org/10.1093/anb/9780198606697.article.1600435; "W. H. Day, A.M., D.D.: The Death of a Noted Colored Man This Morning," *Harrisburg Telegraph*, December 6, 1900, 1, clipping, VF-Howard William Day, Dauphin County Historical Society, Harrisburg, PA.

62. R. J. M. Blackett, *Beating against the Barriers: The Six Lives of Nineteenth-Century Afro-Americans* (Ithaca, NY: Cornell University Press, 1986), 289–294; J. Brent Morris, *Oberlin Hotbed of Abolitionism: College, Community, and the Fight for Freedom and Equality in Antebellum America* (Chapel Hill: University of North Carolina Press, 2014), 146–152, 165–168; W. H. Day, A.M., D.D.: The Death of a Noted Colored Man this Morning."

63. Blackett, *Beating against the Barriers*, 295–310; Lindsay Drapkin, "William Howard Day," Colored Convention Heartland: Black Organizers, Women and the Ohio Movement, exhibit, in Colored Conventions Project: Bringing 19th-century Black Organizing to Digital Life, https://coloredconventions.org/ohio-organizing/biographies/william-howard-day/; Kabria Baumgartner, "Gender Politics and the Manual Labor College Initiative at National Colored Conventions in Antebellum America," in *The Colored Conventions Movement: Black Organizing in the Nineteenth Century*, ed. P. Gabrielle Foreman, Jim Casey, and Sarah Lynn Patterson (Chapel Hill: University of North Carolina Press, 2021), 238–241; Callahan, *Songs of Slavery and Emancipation*, 118.

64. Blackett, "Day, William Howard"; Richard M. Reid, *African Canadians in Union Blue: Volunteering for the Cause in the Civil War* (Kent, OH: Kent State University Press, 2014), 31–32; Blackett, *Beating against the Barriers*, 310–323; Extensive sections of Day's speech was reprinted with some brief commentary by L. A. Bell peppered throughout. See L. A. Bell, *Celebration by the Colored People's Educational Monument Association in Memory of Abraham Lincoln, on the Fourth of July, 1865, in the Presidential Grounds, Washington, DC. Printed by Order of the Board of Directors. L. A. Bell, Recording Secretary* (Washington, DC: McGill and Witherow, Printers and Stereotypers, 1865), 10–18.

65. Blackett, *Beating against the Barriers*, 326–380; Mary Klaus, "Marker Honors Abolition, Editor William Howard Day," *Patriot News*, July 22, 1997, clipping, VF-Howard William Day, Dauphin County Historical Society; "New School Board. Organized Monday Night for the Ensuing Year. Prof. Day Re-elected," *Harrisburg Telegraph*, June 11,

1892, 2; "Professor Day's Address," ca. 1892, clipping and *Program and Handbook of How-
ard Day Testimonial, 1847–1897. Wednesday, April 27th to Monday, May 2, 1898, at Wesley
Union African Methodist Episcopal Zion Church, South Street and Tanner's Avenue, Har-
risburg, PA* accessed in VF-Howard William Day, Dauphin County Historical Society;
Todd Mealy, *Aliened American: A Biography of William Howard Day: 1866–1900*, vol. 2
(Baltimore: Publish America, 2010), 189–215, 221–222, 387.

66. "Our Harrisburg Letter." *The Christian Recorder* correspondent reprinted the
extensive quotes from the Harrisburg *Telegraph* in its report.

67. "Our Harrisburg Letter."

68. "Our Harrisburg Letter."

69. Our Harrisburg Letter." Rev. John Walker Jackson, a white minister at Locust
Street Methodist Church and ally to the Black Harrisburg community, later recalled
his experiences during the Gettysburg campaign and the threat posed by the invading
Confederate army. His allyship contributed to his appearance at Garnet League events,
including the reception. See Rev. John Walker Jackson (1888), "A Pastor Recalls the Gettysburg Campaign," *Annals of Eastern Pennsylvania: Journal of the Historical Society of
the EPA Conference* (2006), 57–61.

70. Blackett, *Thomas Morris Chester, Black Civil War Correspondent*, 48.

71. Andrew K. Diemer, *Vigilance: The Life of William Still, Father of the Underground
Railroad* (New York: Alfred A. Knopf, 2022), 229–236.

72. Diemer, *Vigilance*, 236–237.

73. Diemer, *Vigilance*, 237.

74. Diemer, *Vigilance*, 261.

75. Diemer, *Vigilance*, 295–296, 305–306.

76. Garnet League, *Ceremonies at the Reception of Welcome to the Colored Soldiers of
Pennsylvania*,16–18.

77. Garnet League, *Ceremonies at the Reception of Welcome to the Colored Soldiers of
Pennsylvania*, 16.

78. See "Welcome to Colored Soldiers," *Philadelphia Inquirer*, October 26, 1865, 4;
"Colored Soldiers! Welcome! Welcome!!," advertisement, *Christian Recorder*, October
28, 1865, 3; "State Items," *Pittsburgh Daily Commercial*, November 4, 1865, 1; "Reception
of the Colored Heroes: A Grand Demonstration," *Harrisburg Daily Telegraph*, Novem-
ber 1, 1865, 3, and "Colored Soldiers! Welcome! Welcome!," *Harrisburg Daily Telegraph*,
November 1, 1865, evening edition, 2, clippings in Reception of Colored Troops—Nov.
14, 1865 VF, Dauphin County Historical Society, Harrisburg, PA; "Colored Soldiers!
Welcome! Welcome!!," advertisement, *Anglo American*, November 4, 1865, 3; "Untitled,"
Sunbury Gazette (Sunbury, Pennsylvania), November 4, 1865, 3; "Reception of Colored
Troops. The Plan and Originators of the Ovation," *Philadelphia Inquirer*, November 3,
1865, 1; "Colored Soldiers' Festival," *Daily Evening Express* (Lancaster, PA), November
8, 1865, 2; "The Reception of Colored Soldiers," *Daily Evening Express* (Lancaster, PA),
November 9, 1865, 2; "Welcome to Our Colored Soldiers," *Christian Recorder*, November
11, 1865, 2.

79. L'Overture, "The Reception of Colored Soldiers at Harrisburg," *Christian Recorder*,
November 11, 1865, 1.

80. L'Overture, "The Reception of Colored Soldiers at Harrisburg."

81. P. Gabrielle Foreman, "Black Organizing, Print Advocacy, and Collective Authorship: The Long History of the Colored Conventions Movement," in *The Colored Conventions Movement: Black Organizing in the Nineteenth Century*, ed. P. Gabrielle Foreman, Jim Casey, and Sarah Lynn Patterson (Chapel Hill: University of North Carolina Press, 2021), 36.

82. "Garnet League of Harrisburg," *Pittsburgh Gazette*, October 31, 1865, 4.

83. For other local communities' efforts, see "State Items," *Pittsburgh Daily Commercial*, November 4, 1865, 1; "Untitled," *Sunbury Gazette* (Sunbury, PA), November 4, 1865, 3; "Reception of the Colored Troops," *Reading Times*, October 30, 1865, 2. Foreman, "Black Organizing, Print Advocacy, and Collective Authorship," 36.

84. Luke and Smith, *Soldiering for Freedom*, 30–32, 39–41; "Welcome to Our Colored Soldiers," *Christian Recorder*, November 11, 1865, 2.

85. "From Harrisburg. Grand Review of Pennsylvania Colored Troops To-Day. The Arrangements for the Display," *Philadelphia Inquirer*, November 14, 1865, 1; "Harrisburg. Grand Welcome to Pennsylvania Colored Troops. Imposing Demonstration at the State Capital. Our "American Citizens of African Descent." They Demand the Elective Franchise. Their Addresses and Resolutions. Speeches of White and Colored Orators. Special Telegraphic Dispatches," *Philadelphia Inquirer*, November 15, 1865, 1.

86. "Local Intelligence," *Patriot* (Harrisburg, PA), November 23, 1865, 3.

87. Psyche Williams-Forson, "Where Did They Eat? Where Did They Stay?: Interpreting the Material Culture of Black Women's Domesticity in the Context of the Colored Conventions," in *The Colored Conventions Movement: Black Organizing in the Nineteenth Century*, ed. P. Gabrielle Foreman, Jim Casey, and Sarah Lynn Patterson (Chapel Hill: University of North Carolina Press, 2021), 89–90.

88. "Local Intelligence."

89. "Local Intelligence."

90. Adriana Lima, "William Battis," in *One Hundred Voices*, 9.

91. "Local Intelligence." For Garner's documented occupation in the hotel industry, see *1870 United States Federal Census* (Provo: Ancestry.com Operations, Inc., 2009); *1880 United States Federal Census* (Provo: Ancestry.com Operations, Inc., 2009); and *1900 United States Federal Census* (Provo: Ancestry.com Operations Inc, 2010); Garnet League, *Ceremonies at the Reception of Welcome to the Colored Soldiers of Pennsylvania*, 28.

92. "Local Intelligence." Bradley's barbershop was located in a popular location for other Black Harrisburg barbershops in the Eighth Ward during the nineteenth and early twentieth centuries. See Julie Ann Hurst, "Barbershops in Harrisburg's Old Eighth, 1890–1905," *Pennsylvania History: A Journal of Mid-Atlantic Studies* 72 (Autumn 2005): 446–452.

93. Sarah Myers, "Dr. William M. Jones," in *One Hundred Voices*, 72; Gerald G. Eggert, "The Impact of the Fugitive Slave Law on Harrisburg: A Case Study," *Pennsylvania Magazine of History and Biography* 109 (October 1985): 540–543; Eggert, "'Two Steps Forward, a Step-and-a-Half Back,'" 11; Blackett, *The Captive's Quest for Freedom*, 271–283, 287–291.

94. "Local Intelligence."

95. Eggert, "'Two Steps Forward, a Step-and-a-Half Back,'" 14; Michael Barton, "Almost Our Own Montmartre: Studying Harrisburg's Old Eighth Ward," *Pennsylvania History: A Journal of Mid-Atlantic Studies* 72 (Autumn 2005): 406–407.

96. Foreman," "Black Organizing, Print Advocacy, and Collective Authorship," 36.

97. Garnet League, *Ceremonies at the Reception of Welcome to the Colored Soldiers of Pennsylvania*, 21–22; Brutus, "Grand Day among the Negroes," *Valley Spirit*, November 22, 1865, 3.

98. "Local Intelligence."

99. Mealy, *Aliened American*, 370.

100. "Harrisburg. Reception of the Colored Soldiers. Speech of Cameron. Letters from Generals Meade and Butler," *Press* (Philadelphia, PA), November 15, 1865, 1, in Reception of Colored Troops—Nov. 14, 1865, VF, Dauphin County Historical Society, Harrisburg, PA. Of the newspaper coverage, Thomas Morris Chester's former wartime employer had the most complete remarks delivered at the reception.

101. "Harrisburg."

102. "Harrisburg."

103. "Harrisburg."

104. "Harrisburg."

105. "The Twenty-Second Regiment of Colored Troops," *Philadelphia Inquirer*, February 8, 1864, 8; "Parade of a Colored Regiment," *Philadelphia Inquirer*, February 10, 1864, 8; "Departure of the Twenty-Second Colored Regiment," *Philadelphia Inquirer*, February 11, 1864, 8; "From Harrisburg. Review of the Garrison—Anti-Cholera Measures—Troops Mustered Out of the Service," *Philadelphia Inquirer*, November 7, 1865, 1; Christopher B. Bean, *Too Great a Burden to Bear: The Struggle and Failure of the Freedmen's Bureau in Texas* (New York: Fordham University Press, 2016), 47–110.

106. "The Ovation to Colored Troops at Harrisburg," *Cleveland Daily Leader*, November 17, 1865, 2; "Reception of the Colored Soldiers at Harrisburg," *The Liberator*, November 24, 1865, 2; "Brevet Major-General Kiddoo Relieved from Duty at Harrisburg," *Philadelphia Inquirer*, November 17, 1865, 1; "A Philadelphia Colored Regiment to Be Mustered Out," *Philadelphia Inquirer*, November 20, 1865, 2.

107. Garnet League, *Ceremonies at the Reception of Welcome to the Colored Soldiers of Pennsylvania*, 7.

108. Garnet League, *Ceremonies at the Reception of Welcome to the Colored Soldiers of Pennsylvania*, 9.

109. Garnet League, *Ceremonies at the Reception of Welcome to the Colored Soldiers of Pennsylvania*, 9.

110. "Harrisburg. Grand Welcome to Pennsylvania Colored Troops. Imposing Demonstration at the State Capital. Our 'American Citizens of African Descent.' They Demand the Elective Franchise. Their Addresses and Resolutions. Speeches of White and Colored Orators. Special Telegraphic Dispatches," *Philadelphia Inquirer*, November 15, 1865, 1; "Meade and Butler on Negro Soldiers," *Philadelphia Inquirer*, November 15, 1865, 1; "The Ovation to Colored Troops at Harrisburg," *Cleveland Daily Leader*, November 17, 1865, 2; "Reception of the Colored Soldiers at Harrisburg," *The Liberator*, November 24,

1865, 2; "Untitled," *New Orleans Tribune*, December 21, 1865, 4; Garnet League, *Ceremonies at the Reception of Welcome to the Colored Soldiers of Pennsylvania*, 8.

111. Garnet League, *Ceremonies at the Reception of Welcome to the Colored Soldiers of Pennsylvania*, 7–8; Dobak, *Freedom by the Sword*, 112, 261–262; Luke and Smith, *Soldiering for Freedom*, 28–30, 44–45.

112. Garnet League, *Ceremonies at the Reception of Welcome to the Colored Soldiers of Pennsylvania*, 7–8; Leonard, *Benjamin Francis Butler*, 164–165.

113. Garnet League, *Ceremonies at the Reception of Welcome to the Colored Soldiers of Pennsylvania*, 11.

114. Garnet League, *Ceremonies at the Reception of Welcome to the Colored Soldiers of Pennsylvania*, 11.

115. Garnet League, *Ceremonies at the Reception of Welcome to the Colored Soldiers of Pennsylvania*, 11.

116. Garnet League, *Ceremonies at the Reception of Welcome to the Colored Soldiers of Pennsylvania*, 11.

117. "Closing Exercises," *Harrisburg Daily Telegraph*, November 14, 1865, 3, in Reception of Colored Troops—Nov. 14, 1865, VF, Dauphin County Historical Society, Harrisburg, PA. For the positive coverage, see "Reception of Colored Troops," *Tribune* (Chicago), November 15, 1865, 1; "Reception of Colored Troops—Speech of General Cameron," *Philadelphia (PA) North American and United States Gazette*, November 15, 1865, 1; "From Harrisburg—Reception of Colored Troops," *New York Age*, November 15, 1865, 2; "From Harrisburg. Reception to Colored Troops—What Was Said to Them, &c.," *Cincinnati Daily Inquirer*, November 15, 1865, 3; "The Ovation to Colored Troops at Harrisburg," *Cleveland Daily Leader*, November 17, 1865, 2, and "Reception of the Colored Soldiers at Harrisburg," *The Liberator*, November 24, 1865, 2.

118. "Harrisburg. Reception of the Colored Soldiers. Speech of General Cameron. Letters from Generals Meade and Butler," *Press (Philadelphia, PA)*, November 15, 1865, 1, and "The Reception to the Colored Soldiers," *Harrisburg Daily Telegraph*, November 14, 1865, 3, clippings, Reception of Colored Troops—Nov. 14, 1865, VF, Dauphin Historical Society; "Harrisburg. Grand Welcome to Pennsylvania Colored Troops. Imposing Demonstration at the State Capital. Our 'American Citizens of African Descent.' They Demand the Elective Franchise. Their Addresses and Resolutions. Speeches of White and Colored Orators. Special Telegraphic Dispatches," *Philadelphia Inquirer*, November 15, 1865, 1; Garnet League, *Ceremonies at the Reception of Welcome to the Colored Soldiers of Pennsylvania*, 3–12.

119. "Local Intelligence."

120. "Local Intelligence."

121. "Local Intelligence."

122. "Local Intelligence."

123. "Local Intelligence." For other coverage, see "The Negro Jubilee in Harrisburg. John Brown's Soul A-Marching On. The Parade a Failure. Simon Cameron Promises the Negroes Entire Equality with White Men," *Intelligencer Journal* (Lancaster, PA), November 15, 1865, 2; Brutus, "Grand Day among the Negroes. Reception of the Colored Troops. The Orator of the Day. A Fight at the Depot. Sale of the US Hotel," *Valley Spirit*, November 22, 1865, 3.

124. For the quote, I used the Giesburg edition instead of the comparable Karsonya Wise Whitehead. The latter added punctuation and slightly modified the text for clarity. Both editions are valuable works of recovery. As a pocket diary by a working-class Black Philadelphian youth, I wanted to capture both the gendered and class dimensions of her thoughts. See Judith Giesburg, ed., and transcribed and annotated by the Memorable Days Project *Emilie Davis's Civil War: The Diaries of a Free Black Woman in Philadelphia, 1863–1865* (University Park: The Pennsylvania State University Press, 2014), 187, and Karsonya Wise Whitehead, *Notes from a Colored Girl: The Civil War Pocket Diaries of Emilie Frances Davis* (Columbia: University of South Carolina Press, 2014), 209.

125. Garnet League, *Ceremonies at the Reception of Welcome to the Colored Soldiers of Pennsylvania*, 3–28.

126. Garnet League, *Ceremonies at the Reception of Welcome to the Colored Soldiers of Pennsylvania*, 13–15.

127. Garnet League, *Ceremonies at the Reception of Welcome to the Colored Soldiers of Pennsylvania*, 15–16.

128. Garnet League, *Ceremonies at the Reception of Welcome to the Colored Soldiers of Pennsylvania*, 25–27.

129. Garnet League, *Ceremonies at the Reception of Welcome to the Colored Soldiers of Pennsylvania*, 22.

130. "Untitled," *New York Tribune*, July 2, 1866, 4; "From Harrisburg. The Soldier's Orphans. Execution of Three Murderers, Houser, Buser and Berger. The Garnet League and the Freedmen of the South, &c," *Philadelphia Inquirer*, March 19, 1866, 4; "From Harrisburg," *Philadelphia Inquirer*, August 26, 1867, 1.

131. Blackett, *Thomas Morris Chester, Black Civil War Correspondent*, 50–57.

132. "Harrisburg," *Philadelphia Inquirer*, January 15, 1866, 2

133. "Grand Reception for 'Beast' Butler," *Patriot* [Harrisburg], April 11, 1866, 3; Biographer Elizabeth D. Leonard discusses the origins of these less than flattering nicknames of Butler for his support of slave refugees, USCT soldiers, and African Americans more broadly. See Leonard, *Benjamin Francis Butler*, 70, 127.

134. Eggert, "'Two Steps Forward, a Step-and-a-Half Back,'" 16–17.

135. For previous strategies, such as petitioning, see Christopher James Bonner, *Remaking the Republic: Black Politics and the Creation of American Citizenship* (Philadelphia: University of Pennsylvania Press, 2020), 168.

136. "Pennsylvania State Equal Rights League," *Harrisburg Telegraph*, August 21, 1872, 3.

137. "Pennsylvania State Equal Rights League," *Harrisburg Telegraph*, August 21, 1872, 3.

138. Eggert, "'Two Steps Forward, a Step-and-a-Half Back,'" 26–27.

139. For the formation of Harrisburg GAR post and original namesake, see "Colored Veterans Organize," *Harrisburg Telegraph*, June 16, 1886, 4, "New GAR Post," *Harrisburg Telegraph*, June 23, 1886, 1; "Gustavus V. Catto," *Harrisburg Daily Independent*, June 23, 1886, 4; "Secure a Room," *Harrisburg Daily Independent*, July 16, 1886, 4; Daniel R. Biddle and Murray Dubin, *Tasting Freedom: Octavius Catto and the Battle for Equality in Civil War America* (Philadelphia: Temple University Press, 2010), 288–322, 331–354, 388–440.

The newspapers misspelled Catto's first name. For the change in post name, see "Memorial," *Harrisburg Daily Independent*, May 30, 1887, 1, and "Five Surviving Members in Stevens Post No. 520," *Harrisburg Telegraph*, May 30, 1931, 7. In the Harrisburg newspapers, the post namesake's last name interchangeably appears as Stevens. Barbara Gannon, *The Won Cause: Black and White Comradeship in the Grand Army of the Republic* (Chapel Hill: University of North Carolina Press, 2011), 58–60; Shaffer, *After the Glory*, 171.

140. Gannon, *Won Cause*, 5–9, 145–162; Shaffer, *After the Glory*, 169–173, 188–192.

141. Katie Heiser, "Catherine McClintock," in *One Hundred Voices*, 89; Dylan Goss, "Harriet M. Marshall," in *One Hundred Voices*, 81–82; Lydia Tamrat, Joshua Reid, and Sarah Myers, "Laura Robinson," in *One Hundred Voices*, 113; "Lincoln Cemetery," *State Journal* (Harrisburg, PA), April 5, 1884, 2.

142. "Lincoln Cemetery." For the dedication of Lincoln Cemetery, see "Cemetery Dedication," *Harrisburg Telegraph*, November 13, 1877, 4, and "The Dedication," *Harrisburg Telegraph*, November 19, 1877, 4. Formerly known as East Harrisburg, the cemetery is in the borough of Penbrook.

143. See "Untitled," *State Journal* (Harrisburg, PA), May 31, 1884, 2; "Memorial," *Harrisburg Daily Independent*, May 30, 1887, 1; "Memorial Day," *Harrisburg Daily Independent*, May 30, 1892, 1; "GAR Installations," *Harrisburg Telegraph*, January 10, 1893, 4; "Heroes Honored," *Harrisburg Telegraph*, May 30, 1899, 1; "Colored Knights Hold Parade in Morning," *Evening News* (Harrisburg, PA), May 31, 1920, 3; "City Pays High Tribute to Her Veterans of War," *Harrisburg Telegraph*, May 31, 1921, 2.

144. Ephraim Slaughter is the last Civil War veteran interred at Lincoln Cemetery. Born into slavery in North Carolina, he self-liberated, enlisted under the alias of "Ephraim Newsome," and served in both the 37th USCT and the Third NC Colored Infantry. As the last Dauphin County Black Civil War veteran, his death and interment at Lincoln has garnered much attention. See "Ephraim Slaughter," *Evening News* (Harrisburg, PA), January 16, 1943, 10; "Last Veteran of Civil War Dies," *Evening News* (Harrisburg, PA), February 18, 1943, 13; "Obituaries: Ephraim Slaughter," *Evening News* (Harrisburg, PA), February 19, 1943, 19.

145. Mealy, *Aliened American*, 2:394; City Twenty One (Harrisburg, PA), Dedication of Memorial to William Howard Day program, May 30, 1950, accessed in W. E. B. Du Bois Papers (MS 312), Special Collections and University Archives, University of Massachusetts Amherst Libraries, Amherst, MA; W. E. B. Du Bois, "The World of William Howard Day," May 30, 1950, speech made at Lincoln Cemetery, Penbrook, PA, accessed at Western Reserve Historical Society, Cleveland, OH. For coverage of the dedication and monument text, see "Unveils Memorial," *Evening News*, May 31, 1950, 38, and "Honor Day's Memory," *Patriot*, May 31, 1950, 2, clippings, and "William Howard Day AB AM DD," text of Marker, index card, Howard William Day VF, Dauphin County Historical Society, Harrisburg, PA.

146. Du Bois, "The World of William Howard Day."

147. Blackett, *Beating against The Barriers*, 287, 385; Todd Mealy, "William Howard Day: A Midstate Civil Rights Leader Forgotten by Time," *PennLive*, February 26, 2011, C1, clipping, VF-Howard William Day, Dauphin County Historical Society, Harrisburg, PA.

148. See "US Colored Troops Grand Review," Pennsylvania Historical Marker Program, Pennsylvania Historical and Museum Commission, Harrisburg, PA, https://md .patrailsofhistory.com/historical-markers/us-colored-troops-grand-review; "Harrisburg's Grand Review of Black Troops," Historical Marker Database, https://www.hmdb.org/m .asp?m=121992.

149. Fishlock, "Pennsylvania Will Honor Black Civil War Soldiers Again."

150. Charles Thompson, "The Harrisburg Grand Review Celebrates Civil War History," PennLive.com, November 6, 2010, https://www.pennlive.com/midstate/2010/11/the _harrisburg_grand_review_ce.html.

151. Patriot-News Editorial Board, "Salute Civil War's Black Soldiers," PennLive.com, November 6, 2010, https://www.pennlive.com/editorials/2010/11/salute_civil_wars_black _soldie.html.

152. "Grand Review Times: A Call for the Descendants of USCT Troops from Camp William Penn 1863 to the Harrisburg Grand Review, 1865," supplement to *ShowcaseNow!* Magazine, March 22, 2010, Pennsylvania Grand Review: Honoring African American Patriots, 1865/2010, https://housedivided.dickinson.edu/grandreview/wp-content/ uploads/2010/04/USCT_Supplement.pdf.

153. "From Front and Center: Some Who Served in the United States Colored Troops," June 1, 2010, Pennsylvania Grand Review: Honoring African American Patriots, 1865/2010, https://housedivided.dickinson.edu/grandreview/category/individual -stories/, accessed September 5, 2022.

154. Tom Knapp, "Fought, Died, Forgotten: Speakers Hope That Fate Can Be Avoided for Black War Veterans," *Intelligencer Journal and Lancaster New Era,* November 15, 2010, B1; "A. Lee Brinson Playing Sgt. Jonathan Sweeney (1832–1915), a Black Civil War Soldier," Shreiner-Concord Cemetery, November 14, 2010, video clip, YouTube.com, https:// www.youtube.com/watch?v=d7qLEmSzuaE.

155. "Darlene Colon playing Lydia Hamilton Smith at Ceremony Honoring Black Civil War Soldiers," Shreiner-Concord Cemetery, November 14, 2022, video clip, YouTube.com, https://www.youtube.com/watch?v=0OvrYADVH3E.

156. Knapp, "Fought, Died, Forgotten," B1 and B2.

157. See Harriet Gaston, "Commemoration Ceremony Honoring Six USCT Soldiers Who Fought in the Civil War and Are Buried at Eastern Light Cemetery," November 14, 2010, flyer, Pennsylvania Grand Review: Honoring African American Patriots, 1865/2010, https://housedivided.dickinson.edu/grandreview/wp-content/uploads/ 2011/01/usct_flyer.pdf; Huntingdon County Historical Society, Program of Honoring Civil War Colored Troops at Riverview Cemetery, Sunday, November 14th at 2 p.m.," Pennsylvania Grand Review: Honoring African American Patriots, 1865/2010, https:// housedivided.dickinson.edu/grandreview/wp-content/uploads/2011/01/Riverview _Cemetery_Huntingdon.pdf; Ryan Smith, "County Honors Black Troops of Civil War," *Meadville Tribune,* November 15, 2010, A1 and A2.

158. Becky Ault, "The Commonwealth Memorial: A New Sculpture for the Capitol Grounds," *Pennsylvania History: A Journal of Mid-Atlantic Studies* 87, no. 1 (Winter 2020): 225–232; Todd Mealy, "A Gathering at the Crossroads: Memorializing African American Trailblazers and a Lost Neighborhood in Harrisburg," *Pennsylvania Heritage*

(Spring 2021), http://paheritage.wpengine.com/article/a-gathering-at-the-crossroads-memorializing-african-american-trailblazers-and-a-lost-neighborhood-in-harrisburg/, accessed September 4, 2022; Katie Wingert McArdle, Introduction to *One Hundred Voices*, xxi–xxvi.

3. Joseph Winters's Songs for Self-Made Men

1. Joseph R. Winters, "On the Death of Abraham Lincoln," poem, 1865, VF-African Americans, Franklin County Historical Society, Chambersburg, PA.

2. Winters, "On the Death of Abraham Lincoln."

3. Winters, "On the Death of Abraham Lincoln."

4. Jonathan W. White, ed., *To Address You as My Friend: African American Letters to Abraham Lincoln* (Chapel Hill: University of North Carolina Press, 2021), 235–238; John E. Washington, *They Knew Lincoln*, with a new introduction by Kate Masur (New York: Oxford University Press, 2018), 15.

5. Kathleen Ann Clark, *Defining Moments: African American Commemoration and Political Culture in the South, 1863–1913* (Chapel Hill: University of North Carolina Press, 2005), 92–94.

6. "Red Hot," *Public Weekly Opinion*, March 15, 1870, 3.

7. "Jubilee," *Public Weekly Opinion*, May 3, 1870, 2.

8. "Jubilee," *Public Weekly Opinion*, May 3, 1870, 2.

9. "Jubilee," *Public Weekly Opinion*, May 3, 1870, 2.

10. "They Ought to Be Represented," *Valley Spirit*, June 1, 1870, 2.

11. "They Ought to Be Represented."

12. "Rally the Negroes—Speeches by Whites and Blacks—Address of Thaddeus M. Mahon, Esq., Radical Candidate for the Legislature—He Sucked Abolitionism in With His Mother's Milk—Tell A Story of the "Irishman and the Bull" —Calls Democrats "Bloody Rebel Heathens" —Figure 8599 Majority—Is Reminded of the Story of "Jim and Bill" —Hamman's "Betsy and the Bear," *Valley Spirit*, October 5, 1870, 3.

13. "Rally the Negroes"; Matthew E. Stanley, *Grand Army of Labor: Workers, Veterans, the Meaning of the Civil War* (Urbana: University of Illinois Press, 2021), 31–32.

14. "Rally the Negroes"; Stanley, *Grand Army of Labor*, 28–42; Millington W. Bergeson-Lockwood, *Race over Party: Black Politics and Partisanship in Late Nineteenth-Century Boston* (Chapel Hill: University of North Carolina Press, 2018), 46–52.

15. Steven Hahn, *A Nation under Our Feet: Black Political Struggles in the Rural South from Slavery to the Great Migration* (Cambridge, MA: Belknap Press of Harvard University Press, 2003), 110–111.

16. "Fred. Douglass' Lecture," *Public Weekly Opinion*, February 27, 1872, 3; Mark W. Podvia, "Frederick Douglass in Carlisle," *Unbound: An Annual Review of Legal History and Rare Books* 5 (2012): 19; David W. Blight, *Frederick Douglass: Prophet of Freedom* (New York: Simon and Schuster, 2018), 470.

17. Podvia, "Frederick Douglass in Carlisle," 19.

18. Frederick Douglass, "Self-Made Men," Speech, 1872, in *Frederick Douglass Heritage: The Official Website*, http://www.frederick-douglass-heritage.org/self-made-men/ (accessed on May 28, 2022).

19. Douglass, "Self-Made Men."

20. Douglass, "Self-Made Men."

21. Douglass, "Self-Made Men."

22. Douglass, "Self-Made Men."

23. Quoted in Podiva, "Frederick Douglass in Carlisle," 20.

24. David Smith, "Frederick Douglass in Carlisle," *Cumberland County History* 22 (2005), 55.

25. See Podiva, "Frederick Douglass in Carlisle," 22–23 and Smith, "Frederick Douglass in Carlisle," 54–56. Historian David Smith relied on the Podiva transcriptions for his 2005 essay. Both offer a nice summary of the vocal opposition to the Bentz Hotel incident and postwar Black claims for racial equality and citizenship expressed during the 1872 election season in the border Pennsylvania community.

26. Quoted in Smith, "Frederick Douglass in Carlisle," 57, 59.

27. Compiled Service Record of Ashford Collins, *US, Colored Troops Military Service Records, 1863–1865* (database online). Provo, UT: Ancestry.com Operations, 2007); "Jubilee," *Public Opinion*, May 3, 1870, 2.

28. Bradford's first name alternates between Albert and Alfred from his service record to his death. Compiled Service Record of Albert Bradford, *US, Colored Troops Military Service Records, 1863–1865* (Provo, UT: Ancestry.com Operations, 2007); "Jubilee," *Public Opinion*, May 3, 1870, 2; "Three New Organizations," *Public Weekly Opinion*, September 25, 1885, 3; "The Colored Veterans Elect Officers," *Valley Spirit*, December 6, 1889, 3.

29. See Marriage Record of William H. Middleton and Emma J. Crunkleton, Presbyterian Church of the Upper West Conococheague, Mercersburg, PA, February 6, 1879 (Lehi, UT: Ancestry.com Operations, 2012); "Jubilee," *Public Opinion*, May 3, 1870, 2; "Our Colored Odd Fellows," *Public Opinion*, June 2, 1874, 3; "Untitled," *Valley Spirit*, September 2, 1885, 3; *Valley Spirit*, September 22, 1886, 3; "First Gun of the Campaign," *Public Weekly Opinion*, September 22, 1874, 2.

30. James Lewis, Gilbert Braxton, and John Ukkerd were born enslaved in Virginia, self-liberated, and enlisted out of Pennsylvania before returning to Franklin County after the Civil War. All joined the Chambersburg GAR post. See Compiled Service Record of James Lewis, *US, Colored Troops Military Service Records, 1863–1865* (Provo, UT: Ancestry.com Operations, 2007); "Gilbert Braxton," in *Find a Grave Index, 1600s–Current* (Lehi, UT: Ancestry.com Operations, 2012); "Well Known Negro Is Dead," *Public Opinion*, November 18, 1907, 1; "Service Record of John Ukkerd," in *US, Colored Troops Military Service Records, 1863–1865* (Provo, UT: Ancestry.com Operations, 2007); "Three New Organizations," *Public Weekly Opinion*, September 25, 1885, 3.

31. Compiled Service Record of David Little, *US, Colored Troops Military Service Records, 1863–1865* (Provo, UT: Ancestry.com Operations, 2007); "David Little, Aged 64 Years," *Valley Spirit*, September 6, 1911, 3; Stella M. Fries, Janet Z. Gabler, and C. Bernard Ruffin, eds., *Some Chambersburg Roots: A Black Perspective* (Chambersburg: Stella Fries, 1980), 119–120.

32. Death Certificate of Armstead Baltimore, *Pennsylvania, US, Death Certificates, 1906–1968* (Lehi, UT: Ancestry.com Operations, 2014); "Record of Death," *Franklin*

Repository (Chambersburg, PA), November 28, 1906, 4; "Baltimore," *People's Register* (Chambersburg, PA), November 30, 1906, 5; Death Certificate of Henry Reeves, *Pennsylvania, US, Death Certificates, 1906–1968* (Lehi, UT: Ancestry.com Operations, 2014).

33. Edna Knapper Christian, "Outstanding Colored Citizens of Chambersburg—Past and Present: The Christian Family," *Public Opinion*, May 2, 1956, clipping, VF-African American; C. Bernard Ruffin, "This Is My Story: An Oral History of the African American Community of Chambersburg, Pennsylvania," 1:404–407, accessed at Franklin County Historical Society, Chambersburg, PA.

34. "Grant and Wilson Club," *Public Weekly Opinion*, August 20, 1872, 3.

35. "Grant and Wilson Club," *Public Weekly Opinion*, August 20, 1872, 3.

36. "Grant and Wilson Club," *Public Weekly Opinion*, August 20, 1872, 3.

37. "Grant and Wilson Club," *Public Weekly Opinion*, August 20, 1872, 3.

38. "The Pennsylvania Equal Rights League," *Harrisburg Telegraph*, July 29, 1872, 3. The announcement was reprinted in the *Harrisburg Telegraph*, August 7, 1872, 3.

39. "The Pennsylvania Equal Rights League," *Harrisburg Telegraph*, July 29, 1872, 3.

40. "Untitled," *Harrisburg Telegraph*, August 13, 1872, 3; "Special Orders, No. 2," *Harrisburg Telegraph*, August 20, 1872, 3; "A Gala Day," *Harrisburg Telegraph*, August 21, 1872, 3.

41. "The Colored Grant and Wilson Club," *Public Weekly Opinion*, September 10, 1872, 3.

42. "The Colored Grant and Wilson Club," *Public Weekly Opinion*, September 10, 1872, 3; "Untitled," *Public Weekly Opinion*, October 1, 1872, 3.

43. Elijah W. Smith, "The Colored Voters' Song," Union Republican Congressional Committee, *National Republican Grant and Wilson Song-Book* (Washington, DC: Union Republican Congressional Committee, 1872), 22.

44. Smith, "The Colored Voters' Song," 23; As Catherine Bateson has shown, "Tramp, Tramp, Tramp" gained postwar currency for celebrating Grant's first presidential campaign victory and even advancing proto-Irish nationalism. Smith drew on this popular song for cementing African American political allegiance in a similar manner. See Catherine V. Bateson, *Irish American Civil War Songs: Identity, Loyalty, and Nationhood* (Baton Rouge: Louisiana State University Press, 2022), 149–150.

45. Smith, "The Colored Voters' Vote," 24.

46. W. H. Browne, "Attention, Ye Freemen," and John J. Hood, "Freedom's Flag" attempted to appeal to African American voters. The tropes and images appealed to interests, histories, and understanding of Southern African Americans more than Northern African American voters. Winters's song, therefore, is a noteworthy exception. See Union Republican Congressional Committee, *Hayes & Wheeler Song Book* (Washington, DC: Union Republican Congressional Committee, 1876) in New York Public Library Digital Collections, New York, NY, https://digitalcollections.nypl.org/items/40167000 -6a7a-0135-1677-637d20f65c8f

47. Winters, "About Ten Days after the Battle of Gettysburg."

48. Winters, "At the Time of the Draft for the Civil War."

49. For Rutherford B. Hayes's Civil War military experience in the Twenty-Third Ohio Infantry, see Ari Hoogenboom, *Rutherford B. Hayes: Warrior and President* (Lawrence: University Press of Kansas, 1995), 112–188.

50. Joseph R. Winters, "A Campaign Song," 1876, Charles L. Blockson, Afro American Collection, Temple University, Philadelphia, PA.

51. Matthew Harper, *The End of Days: African American Religion and Politics in the Age of Emancipation* (Chapel Hill: University of North Carolina Press, 2016), 4–5.

52. Harper, *End of Days*, 12–13, 42.

53. Winters, "A Campaign Song," 1876.

54. Winters, "A Campaign Song," 1876.

55. Winters, "A Campaign Song," 1876.

56. Winters, "A Campaign Song," 1876.

57. Blight, *Frederick Douglass*, 574–579.

58. The archival record suggests that Winters only wrote presidential campaign songs. No songs exist for state elections and midterm congressional elections. David M. Jordan, *Winfield Scott Hancock: A Soldier's Life* (Bloomington: Indiana University Press, 1988), 35–175; Perry D. Jamieson, *Winfield Scott Hancock: Gettysburg Hero* (Abilene, TX: McWhiney Foundation Press, 2003), 54–89.

59. Democratic Party Platforms, 1880 Democratic Party Platform Online by Gerhard Peters and John T. Woolley, the American Presidency Project, https://www.presidency.ucsb.edu/node/273182. Accessed on July 13, 2021; Jordan, *Winfield Scott Hancock*, 255–305; Jamieson, *Winfield Scott Hancock*, 164–172.

60. Democratic Party Platforms, 1880 Democratic Party Platform, the American Presidency Project.

61. See Kenneth D. Ackerman, *Dark Horse: The Surprise Election and Political Murder of President James A. Garfield* (New York: Carroll and Graf, 2003), 98–133; and Candice Millard, *Destiny of the Republic: A Tale of Madness, Medicine, and the Murder of a President* (New York: Doubleday, 2011), 10–47; C. W. Goodyear, *President Garfield: From Radical to Unifier* (New York: Simon and Schuster, 2023), 337–362.

62. "James A. Garfield's Letter Accepting the 1880 Republican presidential Nomination," James A. Garfield National Historic Site, National Park Services, https://www.nps.gov/articles/000/james-a-garfield-s-letter-accepting-the-1880-republican-presidential-nomination.htm.

63. Robert J. Cook, "'Hollow Victory': Federal Veterans, Racial Justice, and the Eclipse of the Union Cause in American Memory," *History and Memory* 33, no. 1 (Spring/Summer 2021): 11–12. For other 1880 Republican campaign songs, see Ackerman, *Dark Horse*, 194; Millard, *Destiny of the Republic*, 61–62; L. Fayette Sykes, *Garfield and Arthur Republican Campaign Song Book, 1880* (New York: Republican Central Campaign Club of New York, 1880), in New York Public Library Digital Collections, New York, NY, https://digitalcollections.nypl.org/items/561c6790-6a6a-0135-b002-13bcba4cf674; and Republican Congressional Committee, *Garfield and Arthur Campaign Song Book* (Washington, DC: Republican Congressional Committee, 1880), in Stephen Foster Collection, University of Pittsburgh Digital Collections, https://digital.library.pitt.edu/islandora/object/pitt%3A31735061821041/viewer#page/1/mode/2up.

64. Joseph R. Winters, "A Campaign Song," ca. 1880, MSS Misc 0421, Joseph R. Winters, Songs: broadsides, c. 1881–1912, Department of Special Collections, Stanford University Libraries, Stanford, CA.

65. Winters, "A Campaign Song," 1880.

66. Frederick Douglass, "Men of Color, to Arms!"

67. Douglass, "Men of Color, to Arms!"; Winters, "A Campaign Song," ca. 1880.

68. Winters, "A Campaign Song," 1880.

69. Winters, "A Campaign Song," 1880.

70. Winters, "A Campaign Song," 1880.

71. Winters, "A Campaign Song," 1880.

72. Winters, "A Campaign Song," 1880.

73. Winters, "A Campaign Song," 1880.

74. Winters, "A Campaign Song," ca. 1880.

75. "Information Wanted," *Valley Spirit*, October 25, 1882, 2.

76. "Information Wanted."

77. "Information Wanted."

78. "Information Wanted."

79. "Information Wanted."

80. "Information Wanted."

81. "Information Wanted"; Cooper Wingert, "Fighting for State Citizenship in the US Colored Troops," *Civil War History* 69, no. 3 (September 2023):10, 18–24.

82. "Information Wanted."

83. "The Colored Men Heard From—They Object to the Opinion's Strictures Upon Them," *Valley Spirit*, August 18, 1886, 2.

84. "The Colored Men Heard From—They Object to the Opinion's Strictures Upon Them."

85. "The Colored Men Heard From—They Object to the Opinion's Strictures Upon Them."

86. Andrew K. Diemer, *Vigilance: The Life of William Still, Father of the Underground Railroad* (New York: Alfred A. Knopf, 2022), 282–290, 303–305; Cook, "'Hollow Victory,'" 12.

87. Bergeson-Lockwood, *Race over Party*, 3; Dennis Patrick Halpin, *A Brotherhood of Liberty: Black Reconstruction and Its Legacy in Baltimore, 1865–1920* (Philadelphia: University of Pennsylvania Press, 2019), 12.

88. Halpin, *A Brotherhood of Liberty*, 115.

89. Halpin, *A Brotherhood of Liberty*, 71–91.

90. Bergeson-Lockwood, *Race over Party*, 54, 86–107.

91. Stanley, *Grand Army of Labor*, 14.

92. For some of the third party movements and uses of Civil War memory for mobilizing voters, see Stanley, *Grand Army of Labor*, 67–151.

93. "Ratified," *Valley Spirit*, November 12, 1890, 1.

94. "After the Election," *Valley Spirit*, November 19, 1890, 6.

95. "Colored Democratic Club," *Harrisburg Daily Independent*, October 11, 1912, 16.

96. See "Up the Cumberland Valley," *Harrisburg Telegraph,* January 10, 1877, 4; "Untitled," *Shippensburg News*, April 26, 1879, 3; "Franklin County Items," *Democratic Chronicle* (Shippensburg), February 24, 1882, 3. Joseph R. Winters's Improved Fire Escape and Fire Alarm, advertisement, n.d, VF- Winters; Joseph R. Winters's Improved Fire Escape and Fire Alarm, photograph, Temple University, Philadelphia, PA.

97. See "A New Fund," *Valley Spirit*, July 18, 1889, 3; "Winters, Bentz &, Co., Artesian Well Drillers for Water, Oil or Gas," advertisement, *Valley Spirit*, August 20, 1890, 5; "Reports Valuable Discoveries," *Star and Enterprise* (Newville, PA), August 5, 1903, 5; "Jos. R. Winters Passes; Long Time Town Resident," *People's Register* (Chambersburg, PA), December 7, 1916, 5.

98. Joseph R. Winters, Campaign Song, 1900, and Joseph R. Winters, Campaign Song, 1904, Franklin County Historical Society, Chambersburg, PA; Joseph R. Winters, A Campaign Song, 1912, MSS Misc 0421, Joseph R. Winters, Songs: broadsides, c. 1881–1912, Department of Special Collections, Stanford University Libraries, Stanford, CA; Bateson, *Irish American Civil War Songs*, 35–36.

99. Winters, Campaign Song, 1900; Winters, Campaign Song, 1904; Winters, A Campaign Song, 1912.

100. Stanley, *Grand Army of Labor*, 135–137, 146–151, 184–192.

101. Andre Johnson, *No Future in This Country: The Prophetic Pessimism of Bishop Henry McNeal Turner* (Jackson: University Press of Mississippi, 2020), 31. As a scholar of rhetoric, Johnson extensively quotes Turner's speeches, interviews, and writings, some of which are not readily accessible to scholars, like the Podiva transcriptions of the Douglass speech in Chambersburg. I and other scholars are indebted to his transcriptions. This chapter draws on the substantial quotes in the analysis.

102. Stephen Ward Angell, *Bishop Henry McNeal Turner and African American Religion in the South* (Knoxville: University of Tennessee Press, 1992), 167–170; Johnson, *No Future in This Country*, 33–38.

103. Johnson, *No Future in This Country*, 97–100.

104. Angell, *Bishop Henry McNeal Turner and African American Religion in the South*, 208–214; Johnson, *No Future in This Country*, 129–142.

105. For McKinley's Civil War record, see William H. ;, *Major McKinley: William McKinley and the Civil War* (Kent, OH: Kent State University Press, 2000), 1–106 and Robert W., *President McKinley: Architect of the American Century* (New York: Simon and Schuster, 2017), 20–34.

106. Angell, *Bishop Henry McNeal Turner and African American Religion in the South*, 236; Johnson, *No Future in This Country*, 78–86; Armstrong, *Major McKinley*, 137–140; Cook, "'Hollow Victory,'" 24–25. For African American perceptions of the Spanish-American War as advancing aims and collective understanding of the Civil War generation, see David W. Blight, *Race and Reunion: The Civil War in American Memory* (Cambridge, MA: Belknap Press of Harvard University Press, 2001), 348–352 and Le'trice D. Donaldson, *Duty beyond the Battlefield: African American Soldiers in the Fight for Racial Uplift, Citizenship, and Manhood, 1870–1920* (Carbondale: Southern Illinois University Press, 2020), 40–48.

107. Donaldson, *Duty beyond the Battlefield*, 55–56; quoted in Angell, *Bishop Henry McNeal Turner and African American Religion in the South*, 236. In another strongly worded editorial titled "Shoot the Fool Negroes," Turner further condemned African American soldiers who served in the war. See Johnson, *No Future in This Country*, 83–84.

108. Quoted in Angell, *Bishop Henry McNeal Turner and African American Religion in the South*, 236

109. Johnson, *No Future in This Country*, 103–106; John M. Hilbert, *American Cyclone: Theodore Roosevelt and His 1900 Whistle-Stop Campaign* (Jackson: University Press of Mississippi, 2015), 39–40, 244, 258.

110. Patrick J. Kelly, "The Election of 1896 and the Restructuring of Civil War Memory," *Civil War History* 49 (September 2003): 255–257, 261–262, 275; Stanley, *Grand Army of Labor*, 146–148; Merry, *President McKinley*, 444–448.

111. Johnson, *No Future in This Country*, 106–107.

112. Johnson, *No Future in This Country*, 108–110.

113. Joseph R. Winters, Campaign Song, 1900, Franklin County Historical Society, Chambersburg, PA.

114. Joseph R. Winters, Campaign Song, 1900, Franklin County Historical Society, Chambersburg, PA.

115. Noel Jacob Kent, *America in 1900* (Armonk, NY: M. E. Sharpe, 2002), 63–77.

116. Winters, Campaign Song, 1900.

117. "Jubilee," *Public Weekly Opinion*, May 3, 1870, 2; Blight, *Race and Reunion,* 304.

118. Winters, Campaign Song, 1900.

119. Winters, Campaign Song, 1900.

120. Winters, Campaign Song, 1900.

121. Winters, Campaign Song, 1900.

122. Merry, *President McKinley*, 392; Armstrong, *Major McKinley*, 137–140.

123. Merry, *President McKinley*, 478–482.

124. Johnson, *No Future in This Country*, 169.

125. Democratic Party Platforms, 1904 Democratic Party Platform Online by Gerhard Peters and John T. Woolley, the American Presidency Project, UC Santa Barbara, Santa Barbara, CA, https://www.presidency.ucsb.edu/node/273196.

126. Democratic Party Platforms, 1904 Democratic Party Platform Online by Gerhard Peters and John T. Woolley.

127. Republican Party Platforms, Republican Party Platform of 1904 Online by Gerhard Peters and John T. Woolley, the American Presidency Project, UC Santa Barbara, Santa Barbara, CA, https://www.presidency.ucsb.edu/node/273323.

128. Republican Party Platforms, Republican Party Platform of 1904 Online by Gerhard Peters and John T. Woolley.

129. Joseph R. Winters, Campaign Song, 1904, Franklin County Historical Society, Chambersburg, PA.

130. "1904 Statistics," the American Presidency Project, UC Santa Barbara, Santa Barbara, CA, https://www.presidency.ucsb.edu/statistics/elections/1904.

131. "Colored Democratic Club," *Harrisburg Daily Independent*, October 11, 1912, 16; Winters, Campaign Song, 1912.

132. Don Linky, "Woodrow Wilson and the Election of 1912," Center on the American Governor, Eagleton Institute of Politics, Rutgers University, https://governors.rutgers.edu/woodrow-wilson-and-the-election-of-1912/, accessed on June 22, 2022; James

Chace, *1912: Wilson, Roosevelt, Taft, and Debs: The Election That Changed the Country* (New York: Simon and Schuster, 2004), 194–197; Sidney M. Milkis, *Theodore Roosevelt, the Progressive Party, and the Transformation of American Democracy* (Lawrence: University Press of Kansas, 2009), 202–216.

133. Winters, A Campaign Song, 1912; Winters notably ignored Debs's campaign with the Socialist Party of America. Due to his strong oratory and a divided African American political landscape, Debs received some consideration among disaffected voters. See Chace, *1912*, 67–90, and Milkis, *Theodore Roosevelt, the Progressive Party, and the Transformation of American Democracy*, 193–202, 230–237.

134. Milkis, *Theodore Roosevelt, the Progressive Party, and the Transformation of American Democracy*, 193.

135. Milkis, *Theodore Roosevelt, the Progressive Party, and the Transformation of American Democracy*, 194.

136. Chace, *1912*, 115–123, 161–168; Milkis, *Theodore Roosevelt, the Progressive Party, and the Transformation of American Democracy*, 123–184, 202–216; Winters, A Campaign Song, 1912.

137. Winters, A Campaign Song, 1912.

138. Winters, A Campaign Song, 1912.

139. Winters, A Campaign Song, 1912.

140. Chace, *1912*, 238–239.

141. M. L. Marotte III, *The Story of Joseph Winters, 1816–1916: Citizen, Pioneer, Inventor, Gunsmith, Machinist, Land Owner, and Born a Free Man* (Chambersburg: M. L. Marotte III, 1999), 6; Winters headstone, photograph, c. 1916, VF-Winters; For listing of Black veterans and GAR members buried in the Mt. Lebanon Cemetery, see Fries, Gabler and Ruffin, *Some Chambersburg Roots*, 50–70.

142. "Jos. R. Winters Passes; Long Time Resident," *People's Register* (Chambersburg, PA), December 7, 1916, 5. Beyond Chambersburg, several newspapers covered Winters's death. See "Notable Negro Dies at 104," *Harrisburg Telegraph*, December 1, 1916, 2; "Dies at 104 Years," *Philadelphia Inquirer*, December 1, 1916, 3, and "Their Oldest Man," *Adams County News*, December 2, 1916, 5.

4. Cumberland Valley Veterans and the Grand Army of the Republic

1. Emma Jones Lapansky, "Feminism, Freedom, and Community: Charlotte Forten and Women Activists in Nineteenth-Century Philadelphia," *Pennsylvania Magazine of History and Biography* 113, no. 1 (January 1989): 16; Charlotte Forten Grimké, "The Gathering of the Grand Army" (1890), in *The Portable Nineteenth-Century African American Women Writers*, ed. Hollis Robbins and Henry Louis Gates Jr. (New York: Penguin Books, 2017), 165.

2. Grimké, "The Gathering of the Grand Army" (1890), 165.

3. Brian Matthew Jordan, *Marching Home: Union Veterans and Their Unending Civil War* (New York: Liveright, 2014), 69–70, 162–169; Kelly D. Mezurek, *For Their Own Cause: The 27th United States Colored Troops* (Kent, OH: Kent State University Press, 2016), 246–256; Donald R. Shaffer, *After the Glory: The Struggle of Black Civil War Veterans* (Lawrence: University Press of Kansas, 2004), 143–168; Robert J. Cook, "'Hollow

Victory': Federal Veterans, Racial Justice and the Eclipse of the Union Cause in American Memory," *History and Memory* 33, no. 1 (Spring/Summer 2021): 10–12; Barbara Gannon, *The Won Cause: Black and White Comradeship in the Grand Army of the Republic* (Chapel Hill: University of North Carolina Press, 2011), 5–9, 145–162.

4. Colored Men's Border Convention (1868, Baltimore, MD), "Address of the Colored Men's Border State Convention to the People of the United States, Baltimore, August 5–6, 1868," in *Colored Conventions Project Digital Records,* accessed January 28, 2021, https://omeka.coloredconventions.org/items/show/568.

5. Colored Men's Border Convention (1868. Baltimore, MD), "Address of the Colored Men's Border State Convention to the People of the United States, Baltimore, August 5–6, 1868"; "Colored Border State Convention," *Delaware Tribune* (Wilmington, DE), August 6, 1868, 2; Denise Burger, "Recovering Black Women in the Colored Conventions Movement," *Legacy: A Journal of American Women Writers* 36, no. 2 (2019): 256–262; Martha S. Jones, *Birthright Citizens: A History of Race and Rights in Antebellum America* (Cambridge: Cambridge University Press, 2019), 152; "Colored Border Convention," *Philadelphia Inquirer,* August 11, 1868, 7.

6. Maurice Wallace, "Are We Men?: Prince Hall, Martin Delany, and the Masculine Ideal in Black Freemasonry, 1775–1865," *American Literary History* 9 (Autumn 1997): 397.

7. Wallace, "Are We Men," 407, 415–418.

8. Paul Lawrence Dunbar, "Hidden in Plain Sight: African American Secret Societies and Black Freemasonry," *Journal of African American Studies* 16, no. 4 (December 2012): 630; Stephen Kantrowitz, "'Intended for the Better Government of Man': The Political History of African American Freemasonry in the Era of Emancipation," *Journal of American History* 96 (March 2010): 1011–1012.

9. Brittney C. Cooper, "'They Are Nevertheless Our Brethren': The Order of the Eastern Star and the Battle for Women's Leadership, 1874–1926," in *All Men Free and Brethren: Essays on the History of African American Freemasonry,* ed. Peter P. Hinks and Stephen Kantrowitz (Ithaca, NY: Cornell University Press, 2013), 120–124.

10. Stephen Kantrowitz, "Brotherhood Denied: Black Freemasonry and the Limits of Reconstruction," in *All Men Free and Brethren: Essays on the History of African American Freemasonry,* ed. Peter P. Hinks and Stephen Kantrowitz (Ithaca, NY: Cornell University Press, 2013), 106–109.

11. Gregory Mixon, *Show Thyself A Man: Georgia State Troops, Colored, 1865–1905* (Gainesville: University Press of Florida, 2016), 126–248; Charles Leeds, "Old Military Organization," *The Sentinel* (Carlisle, PA), October 29, 1910, 3.

12. Leeds, "Old Military Organization"; William P. Clarke, *Official History of the Militia and the National Guard of the State of Pennsylvania from the Earliest Period of Record to the Present Time* (Philadelphia: Captain Charles J. Hendler, 1909), 49–51.

13. Ancestry.com, *1890 Veterans Schedules of the US Federal Census* [database online]. Provo, UT: Ancestry.com Operations, 2005; Janet L. Bell, "Corporal Jesse G. Thompson GAR, Post 440," *Cumberland County History* 30 (2013): 92.

14. "Untitled," *Public Weekly Opinion,* July 24, 1885, 2; "That Big Day," *Public Weekly Opinion,* July 17, 1885, 2; "Franklin County Affairs," *Shippensburg Chronicle,* July 17, 1885, 3; "Untitled," *The Sentinel* (Carlisle, PA), August 4, 1885, 4; "By the Way," *Public Weekly*

Opinion, August 7, 1885, 3; "In Twelve Months," *Valley Spirit,* January 6, 1886, 1. This encampment was organized by the posts of Franklin, Cumberland, and Dauphin Counties and served as the inaugural event formally announcing the creation of the African American GAR posts in the respective counties. See Janet L. Bell, "Corporal Jesse G. Thompson GAR, Post 440," *Cumberland County History* 30 (2013): 92.

15. "Reunion of Colored People," *Harrisburg Telegraph,* August 20, 1885, 4; "Three New Organizations," *Public Weekly Opinion,* September 25, 1885, 3.

16. Gannon, *Won Cause,* 58–60; Shaffer, *After the Glory,* 171. Lyon Post is most likely named after Nathaniel Lyon, a white Civil War general who is considered to be the first general killed during the Civil War.

17. Tunde Adeleke, *Without Regard to Race: The Other Martin Robison Delany* (Jackson: University Press of Mississippi, 2003), 40–41; Nell Irvin Painter, "Martin R. Delany: Elitism and Black Nationalism," in *Black Leaders of the Nineteenth Century,* ed. Leon Litwack and August Meier (Urbana: University of Illinois Press, 1988), 150–151, 155; Andre E. Johnson, *No Future in This Country: The Prophetic Pessimism of Henry McNeal Turner* (Jackson: University Press of Mississippi, 2020), 120–121.

18. Painter, "Martin R. Delany," 162–163; Adeleke, *Without Regard to Race,* 76–77. David Demus of the Fifty-Fourth Massachusetts regiment was one possibility. He never fully recovered from an injury received at Fort Wagner. He died shortly after returning to Franklin County at the war's end. See Edward L. Ayers, *The Thin Light of Freedom: The Civil War and Emancipation in the Heart of America* (New York: W. W. Norton, 2017), 91–94, 477–478.

19. "The Officers of Major Martin R. Delany Post," *Valley Spirit,* September 23, 1885, 3; "In Twelve Months," *Valley Spirit,* January 6, 1886, 1. Local newspapers often misspelled Delany's last name by adding an "e".

20. Bell, "Corporal Jesse G. Thompson GAR, Post 440," 92.

21. Bell, "Corporal Jesse G. Thompson GAR, Post 440," 89–91; "A. B. Sharpe's Address," *The Sentinel* (Carlisle, PA), July 6, 1885, 1; "Gen. A. B. Sharpe's Death," *The Sentinel* (Carlisle, PA), December 26, 1891, 3.

22. Bell, "Corporal Jesse G. Thompson GAR, Post 440," 92; "A. B. Sharpe's Address."

23. "Gen. A. B. Sharpe's Address."

24. "Gen. A. B. Sharpe's Address."

25. "Gen. A. B. Sharpe's Address."

26. See "Memorial Service," *The Sentinel* (Carlisle), May 31, 1886, 2; "At Rhial's Grave," *Valley Spirit,* June 23, 1886, 3; "Officers Elected," *The Sentinel* (Carlisle), December 8, 1887, 1.

27. Frederick Douglass, *The Life and Times of Frederick Douglass, Written by Himself: His Early Life as a Slave, His Escape from Bondage, and His Complete History* (Boston: DeWolfe, 1892), 652, accessed at Documenting the American South, http://docsouth.unc.edu/neh/dougl92/dougl92.html.

28. Douglass, *The Life and Times of Frederick Douglass,* 652. For Douglass's views of this case as a failure of Civil War memory and commitment to African Americans' full citizenship, see David Blight, "'For Something beyond the Battlefield': Frederick Douglass and the Memory of the Civil War," *Journal of American History* 75 (March 1989): 1158–1160.

29. Johnson, *No Future in This Country*, 34.

30. Johnson, *No Future in This Country*, 128–129.

31. Michael Bellesiles, *Inventing* Equality: *Reconstructing the Constitution in the Aftermath of the Civil War* (New York: St. Martin's Press, 2020), 257–265; Gannon, *Won Cause*, 79.

32. David K. Graham, *Loyalty on the Line: Civil War Maryland in American Memory* (Athens: University of Georgia Press, 2018), 30.

33. Graham, *Loyalty on the Line*, 30.

34. Gannon, *Won Cause*, 79.

35. "The Monument at Antietam," *Baltimore Sun*, September 17, 1896, 1; Lyon comrades also participated in the 1892 Grand Review in Washington, DC. See "Maryland Divisions," *Baltimore Sun*, September 21, 1892, 1–2.

36. James M. McPherson, *Battle Cry of Freedom: The Civil War Era* (New York: Oxford University Press, 1988), 502–510; Ethan S. Rafuse, *McClellan's War: The Failure of Moderation in the Struggle for the Union* (Bloomington: Indiana University Press, 2005), 337–356; Chester G. Hearn, *Lincoln and McClellan at War* (Baton Rouge: Louisiana State University Press, 2012), 196–206, 209–221.

37. Graham, *Loyalty on the Line*, 42–52, 69–74; Caroline E. Janney, *Remembering the Civil War: Reunion and the Limits of Reconciliation* (Chapel Hill: University of North Carolina Press, 2013), 144–147, 165–167; David W. Blight *Race and Reunion: The Civil War in American Memory* (Cambridge, MA: Belknap Press of Harvard University Press, 2001), 355–366.

38. Blight, *Race and Reunion*, 304; "Gen. McClellan in Hagerstown," *Herald and Torch Light,* May 30, 1885, 1.

39. "Another Memorial Day," *Herald and Torch Light*, June 4, 1885, 2; "Gen. McClellan in Hagerstown."

40. "The War Veterans at Chambersburg," *Scranton Tribune*, June 3, 1896, 1.

41. F. W. Day to O. O. Howard, April 30, 1896, Box 32, Folder 37 1896 Apr 28–1896 Apr 30, Oliver Otis Howard Papers, 1832–1912, George J. Mitchell Department of Special Collections and Archives, Bowdoin College Library, Brunswick, Maine.

42. O. O. Howard, "Campaign of General George G. Meade, including the Battle of Gettysburg, July 1st, 2nd, and 3rd 1865, Delivered by General O. O. Howard, US Army, at the Memorial Exercises of Edward W. Kinsley Post, GAR, Boston, Mass., May 30, 1894," in Oliver Otis Howard Papers.

43. "Veterans Break Camp," *Scranton Tribune*, June 5, 1896, 1.

44. Howard, "Campaign of General George G. Meade," 11.

45. "A Lover's Cut," *Cleveland Gazette,* June 6, 1896, 1; "Veterans Gather in Chambersburg," *Valley Spirit*, October 10, 1888, 3.

46. "Memorial Day," *Herald and Torch Light*, June 4, 1891, 3.

47. Lorenzo D. Blackson, "Sermon to GAR Posts," *The Sentinel*, June 15, 1885, 3; Laurie F. Maffly-Kipp, *Setting Down the Sacred Past: African-American Race Histories* (Cambridge, MA: Belknap Press of Harvard University Press, 2010), 4–6.

48. Maffly-Kipp, *Setting Down the Sacred Past*, 205.

49. Blackson, "Sermon to GAR Posts."

50. Blackson, "Sermon to GAR Posts."

51. Blackson, "Sermon to GAR Posts."

52. Blackson, "Sermon to GAR Posts."

53. "At Rhial's Grave," "Corporal Rhial Honored," *Baltimore Sun*, June 23, 1886, 6; "In Honor of Rhial," *Public Weekly Opinion* (Chambersburg, PA), June 25, 1886, 4.

54. "At Rhial's Grave."

55. "At Rhial's Grave"; Christian McWhirter, *Battle Hymns: The Power and Popularity of Music in the Civil War* (Chapel Hill: University of North Carolina Press, 2012), 168–169.

56. "Waynesboro's Great Day of Celebration," *Philadelphia Inquirer*, September 2, 1897, 5; Benjamin Matthias Nead, *Waynesboro: The history of a Settlement in the County formerly called Cumberland, but later Franklin, in the Commonwealth of Pennsylvania, in its beginnings, through its growth into a village and borough, to its centennial period, and to the close of the present century, including a relation of pertinent topics of general state and county history* (Harrisburg: Harrisburg Publishing, 1900), 335–341.

57. "Burial of Capt. Miles—Disposal of His Effects," *Valley Spirit*, February 4, 1887, 3.

58. Sara Ahmed, *On Being Included: Racism and Diversity in Institutional Life* (Durham, NC: Duke University Press, 2012), 13; Gannon, *Won Cause*, 117–141; Shaffer, *After the Glory*, 143–159.

59. "A Good Sermon," *Carlisle Weekly Herald*, May 29, 1890; "By the Way," *Public Weekly Opinion*, May 20, 1887, 3; Bell, "Corporal Jesse G. Thompson GAR, Post 440," 93.

60. "Lyon Post GAR Officers," *Herald and Torch Light*, December 11, 1884, 3.

61. See "The Officers of Major Martin R. Delaney Post," *Valley Spirit*, September 23, 1885, 3; "In Twelve Months," *Valley Spirit*, January 6, 1886, 1; "Inspection of Grand Army Posts in District No. 21," *Valley Spirit*, June 9, 1887, 3; "Officers Elected," *The Sentinel*, December 8, 1887, 1; "Inspection of Grand Army Posts in Franklin County," *Valley Spirit*, May 9, 1888, 3; "Officers Elected," *Carlisle Weekly Herald*, December 13, 1888, 2; "Post Officers Elected," *Carlisle Weekly Herald*, December 4, 1890, 1; "The Colored Veterans Elect Officers," *Valley Spirit*, December 6, 1889, 3; "Public Installation of Post Officers," *Valley Spirit*, December 26, 1889, 3; "Elected a Delegate," *The Sentinel*, April 24, 1896, 2; "Installation of Officers at Carlisle," *Philadelphia Inquirer*, January 20, 1898, 15; "GAR Officers Installed," *Carlisle Evening Herald*, January 29, 1909, 1 and "Post 440 GAR," *Carlisle Evening Herald*, November 27, 1909, 1.

62. "Brief Bits," *The News*, August 16, 1893, 3.

63. "Washington County," *Baltimore Sun*, July 17, 1895, 2.

64. "Untitled," *Herald and Torch Light*, May 31, 1892, 4.

65. "Chambersburg," *State Journal*, September 27, 1884, 1.

66. James Walker Hood, *One Hundred Years of the African Methodist Episcopal Zion Church; or, The Centennial of African Methodism* (New York: A.M.E. Zion Book Concern, 1895), 618; "Untitled [Rev Ross]," *State Journal*, December 13, 1884, 2.

67. "Untitled [Rev Ross]," 2; "Affairs Around Home," *Valley Spirit*, December 24, 1884, 3.

68. "GAR Officers Installed," *Carlisle Evening Herald*, January 29, 1909, 1.

69. "Bethel A.M.E. Church," *Carlisle Evening Herald*, February 6, 1909, 1; "GAR at Bethel Church," *The Sentinel*, February 6, 1909, 3.

70. "Third Presbyterian—Rev. A. Sellers Mays, pastor," *The Sentinel*, May 24, 1913, 8; "Patriotic Services," *The Sentinel*, February 17, 1896, 2; "West Street A.M.E. Zion," *Carlisle Evening Herald*, May 23, 1908, 1.

71. Matthew Harper, *The End of Days: African American Religion and Politics in the Age of Emancipation* (Chapel Hill: University of North Carolina Press, 2016), 4.

72. Harper, *End of Days*, 4.

73. Harper, *End of Days*, 5.

74. "Rev. John W. Davis," *Valley Spirit*, August 15, 1900, 5.

75. Harper, *End of Days*, 17.

76. Harper, *End of Days*, 42; "About the Churches," *Valley Spirit*, June 1, 1887, 2.

77. See Gannon, *Won Cause*, 48–49; Wendy Hamand Venet, "Faithful Helpmates and Fervent Activists: Northern Women and Civil War Memory," in *Women and the American Civil War: North-South Counterpoints*, ed. Judith Giesburg and Randall M. Miller (Kent, OH: Kent State University Press, 2018), 323–336.

78. Bell, "Corporal Jesse G. Thompson GAR, Post 440," 94.

79. "Will Meet on Monday Evening," *The Sentinel*, April 17, 1896, 3; "Mrs. Jane Williams," *Carlisle Weekly Herald*, May 4, 1900, 1; "Those Who Have Passed beyond the River," *Star and Enterprise* (Newville, PA), May 9, 1900, 4; "Ladies of the GAR," *Valley Spirit*, June 3, 1896, 1; Gannon, *Won Cause*, 53–54.

80. Cooper, "'They Are Nevertheless Our Brethren,'" 118–120.

81. Cooper, "'They Are Nevertheless Our Brethren,'" 126–130; Koritha Mitchell, *From Slave Cabins to the White House: Homemade Citizenship in African American Culture* (Urbana: University of Illinois Press, 2020), 63–66, 90–91.

82. Victoria Wolcott, *Race, Riots, and Roller Coasters: The Struggle over Segregated Recreation in America* (Philadelphia: University of Pennsylvania Press, 2012), 3–4; David Goldberg, *The Retreats of Reconstruction: Race, Leisure, and the Politics of Segregation at the New Jersey Shore, 1865–1920* (New York: Fordham University Press, 2017), 41–45.

83. Wolcott, *Race, Riots, and Roller Coasters*, 5; Goldberg, *Retreats of Reconstruction*, 51–54.

84. Wolcott, *Race, Riots, and Roller Coasters*, 19.

85. For discussion of so-called less respectable forms of entertainment encountered by GAR comrades and members of the Black Victorian middle class, see Tera Hunter, *To 'Joy My Freedom: Southern Black Women's Lives and Labors after the Civil War* (Cambridge, MA: Harvard University Press, 1997), 168–186; Kali N. Gross, *Colored Amazons: Crime, Violence, and Black Women in the City of Brotherly Love, 1880–1910* (Durham, NC: Duke University Press, 2006), 72–100; Cheryl D. Hicks, *Talk with You Like a Woman: African American Women, Justice and Reform in New York, 1890–1935* (Chapel Hill: University of North Carolina Press, 2010), 106–107; Douglas Flowe, *Uncontrollable Blackness: African American Men and Criminality in Jim Crow New York* (Chapel Hill: University of North Carolina Press, 2020), 55–57, 66–72.

86. "Affairs around Home," *Valley Spirit*, August 10, 1881, 3; "Entertainment," *The Sentinel* (Carlisle, PA), March 25, 1885, 1.

87. "Concert Wednesday Night," *The Sentinel* (Carlisle, PA), March 23, 1886, 2.

88. "The Coming Fair of the Post of Colored Veterans," *Valley Spirit*, February 15, 1888, 4; For shifting understandings of the American Revolution before and after the Civil War, see Eric Foner, *The Second Founding: How the Civil War and Reconstruction Remade the Constitution* (New York: W. W. Norton, 2019), 12–17.

89. Daphne Brooks, *Bodies in Dissent: Spectacular Performances of Race and Freedom, 1850–1910* (Durham, NC: Duke University Press, 2005), 220.

90. "Emancipation Celebration," *Baltimore Sun*, September 25, 1885, 1; "Celebrating Emancipation," *Herald and Torch Light* (Hagerstown, MD), October 1, 1885, 3.

91. "Celebrating Emancipation."

92. "Emancipation Celebration"; "Celebrating Emancipation."

93. "Their Day of Freedom," *Valley Spirit*, December 19, 1888, 1; "Emancipation," *The Sentinel*, January 6, 1888, 1; "They Returned Thanks," *Carlisle Weekly Herald*, February 15, 1889, 2.

94. "Colored Excursionists," *Harrisburg Daily Independent*, July 18, 1884, 4.

95. "Colored Excursionists."

96. "Untitled," *Herald and Torch Light*, May 31, 1892, 4; "Brief Bits," *The News*, August 16, 1893, 3.

97. "Affairs around Home," *Valley Spirit*, July 14, 1886, 3.

98. Jill Ogline Titus, *Gettysburg 1963: Civil Rights, Cold War Politics, and Historical Memory in America's Most Famous Small Town* (Chapel Hill, NC: University of North Carolina Press, 2021), 11–12; "Affairs around Home."

99. The cultural renaissance of the New Negro Movement popular among World War I veterans represented a rejection of the earlier recreation and entertainment of the Civil War generation. Veterans and communities embraced newer, modern, and race cognizant forms to connect their communities and deploy their veteran status for cementing their leadership positions. For more about intergenerational entertainment and recreational forms promoting new community ethos and activism, see Treva B. Lindsey, *Colored No More: Reinventing Black Womanhood in Washington, DC* (Urbana: University of Illinois Press, 2017), 111–136; Imani Perry, *May We Forever Stand: A History of the Black National Anthem* (Chapel Hill: University of North Carolina Press, 2018), 25–71.

100. See "Two Band Concerts and Colored Observance Are Parts of Annual Memorial Day Celebration," *News-Chronicle*, May 30, 1935, 1; "Arrangements Are Made for Colored Fete," *News-Chronicle*, May 24, 1938; Le'Trice Donaldson, *Duty beyond the Battlefield: African American Soldiers Fight for Racial Uplift, Citizenship, and Manhood, 1870–1920* (Carbondale: Southern Illinois Press, 2020), 154.

101. For the role of the Victor and Alma Green's essential guide for African American travelers, see Candacy A. Taylor, *Overland Railroad: The Green Book and Roots of Black Travel in America* (New York: Abrams Press, 2020), Gretchen Sorin, *Driving While Black: African American Travel and the Road to Civil Rights* (New York: Liveright, 2020), chap. 7; and Mia Bay, *Traveling Black: A Story of Race and Resistance* (Cambridge, MA: Belknap Press of Harvard University Press, 2021), 141–148.

102. Frank Stephenson, *Chowan Beach: Remembering an African American Resort* (Charleston, SC: History Press, 2006), 11–19; Wolcott, *Race, Riots, and Roller Coasters*, 13–87; Sorin, *Driving While Black*.

103. "Death of Milton Taylor," *Herald and Torch Light*, February 4, 1892, 3.

104. "Obituary Record," *Herald and Torch Light*, April 4, 1895, 6.

105. "Obituary," *Reading Times*, March 3, 1906, 5.

106. "A Sermon in Memory of a Dead Comrade," *Valley Spirit*, March 3, 1887, 3.

107. "Death of Colored Man," *Carlisle Weekly Herald*, August 7, 1890, 1; "Abraham Parker," *Carlisle Evening Herald*, November 28, 1898, 1; "Rev. John W. Davis," *Valley Spirit*, August 15, 1900, 5.

108. "Chambersburg," *State Journal*, January 24, 1888, 1.

109. "Mrs. Jane Williams," *Carlisle Weekly Herald*, May 4, 1900, 1; "Those Who Have Passed beyond the River," *Star and Enterprise* (Newville, PA), May 9, 1900, 4.

110. "Demas," *The Sentinel*, April 6, 1912, 2.

111. "Mrs. Rebecca Demas," *The Sentinel*, April 20, 1927, 8.

112. "Mrs. Rebecca Demas"; The Woman's Club of Mercersburg, *Old Mercersburg Revisited: Civil War to Bicentennial* (Mercersburg, PA: Woman's Club of Mercersburg, 1987), 235–236; Art Heinz, "Brochure Details Mercersburg's Rich African-American Heritage," *Public Opinion*, June 4, 1998, clipping, VF-African Americans, Franklin County Historical Society-Kittochtinny, Chambersburg, PA.

113. Leeds, "Old Military Organization"; "Colored Citizens Will Hold Appropriate Exercises and Parade," *The Sentinel* (Carlisle, PA), May 17, 1913, 8.

114. "Colored Citizens Properly Observe Memorial Day," *The Sentinel* (Carlisle, PA), May 31, 1912, 8; Hood, *One Hundred Years of the African Methodist Episcopal Zion Church*, 238–239.

115. Grimké, "The Gathering of the Grand Army," 166–167.

116. Grimké, "The Gathering of the Grand Army."

Porch Lessons I: Rebel, Father, and Veteran

1. Service Record of Joseph Lane, 22nd US Colored Infantry, United States Civil War Service Records of Union Colored Troops, 1863–1865. Database. Fold3.com, http://www.fold3.com; "The Reception to the Colored Soldiers," *Harrisburg Daily Telegraph*, November 14, 1865, 3, and "Harrisburg. Reception of the Colored Soldiers. Speech of General Cameron. Letters from Generals Meade and Butler," *Press* (*Philadelphia*), November 15, 1865, 1, in Reception of Colored Troops—Nov. 14, 1865, VF, Dauphin County Historical Society, Harrisburg, PA.

2. Barbara Gannon, *The Won Cause: Black and White Comradeship in the Grand Army of the Republic* (Chapel Hill: University of North Carolina Press, 2011), 36–71.

3. Service Record of Joseph Lane.

4. Service Record of Joseph Lane. Reed's fractious racial politics and poor relationship with other men continued after this court-martial. Reflecting on Reed's service as Provost Marshal in Brownsville, Texas, Bvt. Maj. General Giles A. Smith surmised that "the public service would be promoted by his discharge" on December 11, 1865. See Service Record of Joseph B. Reed, 19th US Colored Infantry, United States Civil War Service Records of Union Colored Troops, 1863–1865. Database. Fold3.com, https://www.fold3.com/image/264630194.

5. Service Record of Joseph Lane.

6. William H. Burkhart, Samuel L. Daihl, J. Houston McCulloch, Dr. George Kaluger, Mrs. Elizabeth Roler, and Mrs. Howard A. Ryder, *Shippensburg, Pennsylvania, in the Civil War* (Shippensburg, PA: Burd Street Press, 2003), 223; Black Veterans Binder: Mil Civ Black, Shippensburg Historical Society, October 1960, n.p.

7. "Shot at Midnight," *Philadelphia Times*, December 19, 1878, 1; "Telegraphic Summary, Etc.," *Baltimore Sun*, December 19, 1878, 1; "Hanging of Peter Swingler," *New York Times*, June 6, 1879, 5.

8. Burkhart, Daihl, McCulloch, et al. *Shippensburg, Pennsylvania, in the Civil War*, 223.

9. "Peter Swingler to Hang," *Philadelphia Times*, May 24, 1879, 1; "A Charcoal Cherub," *St. Louis Post-Dispatch*, June 5, 1879, 1; "Hanging of Peter Swingler," *New York Times*, June 6, 1879, 5; "Hanged," *Chicago Daily Tribune*, June 6, 1879, 6; Gail Bederman, *Manliness and Civilization: A Cultural History of Gender and Race in the United States, 1880–1917* (Chicago: University of Chicago Press, 1995), 8, 20–21.

10. "Peter Swingler to Hang"; "A Charcoal Cherub"; "Hanging of Peter Swingler"; "Hanged."

11. Bederman, *Manliness and Civilization*, 29.

12. Bederman, *Manliness and Civilization*, 49–53.

13. Steven B. Burg, "Shippensburg's Locust Grove African-American Cemetery: A Window on Two Centuries of Cumberland County's African American History," *Cumberland County History* 26 (2009): 37.

14. Burg, "Shippensburg's Locust Grove African-American Cemetery," 38; Historic Site Report for Locust Grove Cemetery Shippensburg, Pennsylvania, October 20, 2007, 32–33.

15. Steven B. Burg, "From Troubled Grounds to Common Ground: The Locust Grove African American Cemetery Preservation Project: A Case Study of Service," *Public Historian* 30 (May 2008): 57.

16. Historian Janet Bell has compiled a list of known but incomplete roster of Carlisle post members. It primarily includes those members interred at Lincoln Cemetery and Union Cemetery, both historic African American cemeteries in Carlisle, Pennsylvania. See Janet L. Bell, "Corporal Jesse G. Thompson G.A.R. Post 440," *Cumberland County History* 30 (2013): 96–97, and Stephanie A. Jirard, "US. Colored Troops from Cumberland County Buried in Union Cemetery, Carlisle, Pennsylvania," Special Civil War Edition, *Cumberland County History* 28 (2011): 39–53.

17. Historic Site Report for Locust Grove Cemetery Shippensburg, Pennsylvania, 47.

18. Burkhart, Daihl, McCulloch, et al., *Shippensburg, Pennsylvania, in the Civil War*, 223–229, 247–249, 276–277; Black Veterans Binder, Shippensburg Historical Society, Shippensburg, PA, 22.

19. Burkhart, Daihl, McCulloch, et al., *Shippensburg, Pennsylvania, in the Civil War*, 220–237; Black Veterans Binder, 22–38; The oral tradition was not limited to Shippensburg but included Lane's native community of Chambersburg, PA. See the interviews of Mary Lee Williams Barnett, 1887–1993, Anna Blondine Jones Bruce, 1898–1981, Larry Dean Calimer, b. 1938, Anna Belle Chase (1912–2006), and Vivian Chase Hines (b.

1931) in *Voices of Chambersburg: An Oral History of the African American Community of Franklin County, Pennsylvania,* by C. Bernard Ruffin, vol. 1 of 5—*Interviews* (Greencastle, PA: Allison-Antrim Museum, 2011); Jennifer Rittenhouse, *Growing Up Jim Crow: How Black and White Southern Children Learned Race* (Chapel Hill: University of North Carolina Press, 2006), 88.

20. Rittenhouse, *Growing Up Jim Crow,* 11, 13.

21. Leeann G. Reynolds, *Maintaining Segregation: Children and Racial Instruction in the South, 1920–1955* (Baton Rouge: Louisiana State University, 2017), 40–48, 59–61.

22. Reynolds, *Maintaining Segregation,* 47; see C. Bernard Ruffin, *Voices of Chambersburg: An Oral History of the African American Community of Franklin County, Pennsylvania,* vol. 1 of 5—*Interviews* (Greencastle, PA: Allison-Antrim Museum, 2011).

23. See Evelyn Brooks Higginbotham, *Righteous Discontent: The Women's Movement in the Black Baptist Church, 1880–1920* (Cambridge, MA: Harvard University Press, 1993), Victoria W. Wolcott, *Remaking Respectability: African American Women in Interwar Detroit* (Chapel Hill: University of North Carolina Press, 2001); Treva Lindsey, *Colored No More: Reinventing Black Womanhood in Washington, DC* (Urbana: University of Illinois Press, 2017), and Brittany Cooper, *Beyond Respectability: The Intellectual Thought of Race Women* (Urbana: University of Illinois Press, 2017).

24. Rittenhouse, *Growing Up Jim Crow,* 85.

25. Rittenhouse, *Growing Up Jim Crow,* 85.

26. Rittenhouse, *Growing Up Jim Crow,* 86.

27. Rittenhouse, *Growing Up Jim Crow,* 86.

28. Karen L. Cox, *Dixie's Daughters: The United Daughters of the Confederacy and the Preservation of Confederate Culture.* New Perspectives on the History of the South (Gainesville: University Press of Florida, 2003), 139–140.

29. "Sun Shines Memorial Day," *News-Chronicle,* June 2, 1933; "Colored War Dead to Be Honored Here," *News-Chronicle,* May 30, 1940, 1.

5. The Limits of Emancipationist Memory in Richmond

1. Michael A. Bellesiles, *Inventing Equality: Reconstructing the Constitution in the Aftermath of the Civil War* (New York: St. Martin's Press, 2020), 107; R. J. M. Blackett, *Thomas Morris Chester, Black War Correspondent: His Dispatches from the Virginia Front* (Boston: Da Capo Press, 1989), 289–290.

2. Blackett, *Thomas Morris Chester, Black War Correspondent,* 290.

3. Blackett, *Thomas Morris Chester, Black War Correspondent,* 290.

4. Blackett, *Thomas Morris Chester, Black War Correspondent,* 296–303.

5. Peter Rachleff, *Black Labor in Richmond, 1865–1890* (Urbana: University of Illinois Press, 1984), 36–37; Gregg D. Kimball, *American City, Southern Place: A Cultural History of Antebellum Richmond* (Athens: University of Georgia Press, 2000), 259–260; Elsa Barkley Brown, "Negotiating and Transforming the Public Sphere: African American Political Life in the Transition from Slavery to Freedom," in *Time Longer Than Rope: A Century of African American Activism, 1850–1950,* ed. Charles M. Payne and Adam Green (New York: New York University Press, 2003), 71–73.

6. Kathleen Ann Clark, *Defining Moments: African American Commemoration and Political Culture in the South, 1863–1913* (Chapel Hill: University of North Carolina Press, 2005), 54; "Notice! The Colored People of the city of Richmond would most respectfully inform the public, that they do not intend to celebrate the failure of the Southern confederacy . . . ," broadside, Richmond, VA, April 2, 1866, Virginia Historical Society, Richmond, Virginia.

7. Julia Porter Read to Harriett Sublett (Read) Berry, c. April–May 1865, section 4, Read Family Papers, 1828–1914, Virginia Historical Society; Gaines M. Foster, *Ghosts of the Confederacy: Defeat, the Lost Cause, and the Emergence of the New South, 1865–1913* (New York: Oxford University Press, 1987), 33, 35.

8. "From John H. Gilmer," in *The Papers of Andrew Johnson*, vol. 9, September 1865–January 1866, ed. Paul H. Bergeron (Knoxville: University of Tennessee Press, 1991), 249–250; "From John H. Gilmer," in *The Papers of Andrew Johnson*, vol. 10, February–July 1866, ed. Paul H. Bergeron (Knoxville: University of Tennessee Press, 1992), 337.

9. Eric Foner, *Reconstruction: America's Unfinished Revolution, 1863–1877* (New York: Harper and Row, 1988), 247; The *Papers of Andrew Johnson*, vol. 10, February–July 1866, 41–48, 53–54, 58–59, 120–127; Bellesiles, *Inventing Equality*, 180–184.

10. "The Third of April and the Freedman," *Richmond Whig*, March 27, 1866, 1.

11. "Negro Celebration on the Fall of Richmond," *Evening Star*, March 30, 1866, 3. Following this article, several newspapers circulated misinformation of federal involvement by Major General Terry, the silence of Grant, and an alleged executive order issued by the president. In reviewing the Presidential Papers, I do not see any evidence of the executive order being issued as reported by the media. See "From Washington. Our Special Dispatches," *New York Daily Tribune,* March 31, 1866, 1; "The Celebration of the Third of April by the Negroes of Richmond Prohibited by the President," *Charleston Daily News*, April 3, 1866, 1; "Untitled," *Daily Phoenix*, April 4, 1866, 3; "Negro Celebration," *Staunton Spectator*, April 3, 1866, 3.

12. Quoted in "To Maj. Gen. Alfred H. Terry," in *The Papers of Ulysses S. Grant, vol. 16: 1866*, ed. John Y. Simon (Carbondale: Southern Illinois University Press, 1988), 142.

13. To Maj. Gen. Alfred H. Terry," *The Papers of Ulysses S. Grant*, 142.

14. John T. O'Brien, "Reconstruction in Richmond: White Restoration and Black Protest, April–June 1865," *Virginia Magazine of History and Biography* 89, no. 3 (July 1981): 279.

15. "Notice! The Colored People of the city of Richmond would most respectfully inform the public, that they do not intend to celebrate the failure of the Southern confederacy..."; To Maj. Gen. Alfred H. Terry," *The Papers of Ulysses S. Grant*, 142.

16. To Maj. Gen. Alfred H. Terry," *The Papers of Ulysses S. Grant*, 142–143.

17. Rachleff, *Black Labor in Richmond, 1865–1890*, 39–40.

18. Rachleff, *Black Labor in Richmond, 1865–1890*, 39; William D. Harris to George Whipple, April 6, 1866, microfilm roll 13, AMA Papers, Virginia.

19. "The Negro Celebration on the 3rd of April," *Daily Dispatch*, April 9, 1866, 1; "Negro Celebration on the Third of April," *Richmond Whig*, April 10, 1866, 2.

20. "Negro Celebration on the Third of April," *Richmond Whig*, April 10, 1866, 2.

21. Quoted in "The Negro Celebration on the 3rd of April," *Daily Dispatch*, April 9, 1866, 1.

22. Harris to Whipple, April 6, 1866.

23. Harris to Whipple, April 6, 1866; To Maj. Gen. Alfred H. Terry," *The Papers of Ulysses S. Grant*, 142.

24. "The Negro Celebration on the 3rd of April," *Daily Dispatch*, April 9, 1866, 1; "Telegrams, etc.," *Evening Star*, April 4, 1866, 1; "Negro Celebration on the Third of April," *Richmond Whig*, April 10. 1866. 2; "The Second African Church Burned Down," *Daily Dispatch*, April 10, 1866, 1.

25. Marie Tyler-McGraw, "Southern Comfort Levels: Race, Heritage Tourism, and the Civil War in Richmond," in *Slavery and Public History: The Tough Stuff of American Memory*, ed. James Oliver Horton and Lois E. Horton (New York: New Press, 2006), 155; For African American commemorative traditions after the Civil War, see Clark, *Defining Moments*.

26. Quoted in Rachleff, *Black Labor in Richmond*, 41.

27. "Untitled," *Freeman* (Indianapolis, IN), August 9, 1890, 4; Ellen M. Litwicki, *America's Public Holidays, 1865–1920* (Washington, DC: Smithsonian Institution Press, 2000), 58–59.

28. George Williams Jr., "George Williams Jr., Originator and General Superintendent of the Emancipation Celebration," *Richmond Planet*, October 18, 1890, 1; Litwicki, *America's Public Holidays*, 59.

29. "Virginia Industrial, Mercantile, Building and Loan Association. Capital Stocks," advertisement, *Washington Bee*, June 11, 1892, 3; "Curbstone Chit and Chat: The News of the City Dished Up for the Bee," *Washington Bee*, March 24, 1894, 1; "From Bluefield," *Richmond Planet*, October 9, 1897, 3; "From Bluefield," *Richmond Planet*, November 13, 1897, 3. For tours and success as a tour operator, see "Fair at Charleston, W. Va.," *Freeman* (Indianapolis, IN), September 10, 1892, 5; "Notice," *Richmond Planet*, August 15, 1896, 4; "A Successful Excursion," *Richmond Planet*, September 10, 1898, 8.

30. "The Thanksgiving Celebration. Address to the Public and All Whom It May Concern," *Richmond Planet*, October 11, 1890, 1; "Celebration of the Emancipation Proclamation, 1890," broadside, 189–.C7FF, Special Collections, Library of Virginia, Richmond, Virginia. For a list of Richmond Colored Normal graduates used for gauging event organizers, see Hilary Nicole Green, "Educational Reconstruction: African American Education in the Urban South, 1865–1890" (PhD diss., University of North Carolina at Chapel Hill, 2010), 369–385; Litwicki, *America's Public Holidays*, 60–61.

31. George Williams Jr., "Emancipation Celebration," a letter to the editor, *Freeman* (Indianapolis, IN), September 13, 1890, 6.

32. Williams Jr., "Emancipation Celebration"; "Political Arena," *Freeman* (Indianapolis, IN), September 27, 1890, 10; "Items of *The Age*," *New York Age*, October 25, 1890, 2.

33. "Doings of the Race," *Cleveland Gazette*, October 18, 1890, 3.

34. J.A.G., "Old Dominion. A Chairman Resigns—Delegates to the Richmond Celebration," *Freeman* (Indianapolis, IN), October 18, 1890, 7; "A Visit to Richmond," *New York Age*, October 25, 1890, 1; "The Day for Celebration. The Richmond Conventional Recommends January 1st. Echoes of the Recent Demonstration," *New York Age*, October

25, 1890, 1. Known as the Danville Massacre, the violence resulted in the statewide defeat of the Readjusters and their interracial and cross-class coalition in November 1883 elections. With the violence continuing for several days, the post-election investigations did not offer justice for the largely African American victims. See Jane Dailey, *Before Jim Crow: The Politics of Race in Postemancipation Virginia* (Chapel Hill: University of North Carolina Press, 2000), 119–128.

35. A Visit to Richmond"; "What I Saw and Heard," *Washington Bee*, October 18, 1890, 3.

36. "What I Saw and Heard"; "The Day for Celebration"; Litwicki, *America's Public Holidays*, 61.

37. "A Gala Day," *Richmond Planet*, October 18, 1890, 1.

38. "A Gala Day"; Caroline Janney, *Remembering the Civil War: Reunion and the Limits of Reconciliation* (Chapel Hill: University of North Carolina Press, 2013), 214.

39. "The Day for Celebration."

40. "The Day for Celebration."

41. "The Day for Celebration."

42. "Celebration of the Emancipation Proclamation, 1890"; "The Emancipation Celebration," *Richmond Planet*, October 11, 1890, 1; Janney, *Remembering the Civil War*, 214.

43. "The Emancipation Celebration," *Richmond Planet*, October 11, 1890, 1; Litwicki, *America's Public Holidays*, 64; "A Gala Day," *Richmond Planet*, October 18, 1890, 1.

44. David W. Blight, *Race and Reunion: The Civil War in American Memory* (Cambridge, MA: Belknap Press of Harvard University Press, 2001), 267–270; Janney, *Remembering the Civil War*, 181–182.

45. Blight, *Race and Reunion*, 94–95; Karen L. Cox, *Dixie's Daughters: The United Daughters of the Confederacy and the Preservation of Confederate Culture*. New Perspectives on the History of the South (Gainesville: University Press of Florida, 2003), 63–65; West Virginia, *Biennial Report of the Adjutant General of the State of West Virginia for the Years 1889 and 1890* (Charleston, WVA: Moses W. Donnally, Public Printer, 1890), 4–5, 34; "M. F. Wyckoff and Unidentified African American boy," photograph, n.p., 1890, author's personal collection.

46. Blight, *Race and Reunion*, 284–289; Micki McElya, *Clinging to Mammy: The Faithful Slave in Twentieth-Century America* (Cambridge, MA: Harvard University Press, 2007), 5–13, 38–40; Kevin M. Levin, *Searching for Black Confederates: The Civil War's Most Persistent Myth* (Chapel Hill: University of North Carolina Press, 2019), 97–99; Adam H. Domby, *The False Cause: Fraud, Fabrication, and White Supremacy in Confederate Memory* (Charlottesville: University of Virginia Press, 2020), 104–131.

47. Blight, *Race and Reunion*, 270–272; "The Lee Monument Unveiling," *Richmond Planet*, May 31, 1890, 1.

48. "The Lee Monument Unveiling."

49. "The Day for Celebration"; Janney, *Remembering the Civil War*, 214–215.

50. "A Gala Day."

51. "Emancipation Day Celebration in Richmond," photograph, 1905, Library of Congress, Prints and Photographs Division (LC-DIG-det-4a12513), Washington, DC.

52. Kathy Edwards and Esme Howard, "Monument Avenue: The Architecture of Consensus in the New South, 1890–1930," *Perspectives in Vernacular Architecture* 6 (1997): 92–107; Rebecca B. Watts, *Contemporary Southern Identity: Community through Controversy* (Jackson: University of Mississippi Press, 2007), 49; Koritha Mitchell, *From Slave Cabins to the White House: Homemade Citizenship in African American Culture* (Urbana: University of Illinois Press, 2020), 4–5.

53. Mitchell, *From Slave Cabins to the White House*, 92; Marc Howard Ross, *Slavery in the North: Forgetting History and Recovering Memory* (Philadelphia: University of Pennsylvania Press, 2018), 86.

54. Ross, *Slavery in the North*, 94.

55. Amici Curiae: David W. Blight and Gaines M. Foster (Adam L. Sorensen; Joseph R. Palmore; Morrison & Foerster, on brief), in support of appellees and Amici Curiae: Professors Thomas J. Brown, W. Fitzhugh Brundage, Karen L. Cox, Hilary N. Green, Kirk Savage, and Dell Upton (Blake E. Stafford; Christine C. Smith; Briana M. Clark; Latham & Watkins, on brief), in support of appellees in Supreme Court of Virginia Counsel in Case Decided September 2, 2021: *Helen Marie Taylor, et al. v. Ralph S. Northam, et al.* Record No. 210113, Counsel in Decided Cases, Supreme Court of Virginia, Richmond, Virginia, http://www.courts.state.va.us/courts/scv/counsel.pdf; *Helen Marie Taylor et al. v. Ralph S. Northam et al.* Record No. 210113 (September 2, 2021) and *William C. Gregory v. Ralph S. Northam, et al.*, Record No. 201307 order (September 2, 2021) in Supreme Court of Virginia Opinions and Published Orders, Supreme Court of Virginia, Richmond, Virginia, http://www.courts.state.va.us/scndex.htm; "Workers Remove Richmond's Iconic Statue of Robert E. Lee," *Washington Post*, September 8, 2021.

56. "Great Exposition and Celebration," *Industrial Advocate* (Richmond, VA), October 31, 1914, 1, accessed at Albert and Shirley Small Collections Library, University of Virginia, Charlottesville, Virginia.

57. "Great Exposition and Celebration."

58. Lauranett Lee, "Giles B. Jackson (1853–1924)," *Encyclopedia Virginia*, Virginia Foundation for the Humanities, https://www.encyclopediavirginia.org/Jackson_Giles _B_1853–1924; "Richmond Fair Is Warmly Indorsed," *Denver Star,* June 26, 1915, 4; *1870 United States Federal Census* (database online), Provo, UT: Ancestry.com Operations, 2009; *District of Columbia, Compiled Marriage Index, 1830–1921* (database online), Provo, UT: Ancestry.com Operations, 2014.

59. Lee, "Giles B. Jackson"; *1880 United States Federal Census* (database online) Lehi, UT: Ancestry.com Operations, 2010; Ancestry.com. *1910 United States Federal Census* (database online). Lehi, UT: Ancestry.com Operations, 2006.

60. Brian de Ruiter, "Jamestown Ter-Centennial Exposition of 1907," in *Encyclopedia Virginia*, Virginia Foundation for the Humanities, Richmond, VA, https://www .encyclopediavirginia.org/Jamestown_Ter-Centennial_Exposition_of_1907; "Negro Day at Jamestown," *Evening Star* (Washington, DC), July 29, 1907, 2; "Negro's Gala Day," *Washington Bee*, August 10, 1907, 1.

61. "No. 119, Negro Building, Jamestown Exposition of 1907," official souvenir Jamestown Ter-Centennial postcard, 1907, in author's personal collection. Discoloration caused by the photo corners on the postcard notes the preservation practice;

"Unidentified African American girl and women," Jamestown Ter-Centennial souvenir photograph, Norfolk, 1907, tintype in embossed paper mat, in author's personal collection.

62. John Thornton, "The African Experience of '20 and Odd Negroes' Arriving in Virginia in 1619," *William and Mary Quarterly* 55 (July 1998): 421-434; Ibram X. Kendi, "A Community of Souls: An Introduction," in *Four Hundred Souls: A Community History of African America, 1619-2019*, ed. Ibram X. Kendi and Keisha N. Blain (New York: One World, 2021), xiii-xiv; Nikole Hannah-Jones, "1619-1624: Arrival," in *Four Hundred Souls: A Community History of African America, 1619-2019*, ed. Ibram X. Kendi and Keisha N. Blain (New York: One World, 2021), 3-7; Cathleen D. Cahill, *Recasting the Vote: How Women of Color Transformed the Suffrage Movement* (Chapel Hill: University of North Carolina Press, 2021), 68-69; Carrie Williams Clifford, *The Widening Light* (Boston: Walter Reid, 1922), 23.

63. De Ruiter, "Jamestown Ter-Centennial Exposition of 1907."

64. R. W. Thompson, "A New Page of History on Hampton Roads," *New York Age*, December 5, 1907, 1-2.

65. Thompson, "A New Page of History on Hampton Roads," 2.

66. Lee, "Giles B. Jackson"; Giles B. Jackson and Daniel Webster Davis, *The Industrial History of the Negro Race of the United States* (Richmond: Virginia Press, 1908), 53-137.

67. Giles B. Jackson to Woodrow Wilson, December 23, 1912, *The Papers of Woodrow Wilson*, vol. 25, ed. Arthur S. Link (Princeton, NJ: Princeton University Press, 1978), 619-621; David Blight, *Beyond the Battlefield: Race, Memory, and the American Civil War* (Amherst: University of Massachusetts Press, 2002), 197-198; K. Stephen Prince, "Jim Crow Memory: Southern White Supremacists and the Regional Politics of Remembrance," in *Remembering Reconstruction: Struggles of the Meaning of America's Most Turbulent Era*, ed. Carol Emberton and Bruce E. Baker (Baton Rouge: Louisiana State University Press, 2017), 23, 26; "Great Exposition and Celebration." A few issues survive of this short-lived African American newspaper. Many of the inaugural articles were reprinted on the first two pages of subsequent volumes. The editorials and status updates changed in later editions.

68. "President Wilson Heartily Receives Delegation of Leading Negroes and Accepts Invitation," *Industrial Advocate* (Richmond, VA), November 14, 1914, 1.

69. "Great Exposition and Celebration."

70. "National Government Appropriates $55,000," *Industrial Advocate* (Richmond), October 31, 1914, 1; Giles B. Jackson, "The Advent and Policy of the Industrial Advocate as Proclaimed by Its Editor," *Industrial Advocate* (Richmond, VA), October 31, 1914, 2; "The Negro Historical and Industrial Association," *Industrial Advocate* (Richmond. VA), October 31, 1914, 2; "Gov. H. C. Stuart Writes President Wilson," *Industrial Advocate* (Richmond, VA), October 31, 1914, 2; "Letter from Giles B. Jackson to President Wilson," *Industrial Advocate* (Richmond, VA), October 31, 1914, 2; "The Negro Historical and Industrial Association," Exhibitor Form, *Industrial Advocate* (Richmond, VA), October 31, 1914, 3; "Negro Historical, Industrial Association Busy With Plans for Big Summer Exposition," *Industrial Advocate* (Richmond, VA), October 31, 1914, 3.

71. "Dr. Socrates' Letter," *Industrial Advocate* (Richmond, VA), October 31, 1914, 1.

72. Blight, *Race and Reunion*, 362–366; Janney, *Remembering the Civil War*, 272–275; "Dr. Socrates' Letter."

73. "Dr. Socrates' Letter."

74. "Virginia Colored Exposition," *Industrial Advocate* (Richmond, VA), October 31, 1914, 2.

75. "Virginia Colored Exposition."

76. "Afro-American Cullings," *Uplift* (Pittsburg, Kansas), December 5, 1914, 2; "Planning for National Exposition in Virginia," *Denver Star*, November 28, 1914, 7; "Richmond Fair Is Warmly Indorsed," *Denver Star*, June 26, 1915, 4; "Half Century of Freedom: Progress of Race to Be Shown in Big Celebration," *Cleveland Gazette,* May 8, 1915, 1. See also "Afro-American Cullings," *Tulsa Star*, December 5, 1914, 6 and N. Barnett Dodson, "Milestones in Our History," *Muskogee Cimeter* (Muskogee, Indian Territory, Oklahoma), June 5, 1915, 4.

77. "Rise in Capital of Old Dominion. Success of Our Institutions in Richmond, Va. True Reformers Led Way," *Oakland Sunshine* (Oakland, CA), March 20, 1915, 2.

78. "Negro Exposition in July to Be Held in Richmond," *Herald and News* (Newberry, SC), May 11, 1915.

79. "Untitled," *Freeman* (Indianapolis, IN), January 1, 1915, 4; "Short Flights," *Freeman* (Indianapolis, IN), February 6, 1915, 2.

80. "The Members of the Illinois State Commission, to Celebrate the Fifty Years of Freedom on the Part of the Afro-Americans in This State in 1915, Have Already Expended Seven Thousand, Eight Hundred Twenty-Seven Dollars and Seven Cents of the Twenty-Five Thousand Dollars Appropriated for the Purpose. So Far Nothing Has Been Accomplished by the Commission in That Direction," *Broad Ax* (Chicago), June 27, 1914, 1; "The Fiftieth Anniversary of Negro's Freedom," *Broad Ax* (Chicago), May 15, 1915, 1.

81. "Negro Exposition Attracts Attention," *Richmond Times-Dispatch*, May 6, 1915, 7; "Tobacco Exhibit," *Richmond Times-Dispatch*, May 11, 1915, 4; "Jackson Asks Support of Theodore Roosevelt," *Richmond Times-Dispatch*, May 16, 1915, 15; "Negro Race Opens Great Exposition," *Richmond Times-Dispatch*, July 5, 1915, 1; "Invites White People to Attend Exposition," *Richmond Times-Dispatch*, July 8, 1915, 3.

82. "Negro Fair Closes with Visit of Governor Stuart," *Richmond Times-Dispatch*, July 29, 1915, 7; Giles B. Jackson to Woodrow Wilson, July 23, 1915, *The Papers of Woodrow Wilson*, vol. 34 (Princeton, NJ: Princeton University Press, 1985), 16; "Col. Giles B. Jackson and His Fifty Years of Freedom Celebration at Richmond, Virginia, Has Turned Out to Be a Ranked Failure," *Broad Ax* (Chicago), August 7, 1915, 1.

83. "Col. Giles B. Jackson and His Fifty Years of Freedom Celebration at Richmond, Virginia Has Turned Out to Be a Ranked Failure."

84. "That Richmond Fair," *Freeman* (Indianapolis, IN), July 31, 1915, 4; The *Richmond Times-Dispatch* highlighted the post-exposition investigation of mismanagement charge. See "Charge Mismanagement of Negro Exposition," *Richmond Times-Dispatch*, July 23, 1915, 1 and "Directors Charge Waste of Funds of Exposition," *Richmond Times-Dispatch*, July 30, 1915, 12.

85. See Blight, *Beyond the Battlefield*, 198–208; W. Fitzhugh Brundage, *The Southern Past: A Clash of Race and Memory* (Cambridge, MA: Belknap Press of Harvard

University Press, 2008); Jeffrey Aaron Snyder, *Making Black History: The Color Line, Culture, and Race in the Age of Jim Crow* (Athens: University of Georgia Press, 2018); Treva Lindsey, *Colored No More: Reinventing Black Womanhood in Washington, D.C.* (Urbana: University of Illinois Press, 2017).

86. Burnis R. Morris, *Carter G. Woodson: History, The Black Press and Public Relations* (Jackson: University Press of Mississippi, 2017), 3–6; Jarvis R. Givens, *Fugitive Pedagogy: Carter G. Woodson and the Art of Black Teaching* (Cambridge, MA: Harvard University Press, 2021), 30–43; Snyder, *Making Black History*, 19. For Woodson's reflections his relationships with Civil War veterans, see Carter G. Woodson, "My Recollections of Veterans of the Civil War," *Negro History Bulletin* 7, no. 5 (February 1944): 103–104, 115–118.

87. Snyder, *Making Black History*, 20–21.

88. Morris, *Carter G. Woodson*, xiii–xx; Snyder, *Making Black History*, 33–34; Brundage, *The Southern Past*, 154–157; Givens, *Fugitive Pedagogy*, 66–71.

89. Snyder, *Making Black History*, 39.

90. Snyder, *Making Black History*, 154–155.

91. Snyder, *Making Black History*, 110; Givens, *Fugitive Pedagogy*, 82–92.

92. Givens, *Fugitive Pedagogy*, 159–198; Brundage, *The Southern Past*, 166–177; Snyder, *Making Black History*, 71.

93. Elsa Barkley Brown, "Negotiating and Transforming the Public Sphere: African American Political Life in the Transition from Slavery to Freedom," *Public Culture* 7 (1994): 93–96; Mitchell, *From Slave Cabins to the White House*, 3.

94. Edwards and Howard, "Monument Avenue: The Architecture of Consensus in the New South, 1890–1930," 107; Watts, *Contemporary Southern Identity*, 49, 54–73.

95. Chris Suarez, "With Removal of A. P. Hill Monument Pending, Richmond Officials Still Reviewing Offers for Final Disposition of Its Confederate Monuments," *Richmond Times-Dispatch*, October 24, 2020, https://richmond.com/news/local/govt-and-politics/with-removal-of-a-p-hill-monument-pending-richmond-officials-still-reviewing-offers-for-final/article_4840f7ff-3fc9-5ee3-b25a-5bb0df845a25.html. Accessed December 30, 2020; Emma Davis, "UR Community Reflects on the Removal of Richmond Confederate Monuments," *The Collegian*, September 8, 2020, https://www.thecollegianur.com/article/2020/09/members-of-ur-community-reflect-on-removal-of-confederate-monuments. Accessed December 30, 2020.

96. Amici Curiae: David W. Blight and Gaines M. Foster (Adam L. Sorensen; Joseph R. Palmore; Morrison & Foerster, on brief), in support of appellees and Amici Curiae: Professors Thomas J. Brown, W. Fitzhugh Brundage, Karen L. Cox, Hilary N. Green, Kirk Savage, and Dell Upton (Blake E. Stafford; Christine C. Smith; Briana M. Clark; Latham & Watkins, on brief), in support of appellees in Supreme Court of Virginia Counsel in Case Decided September 2, 2021: *Helen Marie Taylor, et al. v. Ralph S. Northam, et al.* Record No. 210113, Counsel in Decided Cases, Supreme Court of Virginia, Richmond, Virginia, http://www.courts.state.va.us/courts/scv/counsel.pdf; *Helen Marie Taylor, et al. v. Ralph S. Northam, et al.* Record No. 210113 (September 2, 2021) and *William C. Gregory v. Ralph S. Northam, et al.*, Record No. 201307 order (September 2, 2021) in Supreme Court of Virginia Opinions and Published Orders, Supreme Court

of Virginia, Richmond, Virginia, http://www.courts.state.va.us/scndex.htm; "Workers Remove Richmond's Iconic Statue of Robert E. Lee," *Washington Post*, September 8, 2021.

6. Black Women and the Persistence of Memory

1. Carrie Williams Clifford, *Race Rhymes* (Washington, DC: R. L. Pendleton, 1911), 9; Adam H. Domby, *The False Cause: Fraud, Fabrication, and White Supremacy in Confederate Memory* (Charlottesville: University of Virginia Press, 2020), 124–126.

2. Cathleen D. Cahill, *Recasting the Vote: How Women of Color Transformed the Suffrage Movement* (Chapel Hill: University of North Carolina Press, 2020), 111; Clifford, *Race Rhymes*, 22.

3. Clifford, *Race Rhymes*, 17–18; Cahill, *Recasting the Vote*, 124–126; Carrie Williams Clifford, *The Widening Light* (Boston: Walter Reid, 1922), 4, 27, 40, 62.

4. Koritha Mitchell, *From Slave Cabins to the White House: Homemade Citizenship in African American Culture* (Urbana: University of Illinois Press, 2020), 4–5.

5. Drew Gilpin Faust, *The Republic of Suffering: Death and the American Civil War* (New York: Vintage Books, 2008), 212–249; Caroline E. Janney, *Burying the Dead But Not the Past: Ladies' Memorial Association and the Lost Cause* (Chapel Hill: University of North Carolina Press, 2008), 39–164; Karen L. Cox, *Dixie's Daughters: The United Daughters of the Confederacy and the Preservation of Confederate Culture*. New Perspectives on the History of the South (Gainesville: University Press of Florida, 2003), 8–16.

6. Quoted in Kevin Waite, "The 'Lost Cause' Goes West: Confederate Culture and Civil War Memory in California," *California History* 97 (Spring 2020): 36–37.

7. Janney, *Burying the Dead But Not the Past*, 167–178; Cox, *Dixie's Daughters*, 16–48.

8. Cox, *Dixie's Daughters*, 48–158; W. Fitzhugh Brundage, *The Southern Past: A Clash of Race and Memory* (Cambridge, MA: Belknap Press of Harvard University Press, 2005), 27–54.

9. Cox, *Dixie's Daughters*, 49.

10. Adam Domby, "The Cost of a Democratic Memory: Financing North Carolina's Commemorative Landscape," 2012, *Commemorative Landscapes of North Carolina*, https://docsouth.unc.edu/commland/features/essays/domby/; David Silkenat, "'A Company of Gentlemen': Confederate Veterans and Southern Universities," *American Nineteenth Century History* 21, no. 3 (November 2020): 237–253; Domby, *The False Cause*, 12–15.

11. Karen L. Cox, *No Common Ground: Confederate Monuments and the Ongoing Fight for Racial Justice* (Chapel Hill: University of North Carolina Press, 2021), 21–22; For the antebellum role of Southern colleges and universities in advancing pro-slavery thought, see Alfred L. Brophy, *University, Court, and Slave: Pro-Slavery Thought in Southern Colleges and Courts and the Coming of the Civil War* (New York: Oxford University Press, 2016), 48–156.

12. Julian S. Carr, "Unveiling of Confederate Monument at University, June 2, 1913," in the Julian Shakespeare Carr Papers #141, Southern Historical Collection, The Wilson Library, University of North Carolina at Chapel Hill; Domby, *The False Cause*, 17–19.

13. Domby, *The False Cause*, 18–19; Carr, "Unveiling of Confederate Monument at University, June 2, 1913."

14. Micki McElya, *Clinging to Mammy: The Faithful Slave in Twentieth-Century America* (Cambridge, MA: Harvard University Press, 2007), 1–3, 22–32; Kevin M. Levin, *Searching for Black Confederates: The Civil War's Most Persistent Myth* (Chapel Hill: University of North Carolina Press, 2019), 82–96.

15. Kirk Savage, *Standing Soldiers, Kneeling Slaves; Race, War, and Monument in Nineteenth-Century America* (Princeton, NJ: Princeton University Press, 1997), 155–162; Levin, *Searching for Black Confederates*, 97–99; McElya, *Clinging to Mammy*, 116–159; Joan Marie Johnson, "'Ye Gave Them a Stone': African American Women's Clubs, the Frederick Douglass Home, and the Black Mammy Monument," *Journal of Women's History* 17 (Spring 2005): 62–64, 69–79; Alison M. Parker, *Unceasing Militant: The Life of Mary Church Terrell* (Chapel Hill: University of North Carolina Press, 2020), 135–141; Patricia Morton, *Disfigured Images: The Historical Assault on Afro-American Women* (New York: Greenwood Press, 1991), 27–37.

16. Ethan J. Kytle and Blain Roberts, *Denmark Vesey's Garden: Slavery and Memory in the Cradle of the Confederacy* (New York: New Press, 2018), 102, 107–108.

17. Mamie Garvin Fields, *Lemon Swamp and Other Places: A Carolina Memoir* (New York: Free Press, 1983), 57.

18. Fields, *Lemon Swamp and Other Places*, 57.

19. Fields, *Lemon Swamp and Other Places*, 57.

20. Kytle and Roberts, *Denmark Vesey's Garden*, 104–113; Fields, *Lemon Swamp and Other Places*, 57.

21. "Monument Defaced" and "Reward," *Chatham Record*, September 5, 1907, 3; These original articles were combined and published under a new title reprinted throughout the state. See "Hanging Too Good, for Miscreant Who Defaced Confederate Monument," *Raleigh Farmer and Mechanic*, September 10, 1907, 8, and "Hanging Too Good, for Miscreant Who Defaced Confederate Monument," *Messenger and Intelligencer* (Wadesboro, NC), September 12, 1907.

22. "Local Briefs," *North Carolinian*, January 7, 1874, 3; "Untitled," *North Carolinian*, January 4, 1888, 3; Domby, *The False Cause*, 41.

23. Kathleen Ann Clark, *Defining Moments: African American Commemoration and Political Culture in the South, 1863–1913* (Chapel Hill: University of North Carolina Press, 2005), 28–29.

24. "Hertford," *Virginian Pilot*, January 4, 1899, 9; "Emancipation Day," *The Weekly Economist* (Elizabeth City, NC), January 4, 1901, 3; "Colored People Celebrate," *Tar Heel* (Elizabeth City, NC), January 2, 1903, 1; "Negro Veterans of Two Wars Appear in Parade," *Independent* (Elizabeth City, NC), January 2, 1920, 1; Clark, *Defining Moments*, 169.

25. Clark, *Defining Moments*, 210–220; Thavolia Glymph, "'Liberty Dearly Bought': The Making of Civil War Memory in Afro-American Communities in the South," in *Time Longer Than Rope: A Century of African American Activism, 1850–1950*, ed. Charles M. Payne and Adam Green (New York: New York University Press, 2003), 123–127; Elsa Barkley Brown, "Negotiating and Transforming the Public Sphere: African American Political Life in the Transition from Slavery to Freedom," in *Time Longer Than Rope: A Century of African American Activism, 1850–1950*, ed. Charles M. Payne and Adam Green (New York: New York University Press, 2003), 93–96.

26. *Eleventh Census of the United States, 1890: Schedules Enumerating Union Veterans and Widows of Union Veterans of the Civil War, North Carolina, Bundles 119–123*, microfilm (Washington, DC: National Archives, 1948); Dorothy Redford, "Civil War Veterans Alive in 1890," Dorothy Spruill Redford papers; Richard M. Reid, *Freedom for Themselves: North Carolina's Black Soldiers in the Civil War Era* (Chapel Hill: University of North Carolina Press, 2008), 22–109; James K. Bryant II, *The 36th United States Infantry Colored Troops in the Civil War: A History and Roster* (Jefferson, NC: McFarland, 2012), 29–124.

27. Reid, *Freedom for Themselves*, 117–125; Bryant, *The 36th Infantry United States Colored Troops in the Civil War*, 47–56.

28. See "Grand Army Notes," *New York Freeman*, February 26, 1887, 3; "Elizabeth City, NC," *New York Age*, June 13, 1891, 2; "North Carolina GAR Posts: Decorate the Graves of the Dead Who Gave Their Lives in the Sixties," *Atlanta Constitution*, May 31, 1896, 14; Reid, *Freedom for Themselves*, 309.

29. Reid, *Freedom for Themselves*, 307–310; *Proceedings of the Twenty-Seventh Annual Encampment, Department of Virginia and North Carolina. Grand Army of the Republic. Held at the Court House, Elizabeth City, North Carolina, April 27, 1898* (Hampton, VA: N. S. Press, Printer and Binders, 1898), accessed at the Library of Congress, Washington, DC; "Unveiled amid Inspiring Scenes," *Tar Heel* (Elizabeth City, NC), May 12, 1911, 1; "List of Old Soldiers," *Tar Heel* (Elizabeth City, NC), May 12, 1911, 1.

30. Margaret M. Mulrooney, *Race, Place, and Memory: Deep Currents in Wilmington, North Carolina* (Gainesville: University Press of Florida, 2018), 127–145; H. Leon Prather Sr., *We Have Taken a City: Wilmington Racial Massacre and Coup of 1898* (Rutherford, NJ: Fairleigh Dickenson University Press, 1984), 107–150; H. Leon Prather Sr., "We Have Taken A City: A Centennial Essay," in *Democracy Betrayed: The Wilmington Race Riot of 1898 and Its Legacy*, ed. David S. Cecelski and Timothy B. Tyson (Chapel Hill: University of North Carolina Press, 1998), 28–38; Timothy B. Tyson, *Blood Done Sign My Name: A True Story* (New York: Crown, 2004), 271–275; David Zucchino, *Wilmington's Life: The Murderous Coup of 1898 and the Rise of White Supremacy* (New York: Grove Press, 2020), 174–300.

31. Mulrooney, *Race, Place, and Memory*, 121–127, 151–158, 241–243; Richard Yarborough, "Violence, Manhood, and Black Heroism: The Wilmington Riot in Two Turn-of-the-Century African American Novels," in *Democracy Betrayed: The Wilmington Race Riot of 1898 and Its Legacy*, ed. David S. Cecelski and Timothy B. Tyson (Chapel Hill: University of North Carolina Press, 1998), 225–248; Clark, *Defining Moments*, 210–212; Cox, *No Common Ground*, 106–136; Matthew E. Stanley, *Grand Army of Labor: Workers, Veterans, and the Meaning of the Civil War* (Urbana: University of Illinois Press, 2021), 150–151.

32. "Untitled," *North Carolinian*, May 22, 1889; "Federal Memorial Day," *Norfolk Landmark*, May 28, 1893, 1; "Headstones for Union Veterans," *Norfolk Landmark*, March 14, 1897, 1; Barbara Gannon, *The Won Cause: Black and White Comradeship in the Grand Army of the Republic* (Chapel Hill: University of North Carolina Press, 2011), 109–110; Lane Pearson, "African Americans and Their Civil War Legacy in the Albemarle," *The Gateway*, 6, clipping, Dorothy Spruill Redford papers.

33. Cassandra Newby-Alexander, "Remembering Norfolk's African American Cemeteries" (unpublished paper, no date), http://www.racetimeplace.com/cemeteryhistory .htm.

34. Newby-Alexander, "Remembering Norfolk's African American Cemeteries"; "Effort to Erect a Monument," *Norfolk Landmark*, July 24, 1895, 1; Savage, *Standing Soldiers, Kneeling Slaves*, 187–188; Gannon, *Won Cause*, 104–105.

35. David W. Blight, *Beyond the Battlefield: Race, Memory, and the American Civil War* (Amherst: University of Massachusetts Press, 2002), 153–166; Thomas J. Brown, *Civil War Monuments and the Militarization of America* (Chapel Hill: University of North Carolina Press, 2019), 100–105; Savage, *Standing Soldiers, Kneeling Slaves*, 89–128, 186–207.

36. Photograph of Grand Army of the Republic Reunion of African Americans ca. 1910, Accession #1143re6, Albert and Shirley Small Special Collections Library, University of Virginia, Charlottesville, VA; Gannon, *Won Cause*, 37; Courtney R. Baker, *Humane Insight: Looking at Images of African American Suffering and Death* (Urbana: University of Illinois Press, 2015), 37–38; Leigh Raiford, "Photography and the Practices of Critical Black Memory," *History and Theory* 48, no. 4 (December, 2009): 115–118.

37. Pearson, "African Americans and Their Civil War Legacy in the Albemarle," 7; Alberta H. Eason and Elizabeth Hines, eds., *History of First Baptist Church Hertford, North Carolina, 110th Anniversary Celebration*, 1976, p. 6, clipping, accessed in the Dorothy Spruill Redford papers.

38. Known United Daughters of Veterans members primarily represented the families of Stephen Felton, a First USCI veteran; David Skinner, a Fortieth USCI veteran; Augustus Reid, a US Navy veteran; William E. Ferebee, a Thirty-Eighth USCI veteran; Isaac Wood, a Forty-First USCI veteran; and John Sharp, a Thirty-Seventh USCI veteran. See Eason and Hines, eds., *History of First Baptist Church Hertford*; Redford, "Civil War Veterans Alive in 1890"; National Park Services, *Civil War Soldiers, 1861–1865* (database online), Ancestry.com; *US, Colored Troops Military Service Records, 1863–1865* (database online) and African American Civil War Sailor Index, 1861–1865, Ancestry.com.

39. Cox, *No Common Ground*, 24.

40. "Colored Union Soldiers Monument," clipping. Dorothy Spruill Redford included the following handwritten notation listing all of the original members of the Sister Missionary Union who also served in the organization responsible for the Hertford monument: "Church History appears in 1907 when The Sister Missionary was formed." See Dorothy Spruill Redford, "Membership of the Sisters Missionary Union," n.d., Dorothy Spruill Redford papers.

41. Cox, *Dixie's Daughters*, 49.

42. Hertford, NC, June 1916 Sanford Map, photocopy clipping, Dorothy Spruill Redford papers; Cox, *Dixie's Daughters*, 56; "Confederate Soldiers Monument, Hertford," *Commemorative Landscapes of North Carolina*, https://docsouth.unc.edu/commland/ monument/606/.

43. "Colored Union Soldiers Monument"; "Monuments to the United States Colored Troops (USCT) [African American Civil War Soldiers]: The List," *Jubilo! The Emancipation Century*, May 30, 2011, http://jubiloemancipationcentury.wordpress.com/2011/05/30/ monuments-to-the-united-states-colored-troops-usct-the-list/.

44. "Confederate Soldiers Monument, Hertford"; "Colored Union Soldiers Monument."

45. 1894 Deed of Academy Green, clipping, and Herford, NC, June 1916 Sanford Map, Dorothy Spruill Redford Papers.

46. David W. Blight, *Race and Reunion: The Civil War in American Memory* (Cambridge, MA: Belknap Press of Harvard University Press, 2001), 304.

47. Marita Sturken, *Tangled Memories: The Vietnam War, The AIDS Epidemic, and the Politics of Remembering* (Berkeley: University of California Press, 1997), 7–9.

48. Johnson, "'Ye Gave Them a Stone,'" 65.

49. Evelyn Brooks Higginbotham, *Righteous Discontent: The Women's Movement in the Black Baptist Church, 1880–1920* (Cambridge, MA: Harvard University Press, 1993), 171–184, 221–229; Brittney C. Cooper, *Beyond Respectability: The Intellectual Thought of Race Women* (Urbana: University of Illinois Press, 2017), 51–55; Jeffrey Aaron Snyder, *Making Black History: The Color Line, Culture, and Race in the Age of Jim Crow* (Athens: University of Georgia Press, 2018), 110–117.

50. Snyder, *Making Black History*, 154–160.

51. Mitchell, *From Slave Cabins to the White House*, 195.

52. Mitchell, *From Slave Cabins to the White House*, 4–5.

53. Aniko Bodroghkozy, *Equal Time: Television and the Civil Rights Movement* (Urbana: University of Illinois Press, 2012), 17–20.

54. William G. Thomas III, "Television News and the Civil Rights Struggle: The Views in Virginia and Mississippi," *Southern Spaces*, November 3, 2004, https://southernspaces .org/2004/television-news-and-civil-rights-struggle-views-virginia-and-mississippi/; Patrick Novotny, "The Impact of Television on Georgia, 1948–1952," *Georgia Historical Quarterly* 91 (Fall 2007): 324–347; B. J. Hollars, *Opening the Doors: The Desegregation of the University of Alabama and the Fight for Civil Rights in Tuscaloosa* (Tuscaloosa: University of Alabama Press, 2013), 9–51.

55. Bodroghkozy, *Equal Time*, 42–88; Baker, *Humane Insight*, 95–100, 105–108.

56. Barbara Dianne Savage, *Broadcasting Freedom: Race, War, and the Politics of Race, 1936–1948* (Chapel Hill: University of North Carolina Press, 1999), 63–105; Imani Perry, *May We Forever Stand: A History of the Black National Anthem* (Chapel Hill: University of North Carolina Press, 2018), 112–115; Joshua Clark Davis, "The Race to Preserve African American Radio," *Black Perspectives*, December 21, 2017, https://www.aaihs.org/the -race-to-preserve-african-american-radio/.

57. Perry, *May We Forever Stand*, 113.

58. Savage, *Broadcasting Freedom*, 260–270; Ashleigh Lawrence-Sanders, "History, Memory, and the Power of Black Radio," *Black Perspectives*, March 16, 2018, https://www .aaihs.org/history-memory-and-the-power-of-black-radio/.

59. Savage, *Broadcasting Freedom*, 78–81; Snyder, *Making Black History*, 154–158.

60. Perry, *May We Forever Stand*, 7–12, 143–144.

61. C. Bernard Ruffin, "An All-American Town: An Oral History of the African American Community of Franklin County, Pennsylvania," Unpublished manuscript, 2010, 3, accessed at the Franklin County Historical Society, Chambersburg, PA; Snyder, *Making Black History*, 156.

62. Savage, *Broadcasting Freedom*, 275–276.

63. See E. James West, *Ebony Magazine and Lerone Bennett Jr.: Popular Black History in Postwar America* (Urbana: University of Illinois Press, 2020), 17–30; Fred Carroll, *Race News: Black Journalists and the Fight for Racial Justice in the Twentieth Century* (Urbana: University of Illinois Press, 2017), 132–140, 151; John E. Washington, *They Knew Lincoln*, with a new introduction by Kate Masur (New York: Oxford University Press, 2018), 28–32; Carole Emberton, *To Walk About in Freedom: The Long Emancipation of Priscilla Joyner* (New York: W. W. Norton, 2022), xiii–xxiv, 159–177.

64. Royal A. Christian and Pellom McDaniels III, eds., *Porter, Steward, Citizen: An African American's Memoir of World War I* (New York: Oxford University Press, 2017), xx–xxiii; The published 1970s and 1980s interviews of Knapper have been compiled in C. Bernard Ruffin, "This Is My Story: An Oral History of the African American Community of Chambersburg, Pennsylvania," 1:404–407, accessed at Franklin County Historical Society, Chambersburg, PA.

65. Dennis Shaw, "Helping: Once a Teacher, Always a Teacher," *Morning Herald* (Hagerstown, MD), March 19, 1976, 15; Christian and McDaniels III, ed., *Porter, Steward, Citizen*, 1–151; Irv Randolph, "State House Honors Edna Knapper," *Public Opinion*, March 31, 1984, clipping, VF—African Americans, Franklin County Historical Society; "Mrs. Edna Knapper Retires after 38 Teaching Years," *News-Chronicle* (Shippensburg, PA), June 19, 1953, 14; Ruffin, *This Is My Story*, 404–407; Libra R. Hilde, *Slavery, Fatherhood, and Paternal Duty in African American Communities over the Long Nineteenth Century* (Chapel Hill: University of North Carolina Press, 2020), 278–280.

66. Shaw, "Helping: Once a Teacher, Always a Teacher."

67. Kate Masur, "Introduction: John E. Washington and They Knew Lincoln," in *They Knew Lincoln*, with a new introduction by Kate Masur (New York: Oxford University Press, 2018), lxvi.

68. Edna Christian Knapper, "Outstanding Colored Citizens of Chambersburg—Past and Present: Colored Policemen," *Public Opinion* (Chambersburg, PA), April 4, 1956, 11.

69. Edna Christian Knapper, "Outstanding Colored Citizens of Chambersburg—Past and Present: Do You Remember?" *Public Opinion* (Chambersburg, PA), April 11, 1956, 6.

70. Edna Christian Knapper, "Outstanding Colored Citizens of Chambersburg—Past and Present: Isaac Page," *Public Opinion* (Chambersburg, PA), February 22, 1956, 6; Jonathan A. Noyalas, *Slavery and Freedom in the Shenandoah Valley during the Civil War Era* (Gainesville: University Press of Florida, 2021), 46–47, 53, 79–80.

71. Edna Christian Knapper, "Outstanding Colored Citizens of Chambersburg—Past and Present: The Ransom Family," *Public Opinion* (Chambersburg, PA), April 17, 1956, 7; Noyalas, *Slavery and Freedom in the Shenandoah Valley during the Civil War Era*, 52–53; Her praise mirrored that of other children of former enslaved fathers. See Hilde, *Slavery, Fatherhood, and Paternal Duty*, 80.

72. Edna Christian Knapper, "Outstanding Colored Citizens of Chambersburg—Past and Present: The Christian Family," *Public Opinion* (Chambersburg, PA), May 2, 1956, 21.

73. Knapper, "Outstanding Colored Citizens of Chambersburg—Past and Present: The Christian Family."

74. Knapper, "Outstanding Colored Citizens of Chambersburg—Past and Present: Isaac Page."

75. Knapper, "Outstanding Colored Citizens of Chambersburg—Past and Present: Do You Remember?"

76. Like Knapper, Black Gettysburg residents are also turning to Civil War memory, media, and events for shaping the centennial celebration. See Jill Ogline Titus, *Gettysburg 1963: Civil Rights, Cold War Politics, and Historical Memory in America's Most Famous Small Town* (Chapel Hill: University of North Carolina Press, 2021), 36–77.

77. Edna Christian Knapper, "Outstanding Colored Citizens of Chambersburg—Past and Present: Joe Winters," *Public Opinion* (Chambersburg, PA), January 17, 1956, 18.

78. See Stella M. Fries, Janet Z. Gabler, and C. Bernard Ruffin, *Some Chambersburg Roots: A Black Perspective* (Chambersburg, PA: Stella Fries, 1980), 179; "History of Blacks Is Rich: A Conversation with Stella Fries," clipping, VF-African Americans, Franklin County Historical Society, Chambersburg, PA.

79. Snyder, *Making Black History*, 160–163; Zadie Jones, "Life Story of Pioneers of Negro Education Is Told by Relative," *Alabama Citizen*, February 27, 1954, 2; Zadie Jones, "Barnes Story, Continued from Last Week," *Alabama Citizen*, March 6, 1954, 2.

80. Jones, "Life Story of Pioneers of Negro Education Is Told by Relative."

81. Jones, "Life Story of Pioneers of Negro Education Is Told by Relative."

82. Jones, "Life Story of Pioneers of Negro Education Is Told by Relative."

83. Jones, "Life Story of Pioneers of Negro Education Is Told by Relative."

84. Jones, "Life Story of Pioneers of Negro Education Is Told by Relative"; "Golden Wedding Is Celebrated by Darkies," *Tuscaloosa News,* June 23, 1915, 1.

85. Jones, "Barnes Story, Continued from Last Week."

86. Jones, "Barnes Story, Continued from Last Week," For 1910 coverage of Washington's visit, see "Booker T. Washington Coming to Tuscaloosa," *Tuscaloosa Times-Gazette,* December 25, 1909, 6; "B. T. Washington in Tuscaloosa," *Tuscaloosa Times-Gazette,* February 22, 1910, 1, 4, 5, 8; "Booker T. Washington," *Tuscaloosa Times-Gazette*, February 22, 1910, 2 and "Untitled," *Tuscaloosa Times-Gazette*, February 24, 1910, 2.

87. Jones, "Barnes Story, Continued from Last Week."

88. E. S. Smith, "Educational Progress," *Alabama Citizen*, March 6, 1954, 2; Dr. S. B. Hay, "Stillman College History," *Alabama Citizen*, March 6, 1954, 2.

89. "A Name for the New High School," *Alabama Citizen,* February 21, 1953, 2.

90. Hilary Green, *Educational Reconstruction: African American Schools in the Urban South, 1865–1890* (New York: Fordham University Press, 2016), 130–154, 174–184; "A Name for the New High School."

91. "A Name for the New High School."

92. "A Name for the New High School"; "Long Live the Druid High School Dragons," *Tuscaloosa News*, July 5, 2009, https://www.tuscaloosanews.com/opinion/20090705/long-live-the-druid-high-school-dragons.

93. "J. H. Barnes," *Southern Watchman*, July 27, 1901, 1; "Active Career of Noted Educator: Graduate of Tuskegee, 1891," *Tuscaloosa News and Times-Gazette*, May 29, 1916, 7.

94. "New YMCA Branch Here," *Alabama Citizen*, December 26, 1953, 1.

95. "New YMCA Branch Here."

96. Simon Wendt, "God, Gandhi, and Guns: The African American Freedom Struggle in Tuscaloosa, Alabama, 1964–1965," *Journal of African American History* 89, no. 1 (Winter 2004): 38–39; Hollars, *Opening the Doors*, 9–51; 86–96.

97. Wendt, "God, Gandhi, and Guns," 39–52; B. J. Hollars, *Opening the Doors*, 154–161, 193–199.

98. See Kidada E. Williams, *They Left Great Marks on Me: African American Testimonies of Racial Violence from Emancipation to World War I* (New York: New York University Press, 2012), 40–42; Michael W. Fitzgerald, *Reconstruction in Alabama: From Civil War to Redemption in the Cotton South* (Baton Rouge: Louisiana State University Press, 2017), 149–151, 178–180, 195–198, 243–256; G. Ward Hubbs, *Searching for Freedom after the Civil War: Klansman, Carpetbagger, Scalawag, and Freedman* (Tuscaloosa: University of Alabama Press, 2015), 31–50, 144–156.

99. Mitchell, *From Slave Cabins to the White House*, 4–5.

100. Cox, *No Common Ground*, 93–99.

101. Cox, *No Common Ground*, 99–104.

102. Quoted in Cox, *No Common Ground*, 103.

103. Louise Jennings, "Silent Sam's Dignity Restored," *Daily Tar Heel*, April 9, 1968, 5; Corolla 1975, v. 83, 108 accessed at the W. S. Hoole Special Collections, University of Alabama, Tuscaloosa, AL; LeeAnn Whites, *Gender Matters: Civil War, Reconstruction, and the Making of the New South* (New York: Palgrave Macmillan 2005), 95–111; Mary Beth Brown, "The Long History of Civil Rights Activism at Mizzou," Department of History, University of Missouri, July 17, 2020, https://history.missouri.edu/node/148.

104. Cox, *No Common Ground*, 108–120. For ongoing African American resistance, see Peter Stoddard, "New Parks, New Places to Go, New Pride in Neighborhoods," *The Herald* (Rock Hill, SC), June 26, 1973, 12; "Confederate Gravestones Vandalized in Cemetery," *Columbia Record*, April 27, 1977, 7-D; "Vandals Eggs Cars," *The Herald* (Rock Hill, SC), May 1, 1978, 1.

105. Glymph, "'Liberty Dearly Bought,'"127–130; "Hertford," *New Journal and Guide* (Norfolk, VA), July 17, 1976, 18. In the official commemorative program, the women who spearheaded the Colored Union Soldiers Monument are named and the 1910 date included. See Eason and Hines, eds., *History of First Baptist Church Hertford, North Carolina, 110th Anniversary Celebration*.

106. Eason and Hines, eds., *History of First Baptist Church Hertford, North Carolina, 110th Anniversary Celebration*, 28.

107. Erica L. Ball and Kellie Carter Jackson, "Introduction: Reconsidering Roots," in *Reconsidering Roots: Race, Politics and Memory*, ed. Erica L. Ball and Kellie Carter Jackson (Athens: University of Georgia Press, 2017), 1–13; Francesca Morgan, "My Furthest-Back Person: Black Genealogy Before and After Roots," in *Reconsidering Roots: Race, Politics and Memory*, ed. Erica L. Ball and Kellie Carter Jackson (Athens: University of Georgia Press, 2017), 69–74; Robert K. Chester, "The Black Military Image in *Roots: The Next Generation*," in *Reconsidering Roots: Race, Politics and Memory*, ed. Erica L. Ball and Kellie Carter Jackson (Athens: University of Georgia Press, 2017), 129–140; Fries, Gabler, and Ruffin, *Some Chambersburg Roots*, iii, vi.

108. Fries, Gabler, and Ruffin, *Some Chambersburg Roots*, 10–12, 49–72, 93–97, 119–120, 235–239.

109. "History of Blacks Is Rich: A Conversation with Stella Fries," clipping, VF-African Americans, Franklin County Historical Society, Chambersburg, PA.

110. Fries, Gabler, and Ruffin, *Some Chambersburg Roots*, 179.

111. Fries, Gabler, and Ruffin, *Some Chambersburg Roots*, 179.

112. For the Winter slave trader myth, see C. Bernard Ruffin, *Voices of Chambersburg: An Oral History of the African American Community of Franklin County, Pennsylvania*, vol. 1 of 4—*Interviews* (Greencastle, PA: Allison-Antrim Museum, 2011), 112; and C. Bernard Ruffin, "An All-American Town: An Oral History of the African American Community of Franklin County, Pennsylvania," unpublished manuscript, 3, accessed at the Franklin County Historical Society, Chambersburg, PA; For positive recollections, see Fries, Gabler, and Ruffin, *Some Chambersburg Roots*, 192, and Ruffin, *Voices of Chambersburg*, vol. 1 of 4—*Interviews*, 44, accessed in Franklin County Historical Society.

113. Shawn Hardy, "Mercersburg Focusing on Black Heritage," *Record Herald*, April 23, 1994, clipping, VF-African Americans, Franklin County Historical Society.

114. Keesha E. Lawson, "Pastor Emphasizes History of Blacks," *Public Opinion*, n.d, clipping, and Brian Couturier, "Town Home to Free Blacks before War," n.p., May 8, 1992, A1 and A5, clipping, VF-African Americans, Franklin County Historical Society; Jim Namiotka, "Researcher Traces Roots of Blacks in Mercersburg," *Public Opinion*, June 3, 1992, 3.

115. Photograph of original "A Rare Monument" wayside marker, email attachment in Mary K. Vidaurri's email to Dorothy Spruill Redford, January 30, 2007; Dorothy Spruill Redford, email to Jeffrey Crow, February 5, 2007.

116. For her work at Somerset Place, see Dorothy Spruill Redford with Michael D'Orso, *Somerset Homecoming: Recovering a Lost Heritage* (Chapel Hill: University of North Carolina Press, 1988), 81–164, and Dorothy Spruill Redford, *Generations of Somerset Place: From Slavery to Freedom* (Charleston, SC: Arcadia Publishing, 2005), 92–102; Dorothy Spruill Redford, email to Jeffrey Crow, February 5, 2007.

117. Michael Hill, email to Dorothy Spruill Redford, February 5, 2007.

118. Michael Hill, email to Dorothy Spruill Redford, February 5, 2007.

119. John S. Salmon, email to Dorothy Spruill Redford, February 8, 2007.

120. John S. Salmon, email to Dorothy Spruill Redford, February 8, 2007.

121. Dorothy Spruill Redford, email to Jeffrey Crow, January 31, 2008.

122. Dorothy Spruill Redford, email to Jeffrey Crow, January 31, 2008; "John Beaver and Dot Redford Retire," *Carolina Comments* 56, no. 4 (October 2008): 121–122.

123. The Northeastern North Carolina African American Festival, The Black Civil War Memorial in Hertford, NC, June 30, 2007, program, Dorothy Spruill Redford papers.

124. "Civil War Programming at State Historic Sites," *Carolina Comments* 59, no. 2 (April 2011): 21; "*Freedom, Sacrifice, Memory*: Civil War Sesquicentennial Photo Exhibit to Tour the State," *Carolina Comments* 59, no. 2 (April 2011): 10; "African American Heritage Commission Recognizes Black History Month," *Carolina Comments* 59, no. 2 (April 2011): 7–8; "Milestone for Marker Program," *Carolina Comments* 59, no. 2 (April 2011): 14–16.

125. Clifford, *Race Rhymes*, 9.

126. Anna Julia Cooper, *A Voice from the South: By a Black Woman of the South* (Xenia, OH: Aldine Printing House, 1892), 31, accessed in Documenting the American South, https://docsouth.unc.edu/church/cooper/cooper.html.

Porch Lessons II: More Than Names on a Page

1. Epigraph from Frances E. W. Harper, "The Massachusetts Fifty-Fourth," *Anglo-African*, October 10, 1863, 1. Pension File of Joseph Lane, Twenty-Second USCT, Department of Veterans Affairs, Washington, DC, released under the Freedom of Information Act to the author, who is a direct descendant, on March 16, 2022. Some of this porch lesson has been published in an online roundtable of Holly Pinheiro's *The Families' Civil War*. See Hilary Green, *Black Widows and the Struggle for Pensions after the Civil War*, *Black Perspectives*, January 12, 2023, https://www.aaihs.org/black-widows-and-the-struggle-for-pensions-after-the-civil-war/.

2. Holly A. Pinheiro Jr., *The Families' Civil War: Black Soldiers and the Fight for Racial Justice* (Athens: University of Georgia Press, 2022); Brandi C. Brimmer, *Claiming Union Widowhood: Race, Respectability, and Poverty in the Post-Emancipation South* (Durham, NC: Duke University Press, 2020); and James G. Mendez, *A Great Sacrifice: Northern Black Soldiers, Their Families, and the Experience of the Civil War* (New York: Fordham University Press, 2019).

3. Pension Index Card of Joseph Lane, accessed in National Archives and Records Administration, *US Civil War Pension Index: General Index to Pension Files, 1861–1934* (Provo, UT, USA: Ancestry.com Operations, 2000); Pension File of Joseph Lane, Twenty-Second USCT; Gail Bederman, *Manliness and Civilization: A Cultural History of Gender and Race in the United States, 1880–1917* (Chicago: University of Chicago Press, 1995), 20–21; Elizabeth Regosin, *Freedom's Promise: Ex-Slave Families and Citizenship in the Age of Emancipation* (Charlottesville: University of Virginia Press, 2002), 119.

4. Donald R. Shaffer, *After the Glory: The Struggle of Black Civil War Veterans* (Lawrence: University Press of Kansas, 2004), 121–131; Kelly D. Mezurek, *For Their Own Cause: The 27th United States Colored Troops* (Kent: OH: Kent State University Press, 2016), 233–237.

5. Shaffer, *After the Glory*, 122; Mezurek, *For Their Own Cause*, 238–240; Pension File of Joseph Lane, Twenty-Second USCT.

6. Pension File of Joseph Lane, Twenty-Second USCT; "Personal and Social Gossip," *Shippensburg News*, January 28, 1898, 3.

7. Pension File of Joseph Lane, Twenty-Second USCT.

8. Steven B. Burg, "The North Queen Cemetery and the African American Experience in Shippensburg," *Pennsylvania History: A Journal of Mid-Atlantic Studies* 77 (Winter 2010): 21–23.

9. Pension File of Joseph Lane, Twenty-Second USCT.

10. *1900 United States Federal Census*, accessed at Ancestry.com

11. "Another Murder Case," *The Sentinel* (Carlisle, PA), August 9, 1901, 2; "The Prisoner Talks," *The Sentinel* (Carlisle, PA), August 10, 1901, 2; "Negro Killed in a Fight," *Valley Spirit*, August 14, 1901, 6; "Another Murder," *Star and Enterprise*, August 14, 1901, 4;

Douglas J. Flowe, *Uncontrollable Blackness: African American Men and Criminality in Jim Crow New York* (Chapel Hill: University of North Carolina Press, 2020), 33.

12. "The Murder Case," *The Sentinel* (Carlisle, PA), September 13, 1901, 3; "The Shippensburg Murder Case," *Carlisle Evening Herald*, September 16, 1901, 1 and 4; "Shippensburg Murder Case," *Carlisle Evening Herald*, September 17, 1901, 1.

13. "The Murder Case," *The Sentinel* (Carlisle, PA), September 13, 1901, 3; "The Shippensburg Murder Case," *Carlisle Evening Herald*, September 16, 1901, 1 and 4; "Shippensburg Murder Case," *Carlisle Evening Herald*, September 17, 1901, 1; Daniel Thorp, *Facing Freedom: An African American Community in Virginia from Reconstruction to Jim Crow* (Charlottesville: University of Virginia Press, 2017), 227.

14. Flowe, *Uncontrollable Blackness*, 16–17, 57; Kali N. Gross, *Colored Amazons: Crime, Violence, and Black Women in the City of Brotherly Love, 1880–1910* (Durham, NC: Duke University Press, 2006), 107–126.

15. "16 Years for Second Degree Murder," *Philadelphia Inquirer*, September 22, 1901, 4; "Murderer Sentenced," *Pittsburgh Press*, September 22, 1901, 14; "Arthur Robinson Sentenced," *Harrisburg Daily Independent*, September 23, 1901, 4; Gross, *Colored Amazons*, 132.

16. "Oscar Lane's Funeral," *The Sentinel* (Carlisle, PA), August 12, 1901, 3.

17. "Oscar Lane's Funeral," *The Sentinel* (Carlisle, PA), August 12, 1901, 3; "Lane Carried Insurance," *The Sentinel* (Carlisle, PA), August 16, 1901, 2.

18. Sarah Bair, "Continuing to Pay the 'Patriotic Debt': The Establishment of the Pennsylvania Soldiers' Orphans Industrial School, 1893–1912," *Pennsylvania History: A Journal of Mid-Atlantic Studies* 82 (Autumn 2015): 472–473.

19. Bair, "Continuing to Pay the 'Patriotic Debt,'" 474–475; "John Palmer Lane," *Public Opinion* (Chambersburg, PA), March 28, 1961, 4.

20. Pennsylvania Superintendent of Solders' Orphans, *Annual Report of the Pennsylvania Commission of Soldiers' Orphan Schools for the Year Ending May 31, 1905* (Harrisburg: Harrisburg Publishing, State Printer, 1906), 49; Pennsylvania Superintendent of Solders' Orphans, *Annual Report of the Pennsylvania Commission of Soldiers' Orphan Schools for the Year Ending May 31, 1907* (Harrisburg: Harrisburg Publishing, State Printer, 1908), 47.

21. "Items of a Personal Nature," *The Sentinel* (Carlisle, PA), July 22, 1903, 2; "Deaths," *The Sentinel*, December 27, 1899, 3; "Daniel C. Collins," *Public Opinion* (Chambersburg, PA), September 22, 1960, 4.

22. For Collins's military service, see "More Enlistments from Chambersburg," *Public Weekly Opinion* (Chambersburg, PA), May 5, 1899, 1; "Shippensburg Recruit," *The Sentinel* (Carlisle, PA), July 22, 1903, 2; "Harrisburg Sets Recruiting Pace for This State, April 1, 1917, 1; Commonwealth of Pennsylvania Veteran's Compensation Application of Daniel Collins, No. 148041, accessed in Ancestry.com. *Pennsylvania, US, World War I Veterans Service and Compensation Files, 1917–1919, 1934–1948* (Lehi, UT: Ancestry.com Operations, 2015); World War II Draft Registration Card of Daniel Collins, No. 1458, accessed in Ancestry.com. *US, World War II Draft Registration Cards, 1942* (Lehi, UT: Ancestry.com Operations, 2010), "Daniel C. Collins," *Public Opinion* (Chambersburg, PA), September 22, 1960, 4.

23. Le'Trice D. Donaldson, *Duty beyond the Battlefield: African American Soldiers Fight for Racial Uplift, Citizenship, and Manhood, 1870–1920* (Carbondale: Southern Illinois University Press, 2020), 4–8, 43–45, 55–90.

24. *1910 United States Federal Census*, accessed at Ancestry.com; *1920 United States Federal Census*, accessed at Ancestry.com; *1930 United States Federal Census*, accessed at Ancestry.com; *1940 United States Federal Census* [database on-line]. Provo, UT: Ancestry.com Operations, 2012.

25. Pension File of Joseph Lane, Twenty-Second USCT; *1910 United States Federal Census*, accessed at Ancestry.com; *1920 United States Federal Census*, accessed at Ancestry.com; *1930 United States Federal Census*, accessed at Ancestry.com; "Shippensburg Boy Dies Here; Was Mangled by Train," *Public Opinion*, February 25, 1926, 1; "Certificate of Death—Clarence Lane," Commonwealth of Pennsylvania Department of Health, Bureau of Vital Statistics, File number 17567, accessed in Ancestry.com; Certificate of Birth—John Leroy Green, Commonwealth of Pennsylvania Bureau of Vital Statistics, accessed in Ancestry.com.

26. "Fined $12.50 Each," *The Sentinel*, March 10, 1927, 6; "This Afternoon's Proceedings," *The Sentinel*, May 3, 1927, 2.

27. Psyche Williams-Forson, "Where Did They Eat? Where Did They Stay?: Interpreting Material Culture of Black Women's Domesticity in the Context of the Colored Conventions," in *The Colored Conventions Movement: Black Organizing in the Nineteenth Century*, ed. P. Gabrielle Foreman, Jim Casey, and Sarah Lynn Patterson (Chapel Hill: University of North Carolina Press, 2021), 88–100; Flowe, *Uncontrollable Blackness*, 40; David Silkenat, *Moments of Despair: Suicide, Divorce, and Debt in Civil War–Era North Carolina* (Chapel Hill: University of North Carolina Press, 2011), 186–203.

28. "Bessie Lane," photograph, Omwake Photo Box, Photo Collection—Box 1956.91, Shippensburg Historical Society, Shippensburg, PA; *1910 United States Federal Census*, accessed at Ancestry.com; *1920 United States Federal Census*, accessed at Ancestry.com; *1930 United States Federal Census*, accessed at Ancestry.com; *1940 United States Federal Census* (database online). Provo, UT, US: Ancestry.com Operations, 2012; "Special Session of Court," *Carlisle Evening Herald*, July 6, 1909, 4.

29. "Colored Folks Organize," *News-Chronicle,* November 27, 1928, 1; "Our Letter Box," *News-Chronicle,* May 2, 1930, 4. Steven B. Burg, "'From Troubled Ground to Common Ground': The Locust Grove African American Cemetery Preservation Project: A Case Study of Service," *Public Historian* 30 (May 2008): 58–59; Jill Ogline Titus, *Gettysburg 1963: Civil Rights, Cold War Politics, and Historical Memory in America's Most Famous Small Town* (Chapel Hill: University of North Carolina Press, 2021), 15–16.

30. Barbara Gannon, *The Won Cause: Black and White Comradeship in the Grand Army of the Republic* (Chapel Hill: University of North Carolina Press, 2011), 47–56; Libra R. Hilde, *Slavery, Fatherhood, and Paternal Duty in the African American Communities over the Long Nineteenth Century* (Chapel Hill: University of North Carolina Press, 2020), 278–280.

31. Burg, "'From Troubled Ground to Common Ground,'" 57–58; Burg, "The North Queen Cemetery and the African American Experience in Shippensburg," 21–23;

Historic Site Report for Locust Grove Cemetery Shippensburg, Pennsylvania, October 20, 2007, 49, accessed at the Shippensburg Historical Society, Shippensburg, PA.

32. "Untitled," *The Chronicle*, May 24, 1923, 1.

33. Historic Site Report for Locust Grove Cemetery Shippensburg, Pennsylvania, 48; Burg, "The North Queen Cemetery and the African American Experience in Shippensburg," 23–24.

34. Burg, "The North Queen Cemetery and the African American Experience in Shippensburg," 24.

35. "John Smith," *News-Chronicle*, February 8, 1935, 8; 1930 Census, accessed in Ancestry.com.

36. William H. Burkhart, "Shippensburg's Colored Veterans of the Civil War," in *Shippensburg, Pennsylvania in the Civil War*, ed. William H. Burkhart, Samuel L. Daihl, J. Houston McCulloch, Dr. George Kaluger, Mrs. Elizabeth Roler, Mrs. Howard A. Ryder, and Shippensburg Historical Society, 2nd rev. and updated ed. (Shippensburg: Burd Street Press, 2003), 224–225; interviews with Barbara Lane Hill and Millicent Lowman Green, July 6, 2016.

37. Evelyn Brooks Higginbotham, *Righteous Discontent: The Women's Movement in the Black Baptist Church, 1880–1920* (Cambridge, MA: Harvard University Press, 1993), 184.

38. Wendy Hamand Venet, "Faithful Helpmates and Fervent Activists: Northern Women and Civil War Memory," in *Women and the American Civil War: North–South Counterpoints*, ed. Judith Giesburg and Randall M. Miller (Kent, OH: Kent State University Press, 2018), 325; Gannon, *Won Cause*, 47; Carrie Williams Clifford, *Race Rhymes* (Washington, DC: R. L. Pendleton, 1911), 22.

39. Koritha Mitchell, *From Slave Cabins to the White House: Homemade Citizenship in African American Culture* (Urbana: University of Illinois Press, 2020), 2.

40. "Foust Urges Citizens to Employ Vote," *News-Chronicle*, May 31, 1938, 1.

41. "Norris Talks for Colored Service Here," *News-Chronicle*, June 2, 1939, 1.

42. "Norris Talks for Colored Service Here," *News-Chronicle*, June 2, 1939, 6.

43. "Mrs. Daniel Collins Dies; Was Ill Long," *News-Chronicle*, April 10, 1942, 1; "Card of Thanks," *News-Chronicle*, April 14, 1942, 4; "Dedication Service Sunday at St. Peters AME Church," *News-Chronicle*, June 28, 1946, 7; Lillian B. Daniels, "Chatterbox," *News-Chronicle*, July 12, 1946, 5.

44. See Lillian B. Daniels, "Chatterbox," *News-Chronicle*, June 27, 1947, 8; "Chatterbox," *News-Chronicle*, August 12, 1952, 3; "Chatterbox," *News-Chronicle*, June 12, 1953, 18; and "Chatterbox," *News-Chronicle* (Shippensburg, PA), June 11, 1954, 15.

45. Interviews with Barbara Lane Hill and Millicent Green, July 6, 2016.

46. Burg, "'From Troubled Ground to Common Ground,'" 63–64; Burkhart, "Shippensburg's Colored Veterans of the Civil War," 207–208.

47. Burkhart, "Shippensburg's Colored Veterans of the Civil War," 209.

48. William H. Burkhart, "Black Veterans Binder," accessed at the Shippensburg Historical Society, Shippensburg, PA; Burkhart, "Shippensburg's Colored Veterans of the Civil War," 207.

49. Burkhart, "Black Veterans Binder," 22, accessed at the Shippensburg Historical Society, Shippensburg, PA.

50. "John Palmer Lane," *Public Opinion* (Chambersburg, PA), March 28, 1961, 4; "Miss Bessie Lane," *Public Opinion* (Chambersburg, PA), July 16, 1962, 4; "Letters Are Issued in Newville Estate," *The Sentinel* (Carlisle, PA), September 13, 1962, 2; "Mrs. Leonard Robinson," *Public Opinion* (Chambersburg, PA), November 21, 1962, 4; "Miss Avis Lane," *Public Opinion* (Chambersburg, PA), May 25, 1966, 38.

51. Stephen B. Burg, "The North Queen Street Cemetery and the African American Experience in Shippensburg, Pennsylvania," *Pennsylvania History: A Journal of Mid-Atlantic Studies* 77 (Winter 2010): 25–26; Burg, "From Troubled Ground to Common Ground," 52–76.

52. Burg, "'From Troubled Ground to Common Ground,'" 70–71.

53. Interview with Millicent Lowman Green, April 8, 2022.

54. Interview with Barbara Lane Hill, July 6, 2016.

Porch Lessons III: The Other Syllabus

1. Alex Haley, "The Black Scholar Interviews: Alex Haley," *The Black Scholar* 8, no. 1 (September 1976): 39. Haley's plagiarism of Margaret Walker's *Jubilee* has raised questions about his methods, including whether he conducted oral histories. Despite these questions and legal settlements, Haley still held significant cultural power to speak on the matters of Black memory, genealogy, and historical contributions of African-descended people. For many, the phenomenon of *Roots* transcended these issues and began an important cultural movement centered on Black memory, storytelling, and history. Matthew Delmont, *Making Roots: A Nation Captivated* (Oakland: University of California Press, 2016), 132–152, 175–180; Erica L. Ball and Kellie Carter Jackson, "Introduction: Reconsidering Roots," in *Reconsidering Roots: Race, Politics, and Memory*, ed. Erica L. Ball and Kellie Carter Jackson (Athens: University of Georgia Press, 2017), 1–8; For international reception, see Martin Stollery, "The Same, but a Step Removed: Aspects of the British Reception of *Roots*," in *Reconsidering Roots: Race, Politics and Memory*, ed. Erica L. Ball and Kellie Carter Jackson (Athens: University of Georgia Press, 2017), 147–164; "Norvella P. Carter, Warren Chalklen and Bhekuyise Zungu, "Re-Rooting *Roots*: The South African Perspective," in *Reconsidering Roots: Race, Politics and Memory*, ed. Erica L. Ball and Kellie Carter Jackson (Athens: University of Georgia Press, 2017), 165–181; and Dominic Meng-Hsuan Yang, "One Man's Quest: Chiang Ssu-chang, *Roots*, and the Mainlander Homebound Movement in Taiwan," in *Reconsidering Roots: Race, Politics and Memory*, ed. Erica L. Ball and Kellie Carter Jackson (Athens: University of Georgia Press, 2017), 182–201.

2. Elise Chatelain, "The Roots of African American Labor Struggles: Reading *Roots* and *Backstairs at the White House* in a 1970s Storytelling Tradition," in *Reconsidering Roots: Race, Politics and Memory*, ed. Erica L. Ball and Kellie Carter Jackson (Athens: University of Georgia Press, 2017), 108.

3. The national and international reception of *Roots* also shaped new interpretations of the Black Confederates myth by late twentieth-century Lost Cause proponents. See Kevin M. Levin, *Searching for Black Confederates: The Civil War's Most Persistent Myth* (Chapel Hill: University of North Carolina Press, 2019), 129–130.

4. James Weldon Johnson, "Lift Every Voice and Sing," 1900, *Poetry Foundation*, https://www.poetryfoundation.org/poems/48104/lift-evry-voice-and-sing.

5. Mel Watkins, "Thirteen Runaway Slaves and David Bradley," *New York Times*, April 19, 1981, section 7, 7.

6. Watkins, "Thirteen Runaway Slaves and David Bradley."

7. Watkins, "Thirteen Runaway Slaves and David Bradley."

8. Watkins, "Thirteen Runaway Slaves and David Bradley."

9. David Bradley received critical acclaim for *The Chaneysville Incident*. The *New York Times Book Review* considered the novel to be one of the best books published in 1981. Bradley also received the Faulkner Award. See Edwin McDowell, "'Chaneysville Incident' Wins Faulkner Award," *New York Times*, August 11, 1982, sec. 1, 46.

10. David Bradley, *The Chaneysville Incident* (New York: Harper and Row, 1981), 88.

11. Bradley, *The Chaneysville Incident*, 47.

12. Bradley, *The Chaneysville Incident*, 49.

13. Bradley, *The Chaneysville Incident*, 62.

14. Bradley, *The Chaneysville Incident*, 221.

15. Bradley, *The Chaneysville Incident*, 222–223.

16. Bradley, *The Chaneysville Incident*, 323–337, 345.

17. Bradley, *The Chaneysville Incident*, 385–432.

18. Toni Morrison, *Beloved* (1987; New York: Vintage Books, 2004); Nikki M. Taylor, *Driven toward Madness: The Fugitive Slave Margaret Garner and Tragedy on the Ohio* (Athens: Ohio University Press, 2016), 8–23.

19. Taylor, *Driven toward Madness*, 64–87; Toni Morrison, "It Is Like Growing Up Black One More Time," *New York Times*, August 11, 1974, https://www.nytimes.com/1974/08/11/archives/rediscovering-black-history-it-is-like-growing-up-black-one-more.html; Elizabeth Kastor, "In 'Beloved' a Haunting Tale of Love from Toni Morrison," *News and Observer*, October 23, 1987, 3D.

20. Farah Jasmine Griffin, *Read until You Understand: The Profound Wisdom of Black Life and Literature* (New York: W. W. Norton, 2021), 203.

21. Taylor, *Driven toward Madness*, 1-2; "Beloved (1998)," IMDb, https://www.imdb .com/title/tt0120603/.

22. "*Uncle Tom's Cabin* (1987)," IMDb, https://www.imdb.com/title/tt0094213/.

23. John J. O'Connor, "Uncle Tom's Cabin," *New York Times*, June 12, 1987, sec. C, 30, https://www.nytimes.com/1987/06/12/arts/uncle-tom-s-cabin.html.

24. Robert K. Chester, "The Black Military Image in *Roots: The Next Generations*," in *Reconsidering Roots: Race, Politics and Memory*, ed. Erica L. Ball and Kellie Carter Jackson (Athens: University of Georgia Press, 2017), 135–140.

25. Chester, "The Black Military Image in *Roots: The Next Generations*," 140–141.

26. Chatelain, "African American Labor Struggles," 99–100.

27. See R. Blakeslee Gilpin, *John Brown Still Lives!: America's Long Reckoning with Violence, Equality, and Change* (Chapel Hill: University of North Carolina Press, 2011), 1–6, 54–105, 159–180; Benjamin Quarles, *Allies for Freedom*, in *Allies for Freedom and Blacks on John Brown*, with new introduction by William S. McFeely (1974; Boston: Da Capo

Press, 2001), 170–198; Tony Horwitz, *Midnight Rising: John Brown and the Raid That Shaped the Civil War* (New York: Picador, 2011), 258–261, 277–290.

28. James McBride, *The Good Lord Bird: A Novel* (New York: Riverhead Books, 2013).

29. Julie Bosman, "'Good Lord Bird' Is a Surprise Winner for National Book Award in Fiction," *New York Times*, November 20, 2013, A23; McBride, *The Good Lord Bird*, 3.

30. McBride, *The Good Lord Bird*, 237–277; For Brown's recruitment tour for Harpers Ferry, see Gilpin, *John Brown Still Lives*, 32–37, Quarles, *Allies For Freedom*, 63–82 and Louis A. DeCaro, Jr., *The Untold Story of Shields Green: The Life and Death of a Harper's Ferry Raider* (New York: New York University Press, 2020), 23–48.

31. For the events of Harpers' Ferry raid, Quarles, *Allies for Freedom*, 92–105, Louis A. DeCaro Jr., *The Untold Story of Shields Green: The Life and Death of a Harper's Ferry Raider* (New York: New York University Press, 2020), 75–102; McBride, *The Good Lord Bird*, 427.

32. McBride, *The Good Lord Bird*, 459. For the trial, execution, and legacy of Harpers' Ferry in the Black community, see Quarles, *Allies for Freedom*, 108–111, 123–124, 170–198, and DeCaro, *The Untold Story of Shields Green*, 159–176.

33. "The Good Lord Bird (TV Mini Series 2020)," IMDb.com, https://www.imdb .com/title/tt3673480/.

34. Carvell Wallace, "'The Good Lord Bird' Is Good TV. But Mix Art and Slavery at Your Peril," *New York Times*, October 6, 2020 (updated January 15, 2021), https://www .nytimes.com/2020/10/06/magazine/good-lord-bird-tv-slavery.html.

35. Wallace, "'The Good Lord Bird' Is Good TV. But Mix Art and Slavery at Your Peril."

36. Wallace, "'The Good Lord Bird' Is Good TV. But Mix Art and Slavery at Your Peril."

37. *Harriet* (2019), IMDb.com, https://www.imdb.com/title/tt4648786/; Kate Clifford Larson, *Bound for the Promised Land: Harriet Tubman, Portrait of an American Hero* (New York: Ballantine Books, 2004), 212–217.

38. Catherine Clinton, "More Than Ready For Her Close-Up: Harriet Tubman on Screen," *Reviews in American History* 48 (June 2020): 253, 256, 259–260.

39. Wallace, "'The Good Lord Bird' Is Good TV. But Mix Art and Slavery at Your Peril."

40. Wallace, "'The Good Lord Bird' Is Good TV. But Mix Art and Slavery at Your Peril."

41. Wallace, "'The Good Lord Bird' Is Good TV. But Mix Art and Slavery at Your Peril."

42. Wallace, "'The Good Lord Bird' Is Good TV. But Mix Art and Slavery at Your Peril."

43. Kianna Alexander, *Carolina Built: A Novel* (New York: Gallery Books, 2022), xi, xii.

44. Mary Niall Mitchell, *Raising Freedom's Children: Black Children and Visions of the Future after Slavery* (New York: New York University Press, 2010), 5–7; Alexander, *Carolina Built*, 47.

45. Mitchell, *Raising Freedom's Children*, 5.

46. Alexander, *Carolina Built*, 174.

47. Alexander, *Carolina Built*, 88.

48. Alexander, *Carolina Built*, 304–305.

49. Michael Shaara, *The Killer Angels* (1974; New York: Ballantine Books, 1987); Charles Frazier, *Cold Mountain: A Novel* (New York: Atlantic Monthly Press, 1997).

7. Delayed Honor in the Charleston Lowcountry

1. Chris Black, "Bay State Black Union Troops Are Laid to Final Rest in South," *Boston Globe*, May 30, 1989, 3.

2. Black, "Bay State Black Union Troops Are Laid to Final Rest in South."

3. Black, "Bay State Black Union Troops Are Laid to Final Rest in South."

4. Black, "Bay State Black Union Troops Are Laid to Final Rest in South."

5. Black, "Bay State Black Union Troops Are Laid to Final Rest in South."

6. Art Harris, "Salute to a Forgotten Regiment," *Washington Post*, May 30, 1989, https://www.washingtonpost.com/archive/lifestyle/1989/05/30/salute-to-a-forgotten -black-regiment/bfb4ed0d-bf30-42dc-af7e-e34336a61c48/. Of the estimated 2,000 spectators, Coblyn received extended coverage in the press; and in turn, has shaped which USCT descendants' voices are included in recent scholarship on this event. See Douglas R. Egerton, "The Bones of Morris and Folly," in *Final Resting Places: Reflections on the Meaning of Civil War Graves*, ed. Brian Matthew Jordan and Jonathan W. White (Athens: University of Georgia Press, 2023), 87. 89.

7. Wendell M. Patton III, "Time Traveler: Discovery by Charleston Chef Not His First Contact with Past," *The State* (Columbia, SC), June 16, 1988, 2B.

8. Patton, "Time Traveler."

9. Patton, "Time Traveler."

10. Patton, "Time Traveler."

11. Patton, "Time Traveler"; James B. Legg and Steven D. Smith, *"The Best Ever Occupied . . ." Archaeological Investigations of a Civil War Encampment on Folly Island, South Carolina*, South Carolina Institute of Archaeology and Anthropology Research Manuscript Series 209 (Columbia: South Carolina Institute of Archaeology and Anthropology, 1989), 2.

12. Legg and Smith, *"The Best Ever Occupied . . . ,"* 2; South Carolina Institute of Archaeology and Anthropology, *Annual Report for 1987 and 1988* (Columbia: South Carolina State Library, 1990), 15.

13. Legg and Smith, *"The Best Ever Occupied . . . ,"* 2.

14. "Archaeologists Sift through Sand for Remains of Union Soldiers," *Index-Journal* (Greenwood, SC), May 20, 1987, 20; Legg and Smith, *"The Best Ever Occupied . . . ,"* 2.

15. Legg and Smith, *"The Best Ever Occupied . . . ,"* 2–4.

16. Legg and Smith, *"The Best Ever Occupied . . . ,"* 4; "Bodies to Be Moved," *The State* (Columbia, SC), August 27, 1987, 3-C.

17. The official site names are 38CH964, 38CH965, and 38CH966. South Carolina Institute of Archaeology and Anthropology, *Annual Report for 1987 and 1988*, 17; Legg and Smith, *"The Best Ever Occupied . . . ,"* 9–12, 35–97.

18. Legg and Smith, *"The Best Ever Occupied . . . ,"* viii–ix, 4; "Group seeking money to analyze remains of 14 Union soldiers," *The Greenville News*, November 15, 1987, 2B. The *Greenville News*, the *Columbia Record, Sun News* (Myrtle Beach) and *The Item* (Sumter, SC) republished this article for their readership.

19. Legg and Smith, *"The Best Ever Occupied . . . ,"* 7.

20. Margaret M. Wilcox, "Hunley Is Reminder of Important Event in History," clipping, November 26, 1967, SC History, H. L. Hunley, 30-12-225, vertical file, Special Collections—SC Historical Society Archives, College of Charleston, SC; Thomas J. Brown, *Civil War Canon: Sites of Confederate Memory in South Carolina* (Chapel Hill: University of North Carolina Press, 2015), 238–239; Joseph Flanagan, "Raising the Hunley," *Common Ground* (Summer/Fall 2001): 12–24, accessed in H.L. Hunley, 30-12-225, vertical file, Special Collections—SC Historical Society Archives, College of Charleston, SC; "Brian Hicks, "Hunley in the Crosshairs," *Post and Courier*, May 28, 2006, 1A, 6A, and 7A.

21. Brown, *Civil War Canon*, 270–275; Legg and Smith, *"The Best Ever Occupied . . . ,"* ix.

22. Legg and Smith, *"The Best Ever Occupied . . . ,"* ix, 65; South Carolina Institute of Archaeology and Anthropology, *Annual Report for 1987 and 1988*, 17; "Black Soldiers Civil War Remains Found in Folly Island Excavations," *Anderson Independent-Mail*, October 16, 1988, 3; "Civil War Relics Found on Island," *Beaufort Gazette*, October 17, 1988, 5.

23. Legg and Smith, *"The Best Ever Occupied . . . ,"* 36–47.

24. Legg and Smith, *"The Best Ever Occupied . . . ,"* 48.

25. Legg and Smith, *"The Best Ever Occupied . . . ,"* 48; South Carolina Institute of Archaeology and Anthropology, Annual Report *for 1987 and 1988*, 15.

26. Charles Barnard Fox, *Record of the Service of the Fifty-Fifth Regiment of Massachusetts Volunteer Infantry. Printed for the Regimental Association* (Cambridge, MA: John Wilson and Son, 1868), 12–21, 110–111, accessed at the Massachusetts State Archives, Boston, MA. The regiment chose to use Fox's wartime diary as the official regimental history; Legg and Smith, *"The Best Ever Occupied . . . ,"* ix, 57–62; For effects on the First NC Colored Infantry, see Reid, *Freedom for Themselves*, 67–70.

27. Legg and Smith, *"The Best Ever Occupied . . . ,"* 12.

28. Several South Carolina news articles educated residents, primarily white South Carolinians, of the history of the Beaufort National Cemetery and the rationale for the reburial of the recovered USCT remains there. See Noah Jenkins, "Union Cemetery Deserves Care," *Island Packet* (Hilton Head, SC), November 7, 1988, 8A; Tom McCammon, "Union Soldiers' Bodies Moved to Beaufort," *Island Packet* (Hilton Head, SC), November 16, 1988, 8A; Gerhard Spieler, "National Cemetery Created by Lincoln during Occupation," *Beaufort Gazette*, March 14, 1989, 5-B; Lolita Huckaby, "Dukakis to Honor War Dead in Beaufort," *Beaufort Gazette*, April 14, 1989, 1.

29. Huckaby, "Dukakis to Honor War Dead in Beaufort."

30. Mindy S. Lubber, press secretary, "Dukakis Leads Memorial Day Ceremony Honoring Black Civil War Solders," a news release from the Office of Governor Michael S. Dukakis, May 26, 1989, GO11/series 10. Speech files, Dukakis, Box 1, May 29, 1989, Memorial Day Ceremony, Beaufort, SC. Massachusetts State Archives. Boston, Massachusetts; Elizabeth Leland, "In Remembrance: Special Ceremony Commemorates Black Civil War Dead," *Charlotte Observer*, May 29, 1989, 1A.

31. Huckaby, "Dukakis to Honor War Dead in Beaufort"; Lubber, Press Secretary, "Dukakis Leads Memorial Day Ceremony Honoring Black Civil War Solders."

32. Michael S. Dukakis, "Remarks of Governor Michael S. Dukakis, Commonwealth of Massachusetts, Memorial Day Ceremonies, National Cemetery, Beaufort, South Carolina," speech, May 29, 1989, 1, GO11/series 10. Speech files, Dukakis, Box 1, May 29, 1989, Memorial Day Ceremony, Beaufort, SC. Massachusetts State Archives. Boston, Massachusetts.

33. Dukakis, "Remarks of Governor Michael S. Dukakis," 2.

34. Dukakis, "Remarks of Governor Michael S. Dukakis," 2.

35. Dukakis, "Remarks of Governor Michael S. Dukakis," 3.

36. Dukakis, "Remarks of Governor Michael S. Dukakis," 4.

37. Dukakis, "Remarks of Governor Michael S. Dukakis," 5.

38. Dukakis, "Remarks of Governor Michael S. Dukakis," 9.

39. Dukakis, "Remarks of Governor Michael S. Dukakis," 9.

40. Dukakis, "Remarks of Governor Michael S. Dukakis," 10.

41. See "SC National Cemetery Final Resting Place of Black War Dead," *Charlotte Observer*, May 30, 1989, 2B; "Remains Of 19 Black Soldiers Buried in SC," T *Charlotte Observer*, May 30, 1989, 3B; Black, "Bay State Black Union Troops Are Laid to Final Rest in South"; Harris, "Salute to a Forgotten Regiment"; "Black Union Soldiers to Be Reburied," UPI.com, May 28, 1989, https://www.upi.com/Archives/1989/05/28/Black-Union-soldiers-to-be-reburied/8065612331200/.

42. "SC National Cemetery Final Resting Place of Black War Dead."

43. "Bay State Black Union Troops Are Laid to Final Rest in South." The Washington Post also included Coblyn's recounting of the 1938 Gettysburg Reunion. See Harris, "Salute to a Forgotten Regiment."

44. Harris, "Salute to a Forgotten Regiment."

45. Harris, "Salute to a Forgotten Regiment."

46. "Bay State Black Union Troops Are Laid to Final Rest in South." For the 1913 Gettysburg Reunion activities and commentary, see David W. Blight, *Race and Reunion: The Civil War in American Memory* (Cambridge, MA: Belknap Press of Harvard University Press, 2001), 383–391; Caroline E. Janney, *Remembering the Civil War: Reunion and the Limits of Reconciliation* (Chapel Hill: University of North Carolina Press, 2013), 266–269; Barbara Gannon, *The Won Cause: Black and White Comradeship in the Grand Army of the Republic* (Chapel Hill: University of North Carolina Press, 2011), 182–190.

47. *Glory* (1989), IMDb.org, https://www.imdb.com/title/tt0097441/.

48. Gary W. Gallagher, *Causes Won, Lost, and Forgotten: How Hollywood and Popular Art Shape What We Know about the Civil War* (Chapel Hill: University of North Carolina Press, 2008), 95–96.

49. William Thomas, "Historian Who Made 'Glory' Script Authentic Rejected a Role in Film," *Herald-Sun* (Durham, NC), December 26, 1989, 7A; *Glory* (1989); John David Smith, "Glory: 'Heroism Writ Large, from People Whom History Has Made Small,'" in *Writing History With Lightning: Cinematic Representations of Nineteenth-Century America*, ed. Matthew Christopher Hulbert and John C. Inscoe (Baton Rouge: Louisiana State University Press, 2019), 163–165; Douglas R. Egerton, *Thunder at the Gates: The Black*

Civil War Regiments That Redeemed America (New York: Basic Books, 2016), 90–91, and Lorien Foote, *Rites of Retaliation: Civilization, Soldiers and Campaigns in the American Civil War* (Chapel Hill: University of North Carolina Press, 2021), 27–47.

    50. *Glory* (1989).

    51. *Glory* (1989).

    52. *A Soldier's Story,* IMDb.org, https://www.imdb.com/title/tt0088146/.

    53. *Glory* (1989); Michael Cieply, "Denzel Washington Wins Oscar for 'Glory': Academy Awards, He is Named Best Supporting Actor for Role in Civil War Drama about Black Soldiers," *Los Angeles Times*, March 27, 1990, https://www.latimes.com/archives/la-xpm-1990-03-27-mn-2-story.html.

    54. Smith, "Glory," 165; Gallagher, *Causes Won, Lost, and Forgotten*, 95; Laura Blanton, "From Set of *Glory* to the Smithsonian Collections," *O Can You See?: Stories from the Museum*, July 30, 2014, https://americanhistory.si.edu/blog/2014/07/from-the-set-of-glory-to-the-smithsonian-collections.html.

    55. Smith, "Glory," 162–163, 166–168,

    56. *Glory* (1989); "Departure of the Fifty-Fourth Regiment of Massachusetts Volunteers," *The Liberator*, June 5, 1863, 91; David W. Blight, *Frederick Douglass: Prophet of Freedom* (New York; Simon and Schuster, 2018), 396–398.

    57. Gallagher, *Causes Won, Lost, and Forgotten*, 96.

    58. Smith, "Glory," 163.

    59. Gallagher, *Causes Won, Lost, and Forgotten*, 98–100.

    60. Gallagher, *Causes Won, Lost, and Forgotten*, 96–98.

    61. Smith, "Glory," 164.

    62. *Glory* (1989); Smith, "Glory," 168–169.

    63. Smith, "Glory," 162.

    64. Gallagher, *Causes Won, Lost, and Forgotten*, 7; Associated Press, "Re-Enactment," photograph, *Reno Gazette-Journal*, September 13, 1996, 2A; "Services Honored," *Reno Gazette-Journal*, September 13, 1996, 2A.

    65. "Services Honored," *Reno Gazette-Journal*, September 13, 1996, 2A.

    66. Associated Press, "Service Completes First Part of Black Civil War Memorial," *Reno Gazette-Journal*, September 11, 1996, 9A.

    67. Richard W. Stevenson, "Civil War Memorial Honoring Black Soldiers to Be Unveiled in DC," *News and Observer* (Raleigh, NC), July 12, 1998, 3H.

    68. "African American Civil War Memorial," National Park Services, https://www.nps.gov/places/000/african-american-civil-war-memorial-the-spirit-of-freedom.htm.

    69. "African American Civil War Memorial."

    70. "African American Civil War Memorial."

    71. Gallagher, *Causes Won, Lost, and Forgotten*, 7.

    72. Erica L. Ball, "Style Politics and Self-Fashioning in Mamie Garvin Fields' *Lemon Swamp and Other Places*," *WSQ: Women's Studies Quarterly* 46 (Spring/Summer 2018): 55–56; The Fields sisters also wrote of the grandmother, the process of writing her memoir, and challenges of documenting her experiences with the John C. Calhoun monuments in Charleston in a chapter titled "What One Cannot Remember Mistakenly" for their co-authored volume of essays. See Karen E. Fields and Barbara J. Fields, *Racecraft:*

The Soul of Inequality in American Life (London: Verso, 2012),171–192; Ball, "Style Politics and Self-Fashioning," 55–56.

73. Mamie Garvin Fields and Karen Fields, *Lemon Swamp and Other Places: A Carolina Memoir* (New York: Free Press, 1983), 1, 12.

74. Fields, *Lemon Swamp*, 42, 45.

75. Fields, *Lemon Swamp*, 37, 40–42.

76. Fields, *Lemon Swamp*, 45.

77. Fields, *Lemon Swamp*, 48.

78. Fields, *Lemon Swamp*, 48, 57.

79. Fields, *Lemon Swamp*, 55–56.

80. Fields, *Lemon Swamp*, 56–57.

81. Jarvis R. Givens, *Fugitive Pedagogy: Carter G. Woodson and the Art of Black Teaching* (Cambridge, MA: Harvard University Press, 2021), 10–16; Fields, *Lemon Swamp*, 127.

82. Fields, *Lemon Swamp*, 189–241; For more of her activism, specifically speeches, photographs, and ephemera, see Mamie Garvin Fields papers, Avery Research Center, College of Charleston, Charleston, SC, https://lcdl.library.cofc.edu/content/mamie-e -garvin-fields-papers-1894-1987/.

83. Ethan J. Kytle and Blain Roberts, *Denmark Vesey's Garden: Slavery and Memory in the Cradle of the Confederacy* (New York: New Press, 2018), 304–305.

84. Kytle and Roberts, *Denmark Vesey's Garden*, 306–310.

85. Kytle and Roberts, *Denmark Vesey's Garden*, 315–319, 327–331; Ethan J. Kytle and Blain Roberts, "Is It Okay to Talk about Slaves? Segregating the Past in Historic Charleston," in *Destination Dixie: Tourism and Southern Tourism*, ed. Karen L. Cox (Gainesville: University Press of Florida, 2012), 140–144; In his Pulitzer Prize–winning book, Tony Horwitz briefly included a discussion with Joseph McGill, a National Park Service Ranger who shared the revised narrative that included Robert Smalls, *The Planter*, and other nuanced African American Civil War experiences. See Horwitz, *Confederates in the Attic: Dispatches from the Unfinished Civil War* (New York: Pantheon Books, 1998), 47–49.

86. Kytle and Roberts, *Denmark Vesey's Garden*, 327–331; Kytle and Roberts, "Is It Okay to Talk about Slaves?"145–152.

87. Joseph McGill Jr. and Herb Frazier, *Sleeping with the Ancestors: How I Followed the Footprints of Slavery* (New York: Hachette Books, 2023), 47–49; Horwitz, *Confederates in the Attic*, 136–137.

88. "Formation of a 54th Massachusetts Reenactment Regiment," Charleston Chronicle, November 11, 1992, clipping, SC History—Battles, Fort Wagner, 30-11-6W, vertical file, Special Collections—SC Historical Society Archives, College of Charleston, SC.

89. Paul Brownfield, "Black Civil War Re-Enactors Enjoy Glory of Hobby," *The State*, September 15, 1996, E1; McGill and Frazier, *Sleeping with the Ancestors*, 49.

90. "Re-enactors Will Bring History to Life," June 7, 2005, clipping, SC History-Battles, Fort Wagner, 30-11-6W, vertical file, Special Collections--SC Historical Society Archives, College of Charleston, SC.

91. Brownfield, "Black Civil War Re-Enactors Enjoy Glory of Hobby"; Carolyn Grant, "Civil War Re-Enactors Bring World of Black Soldiers to Life," *Island Packet* (Hilton Head Island, SC), September 30, 2001, 14A.

92. Lydia Mattice Brandt, *The South Carolina State House Grounds* (Columbia: University of South Carolina Press, 2021), 121; John Shelton Reed, "The Banner That Won't Stay Furled," *Southern Cultures* 8, no. 1 (Spring 2002): 77; Charles Joyner, "Furling That Banner: The Rise and Fall of the Confederate Flag in South Carolina, 1961–2000," in *Citizen-Scholar: Essays in Honor of Walter Edgar*, ed. Robert H. Brinkmeyer (Columbia: University of South Carolina Press, 2016), 23–33; Brown, *Civil War Canon*, 202–203, 212–215.

93. "Monument to Black History Is Endorsed," *The State*, February 16, 1996, B6; "Monument Would Honor Black Americans," *The State*, B4; Brown, *Civil War Canon*, 215–216.

94. Ross Scoppe, "African American Monument on Hold," *The State*, May 10, 1996, B3; Michael Sponhour and Cindi Ross Scoppe, "Knotts Angers Black Lawmakers," *The State*, May 31, 1996, A8; John M. "Jake" Knotts, "Amendments on Monuments Offered in Interest of Fairness," *The State*, June 12, 1996, A13; "Build Monument, State Says," *The State*, June 28, 1996.

95. "Quote of the Week," *The State*, June 30, 1996, D4.

96. "Build Monument, State Says"; Gary Karr, "RDA, Black Monument OK'd on 'Good Day,'" *Times and Democrat* (Orangeburg, SC), June 28, 1996, 1A and 4A; "Black Monument Vote," *Times and Democrat* (Orangeburg, SC), June 28, 1996, 4A.

97. Pat Butler, "Monumental Task Ahead," *The State*, July 6, 1996, B1; Michael Sponhour, "Written in Stone," *The State*, August 18, 1996, D5.

98. On Our Minds," *The State*, May 29, 1996, B2; Sponhour, "Written in Stone," D1 and D5; Butler, "Monumental Task Ahead."

99. Ernest L. Wiggins, "Monument to African-Americans Is a Nice, But Misguided Gesture," *The State*, July 3, 1996, A13.

100. Wiggins, "Monument to African-Americans Is a Nice, But Misguided Gesture."

101. "The Commission," *The State*, August 18, 1996, D5; Brown, *Civil War Canon*, 211–212.

102. "The Commission."

103. Michael Sponhour, "Panel Ponders Black History Museum," *The State*, September 13, 1996, B1 and B3.

104. Brandt, *The South Carolina State House Grounds*, 122–123; Blain Roberts and Ethan Kytle, "Looking the Thing in the Face: Slavery, Race, and the Commemorative Landscape in Charleston, South Carolina, 1865–2010," *Journal of Southern History* 78, no. 3 (August 2012): 677; Sid Gaulden, "African American Monument Selected," *Post and Courier*, April 10, 1998, 1A and 19A, clipping, in African American, slavery monuments, 30-21-4A, vertical file, Special Collections—SC Historical Society Archives, College of Charleston, SC; Jessie J. Holland, "Colo. Man to Design Statehouse First African-American Monument," *Times and Democrat* (Orangeburg, SC), April 10, 1998, 1B and 2B; "Colorado Artist Chosen to Design Monument to S.C. Blacks," *The Item* (Sumter, SC), April 10, 1998, 2A; Lee Bandy, "Black-History Monument 'Off and Running,'" *The State*, December 15, 1998, A1 and A8.

105. Brandt, *The South Carolina State House Grounds*, 37–71, 117–119, 125–129.

106. Chuck Crumbo, "Event Launches Fund-Raising Blitz," *The State*, May 12, 2000, A1 and A12, clipping, in African American, slavery monuments, 30-21-4A; Brandt, *The*

South Carolina State House Grounds, 125; "Granite, Bronze and Triumph," *The State*, March 25, 2001, A1.

107. "Granite, Bronze and Triumph," A18; Kenneth A. Harris, "Minor, not Monumental, Delays on African-American Marker, *The State*, December 3, 2000, D4.

108. Valerie Bauerlein, "History Embraced: African-American Monument Dedicated. 'There Are So Many Things That Need to Have Been Told,'" *The State*, March 30, 2001, A1 and A12.

109. Bauerlein, "History Embraced"; Brandt, *The South Carolina State House Grounds*, 123–125.

110. Bauerlein, "History Embraced."

111. "New Monument on State House Grounds," *The State*, March 30, 2001, A12; Chuck Crumbo, "Monument Draws Rave Reviews from Crowds," *The State*, March 31, 2001, B1; John Rainey, "A Monument for All," *The State*, July 12, 2001, A17.

112. "African American History Monument," Historic Columbia, https://www .historiccolumbia.org/tour-locations/1100-gervais-street-2.

113. "African American History Monument"; "Monument Panels," *The State*, March 25, 2001, A18.

114. "Monument Panels"; William A. Dobak, *Freedom by the Sword: The US Colored Troops, 1862–1867* (New York: Skyhorse Publishing, 2013), 14, 70; Egerton, *Thunder at the Gates*, 90.

115. "Monument Panels."

116. "Monument Panels."

117. "Dedication Poem," *The State*, March 30, 2001, A12.

118. "Granite, Bronze and Triumph," A18; Kenneth A. Harris, "Cobb-Hunter Boycotts Monument Ceremony," *The State*, March 30, 2001, A12.

119. Harris, "Cobb-Hunter Boycotts Monument Ceremony."

120. Brandt, *The South Carolina State House Grounds*, 121.

121. Brandt, *The South Carolina State House Grounds*, 87–89; Brown, *Civil War Canon*, 231–233; Christopher Frear, Jane O'Boyle, and Sei-Hill Kim, "Regional Media Framing of the Confederate Flag Debate in South Carolina," *Newspaper Research Journal* 40, no. 1 (March 2019): 84, 97–100.

122. Brownfield, "Black Civil War Re-Enactors Enjoy Glory of Hobby," E1.

123. Brownfield, "Black Civil War Re-Enactors Enjoy Glory of Hobby," E1; Grant, "Civil War Re-Enactors Bring World of Black Soldiers to Life," 1A; Carolyn Grant, "Black Re-Enactors to Portray 54th Massachusetts," *Beaufort Gazette*, October 1, 1996, 14A. Walker was the first Black soldier court-martialed, convicted, and executed before his men; his case saw calls for changes in military regulations but also revealed the racial differences in military discipline during the Civil War. See Christian G. Samito, "The Intersection between Military Justice and Equal Rights: Mutinies, Courts-martial, and Black Civil War Soldiers," *Civil War History* 53, no 2 (June 2007), 186–187, 197–202.

124. Grant, "Civil War Re-Enactors Bring World of Black Soldiers to Life," 14A.

125. Almar Flotildes, "Re-enactors Offer Glimpse into History," *Post and Courier*, February 20, 2011, clipping, SC History—Battles, Fort Wagner, 30-11-6W, Special Collections—SC Historical Society Archives, College of Charleston, SC.

126. Flotildes, "Re-enactors Offer Glimpse into History."

127. Flotildes, "Re-enactors Offer Glimpse into History"; Bruce Smith, "Re-enactors Keep Memory of Black Civil War Alive," *Times and Democrat* (Orangeburg, SC), August 28, 2010, A4.

128. Robert Behre, "Massachusetts 54th: 'We Will Not Be a Footnote' to History, Say Union Army re-enactors," *Post and Courier*, July 17, 2010, 1B, SC History—Battles, Fort Wagner, 30-11-6W, Special Collections—SC Historical Society Archives, College of Charleston, SC.

129. Behre, "Massachusetts 54th."

130. Smith, "Re-enactors Keep Memory of Black Civil War Troops Alive," 4; Kevin Allen, "The Second Battle of Fort Sumter: The Debate Over the Politics of Race and Historical Memory at the Opening of the America's Civil War Centennial, 1961," *Public Historian* 33, no. 2 (Spring 2011), 94–109; Brown, *Civil War Canon*, 207–211, 253–258.

131. Behre, "Massachusetts 54th"; Edward C. Fennell, "Depiction of Local Civil War Battle," *Post and Courier*, February 17, 2011, 10ZB, clipping, SC History—Battles, Fort Wagner, 30-11-6W, vertical file, Special Collections—SC Historical Society Archives, College of Charleston, SC.

132. Behre, "Massachusetts 54th."

133. Smith, "Re-enactors Keep Memory of Black Civil War Troops Alive."

134. Thomas Novelly, "Gov Honors Historian Who Found Remains of Black Soldiers," *US News and World Report*, February 21, 2021, https://www.usnews.com/news/best-states/south-carolina/articles/2021-02-20/gov-honors-historian-who-found-remains-of-black-soldiers.

135. Novelly, "Gov Honors Historian Who Found Remains of Black Soldiers."

136. Novelly, "Gov Honors Historian Who Found Remains of Black Soldiers."

137. Novelly, "Gov Honors Historian Who Found Remains of Black Soldiers."

138. Novelly, "Gov Honors Historian Who Found Remains of Black Soldiers."

8. "More Than a Footnote" during the Sesquicentennial

1. Robert Behre, "Massachusetts 54th: 'We will not be a footnote' to history, say Union Army re-enactors," *Post and Courier*, July 17, 2010, 1B, SC History—Battles, Fort Wagner, 30-11-6W, Special Collections—SC Historical Society Archives, College of Charleston, SC.; Stratton Lawrence, "Local Group Reenacts the Glory of the Black Union Soldiers of the 54th Massachusetts," *Charleston City Paper*, July 10, 2013, https://charlestoncitypaper.com/2013/07/10/local-group-reenacts-the-glory-of-the-black-union-soldiers-of-the-54th-massachusetts/.

2. Lawrence, "Local Group Reenacts the Glory of the Black Union Soldiers of the 54th Massachusetts."

3. Lawrence, "Local Group Reenacts the Glory of the Black Union Soldiers of the 54th Massachusetts."

4. Behre, "Massachusetts 54th: 'We will not be a footnote' to history, say Union Army re-enactors."

5. Robert J. Cook, *Troubled Commemoration: The American Civil War Centennial* (Baton Rouge: Louisiana State University Press, 2007), 88–119.

6. Robert K. Sutton, ed., *Rally on the High Ground: The National Park Service Sympo-sium on the Civil War* (Washington, DC: National Park Service, 2001), http://npshistory.com/series/symposia/rally_high_ground/index.htm; Greg Hambrick, "Charleston Plan-ning $90,000 Civil War Sesquicentennial Schedule," *Charleston City Paper*, September 14, 2010, https://charlestoncitypaper.com/2010/09/14/charleston-planning-90000-civil-war-sesquicentennial-schedule/; Will Moredock, "Whitewashing History: Don't Let Neo-Confederates Make a Lie of the Past," *Charleston City Paper*, April 13, 2010, https://charlestoncitypaper.com/2010/04/13/whitewashing-history-dont-let-neo-confederates-make-a-lie-of-the-past/.

7. Jesse Jackson Jr., "A More Perfect Union," in *Rally on the High Ground: The National Park Service Symposium on the Civil War*, ed. Robert K. Sutton (Washington, DC: Na-tional Park Service, 2001), https://www.nps.gov/parkhistory/online_books/rthg/chap1.htm.

8. Jackson, "A More Perfect Union."

9. Robert Sutton, Introduction to *Rally on the High Ground: The National Park Service Symposium on the Civil War*, ed. Robert K. Sutton (Washington: National Park Service, 2001), http://npshistory.com/series/symposia/rally_high_ground/intro.htm.

10. Sutton, Introduction to *Rally on the High Ground*.

11. Sutton, Introduction to *Rally on the High Ground*.

12. See Edward T. Linenthal, "Healing and History: The Dilemmas of Interpretation," in *Rally on the High Ground: The National Park Service Symposium on the Civil War*, ed. Robert K. Sutton (Washington, DC: National Park Service, 2001), http://npshistory.com/series/symposia/rally_high_ground/chap3b.htm; James M. McPherson, "Citizen Soldiers of the Civil War: Why They Fought," in *Rally on the High Ground: The National Park Symposium on the Civil War*, ed. Robert K. Sutton (Washington, DC: National Park Ser-vice, 2001), http://npshistory.com/series/symposia/rally_high_ground/chap4.htm; James Oliver Horton, "Slavery and the Coming of the Civil War: A Matter for Interpretation," in *Rally on the High Ground: The National Park Symposium on the Civil War*, ed. Robert K. Sutton (Washington, DC: National Park Service, 2001), http://npshistory.com/series/symposia/rally_high_ground/chap5.htm.

13. Robert J. Cook, *Civil War Memories: Contesting the Past in the United States since 1865* (Baltimore: Johns Hopkins University Press, 2017), 201–203.

14. Robert Behre, "NAACP to Protest Secession Ball," *Post and Courier*, November 30, 2010; Robert Behre, "NAACP to Protest Secession Event," *Post and Courier*, December 2, 2010; Other South Carolina newspapers, including the Columbia newspaper, reprinted Behre's reporting often under a new title. See Robert Behre, "Secession Ball Stirs Contro-versy," *The State* (Columbia, SC), December 3, 2010, B3; Robert Behre, "NAACP: Group Is Glamorizing Event," *Beaufort Gazette*, December 3, 2010, 5A, and Robert Behre, "Se-cession Ball Stirs Controversy," *Sun-News* (Myrtle Beach, SC), December 3, 2010, C5.

15. Prentiss Findlay, "NAACP Releases Details on Secession Ball Protest," *Post and Courier*, December 9, 2010; Prentiss Findlay, "NAACP Details Protest of Ball," *Post and Courier*, December 10, 2010; Robert Behre, "President Obama Asked by Mayor Riley to Participate in Area's Observance of Start of Civil War," *Post and Courier*, December 15, 2010; Chris Haire, "NAACP President Says Secession Gala Tarnishes Other Events,"

Charleston City Paper, December 14, 2010, https://charlestoncitypaper.com/2010/12/14/naacp-president-says-secession-gala-tarnishes-other-events/; Robert Behre, "Historical Secession Marker Unveiled, Protests Ongoing," *Post and Courier*, December 19, 2010; Wayne Washington, "Approaches to Marking Civil War Vary," *The State* (Columbia, SC), December 16, 2010, B3.

16. Robert Behre and Brian Hicks, "Secession Day: 150 Years Later, Dec. 20, 1860, Still Divides," *Post and Courier*, December 20, 2010; Wayne Washington, "Secession Ball: Celebrators, Protesters Present Opposite Views of History at Event," *The State* (Columbia, SC), December 21, 2010, A1 and A8; Jeffrey Collins, "South Carolina Secession: Dance, Protests Mark 150th Anniversary," *Montgomery Advertiser*, December 21, 2010, 6A; Stephen M. Monroe, *Heritage and Hate: Old South Rhetoric at Southern Universities* (Tuscaloosa: University of Alabama Press, 2021), 2-5.

17. See Behre, "NAACP to Protest Secession Ball"; Behre, "NAACP to Protest Secession Event"; Findlay, "NAACP Releases Details on Secession Ball Protest"; Findlay, "NAACP Details Protest of Ball"; Washington, "Approaches to Marking Civil War Vary"; Chris Haire, "Secession Gala Organizer Says Nothing 'Inappropriate,' About Event," *Charleston City Paper*, December 14, 2010, https://charlestoncitypaper.com/2010/12/14/secession-gala-organizer-says-nothing-inappropriate-about-event/.

18. Ben Busbee, "NAACP Should Mind Its Own Business," letter to the editor, *The State* (Columbia, SC), December 17, 2010, A14; Gail Jarvis, "North Benefited from Slavery Also," letter to the editor, *The State* (Columbia, SC), December 27, 2010, A15.

19. Monroe, *Heritage and Hate*, 5–11; Will Moredock, "What Has SC Learned Since the Civil War Centennial," *Charleston City Paper*, December 15, 2010, https://charlestoncitypaper.com/2010/12/15/what-has-s-c-learned-since-the-civil-war-centennial/; Ben Bentley, "Civil War Never to Be Celebrated," letter to the editor, *The State* (Columbia, SC), December 17, 2010, A14; Tom Turnispeed, "It Doesn't Seem Like Civil War Is Over," letter to the editor, *The State* (Columbia, SC), December 17, 2010, A14; Bill Foltz, "Don't Celebrate; Repent, Reconcile," letter to the editor, *The State* (Columbia, SC), December 19, 2010, D2; David Coble, "NAACP Seems to be Right—This Time," letter to the editor, *The State* (Columbia, SC), December 19, 2010, D2; James M. Holloway, "Secession Articles Well Written," letter to the editor, *The State* (Columbia, SC), December 27, 2010, A15.

20. Chris Haire, "Rocky D Champions Secession Ball, Blasts NAACP," *Charleston City Paper*, December 8, 2010, https://charlestoncitypaper.com/2010/12/08/rocky-d-champions-secession-ball-blasts-naacp/.

21. Washington, "Approaches to Marking Civil War Vary," B1.

22. Washington, "Approaches to Marking Civil War Vary," B1 and B3; Chris Haire, "Mayor Riley Calls Secession Gala 'Unfortunate,' 'the Opposite of Unifying,'" *Charleston City Paper*, December 9, 2010, https://charlestoncitypaper.com/2010/12/09/mayor-riley-calls-secession-gala-unfortunate-the-opposite-of-unifying/.

23. Washington, "Approaches to Marking Civil War Vary," B3.

24. Washington, "Approaches to Marking Civil War Vary," B3.

25. Washington, "Approaches to Marking Civil War Vary," B3.

26. Warren Bolton, "What's There to Celebrate?" *The State*, December 17, 2010, A14.

27. Bolton, "What's There to Celebrate?"

28. Bolton, "What's There to Celebrate?"

29. Bolton, "What's There to Celebrate?"

30. Warren Bolton, "We Tried Seceding; Now Let's Succeed," *The State*, December 19, 2010, D2.

31. Bolton, "We Tried Seceding; Now Let's Succeed."

32. Harvey Elwood Jr., "Another Way to Look At Secession," letter to the editor, *The State* (Columbia, SC), December 17, 2010, A14.

33. Albert Jabs, "SC Understands Need to Repent," letter to the editor, *The State* (Columbia, SC), December 27, 2010, A15.

34. Cook, *Civil War Memories*, 201–203; Robert Cook, Kenneth Noe, Dana Shoaf, Jennifer Weber, and Daniel E. Sutherland, "Historians' Forum: The American Civil War's Centennial vs. the Sesquicentennial," *Civil War History* 57, no. 4 (December 2011): 381–388; Gary Gallagher, "The Civil War at the Sesquicentennial: How Well Do Americans Understand Their Great National Crisis?" *Journal of Civil War Era* 3, no. 2 (June 2013): 295–298, 301–302.

35. Cook, Noe, Shoaf, Weber, and Sutherland, "Historians' Forum," 388–391; Ethan J. Kytle, "Fort Sumter Sesquicentennial: Charleston Changed Its Tune," History News Network, April 18, 2011, https://historynewsnetwork.org/article/138511.

36. Jill Ogline Titus, "Unfinished Struggle: Sesquicentennial Interpretations of Slavery and Emancipation," *Journal of Civil War Era* 4, no. 2 (June 2014): 338, 341–342.

37. Robert Behre, "Obama Receives Invitation— President Asked by Riley to Participate in Area's Sesquicentennial Observance of Start of Civil War," *Post and Courier*, December 16, 2010, A1; Will Moredock, "President Obama Should Stay in DC on April 12," *Charleston City Paper*, January 5, 2011, https://charlestoncitypaper.com/2011/01/05/president-obama-should-stay-in-d-c-on-april-12/.

38. Moredock, "President Obama Should Stay in DC on April 12."

39. Moredock, "President Obama Should Stay in DC on April 12."

40. Brian Hicks, "Civil War Years: Charleston at War—Divided Democrats Set the Stage," SERIES: Civil War: 150 Years, 1 of 20, *Post and Courier*, December 12, 2010, A1; Brian Hicks, "Our City Falls—Confederates Abandon Battered Charleston," SERIES: CIVIL WAR: 150 Years, Final Installment," *Post and Courier*, April 24, 2011, A1.

41. See Brian Hicks, "A Simple Ordinance of Secession," SERIES: Civil War: 150 Years, 2 of 20, *Post and Courier*, December 19, 2010, A1; of 20, *Post and Courier*, January 9, 2011, A1; Brian Hicks, "Union Troops Sets Sights on Morris Island," SERIES: Civil War: 150 Years, 14 of 20, *Post and Courier*, March 13, 2011, A1; Brian Hicks, Hunley creates history . . . and a mystery SERIES: CIVIL WAR: 150 Years, Part 18 of 20, *Post and Courier*, April 10, 2011, B1; Hicks, "Our City Falls."

42. Brian Hicks, "Walking with Ghosts of Secessionville," *Post and Courier*, April 12, 2011, A1.

43. Daniel L. Gidick, "We Need to Remember and Learn from the Civil War, Not Celebrate It," Civil War Issue, *Charleston City Paper*, April 6, 2011, https://charlestoncitypaper.com/2011/04/06/we-need-to-remember-and-learn-from-the-civil-war-not-celebrate-it/.

44. Gidick, "We Need to Remember and Learn from the Civil War, Not Celebrate It."

45. Chris Haire, "The Story of a Boy and His Infatuation with the Rebel Flag," Civil War Issue, *Charleston City Paper*, April 6, 2011, https://charlestoncitypaper.com/2011/04/06/the-story-of-a-boy-and-his-infatuation-with-the-rebel-flag/.

46. Greg Hambrick, "Charleston's Rich Sought Shelter in North Carolina Mountains," Civil War Issue, *Charleston City Paper*, April 6, 2011, https://charlestoncitypaper.com/2011/04/06/charlestons-rich-sought-shelter-in-the-north-carolina-mountains/; David Silkenat, *Driven from Home: North Carolina's Civil War Refugee Crisis* (Athens: University of Georgia Press, 2016), 180, 188–192.

47. Silkenat, *Driven from Home*, 213.

48. Greg Hambrick, "Slavery the Pivotal Issue for Charleston's *Mercury*," Civil War Issue, *Charleston City Paper*, April 6, 2011, https://charlestoncitypaper.com/2011/04/06/slavery-the-pivotal-issue-for-charlestons-mercury/.

49. Michael Smallwood, "The Old Slave Mart Is One of the Few Museums to Expose America's Shameful Past," Civil War Issue, *Charleston City Paper*, April 6, 2011, https://charlestoncitypaper.com/2011/04/06/the-old-slave-mart-is-one-of-the-few-museums-to-expose-americas-shameful-past/; Kytle and Roberts, *Denmark Vesey's Garden*, 245-256, 276-278, 304.

50. Smallwood, "The Old Slave Mart Is One of the Few Museums to Expose America's Shameful Past."

51. Michael Smallwood, "Civil War Voices Bring True Stories to the Stage," Civil War Issue, *Charleston City Paper*, April 6, 2011, https://charlestoncitypaper.com/2011/04/06/civil-war-voices-brings-true-stories-to-the-stage/.

52. Lisa Ryan, "Local Galleries Commemorate the Civil War Sesquicentennial," *Charleston City Paper*, April 6, 2011, https://charlestoncitypaper.com/2011/04/06/local-galleries-commemorate-the-civil-war-sesquicentennial/.

53. The *Post and Courier* also featured coverage of these art exhibits but appealed to its more affluent readership. See Bill Thompson, "Civil War, Past and Present— Exhibits Depict Charleston, Artistic Interpretations," *Post and Courier*, March 27, 2011, E1, and Brian Hicks, "City's Siege, On Canvas—Artist's Charleston Scenes Coming to Gibbes," *Post and Courier*, April 8, 2011, A1.

54. The Lowcountry Civil War Sesquicentennial Observance, "Why They Fought: Reflections on the 150th Anniversary of the American Civil War, April 8–12, 2011," A Lecture Series Produced by the Fort Sumter-Fort Moultrie Historical Trust, Charleston, South Carolina, program, Events, Civil War Sesquicentennial Commemoration, 30-11-12, Special Collections—SC Historical Society Archives, College of Charleston, SC.

55. The Lowcountry Civil War Sesquicentennial Observance, "Why They Fought."

56. The Lowcountry Civil War Sesquicentennial Observance, "Why They Fought."

57. The Lowcountry Civil War Sesquicentennial Observance, "Voices from the Civil War," White Point Garden, "The Battery," Charleston, SC, April 11, 2011, program, Events, Civil War Sesquicentennial Commemoration, 30-11-12, Special Collections—SC Historical Society Archives, College of Charleston, SC.

58. The Lowcountry Civil War Sesquicentennial Observance, "Voices from the Civil War."

59. The Lowcountry Civil War Sesquicentennial Observance, "Voices from the Civil War."

60. The Lowcountry Civil War Sesquicentennial Observance, "Voices from the Civil War."

61. Will Moredock, "Well Done, Charleston! We Staged a World-Class Civil War Commemoration," *Charleston City Paper*, April 20, 2011, clipping, Events, Civil War Sesquicentennial Commemoration, 30-11-12, Special Collections—SC Historical Society Archives, College of Charleston, SC.

62. Fort Sumter National Monument, "A Commemoration of the 150th Anniversary of the First Shots of the Civil War," April 12, 2011, official program, Events, Civil War Sesquicentennial Commemoration, 30-11-12, Special Collections—SC Historical Society Archives, College of Charleston, SC.

63. Fort Sumter National Monument, "A Commemoration of the 150th Anniversary of the First Shots of the Civil War."

64. Moredock, "Well Done, Charleston!"

65. Moredock, "Well Done, Charleston!"

66. Moredock, "Well Done, Charleston!"; Schuyler Kropf and Robert Behre, "Salute to History—Charleston Leads Nation's Civil War Commemoration," *Post and Courier*, April 13, 2011, A1.

67. Bruce Smith, "Blacks Shun War Events," *Post and Courier*, April 16, 2011, 2B, clipping, Events, Civil War Sesquicentennial Commemoration, 30-11-12, Special Collections—SC Historical Society Archives, College of Charleston, SC.

68. Smith, "Blacks Shun War Events."

69. Kevin Allen, "The Second Battle of Fort Sumter: The Debate over the Politics of Race and Historical Memory at the Opening of America's Civil War Centennial, 1961," *Public Historian* 33, no 2 (Spring 2011): 106.

70. Allen, "The Second Battle of Fort Sumter," 106.

71. Allen, "The Second Battle of Fort Sumter," 107.

72. Smith, "Blacks Shun War Events."

73. Smith, "Blacks Shun War Events"; Kytle, "Fort Sumter Sesquicentennial"; "NAACP to Teach 'Truth'—Firing on Fort Called Act of Terrorism," *Post and Courier*, April 12, 2011, A4.

74. Nicholas Watson, "Civil War Commander Gets Saddle Back 151 Years Late," *Post and Courier*, July 5, 2013, 4.

75. Robert N. Rosen, "When Morris Island Was 'the deadliest sandpit on earth,'" *Post and Courier*, July 10, 2013, 13; Robert N. Rosen, "The Storming of Battery Wagner," *Post and Courier*, July 18, 2013, 11; Robert N. Rosen, "Black Soldiers' Epic Courage Changed History at Battery Wagner," *Post and Courier*, July 21, 2013, 11.

76. Brian Hicks, "The Battle That Changed Charleston: Morris Island Feud Began City's Fall during Civil War," *Post and Courier*, July 14, 2013, 1; Bruce Smith, "54th Massachusetts Volunteer Infantry: 150th Anniversary of Black Soldiers' Attack," *The State* (Columbia, SC), July 14, 2013, B8; Bruce Smith, "Events to Mark Attack by Mass. Regiment," *Times and Democrat* (Orangeburg, SC), July 14, 2013, A6.

77. Robert Behre, "City Marks Anniversary of Civil War Skirmish," *Post and Courier*, July 7, 2013, 7; "1863 Campaign for Charleston Remembered with Events," *Times and Democrat* (Orangeburg, SC), July 11, 2013, A8; Lawrence, "Local Group Reenacts the Glory of the Black Union Soldiers of the 54th Massachusetts"; Sam Spence, "The Agenda: 54th Mass. Remembered; SC Hospitals Sue over Vote; Another Dreamliner Turns Back," *Charleston City Paper*, July 19, 2013, https://charlestoncitypaper.com/2013/07/19/the-agenda-54th-mass-remembered-s-c-hospitals-sue-state-over-veto-another-dreamliner-turns-back/; Bruce Smith, "'Glory': Civil War Fight by Troops Recalled," *Times and Democrat* (Orangeburg, SC), July 19, 2013, A2.

78. Lawrence, "Local Group Reenacts the Glory of the Black Union Soldiers of the 54th Massachusetts."

79. Lawrence, "Local Group Reenacts the Glory of the Black Union Soldiers of the 54th Massachusetts."

80. Lawrence, "Local Group Reenacts the Glory of the Black Union Soldiers of the 54th Massachusetts."

81. Bruce Smith, "Events to Mark Attack by Mass. Regiment," *Times and Democrat* (Orangeburg, SC), July 14, 2013.

82. Behre, "City Marks Anniversary of Civil War Skirmish."

83. Lawrence, "Local Group Reenacts the Glory of the Black Union Soldiers of the 54th Massachusetts."

84. Behre, "City Marks Anniversary of Civil War Skirmish."

85. Lawrence, "Local Group Reenacts the Glory of the Black Union Soldiers of the 54th Massachusetts."

86. Lawrence, "Local Group Reenacts the Glory of the Black Union Soldiers of the 54th Massachusetts."

87. Elizabeth Pandolfi, "The Heart of Sol Legare," *Charleston City Paper*, February 6, 2013, https://charlestoncitypaper.com/2013/02/06/the-heart-of-sol-legare/; Lawrence, "Local Group Reenacts the Glory of the Black Union Soldiers of the 54th Massachusetts." Ernest Parks initially reenacted as an unknown Black soldier who enlisted from the Charleston lowcountry. After several years in the group, Parks currently re-creates the life and experiences of his paternal great-great-grandfather Harrison Wilder who escaped from Sumter, South Carolina, and enlisted in the 104th USCI. For more of his biography, see Joseph McGill Jr. and Herb Frazier, *Sleeping with the Ancestors: How I Followed the Footprints of Slavery* (New York: Hachette Books, 2023), 50–55.

88. Lawrence, "Local Group Reenacts the Glory of the Black Union Soldiers of the 54th Massachusetts."

89. Nicholas Watson, "Living History in All Its Glory at Battery Wagner Anniversary," *Post and Courier*, July 19, 2013, 3; Smith, "'Glory.'"

90. Smith, "'Glory'"; Watson, "Living History in All Its Glory at Battery Wagner Anniversary."

91. Watson, "Living History in All Its Glory at Battery Wagner Anniversary."

92. "Mass. Governor Honors 54th," *Times and Democrat* (Orangeburg, SC), July 19, 2013, A2; Alyssa A. Botelho, "Valor of Black Regiment Is Honored," *Boston Globe*, July 19, 2013, B2.

93. Botelho, "Valor of Black Regiment Is Honored."
94. Botelho, "Valor of Black Regiment Is Honored."
95. Botelho, "Valor of Black Regiment Is Honored."
96. Botelho, "Valor of Black Regiment Is Honored."
97. F. C. Hacker, "The 'Ring of Fire' Tightens," *News and Courier*, July 14, 1963, 6C, clipping, SC History—Battles, Fort Wagner, 30-11-6W, Special Collections—SC Historical Society Archives, College of Charleston, SC.
98. Cook, *Troubled Commemoration*, 88–119; Cook, *Civil War Memories*, 181–182, 204–205.
99. Ethan J. Kytle, "Fact, Fancy, and Nat Fuller's Feast in 1865 and 2015," in *Freedoms Gained and Lost: Reconstruction and Its Meanings 150 Years Later*, ed. Adam H. Domby and Simon Lewis (New York: Fordham University Press, 2022), 276.
100. Kytle, "Fact, Fancy, and Nat Fuller's Feast in 1865 and 2015," 276–277; Kinsey Gidick, "Historic Nat Fuller Dinner Menu Released," *Charleston City Paper*, March 19, 2015, https://charlestoncitypaper.com/2015/03/19/historic-nat-fuller-dinner-menu-released/.
101. See Hannah Raskin, "Breaking Bread Together," *Post and Courier*, April 21, 2015, https://www.postandcourier.com/food/breaking-bread-together/article_63669d9a-a220-5c80-800e-2226562f4c72.html; Robert F. Moss, "The Nat Fuller Feast Opens a New Chapter in Charleston's Forgotten Culinary History," *Charleston City Paper*, April 29, 2015, https://charlestoncitypaper.com/2015/04/29/the-nat-fuller-feast-opens-a-new-chapter-in-charlestons-forgotten-culinary-history/; "Celebrating Civility," *The State* (Columbia, SC), April 15, 2015, C3 and C10; Harrison Cahill, "Breaking Bread Together: After 150 Years, Another Feast of Cuisine, Conversation," *The State* (Columbia, SC), April 15, 2015, A3 and A7; Helen Schwab, "Nat Fuller Feast Honors Star Chef, Slave, Herald of Unity," *Charlotte Observer*, May 6, 2015, 1C and 6C; John Kessler, "Feast of Reconciliation," *Atlanta Constitution*, April 15, 2015, D1 and D5.
102. Kytle, "Fact, Fancy, and Nat Fuller's Feast in 1865 and 2015," 277, 281, 289–290.
103. Kytle, "Fact, Fancy, and Nat Fuller's Feast in 1865 and 2015," 276.
104. Kytle, "Fact, Fancy, and Nat Fuller's Feast in 1865 and 2015," 278–279.
105. Kytle, "Fact, Fancy, and Nat Fuller's Feast in 1865 and 2015," 283–287.
106. Kytle, "Fact, Fancy, and Nat Fuller's Feast in 1865 and 2015," 290–291.
107. Kytle, "Fact, Fancy, and Nat Fuller's Feast in 1865 and 2015," 293–294.
108. See Frances Robles, "Dylann Roof Photos and a Manifesto Are Posted on Website," *New York Times*, June 20, 2015, https://www.nytimes.com/2015/06/21/us/dylann-storm-roof-photos-website-charleston-church-shooting.html; Lenny Bernstein, Sari Horwitz and Peter Holley, "Dylann Roof's Racist Manifesto: 'I have no choice,'" *Washington Post*, June 20, 2015, https://www.washingtonpost.com/national/health-science/authorities-investigate-whether-racist-manifesto-was-written-by-sc-gunman/2015/06/20/f0bd3052-1762-11e5-9ddc-e3353542100c_story.html; David Wren and Doug Pardue, "Dylann Roof Had Outlined Racist Views on Website Prior to Church Shooting," *Post and Courier* (web edition), June 19, 2015; John Monk, "Alleged Shooter's 'Manifesto' Found on Online?," *The State*, June 20, 2015, A1 and A6; "Purported to Be the Dylann Roof 'Manifesto,'" *The State*, June 20, 2015, http://media.thestate.com/

static/roofmanifesto.pdf; "Dylann Roof's Journal," *Post and Courier*, December 6, 2016, https://www.postandcourier.com/dylann-roofs-journal/pdf_c5f6550c-be72-11e6-b869 -7bdf860326f5.html. South Carolina and national newspapers published parts of Roof's words in their initial coverage. Several South Carolina newspapers published a transcript of the digitized manifesto and then a handwritten version during his first trial in their digital editions. Comparing the handwritten text and digitized copy, the texts are similar to each other. My analysis draws on both versions of the text and the published account. Kathleen Belew, *Bring the War Home: The White Power Movement and Paramilitary America* (Cambridge, MA: Harvard University Press, 2018), 3–11.

109. "Purported to Be the Dylann Roof 'Manifesto'"; Belew, *Bring the War Home*, 156–170.

110. "Purported to Be the Dylann Roof 'Manifesto.'"

111. "Purported to Be the Dylann Roof 'Manifesto.'" Roof's disdain for the national reverence of post–Vietnam War veterans aligns with the broader national white power movement. See Belew, *Bring the War Home*, 19–32.

112. Chad Williams, Kidada Williams, and Keisha Blain, Introduction to *Charleston Syllabus: Readings on Race, Racism, and Racial Violence*), ed. Chad Williams, Kidada E. Williams, and Keisha N. Blain (Athens: University of Georgia Press, 2016), 1–2; "Purported to Be the Dylann Roof 'Manifesto'"; Robles, "Dylann Roof Photos and a Manifesto Are Posted on Website"; Monk, "Alleged Shooter's 'Manifesto' Found on Online?"

113. "Purported to Be the Dylann Roof 'Manifesto.'"

114. David Wren and Doug Pardue, "Dylann Roof Had Outlined Racist Views on Website Prior to Church Shooting"; Robles, "Dylann Roof Photos and a Manifesto Are Posted on Website"; Monk, "Alleged Shooter's 'Manifesto' Found on Online?"; Belew, *Bring the War Home*, 238.

115. Williams, Williams, and Blain, Introduction to *Charleston Syllabus*, 1.

116. Williams, Williams, and Blain, Introduction to *Charleston Syllabus*, 1–2, 7.

117. Cook, *Civil War Memories*, 197–201. Robert J. Cook defines Obama's influence as a subheading title in the 2017 monograph. This notion becomes useful in understanding not only the Charleston Massacre but the entire sesquicentennial, including the lack of a federal commission, reception, and framing of the multi-year commemorative events.

118. Barack Obama, "Remarks by the President in Eulogy for the Honorable Reverend Clementa Pinckney, College of Charleston, Charleston, South Carolina (June 29, 2015)," in *Charleston Syllabus: Readings on Race, Racism, and Racial Violence*), ed. Chad Williams, Kidada E. Williams, and Keisha N. Blain (Athens: University of Georgia Press, 2016), 273–279.

119. Obama, "Remarks by the President in Eulogy for the Honorable Reverend Clementa Pickney," 274.

120. Obama, "Remarks by the President in Eulogy for the Honorable Reverend Clementa Pinckney," 274.

121. Obama, "Remarks by the President in Eulogy for the Honorable Reverend Clementa Pinckney," 274.

122. Obama, "Remarks by the President in Eulogy for the Honorable Reverend Clementa Pinckney," 274.

123. Obama, "Remarks by the President in Eulogy for the Honorable Reverend Clementa Pinckney," 275.

124. Obama, "Remarks by the President in Eulogy for the Honorable Reverend Clementa Pinckney," 275.

125. Obama, "Remarks by the President in Eulogy for the Honorable Reverend Clementa Pinckney," 275.

126. Obama, "Remarks by the President in Eulogy for the Honorable Reverend Clementa Pinckney," 275.

127. Obama, "Remarks by the President in Eulogy for the Honorable Reverend Clementa Pinckney," 276–277.

128. Obama, "Remarks by the President in Eulogy for the Honorable Reverend Clementa Pinckney," 278–279.

129. Obama, "Remarks by the President in Eulogy for the Honorable Reverend Clementa Pinckney," 279.

130. Cynthia Roldan, "Confederate Battle Flag Controversy Renewed," *Post and Courier* (web edition), June 18, 2015.

131. Christopher Frear, Jane O'Boyle and Sel-Hill Kim, "Regional Media Framing of the Confederate Flag Debate in South Carolina," *Newspaper Research Journal* 40, no. 1 (March 2019): 94.

132. "Time to Furl the Confederate Flag," *Post and Courier* (web edition), June 21, 2015.

133. Frear, O'Boyle, and Kim, "Regional Media Framing of the Confederate Flag Debate in South Carolina," 97.

134. Frear, O'Boyle, and Kim, "Regional Media Framing of the Confederate Flag Debate in South Carolina," 97.

135. Frear, O'Boyle, and Kim, "Regional Media Framing of the Confederate Flag Debate in South Carolina," 98–99; quoted in Lydia Mattice Brandt, *The South Carolina State House Grounds* (Columbia: University of South Carolina Press, 2021), 89; Cynthia Roldan, "Haley Says She Won't Violate Law by Temporarily Removing Confederate Flag," *Post and Courier* (web edition), June 23, 2015; Cynthia Roldan, "As the Legislature Returns to Tackle the Confederate Flag, Haley Reflects on Her Decision to Call for Its Removal," *Post and Courier* (web edition), July 4, 2015.

136. Frear, O'Boyle, and Kim, "Regional Media Framing of the Confederate Flag Debate in South Carolina," 99; Cynthia Roldan and Diane Knich, "Flag's Defenders Prepare Last Stand," *Post and Courier* (web edition), July 6, 2015.

137. Cynthia Roldan, "Woman Takes Down Confederate Flag on Statehouse Grounds," *Post and Courier* (web edition), June 26, 2015; "Woman Charged with Removing Confederate Flag from State House Grounds Appears in Court," *The State*, June 28, 2015, A3; Ann Doss Helms, "The Woman on the Flagpole: Who Is the Activist Who Furled Flag," *The State*, June 29, 2015, A3; Brittney Cooper, "On the Pole for Freedom: Bree Newsome's Politics, Theory, and Theology of Resistance (June 29, 2015)," in *Charleston Syllabus: Readings on Race, Racism, and Racial Violence*, ed. Chad Williams, Kidada E. Williams, and Keisha N. Blain (Athens: University of Georgia Press, 2016), 303.

138. Cooper, "On the Pole for Freedom," 302.

139. Cooper, "On the Pole for Freedom," 304.

140. "The Confederate Flag: The Pressure Builds in Flag Debate's Final Days," *The State*, July 8, 2015, A1 and A7; "Breaking: SC House Votes to Remove," *The State*, July 9, 2015, A1 and A7; "A New Day Dawns," *The State*, July 10, 2015, A1; Cassie Cope, "Haley Signs Bill Furling Flag of Capitol Grounds," *The State,* July 10, 2015, A3 and A5; Cassie Cope and Andrew Shain, "The Flag Comes Down; SC Moves Forward," *The State*, July 11, 2015, A4; Cynthia Roldan, "Palmetto Sunrise: It's A Wrap," *Post and Courier* (web edition), July 12, 2015.

141. "A New Day Dawns," *The State*, July 10, 2015, A1; "About Poet Nikky Finney, Author of 'A New Day Dawns,'" *The State*, July 10, 2015, A2.

142. Brandt, *The South Carolina State House Grounds*, 89.

143. Hilary Green, "2 Shifting Landscapes and the Monument Removal Craze, 2015–20," *Patterns of Prejudice* 54, no. 5 (2020): 486–490; Roger C. Hartley, *Monumental Harm: Reckoning with Jim Crow Era Confederate Monuments* (Columbia: University of South Carolina Press, 2021), 127–180; Karen L. Cox, *No Common Ground: Confederate Monuments and the Ongoing Fight for Racial Justice* (Chapel Hill: University of North Carolina Press, 2021), 160–174; James Gill and Howard Hunter, *Tearing Down the Lost Cause: The Removal of New Orleans's Confederate Statues* (Jackson: University Press of Mississippi, 2021), 130–163; Margaret Edds, *What The Eyes Can't See: Ralph Northam, Black Resolve, and a Racial Reckoning in Virginia* (Columbia: University of South Carolina Press, 2021), 147–165, 202–206.

Toward Black Civil War Memory Studies: A Conclusion

1. See David W. Blight, *Race and Reunion: The Civil War in American Memory* (Cambridge, MA: Belknap Press of Harvard University Press, 2001), and Barbara Gannon, *The Won Cause: Black and White Comradeship in the Grand Army of the Republic* (Chapel Hill: University of North Carolina Press, 2011).

2. See Annette Gordon-Reed, *On Juneteenth* (New York: Liveright, 2021).

3. Michel-Rolph Trouillot, *Silencing the Past: Power and the Production of History*, with a new foreword by Hazel V. Carby (Boston: Beacon Press, 2015), 70–107.

Locating Neal, Crawford, and Gabe: An Epilogue

1. B. J. Hollars, *Opening the Doors: The Desegregation of the University of Alabama and the Fight for Civil Rights in Tuscaloosa* (Tuscaloosa: University of Alabama Press, 2013), 26–49, 86–96.

2. Faculty Senate, Minutes, March 16, 2004, and April 20, 2004, University of Alabama, Tuscaloosa, AL; Alfred Brophy, "The University and the Slaves: Apology and Its Meaning," in *The Age of Apology: Facing Up to the Past*, ed. Mark Gibney, Rhoda E. Howard-Hassmann, Jean-Marc Coicaud, and Niklaus Steiner (Philadelphia: University of Pennsylvania Press, 2008), 109–117; "The Little Round House," Historical Marker Database, https://www.hmdb.org/marker.asp?marker=25387.

3. Brophy, "The University and the Slaves: Apology and Its Meaning," 112–118; Max Clarke and Gary Alan Fine, "'A' for Apology: Slavery and the Collegiate Discourses of

Remembrance—Cases of Brown University and the University of Alabama," *History and Memory* 22, no. 1 (Spring/Summer 2010): 103–104.

4. Vincent Brown, "Mapping a Slave Revolt: Visualizing Spatial History through the Archives of Slavery," *Social Text* 125 (December 2015): 134.

5. Brundage, *The Southern Past*, 106–107, 119.

6. Marissa J. Fuentes, *Dispossessed Lives: Enslaved Women, Violence, and the Archive* (Philadelphia: University of Pennsylvania Press, 2016), 1–45; Tara McPherson, "Why Are the Digital Humanities So White? or Thinking the Histories of Race and Computation," in *Debates in the Digital Humanities*, ed. Matthew K. Gold (Minneapolis: University of Minnesota Press, 2012); Moya Z. Bailey, "All the Digital Humanists Are White, All the Nerds Are Men, but Some of Us Are Brave," *Journal of Digital Humanities* 1 (Winter 2011), http://journalofdigitalhumanities.org/1-1/all-the-digital-humanists-are-white-all-the-nerds-are-men-but-some-of-us-are-brave-by-moya-z-bailey/; Jessica Marie Johnson, "Markup Bodies: Black [Life] Studies and Slavery [Death] Studies at the Digital Crossroads," *Social Text* 137 (December 2018): 57–79.

7. James Baldwin, "Black English: A Dishonest Argument," in *The Cross of Redemption: Uncollected Writings*, ed. Randall Kenan (New York: Pantheon Books, 2010), 125.

8. See James Sellers, *History of the University of Alabama*, vol. 1: *1818–1902* (Tuscaloosa: University of Alabama Press, 1953); Alfred L. Brophy, *The University, Court, and Slave: Pro-Slavery Thought in Southern Colleges and Courts and the Coming of the Civil War* (New York: Oxford University Press, 2016); A. James Fuller, *Chaplain to the Confederacy: Basil Manly and Baptist Life in the Old South* (Baton Rouge: Louisiana State University Press, 2000); Robert Oliver Mellown, *The University of Alabama: A Guide to the Campus and Its Architecture* (Tuscaloosa: University of Alabama Press, 2013).

9. L. C. Garland, A Slave Pass for Gabe and Neal, Mrs. H. W. Watson, June 15, 1863, 387 in Letterbook of Landon Cabell Garland President of University of Alabama, 1855–1865, vol.1: 1862–1863; L. C. Garland to Mrs. N. J. Watson, October 21, 1863, 75; L. C. Garland to General McIver, October 30, 1863, 86–89, and L. C. Garland to Mrs. N. J. Watson, November 27, 1863, 146, in Letterbook of Landon Cabell Garland President of University of Alabama, 1855–1865, vol. 2, pt. 1, 1863–1864, in the Landon Cabell Garland letters, W. S. Hoole Special Collections, University of Alabama, Tuscaloosa, AL.

10. Appropriation and expenditures for Quartermaster's Dept., contingent fund, subsistence dept., servants fund, library fund, chemical fund, general assessment fund, salary of teachers, accounts of students, expenses of cadets in state, 1861–1863, Early Administrative Records RG 1, W. S. Hoole Special Collections, Tuscaloosa, Alabama.

11. Bennett Burks, Report of the Superintendent of Defenses, 1864, Early Administrative Records RG 1, box 3, folder 96.

12. "List of Boarding Students," January 8, 1861, Early Administrative Records RG 1, box 1, folder 20; Mellown, *The University of Alabama*, 57–58.

13. L. C. Garland to Gov. Watts, September 3, 1864, 74–75, in Letterbook of Landon Cabell Garland President of University of Alabama, 1855–1865, vol. 3, pt. 1, 1863–1864.

14. *The Corolla, 1893–2014*, W. S. Hoole Special Collections, University of Alabama, Tuscaloosa, AL. The 1913, 1923, and 1961 *Corolla* covers feature the Little Round House/Guardhouse. As a peer institution, the University of Mississippi yearbooks also proved

instrumental in advancing Lost Cause logics under the guise of campus traditions before desegregation. After desegregation, the yearbooks reveal the malleability and persistence of Confederate rhetoric. See Stephen M. Monroe, *Heritage and Hate: Old South Rhetoric at Southern Universities* (Tuscaloosa: University of Alabama Press, 2021), 25–57.

15. *Corolla 1912*, vol. 20, 304.

16. *Corolla 1894*, vol. 2, 64–70; *Corolla 1902*, vol. 10, 211–214; *Corolla 1927*, vol. 34.

17. *Corolla 1930*, vol. 37, 98; *Corolla 1948*, vol. 56, 18; *Corolla 1966*, vol. 74, 278, 326, 329.

18. "In Memory of Ed," *Corolla 1908*, vol. 16, 173; "Memorial Day Observance at Greenwood Cemetery," *Tuscaloosa News,* April 27, 1907, 2; "Death of Ed Gould, An Old and Well Liked Darkey Passes Away," *Tuscaloosa News,* April 7, 1908, 7; M. H. J., "Old Dan Spencer," *Corolla 1900*, vol. 8, 166–167.

19. Ormond O. Black, "Campus of Alabama Abounds with Remains of Old University in Mound, Guard House, Bowlder, Observatory," *Crimson White*, September 27, 1923, 1.

20. "UDC Monument to Be Dedicated in May," *Crimson White*, May 6, 1914, 1; "Honorary Degrees Given to Old Confederate Cadets," *Crimson White*, May 13, 1914, 1; "1912 Class Memorial," *Crimson White*, May 13, 1914, 1; Alabama Division, United Daughters of the Confederacy, *Minutes of the Eighteenth Annual Convention. Alabama Division United Daughters of the Confederacy Held at Tuscaloosa, Alabama, May 13, 14, 15, 1914. Organized in Montgomery, April 30, 1897. Mrs. L. M. Bashinsky, President, Mrs. E. M. Trimble, Secretary* (Opelika: Post, 1914), 9, clipping, Alabama Division, United Daughters of the Confederacy, *History of the Alabama Division of the United Daughters of the Confederacy* (1937), 339–340, clipping; accessed in W. S. Hoole Special Collections; R. E. Rodes UDC Chapter, *Yearbook of the R. E. Rodes Chapter United Daughters of the Confederacy, 1933–1934* (Tuscaloosa, AL), in Author's Personal Collection. The author purchased this Lost Cause artifact in a Tuscaloosa antique store.

21. "The Jasons," *Corolla 1915*, vol. 22, 171; Mellown, *The University of Alabama*, 60; Starting with the *Corolla 1938*, students commonly refer to the Little Round House/Guardhouse as Jason's Shrine. See *Corolla 1938*, vol. 46, 18, 74.

22. Bessie Leach Hayden, "Biography of James Austin Anderson," December 11, 1951, and James A. Anderson, "Military History of the University of Alabama, speech before the Alabama State Convention of the Reserve Officers of the United States at the University of Alabama, May 3, 1941," 3, in James Austin Anderson Papers, University of Alabama Libraries Digital Collections, Tuscaloosa, AL.

23. See James Austin Anderson, "Major Caleb Huse, The Forgotten Man of the University of Alabama and the Southern Confederacy, ca. 1930, "Transcription, University of Alabama's Military History Broadcast via WJRD radio, read by James A. Anderson," April 21, 1941, and James Austin Anderson, "Speech Given to Tuscaloosa Study Club," March 30, 1940, in the James Austin Anderson Papers.

24. Sellers, *History of the University of Alabama*, 282–284.

25. Thomas P. Clinton, James A. Anderson, and Samuel Williamson John, The Federal Invasion of Tuscaloosa, 1865. Compiled by Matthew W. Clinton (1965; Tuscaloosa, 2015) in author's personal collection.

26. Hollars, *Opening the Doors,* 31–33; Robert J. Cook, *Troubled Commemoration: The American Civil War Centennial, 1961–1965* (Baton Rouge: Louisiana State University Press, 2007), 71, 79–83; Albert B. Moore, *Reasons for the National Centennial Commemoration of the Civil War: Its Basic Objectives and Potential Values* (Tuscaloosa: Alabama Civil War Centennial Commission, 1963); and Albert B. Moore and Alabama Civil War Centennial Commission, *Alabama Civil War Centennial: Manual for Alabamians* (Montgomery: Alabama Civil War Centennial Commission, 1960), in author's personal collection.

27. "Cover," *Corolla 1961.*

28. "Dedication," *Corolla 1961,* 7.

29. "Student Life," *Corolla 1961,* 35–38.

30. Hollars, *Opening the Doors,* 86–113.

31. R. E. Rodes UDC Chapter, *Yearbook of 1933–1934.*

32. Reconstruction Letters, Early Administrative Records RG 1, box 3, folder 86; Benjamin H. Barnes, "Professor Jeremiah Barnes," *Tuscaloosa News,* May 29, 1916, 6; "Clabe Garland, A Respected Colored Citizen, Departed for that Undiscovered Country," *Tuscaloosa Times Weekly,* July 9, 1891, 1; "Mortgage Sale," *Tuscaloosa Weekly Times,* April 27, 1892, 3; "Emancipation Celebration and Patriotic Meeting," *Tuscaloosa News,* December 28, 1917, 6; Zadie Jones, "Life Story of Pioneers of Negro Education as Told by Relative," *Alabama Citizen,* February 27, 1954, 2.

33. Karen L. Cox, *Dixie's Daughters: The United Daughters of the Confederacy and the Preservation of Confederate Culture.* New Perspectives on the History of the South. (Gainesville: University Press of Florida, 2003), 49.

34. Rochelle Riley, ed., *The Burden: African Americans and the Enduring Impact of Slavery* (Detroit: Wayne State University Press, 2018), 6.

35. The University of Alabama System Board of Trustees, UA President Stuart Bell, and Chancellor Finis St. John, "Joint Statement Regarding Plaque Removals at UA and Formation of Building Names Review Committee," June 8, 2020, University of Alabama System Office, Tuscaloosa, AL.

36. Stephanie Taylor, "University of Alabama Removes Confederate Monument," *Tuscaloosa News,* June 9, 2020; Grace Schepis, "Board of Trustees Rename the Ferg, Moore Hall," *Crimson White,* September 17, 2021, https://thecrimsonwhite.com/82852/news/board-of-trustees-rename-the-ferg-moore-hall/; Brian Lyman, "University of Alabama Will Take Klansman's Name Off Building, Now Named for Civil Rights Hero," *Montgomery Advertiser,* February 11, 2022, https://www.montgomeryadvertiser.com/story/news/2022/02/11/university-alabama-take-klansmans-name-off-building-named-civil-rights-hero/6742689001/.

37. As part of the Hallowed Ground Project, I have published several publications that contribute to the growing interdisciplinary field of Critical Universities Studies. These publications reflect the tension between institutional assessment of scholarly production and personal responsibility to community needs. By community, I mean the intersecting communities in which I find myself—a professor to students and descendants who desire this knowledge, a former Tuscaloosa resident, and scholar. See Hilary Green, "The

Burden of the University of Alabama's Hallowed Grounds," *Public Historian* 42, no. 4 (November 2020): 28–40; Hilary Green, "The Hallowed Grounds Tour: Revising and Reimagining Landscapes of Race and Slavery at the University of Alabama," in *Segregation and Resistance in America's Urban Landscapes*, ed. Thaisa Way and Eric Avila (Washington, DC: Dumbarton Oaks Press, Trustees for Harvard University, 2023), 297–323; Hilary Green, "The Slave Cemetery and Apology Marker at the University of Alabama," in *Final Resting Places: Reflections on the Meaning of Civil War Graves*, ed. Brian Jordan and Jonathan White (Athens: University of Georgia Press, 2023), 248–256.

Bibliography

Manuscript Collections

W. S. Hoole Special Collections, University of Alabama, Tuscaloosa, AL

The Corolla, 1893–2014.
James Austin Anderson Papers.
Landon Cabell Garland letters.
University of Alabama Early Administrative Records RG 1.
VF—Alabama Division, United Daughters of the Confederacy.

Department of Special Collections, Stanford University Libraries, Stanford University, Stanford, CA

MSS Misc 0421, Joseph R. Winters, Songs: broadsides, c. 1881–1912.

Library of Congress, Washington, DC

Frederick Douglass papers.
"Emancipation Day Celebration in Richmond," photograph, 1905.
Proceedings of the Twenty Seventh Annual Encampment, Department of Virginia and North Carolina. Grand Army of the Republic. Held at the Court House, Elizabeth City, North Carolina, April 27, 1898. Hampton, VA: N. S. Press, Printer and Binders, 1898.

National Archives, Washington, DC

Correspondence and Reports Relating to Federal Citizens, Clerks, and Sutlers Confined in Castle Thunder Prison, RG 249 Records of the Commissary General of Prisoners, box 1, NM 68 131

National Archives at Atlanta, Morrow, GA

Records of the Field Offices for the State of Virginia, Bureau of Refugees, Freedmen, and Abandoned Lands, 1865-1872, M1913. Washington, DC: National Archives and Records Administration, 2006.

Amistad Research Center, Tulane University, New Orleans, LA

American Missionary Association Papers.

Special Collections and University Archives, University of Massachusetts Amherst Libraries, Amherst, MA

City Twenty One (Harrisburg, PA), Dedication of Memorial to William Howard Day program, May 30, 1950, accessed in W. E. B. Du Bois Papers (MS 312).

Massachusetts State Archives, Boston, MA

Michael S. Dukakis, "Remarks of Governor Michael S. Dukakis, Commonwealth of Massachusetts, Memorial Day Ceremonies, National Cemetery, Beaufort, South Carolina," speech, May 29, 1989, GO11/series 10. Speech files, Dukakis, Box 1, May 29, 1989, Memorial Day Ceremony, Beaufort, SC.

Mindy S. Lubber, Press Secretary, "Dukakis Leads Memorial Day Ceremony Honoring Black Civil War Solders," a news release from the Office of Governor Michael S. Dukakis, May 26, 1989, GO11/series 10. Speech files, Dukakis, Box 1, May 29, 1989, Memorial Day Ceremony, Beaufort, SC.

Charles Barnard Fox, *Record of the Service of the Fifty-Fifth Regiment of Massachusetts Volunteer Infantry. Printed for the Regimental Association.* Cambridge, MA: John Wilson and Son, 1868.

George J. Mitchell Department of Special Collections and Archives, Bowdoin College Library, Brunswick, ME

Oliver Otis Howard Papers, 1832–1912.

Southern Historical Collection, The Wilson Library, University of North Carolina at Chapel Hill, Chapel Hill, NC

Julian S. Carr, "Unveiling of Confederate Monument at University. June 2, 1913," in the Julian Shakespeare Carr Papers #141.

David M. Rubenstein Rare Book & Manuscript Library, Duke University, Durham, NC

Samuel Nickless, "The New Version of the Colored Volunteer," American Song Sheets collection.

ECSU Archives, Elizabeth City State University, Elizabeth City, NC

P. W. Moore Collection.

State Archives of North Carolina, Raleigh, NC

North Carolina Freedman's Savings and Trust Company Records
Whedbee Freedmen Papers, 1854–1882.

New York Public Library Digital Collections, New York, NY

L. Fayette Sykes, *Garfield and Arthur Republican Campaign Song Book, 1880.* New York: Republican Central Campaign Club of New York, 1880.

Western Reserve Historical Society, Cleveland, OH

W. E. B. Du Bois, "The World of William Howard Day," May 30, 1950, typewritten copy
  of speech made at the dedication of the marker erected over the grave of William
  Howard Day on May 30, 1950, in the Lincoln Cemetery, Penbrook, PA.

Franklin County Historical Society, Chambersburg, PA

VF—African Americans.
VF—Joseph Winters.
Marotte, M. L., III. *The Story of Joseph Winters, 1816–1916: Citizen, Pioneer, Inventor, Gun-
  smith, Machinist, Land Owner, and Born a Free Man*. Chambersburg: M. L. Marotte
  III, 1999.
Ruffin, C. Bernard. "An All-American Town: An Oral History of the African American
  Community of Franklin County, Pennsylvania." Unpublished manuscript, 2010. Ac-
  cessed at the Franklin County Historical Society, Chambersburg, PA.
Ruffin, C. Bernard. "This Is My Story: An Oral History of African American Commu-
  nity of Chambersburg, PA." Unpublished manuscript, n.d. Accessed at the Franklin
  County Historical Society, Chambersburg, PA.

Gettysburg National Park Library and Research Center, Gettysburg, PA

Major Charles Blacknall, 23rd NC Infantry to brother George, June 18, 1863, printed in the
  (NC) Carolina Watchman, July 13, 1863, 2, Gettysburg Library File V7-NC23.

Dauphin County Historical Society, Harrisburg, PA

William Howard Day—VF
Thomas Morris Morris—VF
Reception of Colored Troops, Nov. 14, 1865—VF.
Mealy, Todd. *Aliened American: A Biography of William Howard Day, 1825–1865*, volume
  1. Baltimore: Publish America, 2010.

Pennsylvania Historical and Museum Commission, Harrisburg, PA

Pennsylvania Historical Marker Program.
A Gathering at the Crossroads monument photograph.

Pennsylvania State Archives, Harrisburg, PA

RG-2, Damage Claims Applicants for Cumberland and Franklin Counties
Simon Cameron Papers, 1824–ca. 1919.
Ron Gancas, *Fields of Freedom: United States Colored Troops from Southwestern Pennsyl-
  vania*. Soldiers and Sailors Memorial Hall and Trust, 2004.
MG-379 State Fencibles Collection, Scrapbooks,1813–1926.
Charles L. Blockson, Afro American Collection, Temple University, Philadelphia, PA.
Winters, Joseph R. documents.

Stephen Foster Collection, University of Pittsburgh Digital Collections, Pittsburgh, PA

Republican Congressional Committee, *Garfield and Arthur Campaign Song Book*. Washington, DC: Republican Congressional Committee, 1880.

Shippensburg Historical Society, Shippensburg, PA

Black Veterans Binder: Mil Civ Black, Shippensburg Historical Society, October 1960), n.p.

Historic Site Report for Locust Grove Cemetery Shippensburg, Pennsylvania, October 20, 2007.

Special Collections—South Carolina Historical Society Archives, College of Charleston, Charleston, SC

African American, cemeteries, 30-21-10, vertical file.

African American, slavery monuments, 30-21-4A, vertical file.

Events, Civil War Sesquicentennial Commemoration, 30-11-12, vertical file.

SC History – Battles, Fort Wagner, 30-11-6W, vertical file.

SC History, H.L. Hunley, 30-12-225, vertical file.

Special Collections, Albert and Shirley Small Collections Library, University of Virginia, Charlottesville, VA

Photograph of Grand Army of the Republic Reunion of African Americans, 1910.

Detail! Victory! Victory!!! We celebrate the fall of Richmond, April 3d, 1865, broadside, Elizabeth Cocke Coles Fund (Broadside 1865, V53).

Philena Carkin, "Reminiscences of my Life and Work among the Freedmen of Charlottesville, Virginia, from March 1, 1866, to July 1, 1875.

Robert Larimer, Diary, 1865, MSS 38-129.

Clara Shafer, Diary 1865.

Diary of Benson J. Lossing, manuscript, 1865 April 12–May 2.

Henry Chapin, Letter to his father, April 26, 1865.

Edward A. Wild, Letter to Edward W. Kinsley, November 19, 1863.

Robert Hutson Milroy, "Freedom to Slaves," January 5, 1863.

Concert of Negro Music Composed and Rendered Exclusively by Colored Musicians Carnegie Hall Lincoln's Birthday, February 12, 1913, at 8.15 in Commemoration of the 50th Anniversary of the Emancipation Proclamation.

C. H. Perkins' Celebrated Colored Virginia and Texas Jubilee Singers of Norfolk, Va., and Waco Texas Will Give One of their Pleasing Concerts, broadside.

John Gilmer Letters, 1861, 1867.

Letter from Malcolm N. Fleming, manuscript, 1864 August 10, MSS 38-651.

J. E. B. Stuart to Robert E. Lee, October 12, 1862.

Addresses of the Hon. W. D. Kelley, Miss Anna E Dickinson, and Mr. Frederick Douglass, at a Mass Meeting held at National Hall, Philadelphia, July 6, 1863, for the Promotion of Colored Enlistments.

Virginia Historical Society, Richmond, VA

"Notice! The Colored People of the city of Richmond would most respectfully inform the public, that they do not intend to celebrate the failure of the Southern confederacy . . . ," broadside, Richmond, VA, April 2, 1866.

Read Family Papers, 1828–1914.

Published Primary Sources

Adams, John Quincy. *Narrative of the Life of John Quincy Adams, When in Slavery, and Now as a Freeman*. Harrisburg, PA: Sieg, Printer and Stationer, 1872.

Alexander, Kianna. *Carolina Built: A Novel*. New York: Gallery Books, 2022.

Bates, Samuel P., and J. Fraise Richard. *History of Franklin County, Pennsylvania: Containing a History of the County, its Townships, Towns, Villages, Schools, Churches, Industries, etc.; Portraits of Early Settlers and Prominent men; Biographies; History of Pennsylvania, Statistical and Miscellaneous Matter, etc.* Chicago: Warner Beers, 1887.

Bell, L. A. *Celebration by the Colored People's Educational Monument Association in Memory of Abraham Lincoln, on the Fourth of July, 1865, in the Presidential Grounds, Washington, DC. Printed by Order of the Board of Directors. L. A. Bell, Recording Secretary*. Washington, DC: McGill and Witherow, Printers and Stereotypers, 1865.

Bradley, David. *The Chaneysville Incident*. New York, 1981.

Brown, William Wells. *The Negro in the American Rebellion: His Heroism and His Fidelity*. Boston: Lee and Shepard, 1867.

Christian, Royal A., and Pellom McDaniels III, eds. *Porter, Steward, Citizen: An African American's Memoir of World War I*. New York: Oxford University Press, 2017.

Clarke, William P. *Official History of the Militia and the National Guard of the State of Pennsylvania from the Earliest Period of Record to the Present Time*. Philadelphia: Captain Charles J. Hendler, 1909.

Clifford, Carrie Williams. *Race Rhymes*. Washington, DC: R. L. Pendleton, 1911.

Clifford, Carrie Williams. *Widening Light*. Boston: Walter Reid, 1922.

Cochran, Thomas E. *Address delivered at McSherrysville, Lower Chanceford Twp., York County, Pennsylvania, on the fourth day of July, 1865, by Thomas E. Cochran*. Lancaster: Pearsol & Geist, Printers, 1865.

Cooper, Anna Julia. *A Voice from the South: By a Black Woman of the South*. Xenia, OH: Aldine Printing House, 1892. https://docsouth.unc.edu/church/cooper/cooper.html.

Douglass, Frederick. *The Life and Times of Frederick Douglass, Written by Himself: His Early Life as a Slave, His Escape from Bondage, and His Complete History*. Boston: DeWolfe, 1892.

Douglass, Frederick. "Self-Made Men," Speech, 1872. In *Frederick Douglass Heritage The Official Website*. http://www.frederick-douglass-heritage.org/self-made-men/, accessed on May 28, 2022.

Dunbar, Paul Laurence. "The Colored Soldiers." In *African American Poetry (1870–1927): A Digital Anthology*, edited by Amardeep Singh (Bethlehem, PA: Lehigh University, 2023). https://scalar.lehigh.edu/african-american-poetry-a-digital-anthology/paul-laurence-dunbar-the-colored-soldiers-1895.

Early, Jubal Anderson. *Lieutenant General Jubal Anderson Early C.S.A.: Autobiographical Sketch and Narrative of the War Between the States with notes by R. H. Early.* Philadelphia: J. B. Lippincott, 1912.

Emilio, Luis F. *The Assault on Fort Wagner, July 18, 1865, the Memorable Charge of the Fifty-fourth Regiment of Massachusetts Volunteers, Written for "The Springfield Republican."* Boston: Rand Avery, 1887.

Fields, Mamie Garvin. *Lemon Swamp and Other Places: A Carolina Memoir.* New York: Free Press, 1983.

Finney, Nikky. *Love Child's Hotbed of Occasional Poetry.* Evanston, IL: TriQuarterly Books/Northwestern University Press, 2020.

Frazier, Charles. *Cold Mountain: A Novel.* New York: Atlantic Monthly Press, 1997.

Fremantle, Sir Arthur James Lyon. *Three Months in the Southern States: April, June 1863 by Lieut-Col. Fremantle, Coldstream Guards.* Mobile: S. H. Goetzel, 1864.

Garfield, James A. "James A. Garfield's Letter Accepting the 1880 Republican Presidential Nomination." James A. Garfield National Historic Site, National Park Services. https://www.nps.gov/articles/000/james-a-garfield-s-letter-accepting-the-1880-republican-presidential-nomination.htm.

Garnet League. *Ceremonies at the Reception of Welcome to the Colored Soldiers of Pennsylvania, in the City of Harrisburg, Nov. 14th, 1865, by the Garnet League; together with the report of the Committee of Arrangements, and Resolutions of Vindication by the Garnet League, defending its position with reference to the Pennsylvania State Equal Rights League.* Harrisburg: Telegraph Steam Book, 1866.

Gordon, John B. *Reminiscences of the Civil War.* New York: Charles Scribner's Sons, 1904.

Grant, Ulysses S. *The Papers of Ulysses S. Grant,* vol. 16: *1866.* Edited by John Y. Simon. Carbondale: Southern Illinois Press, 1988.

Grimes, Bryan. *Extracts of Letters of Major-Gen'l Bryan Grimes to His Wife: Written While in Active Service in the Army of Northern Virginia. Together with some Personal Recollections of the War, Written by Him after its Close, etc. Bryan Grimes Compiled from original manuscripts by Pulaski Cowper.* Raleigh, NC: E. Broughton,1883.

Haley, Alex. "The Black Scholar Interviews: Alex Haley." *Black Scholar* 8, no. 1 (September 1976): 33–40.

Harper, Frances E. W. "The Massachusetts Fifty-Fourth." *Anglo-African,* October 10, 1863.

Hoke, Jacob. *Historical Reminiscences of the War: Incidents Which Transpired in and about Chambersburg, During the War of the Rebellion.* Chambersburg, PA: M. A. Foltz, Printer and Publisher, 1884.

Hood, James Walker. *One Hundred Years of the African Methodist Episcopal Zion Church; or, The Centennial of African Methodism.* New York: A.M.E. Zion Book Concern, 1895.

Jackson Giles B., and Daniel Webster Davis. *The Industrial History of the Negro Race of the United States.* Richmond: Virginia Press, 1908.

Jackson, Rev. John Walker. "A Pastor Recalls the Gettysburg Campaign." *Annals of Eastern Pennsylvania: Journal of the Historical Society of the Eastern Pennsylvania Conference* (2006): 57–63.

Johnson, Andrew. *The Papers of Andrew Johnson*, vol. 9, September 1865–January 1866. Edited by Paul H. Bergeron. Knoxville: University of Tennessee Press, 1991.

Johnson, Andrew. *The Papers of Andrew Johnson*, vol. 10, February–July 1866. Edited by Paul H. Bergeron. Knoxville: University of Tennessee Press, 1992.

Johnson, James Weldon. "Lift Every Voice and Sing." 1900. *Poetry Foundation*. https://www.poetryfoundation.org/poems/46549/lift-every-voice-and-sing.

Johnson, James Weldon. *Fifty Years and Other Poems*. Boston: Cornhill, 1917.

Johnston, David E. *The Story of a Confederate Boy in the Civil War*. Portland, OR: Glass and Prudhomme, 1914.

Leon, Louis. *Diary of a Tar Heel Confederate Soldier*. Charlotte, NC: Stone Publishing Company, 1913.

McBride, James. *The Good Lord Bird: A Novel*. New York: Riverhead Books, 2013.

McGill, Joseph, Jr., and Herb Frazier. *Sleeping with the Ancestors: How I Followed the Footprints of Slavery*. New York: Hachette Books, 2023.

Morrison, Toni. *Beloved*. 1987. New York: Vintage Books, 2004.

Mosby, John Singleton. *The Memoirs of Colonel John S. Mosby, Edited by Charles Wells Russell with Illustrations*. Boston: Little, Brown, 1917.

Nead, Benjamin Matthias. *Waynesboro: The History of a Settlement in the County Formerly Called Cumberland, but later Franklin, in the Commonwealth of Pennsylvania, in its Beginnings, Through its Growth into a Village and Borough, to its Centennial Period, and to the Close of the Present Century, Including a Relation of Pertinent Topics of General State and County history*. Harrisburg: Harrisburg Publishing Company, 1900.

North Carolina Freedman's Savings and Trust Company Records. Abstracted by Bill Reaves. Raleigh, NC: North Carolina Genealogical Society, 1992.

Obama, Barack. Establishment of the Reconstruction Era National Monument by the President of the United States of America: A Proclamation, January 12, 2017. https://obamawhitehouse.archives.gov/the-press-office/2017/01/12/presidential-proclamations-establishment-reconstruction-era-national.

Obama, Barack. "Remarks by the President in Eulogy for the Honorable Reverend Clementa Pinckney, College of Charleston, Charleston, South Carolina (June 29, 2015)." In *Charleston Syllabus: Readings on Race, Racism, and Racial Violence*, edited by Chad Williams, Kidada E. Williams, and Keisha N. Blain, 273–279. Athens: University of Georgia Press, 2016.

Shaara, Michael. *The Killer Angels*. 1974. New York: Ballantine Books, 1987.

Sykes, L. Fayette. *Garfield and Arthur Republican Campaign Song Book, 1880*. New York: Republican Central Campaign Club of New York, 1880.

Taylor, Susie King. *Reminiscences of My Life in Camp With the 3rd United States Colored Troops Late 1st S.C. Volunteers*. Boston: Self-Published, 1902.

Union Republican Congressional Committee. *National Republican Grant and Wilson Song-Book*. Washington, DC: Union Republican Congressional Committee, 1872.

Union Republican Congressional Committee. *Hayes & Wheeler Song Book*. Washington, DC: Union Republican Congressional Committee, 1876.

Washington, John E. *They Knew Lincoln*. With a new introduction by Kate Masur. New York: Oxford University Press, 2018.

Wilson, Joseph T. *The Black Phalanx: A History of the Negro Soldiers of the United States in the War of Independence, the War of 1812 and the Civil War*. Hartford, CT: American Publishing Company, 1888.

Wilson, Woodrow. *The Papers of Woodrow Wilson*, vol. 25. Edited by Arthur S. Link. Princeton, NJ: Princeton University Press, 1978.

Wilson, Woodrow. *The Papers of Woodrow Wilson*, vol. 34. Edited by Arthur S. Link. Princeton, NJ: Princeton University Press, 1985.

Woodson, Carter G. "My Recollections of Veterans of the Civil War." *Negro History Bulletin* 7, no. 5 (February 1944): 103–104, 115–118.

Author's Personal Collection

"M. F. Wyckoff and Unidentified African American boy." Photograph, n.p., 1890.

"No. 119, Negro Building, Jamestown Exposition of 1907." Official souvenir Jamestown Ter-Centennial postcard, 1907.

"Unidentified African American girl and women." Jamestown Ter-Centennial souvenir photograph, Norfolk, 1907, tintype in embossed paper mat.

Dorothy Spruill Redford papers.

Interview with Barbara Lane Hill, July 6, 2016.

Interview with Millicent Lowman Green, July 6, 2016.

Interview with Millicent Lowman Green, April 8, 2022.

Moore, Albert B. *Reasons for the National Centennial Commemoration of the Civil War; Its Basic Objectives and Potential Values*. Tuscaloosa: Alabama Civil War Centennial Commission, 1963.

Moore, Albert B., and Alabama Civil War Centennial Commission. *Alabama Civil War Centennial: Manual for Alabamians*. Montgomery, Alabama Civil War Centennial Commission, 1960.

Photograph of author, brother, and grandmother. Waynesboro, PA. c. 1983.

R. E. Rodes UDC Chapter, *Yearbook of the R. E. Rodes Chapter United Daughters of the Confederacy, 1933–1934*. Tuscaloosa, AL.

Thomas P. Clinton, James A. Anderson, Samuel Williamson John, The Federal Invasion of Tuscaloosa, 1865. Compiled by Matthew W. Clinton. 1965. Tuscaloosa, 2015s.

Newspapers and Periodicals

Adams County News (Gettysburg, PA)
Afro-American Sentinel
Al.com
Alabama Citizen (Tuscaloosa, AL)
The Anderson Independent-Mail (Anderson, SC)
Anglo-African
The Atlanta Constitution
Baltimore Sun
The Beaufort Gazette (Beaufort, SC)
The Boston Globe

Broad Ax (Chicago, IL)
Carlisle Evening Herald
Charlotte Observer
Charleston City Paper
Charleston Daily News
Chatham Record
Chicago Tribune
The Christian Recorder
Cleveland Daily Leader
Cleveland Gazette
The Collegian (Richmond, VA)
The Columbia Record (Columbia, SC)
Crimson White (Tuscaloosa, AL)
Daily Alta California
Daily National Intelligencer (Washington, DC)
Daily Phoenix
The Daily Picayune
Denver Star
Edgefield Advertiser
Evening Star (Washington, DC)
Evening Union (Washington, DC)
The Evening News (Harrisburg, PA).
Frank Leslie's Illustrated Newspaper
Franklin Repository
Freeman (Indianapolis)
The Freemont Journal
The Greenville News (Greenville, SC)
Harrisburg Daily Independent
Harrisburg Telegraph
Harper's Weekly
The Herald and News (Newberry, SC)
Herald and Torch Light (Hagerstown, MD)
Herald Sun (Durham, NC)
Index-Journal (Greenwood, SC)
Industrial Advocate (Richmond, VA)
Intelligencer Journal (Lancaster, PA)
The Item (Sumter, SC)
The Jeffersonian (Stroudsburg, PA)
The Island Packet (Hilton Head, SC)
L'Union
The Lexington Gazette
The Liberator
Los Angeles Times
The Meadville Tribune

The Messenger and Intelligencer (Wadesboro, NC)
Muskogee Cimeter (Muskogee, Indian Territory, Oklahoma)
The National Tribune
New Journal and Guide (Norfolk, VA)
New Orleans Tribune
New York Age
New York Daily Tribune
New York Freeman
New York Herald
New York Times
News and Observer (Raleigh, NC)
The News-Chronicle (Shippensburg, PA)
The North Carolinian
Oakland Sunshine (Oakland, CA)
Pacific Appeal
Patriot and Union
Patriot (Harrisburg, PA)
PennLive.com
People's Register (Chambersburg, PA)
The Philadelphia Inquirer
Pilot (Greencastle, PA)
Pittsburgh Press
Plain Dealer
Portland New Age
Post and Courier (Charleston, SC)
Press (Philadelphia, PA)
Public Opinion (Chambersburg, PA)
Public Weekly Opinion (Chambersburg, PA)
Raleigh Farmer and Mechanic
Reno Gazette-Journal
Richmond Dispatch
Richmond Planet
Richmond Times-Dispatch
Richmond Whig
Sacramento Daily Union
St. Louis Post-Dispatch
San Francisco Bulletin
Scranton Tribune
Savannah Tribune
Scranton Tribune
The Sentinel
Shippensburg News
The Southern Watchman (Tuskegee, AL)
Star and Enterprise (Newville, PA)

The State (Columbia, SC)
State Journal (Harrisburg, PA)
Staunton Spectator
The Sun
The Sun News (Myrtle Beach, SC)
Sunbury American (Sunbury, PA)
Tar Heel (Elizabeth City, NC)
Times-Dispatch (Richmond, VA)
Times and Democrat (Orangeburg, SC)
Tuscaloosa News
The Tuscaloosa Times-Gazette
Uplift (Pittsburg, Kansas)
US News and World Report
Valley Spirit
Village Record
Washington Bee
Washington Herald
Washington Post

State and Federal Government Documents

Lane, Joseph, pension file. Twenty-Second, USCT, Department of Veterans Affairs. Washington, DC. Released under a Freedom of Information Act to the author who is a direct descendant.

Legg, James B., and Steven D. Smith. *"The Best Ever Occupied . . ." Archaeological Investigations of a Civil War Encampment on Folly Island, South Carolina."* South Carolina Institute of Archaeology and Anthropology Research Manuscript Series 209. Columbia: South Carolina Institute of Archaeology and Anthropology, 1989.

North Carolina Department of Archives and History. "John Beaver and Dot Redford Retire." *Carolina Comments* 56, no. 4 (October 2008): 121–122.

North Carolina Department of Archives and History. "Civil War Programming at State Historic Sites." *Carolina Comments* 59, no. 2 (April 2011): 21.

North Carolina Department of Archives and History. *"Freedom, Sacrifice, Memory*: Civil War Sesquicentennial Photo Exhibit to Tour the State." *Carolina Comments* 59, no. 2 (April 2011): 10.

North Carolina Department of Archives and History. "African American Heritage Commission Recognizes Black History Month. *Carolina Comments* 59, no. 2 (April 2011): 7–8.

North Carolina Department of Archives and History, "Milestone for Marker Program," *Carolina Comments* 59, no. 2 (April 2011): 14–16.

Pennsylvania Superintendent of Solders' Orphans. *Annual Report of the Pennsylvania Commission of Soldiers' Orphan Schools for the Year Ending May 31, 1905.* Harrisburg, PA: Harrisburg Publishing Co., State Printer, 1906.

Pennsylvania Superintendent of Solders' Orphans. *Annual Report of the Pennsylvania Commission of Soldiers' Orphan Schools for the Year Ending May 31, 1907.* Harrisburg, PA: Harrisburg Publishing Co., State Printer, 1908.

Sutton, Robert K, ed. *Rally on the High Ground: The National Park Service Symposium on the Civil War*. Washington, DC: National Park Service, 2001. http://npshistory.com/series/symposia/rally_high_ground/index.htm.

United States Census Office. *Eleventh Census of the United States, 1890: Schedules Enumerating Union Veterans and Widows of Union Veterans of the Civil War, North Carolina, Bundles 119–123*, microfilm, Washington, DC: National Archives, 1948.

United States War Department. *The War of the Rebellion: A Compilation of the Official Records of the Union and Confederate Armies*, the *Official Records*. Washington, DC: Government Printing Office, 1880–1901.

University of Alabama Faculty Senate. Minutes, March 16, 2004, and April 20, 2004. University of Alabama, Tuscaloosa, AL.

The University of Alabama System Board of Trustees, UA President Stuart Bell and Chancellor Finis St. John. "Joint statement regarding plaque removals at UA and formation of Building Names Review Committee," June 8, 2020. University of Alabama System Office, Tuscaloosa, AL.

West Virginia. *Biennial Report of the Adjutant General of the State of West Virginia for the Years 1889 and 1890*. Charleston, WV: Moses W. Donnally, Public Printer, 1890.

Legal Documents

Amici Curiae: David W. Blight and Gaines M. Foster (Adam L. Sorensen; Joseph R. Palmore; Morrison & Foerster, on brief), in support of appellees and Amici Curiae: Professors Thomas J. Brown, W. Fitzhugh Brundage, Karen L. Cox, Hilary N. Green, Kirk Savage, and Dell Upton (Blake E. Stafford; Christine C. Smith; Briana M. Clark; Latham & Watkins, on brief), in support of appellees in Supreme Court of Virginia Counsel in Case Decided September 2, 2021.

Helen Marie Taylor et al. v. Ralph S. Northam et al. Record No. 210113, Counsel in Decided Cases, Supreme Court of Virginia, Richmond, Virginia. http://www.courts.state.va.us/courts/scv/counsel.pdf.

Helen Marie Taylor et al. v. Ralph S. Northam et al. Record No. 210113 (September 2, 2021) and William C. Gregory v. Ralph S. Northam et al, Record No. 201307 order (September 2, 2021) in Supreme Court of Virginia Opinions and Published Orders, Supreme Court of Virginia, Richmond, Virginia. http://www.courts.state.va.us/scndex.htm.

Digital Humanities Projects and Collections

Gerhard Peters and John T. Woolley, The American Presidency Project, UC Santa Barbara, Santa Barbara, CA. https://www.presidency.ucsb.edu.

Democratic Party Platforms, 1880 Democratic Party Platform.

Democratic Party Platforms, 1904 Democratic Party Platform.

Republican Party Platforms, Republican Party Platform of 1904.

1904 Statistics.

Ancestry.com, Ancestry.com Operations Inc, Provo, Utah

Fold3. https://www.fold3.com/.

US Colored Infantry, United States Civil War Service Records of Union Colored Troops, 1863–1865.

Commemorative Landscapes of North Carolina, Documenting the American South, University of North Carolina at Chapel Hill, Chapel Hill, NC. https://docsouth.unc .edu/commland/.

Pennsylvania Grand Review: Honoring African American Patriots 1865/2019, House Divided Project at Dickinson College, Carlisle, PA. https://housedivided.dickinson .edu/grandreview/.

Colored Conventions Project, Penn State University, State College, PA. https:// coloredconventions.org.

The Historical Marker Database, Springfield, VA. http://www.hmdb.org.

The Valley of the Shadow: Two Communities during the Civil War, University of Virginia Library, Charlottesville, Virginia. http://valley.lib.virginia.edu/.

Secondary Books

Ackerman, Kenneth D. *Dark Horse: The Surprise Election and Political Murder of President James A. Garfield.* New York: Carroll and Graf, 2003.

Adeleke, Tunde. *Without Regard to Race: The Other Martin Robison Delany.* Jackson: University Press of Mississippi, 2003.

Angell, Stephen Ward. *Bishop Henry McNeal Turner and African American Religion in the South.* Knoxville: University of Tennessee Press, 1992.

Armstrong, William H. *Major McKinley: William McKinley and the Civil War.* Kent, OH: Kent State University Press, 2000.

Ayers, Edward L. *In the Presence of Mine Enemies: The Civil War in the Heart of America, 1859–1863.* New York: W. W. Norton, 2003.

Ayers, Edward L. *The Thin Light of Freedom: The Civil War and Emancipation in the Heart of America.* New York: W. W. Norton, 2017.

Baker, Bruce E. *What Reconstruction Meant: Historical Memory in the American South.* Charlottesville: University of Virginia Press, 2009.

Baker, Courtney R. *Humane Insight: Looking at Images of African American Suffering and Death.* Urbana: University of Illinois Press, 2015.

Baldwin, James. *The Fire Next Time.* 1963. New York: Vintage International, 1993.

Bateson, Catherine V. *Irish American Civil War Songs: Identity, Loyalty, and Nationhood.* Baton Rouge: Louisiana State University Press, 2022.

Bay, Mia. *Traveling Black: A Story of Race and Resistance.* Cambridge, MA: Belknap Press of Harvard University Press, 2021.

Bean, Christopher B. *Too Great a Burden to Bear: The Struggle and Failure of the Freedmen's Bureau in Texas.* New York: Fordham University Press, 2016.

Bederman, Gail. *Manliness and Civilization: A Cultural History of Gender and Race in the United States, 1880–1917.* Chicago: University of Chicago Press, 1995.

Belew, Kathleen. *Bring the War Home: The White Power Movement and Paramilitary America.* Cambridge, MA: Harvard University Press, 2018.

Bellesiles, Michael. *Inventing Equality: Reconstructing the Constitution in the Aftermath of the Civil War.* New York: St. Martin's Press, 2020.

Bergeson-Lockwood, Millington W. *Race over Party: Black Politics and Partisanship in Late Nineteenth-Century Boston.* Chapel Hill: University of North Carolina Press, 2018.

Berlin, Ira, Barbara Fields, Steven F. Miller, Joseph P. Reidy, and Leslie S. Rowland. *Free at Last: A Documentary History of Slavery, Freedom, and the Civil War.* New York: New Press, 1992.

Berry, Stephen A. *The Jim Crow Routine: Everyday Performances of Race, Civil Rights, and Segregation in Mississippi.* Chapel Hill: University of North Carolina Press, 2015.

Biddle, Daniel R., and Murray Dubin. *Tasting Freedom: Octavius Catto and the Battle for Equality in Civil War America.* Philadelphia: Temple University Press, 2010.

Blackett, R. J. M. *Beating against the Barriers: The Six Lives of Nineteenth-Century Afro-Americans.* Ithaca, NY: Cornell University Press, 1986.

Blackett, R. J. M. *The Captive's Quest for Freedom: Fugitive Slaves, the 1850 Fugitive Slave Law, and the Politics of Slavery.* New York: Cambridge University Press, 2018.

Blackett, R. J. M. *Thomas Morris Chester, Black Civil War Correspondent: His Dispatches from the Virginia Front.* Boston: Da Capo Press, 1989.

Blair, William. *Cities of the Dead: Contesting the Memory of the Civil War in the South, 1865–1914.* Chapel Hill: University of North Carolina Press, 2004.

Blight, David W. *Beyond the Battlefield: Race, Memory, and the American Civil War.* Amherst: University of Massachusetts Press, 2002.

Blight, David W. *Frederick Douglass: Prophet of Freedom.* New York: Simon and Schuster, 2018.

Blight, David W. *Race and Reunion: The Civil War in American Memory.* Cambridge, MA: Belknap Press of Harvard University Press, 2001.

Bodroghkozy, Aniko. *Equal Time: Television and the Civil Rights Movement.* Urbana: University of Illinois Press, 2012.

Bonner, Christopher James. *Remaking the Republic: Black Politics and the Creation of American Citizenship.* Philadelphia: University of Pennsylvania Press, 2020.

Brandt, Lydia Mattice. *The South Carolina State House Grounds.* Columbia: University of South Carolina Press, 2021.

Brimmer, Brandi. *Claiming Union Widowhood: Race, Respectability, and Poverty in the Post-Emancipation South.* Durham, NC: Duke University Press, 2020.

Brooks, Daphne. *Bodies in Dissent: Spectacular Performances of Race and Freedom, 1850–1910.* Durham, NC: Duke University Press, 2005.

Brown, Joshua. *Beyond the Lines: Pictorial Reporting, Everyday Life, and the Crisis of Gilded Age America.* Berkeley: University of California Press, 2002.

Brown, Thomas J. *Civil War Canon: Sites of Confederate Memory in South Carolina.* Chapel Hill: University of North Carolina Press, 2015.

Brown, Thomas J. *Civil War Monuments and the Militarization of America.* Chapel Hill: University of North Carolina Press, 2019.

Brophy, Alfred L. *The University, Court, and Slave: Pro-Slavery Thought in Southern Colleges and Courts and the Coming of Civil War.* New York: Oxford University Press, 2016.

Brundage, W. Fitzhugh. *The Southern Past: A Clash of Race and Memory.* Cambridge, MA: Belknap Press of Harvard University Press, 2005.

Brundage, W. Fitzhugh, ed. *Where These Memories Grow: History, Memory, and Southern Identity*. Chapel Hill: University of North Carolina Press, 2000.

Bryant, James K., II *The 36th Infantry United States Colored Troops in the Civil War: A History and Roster*. Jefferson, NC: McFarland, 2012.

Burkhart, William H., Samuel L. Daihl, J. Houston McCulloch, Dr. George Kaluger, Mrs. Elizabeth Roler, and Mrs. Howard A. Ryder. *Shippensburg, Pennsylvania in the Civil War*. Shippensburg, PA: Burd Street Press, 2003.

Cahill, Cathleen D. *Recasting the Vote: How Women of Color Transformed the Suffrage Movement*. Chapel Hill: University of North Carolina Press, 2020.

Callahan, Mat. *Songs of Slavery and Emancipation*. Introduction by Robin D. G. Kelley. Jackson: University Press of Mississippi, 2022.

Carroll, Fred. *Race News: Black Journalists and the Fight for Racial Justice in the Twentieth Century*. Urbana: University of Illinois Press, 2017.

Cecelski, David S. *The Fire of Freedom: Abraham Galloway and the Slave Civil War*. Chapel Hill: University of North Carolina Press, 2012.

Chace, James. *1912: Wilson, Roosevelt, Taft, and Debs: The Election That Changed the Country*. New York: Simon and Schuster, 2004.

Cimbala, Paul A., and Randall M. Miller, eds. *The Freedmen's Bureau and Reconstruction: Reconsiderations*. New York: Fordham University Press, 1999.

Clark, Kathleen Ann. *Defining Moments: African American Commemoration and Political Culture in the South, 1863–1913*. Chapel Hill: University of North Carolina Press, 2005.

Coates, Ta-Nehisi. *Between the World and Me*. New York: Spiegel and Grau, 2015.

Cocks, Catherine. *Doing the Town: The Rise of Urban Tourism in the United States, 1850–1915*. Berkeley: University of California Press, 2001.

Coddington, Edwin B. *The Gettysburg Campaign: A Study in Command*. New York: Charles Scribner's Sons, 1984.

Cook, Robert J. *Civil War Memories: Contesting the Past in the United States since 1865*. Baltimore: Johns Hopkins University Press, 2017.

Cook, Robert J. *Troubled Commemoration: The American Civil War Centennial*. Baton Rouge: Louisiana State University Press, 2007.

Cooper, Brittney. *Beyond Respectability: The Intellectual Thought of Race Women*. Urbana: University of Illinois Press, 2017.

Cox, Karen L. *Dixie's Daughters: The United Daughters of the Confederacy and the Preservation of Confederate Culture*. New Perspectives on the History of the South. Gainesville: University Press of Florida, 2003.

Cox, Karen L., ed. *Destination Dixie: Tourism and Southern History*. Gainesville: University Press of Florida, 2012.

Cox, Karen L. *Dreaming of Dixie: How the South Was Created in American Popular Culture*. Chapel Hill: University of North Carolina Press, 2013.

Cox, Karen L. *No Common Ground: Confederate Monuments and the Ongoing Fight for Racial Justice*. Chapel Hill: University of North Carolina Press, 2021.

Dailey, Jane. *Before Jim Crow: The Politics of Race in Postemancipation Virginia*. Chapel Hill: University of North Carolina Press, 2000.

DeCaro, Louis A., Jr. *The Untold Story of Shields Green: The Life and Death of a Harper's Ferry Raider.* New York: New York University Press, 2020.

Delmont, Matthew F. *Making Roots: A Nation Captivated.* Oakland: University of California Press, 2016.

Diemer, Andrew K. *Vigilance: The Life of William Still, Father of the Underground Railroad.* New York: Alfred A. Knopf, 2022.

Diouf, Sylviane A. *Slavery's Exiles: The Story of American Maroons.* New York: New York University Press, 2014.

Dobak, William A. *Freedom by the Sword: The US Colored Troops, 1862–1867.* New York: Skyhorse, 2013.

Domby, Adam H. *The False Cause: Fraud, Fabrication, and White Supremacy in Confederate Memory.* Charlottesville: University of Virginia Press, 2020.

Donaldson, Le'trice D. *Duty beyond the Battlefield: African American Soldiers Fight for Racial Uplift, Citizenship, and Manhood, 1870–1920.* Carbondale: Southern Illinois University Press, 2020.

Downs, Jim. *Sick from Freedom: African-American Illness and Suffering During the Civil War and Reconstruction.* Oxford: Oxford University Press, 2015.

Du Bois, W. E. B., ed. *The Negro Church Report of a Social Study made under the direction of Atlanta University; together with the Proceedings of the Eighth Conference for the Study of the Negro Problems, held at Atlanta University, May 26th, 1903.* Atlanta: Atlanta University Press, 1903.

Dunbar, Erica Armstrong. *A Fragile Freedom: African American Women and Emancipation in the Antebellum City.* New Haven, CT: Yale University Press, 2008.

Edds, Margaret. *What the Eyes Can't See: Ralph Northam, Black Resolve, and a Racial Reckoning in Virginia.* Columbia: University of South Carolina Press, 2022.

Egerton, Douglas R. *Thunder at the Gates: The Black Civil War Regiments That Redeemed America.* New York: Basic Books, 2016.

Emberton, Carole. *To Walk About in Freedom: The Long Emancipation of Priscilla Joyner.* New York: W. W. Norton, 2022.

Faust, Drew Gilpin. *The Republic of Suffering: Death and the American Civil War.* New York: Vintage Books, 2008.

Field, Kendra Taira. *Growing Up with the Country: Family, Race, and Nation after the Civil War.* New Haven, CT: Yale University Press, 2018.

Fields, Karen E., and Barbara J. Fields, *Racecraft: The Soul of Inequality in American Life.* London: Verso, 2012.

Fitzgerald, Michael W. *Reconstruction in Alabama: From Civil War to Redemption in the Cotton South.* Baton Rouge: Louisiana State University Press, 2017.

Flowe, Douglas. *Uncontrollable Blackness: African American Men and Criminality in Jim Crow New York.* Chapel Hill: University of North Carolina Press, 2020.

Foner, Eric. *Reconstruction: America's Unfinished Revolution, 1863–1877.* New York: Harper and Row, 1988.

Foner, Eric. *The Second Founding: How the Civil War and Reconstruction Remade the Constitution.* New York: W. W. Norton, 2019.

Foote, Lorien. *Rites of Retaliation: Civilization, Soldiers, and Campaigns in the American Civil War.* Chapel Hill: University of North Carolina Press, 2021.

Foster, Gaines M. *Ghosts of the Confederacy: Defeat, the Lost Cause, and the Emergence of the New South, 1865–1913*. New York: Oxford University Press, 1987.

Fries, Stella M., Janet Z. Gabler, and C. Bernard Ruffin. *Some Chambersburg Roots: A Black Perspective*. Chambersburg, PA: Stella Fries, 1980.

Fuentes, Marissa J. *Dispossessed Lives: Enslaved Women, Violence, and the Archive*. Philadelphia: University of Pennsylvania Press, 2016.

Fuller, A. James. *Chaplain to the Confederacy: Basil Manly and Baptist Life in the Old South*. Baton Rouge: Louisiana State University Press, 2000.

Gallagher, Gary W. *Causes Won, Lost, and Forgotten: How Hollywood and Popular Art Shape What We Know about the Civil War*. Chapel Hill: University of North Carolina Press, 2008.

Gannon, Barbara. *The Won Cause: Black and White Comradeship in the Grand Army of the Republic*. Chapel Hill: University of North Carolina Press, 2011.

Giesburg, Judith, ed. Transcribed and annotated by the Memorable Days Project Editorial Team. *Emile Davis's Civil War: The Diaries of a Free Black Woman in Philadelphia, 1863–1865*. University Park: Pennsylvania State University Press, 2014.

Gill, James, and Howard Hunter. *Tearing Down the Lost Cause: The Removal of New Orleans's Confederate Statues*. Jackson: University Press of Mississippi, 2021.

Gilpin, R. Blakeslee. *John Brown Still Lives!: America's Long Reckoning with Violence, Equality, and Change*. Chapel Hill: University of North Carolina Press, 2011.

Givens, Jarvis R. *Fugitive Pedagogy: Carter G. Woodson and the Art of Black Teaching*. Cambridge, MA: Harvard University Press, 2021.

Goldberg, David. *The Retreats of Reconstruction: Race, Leisure, and the Politics of Segregation at the New Jersey Shore, 1865–1920*. New York: Fordham University Press, 2017.

Goodyear, C. W. *President Garfield: From Radical to Unifier*. New York: Simon and Schuster, 2023.

Gordon-Reed, Annette. *On Juneteenth*. New York: Liveright, 2021.

Gosse, Van. *The First Reconstruction: Black Politics in America from the Revolution to the Civil War*. Chapel Hill: University of North Carolina Press, 2021.

Graham, David K. *Loyalty on the Line: Civil War Maryland in American Memory*. Athens: University of Georgia Press, 2018.

Green, Hilary. *Educational Reconstruction: African American Schools in the Urban South, 1865–1890*. New York: Fordham University Press, 2016.

Griffin, Farah Jasmine. *Read Until You Understand: The Profound Wisdom of Black Life and Literature*. New York: W. W. Norton, 2021.

Gross, Kali N. *Colored Amazons: Crime, Violence, and Black Women in the City of Brotherly Love, 1880–1910*. Durham, NC: Duke University Press, 2006.

Hahn, Steven. *A Nation under Our Feet: Black Political Struggles in the Rural South from Slavery to the Great Migration*. Cambridge, MA: Belknap Press of Harvard University Press, 2003.

Halpin, Dennis Patrick. *A Brotherhood of Liberty: Black Reconstruction and Its Legacy in Baltimore, 1865–1920*. Philadelphia: University of Pennsylvania Press, 2019.

Harper, Matthew. *The End of Days: African American Religion and Politics in the Age of Emancipation*. Chapel Hill: University of North Carolina Press, 2016.

Hartley, Roger C. *Monumental Harm: Reckoning with Jim Crow Era Confederate Monuments*. Columbia: University of South Carolina Press, 2021.

Hearn, Chester G. *Lincoln and McClellan at War*. Baton Rouge: Louisiana State University Press, 2012.

Hess, Earl J. *Trench Warfare under Grant and Lee: Field Fortifications in the Overland Campaign*. Chapel Hill: University of North Carolina Press, 2007.

Hicks, Cheryl D. *Talk with You Like a Woman: African American Women, Justice, and Reform in New York, 1890–1935*. Chapel Hill: University of North Carolina Press, 2010.

Higginbotham, Evelyn Brooks. *Righteous Discontent: The Women's Movement in the Black Baptist Church, 1880–1920*. Cambridge, MA: Harvard University Press, 1993.

Hilde, Libra R. *Slavery, Fatherhood, and Paternal Duty in African American Communities over the Long Nineteenth Century*. Chapel Hill: University of North Carolina Press, 2020.

Hillyer, Reiko. *Designing Dixie: Tourism, Memory, and Urban Space in the New South*. Charlottesville: University of Virginia Press, 2014.

Hilbert, John M. *American Cyclone: Theodore Roosevelt and His 1900 Whistle-Stop Campaign*. Jackson: University Press of Mississippi, 2015.

Hollars, B. J. *Opening the Doors: The Desegregation of the University of Alabama and the Fight for Civil Rights in Tuscaloosa*. Tuscaloosa: University of Alabama Press, 2013.

Holt, Sharon Ann. *Making Freedom Pay: North Carolina Freedpeople Working for Themselves, 1865–1900*. Athens: University of Georgia Press, 2000.

Hood, James Walker. *One Hundred Years of the African Methodist Episcopal Zion Church; or, The Centennial of African Methodism*. New York: A.M.E. Zion Book Concern, 1895.

Hoogenboom, Ari. *Rutherford B. Hayes: Warrior and President*. Lawrence: University Press of Kansas, 1995.

Horton, James Oliver. *Free People of Color: Inside the African American Community*. Washington, DC: Smithsonian Institution Press, 1993.

Horton, James Oliver, and Lois E. Horton, eds., *Slavery and Public History: The Tough Stuff of American Memory*. Chapel Hill: University of North Carolina Press, 2006.

Horwitz, Tony. *Confederates in the Attic: Dispatches from the Unfinished Civil War*. New York: Pantheon Books, 1998.

Horwitz. *Midnight Rising: John Brown and the Raid That Shaped the Civil War*. New York: Picador, 2011.

Hubbs, G. Ward. *Searching for Freedom after the Civil War: Klansman, Carpetbagger, Scalawag and Freedman*. Tuscaloosa: University of Alabama Press, 2015.

Hull, Ann and Franklin County Historical Society-Kittochtinny. *Cumberland Valley: From Tuscarora to Chambersburg to Blue Ridge*. Charleston, SC: Arcadia Publishing, 2011.

Hunter, Tera. *To 'Joy My Freedom: Southern Black Women's Lives and Labors after the Civil War*. Cambridge, MA: Harvard University Press, 1997.

Jackson, Calobe, Jr., Katie McArdle, and David Pettegrew. *One Hundred Voices: Harrisburg's Historic African American Community, 1850–1920*. Grand Forks: Digital Press at the University of North Dakota, 2020.

Jamieson, Perry D. *Winfield Scott Hancock: Gettysburg Hero.* Abilene, TX: McWhiney Foundation Press, 2003.

Janney, Caroline E. *Burying the Dead But Not the Past: Ladies' Memorial Association and the Lost Cause.* Chapel Hill: University of North Carolina Press, 2008.

Janney, Caroline E. *Remembering the Civil War: Reunion and the Limits of Reconciliation.* Chapel Hill: University of North Carolina Press, 2013.

Johnson, Andre E. *No Future in This Country: The Prophetic Pessimism of Bishop Henry McNeal Turner.* Jackson: University Press of Mississippi, 2020.

Jones, Martha S. *Birthright Citizens: A History of Race and Rights in Antebellum America.* Cambridge: Cambridge University Press, 2019.

Jordan, Brian Matthew. *Marching Home: Union Veterans and Their Unending Civil War.* New York: Liveright, 2014.

Jordan, David M. *Winfield Scott Hancock: A Soldier's Life.* Bloomington: Indiana University Press, 1988.

Kantrowitz, Stephen. *More Than Freedom: Fighting for Black Citizenship in a White Republic, 1829–1889.* New York: Penguin Books, 2013.

Kelman, Ari. *A Misplaced Massacre: Struggling over the Memory of Sand Creek.* Cambridge: Harvard University Press, 2013.

Kent, Noel Jacob. *America in 1900.* Armonk, NY: M. E. Sharpe, 2002.

Kimball, Gregg D. *American City, Southern Place: A Cultural History of Antebellum Richmond.* Athens: University of Georgia Press, 2000.

King, Wilma. *Stolen Childhood: Slave Youth in Nineteenth-Century America.* Bloomington: Indiana University Press, 1997.

Krauthamer, Barbara. *Black Slaves, Indian Masters: Slavery, Emancipation, and Citizenship in the Native American South.* Chapel Hill: University of North Carolina Press, 2013.

Kytle, Ethan J., and Blain Roberts. *Denmark Vesey's Garden: Slavery and Memory in the Cradle of the Confederacy.* New York: New Press, 2018.

Larson, Kate Clifford. *Bound for the Promised Land: Harriet Tubman, Portrait of An American Hero.* New York: Ballantine Books, 2004.

Leonard, Elizabeth D. *Benjamin Francis Butler: A Noisy, Fearless Life.* Chapel Hill: University of North Carolina Press, 2022.

Lewis, David Levering. *W. E. B. Du Bois: Biography of a Race, 1868–1919.* New York: Henry Holt, 1993.

Levin, Kevin M. *Remembering the Battle of the Crater: War as Murder.* Lexington; University of Kentucky Press, 2017.

Levin, Kevin M. *Searching for Black Confederates: The Civil War's Most Persistent Myth.* Chapel Hill: University of North Carolina Press, 2019.

Lindsey, Treva B. *Colored No More: Reinventing Black Womanhood in Washington, DC.* Urbana: University of Illinois Press, 2017.

Litwack, Leon. *Been in the Storm So Long: The Aftermath of Slavery.* New York: Alfred A. Knopf, 1979.

Litwicki, Ellen M. *America's Public Holidays, 1865–1920.* Washington, DC: Smithsonian Institution Press, 2000.

Luke, Bob, and John David Smith, *Soldiering for Freedom: How the Union Army Recruited, Trained, and Deployed the US Colored Troops*. Baltimore: Johns Hopkins University Press, 2014.

Maffly-Kipp, Laurie F. *Setting Down the Sacred Past: African-American Race Histories*. Cambridge, MA: Belknap Press of Harvard University Press, 2010.

Marshall, Anne E. *Creating a Confederate Kentucky: The Lost Cause and Civil War Memory in a Border State*. Chapel Hill: University of North Carolina Press, 2013.

Masur, Kate. *Until Justice Be Done: America's First Civil Rights Movement*. New York: W. W. Norton, 2021.

McElya, Micki. *Clinging to Mammy: The Faithful Slave in Twentieth-Century America*. Cambridge, MA: Harvard University Press, 2007.

McPherson, James M. *Battle Cry of Freedom: The Civil War Era*. New York: Oxford University Press, 1988,

McWhirter, Christian. *Battle Hymns: The Power and Popularity of Music in the Civil War*. Chapel Hill: University of North Carolina Press, 2012.

Mealy, Todd. *Aliened American: A Biography of William Howard Day: 1866–1900*, vol. 2.. Baltimore: Publish America, 2010.

Meier, August, and Elliott Rudwick. *From Plantation to Ghetto*. Rev. ed. New York: Hill and Wang, 1970.

Mellown, Robert Oliver. *The University of Alabama: A Guide to the Campus and Its Architecture*. Tuscaloosa: University of Alabama Press, 2013.

Merry, Robert W. *President McKinley: Architect of the American Century*. New York: Simon and Schuster, 2017.

Mezurek, Kelly D. *For Their Own Cause: The 27th United States Colored Troops*. Kent, OH: Kent State University Press, 2016.

Miles, Tiya. *Tales from the Haunted South: Dark Tourism and Memories of Slavery from the Civil War Era*. Chapel Hill: University of North Carolina Press, 2015.

Milkis, Sidney M. *Theodore Roosevelt, the Progressive Party, and the Transformation of American Democracy*. Lawrence: University Press of Kansas, 2009.

Millard, Candice. *Destiny of the Republic: A Tale of Madness, Medicine, and the Murder of a President*. New York: Doubleday, 2011.

Minow, Martha. *Between Vengeance and Forgiveness: Facing History after Genocide and Mass Violence*. Boston: Beacon Press, 1998.

Mitchell, Koritha. *From Slave Cabins to the White House: Homemade Citizenship in African American Culture*. Urbana: University of Illinois Press, 2020.

Mitchell, Mary Niall. *Raising Freedom's Children: Black Children and Visions of the Future After Slavery*. New York: New York University Press, 2010.

Mixon, Gregory. *Show Thyself a Man: Georgia State Troops, Colored, 1865–1905*. Gainesville: University Press of Florida, 2016.

Monroe, Stephen M. *Heritage and Hate: Old South Rhetoric at Southern Universities*. Tuscaloosa: University of Alabama Press, 2021.

Morris, Burnis R. *Carter G. Woodson: History, the Black Press, and Public Relations*. Jackson: University Press of Mississippi, 2017.

Morris, J. Brent. *Oberlin Hotbed of Abolitionism: College, Community, and the Fight for Freedom and Equality in Antebellum America*. Chapel Hill: University of North Carolina Press, 2014.

Morton, Patricia. *Disfigured Images: The Historical Assault on Afro-American Women*. New York: Greenwood Press, 1991.

Mulrooney, Margaret M. *Race, Place, and Memory: Deep Currents in Wilmington, North Carolina*. Gainesville: University Press of Florida, 2018.

Neely, Mark E., Jr. *Southern Rights: Political Prisoners and the Myth of Confederate Constitutionalism*. Charlottesville: University Press of Virginia, 1999.

Nelson, Louis P., and Claudrena N. Harold, eds. *Charlottesville 2017: The Legacy of Race and Inequity*. Charlottesville: University of Virginia Press, 2018.

Nelson, Megan Kate. *Ruin Nation: Destruction and the American Civil War*. Athens: University of Georgia Press, 2012.

Noyalas, Jonathan A. *Slavery and Freedom in the Shenandoah Valley during the Civil War Era*. Gainesville: University Press of Florida, 2021.

Parker, Alison M. *Unceasing Militant: The Life of Mary Church Terrell*. Chapel Hill: University of North Carolina Press, 2020.

Perry, Imani. *May We Forever Stand: A History of the Black National Anthem*. Chapel Hill: University of North Carolina Press, 2018.

Phillips, Christopher. *The Rivers Ran Backward: The Civil War and the Remaking of the American Middle Border*. New York: Oxford University Press, 2016.

Pinheiro, Holly A., Jr. *The Families' Civil War: Black Soldiers and the Fight for Racial Justice*. Athens: University of Georgia Press, 2022.

Prather, H. Leon, Sr. *We Have Taken a City: Wilmington Racial Massacre and Coup of 1898*. Rutherford, NJ: Fairleigh Dickinson University Press, 1984.

Quarles, Benjamin. *Allies for Freedom and Blacks on John Brown*. With new introduction by William S. McFeely. 1974. Boston: Da Capo Press, 2001.

Rachleff, Peter. *Black Labor in Richmond, 1865–1890*. Urbana: University of Illinois Press, 1984.

Rafuse, Ethan S. *McClellan's War: The Failure of Moderation in the Struggle for the Union*. Bloomington: Indiana University Press, 2005.

Rainville, Lynn. *Hidden History: African American Cemeteries in Central Virginia*. Charlottesville: University of Virginia Press, 2014.

Redford, Dorothy Spruill. *Generations of Somerset Place: From Slavery to Freedom*. Charleston: Arcadia Publishing, 2005.

Redford, Dorothy Spruill, and Michael D'Orso. *Somerset Homecoming: Recovering a Lost Heritage*. Chapel Hill: University of North Carolina Press, 1988.

Regosin, Elizabeth. *Freedom's Promise: Ex-Slave Families and Citizenship in the Age of Emancipation*. Charlottesville: University of Virginia Press, 2002.

Reid, Richard M. *African Canadians in Union Blue: Volunteering for the Cause in the Civil War*. Kent, OH: Kent State University Press, 2014.

Reid, Richard M. *Freedom for Themselves: North Carolina's Black Soldiers in the Civil War*. Chapel Hill: University of North Carolina Press, 2008.

Reynolds, Leeann G. *Maintaining Segregation: Children and Racial Instruction in the South, 1920–1955*. Baton Rouge: Louisiana State University, 2017.

Rittenhouse, Jennifer. *Growing Up Jim Crow: How Black and White Southern Children Learned Race*. Chapel Hill: University of North Carolina Press, 2006.

Robbins, Hollis, and Henry Louis Gates Jr., eds. *The Portable Nineteenth-Century African American Women Writers*. New York: Penguin Books, 2017.

Roberts, Alaina E. *I've Been Here All the While: Black Freedom on Native Land.* Philadelphia: University of Pennsylvania Press, 2021.

Romeo, Sharon. *Gender and the Jubilee: Black Freedom and the Reconstruction of Citizenship in Civil War Missouri.* Athens: University of Georgia Press, 2016.

Ross, Marc Howard. *Slavery in the North: Forgetting History and Recovering Memory.* Philadelphia: University of Pennsylvania Press, 2018.

Rubin, Anne Sarah. *Through the Heart of Dixie: Sherman's March and American Memory.* Chapel Hill: University of North Carolina, 2014.

Ruffin, C. Bernard. *Voices of Chambersburg: An Oral History of the African American Community of Franklin County, Pennsylvania,* vol. 1 of 4— *Interviews.* Greencastle, PA: Allison-Antrim Museum, 2011.

Savage, Barbara Dianne. *Broadcasting Freedom: Race, War, and the Politics of Race, 1936–1948.* Chapel Hill: University of North Carolina Press, 1999.

Savage, Kirk. *Standing Soldiers, Kneeling Slaves; Race, War, and Monument in Nineteenth-Century America.* Princeton, NJ: Princeton University Press, 1997.

Savoy, Lauret. *Trace: Memory, History, Race, and the American Landscape.* Berkeley, CA: Counterpoint, 2015.

Schaffer, Marguerite S. *See America First: Tourism and National Identity, 1880-1940.* Washington, DC: Smithsonian Institution Press, 2001.

Schwalm, Leslie A. *Emancipation's Diaspora: Race and Reconstruction in the Upper Midwest.* Chapel Hill: University of North Carolina Press, 2009.

Sellers, James B. *History of the University of Alabama,* vol. 1: *1818–1902.* Tuscaloosa: University of Alabama Press, 1953.

Shaffer, Donald R. *After the Glory: The Struggles of Black Civil War Veterans.* Lawrence: University Press of Kansas, 2004.

Silkenat, David. *Driven from Home: North Carolina's Civil War Refugee Crisis.* Athens: University of Georgia Press, 2016.

Silkenat, David. *Moments of Despair: Suicide, Divorce, and Debt in Civil War Era North Carolina.* Chapel Hill: University of North Carolina Press, 2011.

Smith, Clint. *How The Word Is Passed: A Reckoning with the History of Slavery across America.* New York: Little, Brown, 2021.

Smith, David G. *On the Edge of Freedom: The Fugitive Slave Issue in South Central Pennsylvania, 1820–1870.* New York: Fordham University Press, 2013.

Snyder, Jeffrey Aaron. *Making Black History: The Color Line, Culture, and Race in the Age of Jim Crow.* Athens: University of Georgia Press, 2018.

Sorin, Gretchen. *Driving While Black: African American Travel and the Road to Civil Rights.* New York: Liveright, 2020.

Stack, Carol B. *All Our Kin: Strategies for Survival in a Black Community.* New York: Harper and Row, 1974.

Stanonis, Anthony J., ed. *Dixie Emporium: Tourism, Foodways, and Consumer Culture in the American South.* Athens: University of Georgia Press, 2008.

Stanley, Matthew E. *Grand Army of Labor: Workers, Veterans, and the Meaning of the Civil War.* Urbana: University of Illinois Press, 2021.

Stanley, Matthew E. *The Loyal West: Civil War and Reunion in Middle America.* Urbana: University of Illinois Press, 2017.

Stephens, Robert Grier. *Intrepid Warrior: Clement Anselm Evans Confederate General from Georgia: Life, Letters, and Diaries of the War Years*. Dayton, OH: Morningside House, 1992.

Stephenson, Frank. *Chowan Beach: Remembering an African American Resort*. Charleston, SC: History Press, 2006.

Sternhall, Yael A. *War on Record: The Archive and the Afterlife of the Civil War*. New Haven, CT: Yale University Press, 2023.

Stuckey, Sterling. *Slave Culture: Nationalist Theory and the Foundations of Black America*. New York: Oxford University Press, 1987.

Sturken, Marita. *Tangled Memories: The Vietnam War, the AIDS Epidemic, and the Politics of Remembering*. Berkeley: University of California Press, 1997.

Sweet, Timothy. *Traces of War: Poetry, Photography, and the Crisis of the Union*. Baltimore: Johns Hopkins University Press, 1990.

Taylor, Amy Murrell. *Embattled Freedom: Journeys through the Civil War's Slave Refugee Camps*. Chapel Hill: University of North Carolina Press, 2018.

Taylor, Candacy A. *Overland Railroad: The Green Book and Roots of Black Travel in America*. New York: Abrams Press, 2020.

Taylor, Nicki M. *Driven toward Madness: The Fugitive Slave Margaret Garner and Tragedy on the Ohio*. Athens: Ohio University Press, 2016.

Thorp, Daniel. *Facing Freedom: An African American Community in Virginia from Reconstruction to Jim Crow*. Charlottesville: University of Virginia Press, 2017.

Titus, Jill Ogline. *Gettysburg 1963: Civil Rights, Cold War Politics, and Historical Memory in America's Most Famous Small Town*. Chapel Hill: University of North Carolina Press, 2021.

Trouillot, Michel-Rolph. *Silencing the Past: Power and the Production of History*. With a new foreword by Hazel V. Carby. Boston: Beacon Press, 2015.

Trudeau, Noah Andre. *Like Men of War: Black Troops in the Civil War, 1862–1865*. Boston: Back Bay Books, 1998.

Tyson, Timothy B. *Blood Done Sign My Name: A True Story*. New York: Crown, 2004.

Watts, Rebecca B. *Contemporary Southern Identity: Community through Controversy*. Jackson: University of Mississippi Press, 2007.

West, E. James. *Ebony Magazine and Lerone Bennett Jr.: Popular Black History in Postwar America*. Urbana: University of Illinois Press, 2020.

West, E. James. *Our Kind of Historian: The Work and Activism of Lerone Bennett Jr.* Amherst: University of Massachusetts Press, 2022.

White, Jonathan W., ed. *To Address You as My Friend: African American Letters to Abraham Lincoln*. Foreword by Edna Greene Medford. Chapel Hill: University of North Carolina Press, 2021.

Whites, LeeAnn. *Gender Matters: Civil War, Reconstruction, and the Making of the New South*. New York: Palgrave Macmillan, 2005.

Whitehead, Karsonya Wise. *Notes from a Colored Girl: The Civil War Pocket Diaries of Emilie Frances Davis*. Columbia: University of South Carolina Press, 2014.

Williams, Chad, Kidada E. Williams, and Keisha N. Blain. *Charleston Syllabus: Readings on Race, Racism, and Racial Violence*. Athens: University of Georgia Press, 2016.

Williams, Heather A. *Help Me to Find My People: The African American Search for Family Lost in Slavery*. Chapel Hill: University of North Carolina Press, 2012.

Williams, Heather A. *Self-Taught: African American Education in Slavery and Freedom*. Chapel Hill: University of North Carolina Press, 2005.

Williams, Kidada E. *They Left Great Marks on Me: African American Testimonies of Racial Violence from Emancipation to World War I*. New York: New York University Press, 2012.

Willis, Deborah, and Barbara Krauthamer. *Envisioning Emancipation: Black Americans and the End of Slavery*. Philadelphia: Temple University Press, 2013.

Wolcott, Victoria. *Race, Riots, and Roller Coasters: The Struggle over Segregated Recreation in America*. Philadelphia: University of Pennsylvania Press, 2012.

Wolcott, Victoria. *Remaking Respectability: African American Women in Interwar Detroit*. Chapel Hill: University of North Carolina Press, 2001.

Woman's Club of Mercersburg. *Old Mercersburg Revisited: Civil War to Bicentennial*. Mercersburg, PA: Woman's Club of Mercersburg, 1987.

Woodward, Colin Edward. *Marching Masters: Slavery, Race, and the Confederate Army during the Civil War*. Charlottesville: University of Virginia Press, 2014.

Yarbrough, Fay. *Choctaw Confederates: The American Civil War in Indian Country*. Chapel Hill: University of North Carolina Press, 2021.

Zucchino, David. *Wilmington's Life: The Murderous Coup of 1898 and the Rise of White Supremacy*. New York: Grove Press, 2020.

Scholarly Articles and Book Chapters

Alexander, Ted. "A Regular Slave Hunt: The Army of Northern Virginia and Black Civilians in the Gettysburg Campaign." *North and South* 4, no. 7 (September 2001): 82–89.

Allen, Kevin. "The Second Battle of Fort Sumter: The Debate over the Politics of Race and Historical Memory at the Opening of America's Civil War Centennial, 1961." *Public Historian* 33, no. 2 (Spring 2011): 94–109.

Ault, Becky. "The Commonwealth Memorial: A New Sculpture for the Capitol Grounds." *Pennsylvania History: A Journal of Mid-Atlantic Studies* 87, no. 1 (Winter 2020): 225–232.

Babbitt, Bruce. Foreword to *Rally on the High Ground: The National Park Service Symposium on the Civil War*, ed. Robert K. Sutton. Washington, DC: National Park Service, 2001. http://npshistory.com/series/symposia/rally_high_ground/foreword.htm.

Bair, Sarah. "Continuing to Pay the 'Patriotic Debt': The Establishment of the Pennsylvania Soldiers' Orphans Industrial School, 1893–1912." *Pennsylvania History: A Journal of Mid-Atlantic Studies* 82 (Autumn 2015): 460–488.

Bailey, Moya Z. "All the Digital Humanists Are White, All the Nerds Are Men, but Some of Us Are Brave." *Journal of Digital Humanities* 1 (Winter 2011). http://journalofdigitalhumanities.org/1-1/all-the-digital-humanists-are-white-all-the-nerds-are-men-but-some-of-us-are-brave-by-moya-z-bailey/.

Baldwin, James. "Black English: A Dishonest Argument." In *The Cross of Redemption: Uncollected Writings*, edited by Randall Kenan, 125–130. New York: Pantheon Books, 2010.

Ball, Erica L. "Style Politics and Self-Fashioning in Mamie Garvin Fields' *Lemon Swamp and Other Places*." *WSQ: Women's Studies Quarterly* 46 (Spring/Summer 2018): 53–69.

Ball, Erica L., and Kellie Carter Jackson. "Introduction: Reconsidering Roots." In *Reconsidering Roots: Race, Politics, and Memory*, edited by Erica L. Ball and Kellie Carter Jackson, 1–21. Athens: University of Georgia Press, 2017.

Barton, Michael. "Almost Our Own Montmartre: Studying Harrisburg's Old Eighth Ward." *Pennsylvania History: A Journal of Mid-Atlantic Studies* 72 (Autumn 2005): 405–418.

Baumgartner, Kabria. "Gender Politics and the Manual Labor College Initiative at National Colored Conventions in Antebellum America." In *The Colored Conventions Movement: Black Organizing in the Nineteenth Century*, edited by P. Gabrielle Forman, Jim Casey, and Sarah Lynn Patterson, 230–245. Chapel Hill: University of North Carolina Press, 2021.

Bell, Janet L. "Corporal Jesse G. Thompson G.A.R. Post 440." *Cumberland County History* 30 (2013): 89–97.

Blackett, R. J. M. "Day, William Howard, Educators, Newspaper Editors/Publishers." *American National Biography Online*. New York: Oxford University Press, 2000. https://doi.org/10.1093/anb/9780198606697.article.1600435.

Blanton, Laura. "From Set of "Glory" to the Smithsonian Collections." *O Can You See?: Stories from the Museum*, July 30, 2014. https://americanhistory.si.edu/blog/2014/07/from-the-set-of-glory-to-the-smithsonian-collections.html.

Blight, David. "'For Something beyond the Battlefield': Frederick Douglass and the Memory of the Civil War." *Journal of American History* 75 (March 1989): 1156–1178.

Brophy, Alfred L. "The University and the Slaves: Apology and Its Meaning." In *The Age of Apology: Facing Up to the Past*, edited by Mark Gibney, Rhoda E. Howard-Hassmann, Jean-Marc Coicaud, and Niklaus Steiner, 109–119. Philadelphia: University of Pennsylvania Press, 2008.

Brown, Elsa Barkley. "Negotiating and Transforming the Public Sphere: African American Political Life in the Transition from Slavery to Freedom." In *Time Longer Than Rope: A Century of African American Activism, 1850–1950*, edited by Charles M. Payne and Adam Green, 68–110. New York: New York University Press, 2003.

Brown, Vincent. "Mapping a Slave Revolt: Visualizing Spatial History through the Archives of Slavery." *Social Text* 125 (December 2015): 134–141.

Burg, Steven B. "'From Troubled Grounds to Common Ground': The Locust Grove African American Cemetery Preservation Project: A Case Study of Service." *Public Historian* 30 (May 2008): 51–82.

Burg, Steven B. "The North Queen Cemetery and the African American Experience in Shippensburg." *Pennsylvania History: A Journal of Mid-Atlantic Studies* 77 (Winter 2010): 1–36.

Burg, Steven B. "Shippensburg's Locust Grove African-American Cemetery: A Window on Two Centuries of Cumberland County's African American History." *Cumberland County History* v. 26 (2009): 33–47.

Burger, Denise. "Recovering Black Women in the Colored Conventions Movement." *Legacy: A Journal of American Women Writers* 36, no. 2 (2019): 256–262.

Burkhart, William H. "Shippensburg's Colored Veterans of the Civil War," in *Shippensburg, Pennsylvania in the Civil War*, ed. William H. Burkhart, Samuel L. Daihl, J. Houston McCulloch, Dr. George Kaluger, Mrs. Elizabeth Roler, Mrs. Howard A. Ryder, and Shippensburg Historical Society, 2nd rev. and updated ed. Shippensburg: Burd Street Press, 2003.

Chester, Robert K. "The Black Military Image in *Roots: The Next Generation*." In *Reconsidering Roots: Race, Politics, and Memory*, edited by Erica L. Ball and Kellie Carter Jackson, 129–143. Athens: University of Georgia Press, 2017.

Clarke, Max, and Gary Alan Fine. "'A' for Apology: Slavery and the Collegiate Discourses of Remembrance—Cases of Brown University and the University of Alabama." *History and Memory* 22, no. 1 (Spring/Summer 2010): 81–112.

Clinton, Catherine. "More Than Ready for Her Close-Up: Harriet Tubman on Screen." *Reviews in American History* 48 (June 2020): 253–263.

Cook, Robert J. "'Hollow Victory': Federal Veterans, Racial Justice, and the Eclipse of the Union Cause in American Memory." *History and Memory* 33, no. 1 (Spring/Summer 2021): 3–33.

Cook, Robert, Kenneth Noe, Dana Shoaf, Jennifer Weber, and Daniel E. Sutherland. "Historian's Forum: The American Civil War's Centennial vs. the Sesquicentennial." *Civil War History* 57, no. 4 (December 2011): 380–402.

Cooper, Brittney C. "'They Are Nevertheless Our Brethren': The Order of the Eastern Star and the Battle for Women's Leadership, 1874–1926." In *All Men Free and Brethren: Essays on the History of African American Freemasonry*, edited by Peter P. Hinks and Stephen Kantrowitz, 114–130. Ithaca, NY: Cornell University Press, 2013.

Crenshaw, Kimberlé. "Mapping the Margins: Intersectionality, Identity Politics, and Violence against Women of Color." *Stanford Law Review* 43 (July 1991): 1241–1299.

Davis, Joshua Clark. "The Race to Preserve African American Radio." *Black Perspectives*, December 21, 2017. https://www.aaihs.org/the-race-to-preserve-african-american-radio/.

de Ruiter, Brian. "Jamestown Ter-Centennial Exposition of 1907." In *Encyclopedia Virginia*. Virginia Foundation for the Humanities, Richmond, VA. https://www.encyclopediavirginia.org/Jamestown_Ter-Centennial_Exposition_of_1907.

Domby, Adam. "The Cost of a Democratic Memory: Financing North Carolina's Commemorative Landscape." 2012. *Commemorative Landscapes of North Carolina*. https://docsouth.unc.edu/commland/features/essays/domby/.

Drapkin, Lindsay, "William Howard Day." Colored Convention Heartland: Black Organizers, Women and the Ohio Movement, exhibit, in Colored Conventions Project: Bringing 19th-century Black Organizing to Digital Life. https://coloredconventions.org/ohio-organizing/biographies/william-howard-day/.

Dunbar, Paul Lawrence. "Hidden in Plain Sight: African American Secret Societies and Black Freemasonry." *Journal of African American Studies* 16, no. 4 (December 2012): 622–637.

Edwards, Kathy, and Esmé Howard. "Monument Avenue: The Architecture of Consensus in the New South, 1890–1930." *Perspectives in Vernacular Architecture* 6 (1997): 92–110.

Eggert, Gerald G. "The Impact of the Fugitive Slave Law on Harrisburg: A Case Study." *Pennsylvania Magazine of History and Biography* 109 (October 1985): 537–569.

Eggert, Gerald G. "'Two Steps Forward, a Step-and-a-Half Back': Harrisburg's African American Community in the Nineteenth Century." *Pennsylvania History: A Journal of Mid-Atlantic Studies* 58 (January 1991): 1–36.

Egerton, Douglas R. "The Bones of Morris and Folly." In *Final Resting Places: Reflections on the Meaning of Civil War Graves*, edited by Brian Matthew Jordan and Jonathan W. White, 81–90. Athens: University of Georgia Press, 2023.

Flanagan, Joseph. "Raising the Hunley." *Common Ground* (Summer/Fall 2001): 12–24.

Forman, P. Gabrielle. "Black Organizing, Print Advocacy, and Collective Authorship: The Long History of the Colored Conventions Movement." In *The Colored Conventions Movement: Black Organizing in the Nineteenth Century*, edited by P. Gabrielle Forman, Jim Casey, and Sarah Lynn Patterson, 21–71. Chapel Hill: University of North Carolina Press, 2021.

Frear, Christopher, Jane O'Boyle, and Sel-Hill Kim. "Regional Media Framing of the Confederate Flag Debate in South Carolina." *Newspaper Research Journal* 40, no. 1 (March 2019): 83–105.

Gallagher, Gary W. "The Civil War at the Sesquicentennial: How Well Do Americans Understand Their Great National Crisis?" *Journal of Civil War Era* 3, no. 2 (June 2013): 295–303.

Glymph, Thavolia. "'Liberty Dearly Bought': The Making of Civil War Memory in Afro-American Communities in the South." In *Time Longer Than Rope: A Century of African American Activism, 1850–1950*, edited by Charles M. Payne and Adam Green, 111–139. New York: New York University Press, 2003.

Green, Hilary. "The Burden of the University of Alabama's Hallowed Grounds." *Public Historian* 42, no. 4 (November 2020): 28–40.

Green, Hilary. "The Hallowed Grounds Tour: Revising and Reimagining Landscapes of Race and Slavery at the University of Alabama." In *Segregation and Resistance in America's Urban Landscapes*, edited by Thaisa Way and Eric Avila, 297–323. Washington, DC: Dumbarton Oaks Press, Trustees for Harvard University, 2023.

Green, Hilary. "The Slave Cemetery and Apology Marker at the University of Alabama." In *Final Resting Places: Reflections on the Meaning of Civil War Graves*, edited by Brian Jordan and Jonathan White, 248–256. Athens: University of Georgia Press, 2023.

Green, Hilary. "2 Shifting Landscapes and the Monument Removal Craze, 2015–20." *Patterns of Prejudice* 54, no. 5 (December 2020): 485–491.

Griffin, Stanley H. "Noises in the Archives: Acknowledging the Present Yet Silenced Presence in Caribbean Archival Memory." In *Archival Silences: Missing, Lost, and Uncreated Archives*, edited by Michael Moss and David Thomas, 81–99. London: Routledge, 2021.

Hannah-Jones, Nikole. "1619–1624: Arrival." In *Four Hundred Souls: A Community History of African America, 1619–2019*, edited by Ibram X. Kendi and Keisha N. Blain, 3–7. New York: One World, 2021.

Hartman, Saidiya. "Venus in Two Acts." *Small Axe* 12 (June 2008): 1–14.

Historic Columbia. "African American History Monument." Accessed February 14, 2023. https://www.historiccolumbia.org/tour-locations/1100-gervais-street-2.

Horton, James Oliver. "Slavery and the Coming of the Civil War: A Matter for Interpretation." In *Rally on the High Ground: The National Park Service Symposium on the Civil War*, edited by Robert K. Sutton. Washington, DC: National Park Service, 2001. http://npshistory.com/series/symposia/rally_high_ground/chap5.htm.

Hurst, Julie Ann. "Barbershops in Harrisburg's Old Eighth, 1890–1905." *Pennsylvania History: A Journal of Mid-Atlantic Studies* 72 (Autumn 2005): 443–453.

Jackson, Jesse L., Jr. "A More Perfect Union." In *Rally on the High Ground: The National Park Service Symposium on the Civil War*, edited by Robert K. Sutton. http://npshistory.com/series/symposia/rally_high_ground/chap1.htm. Washington, DC: National Park Service, 2001.

Jirard, Stephanie A. "U.S. Colored Troops from Cumberland County Buried in Union Cemetery, Carlisle, Pennsylvania." Special Civil War Edition, *Cumberland County History* 28 (2011): 39–53.

Johnson, Jessica Marie. "Markup Bodies: Black [Life] Studies and Slavery [Death] Studies at the Digital Crossroads." *Social Text* 137 (December 2018): 57–79.

Johnson, Joan Marie. "'Ye Gave Them a Stone': African American Women's Clubs, the Frederick Douglass Home, and the Black Mammy Monument." *Journal of Women's History* 17 (Spring 2005): 62–86.

Joyner, Charles. "Furling That Banner: The Rise and Fall of the Confederate Flag in South Carolina, 1961–2000." In *Citizen-Scholar: Essays in Honor of Walter Edgar*, edited by Robert H. Brinkmeyer, 21–33. Columbia: University of South Carolina Press, 2016.

Kantrowitz, Stephen. "Brotherhood Denied: Black Freemasonry and the Limits of Reconstruction." In *All Men Free and Brethren: Essays on the History of African American Freemasonry*, edited by Peter P. Hinks and Stephen Kantrowitz, 95–113. Ithaca, NY: Cornell University Press, 2013.

Kantrowitz, Stephen. "'Intended for the Better Government of Man': The Political History of African American Freemasonry in the Era of Emancipation." *Journal of American History* 96 (March 2010): 1001–1026.

Kelly, Patrick J. "The Election of 1896 and the Restructuring of Civil War Memory." *Civil War History* 49 (September 2003): 254–280.

Kendi, Ibram X. "A Community of Souls: An Introduction." In *Four Hundred Souls: A Community History of African America, 1619–2019*, edited by Ibram X. Kendi and Keisha N. Blain, xiii–xvii. New York: One World, 2021.

Kytle, Ethan J. "Fact, Fancy, and Nat Fuller's Feast in 1865 and 2015." In *Freedoms Gained and Lost: Reconstruction and Its Meanings 150 Years Later*, edited by Adam H. Domby and Simon Lewis, 276–303. New York: Fordham University Press, 2022.

Kytle, Ethan J. "Fort Sumter Sesquicentennial: Charleston Changed Its Tune." *History News Network*, April 18, 2011. https://historynewsnetwork.org/article/138511.

Kytle, Ethan J., and Blain Roberts, "Is It Okay to Talk about Slaves? Segregating the Past in Historic Charleston." In *Destination Dixie: Tourism and Southern Tourism*, edited by Karen L. Cox, 137–159. Gainesville: University Press of Florida, 2012.

Lande, Jonathan. "Trials of Freedom: African American Deserters during the US Civil War." *Journal of Social History* 49, no. 3 (Spring 2016): 693–709.

Lapansky, Emma Jones. "Feminism, Freedom, and Community: Charlotte Forten and Women Activists in Nineteenth-Century Philadelphia." *Pennsylvania Magazine of History and Biography* 113, no. 1 (January 1989): 3–19.

Lawrence-Sanders, Ashleigh. "History, Memory, and the Power of Black Radio." *Black Perspectives*, March 16, 2018. https://www.aaihs.org/history-memory-and-the-power -of-black-radio/.

Lee, Lauranett. "Giles B. Jackson (1853–1924)." In *Encyclopedia Virginia*. Virginia Foundation for the Humanities, Richmond, VA. https://www.encyclopediavirginia.org/ Jackson_Giles_B_1853-1924.

Linenthal, Edward T. "Healing and History: The Dilemmas of Interpretation." In *Rally on the High Ground: The National Park Service Symposium on the Civil War*, edited by Robert K. Sutton. Washington, DC: National Park Service, 2001. http://npshistory .com/series/symposia/rally_high_ground/chap3b.htm.

Linky, Don. "Woodrow Wilson and the Election of 1912." Center on the American Governor, Eagleton Institute of Politics, Rutgers University. https://governors.rutgers .edu/woodrow-wilson-and-the-election-of-1912/.

Masur, Kate. Introduction to *They Knew Lincoln*, by John E. Washington with a new introduction by Kate Masur, edited by Kate Masur, ix–lxxx. New York: Oxford University Press, 2018.

McPherson, James M. "Citizen Soldiers of the Civil War: Why They Fought." In *Rally on the High Ground: The National Park Service Symposium on the Civil War*, edited by Robert K. Sutton. Washington, DC: National Park Service, 2001. http://npshistory .com/series/symposia/rally_high_ground/chap4.htm.

McPherson, Tara. "Why Are the Digital Humanities So White? or Thinking the Histories of Race and Computation." In *Debates in the Digital Humanities*, edited by Matthew K. Gold. Minneapolis: University of Minnesota Press, 2012.

Mealy, Todd. "A Gathering at the Crossroads: Memorializing African American Trailblazers and a Lost Neighborhood in Harrisburg." *Pennsylvania Heritage* (Spring 2021). http://paheritage.wpengine.com/article/a-gathering-at-the-crossroads -memorializing-african-american-trailblazers-and-a-lost-neighborhood-in -harrisburg/.

Morgan, Francesca. "My Furthest-Back Person: Black Genealogy Before and After Roots." In *Reconsidering Roots: Race, Politics, and Memory*, edited by Erica L. Ball and Kellie Carter Jackson, 63–78. Athens: University of Georgia Press, 2017.

National Park Service. "African American Civil War Memorial." Accessed February 14, 2023. https://www.nps.gov/places/000/african-american-civil-war-memorial-the -spirit-of-freedom.htm.

Nelson, Margaret K. "Fictive Kin, Families We Choose, and Voluntary Kin: What Does the Discourse Tell Us?" *Journal of Family Theory and Review* 5 (December 2013): 259–281.

Novotny, Patrick. "The Impact of Television on Georgia, 1948–1952." *Georgia Historical Quarterly* 91 (Fall 2007): 324–347.

O'Brien, John T. "Reconstruction in Richmond: White Restoration and Black Protest, April–June 1865." *Virginia Magazine of History and Biography* 89, no. 3 (July 1981): 259–281.

Painter, Nell Irvin. "Martin R. Delany: Elitism and Black Nationalism." In *Black Leaders of the Nineteenth Century,* edited by Leon Litwack and August Meier, 149–171. Urbana: University of Illinois Press, 1988.

Prather, H. Leon, Sr. "We Have Taken A City: A Centennial Essay." In *Democracy Betrayed: The Wilmington Race Riot of 1898 and Its Legacy,* edited by David S. Cecelski and Timothy B. Tyson, 15–41. Chapel Hill: University of North Carolina Press, 1998.

Prince, K. Stephen. "Jim Crow Memory: Southern White Supremacists and the Regional Politics of Remembrance." In *Remembering Reconstruction: Struggles of the Meaning of America's Most Turbulent Era,* edited by Carol Emberton and Bruce E. Baker, 17–34. Baton Rouge: Louisiana State University Press, 2017.

Podvia, Mark W. "Frederick Douglass in Carlisle." *Unbound: An Annual Review of Legal History and Rare Books* 5 (2012): 17–28.

Raiford, Leigh. "Photography and the Practices of Critical Black Memory." *History and Theory* 48, no. 4 (December 2009): 112–129.

Reed, John Shelton. "The Banner That Won't Stay Furled." *Southern Cultures* 8, no. 1 (Spring 2002): 76–100.

Riley, Rochelle, ed. *The Burden: African Americans and the Enduring Impact of Slavery.* Detroit: Wayne State University Press, 2018.

Roberts, Blain, and Ethan Kytle. "Looking the Thing in the Face: Slavery, Race, and the Commemorative Landscape in Charleston, South Carolina, 1865–2010." *Journal of Southern History* 78, no. 3 (August 2012): 639–684.

Rosenthal, Carolyn J. "Kinskeeping in the Familial Division of Labor." *Journal of Marriage and Family* 47, no. 4 (November 1985): 965–974.

Samito, Christian G. "The Intersection between Military Justice and Equal Rights: Mutinies, Courts-martial, and Black Civil War Soldiers." *Civil War History* 53, no. 2 (June 2007): 170–202.

Silkenat, David. "'A Company of Gentlemen': Confederate Veterans and Southern Universities." *American Nineteenth Century History* 21, no. 3 (November 2020): 237–253.

Smith, David L. "Frederick Douglass in Carlisle." *Cumberland County History* 22 (2005): 53–60.

Smith, John David. "Glory: 'Heroism Writ Large, from People Whom History Had Made Small'.<HS" In *Writing History with Lightning: Cinematic Representations of Nineteenth-Century America,* edited by Matthew Christopher Hulbert and John C. Inscoe, 162–171. Baton Rouge: Louisiana State University Press, 2019.

Sutton, Robert. Introduction to *Rally on the High Ground: The National Park Service Symposium on the Civil War,* edited by Robert K. Sutton. Washington, DC: National Park Service, 2001. http://npshistory.com/series/symposia/rally_high_ground/intro.htm.

Thomas, William G., III. "Television News and the Civil Rights Struggle: The Views in Virginia and Mississippi." *Southern Spaces,* November 3, 2004. https://southernspaces .org/2004/television-news-and-civil-rights-struggle-views-virginia-and-mississippi/.

Thornton, John. "The African Experience of '20 and Odd Negroes' Arriving in Virginia in 1619." *William and Mary Quarterly* 55 (July 1998): 421–434.

Titus, Jill Ogline. "An Unfinished Struggle: Sesquicentennial Interpretations of Slavery and Emancipation." *Journal of the Civil War Era* 4, no. 2 (June 2014): 338–347.

Tyler-McGraw, Marie. "Southern Comfort Levels: Race, Heritage Tourism, and the Civil War in Richmond." In *Slavery and Public History: The Tough Stuff of American Memory*, edited by James Oliver Horton and Lois E. Horton, 151–167. New York: New Press, 2006.

Venet, Wendy Hamand. "Faithful Helpmates and Fervent Activists: Northern Women and Civil War Memory." In *Women and the American Civil War: North-South Counterpoints*, edited by Judith Giesburg and Randall M. Miller, 323–339. Kent, OH: Kent State University Press, 2018.

Waite, Kevin. "The 'Lost Cause' Goes West: Confederate Culture and Civil War Memory in California." *California History* 97 (Spring 2020): 33–49.

Wallace, Maurice. "Are We Men?: Prince Hall, Martin Delany, and the Masculine Ideal in Black Freemasonry, 1775–1865." *American Literary History* 9 (Autumn 1997): 396–424.

Wendt, Simon. "God, Gandhi, and Guns: The African American Freedom Struggle in Tuscaloosa, Alabama, 1964–1965." *Journal of African American History* 89, no. 1 (Winter 2004): 36–56.

White, Jonathan W., Katie Fisher, and Elizabeth Wall. "The Civil War Letters of Tillman Valentine, Third US Colored Troops." *Pennsylvania Magazine of History and Biography* 139, no. 2 (April 2015): 171–188.

Williams-Forson, Psyche. "Where Did They Eat? Where Did They Stay?: Interpreting the Material Culture of Black Women's Domesticity in the Context of the Colored Conventions." In *The Colored Conventions Movement: Black Organizing in the Nineteenth Century*, edited by P. Gabrielle Forman, Jim Casey, and Sarah Lynn Patterson, 86–104. Chapel Hill: University of North Carolina Press, 2021.

Wingert, Cooper. "Fighting for State Citizenship in the US Colored Troops." *Civil War History* 69, no. 3 (September 2023): 9–31.

Yarborough, Richard. "Violence, Manhood, and Black Heroism: The Wilmington Riot in Two Turn-of-the-Century African American Novels." In *Democracy Betrayed: The Wilmington Race Riot of 1898 and Its Legacy*, edited by David S. Cecelski and Timothy B. Tyson, 225–252. Chapel Hill: University of North Carolina Press, 1998.

Zander, Cecily N. "'Victory's Long Review': The Grand Review of Union Armies and the Meaning of the Civil War." *Civil War History* 66, no. 1 (March 2020): 45–77.

Dissertations, Theses, and Unpublished Papers

Green, Hilary Nicole. "Educational Reconstruction: African American Education in the Urban South, 1865–1890." PhD diss. University of North Carolina at Chapel Hill, 2010.

Newby-Alexander, Cassandra. "Remembering Norfolk's African American Cemeteries" (unpublished paper, no date). http://www.racetimeplace.com/cemeteryhistory.htm.

Index

Abraham Obama, 239

"About Ten Days after Battle of Gettysburg," 1, 21

activism, 7, 45, 56, 57, 67, 87–88, 92, 103, 138, 141, 146, 154, 157–158, 167, 181, 210, 247–248, 260, 294n100, 325n82

activists, 38, 55, 58–59, 104, 140, 143, 146–147, 157, 158, 163–167, 171–172, 188, 197, 213, 232

African American Civil War memorial, 208

African American community, xiv, 75, 122, 138, 140, 146, 155, 165, 169, 171, 181–182, 214, 226, 252, 266n36

African American heritage tours, 211

African American leaders, 63, 123, 127–130, 132, 137, 140. *See also* Black leaders

African American leadership, 11, 102, 142. *See also* Black leadership

African American memory, 3, 4, 5, 11, 35–36, 71, 77, 143, 146–147, 153–154, 160, 162–163, 171–172. *See also* Black memory

African American parents, 115–116

African American porches, 1, 3, 6, 147, 157, 182, 187–189, 193, 197, 200, 245, 248

African American press, 143. *See also* Black press

African Americans, xi, xiii, xiv, 3–10, 12–13, 18–19, 23–24, 27, 31, 33, 35–36, 38–41, 43, 45, 47, 52, 57, 62–67, 71, 73, 75, 77, 78, 82–84, 95–96, 98, 102, 104, 107, 112–113, 115, 121–124, 126–127, 131–133, 135–136, 138–142, 148–151, 155–156, 158, 160–162, 166–167, 169–171, 189, 192–193, 207, 212–213, 220–222, 227, 240–241, 243–248, 250–251, 254, 258, 270n16, 278n133, 283n46, 290n28. *See also* Black Americans

African Methodist Episcopal (AME) Church, xiii, 2, 41, 72, 80–81, 82, 100, 102, 103, 108, 114, 160, 176–177, 179, 181, 230, 238–239, 241

African Methodist Episcopal Zion (AMEZ) Church, 45–46, 50, 72, 99, 101–103, 109, 160

Afro-Canadians, 46,

Alesouth, Eliza, 30, 34

Alexander, Kianna, 195–196

Allen, Michael, 234

allies, 6, 42–43, 45, 52, 56, 58, 63, 66, 73, 78, 92, 125, 127, 166–167, 194, 209, 213, 220, 225, 232, 242, 248

allyship, 42, 248, 257, 274n69

American Colonization Society (ACS), 43

American Legion, 109, 114, 168, 179

Anderson, James A., 254

Anderson, James Harvey, 109

Anderson, John, 113

Andrew, John, 204, 207, 235–236

anti-Black commemorative traditions, 188

anti-Black policies, 72, 124, 247

anti-Black violence, 166, 241

anti-Blackness, 38, 42, 56, 66, 133, 192, 240

Antietam National Cemetery, 96–97

April 3 commemoration, 121–125, 127, 130–133, 136, 143, 246, 253

archival practices, 6–8, 61

archival record, 3, 50, 284n58

archival traces, 87, 184, 189–190, 237

archives, 10, 13, 87, 143, 148, 169, 173, 184, 245, 248, 251, 257, 260; community archives, 7, 87, 247; porch archives, vii, xiv, 6–8, 12–13, 159, 174, 184, 190, 248, 263n22; traditional archives, xiii, 7–8, 174, 184, 197, 248

Hallowell, Norwood Penrose, 236
Hamilton, Ed, 208–209
Hampton Roads, Virginia, 152–153, 155
Hancock, Winfield Scott, 74–75, 98
Harper, Frances E. W., 60, 91, 173
Harpers Ferry xiii, 29, 193
Harriet (2019), 194
Harris, William D., 125–126
Harrisburg, Pennsylvania, 11, 25, 37–39, 40,
    43–60, 69, 70, 77, 105–106, 111, 158, 161,
    245, 266n36, 270n16, 274n69
Harrisburg reception, 40, 45, 53, 58. *See
    also* Grand Review of Colored Troops,
    November 1865 reception; November
    1865 event; November 1865 celebration
Harrison, Benjamin, 128
Harrison, Richard, 108
Hayes, Rutherford B., 71–74, 80–81, 260
headstones, 87, 147, 153, 155, 173, 175,
    182–183
Henry, Thomas E. W., 108
Herr Street cemetery, 57
Hertford, North Carolina, 146, 148,
    152–156, 169, 195
Hertford monument, 151, 169, 170.
    See also Monument, Colored Union
    Soldiers
Hicks, Brian, 227, 231, 233
Hill, Barbara Lane (author's aunt), 184
Hill, Michael, 170
Hinton, John, 178
Hoke, Jacob, 20, 31–32
Holsclaw, Fred, 212
homemade citizenship, 103, 143,
    158, 247
Hood, James, 255
Hope Presbyterian Church, 68, 87
Hopkins, Leroy, 60
Colonel Peter B. Housum GAR post, No.
    309, 100
Howard, Oliver Otis (O. O), 97–98, 208
Hudgins, A. L., 154
Hughes, Langston, 159
Hunnicutt, J. W., 126–127
Hurd, Cynthia, 241

identity, 7, 31, 33, 35, 74–75, 91, 116, 142, 184,
    190
Industrial Advocate, 133–134, 136, 138–139
Information Wanted advertisements, 29
Information Wanted editorial, 76
interdisciplinary, 4, 248, 341n37
intersectional approach and framework,
    4, 36, 248
interpretations, 41, 171, 192, 211, 222–223,
    227, 229, 318n3
invasions, 2, 3, 26, 27, 35, 48, 51, 62–63,
    72, 75, 77, 88, 92–93, 96, 100, 161, 187,
    268n88

Jackson, Calobe Jr., 37
Jackson, Darrell, 213–214
Jackson, Eliza, 103
Jackson, Giles B., 134–140
Jackson, Jesse Jr., 222–223
Jackson, John Walker, 47, 52, 54, 274n69
Jackson, Rose, 29
Jackson, Susie, 241
James Island, South Carolina, 207, 219,
    228, 229, 238
Jamestown Ter-Centennial Exposition of
    1907, 135–136, 139, 301n61
Jenkins, Albert, 19, 21, 23, 30–32, 98, 100
Jim Crow, 12, 84, 85, 87, 115, 122, 133–134,
    136, 141–142, 145, 147–151, 154, 158,
    163–164, 166, 177, 192, 200, 210, 215, 222,
    238, 251, 253–254, 257, 262n10
Jim Crow segregation, 133, 142, 147–148,
    154, 158, 257, 262n10
"John Brown's Body," 17, 47
Jones, William H. "Pap," 50
Jones, Zadie, 157–159, 163–166, 172, 188
Jones House, 50
Journal of Negro History, 141, 143
Jubilee, 17, 71, 83, 121, 123, 137, 207, 245
Juneteenth, 122, 246

Kiddoo, Joseph B., 48, 52
kinkeepers, 10–12, 15, 117, 119, 143, 161, 173,
    184–185, 188, 197–198, 247–248, 260,
    263n22

About the Authors

Hilary N. Green is the James B. Duke Professor of Africana Studies at Davidson College. Professor Green is a distinguished scholar whose research explores the intersections of race, memory, and education in the post–Civil War American South. She is the author of *Educational Reconstruction: African American Schools in the Urban South, 1865–1890*, co-author of the *NPS-OAH Historic Resource Study of African American Schools in the South, 1865–1900*, and co-editor of *The Civil War and the Summer of 2020* (Fordham).

Edda L. Fields-Black is a Professor in the Department of History and Director of the Dietrich College Humanities Center at Carnegie Mellon University. Her latest book, *COMBEE: Harriet Tubman, the Combahee River Raid, and Black Freedom during the Civil War* (2024) uses US Civil War Pension Files to tell the story of the Combahee River Raid, when in June 1863 Harriet Tubman, her ring of spies, scouts, and pilots piloted Colonel James Montgomery, the 2nd SC Volunteers, and one battery of the 3rd Rhode Island Heavy Artillery up the Combahee River to raid seven rice plantations and bring liberation to 756 enslaved people, through the words and using the voices of the Combahee freedom seekers who self-liberated in the raid. One of Fields-Black's many specialties is identifying new sources and methods to recover the voices of historical actors (particularly peasant rice farmers in early and precolonial West Africa's Upper Guinea Coast and Blacks forced to labor on rice plantations in the antebellum South Carolina and Georgia Lowcountry) who did not author their own written sources.

RECONSTRUCTING AMERICA
Andrew L. Slap, series editor

Hans L. Trefousse, *Impeachment of a President: Andrew Johnson, the Blacks, and Reconstruction.*

Richard Paul Fuke, *Imperfect Equality: African Americans and the Confines of White Ideology in Post-Emancipation Maryland.*

Ruth Currie-McDaniel, *Carpetbagger of Conscience: A Biography of John Emory Bryant.*

Paul A. Cimbala and Randall M. Miller, eds., *The Freedmen's Bureau and Reconstruction: Reconsiderations.*

Herman Belz, *A New Birth of Freedom: The Republican Party and Freedmen's Rights, 1861 to 1866.*

Robert Michael Goldman, *"A Free Ballot and a Fair Count": The Department of Justice and the Enforcement of Voting Rights in the South, 1877–1893.*

Ruth Douglas Currie, ed., *Emma Spaulding Bryant: Civil War Bride, Carpetbagger's Wife, Ardent Feminist—Letters, 1860–1900.*

Robert Francis Engs, *Freedom's First Generation: Black Hampton, Virginia, 1861–1890.*

Robert F. Kaczorowski, *The Politics of Judicial Interpretation: The Federal Courts, Department of Justice, and Civil Rights, 1866–1876.*

John Syrett, *The Civil War Confiscation Acts: Failing to Reconstruct the South.*

Michael Les Benedict, *Preserving the Constitution: Essays on Politics and the Constitution in the Reconstruction Era.*

Andrew L. Slap, *The Doom of Reconstruction: The Liberal Republicans in the Civil War Era.*

Edmund L. Drago, *Confederate Phoenix: Rebel Children and Their Families in South Carolina.*

Mary Farmer-Kaiser, *Freedwomen and the Freedmen's Bureau: Race, Gender, and Public Policy in the Age of Emancipation.*

Paul A. Cimbala and Randall Miller, eds., *The Great Task Remaining Before Us: Reconstruction as America's Continuing Civil War.*

John A. Casey Jr., *New Men: Reconstructing the Image of the Veteran in Late-Nineteenth-Century American Literature and Culture.*

Hilary N. Green, *Educational Reconstruction: African American Schools in the Urban South, 1865–1890.*

Christopher B. Bean, *Too Great a Burden to Bear: The Struggle and Failure of the Freedmen's Bureau in Texas.*

David E. Goldberg, *The Retreats of Reconstruction: Race, Leisure, and the Politics of Segregation at the New Jersey Shore, 1865–1920.*

David Prior, ed., *Reconstruction in a Globalizing World.*

Jewel L. Spangler and Frank Towers, eds., *Remaking North American Sovereignty: State Transformation in the 1860s.*

Adam H. Domby and Simon Lewis, eds., *Freedoms Gained and Lost: Reconstruction and Its Meanings 150 Years Later.*

David Prior, ed., *Reconstruction and Empire: The Legacies of Abolition and Union Victory for an Imperial Age.*

Sandra M. Gustafson and Robert S. Levine, eds., *Reimagining the Republic: Race, Citizenship, and Nation in the Literary Work of Albion W. Tourgée.* Foreword by Carolyn L. Karcher.

Brian Schoen, Jewel L. Spangler, and Frank Towers, eds., *Continent in Crisis: The U.S. Civil War in North America.*

Raymond James Krohn, *Abolitionist Twilights: History, Meaning, and the Fate of Racial Egalitarianism, 1865–1909.*

Hilary N. Green and Andrew L. Slap, eds., *The Civil War and the Summer of 2020*.

Ian Delahanty, *Embracing Emancipation: A Transatlantic History of Irish Americans, Slavery, and the American Union, 1840–1865*.

AnneMarie Brosnan, *A Contested Terrain: Freedpeople's Education in North Carolina During the Civil War and Reconstruction*.

Hilary N. Green, *Unforgettable Sacrifice: How Black Communities Remembered the Civil War*. Foreword by Edda L. Fields-Black.